Volume 2

# AGITATORS AND PROMOTERS IN THE AGE OF GLADSTONE AND DISRAELI

# AGITATORS AND PROMOTERS IN THE AGE OF GLADSTONE AND DISRAELI

A Biographical Dictionary of the Leaders of British Pressure Groups
Founded between 1865 and 1886

HOWARD LEROY MALCHOW

Routledge
Taylor & Francis Group

LONDON AND NEW YORK

First published in 1983 by Garland Publishing Inc.

This edition first published in 2018
by Routledge
2 Park Square, Milton Park, Abingdon, Oxon OX14 4RN

and by Routledge
711 Third Avenue, New York, NY 10017

*Routledge is an imprint of the Taylor & Francis Group, an informa business*

*British Library Cataloguing in Publication Data*
A catalogue record for this book is available from the British Library

ISBN: 978-1-138-48265-4 (Set)
ISBN: 978-1-351-05698-4 (Set) (ebk)
ISBN: 978-1-138-48258-6 (Volume 2) (hbk)
ISBN: 978-1-138-48260-9 (Volume 2) (pbk)
ISBN: 978-1-351-05738-7 (Volume 2) (ebk)

**Publisher's Note**
The publisher has gone to great lengths to ensure the quality of this reprint but points out that some imperfections in the original copies may be apparent.

**Disclaimer**
The publisher has made every effort to trace copyright holders and would welcome correspondence from those they have been unable to trace.

# AGITATORS AND PROMOTERS IN THE AGE OF GLADSTONE AND DISRAELI

*A Biographical Dictionary of the Leaders of British Pressure Groups Founded between 1865 and 1886*

Howard LeRoy Malchow

GARLAND PUBLISHING, INC. • NEW YORK & LONDON
1983

**Library of Congress Cataloging in Publication Data**

Malchow, Howard L.
  Agitators and promoters in the age of Gladstone and Disraeli.

  (Garland reference library of social science ;
v. 176)
  1. Pressure group members—Great Britain—Biography.
2. Pressure groups—Great Britain—History—19th
century.  I. Title.  II. Series.
JN329.P7M34  1983    322.4′3′0941    82-49263
ISBN 0-8240-9130-2

Printed on acid-free, 250-year-life paper
Manufactured in the United States of America

For Mother and A.J.

# CONTENTS

# PREFACE

This book brings together the lives of thousands of persons, some famous, most modest and obscure, who were joined a century ago in pursuit of causes promising, it seemed to them, a better, more just world. If many of these crusades (for they were pursued with passion and commitment) strike us as odd or faddist, if many were complete failures and others only partial successes, they nevertheless embodied much of the life and substance of the politics of an important era of transition.

Here we have not simply the political Establishment, the members of government and legislature with their paid functionaries and party hacks, but much of the politicized sub-elite of a generation—some three thousand persons from many layers of Victorian life. These are the organizers and leaders, the agitators and promoters of a host of causes. Reconstruction of this world of "pressure from without" has been a labor-intensive process of several years, a process necessarily incomplete. Where published membership lists have survived in annual reports, tracts, and leaflets, they have been painstakingly accumulated, disaggregated, and each name researched in a number of biographical sources.

Many have assisted in this work. Thanks is first due to the patience of those librarians and their helpers at the British Library, the London School of Economics, the Universities of London, Oxford, and Cambridge, and other British archives, where the characteristic resourcefulness of the British public servant has made all the difference. At Tufts University I have had the considerable advantage of not only much-needed financial support in the form of opportune faculty research grants but the comradely assistance of students and colleagues over half a decade. A work such as this is necessarily a collective effort. I must thank Richard Goodwin, Kelly Cameron, Bruce Rosenthal, Richard Rapp, Diane Damplo, Jerry Ziegler, Edward McMorrow, Jeffrey Hamilton, Warren Sidikman, and Eric Truebenbach. Special thanks are due to George Stalker, without whose knowledge of the possibilities offered by computer science as a tool for the humanities this project could not have been accomplished in its present form. The shortcomings of such an attempt—the inevitable omissions and inaccuracies—are of course my responsibility alone.

*Howard Malchow*
*Medford, Massachusetts*
*11 January 1983*

# INTRODUCTION

## General Purpose

This project includes some three thousand individuals who founded and led seventy-two political pressure groups organized in an era of significant political change: the twenty years between the death of Palmerston in 1865 and the fall of Gladstone's third government in 1886. At each end, these years saw a franchise reform act which propelled British society into the modern world of mass democracy and party discipline. It was an age of transition, of the adaptation of earlier forms of political participation to a new and unpredictable environment. Earlier, extra-parliamentary groups had had to struggle for legitimacy. Success made them, by the 1860s, an established part of the system. After the 1880s, their position was rapidly undermined by the reorganization and strengthening of parties and changes in the system itself. The nineteenth century pressure group, dominated by amateurs, philanthropists, and back-benchers, was largely a manifestation of the professional and leisured middle classes, a part of society never more clearly central to the political culture than in the two decades covered here.

It is not the purpose of this work to compete with the full biographical treatment of many of these individuals which can be found in such general publications as the *Dictionary of National Biography*. Rather, the objective is to create a reference guide to a particular kind of political activity and a particular part of the Victorian political community. By giving the user both information about an individual's pressure group affiliations and significant biographical information, it is hoped that investigation into the important connections between social structure and political activity will be advanced, as well as making clearer the affinities among group leaderships, thus providing one kind of evidence for the inter-relatedness of much of Victorian lobbying.

## Definitions

The quantity and variety of extra-parliamentary participation in a society as populous, educated, and articulate as Victorian Britain were enormous. Limits have had to be drawn because of the labor-intensive nature of biographical dictionaries and, perhaps more importantly, because some definition (and hence restriction) of purpose seemed necessary if the results were to have more significance than a modern telephone book. Not all pressure groups for which membership information exists have been included.

First, this project was limited to what appeared to be at least overtly non-partisan "cause" (as opposed to "special interest") lobbies. Excluded are party organizations like the National Liberal Federation or the Primrose League. Also excluded were many groups, among them most charities and temperance organizations, which did not seem to have a clear political objective. Groups that appeared to fall under the description of interest groups, that is, the more or less permanent spokesman organizations established as watchdogs for some vested interest were also removed. Examples here are the Railway Companies' Association or the Parliamentary Committee of the T.U.C. This sometimes called for rather arbitrary judgment. The rule followed was that groups which *de facto* seemed to represent an interest (for instance, the Central Brewers' License Repeal Association) were nevertheless included so long as the organization was ostensibly an open body addressing a single issue arguably of general interest and was not formally allied to those whom it seemed most to serve. Finally, groups which challenged the basic constitutional structure of politics—franchise expansion groups, home rule associations, and anti-parliamentary or revolutionary societies—were generally omitted. A few which might have qualified for exclusion under this rubric, however, were retained as being insufficiently subversive of the political order (the London Municipal Reform League, the Proportional Representation Society, and the Imperial Federation League). Of central interest in this project were those who by and large accepted the system and attempted to work inside it through the application of legitimate pressure. The premise here is that, broadly considered, the Victorian representative political system, though excluding the majority of the nation from direct participation, nevertheless—or perhaps as a result—possessed a powerful socially conservative mechanism in addition to the franchise for involving the energies and flattering the aspirations of many of those who existed outside the privileged precincts of Mayfair.

Second, it has been necessary to restrict the dictionary to the leaders of those groups which were *founded* between the years 1865 and 1886. This means, of course, that many well-established lobbying organizations, like the United Kingdom Alliance or the Liberation Society, whose foundation pre-dates 1865 but which were active within our period, have not been included. Again, resources demanded some limitation. However, this rule also has the logic that the groups which were organized within the period may have most to tell us of the kinds of people involved in generating extra-parliamentary pressure.

Third, only those groups which left a *published* record of their membership, usually in annual reports, could be included. The scope of the project precluded, at this stage, the kind of manuscript searching necessary to attempt to fill in the gaps. What we have here are the groups which chose to publicize their memberships, and whose publications have survived in the major British libraries. Fortunately, pressure groups needed to advertise their memberships to secure support in an age when such lists were scrutinized [for some surety of genuineness and respectability] by prospective supporters with many demands on their time and money. Rarely does published propaganda not include some mention of officers, patrons, or executive committee.

Finally, the individuals chosen from these lists are not the rank and file members (though in some groups the executive seems identical to general membership) but the leadership. This is defined as those persons who can be identified as founders, officers, executive committeemen, or patrons. Again, this seemed dictated both by the limits of time and resources and by logic. A name on a membership list may mean very little. Clearly an individual's assumption of an official position is a surer indication (if no guarantee) of a depth of commitment to an issue.

## *Biographical Information*

This book is divided into two sections. The major part is a consolidated biographical dictionary of the men and women who led the groups we have investigated. Following this will be found an Appendix which provides an index of names only, arranged by group. This should enable the reader to discover at a glance an individual's colleagues within a particular organization.

Biographical information has been consistently provided in the order indicated below.

```
                                              SMITH, SIR JOHN (1819–1905)
School ————————
College ————————                  Eton; Kings, Camb; Inner Temple.
└ Professional education                   Q.C. 64; Barrister 44.
  Occupation —————————             Liberal. MP Hackney 68–74. Charity
  Political party —————————              Commissioner 71–74, JP.
  Public Office —————————           KCB 74.
  Honors —————————                Fellow Society of Antiquaries.
  Learned & professional societies ———     West London; Berkshire.
  Residence —————————              [DNB, WWW, Fosters]
  Source —————————
  Group affiliation ——————————— Commons Preservation Society (F) 65–86, Exec.
                                          Sunday Society 78–90, Treas., V-Pres.
```

*Name.* Persons are to be found under their family names, not titles, throughout. In all cases where hyphenated or double names occur, the last name has been used for alphabetizing (e.g., GOWER, GEORGE GRANVILLE LEVESON-, not LEVESON-GOWER, GEORGE GRANVILLE) regardless of family usage.

*Birth and death dates.* In a few cases birth date could only be calculated from age at matriculation, and so may involve an error of ± one year.

*Occupation.* Both successive professional rank and occupational change is reflected. The first citation will generally be the occupation or rank held when the individual became an active group leader. The following citations will be arranged, when possible, in chronological order, followed by a two-digit date (e.g., Vicar 72; Curate 41; Priest ⟨CE⟩ 42; Rector 81). In the case of landowners, five categories based on approximate acreage owned were used:

| | | |
|---|---|---|
| Very large landowner | = | 10,001+ acres |
| Large landowner | = | 5,001 to 10,000 acres |
| Substantial landowner | = | 1,001 to 5,000 acres |
| Small landowner | = | 1 to 1,000 acres |
| Landowner | = | acreage unknown |

*Residence.* Domestic residence roughly corresponding to the period of group membership is used when possible. London residence is cited first. In cases of multiple residences, no more than three of the principal ones could be cited.

*Sources.* Within brackets are the codes indicating the various sources from which biographical information has been taken, and where more detail may be found. These codes are:

| | |
|---|---|
| Alum Cantab | = J.A. Venn, *Alumni Cantabrigienses* |
| Alum Oxon | = Joseph Foster, *Alumni Oxonienses* |
| Army List | |
| Aust Dict Biog | = *Australian Dictionary of Biography* |
| Bateman | = John Batemen, *The Great Landowners of Great Britain and Ireland* |
| BP | = *Burke's Peerage* |
| Bryan's Painters | = *Bryan's Dictionary of Painters and Engravers* |
| Crockfds | = *Crockford's Clerical Directory* |
| Dic Lab Biog | = *Dictionary of Labour Biography* |
| Dict New Zealand Biog | = *Dictionary of New Zealand Biography* |
| Direc Direcs | = *The Directory of Directors* |
| DNB | = *Dictonary of National Biography* |
| Dods | = *Dod's Parliamentary Companion* |
| Fosters | = Joseph Foster, *Men-at-the-Bar* |
| Friends | = William Robinson, *Friends of a Half Century* |
| Indian Dic Nat Biog | = *Dictionary of National Biography* (India) |
| MEB | = *Modern English Biography* |
| Navy List | |
| Walfords | = Edward Walford, *The County Families of the United Kingdom* |
| Wesl Min | = William Hill, *An Alphabetical Arrangement of All the Wesleyan Methodist Ministers . . .* |
| WWW | = *Who Was Who* |

*Group affiliation.* [See below for information about specific groups.] Under the source codes (if any) will be found the names of pressure groups to which the individual belonged. This information is organized in the following manner: the group name, followed by (F) if the person was a founder (i.e., joined in the first year of the organization), followed by two dates. These indicate, not necessarily when the individual joined and retired from the group, but rather the dates of the documents where earliest and latest mention were found. Hence, in many cases where surviving records were scarce, only a single date may be available. Finally, there will appear some indication of the office or offices held by the individual within these dates. These include:

| | |
|---|---|
| Chairman | Secretary |
| Exec[utive Committee] | Treas[urer] |
| Hon[orary] Sec[retary] | V[ice]-Chairman |
| Patron | V[ice]-Pres[ident] |
| President | |

[*Note*: the designation "Executive Committee" is somewhat ambiguous. This includes bodies labelled as such, but also "national councils" when these were small and apparently functional rather than synonymous with general membership. In a few cases (Jamaica Committee, Smoke Abatement Committee), the entire memberships of groups labelled as "committees" were included if there was no convenient way to distinguish from the documents available an inner circle or executive. *Also Note*: only the officers of the provincial committees of national organizations have been treated as members of the national executives.]

## *The Groups*

The following are the pressure groups whose leaderships have been included in this dictionary, along with some relevant information about their objectives and dates of foundation.

### *Allotments and Small Holdings Association*
Founded ca. 1884 to secure compliance with the Allotments Act (1882), extend allotment legislation, protect the rights of laborers from enclosure, and "generally to facilitate by all legitimate methods the restoration of the rural population to direct connection with the soil."

### *Anglo-Armenian Association*
Founded in 1878 to promote the execution of the 61st Article of the Treaty of Berlin and to encourage European Powers generally to exert pressure on the government of Turkey to grant greater independence to the inhabitants of Armenia [no membership lists available before 1886].

### *Anglo-French Intervention Committee*
Founded in 1870 by positivists and the Land and Labour League to agitate in support of the French republican movement and advocate "a defensive alliance with France against Prussia."

### *Anglo-Oriental Society for the Suppression of the Opium Trade*
Founded in 1875 to urge the British government to discourage the opium traffic and "restore to the Chinese Government perfect independence of action to deal with opium," through parliamentary action and "a vigorous appeal to the country."

### *Association for the Improvement of London Workhouse Infirmaries*
Founded in 1866 to promote the removal of the sick from workhouses, the establishment by local authorities of central infirmaries, and the creation of a general metropolitan rate for these purposes.

### *Association for the Improvement of Public Morals*
Founded in 1878 to raise the tone of public morality, assist prostitutes "to enter again upon an honourable mode of life," and reform laws "corrupting in their effects." [Part of the Anti-Contagious Diseases Acts movement.]

### *Association for Promoting the Extension of the Contagious Diseases Act, 1866, to the Civil Population of the United Kingdom*
Founded in 1867 to extend the medical inspection of prostitutes beyond military towns.

*Association of the Revivers of British Industry*
Founded in 1869 to advocate protective duties on manufactured imports.

*British Women's Temperance Association*
Founded in 1876 to promote temperance generally and to secure legislation to enforce the Sunday closing of public houses.

*Central Association for Stopping the Sale of Intoxicating Liquors on Sunday* (Later, the Sunday Closing Association)
Founded in 1866 to secure legislation prohibiting the sale of alcoholic beverages on Sunday.

*Central Brewers' License Repeal Association*
Founded in 1873 to agitate for repeal of brewing license legislation. Disbanded when its object was accomplished in 1880 [no membership lists].

*Central Vigilance Committee for the Suppression of Immorality*
Founded in 1883 to promote better enforcement of the laws and their amendment to facilitate the suppression of prostitution.

*Church Association*
Founded in 1865 as an evangelical watchdog group to encourage and support legal proceedings against ritualists and to secure stronger legislation against "Romanism" in the Church of England.

*Church League for the Separation of Church and State*
Founded in 1877 by High Churchmen to resist the subordination of the Church of England to lay courts, and in particular to agitate for the repeal or amendment of the Public Worship Regulation Act of 1874 [no membership lists].

*Church and State Defense Society*
Founded in 1868 to resist disestablishment and disendowment of the Church of England and the Church of Ireland [no membership lists].

*City Church and Churchyard Protection Society*
Founded in 1880 to oppose the demolition of London churches and churchyards by raising public agitation and opposing legislation to facilitate such destruction.

*Commons Preservation Society*
Founded in 1865 to oppose the enclosure of commons by public agitation, legal proceedings, and legislation.

*Eastern Question Association*
Founded in 1876 to oppose Disraeli's foreign policy and continued Turkish misrule of its Eastern European provinces.

*English Land Restoration League* (later, the English League for the Taxation of Land Values)
Founded in 1883 to support Henry George's "single tax" on land values, until "the whole annual value" of land "is taken for the public benefit" and "the English people themselves" become "the landlords of England."

*Financial Reform Union*
Founded in 1868 to campaign for "a large reduction in national expenditure" and "the further remission of duties on articles of general consumption."

*Free Land League*

Founded ca. 1885 to secure "free trade in land" by abolition of primogeniture, copyhold and customary tenure, manorial rights, and strict settlement and the promotion of title registration, commons preservation, enfranchisement of long leaseholds, and tenant right. Also promoted "the acquirement of land by the people for residence and cultivation, both by general laws and by the instrumentality of municipal bodies."

*Howard Association for Promoting the Most Efficient Means of Penal Treatment and Crime Prevention*
(later, the Howard League for Penal Reform)
Founded in 1866 to promote prison reform and the abolition of capital punishment.

*Imperial Federation League*

Founded in 1884 to "use every constitutional means" and "the support of men of all political parties" to "secure by Federation the permanent unity of the Empire."

*Indian Reform Association*

Founded ca. 1884(?) to promote reform of Indian administration generally and in particular the Indian civil service.

*Infant Life Protection Society*

Founded in 1870 to promote legislation regulating baby-farming, remove destitute children from workhouse nurseries, and amend the laws of bastardy, birth and death registration, and evidence in cases of infanticide.

*International Arbitration and Peace Association*

Founded in 1880 to agitate for a system of international arbitration, an international congress to frame an international code, and an international tribunal, and the reduction of standing armies and navies.

*International Law Association* (also, the Association for the Reform and Codification of the Law of Nations)
Founded in 1873 to promote international law and arbitration.

*Jamaica Committee*

Founded in 1866 to press for an official inquiry into the suppression of the Jamaican rebellion of 1865 and the criminal prosecution of Governor Eyre.

*Kyrle Society*

Founded in 1877 to "place objects of beauty within reach of the poor," and later extended its activities to agitation for preservation of disused burial grounds and other open spaces.

*Ladies' National Association for the Repeal of the Contagious Diseases Acts* (later, the Ladies' National Association for the Abolition of State Regulation of Vice and for the Promotion of Social Purity)
Founded in 1869 to fight further extension and promote the repeal of legislation providing for mandatory medical inspection of prostitutes.

*Land Law Reform League*

Founded ca. 1881 to bring public pressure on parliament for the amendment of the land laws. Sought to end primogeniture and entail, make land transfer cheap and easy, require registration of all dealings in land, abolish the game laws, and end preferential rights of landlords over other creditors. Also promoted tenant right, a graduated land tax, and the cultivation of "all lands now uncultivated" which were cultivable.

*Land Nationalisation Society*

Founded in 1881 to restore the "land and all below it to the Crown in trust for the nation" and the guarantee of "universal rights to small holdings for cultivation or residential occupation," security of tenure, revaluation of land every thirty years to secure the "unearned increment" to the community, and the extinction of present landlords' legal claims by terminable annuities.

*Land Tenure Reform Association*

Founded in 1869 (first public meeting in 1871) to secure "free trade in land, just as we had a League for free trade in Corn." Advocated abolition of primogeniture, taxation of unearned increment, cooperative agriculture, easy land transfer, and peasant proprietorship. Sought to empower the State to take control of waste land for national use and "objects of historical, scientific, or artistic interest," with compensation of owners.

*League for the Defense of Constitutional Rights*

Founded in 1881 to agitate against the exclusion of Charles Bradlaugh from the House of Commons.

*Liberty and Property Defense League*

Founded in 1882 to oppose "all attempts to introduce the State as competitor or regulator into the various departments of social activity and industry, which would otherwise be spontaneously and adequately conducted by private enterprise."

*Local Taxation Committee*

Founded in 1869 by the Central Chamber of Agriculture to press for reduction of the land tax and to guard against legislation which would increase the burden of the local rates on agriculture.

*London Committee for the Exposure and Suppression of the Foreign Traffic in British Girls for Purposes of Continental Prostitution*

Founded in 1880 to press for changes in English and Belgian law and to bring criminal prosecutions against those connected with the traffic.

*London Municipal Reform League*

Founded in 1881 to promote representative municipal government for the whole of London.

*London Society for the Abolition of Compulsory Vaccination*

Founded ca. 1880.

*Malthusian League*

Founded in 1877 to agitate against all penalties for publishing or discussing birth control, and to spread knowledge of the methods of birth control

*Metropolitan Free Libraries Association* (originally, the Metropolitan Free Libraries Committee)

Founded in 1877 to promote reference and lending libraries by "the further adoption of the Public Libraries Act" and its amendment.

*Metropolitan Public Gardens Association* (originally, the Metropolitan Public Garden, Boulevard, and Playground Association)

Founded in 1883 to promote the preservation and creation of open spaces both by philanthropic action and by bringing pressure to bear on both local and national authorities.

*National Association for Promoting State Colonization* (also, the National Association for the Promotion of State-directed Emigration and Colonization).

Founded in 1883 to agitate for a national program to finance and organize large-scale emigration from England and colonization in British colonies.

*National Association for Repeal of the Blasphemy Laws*
Founded in 1883.

*National Association for Repeal of the Contagious Diseases Acts* (also, the National Anti-Contagious Diseases Acts Association; also, the National Association for the Abolition of the State Regulation of Vice)
Founded in 1869 to fight further extension and promote repeal of legislation providing for the compulsory medical inspection of prostitutes.

*National Education League*
Founded in 1869 to promote free, unsectarian, and compulsory public education.

*National Education Union*
Founded in 1869 to promote a complete system of national education "to harmonize with the existing framework." Opposed "throwing the whole burden of education on the rates."

*National Emigration League*
Founded in 1870 to press for a program of state-subsidized emigration.

*National Fair Trade League*
Founded in 1881 to raise support for the reimposition of tariffs on manufactured goods from those foreign states which levied tariffs on English goods. Also advocated "imperial preference."

*National Footpaths Preservation Society*
Founded in 1884 to protect all rights of way by land and water and preserve open spaces by bringing legal action against encroaching landlords and promoting changes in the law. Amalgamated with the Commons Preservation Society in 1899.

*National Secular Society*
Founded in 1866 to promote repeal of the blasphemy laws, the removal of religious instruction from schools, and the dissemination of free-thought principles. Also advocated compulsory secular education, disestablishment and disendowment of the Church of England, reform of the land laws, and abolition of the House of Lords.

*National Society for Preserving the Memorials of the Dead*
Founded in 1881 to protect church and churchyard memorials by "carefully watching" restoration and rebuilding of churches and guarding against encroachment of churchyards, and by obtaining "legislation on behalf of the objects of the society."

*National Vigilance Association*
Founded in 1885 to "enforce and improve the laws for the repression of criminal vice and public immorality, to check the causes of vice, and to protect minors."

*Patrons Defense Association*
Founded ca. 1876 to resist the transference of livings from lay patrons to the bishops.

*Plimsoll and Seamen's Fund Committee*
Founded in 1873 to support Samuel Plimsoll's campaign to protect the lives and working conditions of seamen. Advocated legislation to prevent overloading and the sending of unseaworthy vessels to sea.

*Proportional Representation Society*
Founded in 1884 to agitate for the adoption of proportional representation balloting in national elections.

*Public Museums and Free Libraries Association*
Founded ca. 1868 to press for the opening of "the national collections" on week-day evenings and the adoption of the Free Libraries and Museums Acts.

*Railway Passengers Protection Association*
Founded ca. 1882 to agitate for the removal of "unjust or vexatious" regulations made by railway companies and to obtain redress for loss or inconvenience. Advocated legislation for better regulation of railway and canal traffic.

*Sanitary Institute of Great Britain*
Founded in 1876 to advance all subjects bearing upon public health by collecting information, encouraging public discussion, and promoting legislation.

*Smoke Abatement Committee* (later, the National Smoke Abatement Institution)
Founded in 1881 by the National Health Society and the Kyrle Society to promote the abatement of noxious smoke by encouraging public discussion and technical innovation, conducting practical trials, and promoting enactment and enforcement of legislation and regulations.

*Society for the Abolition of Vivisection*
Founded in 1875. Amalgamated in 1876 with the Society for the Total Abolition and Utter Suppression of Vivisection.

*Society for Promoting the Increase of the Home Episcopate*
Founded ca. 1866 to promote legislation creating new sees for the Church of England.

*Society for the Protection of Ancient Buildings*
Founded in 1877 to halt the destruction or drastic "restoration" of historically and aesthetically important buildings by bringing pressure to bear on the responsible authorities and arousing public opinion (first annual meeting, June, 1878).

*State Resistance Union*
Founded in 1882 to "coordinate the political forces at its disposal" to resist the interference of the State "outside its proper limits."

*Sunday Society*
Founded in 1875 to obtain the opening of museums, art galleries, libraries, aquariums, and gardens on Sundays.

*Travelling Tax Abolition Committee*
Founded in 1877 to agitate for the "unconditional abolition" of the railway passenger duty.

*Victoria Street Society for the Protection of Animals from Vivisection*
Founded in 1876 to promote legislation banning vivisection.

*Vigilance Association for the Defense of Personal Rights and the Amendment of the Law Wherein It Is Injurious to Women* (later, the Personal Rights Association)
Founded in 1871 "to uphold the principle of the perfect equality of all persons before the law, irrespective of sex or class."

*Working Men's Committee for Promoting the Separation of Church and State*
Founded in 1871 by the Liberation Society to create working class support for the disestablishment of the Church of England.

*Working Men's National League for the Abolition of the State Regulation of Vice*
   Founded in 1875. Part of the Anti-Contagious Diseases Acts movement.

*Working Men's Protestant League*
   Organized in the 1870s by evangelicals to oppose ritualism in the Church of England.

*Workmen's National Association for the Abolition of the Foreign Sugar Bounties*
   Active in the early 1880s. Promoted retaliation with duties against sugar grown in countries where growers received state subsidies.

*Workmen's Peace Association*
   Founded in 1871 to promote international arbitration and the abolition of armed forces.

# AGITATORS AND PROMOTERS
# IN THE AGE OF GLADSTONE AND DISRAELI

ABBOT, REGINALD CHARLES EDWARD, 3RD BARON COLCHESTER
    (1842-1919)

    Eton;  Christ Church, Oxf;  Lincoln's Inn.
    Barrister 67;  College Fellow 64.
    Conservative.  Charity Commissioner 80-83, DL, JP.
    Baron 67.
    Fellow Society of Antiquaries;  Fellow Royal
        Geograph Society.
    Southwest London;  Sussex.
    [WWW, BP, Walfords, Alum Oxon, Fosters]

    Natl Education Union 71-79, Exec.
    Natl Emigration League (F) 70-70, V-Pres.


ABBOTT, SIR FREDERICK (1805-1892)

    Warfield School, Berks;  U Munich;  Addiscombe Mil
        College.
    Maj. General, RE 58;  Lieutenant, RE 24;  Captain,
        RE 32;  Major, RE 43;  Lt. Colonel, RE 46;
        College Head 51.
    CB 46;  Kt 54.
    Kent.
    [DNB, MEB, BP, Walfords]

    Church Assn 80-80, Exec.


ABEL, SIR FREDERICK AUGUSTUS, 1ST BT. (1827-1902)

    Royal Polytec Instn;  U Munich;  Royal College
        Chemistry.
    Analytical Chemist 46;  College Lecturer 52;  War
        Dept Chemist 56.
    CB 77;  Kt 83;  KCB 91;  Baronet 93;  GCVO 01.
    Fellow Royal Society;  Society of the Arts;  Br
        Assn;  Fellow Chemical Society;  Inst of
        Chemistry;  Inst of Elec Engineers.
    Southeast London.
    [DNB, WWW, Alum Oxon, Alum Cantab]

    Smoke Abatement Committee (F) 81-81, Exec.


ABLEY, EDWARD

    Hereford.

    Jamaica Committee (F) 66-66.


ACHESON, ARCHIBALD BRABAZON SPARROW, 4TH EARL OF GOSFORD
    (1841-1922)

    Harrow.
    Very Large Landowner 64.
    Lord of the Bedchamber, P of W 86-01, V-Chamberlain
        Royal Household 01-  , JP.
    KP;  Earl 64.
    West London;  Co Armagh.
    [WWW, BP, Walfords, Bateman]

    Natl Assn for Promotion of State Colonization
        86-86, Patron.


ACLAND, SIR HENRY WENTWORTH, 1ST BT.  (1815-1900)

    Harrow;  Christ Church, Oxf;  St George's Hospital
        Lond.
    Aldrichian Professor of Clinical Medicine, Oxford
        51;  College Fellow 40.
    CB 83;  KCB 84;  Baronet 90.
    Fellow Royal Society;  Fellow Royal Col Physicians;
        Br Medical Assn.
    Oxford.
    [DNB, MEB, WWW, BP, Alum Cantab, Alum Oxon]

    Assn for Promoting Extension of Contagious Diseases
        Act 68-70, Exec.


ACLAND, SIR THOMAS DYKE, 11TH BT.  (1809-1898)

    Harrow;  Christ Church, Oxf.
    Very Large Landowner 71;  College Fellow 31.
    Liberal.  MP Somersetshire West 37-47, Devonshire
        North 65-85, Wellington<Som> 85-86.  Church
        Estates Commissioner 69-74.
    Baronet 71;  PC 83.
    Devonshire;  Somersetshire.
    [DNB, MEB, WWW, BP, Bateman, Alum Oxon, Dods]

    Assn for Improvement of London Workhouse
        Infirmaries 66-66, Exec.


ACTON, ROGER

    London.

    Jamaica Committee (F) 66-66.


ACWORTH, SIR WILLIAM MITCHELL (1850-1925)

    Uppingham;  Christ Church, Oxf;  Inner Temple.
    School Asst Head 75;  Barrister 90;  College
        Lecturer.
    Conservative.
    Kt 21;  KCSI 22.
    Royal Economic Society.
    Southeast London;  Devonshire.
    [DNB, WWW, Alum Cantab, Alum Oxon]

    Railway Passengers' Protection Assn 86-86, Exec.


ADAMS, -

    Northampton.

    League for Defense of Constitutional Rights 84-84,
        V-Pres.


ADAMS, ANNIE

    Chester.

    British Women's Temperance Assn 85-85, Exec.

ADAMS, CHARLES

> Victoria Street Soc for Protection of Animals from
>   Vivisection 82-82, Secretary.

ADAMS, COLE A.

> Kyrle Soc 84-90, Exec.

ADAMS, FRANCIS

> Author.
> Birmingham.

> Natl Education League (F) 69-77, Secretary.

ADAMS, G. E. D'ARCY

> Physician.
> West London.

> Sanitary Institute 81-84, Exec.

ADAMSON, JOSEPH SAMUEL

> Lt. Colonel 55; Ensign, Army 31; Lieutenant,
>   Army 33; Captain, Army 37; Major 51.
> Dublin.
> [Army List]

> Assn for Promoting Extension of Contagious Diseases
>   Act 68-70, V-Pres.

ADAMSON, WILLIAM

> Ordained Priest<CE>.

> Church Assn 80-80, Exec.

ADDERLEY, CHARLES BOWYER, 1ST BARON NORTON (1814-1905)

> Christ Church, Oxf.
> Substantial Landowner 26; Colliery Owner 26.
> Conservative. MP Staffordshire North 41-78. Pres
>   Board of Health 58-59, V-P Education Committee
>   58-59, Parl U-Sec Col Off 66-68, Pres Board of
>   Trade 74-78, Education Committee 83-84,
>   Education Committee 87-87, DL, JP.
> KCMG 69; Baron 78; PC 58.
> Southwest London; Warwickshire.
> [DNB, WWW, BP, Walfords, Bateman, Alum Oxon, Dods]

> Central Vigilance Comtee for Repression Immorality
>   (F) 83-84, V-Pres.

ADDINGTON, WILLIAM WELLS, 3RD VISCOUNT SIDMOUTH
  (1824-1913)

> Large Landowner 64; Lieutenant, RN 46.
> Conservative. MP Devizes 63-64. DL, JP.
> Viscount 64.
> Southwest London; Devonshire; Berkshire.
> [WWW, BP, Walfords, Bateman, Dods]

> Victoria Street Soc for Protection of Animals from
>   Vivisection 82-85, V-Pres.

Natl Education Union 70-79, Exec.

ADLAM, SOPHIA HARFORD <MRS. WILLIAM ADLAM, nee PARKER>

> Somersetshire.

> Victoria Street Soc for Protection of Animals from
>   Vivisection 80-85, Exec.

ADLAM, WILLIAM (1814- )

> Landowner 58.
> JP.
> Fellow Society of Antiquaries.
> Somersetshire.
> [Walfords]

> Victoria Street Soc for Protection of Animals from
>   Vivisection 84-85, V-Pres.

AGNEW, WILLIAM (1825-1910)

> Swedenborgian School, Salford.
> Publisher 70; Art Dealer 50.
> Liberal. MP Lancashire SE 80-85, Stretford, Lancs
>   SE 85-86. JP.
> Baronet 95.
> West London; Lancashire.
> [DNB, WWW, Dods]

> Free Land League 86-86, V-Pres.
> Intl Arbitration & Peace Assn 81-81, V-Pres.

AITCHISON, GEORGE (1825-1910)

> Merchant Taylors; University Col London; Royal
>   Academy Sch.
> Architect 59.
> Royal Academy; Fellow Royal Inst Br Architects.
> West London.
> [DNB, WWW]

> Soc for Protection of Ancient Buildings (F) 78-80,
>   Exec.

AITKEN, D.

> Clergyman<Sect Unkn>.
> Derbyshire.

> Jamaica Committee (F) 66-66.

AKROYD, EDWARD HALIFAX (1810-1887)

> Textile Manufacturer.
> Liberal. MP Huddersfield 57-59, Halifax 65-74.
>   DL, JP.
> Fellow Society of Antiquaries.
> Southwest London; Halifax.
> [MEB, Walfords, Dods]

> Natl Education Union (F) 69-79, Treas, Exec.

ALBRIGHT, ARTHUR (1810-1900)

    Phosphorus Manufacturer.
    Radical.
    Birmingham.
    [MEB, Direc Direcs]

    Allotments & Small Holdings Assn 85-88, V-Pres.
    Anglo-Oriental Soc for Suppression Opium Trade (F)
        75-75, Exec.


ALCOCK, SIR RUTHERFORD (1809-1897)

    Consul-General 58;  Consul 44;  Army Medical
        Service 32.
    Ambassador 59-71.
    CB 60;  KCB 62.
    Fellow Royal Geograph Society;  Royal Asiatic
        Society;  Fellow Royal Col Surgeons.
    Southwest London.
    [DNB, MEB, WWW, Direc Direcs, Alum Oxon]

    Plimsoll and Seamen's Fund Committee (F) 73-73,
        Exec.


ALCOCK, THOMAS ST. LEGER ( -1882)

    Major 44;  Ensign, Army 22;  Lieutenant, Army 26;
        Captain, Army 32.
    West London.
    [MEB, Army List]

    Commons Preservation Soc 69-82, Exec.


ALDER, THOMAS P.

    Newington<?>.

    Jamaica Committee (F) 66-66.


ALDER, WILLIAM S.

    Sunday Society 76-76, Exec.


ALDIS, WILLIAM STEADMAN (1839-1928)

    City of London School;  Trinity, Camb.
    Private Tutor;  College Professor 70.
    Cambridge.
    [Alum Cantab]

    Jamaica Committee (F) 66-66.


ALDRIDGE, JOHN H.

    Physician.
    Southampton.

    Assn for Promoting Extension of Contagious Diseases
        Act 68-68, Exec.


ALEXANDER, EDWARD, JUN.

    Glasgow.

    Jamaica Committee (F) 66-66.


ALEXANDER, J.

    Jamaica Committee (F) 66-66.


ALEXANDER, JOSEPH GUNDRY (1848-1918)

    Lincoln's Inn.
    Barrister 74.
    Liberal.  JP.
    West Central London;  Croydon.
    [WWW, Fosters]

    Anglo-Oriental Soc for Suppression Opium Trade
        83-83, Hon Sec, Exec.
    Intl Law Assn 83-05, Hon Sec.


ALEXANDER, ROBERT (1798-1879)

    General 70;  Lieutenant, Army 19;  Captain, Army
        26;  Major 36;  Colonel 51;  Maj. General 54;
        Lt. General 65.
    Southwest London.
    [MEB, Army List]

    Anglo-Oriental Soc for Suppression Opium Trade (F)
        75-75, Exec.


ALEXANDER, WILLIAM CLEVERLY (1840-1916)

    West London;  Sussex.
    [WWW, Walfords]

    Soc for Protection of Ancient Buildings (F) 78-85,
        Exec.


ALFORD, CHARLES RICHARD (1816-1898)

    St Paul's, London;  Trinity, Camb.
    Vicar 74;  Ordained Priest<CE> 40;  Curate 39;
        Perp. Curate 43;  College Head 54;  Bishop
        Victoria 67.
    Lancashire;  Kent;  Canada.
    [MEB, WWW, Alum Cantab, Crockfds]

    Church Assn 75-80, V-Pres.


ALFRED ERNEST ALBERT, DUKE OF EDINBURGH AND OF
SAXE-COBURG AND GOTHA (1844-1900)

    Vice-Admiral 82;  Midshipman, RN 58;  Lieutenant,
        RN 63;  Captain, RN 66;  Rear Admiral 78;
        Admiral 87;  Admiral of the Fleet 93.
    KG 63;  KT 64;  Duke 66;  GCMG 69;  GCSI 70;  KP
        80;  GCB 89.
    Southwest London.
    [DNB, MEB, BP, Navy List]

    Kyrle Soc 84-94, President.

ALLAN, WILLIAM (1837- )

    Worcester, Oxf.
    Vicar 74;  Curate 60;  Ordained Priest<CE> 61.
    Southeast London.
    [Alum Oxon, Crockfds]

    Church Assn 75-85, V-Pres, Exec.


ALLBUTT, H. ARTHUR

    Physician.
    Member Royal Col Physicians, Edinburgh.
    Leeds.

    Malthusian League 79-84, V-Pres, Exec.


ALLCROFT, JOHN DERBY (1822-1893)

    Clothing Manufacturer;  Large Landowner 67.
    Conservative.  MP Worcestershire 78-80.
    Fellow Royal Geograph Society;  Royal Agricultural
        Society;  Assoc Royal Academy.
    West London;  Shropshire.
    [MEB, Bateman, Dods]

    Church Assn 75-85, V-Pres.


ALLEN, GEORGE

    Kings Col London.
    Vicar 60;  Curate 55;  Ordained Priest<CE> 56;
        Chaplain 57;  Perp. Curate 59.
    North London.
    [Crockfds]

    Natl Education Union 70-79, Exec.


ALLEN, H. G.

    Free Land League 86-86, V-Pres.


ALLEN, HUGH (1806-1877)

    Trin Col, Dublin.
    Rector 59;  Ordained Priest<CE> 35;  Curate 38;
        Vicar 48;  Newspaper Editor 62.
    Southeast London.
    [MEB, Alum Cantab]

    Assn for Improvement of London Workhouse
        Infirmaries 66-66, Exec.
    Natl Emigration League (F) 70-70, V-Pres.


ALLEN, RICHARD (1803-1886)

    Textile Manufacturer 19.
    Dublin.
    [MEB, Friends]

    Howard Assn 78-82, Exec.
    Jamaica Committee (F) 66-66.


ALLEN, STAFFORD (1806-1889)

    Drug Miller 33.
    Radical.
    North London.
    [MEB, Friends]

    Howard Assn 67-84, Exec.
    Jamaica Committee (F) 66-66.


ALLEN, WILLIAM SHEPHERD (1831-1915)

    Wadham, Oxf.
    Liberal.  MP Newcastle-under-Lyme 65-86.  DL, JP.
    West Central London;  Newcastle-under-Lyme;
        Staffordshire.
    [WWW, Alum Oxon, Dods, Direc Direcs]

    Central Assn for Stopping Sale Intox Liquors on
        Sunday 75-85, V-Pres.


ALLIES, THOMAS WILLIAM (1813-1903)

    Eton;  Wadham, Oxf.
    Professor of Modern History, Catholic U of Ireland,
        Dublin 55;  College Fellow 33;  Ordained
        Priest<CE> 38;  Curate 39;  Chaplain 40;  Vicar
        42;  Private Tutor 50.
    West London.
    [DNB, Alum Oxon]

    Natl Education Union (F) 69-79, Exec.


ALLISON, SIR ROBERT ANDREW (1838-1926)

    Rugby;  Trinity, Camb.
    Landowner 62.
    Radical.  MP Cumberland North 85-00.  DL, JP.
    Kt 10.
    Southwest London;  Cumberland.
    [WWW, Walfords, Alum Cantab, Dods, Direc Direcs]

    Free Land League 86-86, V-Pres.


ALLNUTT, HENRY (1813-1898)

    Drainage Engineer 57.
    West London.
    [MEB]

    Natl Footpaths Preservation Soc (F) 84-98,
        Secretary.


ALSOP, ROBERT ( -1875)

    "In business".
    North London.
    [Friends]

    Howard Assn 67-75, Exec.

AMOS, SHELDON (1835-1886)

Charterhouse; Clare, Camb; Middle Temple.
Professor of Jurisprudence, U Col London 69;
    Barrister 62; Court of Appeal Judge, Egypt 79.
West Central London; Egypt.
[DNB, MEB, Fosters, Alum Cantab]

Anglo-Oriental Soc for Suppression Opium Trade (F)
    75-84, Exec.
Sunday Society 76-85, V-Pres.
Intl Law Assn 74-74, Exec.


ANCRUM, W. R.

Physician.
Gloucester.

Assn for Promoting Extension of Contagious Diseases
    Act 68-70, V-Pres.


ANDERSEN, GEORGE

Civil Engineer.

Malthusian League 78-84, V-Pres.


ANDERSON, A.

Lancashire.

Jamaica Committee (F) 66-66.


ANDERSON, CHARLES HENRY (1838-1889)

Inner Temple.
Q.C. 85; Barrister 67.
Radical. MP Elgin & Nairn 86-89.
West London.
[Dods]

Free Land League 86-86, V-Pres.


ANDERSON, DAVID (1814-1885)

Edinburgh Academy; Exeter, Oxf.
Vicar 64; Ordained Priest<CE> 37; Curate 37;
    College V-Principal 41; Perp. Curate 48;
    Bishop Rupert's Land 49.
Bristol.
[MEB, Alum Oxon, Crockfds]

Assn for Promoting Extension of Contagious Diseases
    Act 68-70, V-Pres.
Church Assn 75-80, V-Pres.


ANDERSON, GEORGE (1819-1896)

Edinburgh High School; U St Andrews.
Merchant; Deputy Master, Melbourne Mint 85.
Radical. MP Glasgow 68-85.
Fifeshire.
[MEB, Walfords, Dods]

Intl Arbitration & Peace Assn 81-81, V-Pres.


ANDERSON, GEORGE

Gas Engineer.
Southwest London.
[Direc Direcs]

Natl Secular Soc 81-84, V-Pres.


ANDERSON, SIR HENRY LACON (1817-1879)

St Paul's, London; St Johns, Oxf; Lincoln's Inn.
India Civil Service 40; Judge, India 53; Sec,
    Govt of Bombay 54; Chief Sec, Govt of Bombay
    60; Sec, India Board 66.
Council of India 63-65.
KCSI 67.
Fellow Royal Geograph Society.
West London.
[MEB, Walfords]

Assn for Promoting Extension of Contagious Diseases
    Act 68-70, V-Pres.


ANDERSON, WILLIAM (1799-1873)

Presbyterian Minister 22.
Radical.
Glasgow.
[DNB, MEB]

Jamaica Committee (F) 66-66.


ANDREWS, H. GENGE

Local Taxation Comtee [of Central Chamber of
    Agriculture] 71-71, Exec.


ANDREWS, THOMAS R.

Church Assn 67-80, V-Chairman, Chairman.


ANGUS, H.

Newcastle-upon-Tyne.

Assn for Promoting Extension of Contagious Diseases
    Act 68-68, V-Pres.


ANNESLEY, HUGH, 5TH EARL ANNESLEY (1831-1908)

Eton; Trin Col, Dublin.
Lt. Colonel 60; Ensign, Army 51; Lieutenant,
    Army 53; Captain, Army 55; Very Large
    Landowner 74.
Conservative. MP Cavan 57-74. DL, JP.
Earl 74.
West London; Co Down.
[WWW, BP, Bateman, Dods, Army List]

Assn for Promoting Extension of Contagious Diseases
    Act 68-70, V-Pres.

6

ANNINGSON, BUSHELL (1838-1916)

King's College School; Gonville & Caius, Camb.
College Lecturer 78; Surgeon 77.
Med Off of Health 75- .
Member Royal Col Surgeons.
Cambridge.
[WWW, Alum Cantab]

Sanitary Institute (F) 76-84, Exec.

ANSON, THOMAS GEORGE, 2ND EARL OF LICHFIELD (1825-1892)

Very Large Landowner 54.
Liberal. MP Lichfield, Staffs 47-54. Lord
Lieutenant 63-71.
Earl 54.
Fellow Royal Geograph Society.
West London; Staffordshire.
[BP, Dods, Bateman]

Public Museums & Free Libraries Assn 68-68, V-Pres.
Central Assn for Stopping Sale Intox Liquors on
Sunday 85-85, V-Pres.
Central Vigilance Comtee for Repression Immorality
(F) 83-84, V-Pres.
Howard Assn 68-84, Patron.
Plimsoll and Seamen's Fund Committee (F) 73-73,
Exec.

ANSTIE, FRANCIS EDMUND (1833-1874)

Kings College(Medical).
Physician 59; Journal Editor 68.
Member Royal Col Surgeons; Fellow Royal Col
Physicians.
West London.
[DNB, MEB]

Assn for Improvement of London Workhouse
Infirmaries 66-66, Hon Sec.

ANTROBUS, W. D. B.

Blackley.

Central Assn for Stopping Sale Intox Liquors on
Sunday (F) 67-70, Exec.

APPLEGARTH, ROBERT (1834-1924)

Trade Union Leader 62; Carpenter 58; Commercial
Traveller 72; Elec Light Merchant 80.
Radical.
Inst of Elec Engineers.
South London.
[WWW, Dic Lab Biog]

Natl Education League (F) 69-71, Exec.
Natl Emigration League (F) 70-70, Exec.
Working Men's Comtee Promoting Separation Church
and State (F) 71-71, Exec.

APPLETON, LEWIS

Intl Arbitration & Peace Assn 81-84, Secretary.

ARCH, JOSEPH (1826-1919)

Trade Union Leader 72; Agricultural Worker 35.
Radical. MP Norfolk Northwest 85-86, Norfolk
Northwest 92-00.
Warwickshire.
[DNB, WWW, Dods, Dic Lab Biog]

Allotments & Small Holdings Assn 85-88, Exec.
Free Land League 86-86, V-Pres.
Land Law Reform League (F) 81-84, V-Pres.
League for Defense of Constitutional Rights 84-84,
V-Pres.
Vigilance Assn for Defense of Personal Rights
83-83, Exec.

ARDEN, DOUGLAS

Vigilance Assn for Defense of Personal Rights
83-83, Exec.

ARKWRIGHT, AUGUSTUS PETER (1821-1887)

Royal Naval College, Portsmouth.
Commander, RN 59; Captain, RN 74; Sub-Lieutenant,
RN 40.
Conservative. MP Derbyshire North 68-80.
Southwest London; Derbyshire.
[MEB, Walfords, Dods, Navy List]

Natl Education Union 71-79, Exec.

ARMITAGE, BENJAMIN (1823-1899)

Barton Hall.
Cotton Manufacturer.
Liberal. MP Salford 80-85, Salford West 85-86.
JP.
West London; Lancashire.
[MEB, Dods]

Sunday Society 80-90, V-Pres.
Free Land League 86-86, V-Pres.

ARMITAGE, EDWARD (1817-1896)

Artist.
Royal Academy; Fellow Royal Geograph Society.
Tunbridge Wells.
[MEB, DNB]

Sunday Society 86-90, V-Pres.

ARMITAGE, SIR ELKANAH (1794-1876)

Cotton Manufacturer 27; Handloom Weaver.
Kt 49.
Manchester; Lancashire.
[MEB]

Assn for Promoting Extension of Contagious Diseases
Act 68-70, V-Pres.

ARMITSTEAD, GEORGE, 1ST BARON ARMITSTEAD (1824-1915)

> U Heidelberg.
> Merchant.
> Liberal. MP Dundee 68-73, Dundee 80-85. DL, JP.
> Baron 06.
> Fellow Royal Geograph Society.
> Southwest London; Perthshire.
> [BP, Walfords, Dods, Direc Direcs]

> Natl Assn for Repeal Contagious Diseases Acts
>     81-81, V-Pres.

ARMSTRONG, SIR ALEXANDER (1818-1899)

> Edinburgh(Medical).
> Dir Gen, RN Medical Serv 69; Asst Surgeon, RN
>     Medical Serv 42; Surgeon, RN Medical Serv 49;
>     Dep Insp Gen, RN Medical Serv 58; Insp Gen, RN
>     Medical Serv 66.
> KCB 71.
> Member Royal Col Physicians; Fellow Royal Col
>     Physicians; Fellow Royal Society.
> Chatham; West London; Nottinghamshire.
> [DNB, MEB, WWW, BP, Direc Direcs]

> Assn for Promoting Extension of Contagious Diseases
>     Act 68-70, V-Pres.

ARMSTRONG, JOHN

> Physician.
> Gravesend.

> Assn for Promoting Extension of Contagious Diseases
>     Act 68-70, V-Pres.

ARMSTRONG, THOMAS (1832-1911)

> Artist 53; Dir Art, South Kensington 81.
> CB 98.
> West London; Hertfordshire.
> [DNB, WWW]

> Soc for Protection of Ancient Buildings (F) 78-85,
>     Exec.

ARNEY, SIR GEORGE ALFRED (1806-1883)

> Winchester College; Brasenose, Oxf; Lincoln's
>     Inn.
> Barrister 37; Chief Justice, New Zealand 58;
>     Landowner 79.
> Kt 62.
> Torquay.
> [MEB, BP, Walfords, Alum Oxon, Dict New Zealand
>     Biog]

> Howard Assn 78-82, Patron.

ARNISON, WILLIAM CHRISTOPHER (1837-1899)

> Durham(Medical).
> Surgeon 62; Medical School Professor 92.
> Member Royal Col Surgeons.
> Newcastle-upon-Tyne.
> [MEB, WWW]

> Assn for Promoting Extension of Contagious Diseases
>     Act 68-68, Exec.

ARNOLD, A. J.

> Central Assn for Stopping Sale Intox Liquors on
>     Sunday 75-75, Secretary.

ARNOLD, SIR ARTHUR (1833-1902)

> Newspaper Editor 68; Surveyor; Novelist;
>     Inspector of Public Works 63; Harbour
>     Commissioner.
> Radical. MP Salford 80-85. JP.
> Kt 95.
> West London.
> [DNB, WWW, Alum Cantab, Dods]

> Free Land League 85-86, Chairman, President.
> Intl Arbitration & Peace Assn 81-81, V-Pres.
> Natl Assn for Repeal Contagious Diseases Acts
>     81-81, V-Pres.
> Plimsoll and Seamen's Fund Committee (F) 73-73,
>     Exec.

ARTHUR, WILLIAM (1819-1901)

> Hoxton Academy.
> Wesleyan Minister 42; College Head 68.
> West Central London; Belfast; West Central
>     London.
> [DNB, Wesl Min]

> Jamaica Committee (F) 66-66.
> Natl Assn for Repeal Contagious Diseases Acts
>     84-84, V-Pres.

ASHBURNHAM, THOMAS (1807-1872)

> Lt. General 60; Lieutenant, Army 23; Captain,
>     Army 26; Lt. Colonel 35; Colonel 46; Maj.
>     General 54; General 68.
> CB 46.
> West London.
> [MEB, BP, Walfords, Army List]

> Assn for Improvement of London Workhouse
>     Infirmaries 66-66, Exec.

ASHBY, RICHARD C.

> Central Vigilance Comtee for Repression Immorality
>     (F) 83-84, Hon Sec.

ASHBY, THOMAS, JUN.

> Surrey.

> Jamaica Committee (F) 66-66.

ASHLEY, ANTHONY EVELYN MELBOURNE (1836-1907)

> Harrow; Trinity, Camb; Lincoln's Inn.
> Barrister 63.
> Liberal(Unionist). MP Poole 74-80, Isle Of Wight
>     80-85. Parl Sec Board of Trade 80-82, Parl
>     U-Sec Col Off 82-85, Ecclesiastical
>     Commissioner 80-85, Church Estates Commissioner
>     80-85, DL, JP.
> PC 91.

Southwest London;  Hampshire.
[DNB, WWW, BP, Bateman, Alum Cantab, Fosters, Dods,
    Direc Direcs]

Victoria Street Soc for Protection of Animals from
    Vivisection 80-85, Treas, Exec.


ASHLEY, ANTHONY WILLIAM (1803-1877)

Christ Church, Oxf.
Hospital Head 59;  Attache, Dip Serv 30.
Treas Royal Household 34-49.
[MEB, BP, Alum Cantab]

Church Assn 75-75, V-Pres.


ASHLEY, LADY EDITH FLORENCE (1847-1913)

West London.
[BP]

Victoria Street Soc for Protection of Animals from
    Vivisection 82-85, Exec.


ASHURST, WILLIAM (1819-1879)

General Post Office Solicitor 62;  Solicitor 43.
West London.
[MEB]

Assn for Improvement of London Workhouse
    Infirmaries 66-66, Treas.
Infant Life Protection Soc 71-71, Exec.


ASHWORTH, EDMUND

Rochdale.

Jamaica Committee (F) 66-66.


ASTLEY, JOHN

Coventry.

Natl Soc for Preserving Memorials of Dead (F)
    81-82, Exec.


ASTON, JOHN WALTER (1853-1881)

St Johns, Oxf.
Curate 76;  Ordained Priest<CE> 77;  Vicar 78.
Cheltenham;  Westmorland.
[Alum Oxon, Crockfds]

Church Assn 78-78, Exec.


ATCHISON, ARTHUR TURNOUR (1846-1891)

Brighton College;  Christ's, Camb.
Civil Engineer.
Assoc Inst Civ Engineers.
Southwest London.
[Alum Cantab, Direc Direcs]

Smoke Abatement Committee 81-81, Exec.
Sunday Society 79-80, Exec.


ATHILL, CHARLES HAROLD ( -1922)

Heraldist 82.
MVO 11.
Fellow Society of Antiquaries.
Northwest London.
[WWW]

Natl Soc for Preserving Memorials of Dead (F)
    81-84, Exec.


ATKINSON, - <MRS. BEAVINGTON ATKINSON>

Kyrle Soc 84-90, Exec.


ATLAY, JAMES (1817-1894)

Oakham;  St John's, Camb.
Bishop Hereford 68;  College Fellow 42;  Ordained
    Priest<CE> 43;  Curate 43;  Vicar 47;  Rural
    Dean 59;  Canon 61.
Conservative.
Hereford.
[DNB, MEB, Alum Cantab, Crockfds]

Central Assn for Stopping Sale Intox Liquors on
    Sunday 70-85, V-Pres.
Soc for Promoting Increase of the Home Episcopate
    72-74, V-Pres.


ATTENBOROUGH, GEORGE

London.

Jamaica Committee (F) 66-66.


AURIOL, EDWARD (1835-1880)

Christ Church, Oxf.
Prebendary 65;  Rector 38.
West Central London.
[MEB, Alum Oxon, Crockfds]

Church Assn 67-78, Exec.


AUSTIN, JOHN SOUTHGATE

Trinity, Oxf.
Vicar 51;  Ordained Priest<CE> 40.
Bath.
[Alum Oxon, Crockfds]

Church Assn 85-85, Exec.


AVELING, EDWARD BIBBONS (1851-1898)

Independent College, Taunton;  University Col
    London;  London U(Medical).
College Fellow;  Medical School Professor 75;
    Author.
Radical.
West London.
[MEB]

Land Law Reform League (F) 81-84, V-Pres.
League for Defense of Constitutional Rights 84-84,
    V-Pres.
Natl Secular Soc 81-84, V-Pres.

AXON, WILLIAM EDWARD ARMYTAGE (1846-1913)

    Librarian; Journalist.
    Fellow Royal Society Literature.
    Manchester.
    [WWW]

    Sunday Society 79-90, V-Pres.

AYLMER, HENRY

    Maj. General, RA 64; Ensign, RA 31; Lieutenant,
       RA 33; Captain, RA 43; Major, RA 54; Lt.
       Colonel, RA 54; Colonel, RA 57.
    [Army List]

    Church Assn 85-85, V-Pres.

AYTON, WILLIAM ALEXANDER (1816-1909)

    Charterhouse; Trinity Hall, Camb.
    Vicar 68; Ordained Priest<CE> 43; Curate 46;
       Rector 50; Perp. Curate 63.
    Northamptonshire.
    [Alum Cantab, Crockfds]

    London Soc for Abolition of Compulsory Vaccination
       81-81, V-Pres.

BACKHOUSE, EDMUND (1824-1906)

    Friends' School, Tottenham.
    Banker.
    Liberal. MP Darlington 68-80. JP.
    West London; Yorks, North Riding.
    [Walfords, Dods]

    Howard Assn 72-80, Patron.
    Local Taxation Comtee [of Central Chamber of
       Agriculture] 71-85, Exec.

BACKHOUSE, EDWARD (1808-1879)

    Banker; Colliery Owner.
    Liberal. JP.
    Sunderland.
    [DNB, MEB, Friends]

    Assn for Improvement of Public Morals (F) 79-79,
       Exec.
    Central Assn for Stopping Sale Intox Liquors on
       Sunday 75-75, V-Pres.
    Jamaica Committee (F) 66-66.

BACKHOUSE, JAMES (1794-1869)

    Tatham's School, Leeds.
    Nursery Owner 16.
    York.
    [MEB, Friends]

    Jamaica Committee (F) 66-66.

BACKHOUSE, JAMES, JUN.

    York.

    Jamaica Committee (F) 66-66.

BACKHOUSE, KATHERINE E. <MRS. EDWARD BACKHOUSE, nee
    MOUNSEY>

    Sunderland.

    Assn for Improvement of Public Morals (F) 79-81,
       Exec.
    Ladies' Natl Assn for Repeal of Contagious Diseases
       Acts 70-72, Exec.

BACON, HENRY F.

    Bury St Edmunds.

    Natl Soc for Preserving Memorials of Dead (F)
       81-82, Exec.

BACON, J. P.

    London.

    Jamaica Committee (F) 66-66.

BAGEHOT, WALTER (1826-1877)

    University Col London; Lincoln's Inn.
    Journal Editor 55; Banker 52; Author.
    Liberal. JP.
    Somersetshire.
    [DNB, MEB]

    Assn for Improvement of London Workhouse
       Infirmaries 66-66, Exec.

BAGGE, SIR WILLIAM, 1ST BT. (1810-1880)

    Charterhouse; Balliol, Oxf.
    Landowner.
    Conservative. MP Norfolk West 37-57, Norfolk West
       65-80. DL, JP.
    Baronet 67.
    Southwest London; Norfolk.
    [MEB, BP, Walfords, Alum Oxon, Dods]

    Assn for Promoting Extension of Contagious Diseases
       Act 70-70, V-Pres.

BAGSHAWE, WILLIAM HENRY GUNNING (1825-1901)

    St Mary's, Oscott; University Col London; Middle
       Temple.
    Q.C. 74; Barrister 48; County Court Judge 81.
    JP.
    Northwest London.
    [WWW, Fosters]

    Soc for Abolition of Vivisection (F) 75-76, Exec.

BAHNS, -

   Workmen's Peace Assn 75-75, Exec.


BAILEY, -

   Workmen's Peace Assn 75-75, Exec.


BAILEY, JOSEPH GREENOAK

   Lincoln, Oxf.
   Chaplain 67;  Curate 62;  Ordained Priest<CE> 63;
      Vicar 78.
   Rochester.
   [Alum Oxon, Crockfds]

   Assn for Promoting Extension of Contagious Diseases
      Act 68-68, Exec.


BAILHACHE, CLEMENT (1830-1878)

   Stepney College.
   Baptist Minister 55.
   North London.
   [MEB]

   Jamaica Committee (F) 66-66.


BAILLIE, ALEXANDER DUNDAS ROSS COCHRANE-WISHEART-, 1ST
   BARON LAMINGTON (1816-1890)

   Eton;  Trinity, Camb.
   Very Large Landowner.
   Conservative.  MP Bridport 41-46, Bridport 47-52,
      Lanarkshire 57-57, Honiton 59-68, Isle Of Wight
      70-80.
   Baron 80.
   Southwest London;  Lanarkshire.
   [DNB, MEB, BP, Bateman, Alum Cantab, Dods]

   Natl Assn for Promotion of State Colonization
      86-86, V-Pres.


BAILY, J.  S.

   Vigilance Assn for Defense of Personal Rights
      83-83, Secretary.


BAIN, ALEXANDER (1818-1903)

   Marischal College.
   Professor of Logic and English, Aberdeen 60;
      College Lecturer 45;  Asst Sec, Board of Health
      48;  Ld Rector, U Aberdeen 81.
   Aberdeen.
   [DNB, WWW]

   Sunday Society (F) 75-90, V-Pres.


BAINES, SIR EDWARD (1800-1890)

   New College, Manchester.
   Newspaper Proprietor 27.
   Liberal.  MP Leeds 59-74.  DL, JP.
   Kt 80.
   Burley;  West London.
   [DNB, MEB, BP, Walfords, Dods]

   Central Assn for Stopping Sale Intox Liquors on
      Sunday 70-85, V-Pres.
   Jamaica Committee (F) 66-66.
   Natl Education Union 70-70, Exec.


BAINES, FREDERICK (1811-1893)

   Newspaper Proprietor.
   Leeds.
   [MEB]

   Jamaica Committee (F) 66-66.


BAIRD, JAMES (1802-1876)

   U Glasgow.
   Iron Manufacturer 30;  Colliery Owner 30;
      Landowner 53.
   Conservative.  MP Falkirk 51-57.  DL, JP.
   Glasgow;  Lanarkshire.
   [DNB, Walfords, Dods]

   Natl Education Union 75-76, Exec.


BAKER, - (MISS)

   Natl Vigilance Assn (F) 85-85, Exec.


BAKER, DANIEL

   Birmingham.

   Travelling Tax Abolition Committee (F) 77-85.


BAKER, GEORGE

   Birmingham.

   Natl Emigration League (F) 69-69, Exec.


BAKER, LAWRENCE JAMES (1827-1921)

   Stock Broker.
   Liberal.  MP Somersetshire Frome 85-86.
   Southwest London;  Surrey.
   [WWW, Dods, Direc Direcs]

   Free Land League 86-86, V-Pres.


BAKER, ROBERT (1803-1880)

   Factory Inspector 58;  Factory Sub-Inspector 34;
      Physician.
   CB 77.
   Leamington.
   [MEB]

   Natl Education Union 70-79, Exec.

BAKER, THOMAS (1819- )

    Inner Temple.
    Barrister 54;  Sec, Board of Health 50;  Sec, Home
       Office Burials Dept 54;  Sec, Salmon Fisheries
       Dept, Home Office 65.
    Wokingham.
    [Fosters]

    London Soc for Abolition of Compulsory Vaccination
       81-81, V-Pres.


BALFOUR, ALEXANDER (1824-1886)

    Shipowner.
    Liberal.
    Liverpool;  Wrexham.
    [MEB]

    Central Assn for Stopping Sale Intox Liquors on
       Sunday 75-80, V-Pres.
    Plimsoll and Seamen's Fund Committee (F) 73-73,
       Exec.


BALFOUR, EUSTACE JAMES ANTHONY (1854-1911)

    Harrow;  Trinity, Camb.
    Architect.
    Conservative.
    Fellow Society of Antiquaries;  Fellow Royal Inst
       Br Architects;  Fellow Zoological Society.
    West London;  East Lothian.
    [WWW, BP, Direc Direcs]

    Soc for Protection of Ancient Buildings (F) 78-85,
       Hon Sec.


BALL, GEORGE V.

    Banbury.

    Jamaica Committee (F) 66-66.


BALLANTINE, ROBERT FREDERICK

    Captain, RA 72;  Ensign, RA 62;  Lieutenant, RA 66.
    Glamorganshire.
    [Army List]

    Central Assn for Stopping Sale Intox Liquors on
       Sunday 85-85, Exec.


BALLISTON. W. H. T.

    "Admiralty".
    Southwest London.

    Railway Passengers' Protection Assn 86-86, Exec.


BANCROFT, GEORGE

    Central Assn for Stopping Sale Intox Liquors on
       Sunday (F) 67-70, Exec.


BANKS, - <MRS. FREDERICK CHARLES BANKS>

    Natl Assn for Repeal Contagious Diseases Acts
       84-84, Exec.


BANKS, FREDERICK CHARLES

    Natl Assn for Repeal Contagious Diseases Acts
       81-84, Secretary.


BANKS, SIR JOHN THOMAS (1812-1908)

    Trin Col, Dublin;  Royal College Surgeons Med Sch.
    Physician 43;  Medical School Professor 49.
    DL, JP.
    KCB 89.
    Royal Col Physicians, Ireland;  Dublin Pathological
       Society;  Royal Academy of Medicine, Ire.
    Dublin.
    [DNB, WWW]

    Assn for Promoting Extension of Contagious Diseases
       Act 68-70, V-Pres.


BANNISTER, EDWARD

    Church Assn 75-85, Exec.


BARBOUR, ROBERT (1797-1885)

    U Glasgow.
    Merchant;  Substantial Landowner 57.
    DL, JP.
    Cheshire.
    [MEB, Walfords, Bateman]

    Central Assn for Stopping Sale Intox Liquors on
       Sunday 75-80, V-Pres.


BARBOUR, WILLIAM BOYLE (1828-1891)

    Merchant.
    Radical.  MP Paisley 85-91.
    Paisley.
    [MEB, Dods]

    Free Land League 86-86, V-Pres.


BARCLAY, A. C.

    Assn for Improvement of London Workhouse
       Infirmaries 66-66, Exec.


BARCLAY, JAMES WILLIAM (1832-1907)

    Aberdeen Grammar School;  U Aberdeen.
    Merchant;  Shipowner;  Farmer.
    Liberal(Unionist).  MP Forfarshire 72-92.
    West London.
    [Dods, Direc Direcs]

    Natl Assn for Promotion of State Colonization
       86-86, V-Pres.

BARFOOT, WILLIAM (1828-1916)

    Yarn Manufacturer;  Hosiery Manufacturer.
    JP.
    Leicester.
    [Direc Direcs]

    Sunday Society 76-90, V-Pres.

BARLOW, JAMES

    Bolton.

    Central Assn for Stopping Sale Intox Liquors on
       Sunday (F) 67-70, V-Pres.

BARNARD, J.  E.

    Stroud.

    Jamaica Committee (F) 66-66.

BARNARD, JABEZ

    Jamaica Committee (F) 66-66.

BARNARD, W.

    North London.

    Jamaica Committee (F) 66-66.

BARNES, F.  W.

    Croydon.

    London Municipal Reform League 82-85, Exec.

BARNES, J.  W.

    Durham[City].

    Soc for Protection of Ancient Buildings (F) 78-85,
       Exec.

BARNES, ROBERT

    DL, JP.

    Central Assn for Stopping Sale Intox Liquors on
       Sunday 70-70, V-Pres.

BARNES, THOMAS (1813- )

    Cotton Manufacturer;  Merchant.
    Liberal.  MP Bolton 52-57, Bolton 61-68.  DL, JP.
    Denbighshire;  Lancashire.
    [Walfords, Dods]

    Jamaica Committee (F) 66-66.

BARNETT, HENRY (1815-1896)

    Eton;  Christ Church, Oxf.
    Banker.
    Conservative.  MP Woodstock 65-74.  DL, JP.
    West London;  Berkshire.
    [MEB, Alum Oxon, Direc Direcs]

    Assn for Promoting Extension of Contagious Diseases
       Act 68-70, V-Pres.

BARR, WILLIAM ALEXANDER

    Physician.
    Member Royal Col Surgeons.
    Northampton.

    Assn for Promoting Extension of Contagious Diseases
       Act 68-68, Exec.

BARRAN, SIR JOHN, 1ST BT.  (1821-1905)

    Merchant;  Clothing Manufacturer.
    Liberal.  MP Leeds 76-85, Otley, Yorks WR E 86-95.
       JP.
    Baronet 95.
    Southwest London;  Leeds.
    [WWW, BP, Dods]

    Howard Assn 78-84, Patron.

BARRETT, RICHARD

    Howard Assn 82-84, Exec.

BARROW, C.

    Lancaster.

    Jamaica Committee (F) 66-66.

BARRY, ALFRED (1826-1910)

    King's College School;  Trinity, Camb;  Inner
       Temple.
    College Head 68;  School Asst Head 49;  Ordained
       Priest<CE> 53;  School Head 54;  Canon 71;
       Bishop Sydney 84;  Rector 95.
    Northwest London.
    [DNB, WWW, Alum Cantab, Alum Oxon, Crockfds]

    Assn for Promoting Extension of Contagious Diseases
       Act 70-70, V-Pres.
    Natl Education Union (F) 69-79, Hon Sec.

BARRY, CHARLES (1823-1900)

    Architect 40.
    Fellow Royal Inst Br Architects;  Fellow Society of
       Antiquaries.
    West London.
    [MEB]

    City Church & Churchyard Protection Soc (F) 80-83,
       Exec.

BARTLETT, G. D.

North London.

Jamaica Committee (F) 66-66.

BARTLETT, H. CRITCHETT

Fellow Chemical Society.
West London.

Sanitary Institute 78-86, Exec.

BARTON, EDWARD

Central Assn for Stopping Sale Intox Liquors on
Sunday (F) 67-70, Secretary.

BARTON, F. B.

Anglo-French Intervention Committee (F) 70-70,
Exec.

BASS, HAMAR ALFRED (1842-1898)

Harrow.
Brewer.
Liberal(Unionist). MP Tamworth 78-85,
Staffordshire West 85-98. DL, JP.
West London; Staffordshire.
[MEB, WWW, BP, Dods, Direc Direcs]

Free Land League 86-86, V-Pres.

BASS, MICHAEL ARTHUR, 1ST BARON BURTON (1837-1909)

Harrow; Trinity, Camb.
Brewer 63; Substantial Landowner 84.
Liberal(Unionist). MP Stafford 65-68,
Staffordshire East 68-85, Staffordshire South
86-86. DL, JP.
Baronet 82; Baron 86; KCVO 04.
West London; Staffordshire.
[DNB, WWW, BP, Alum Cantab, Dods, Direc Direcs]

Free Land League 86-86, V-Pres.

BASSANO, W.

JP.
North London.

Church Assn 80-80, Exec.

BASSETT, FRANCIS (1820-1899)

Grove House School, Tottenham.
Banker.
Liberal. MP Bedfordshire 72-75. JP.
Leighton Buzzard.
[MEB, Dods, Direc Direcs]

Howard Assn 72-74, Patron.

BASTIN, EDWARD PHILIP

West Drayton.

London Comtee Exposure & Suppresn Traffic In Girls
(F) 80-85, Exec.

BATCHELOR, HENRY

Clergyman<Sect Unkn>.
Glasgow.

Jamaica Committee (F) 66-66.

BATE, JOHN

Natl Emigration League (F) 70-70, Exec.

BATE, S. S.

Newcastle-under-Lyme.

Church Assn 70-70, Exec.

BATEMAN, JAMES (1811-1897)

Magdalen, Oxf.
Botonist; Landowner 58.
DL, JP.
Fellow Royal Society; Fellow Linnean Society;
Fellow Royal Horticult Society; Fellow Royal
Geograph Society.
Manchester; Staffordshire.
[DNB, MEB, Walfords, Alum Oxon]

Church Assn 70-80, Exec.

BATEMAN, JOHN (1839-1910)

Brighton College; Trinity, Camb.
Substantial Landowner.
Conservative. DL, JP.
Essex.
[MEB, WWW, Bateman, Alum Cantab]

Church Assn 78-78, Exec.

BATTEN, JOHN WINTERBOTHAM (1831-1901)

Mill Hill School; Inner Temple.
Barrister 72; Q.C.
Liberal.
West London.
[WWW, Fosters, Direc Direcs]

Assn for Promoting Extension of Contagious Diseases
Act 68-68, Exec.

BATTEN, RAYNER W.

Physician.
Gloucester.

Assn for Promoting Extension of Contagious Diseases
Act 68-68, Exec.

BAXTER, R.

    Church Assn 85-85, Exec.


BAXTER, ROBERT (1802-1889)

    Solicitor 23.
    North London.
    [MEB]

    Central Assn for Stopping Sale Intox Liquors on
        Sunday 75-85, V-Pres.
    Anglo-Oriental Soc for Suppression Opium Trade (F)
        75-75, Exec.


BAXTER, THOMAS PRESTON NOWELL (1827-1896)

    St Catherine's, Camb.
    Rector 67;  College Fellow;  Curate 49;  Ordained
        Priest<CE> 50;  Rural Dean 75.
    Great Grimsby.
    [Alum Cantab, Crockfds]

    Natl Soc for Preserving Memorials of Dead (F)
        81-82, Exec.


BAXTER, WILLIAM EDWARD (1825-1890)

    Dundee High School;  U Edinburgh.
    Merchant;  Substantial Landowner.
    Liberal.  MP Montrose 55-85.  Parl Sec Admiralty
        68-71, Sec Treasury 71-73, DL, JP.
    PC 73.
    Southwest London;  Forfarshire.
    [DNB, MEB, Walfords, Bateman, Dods]

    Jamaica Committee (F) 66-66.


BAYLEY, EDWARD HODSON (1841-1938)

    "In business".
    Liberal.  MP Camberwell North 92-95.  JP.
    Northwest London.
    [Dods, Direc Direcs]

    London Municipal Reform League 82-85, Exec.


BAYLEY, JONATHAN (1810-1879)

    Tubingen.
    Swedenborgian Minister 34.
    West London.
    [MEB]

    Natl Emigration League (F) 70-70, V-Pres.


BAYLY, JOHN

    Intl Arbitration & Peace Assn 81-81, V-Pres.


BAYNES, W. W.

    JP.

    Howard Assn 83-84, Exec.


BAZETT, - <"COL.">

    Reading.

    Church Assn 70-75, Exec.


BAZLEY, C. H.

    JP.
    Manchester.

    Natl Education League 71-71, Exec.


BAZLEY, SIR THOMAS, 1ST BT.  (1797-1885)

    Bolton Grammar School.
    Cotton Manufacturer 18;  Large Landowner.
    Liberal.  MP Manchester 58-80.  DL, JP.
    Baronet 69.
    West London;  Gloucestershire.
    [DNB, MEB, BP, Walfords, Bateman, Dods]

    Central Assn for Stopping Sale Intox Liquors on
        Sunday (F) 67-80, V-Pres, President.


BEACH, MICHAEL EDWARD HICKS-, 1ST EARL ST.  ALDWYN
(1837-1916)

    Eton;  Christ Church, Oxf.
    Very Large Landowner 54.
    Conservative.  MP Gloucestershire East 64-85,
        Bristol West 85-06.  Parl Sec Poor Law Board
        68-68, Parl U-Sec Home Off 68-68, Chief Sec
        Ireland 74-78, Sec St Colonial Off 78-80,
        Chancellor Exchequer 85-86, Chief Sec Ireland
        86-87, Pres Board of Trade 88-92, Chancellor
        Exchequer 95-02.
    Baronet 54;  PC 74;  Viscount 06;  Earl 15.
    Southwest London;  Gloucestershire.
    [DNB, WWW, BP, Walfords, Bateman, Alum Oxon, Dods]

    Local Taxation Comtee [of Central Chamber of
        Agriculture] 71-85, Exec.
    Soc for Promoting Increase of the Home Episcopate
        72-74, Exec.


BEAL, JAMES (1829-1891)

    Auctioneer 51;  Estate Agent.
    Radical.
    Southwest London.
    [MEB]

    Sunday Society (F) 75-80, V-Pres.
    Financial Reform Union (F) 68-69, Exec.

BEAL, MICHAEL

 Sheffield.

 Travelling Tax Abolition Committee 80-85, Exec.

BEALE, GEORGE C.

 Co Cork.

 London Soc for Abolition of Compulsory Vaccination
  81-81, V-Pres.

BEALE, SOPHIA

 Sunday Society 80-90, V-Pres.

BEALE, WILLIAM JOHN (1807-1883)

 Solicitor.
 Birmingham.
 [MEB]

 Natl Education League (F) 69-69, Exec.

BEALES, EDMOND (1803-1881)

 Eton; Trinity, Camb; Middle Temple.
 Barrister 30; County Court Judge 70.
 Radical.
 Southwest London.
 [DNB, MEB, Alum Cantab]

 Jamaica Committee (F) 66-66.
 Workmen's Peace Assn 75-78, President, Chairman.
 Natl Emigration League (F) 70-70, Exec.

BEAUCHAMP, SIR THOMAS WILLIAM BROGRAVE PROCTOR-, 4TH BT.
 (1815-1874)

 Large Landowner 61; Lieutenant, Army.
 DL, JP.
 Baronet 61.
 Norfolk.
 [BP, Walfords]

 Plimsoll and Seamen's Fund Committee (F) 73-73,
  Exec.

BECKER, LYDIA ERNESTINE (1827-1890)

 Journal Editor 70.
 Manchester.
 [DNB, MEB]

 Ladies' Natl Assn for Repeal of Contagious Diseases
  Acts 70-72, Exec.

BEDDOE, JOHN (1826-1911)

 Bridgnorth School; University Col London;
  Edinburgh(Medical).
 Physician 53.
 Fellow Royal Society; Br Assn; Anthropological
  Institute; Ethnological Society; Fellow Royal
  Col Physicians.
 Bristol.

[DNB, WWW]

 Assn for Promoting Extension of Contagious Diseases
  Act 68-68, Exec.

BEDFORD, JOHN THOMAS (1812-1900)

 Undertaker.
 Thames Conserv Board.
 West Central London.
 [MEB]

 Metro Public Gardens Assn (F) 83-90, V-Chairman.

BEECHAM, JOHN

 Cirencester.

 Jamaica Committee (F) 66-66.

BEESLY, EDWARD SPENCER (1831-1915)

 Wadham, Oxf.
 Professor of History, U Col London 60; Journal
  Editor; Asst School Master 54.
 Radical.
 West Central London.
 [WWW, Alum Oxon]

 Jamaica Committee (F) 66-66.
 Anglo-French Intervention Committee (F) 70-70,
  Exec.

BEGG, JAMES (1808-1883)

 U Glasgow.
 Free Church Minister 43; Church of Scotland
  Minister 29.
 Edinburgh.
 [DNB, MEB]

 Natl Education Union 71-79, Exec.

BEITH, GILBERT (1827-1904)

 Stirling Academy.
 Merchant.
 Liberal. MP Glasgow Central 85-86, Inverness
  District 92-95.
 Glasgow.
 [Dods, Direc Direcs]

 Free Land League 86-86, V-Pres.

BELCHER, BRYMER

 Wadham, Oxf.
 Vicar 53; Curate 43; Ordained Priest<CE> 44.
 Southwest London.
 [Alum Oxon, Crockfds]

 Soc for Promoting Increase of the Home Episcopate
  72-74, Exec.

BELL, -

    Malthusian League (F) 77-79, Exec.

BELL, CHARLES W.

    Southwest London;  Sussex.

    Sanitary Institute 78-84, Exec.

BELL, ERNEST (1851-1933)

    St Paul's, London;  Trinity, Camb.
    Publisher.
    North London.
    [WWW, Alum Cantab]

    Victoria Street Soc for Protection of Animals from
        Vivisection 84-85, Exec.

BELL, HENRY THOMAS MACKENZIE (1856-1930)

    Poet.
    Radical.
    West London.
    [WWW]

    Natl Assn for Promotion of State Colonization
        86-86, Exec.
    Imperial Federation League (F) 84-84, Exec.

BELL, THOMAS EVANS (1825-1887)

    Major 62;  Ensign, Army 42;  Lieutenant, Army 45;
        Captain, Army 56.
    West London.
    [MEB, Army List]

    Indian Reform Assn 84-84, Exec.
    League for Defense of Constitutional Rights 84-84,
        V-Pres.
    Travelling Tax Abolition Committee (F) 77-85, Exec.

BENDIX, PAUL

    Intl Arbitration & Peace Assn 81-81, Exec.

BENHAM, WILLIAM (1831-1910)

    St Mark's College, Chelsea;  Kings Col London.
    Vicar 67;  Ordained Priest<CE> 58;  School Teacher
        58;  College Professor 65;  Rector 82;  Hon.
        Canon 85.
    Fellow Society of Antiquaries.
    Margate.
    [DNB, WWW, Crockfds]

    City Church & Churchyard Protection Soc 83-83,
        Exec.

BENNETT, ALFRED WILLIAM (1833-1902)

    University Col London.
    Bookseller 58;  Private Tutor 53;  College Lecturer
        68.
    Fellow Linnean Society;  Royal Microscop Society.
    Northwest London.
    [DNB, WWW]

    Jamaica Committee (F) 66-66.

BENNETT, JAMES RISDON (1809-1891)

    Rotherham College, Yorks;  Edinburgh(Medical).
    Physician 33.
    Kt 81.
    Fellow Royal Col Physicians;  Fellow Royal Society.
    East Central London;  West London.
    [DNB, MEB, BP]

    Anglo-Oriental Soc for Suppression Opium Trade
        80-80, V-Pres.
    Assn for Promoting Extension of Contagious Diseases
        Act 70-70, V-Pres.

BENNETT, JOHN

    Ordained Priest<CE>.

    Church Assn 80-80, Exec.

BENNETT, SIR JOHN (1814-1897)

    Colfe's Grammar School, Lewisham.
    Retail Watchmaker.
    Kt 72.
    Fellow Royal Astronomical Society.
    London.
    [DNB, MEB, WWW, BP]

    Metro Free Libraries Assn 77-77, Exec.

BENNETT, JOSEPH (1829-1908)

    Wesley College, Sheffield.
    Merchant.
    Liberal.  MP Lindsey West, Lincs 85-86, Lindsey
        West, Lincs 92-95.  JP.
    Louth.
    [Dods]

    Free Land League 86-86, V-Pres.

BENNETT, SAMUEL R.

    Intl Arbitration & Peace Assn 81-81, Exec.

BENSON, EDWARD WHITE (1829-1896)

    King Edward's School, Birm;  Trinity, Camb.
    Bishop Truro 77;  Archbishop Canterbury 83;  Asst
        School Master 52;  College Fellow 53;  Ordained
        Priest<CE> 57;  School Master 59;  Canon 72.
    Conservative.
    PC 83.
    Truro;  South London.
    [DNB, MEB, Alum Cantab, Alum Oxon, Crockfds]

Commons Preservation Soc 83-86, Exec.
Natl Soc for Preserving Memorials of Dead (F)
    81-84, Patron.
Soc for Protection of Ancient Buildings (F) 78-78,
    Exec.
Central Assn for Stopping Sale Intox Liquors on
    Sunday 83-85, V-Pres.


BENTINCK, GEORGE AUGUSTUS FREDERICK CAVENDISH
    (1821-1891)

Westminster School; Trinity, Camb; Lincoln's Inn.
Barrister 46; Ensign, Army 40.
Conservative. MP Taunton 59-65, Whitehaven 65-91.
    Parl Sec Board of Trade 74-75, Judge Advocate
    General 75-80.
PC 75.
West London; Dorsetshire.
[MEB, Walfords, Alum Cantab, Dods, Direc Direcs]

City Church & Churchyard Protection Soc (F) 80-81,
    V-Pres.
Soc for Protection of Ancient Buildings (F) 78-78,
    Exec.
Assn for Promoting Extension of Contagious Diseases
    Act 68-70, V-Pres.
Plimsoll and Seamen's Fund Committee (F) 73-73,
    Exec.


BENTLEY, JOHN FRANCIS (1839-1902)

Architect 62.
Southwest London.
[DNB]

Soc for Protection of Ancient Buildings (F) 78-85,
    Exec.


BENTLY, SEYMOUR

Rossall; U Col, Durham.
Vicar 72; Curate 70; Ordained Priest<CE> 72.
Nottinghamshire.
[Alum Cantab, Crockfds]

Natl Soc for Preserving Memorials of Dead (F)
    81-82, Exec.


BERDOE, EDWARD

Physician.

Victoria Street Soc for Protection of Animals from
    Vivisection 82-85, Exec.


BERESFORD, MARCUS (1818- )

King's College School.
Conservative. MP Southwark 70-80. JP.
West London; Surrey.
[Walfords, Dods, Direc Direcs]

Plimsoll and Seamen's Fund Committee (F) 73-73,
    Exec.


BERGUER, HENRY JOHN

Kings Col London.
Vicar 71; Curate 57; Ordained Priest<CE> 58.
North London.
[Crockfds]

Church Assn 85-85, Exec.


BERNARD, FRANCIS, 3RD EARL OF BANDON (1810-1877)

Eton; Oriel, Oxf.
Very Large Landowner 56.
Conservative. MP Bandon 31-32, Bandon 42-56. Lord
    Lieutenant, DL, JP.
Earl 56.
Southwest London; Co Cork.
[MEB, BP, Walfords, Alum Oxon, Dods]

Church Assn 67-75, V-Pres.


BERNARD, JAMES FRANCIS, 4TH EARL OF BANDON (1850-1924)

Eton.
Very Large Landowner 77.
Conservative. Lord Lieutenant.
KP; Earl 77.
Co Cork.
[WWW, BP, Bateman]

Church Assn 78-85, V-Pres.


BERNARD, MONTAGUE (1820-1882)

Sherborne; Trinity, Oxf; Lincoln's Inn.
Barrister 46; Professor of International Law and
    Diplomacy, Oxford 59.
PC 71.
London; Herefordshire.
[DNB, MEB, Alum Oxon]

Intl Law Assn (F) 73-74, V-Pres.


BESANT, ANNIE (1847-1933)

Journal Editor.
Radical.
Northwest London.
[DNB, WWW]

Land Law Reform League (F) 81-84, V-Pres.
League for Defense of Constitutional Rights 84-84,
    V-Pres.
Malthusian League (F) 77-84, Hon Sec.
Natl Secular Soc 74-84, V-Pres.


BEVAN, FRANCIS AUGUSTUS (1840-1919)

Harrow.
Banker.
JP.
West London; Hertfordshire.
[WWW, Direc Direcs]

Church Assn 67-85, Treas.

BEVAN, ROBERT COOPER LEE (1809-1890)

    Harrow;  Trinity, Oxf.
    Banker;  Substantial Landowner 46.
    JP.
    Southwest London;  Wiltshire;  Hertfordshire.
    [MEB, Walfords, Bateman, Alum Oxon]

    Church Assn 70-85, V-Pres.


BEWICKE, ALICIA E.  N.  <MISS>

    West London.

    Assn for Improvement of Public Morals 81-81, Hon
        Sec.
    Natl Vigilance Assn (F) 85-85, Exec.


BHOWNAGGREE, SIR MANCHERJEE MERWANJEE (1851-1933)

    Elphinstone College, Bombay;  U Bombay;  Lincoln´s
        Inn.
    Journalist 72;  Barrister 85.
    Conservative.  MP Bethnal Green NE 95-06.  JP.
    CIE 86;  KCIE 97.
    Society of the Arts.
    Southwest London.
    [DNB, WWW, Dods]

    Indian Reform Assn 84-84, Exec.


BICKERSTETH, EDWARD (1814-1892)

    Trinity, Camb;  Durham Theo.
    Vicar 53;  Dean 75;  Curate 38;  Ordained
        Priest<CE> 39;  Perp. Curate 49;  Rural Dean
        49;  Archdeacon 53.
    Fellow Royal Geograph Society.
    Aylesbury;  Lichfield.
    [DNB, MEB, Alum Cantab, Crockfds]

    Natl Soc for Preserving Memorials of Dead (F)
        81-84, Exec.
    Soc for Promoting Increase of the Home Episcopate
        72-74, Exec.


BICKERSTETH, ROBERT (1816-1884)

    Queens´, Camb.
    Bishop Ripon 57;  Curate 41;  Ordained Priest<CE>
        42;  Perp. Curate 45;  Vicar;  Rector 51;
        Canon 54.
    Liberal.
    Fellow Royal Society.
    Ripon;  Southwest London.
    [DNB, MEB, Alum Cantab, Crockfds]

    Anglo-Oriental Soc for Suppression Opium Trade
        79-84, V-Pres.


BICKNELL, HENRY S.

    JP.

    Sunday Society 78-80, V-Pres.


BIDDULPH, MICHAEL, 1ST BARON BIDDULPH (1834-1923)

    Harrow.
    Banker.
    Liberal(Unionist).  MP Herefordshire 65-85,
        Herefordshire South 85-00.  DL, JP.
    Baron 03.
    Southwest London;  Herefordshire.
    [WWW, BP, Walfords, Dods, Direc Direcs]

    Proportional Representation Soc (F) 84-88, Exec.


BIGG, HENRY HEATHER (1826-1881)

    St George´s Hospital Lond.
    Surgical Instruments Maker.
    Assoc Inst Civ Engineers.
    West London.
    [MEB]

    Assn for Improvement of London Workhouse
        Infirmaries 66-66, Exec.


BIGG, LOUISA <MISS>

    Intl Arbitration & Peace Assn 81-81, Exec.


BIGGS, -

    Colonel.
    Bristol.

    Church Assn 75-75, Exec.


BIGGS, R.  W.

    Devizes.

    Jamaica Committee (F) 66-66.


BIGNOLD, CHARLES EDWARD <"COL.">

    Insurance Co Manager.
    Norwich.
    [Direc Direcs]

    Natl Soc for Preserving Memorials of Dead (F)
        81-82, Treas.


BILLCLIFFE, J.

    New Zealand.

    Natl Secular Soc 84-84, V-Pres.


BILLING, ROBERT CLAUDIUS (1834-1898)

    Wye Grammar;  Worcester, Oxf.
    Vicar 63;  Rector 78;  Curate 57;  Ordained
        Priest<CE> 58;  Prebendary 86;  Bishop
        Bedford<Suffragan> 88.
    North London;  East London;  Surrey.
    [MEB, WWW, Alum Oxon, Crockfds]

    Church Assn 75-78, Exec.

BINGHAM, CHARLES WILLIAM (1810-1881)

> New College, Oxf.
> Rector 42;  Prebendary 76;  Ordained Priest<CE> 36;
>     Vicar 38;  Rural Dean 63.
> Dorsetshire.
> [MEB, Alum Oxon, Crockfds]
>
> Church Assn 75-78, Exec.

BINNS, WILLIAM

> Clergyman<Sect Unkn>.
> Birkenhead.
>
> Sunday Society 79-90, V-Pres.

BIRCH, GEORGE HENRY (1842-1904)

> Architect;  Curator, Soan's Museum 94.
> Assoc Royal Inst Br Architects;  Architectural
>     Assn;  Fellow Society of Antiquaries;  Assoc
>     Royal Academy.
> West Central London.
> [DNB, WWW]
>
> City Church & Churchyard Protection Soc (F) 80-83,
>     Exec.

BIRCH, HENRY MILDRED (1820-1884)

> Eton;  King's, Camb.
> Canon 68;  College Fellow 41;  Asst School Master
>     44;  Rector 52.
> Blackburn.
> [MEB, Alum Cantab, Crockfds]
>
> Central Assn for Stopping Sale Intox Liquors on
>     Sunday 70-75, V-Pres.

BIRCH, WILLIAM JOHN

> Balliol, Oxf;  Lincoln's Inn.
> [Alum Oxon]
>
> Malthusian League 78-84, V-Pres.

BIRDWOOD, SIR GEORGE CHRISTOPHER MOLESWORTH (1832-1917)

> Dollar Academy;  U Edinburgh;  Edinburgh(Medical).
> Special Asst, India Office 78;  Army Medical
>     Service 54.
> JP.
> Kt 81;  KCIE 87;  CSI.
> Royal Asiatic Society.
> West London.
> [DNB, WWW, Alum Cantab]
>
> Soc for Protection of Ancient Buildings 80-80,
>     Exec.

BIRKETT, PERCIVAL

> Solicitor.
> West Central London.
>
> Metro Public Gardens Assn (F) 83-90, Exec.

BIRKS, THOMAS RAWSON (1810-1883)

> Mill Hill School;  Trinity, Camb.
> Professor of Moral Philosophy, Cambridge 72;
>     College Fellow 34;  Curate;  Ordained
>     Priest<CE> 41;  Rector 44;  Vicar 66;  Hon.
>     Canon 71.
> Cambridge.
> [DNB, MEB, Alum Cantab, Crockfds]
>
> Church Assn 78-80, V-Pres.

BIRLEY, HUGH (1817-1883)

> Winchester College.
> Rubber Manufacturer.
> Conservative.  MP Manchester 68-83.  JP.
> Manchester;  West London.
> [MEB, Walfords, Dods]
>
> Central Assn for Stopping Sale Intox Liquors on
>     Sunday 70-80, V-Pres.
> Howard Assn 72-82, Patron.
> Natl Education Union (F) 69-83, Chairman.

BIRLEY, ROBERT (1825- )

> Balliol, Oxf.
> Hon. Canon;  Curate 50;  Ordained Priest<CE> 52;
>     Rector 60;  Rural Dean 70.
> Manchester.
> [Alum Oxon, Crockfds]
>
> Central Assn for Stopping Sale Intox Liquors on
>     Sunday 85-85, Exec.

BISHOP, EDWARD

> Clergyman<Sect Unkn>.
>
> Central Assn for Stopping Sale Intox Liquors on
>     Sunday (F) 67-70, Exec.

BLACK, WILLIAM GEORGE (1857-1932)

> Author.
> Conservative.  JP.
> CBE 19.
> Fellow Society of Antiquaries;  Ophthalmic Inst.
> Glasgow;  Dumbartonshire.
> [WWW]
>
> Natl Soc for Preserving Memorials of Dead (F)
>     81-82, Exec.

BLACKBURN, CATHERINE <MRS.>

    Southport.

    Ladies' Natl Assn for Repeal of Contagious Diseases
       Acts 70-72, Exec.


BLACKBURN, HELLEN (1842-1903)

    Journal Editor 81.
    Southwest London.
    [DNB]

    Vigilance Assn for Defense of Personal Rights (F)
       71-71, Exec.


BLACKLOCK, WILLIAM THOMAS (1815-1870)

    Engraver;  Publisher.
    JP.
    Assoc Inst Civ Engineers.
    Lancashire.
    [MEB]

    Central Assn for Stopping Sale Intox Liquors on
       Sunday (F) 67-67, V-Pres.


BLACKMORE, JOHN CHANTER

    U Col, Durham.
    Rector 78;  Curate 72;  Ordained Priest<CE> 74;
       Vicar 76;  Curate 77.
    East Dereham.
    [Crockfds]

    Natl Soc for Preserving Memorials of Dead (F)
       81-82, Exec.


BLADES, JOHN HORTON (1841- )

    Brick Manufacturer 62.
    Radical. MP West Bromwich 85-86.
    West Bromwich.
    [Dods]

    Free Land League 86-86, V-Pres.


BLAIR, ROBERT

    Solicitor.
    South Shields.

    Natl Soc for Preserving Memorials of Dead (F)
       81-82, Exec.


BLAKE, THOMAS (1825-1901)

    Estate Agent;  Accountant.
    Liberal. MP Leominster 75-80, Forest of Dean
       85-87. JP.
    Leominster;  Herefordshire.
    [Dods]

    Central Assn for Stopping Sale Intox Liquors on
       Sunday 80-85, V-Pres.
    Howard Assn 79-79, Patron.
    Intl Arbitration & Peace Assn 81-81, V-Pres.
    Free Land League 86-86, V-Pres.


BLAKENEY, RICHARD PAUL (1820-1884)

    Trin Col, Dublin.
    Vicar 74;  Rural Dean 76;  Canon 82;  Curate 43;
       Ordained Priest<CE> 44;  Perp. Curate 44.
    Bridlington.
    [DNB, MEB, Crockfds]

    Church Assn 70-80, V-Pres.


BLANCHARD, - <MRS. EDWARD LITT LEMAN BLANCHARD>

    Natl Assn for Promotion of State Colonization (F)
       83-86, V-Pres.


BLANDY, -

    JP.
    Reading.

    Assn for Promoting Extension of Contagious Diseases
       Act 68-68, V-Pres.


BLAYDES, F. A.

    Bedfordshire.

    Natl Soc for Preserving Memorials of Dead (F)
       81-82, Exec.


BLEAZBY, WILLIAM

    Trin Col, Dublin.
    Curate;  Ordained Priest<CE> 38.
    St Leonards.
    [Crockfds]

    Church Assn 80-80, Exec.


BLENNERHASSETT, ROWLAND PONSONBY (1850-1913)

    Christ Church, Oxf;  Inner Temple.
    Barrister 78;  Q.C.  94.
    Liberal.  MP Kerry 72-85.  JP.
    Southwest London;  Co Kerry.
    [WWW, Alum Oxon, Fosters, Dods]

    Commons Preservation Soc 86-86, Exec.
    London Soc for Abolition of Compulsory Vaccination
       81-81, V-Pres.
    Proportional Representation Soc (F) 84-88, Exec.


BLIGH, EDWARD HENRY STUART, 7TH EARL OF DARNLEY
(1851-1900)

    Eton;  Christ Church, Oxf.
    Very Large Landowner 96.
    Earl 96.
    Kent.
    [MEB, WWW, BP, Alum Oxon]

    London Soc for Abolition of Compulsory Vaccination
       81-81, V-Pres.

BLIGH, JOHN STUART, 6TH EARL OF DARNLEY (1827-1896)

    Eton;  Christ Church, Oxf.
    Very Large Landowner 35.
    Conservative.  DL, JP.
    Earl 35.
    West London;  Co Meath;  Kent.
    [MEB, BP, Walfords, Bateman, Alum Oxon]

    Assn for Promoting Extension of Contagious Diseases
        Act 68-70, V-Pres.
    Victoria Street Soc for Protection of Animals from
        Vivisection 80-85, V-Pres.


BLINKHORN, OCTAVIUS

    North London.

    Central Assn for Stopping Sale Intox Liquors on
        Sunday 80-85, Exec.


BLISSARD, JOHN CHARLES (1835-1904)

    St John's, Camb.
    Vicar 68;  Curate 60;  Ordained Priest<CE> 63;
        Rural Dean 92.
    Birmingham.
    [Alum Cantab, Crockfds]

    Assn for Promoting Extension of Contagious Diseases
        Act 68-68, Exec.


BLUNT, RICHARD FREDERICK LEFEVRE (1833-1910)

    Merchant Taylors;  Kings Col London.
    Archdeacon 73;  Curate 57;  Ordained Priest<CE> 58;
        Vicar 64;  Prebendary 71;  Canon 82;  Suffragan
        Bishop 91.
    Scarborough.
    [WWW, Crockfds]

    Central Assn for Stopping Sale Intox Liquors on
        Sunday 85-85, V-Pres.


BLYTH, ALEXANDER WYNTER ( -1921)

    Kings Col London;  Lincoln's Inn.
    Physician.
    Med Off of Health.
    Member Royal Col Surgeons;  Society Med Officers of
        Health;  Fellow Chemical Society.
    Northwest London;  Berkshire.
    [WWW]

    Smoke Abatement Committee 81-81.
    Sanitary Institute 84-89, Exec.


BOARDMAN, C.

    Cheltenham.

    Jamaica Committee (F) 66-66.


BOLINGBROKE, NATHANIEL

    Queens', Camb.
    Curate 71;  Ordained Priest<CE> 73;  Vicar 82.
    Norfolk.
    [Alum Cantab, Crockfds]

    Natl Soc for Preserving Memorials of Dead (F)
        81-82, Exec.


BOLTON, JOSEPH CHENEY (1819-1901)

    Merchant.
    Liberal.  MP Stirlingshire 80-92.  DL, JP.
    West London;  Stirlingshire.
    [WWW, Dods, Direc Direcs]

    Free Land League 86-86, V-Pres.


BOLTON, THOMAS DOLLING (1841-1906)

    Solicitor 66.
    Liberal.  MP Derbyshire NE 86-06.  JP.
    London;  Berkshire.
    [WWW, Dods, Direc Direcs]

    Free Land League 86-86, V-Pres.


BOLTON, THOMAS HENRY (1841-1916)

    Solicitor 69;  Supreme Court Master;  Chancery
        Taxing Master 96.
    Liberal(Unionist).  MP St Pancras North 85-86, St
        Pancras North 90-95.
    Sussex;  West Central London.
    [WWW, Dods]

    Free Land League 86-86, V-Pres.
    Financial Reform Union (F) 68-69, Exec.


BONAPARTE, LOUIS LUCIEN, PRINCE (1813-1891)

    Philologist;  Author.
    West London.
    [MEB]

    Victoria Street Soc for Protection of Animals from
        Vivisection 80-85, V-Pres.


BONAR, A.

    West London.

    Church Assn 67-70, Exec.


BOND, C. R.

    Physician.
    Kingston-upon-Thames.

    Malthusian League 80-84, V-Pres.

BOND, EDWARD (1845-1920)

>    Merchant Taylors; St Johns, Oxf; Lincoln's Inn.
>    Barrister 71; College Fellow 69.
>    Conservative. MP Nottingham East 95-06. Asst
>       Charity Commissioner 84-91.
>    Northwest London.
>    [WWW, Alum Oxon, Fosters, Dods, Direc Direcs]
>
>    Commons Preservation Soc 76-86, Exec.

BONE, J. W.

>    Fellow Society of Antiquaries.
>    West Central London.
>
>    Natl Footpaths Preservation Soc 86-86, Exec.

BOOCOCK, - <MRS. S. G. BOOCOCK>

>    British Women's Temperance Assn 84-85, Hon Sec.

BOORNE, JAMES

>    JP.
>    Reading.
>
>    Jamaica Committee (F) 66-66.

BOOTH, JAMES (1796-1880)

>    St John's, Camb; Lincoln's Inn.
>    Barrister 24; Counsel to Speaker, Commons 39;
>       Sec, Board of Trade 50.
>    CB 66.
>    Southwest London.
>    [DNB, MEB, Alum Cantab]
>
>    Sunday Society 78-80, V-Pres.

BOOTH, WILLIAM BRAMWELL (1856-1929)

>    City of London School.
>    Salvation Army Officer 70.
>    CH 29.
>    East Central London.
>    [DNB, WWW]
>
>    Natl Vigilance Assn (F) 85-85, Exec.

BORLASE, WILLIAM COPELAND (1848-1899)

>    Winchester College; Trinity, Oxf; Inner Temple.
>    Barrister 82.
>    Liberal. MP Cornwall East 80-85, St Austell 85-87.
>       Parl Sec Loc Govt Board 86-86, JP.
>    Fellow Society of Antiquaries; Pipe Roll Society.
>    West London; Cornwall.
>    [MEB, Alum Oxon, Fosters, Dods]
>
>    Intl Arbitration & Peace Assn 81-81, V-Pres.
>    Indian Reform Assn 84-84, Exec.

BORTHWICK, ALICE BEATRICE <MRS. A. BORTHWICK, LATER
    LADY GLENESK, nee LISTER> (1841-1898)

>    Southwest London.
>    [BP]
>
>    Smoke Abatement Committee 81-81.

BOSANQUET, HORACE JAMES SMITH- (1824- )

>    Landowner 67.
>    JP.
>    Hertfordshire.
>    [Walfords]
>
>    Church Assn 67-85, V-Pres, Exec.

BOSHER, W.

>    East Central London.
>
>    Jamaica Committee (F) 66-66.

BOSTOCK, - <MISS>

>    Kyrle Soc 85-90, Exec.

BOTT, THOMAS

>    Birkenhead.
>
>    Travelling Tax Abolition Committee 80-82, Exec.

BOULNOIS, H. PERCY

>    Borough Engineer.
>    Member Inst Civ Engineers.
>    Exeter; Portsmouth.
>
>    Sanitary Institute 80-87, Exec.

BOULTBEE, THOMAS POWNALL (1818-1884)

>    Uppingham; St John's, Camb.
>    College Head 63; College Fellow 42; Ordained
>       Priest<CE> 45; Curate; School Master 53.
>    North London.
>    [DNB, MEB, Alum Cantab, Crockfds]
>
>    Church Assn 75-80, V-Pres.

BOURDILLON, JAMES DEWAR (1811-1883)

>    Haileybury College.
>    India Civil Service 29.
>    Tunbridge Wells.
>    [DNB, MEB]
>
>    Church Assn 70-70, Exec.

BOURNE, HENRY RICHARD FOX (1837-1909)

> University Col London.
> Newspaper Proprietor 70;  Civ Serv, War Office 55;
>     Newspaper Editor 76;  Author.
> Radical.
> London.
> [DNB]

> Land Tenure Reform Assn 73-73, Exec.


BOURNE, T.  J.

> Travelling Tax Abolition Committee 79-85, Exec.


BOUSFIELD, C.  H.

> Church Assn 78-85, Exec.


BOUVERIE, EDWARD PLEYDELL (1818-1889)

> Harrow;  Trinity, Camb;  Inner Temple.
> Barrister 43;  Substantial Landowner.
> Liberal.  MP Kilmarnock 44-74.  Parl U-Sec Home Off
>     50-52, Chairman of Committees 53-55, V-P Board
>     of Trade 55-55, Pres Poor Law Board 55-58,
>     Education Committee 57-  , Church Estates
>     Commissioner 59-65, Ecclesiastical Commissioner
>     69-  , JP.
> PC.
> Fellow Royal Society.
> Southwest London;  Wiltshire.
> [DNB, BP, Walfords, Bateman, Alum Cantab, Fosters,
>     Dods]

> Assn for Promoting Extension of Contagious Diseases
>     Act 68-70, V-Pres.


BOUVERIE, WILLIAM PLEYDELL, 5TH EARL OF RADNOR
(1841-1900)

> Harrow;  Trinity, Camb.
> Very Large Landowner 89.
> Conservative.  MP Wiltshire South 74-85, Middlesex
>     Enfield 85-89.  Treas Royal Household 85-92,
>     DL, JP.
> PC 85;  Earl 89.
> West London;  Wiltshire;  Kent.
> [MEB, WWW, BP, Alum Cantab, Dods]

> Natl Assn for Promotion of State Colonization
>     86-86, V-Pres.
> Proportional Representation Soc (F) 84-88, Exec.


BOVILLE, E.  C.

> JP.
> Chiswick.

> Church Assn 78-85, Exec, V-Chairman.


BOWES, JAMES LORD (1834-1899)

> Wool Broker 59.
> Liverpool.
> [MEB]

> Sunday Society 76-80, V-Pres.


BOWKER, CHARLES E.  B.

> Saffron Walden.

> Natl Soc for Preserving Memorials of Dead (F)
>     81-82, Exec.


BOWKER, HENRY F.

> Church Assn 70-75, Exec.


BOWLES, THOMAS GIBSON (1844-1922)

> Kings Col London.
> Journalist.
> Conservative.  MP King's Lynn 92-06, King's Lynn
>     10-10.
> Southwest London;  Wiltshire.
> [DNB, WWW, Dods]

> Assn for Promoting Extension of Contagious Diseases
>     Act 68-68, Exec.


BOWLY, SAMUEL (1802-1884)

> Cheese Merchant 29.
> Gloucester.
> [DNB, MEB, Friends]

> Central Assn for Stopping Sale Intox Liquors on
>     Sunday 70-80, V-Pres.


BOWRING, - <LADY>

> Sunday Society 79-90, V-Pres.


BOWRING, EDGAR ALFRED (1826-1911)

> Univ College School;  University Col London.
> Author;  Private Secretary 46;  Registrar, Board of
>     Trade 49.
> Liberal.  MP Exeter 68-74.
> CB 82.
> West London.
> [WWW, Walfords, Dods]

> Natl Emigration League (F) 70-70, V-Pres.


BOWRING, SIR JOHN (1792-1872)

> Journal Editor 24;  Author;  Merchant 15.
> Radical.  MP Kilmarnock 35-37, Bolton 41-49.
>     Ambassador 54-59, DL, JP.
> Kt 54.
> Fellow Royal Society;  Br Assn;  Fellow Linnean
>     Society;  Royal Asiatic Society.
> West Central London;  Devonshire.
> [DNB, MEB, Walfords, Dods]

Assn for Promoting Extension of Contagious Diseases
    Act 68-70, V-Pres.
Howard Assn 67-72, Patron.
Natl Emigration League (F) 70-70, V-Pres.


BOYCE, GEORGE PRICE (1826-1897)

Artist 52.
Royal Society Water Colour Painters.
Southwest London.
[MEB]

Soc for Protection of Ancient Buildings (F) 78-85,
    Exec.


BOYD, ARCHIBALD (1803-1883)

Londonderry Diocesan College;  Trin Col, Dublin.
Dean 67;  Curate 27;  Ordained Priest<CE> 29;
    Perp. Curate 42;  Hon. Canon 57;  Vicar 59;
    Rural Dean 60.
Exeter.
[DNB, MEB, Alum Oxon, Crockfds]

Central Assn for Stopping Sale Intox Liquors on
    Sunday 80-80, V-Pres.


BOYD, JAMES

Manchester.

Central Assn for Stopping Sale Intox Liquors on
    Sunday (F) 67-75, Exec.


BOYD, THOMAS LUNHAM

Tunbridge Wells.

London Comtee Exposure & Suppresn Traffic In Girls
    (F) 80-85, Exec.


BOYDEN, KATE <MISS>

Sunday Society 76-78, Exec.


BOYLE, GEORGE FREDERICK, 6TH EARL OF GLASGOW (1825-1890)

Christ Church, Oxf.
Very Large Landowner 69.
Conservative. MP Buteshire 65-65. DL, JP.
Earl 69.
West London;  Gt Cumbrae Island.
[BP, Walfords, Bateman, Alum Oxon, Dods]

City Church & Churchyard Protection Soc (F) 80-83,
    V-Pres.
Natl Soc for Preserving Memorials of Dead (F)
    81-84, Patron.


BRABAZON, REGINALD, 12TH EARL OF MEATH (1841-1929)

Eton.
Very Large Landowner 87;  Clerk, FO 63;  Diplomatic
    Service 68.
Liberal(Unionist). Lord Lieutenant.
Earl 87;  PC 87;  KP 05;  GBE 20;  GCVO 23.
West London;  Co Wicklow;  Surrey.
[DNB, WWW, BP, Walfords, Bateman]

Metro Public Gardens Assn (F) 83-29, Chairman,
    Treas.
Sanitary Institute 78-88, V-Pres.
Natl Soc for Preserving Memorials of Dead 84-84,
    Patron.
Kyrle Soc 84-90, Exec.
Natl Assn for Promotion of State Colonization (F)
    83-91, President.
Central Vigilance Comtee for Repression Immorality
    (F) 83-84, V-Pres.


BRABY, ALFRED

Southwest London.

Jamaica Committee (F) 66-66.


BRACEY, CHARLES J.

Physician.
Birmingham.

Assn for Promoting Extension of Contagious Diseases
    Act 68-68, Exec.


BRADLAUGH, ALICE

St Johns Wood.

Natl Secular Soc 84-84, V-Pres.


BRADLAUGH, CHARLES (1833-1891)

Journalist;  Soldier 50;  Solicitor's Clerk 54;
    Newspaper Editor 60;  Newspaper Proprietor 62.
Radical. MP Northampton 85-91.
St Johns Wood.
[DNB, MEB, Dods]

Free Land League 86-86, V-Pres.
Land Law Reform League (F) 81-84, President.
Malthusian League (F) 77-84, Exec, V-Pres.
Natl Secular Soc (F) 66-90, President.


BRADLAUGH, HYPATIA

St Johns Wood.

Natl Secular Soc 84-84, V-Pres.


BRADLEY, - <MRS. J. W. BRADLEY>

West London.

Assn for Improvement of Public Morals 81-81, Exec.
Natl Vigilance Assn (F) 85-85, Exec.

BRADLEY, FRANCIS JOHN

> Soc for Abolition of Vivisection (F) 75-76,
>     Secretary.

BRADLEY, J. W.

> West London.

> Assn for Improvement of Public Morals 81-81, Exec.

BRADY, SIR ANTONIO (1811-1881)

> Colfe's Grammar School, Lewisham.
> Supt, Admiralty ContrAct Dept 69;  Jun Clerk, Civ
>     Serv 28;  Registrar of ContrAct 64.
> JP.
> Kt 70.
> Fellow Royal Meteorlog Society;  Ray Society;
>     Fellow Geological Society;  Paleontographical
>     Society.
> East London.
> [MEB, BP, Walfords]

> Railway Passengers' Protection Assn 74-74, Hon Sec.
> Smoke Abatement Committee 81-81.
> Sanitary Institute 79-81, Exec.

BRADY, JOHN (1812-1887)

> Clones Grammar School.
> Physician.
> Liberal.  MP Leitrim 52-80.  DL, JP.
> Member Royal Col Physicians;  Member Royal Col
>     Surgeons.
> Southwest London;  Ely.
> [MEB, Walfords, Dods]

> Assn for Promoting Extension of Contagious Diseases
>     Act 68-70, V-Pres.

BRAITHWAITE, G. F.

> JP.
> Kendal.

> Central Assn for Stopping Sale Intox Liquors on
>     Sunday 75-85, V-Pres.

BRAMWELL, SIR FREDERICK JOSEPH, 1ST BT. (1818-1903)

> Palace School, Enfield.
> Civil Engineer.
> Ordnance Committee 81-03.
> Kt 81;  Baronet 89.
> Fellow Royal Society;  Fellow Inst Civ Engineers;
>     Inst of Mech Engineers;  Society of the Arts;
>     Fellow British Assn.
> Southwest London;  Kent.
> [DNB, WWW, BP, Alum Cantab, Alum Oxon, Direc
>     Direcs]

> Smoke Abatement Committee 81-81.

BRAMWELL, GEORGE WILLIAM WILSHERE, 1ST BARON BRAMWELL
    (1808-1892)

> Palace School, Enfield;  Inner Temple.
> Judge, Court of Appeal 76;  Barrister 38;  Q.C.
>     51;  Baron, Exchequer 56.
> PC Judicial Committee 76-  .
> Kt 56;  PC 76;  Baron 82.
> Fellow Royal Society.
> Southwest London;  Kent.
> [DNB, MEB, BP, Walfords, Fosters]

> Sunday Society 86-90, V-Pres.
> Liberty & Property Defense League (F) 82-84, Exec.

BRAND, HENRY ROBERT, 2ND VISCOUNT HAMPDEN AND 24TH BARON
    DACRE (1841-1906)

> Rugby.
> Lieutenant, Army 58;  Captain, Army 63;  Landowner
>     92;  Gov, New South Wales 95.
> Liberal(Unionist).  MP Hertfordshire 68-74, Stroud
>     74-74, Stroud 80-86.  Surveyor General Ordnance
>     83-85, DL, JP.
> Viscount 92;  GCMG 99.
> Southwest London;  Hertfordshire.
> [DNB, WWW, BP, Dods, Direc Direcs, Army List]

> Plimsoll and Seamen's Fund Committee (F) 73-73,
>     Exec.

BRANTHWAITE, HARRISON

> Physician.
> Fellow Royal Col Surgeons.
> Northwest London;  Southwest London.

> Railway Passengers' Protection Assn 86-86, Exec.

BRASSEY, HENRY ARTHUR (1840-1891)

> Harrow;  University Col, Oxf;  Lincoln's Inn.
> Barrister 68;  Substantial Landowner.
> Liberal.  MP Sandwich 68-85.  DL, JP.
> Southwest London;  Kent.
> [MEB, Bateman, Alum Oxon, Dods, Direc Direcs]

> Natl Emigration League (F) 70-70, V-Pres.

BRASSEY, THOMAS (1805-1870)

> Railway Contractor 36;  Surveyor 26.
> London.
> [DNB, MEB]

> Natl Emigration League (F) 70-70, V-Pres.

BRASSEY, THOMAS, 1ST EARL BRASSEY (1836-1918)

> Rugby;  University Col, Oxf;  Lincoln's Inn.
> Barrister 66;  Substantial Landowner;  Gov,
>     Victoria 95.
> Liberal.  MP Devonport 65-65, Hastings 68-86.  Lord
>     Admiralty 80-84, Parl Sec Admiralty 84-85, Lord
>     Warden Cinque Ports 08-13, DL, JP.
> KCB 81;  Baron 86;  GCB 06;  Earl 11.
> Assoc Inst Civ Engineers;  Inst Naval Architcts;
>     Fellow Royal Statistical Society.
> West London;  Sussex;  Cheshire.
> [DNB, WWW, BP, Bateman, Fosters, Dods, Direc
>     Direcs]

Natl Emigration League (F) 70-70, V-Pres.
Natl Assn for Promotion of State Colonization
    86-86, V-Pres, Exec.
Natl Footpaths Preservation Soc 86-90, V-Pres.
Free Land League 86-86, V-Pres.


BRAY, – <MRS. CHARLES BRAY>

    Coventry.

    Sunday Society (F) 75-90, V-Pres.


BRAY, W.

    Bible Christian Minister.

    Central Assn for Stopping Sale Intox Liquors on
        Sunday 85-85, V-Pres.


BREWER, H. W.

    West London.

    City Church & Churchyard Protection Soc (F) 80-83,
        Exec.
    Soc for Protection of Ancient Buildings (F) 78-80,
        Exec.


BREWER, JOHN SHERREN (1810-1879)

    Queen's, Oxf.
    Rector 76;  Chaplain 37;  College Lecturer 39;
        Journalist 54;  College Professor 55;  College
        Head 72.
    Essex.
    [DNB, MEB, Alum Oxon, Crockfds]

    Soc for Protection of Ancient Buildings (F) 78-79,
        Exec.


BRIDGEMAN, GEORGE CECIL ORLANDO, 4TH EARL OF BRADFORD
    (1845-1915)

    Harrow;  Trinity, Camb.
    Ensign, Army 64;  Lieutenant, Army 67;  Very Large
        Landowner 98.
    Conservative.  MP Shropshire North 67-85.  DL, JP.
    Earl 98.
    Southwest London.
    [WWW, BP, Alum Cantab, Dods]

    Assn for Promoting Extension of Contagious Diseases
        Act 68-70, V-Pres.


BRIDGER, JOHN ( -1911)

    Vicar;  Curate 78;  Assoc Sec, Irish Church
        Mission.
    Liverpool.
    [WWW, Crockfds]

    Natl Assn for Promotion of State Colonization
        86-86, V-Pres.


BRIDGES, ALEXANDER HENRY (1811-1891)

    Winchester College;  Oriel, Oxf.
    Rector 64;  Curate 36;  Ordained Priest<CE> 37;
        Perp. Curate 58;  Rural Dean 73;  Hon. Canon
        73;  Substantial Landowner 61.
    Surrey.
    [Walfords, Bateman, Alum Cantab, Alum Oxon,
        Crockfds]

    Natl Soc for Preserving Memorials of Dead (F)
        81-88, Exec.


BRIDGES, SIR BROOK WILLIAM, 5TH BT.  AND 1ST BARON
    FITZWALTER (1801-1875)

    Winchester College;  Oriel, Oxf.
    Substantial Landowner 29.
    Conservative.  MP Kent East 52-52, Kent East 57-68.
        DL, JP.
    Baronet 29;  Baron 68.
    West London;  Kent.
    [MEB, BP, Walfords, Alum Oxon, Dods]

    Church Assn 67-70, V-Pres.


BRIDGES, JOHN HENRY (1832-1906)

    Rugby;  Wadham, Oxf;  St George's Hospital Lond.
    Medical Inspector, LGB 69;  Factory Inspector 69;
        College Fellow 55;  Physician 61.
    Member Royal Col Surgeons;  Fellow Royal Col
        Physicians.
    West London.
    [DNB, WWW]

    Anglo-French Intervention Committee (F) 70-70,
        Exec.


BRIGGS, E. A.

    Daventry.

    Jamaica Committee (F) 66-66.


BRIGGS, N.

    Bradford.

    Jamaica Committee (F) 66-66.


BRIGGS, THOMAS

    English Land Restoration League 85-85, Exec.
    Land Nationalization Soc (F) 81-84, Exec.


BRIGGS, THOMAS

    Salford.

    Travelling Tax Abolition Committee (F) 77-85, Exec.

BRIGHT, JACOB (1821-1899)

    Friends' School, York.
    Cotton Manufacturer; Carpet Manufacturer.
    Radical. MP Manchester 67-74, Manchester 76-85,
       Manchester Southwest 86-95. JP.
    PC 95.
    Southwest London; Manchester; Rochdale.
    [DNB, MEB, WWW, Walfords]

    Sunday Society 76-90, V-Pres.
    Central Assn for Stopping Sale Intox Liquors on
       Sunday 70-85, V-Pres.
    Howard Assn 69-73, Patron.
    Jamaica Committee (F) 66-66.
    Natl Assn for Repeal Contagious Diseases Acts
       81-81, V-Pres.
    Vigilance Assn for Defense of Personal Rights
       83-83, Exec.


BRIGHT, JOHN (1811-1889)

    Cotton Manufacturer.
    Radical. MP Durham County 43-47, Manchester 47-57,
       Birmingham 57-85, Birmingham Central 85-89.
       Pres Board of Trade 68-70, Chanc Duchy
       Lancaster 73-74, Chanc Duchy Lancaster 80-82.
    PC 68.
    Rochdale.
    [DNB, MEB, Dods]

    Howard Assn 69-84, Patron.
    Jamaica Committee (F) 66-66.


BRIGHT, URSULA M.  <MRS. JACOB BRIGHT, nee MELLOR>

    Manchester.

    Ladies' Natl Assn for Repeal of Contagious Diseases
       Acts 70-72, Exec.
    Vigilance Assn for Defense of Personal Rights (F)
       71-83, Exec.


BRINTON, JOHN

    Carpet Manufacturer.
    Liberal. MP Kidderminster 80-86. JP.
    Southwest London; Worcestershire.
    [Dods]

    Free Land League 86-86, V-Pres.
    Intl Arbitration & Peace Assn 81-81, V-Pres.


BRITTEN, BENJAMIN

    Workmen's Peace Assn 75-82, Treas.


BRITTEN, J.

    Natl Vigilance Assn (F) 85-85, Exec.


BROADHURST, HENRY (1840-1911)

    Trade Union Leader 72; Mason 53.
    Liberal. MP Stoke-on-Trent 80-85, Birmingham
       Bordesley 85-86, Nottingham West 86-92,
       Leicester 94-06. Parl U-Sec Home Off 86-86,
       JP.
    West Central London.
    [DNB, WWW, Dods, Dic Lab Biog]

    Free Land League 86-86, Exec.
    Intl Arbitration & Peace Assn 81-81, V-Pres.
    Working Men's Comtee Promoting Separation Church
       and State (F) 71-71, Exec.
    Travelling Tax Abolition Committee 82-85, Exec.


BRODRICK, GEORGE CHARLES (1831-1903)

    Eton; Balliol, Oxf; Lincoln's Inn.
    Journalist 60; College Fellow 55; Barrister 59;
       College Head 81.
    Liberal(Unionist). JP.
    Southwest London.
    [DNB, WWW, BP, Alum Oxon, Fosters]

    Assn for Improvement of London Workhouse
       Infirmaries 66-66, Exec.


BROGDEN, ALEXANDER (1825-1892)

    Kings Col London.
    Iron Manufacturer.
    Liberal. MP Wednesbury 68-85. JP.
    Southwest London; Lancashire.
    [MEB, Walfords, Dods, Direc Direcs]

    Natl Assn for Repeal Contagious Diseases Acts
       81-81, V-Pres.


BROOKE, SIR RICHARD, 7TH BT.  (1814-1888)

    Eton.
    Large Landowner 65; Cornet, Army 32; Lieutenant,
       Army 35.
    DL, JP.
    Baronet 65.
    Cheshire.
    [MEB, BP, Walfords, Bateman, Army List]

    Natl Assn for Promotion of State Colonization
       86-86, Patron.


BROOKE, STOPFORD AUGUSTUS (1832-1916)

    Kidderminster School, Kingston; Trin Col, Dublin.
    Perp. Curate 76; Author; Curate 57; Ordained
       Priest<CE> 58; College Head 81.
    West London.
    [DNB, WWW, Crockfds]

    Sunday Society (F) 75-90, V-Pres.
    Soc for Protection of Ancient Buildings (F) 78-85,
       Exec.

BROOKES, W.  M.

    Yorks, West Riding.

    Natl Soc for Preserving Memorials of Dead (F)
       81-82, Exec.


BROOMHALL, B.

    Anglo-Oriental Soc for Suppression Opium Trade
       83-83, Exec.


BROUGH, JOSHUA

    Intl Arbitration & Peace Assn 81-81, V-Pres.


BROUGHAM, HENRY PETER, 1ST BARON BROUGHAM AND VAUX
    (1778-1868)

    Edinburgh High School;  U Edinburgh;  Lincoln's
       Inn.
    Law Lord 30;  Advocate 00;  Barrister 08;  K.C.
       27;  Journalist;  Very Large Landowner.
    Radical.  MP Camelford 10-12, Winchelsea 15-30,
       Yorkshire W Riding 30-30.  Lord Chancellor
       30-34, PC Judicial Committee.
    Baron 30;  PC 30.
    Fellow Royal Society.
    London;  Westmorland.
    [DNB, MEB, BP, Alum Oxon]

    Howard Assn (F) 66-67, Patron.


BROWN, -

    Malthusian League (F) 77-79, Exec.


BROWN, SIR ALEXANDER HARGREAVES, 1ST BT.  (1844-1922)

    "In business";  Cornet, Army.
    Liberal(Unionist).  MP Wenlock 68-85,
       Wellington<Salop> 85-06.  JP.
    Baronet 03.
    Southwest London;  Surrey.
    [WWW, BP, Walfords]

    Commons Preservation Soc 80-86, Exec.
    Natl Assn for Repeal Contagious Diseases Acts
       81-81, V-Pres.


BROWN, ALEXANDER LAING (1851-1936)

    Textile Manufacturer.
    Radical.  MP Hawick 86-92.
    Galashiels.
    [Dods]

    Free Land League 86-86, V-Pres.


BROWN, HENRY

    Bradford.

    Jamaica Committee (F) 66-66.


BROWN, J. JENKYN

    Clergyman<Sect Unkn>.
    Birmingham.

    Natl Education League 71-71, Exec.


BROWN, JOHN

    JP.

    Intl Arbitration & Peace Assn 81-81, V-Pres.


BROWN, JOSEPH (1809-1902)

    Camberwell Grammar School;  Queens', Camb;  Middle
       Temple.
    Q.C.  65;  Barrister 45.
    CB.
    Fellow Geological Society.
    Northwest London.
    [DNB, WWW, Fosters]

    Intl Law Assn 74-74, Exec.


BROWNE, EDWARD HAROLD (1811-1891)

    Eton;  Emmanuel, Camb.
    Bishop Ely 64;  Bishop Winchester 73;  Ordained
       Priest<CE> 37;  Perp. Curate 37;  Rector 47;
       Vicar 50;  Norrisian Professor Divinity,
       Cambridge 54.
    Ely;  Winchester;  Surrey.
    [DNB, MEB, Alum Cantab, Alum Oxon, Crockfds]

    Natl Soc for Preserving Memorials of Dead (F)
       81-85, Patron.
    Central Assn for Stopping Sale Intox Liquors on
       Sunday 75-85, V-Pres.
    Victoria Street Soc for Protection of Animals from
       Vivisection 80-85, V-Pres.
    Soc for Promoting Increase of the Home Episcopate
       72-74, V-Pres.


BROWNE, H.  D.

    London.

    Jamaica Committee (F) 66-66.


BROWNE, HAROLD CARLYON GORE (1844-1919)

    Rugby;  Emmanuel, Camb;  Lincoln's Inn.
    Barrister 71.
    West London.
    [Alum Cantab, Fosters]

    Natl Fair Trade League (F) 81-82, Hon Sec.

BROWNE, PHILIP ( -1884)

Corpus Christi, Camb.
Perp. Curate 52;  Curate 42;  Ordained Priest<CE>
   43.
Birmingham.
[Alum Cantab, Crockfds]

Church Assn 80-80, Exec.


BROWNE, SAMUEL W.

Bristol.

Jamaica Committee (F) 66-66.


BROWNING, BENJAMIN

Physician.
Member Royal Col Physicians;  Fellow Chemical
   Society.
Southeast London.

Sanitary Institute 79-84, Exec.


BROWNING, G.

Fellow Royal Historical Society.
London.

Sunday Society 76-76, V-Pres.


BROWNING, ROBERT (1812-1889)

Poet.
West London.
[DNB, MEB, Alum Oxon]

Victoria Street Soc for Protection of Animals from
   Vivisection 80-85, V-Pres.


BRUCE, LORD CHARLES WILLIAM BRUDENELL (1834-1897)

Eton;  Christ Church, Oxf.
Captain, Army 59;  Cornet, Army 54;  Lieutenant,
   Army 56.
Liberal.  MP Wiltshire North 65-74, Marlborough
   78-85.  V-Chamberlain Royal Household 80-85,
   JP.
PC.
West London.
[BP, Walfords, Alum Cantab, Alum Oxon, Dods, Army
   List]

Assn for Improvement of London Workhouse
   Infirmaries 66-66, Exec.
Assn for Promoting Extension of Contagious Diseases
   Act 70-70, V-Pres.


BRUCE, ERNEST AUGUSTUS CHARLES BRUDENELL, 3RD MARQUIS OF
   AILESBURY (1811-1886)

Eton;  Trinity, Camb.
Very Large Landowner 78.
Conservative, then Liberal.  MP Marlborough 32-78.
   Lord Bedchamber 34-35, V-Chamberlain Royal
   Household 41-46, V-Chamberlain Royal Household
   52-58, Lord Lieutenant, DL, JP.
PC 41;  Marquis 78.

London;  Wiltshire.
[BP, Bateman, Alum Cantab, Alum Oxon, Dods]

Victoria Street Soc for Protection of Animals from
   Vivisection 80-85, V-Pres.


BRUCE, HENRY AUSTIN, 1ST BARON ABERDARE (1815-1895)

Swansea Grammar School;  Lincoln's Inn.
Colliery Owner;  Barrister 37;  Police Court
   Magistrate 47.
Liberal.  MP Merthyr-Tydvil 52-68, Renfrewshire
   69-73.  Parl U-Sec Home Off 62-64, V-P
   Education Committee 64-66, Charity Commissioner
   64-66, Church Estates Commissioner 65-66, Sec
   St Home Office 69-73, Ecclesiastical
   Commissioner 69-74, Lord Pres Council 73-74.
PC 64;  Baron 73;  GCB 85.
Fellow Royal Society;  Fellow Royal Geograph
   Society;  Royal Historical Society.
West London;  Glamorganshire.
[DNB, MEB, BP, Walfords, Alum Oxon, Fosters, Dods,
   Direc Direcs]

Smoke Abatement Committee 81-81.
Metro Free Libraries Assn 78-78, V-Pres.


BRUCE, JOHN COLLINGWOOD (1805-1892)

Mill Hill School;  U Glasgow.
Author;  Asst School Master 31;  School Head 34.
Fellow Society of Antiquaries.
Newcastle-upon-Tyne.
[DNB, MEB]

Assn for Promoting Extension of Contagious Diseases
   Act 68-68, V-Pres.


BRUCE, MICHAEL (1823-1883)

Maj. General 68;  Ensign, Army 40;  Captain, Army
   45;  Lt. Colonel 54;  Colonel 62;  Lt.
   General 80.
West London.
[MEB, Army List]

Assn for Promoting Extension of Contagious Diseases
   Act 68-70, V-Pres.


BRUCE, THOMAS JOHN HOVELL THURLOW-CUMMING-, 5TH BARON
   THURLOW (1838-1916)

Very Large Landowner 74;  Diplomatic Service 58.
Liberal.  Paymaster General 86-86, DL, JP.
Baron 74;  PC 86.
Fellow Royal Society.
Southwest London;  Morayshire.
[WWW, BP, Walfords, Bateman, Alum Oxon, Direc
   Direcs]

Sunday Society 79-90, V-Pres.
Free Land League 86-86, V-Pres, Exec.

BRUNNER, SIR JOHN TOMLINSON, 1ST BT. (1842-1919)

Everton School.
Alkali Manufacturer 73.
Liberal. MP Northwich, Cheshire 85-86, Northwich,
    Cheshire 87-10. DL, JP.
Baronet 95; PC 06.
Fellow Royal Society.
Southwest London; Northwich.
[WWW, BP, Dods, Direc Direcs]

Allotments & Small Holdings Assn 85-88, V-Pres.
Sunday Society 86-90, V-Pres.
Free Land League 86-86, V-Pres.


BRYAN, BENJAMIN

Victoria Street Soc for Protection of Animals from
    Vivisection 84-85, Secretary.


BRYANT, OLIVE <MISS>

Victoria Street Soc for Protection of Animals from
    Vivisection 84-85, Exec.


BRYCE, JAMES, 1ST VISCOUNT BRYCE (1838-1922)

Belfast Academy; Trinity, Oxf; Lincoln's Inn.
Regius Professor of Law, Oxford 70; College Fellow
    62; Barrister 67.
Liberal. MP Tower Hamlets 80-85, Aberdeen South
    85-06. Parl U-Sec For Off 86-86, Chanc Duchy
    Lancaster 92-94, Pres Board of Trade 94-95,
    Chief Sec Ireland 05-06, Ambassador 07-13, DL.
PC 92; OM 07; Viscount 14; GCVO 17.
Fellow Royal Society; British Academy; Fellow
    Royal Geograph Society.
West London.
[DNB, WWW, BP, Alum Cantab, Fosters, Dods]

Commons Preservation Soc 80-86, V-Pres, Chairman.
Soc for Protection of Ancient Buildings (F) 78-85,
    Exec.
Anglo-Armenian Assn (F) 78-78, President.


BRYSON, ALEXANDER (1802-1869)

Glasgow(Medical).
Dir Gen, RN Medical Serv 64; Med Service, RN 27;
    Dep Insp Gen, RN Medical Serv 54; Insp Gen, RN
    Medical Serv 55.
Fellow Royal Society; Fellow Royal Col Physicians.
Surrey.
[DNB, MEB]

Assn for Promoting Extension of Contagious Diseases
    Act 68-70, V-Pres.


BRYSON, JOHN

Pres, Northumberland Miners' Association.
Newcastle-upon-Tyne.

Land Law Reform League (F) 81-81, V-Pres.


BUCHANAN, GEORGE

Intl Arbitration & Peace Assn 84-87, Treas.


BUCHANAN, GEORGE (1827-1905)

U Glasgow; Andersonian U(Medical).
Surgeon 49; Medical School Professor 60.
Glasgow.
[DNB, WWW]

Assn for Promoting Extension of Contagious Diseases
    Act 68-68, V-Pres.


BUCKE, BENJAMIN WALTER (1821-1906)

King's College School; St John's, Camb.
Vicar 63; Ordained Priest<CE> 52; Curate 55.
Southeast London.
[Alum Cantab, Crockfds]

Church Assn 75-80, Exec.


BUCKLER, C. A.

Natl Soc for Preserving Memorials of Dead (F)
    81-84, Exec.


BUCKLEY, J. W.

Croydon.

Jamaica Committee (F) 66-66.


BUCKMASTER, J. C.

Science Examiner, So Kensington.
Fellow Geological Society; Fellow Chemical
    Society.
Southwest London.

Sunday Society (F) 75-90, V-Pres.


BUDGETT, JAMES S.

"In business".
London; Surrey.
[Direc Direcs]

Natl Assn for Repeal Contagious Diseases Acts
    84-84, V-Pres.


BUDGETT, SAMUEL

Bristol.

Natl Assn for Repeal Contagious Diseases Acts
    84-84, V-Pres.

BUDWORTH, PHILIP JOHN (1818- )

    Jesus, Camb;  Inner Temple.
    Landowner 61.
    DL, JP.
    West London;  Essex.
    [Walfords, Alum Cantab]

    Sunday Society 79-85, V-Pres.

BULLER, SPENCER <"CAPT.">

    Cheltenham.

    Church Assn 75-75, Exec.

BULLEY, FREDERIC (1810-1885)

    Magdalen, Oxf.
    College Head 55;  Ordained Priest<CE> 34;  College
       Fellow;  College Tutor.
    Oxford.
    [MEB, Alum Oxon, Crockfds]

    City Church & Churchyard Protection Soc (F) 80-83,
       V-Pres.

BUNCE, JOHN THACKRAY (1828-1899)

    King Edward's School, Birm.
    Newspaper Editor.
    JP.
    Fellow Royal Statistical Society;  Fellow Inst
       Journalists.
    Birmingham.
    [MEB, WWW]

    Natl Education League (F) 69-71, Exec.

BUNTING, - <MRS.>

    Natl Vigilance Assn (F) 85-85, Exec.

BUNTING, MARY HYETT <MRS. PERCY BUNTING, nee LIDGETT>

    West Central London.

    London Comtee Exposure & Suppresn Traffic In Girls
       (F) 80-85, Exec.
    Natl Vigilance Assn (F) 85-85, Exec.

BUNTING, SIR PERCY WILLIAM (1836-1911)

    Owens Col, Manch;  Lincoln's Inn.
    Barrister 62;  Journal Editor 82.
    Liberal.
    Kt 08.
    Northwest London.
    [DNB, WWW, Alum Cantab, Fosters]

    Natl Vigilance Assn (F) 85-85, Exec.

BURBIDGE, JOHN

    Perp. Curate 58;  Ordained Priest<CE> 56;  Curate
       56.
    Sheffield.
    [Crockfds]

    Church Assn 70-70, Exec.

BURBURY, - <MRS. WILLIAM BURBURY>

    London.

    Sunday Society (F) 75-90, V-Pres.

BURDETT, HENRY C.

    Fellow Royal Statistical Society.
    Northwest London.

    Sanitary Institute 78-84, Exec.

BURGES, YNYR HENRY (1834-1908)

    Christ Church, Oxf;  Lincoln's Inn.
    Substantial Landowner 89.
    Conservative. DL, JP.
    West London;  Co Tyrone.
    [WWW, Walfords, Alum Oxon, Army List]

    Metro Public Gardens Assn (F) 83-90, V-Chairman.

BURN, HENRY W.

    Sunday Society 76-76, Exec.

BURNEY, GEORGE

    West Central London.

    Commons Preservation Soc 69-84, Exec.
    Jamaica Committee (F) 66-66.

BURNLEY, W. F.

    Church Assn 67-85, V-Pres.

BURNS, DAWSON (1828-1909)

    General Baptist College.
    Baptist Minister 51.
    North London.
    [DNB]

    Public Museums & Free Libraries Assn 68-68, Exec.
    Jamaica Committee (F) 66-66.

BURNS, JOHN

    Glasgow.

    Plimsoll and Seamen's Fund Committee (F) 73-73,
       Exec.


BURROUGHS, S. M.

    English Land Restoration League 85-85, Exec.


BURROWS, SIR GEORGE, 1ST BT. (1801-1887)

    Ealing School; Gonville & Caius, Camb; St
       Bartholomew's Hosp.
    Physician 41.
    Baronet 74.
    Fellow Royal Society; Fellow Royal Col Physicians;
       Royal Med & Chir Society; Br Medical Assn.
    West London.
    [DNB, MEB, BP, Alum Cantab, Alum Oxon]

    Assn for Promoting Extension of Contagious Diseases
       Act 68-70, V-Pres.


BURROWS, HERBERT

    Land Nationalization Soc (F) 81-81, Exec.
    Natl Assn for Repeal Blasphemy Laws (F) 84-84,
       Exec.


BURROWS, SIR JOHN CORDY (1813-1876)

    Ipswich Grammar School; St Thomas's Hospital Lond.
    Physician 39.
    Kt 73.
    Fellow Royal Col Surgeons; Society of
       Apothecaries; Fellow Linnean Society; Fellow
       Zoological Society; Fellow Royal Geograph
       Society.
    Brighton.
    [DNB, MEB]

    Sunday Society (F) 75-75, V-Pres.


BURT, JAMES

    Worthing.

    Natl Soc for Preserving Memorials of Dead (F)
       81-82, Exec.


BURT, THOMAS (1837-1922)

    Trade Union Leader 65; Miner 47.
    Radical. MP Morpeth 74-18. Parl Sec Board of
       Trade 92-95.
    PC 06.
    Southwest London; Newcastle-upon-Tyne.
    [DNB, WWW, Dods, Dic Lab Biog]

    Sunday Society (F) 75-90, V-Pres, President.
    Anglo-Oriental Soc for Suppression Opium Trade
       83-86, Exec.
    Free Land League 86-86, V-Pres.
    Intl Arbitration & Peace Assn 81-81, V-Pres.
    Land Law Reform League (F) 81-84, V-Pres.

    London Soc for Abolition of Compulsory Vaccination
       81-81, V-Pres.
    Workmen's Peace Assn 75-82, President.
    Natl Assn for Repeal Contagious Diseases Acts
       81-81, V-Pres.
    Travelling Tax Abolition Committee (F) 77-85, Exec.


BURTON, SIR FREDERIC WILLIAM (1816-1900)

    Director, Natl Gallery 74; Artist.
    Kt 84.
    Fellow Society of Antiquaries; Royal Hibernian
       Society; Royal Society Water Colour Painters;
       Royal Irish Academy.
    West London.
    [DNB, MEB, WWW]

    Soc for Protection of Ancient Buildings (F) 78-85,
       Exec.


BUSK, E. S. <MISS>

    Kyrle Soc 85-89, Exec.


BUSZARD, MARSTON CLARKE (1837-1921)

    Rugby; Trinity, Camb; Inner Temple.
    Q.C. 77; Barrister 62.
    Liberal(Unionist). MP Stamford 80-85. JP.
    West London; Lutterworth.
    [WWW, Alum Cantab, Fosters, Dods]

    Sunday Society 84-90, V-Pres.


BUTLER, GEORGE (1819-1890)

    Harrow; Exeter, Oxf.
    College Head 66; College Fellow 42; Curate 54;
       Ordained Priest<CE> 55; School Head 55;
       College V-Principal 58; Canon 82.
    Liverpool; Winchester.
    [DNB, MEB, Alum Cantab, Alum Oxon, Crockfds]

    Assn for Improvement of Public Morals (F) 79-81,
       Exec.
    Vigilance Assn for Defense of Personal Rights (F)
       71-71, Exec.
    Natl Vigilance Assn (F) 85-85, Exec.


BUTLER, GEORGE GREY (1852-1935)

    Cheltenham College; Trinity, Camb; Inner Temple.
    Barrister 83; Asst Civ Serv Examiner 76; Sen Civ
       Serv Examiner 82.
    JP.
    Fellow Royal Geograph Society; Fellow Geological
       Society.
    West London; Northumberland.
    [WWW, Alum Cantab, Fosters]

    London Comtee Exposure & Suppresn Traffic In Girls
       85-85, Exec.

BUTLER, HENRY MONTAGUE (1833-1918)

Harrow; Trinity, Camb.
School Head 59; College Fellow 55; Ordained
    Priest<CE> 59; Curate; Prebendary 82; Dean
    85; Hon. Canon 97.
Harrow-on-the-Hill.
[WWW, Alum Cantab, Crockfds]

Plimsoll and Seamen's Fund Committee (F) 73-73,
    Exec.


BUTLER, JOSEPHINE E.  <MRS. GEORGE BUTLER, nee GREY>
(1828-1906)

Liverpool.
[DNB, WWW]

Assn for Improvement of Public Morals (F) 79-81,
    Exec.
Ladies' Natl Assn for Repeal of Contagious Diseases
    Acts (F) 69-85, Hon Sec.
London Comtee Exposure & Suppresn Traffic In Girls
    (F) 80-80, Exec.
London Soc for Abolition of Compulsory Vaccination
    81-81, V-Pres.
Vigilance Assn for Defense of Personal Rights (F)
    71-71, Exec.
Natl Vigilance Assn (F) 85-85, Exec.


BUTTERWORTH, EDWIN

Manchester.

Jamaica Committee (F) 66-66.


BUTTIFANT, A.  G.


Land Nationalization Soc 85-85, Exec.


BUXTON, CHARLES (1823-1871)

Trinity, Camb.
Brewer; Landowner.
Liberal.  MP Newport[I Of W] 57-59, Maidstone
    59-65, Surrey East 65-71.  JP.
Southwest London;  Surrey.
[DNB, MEB, Walfords, Alum Cantab, Dods]

Commons Preservation Soc 69-69, Exec.
Public Museums & Free Libraries Assn 68-68, V-Pres.
Assn for Promoting Extension of Contagious Diseases
    Act 70-70, V-Pres.
Howard Assn 70-70, Patron.
Jamaica Committee (F) 66-66, Chairman.


BUXTON, EDWARD NORTH (1840-1924)

Trinity, Camb.
Brewer.
Liberal.  MP Walthamstow 85-86.  DL, JP.
Fellow Royal Geograph Society.
Essex.
[WWW, Walfords, Alum Cantab, Dods, Direc Direcs,
    BP]

Natl Assn for Promotion of State Colonization
    86-86, Exec, V-Pres.
Commons Preservation Soc (F) 65-86, Exec, V-Pres.


BUXTON, FRANCIS WILLIAM (1847-1911)

Trinity, Camb;  Lincoln's Inn.
Barrister 74;  Banker;  Public Works Loan
    Commissioner 93.
Liberal.  MP Andover 80-85.  JP.
Royal Economic Society;  Royal Institution;  Fellow
    Royal Geograph Society.
Southwest London;  Sussex.
[WWW, BP, Alum Cantab, Fosters, Dods, Direc Direcs]

Commons Preservation Soc 80-86, Exec.


BUXTON, GERALD (1862-1928)

Harrow;  Trinity, Camb.
Brewer.
JP.
Essex.
[BP, Alum Cantab, Direc Direcs]

Commons Preservation Soc 85-86, Exec.


BUXTON, SAMUEL GURNEY (1838-1909)

Harrow;  Trinity, Camb.
Banker.
DL, JP.
Norfolk.
[BP, Walfords, Alum Cantab, Direc Direcs]

Commons Preservation Soc 69-76, Exec.


BUXTON, SYDNEY CHARLES, 1ST EARL BUXTON (1853-1934)

Clifton College;  Trinity, Camb.
Governor General, U South Africa 14.
Radical.  MP Peterborough 83-85, Twr Hmlts Poplar
    86-14.  Parl U-Sec Col Off 92-95, Postmaster
    General 05-10, Pres Board of Trade 10-14.
PC 05;  Viscount 14;  GCMG 14;  Earl 20.
Southwest London;  Sussex.
[DNB, WWW, BP, Alum Cantab, Dods]

Commons Preservation Soc 81-86, Exec.
Natl Footpaths Preservation Soc (F) 85-90, V-Pres.
Free Land League 86-86, V-Pres.
London Municipal Reform League 82-85, Exec,
    V-Chairman.


BUXTON, THOMAS FOWELL (1822-1908)

Trinity, Camb.
Brewer;  Landowner.
JP.
Hertfordshire;  Norfolk.
[BP, Walfords, Alum Cantab]

Jamaica Committee (F) 66-66.


BUXTON, SIR THOMAS FOWELL, 3RD BT.  (1837-1915)

Harrow;  Trinity, Camb.
Brewer;  Substantial Landowner 58;  Gov, South
    Australia 95.
Liberal.  MP King's Lynn 65-68.  DL, JP.
Baronet 58;  KCMG 95;  GCMG 99.
Fellow Royal Geograph Society.
Southwest London;  Norfolk;  Essex.
[DNB, BP, Walfords, Bateman, Alum Cantab, Dods,
    Direc Direcs]

Commons Preservation Soc (F) 65-86, Exec.
Howard Assn 71-84, Patron.
Jamaica Committee (F) 66-66.


BYNG, GEORGE HENRY CHARLES, 3RD EARL OF STRAFFORD
(1830-1898)

Eton;  Christ Church, Oxf.
Very Large Landowner 86;  First Civil Service
    Commssioner.
Liberal.  MP Tavistock 52-57, Middlesex 57-74.
    Parl Sec Poor Law Board 65-66, Parl U-Sec For
    Off 70-74, Parl U-Sec India 80-82, Dep
    Commissioner Board of Works, Lord Lieutenant,
    DL, JP.
Baron 74;  Earl 86.
West London;  North London.
[MEB, WWW, BP, Walfords, Alum Oxon, Dods]

Natl Footpaths Preservation Soc 86-90, V-Pres.


BYRNE, THOMAS

Dublin.

Assn for Promoting Extension of Contagious Diseases
    Act 70-70, V-Pres.


BYRON, GEORGE FREDERICK WILLIAM, 9TH BARON BYRON
(1855-1917)

Harrow;  Christ Church, Oxf.
Landowner.
Conservative.
Baron 70.
Northwest London;  Derbyshire.
[WWW, BP, Walfords, Alum Oxon]

Natl Assn for Promotion of State Colonization
    86-86, V-Pres.


BYWATER, INGRAM (1840-1914)

King's College School;  Queen's, Oxf.
Librarian;  College Fellow 63;  College Reader 84;
    Regius Professor of Greek, Oxford 93.
Liberal.
British Academy.
Oxford.
[DNB, WWW, Alum Cantab, Alum Oxon]

Soc for Protection of Ancient Buildings (F) 78-85,
    Exec.


CAINE, WILLIAM (1825-1886)

Trin Col, Dublin.
Rector 72;  Curate 55;  Ordained Priest<CE> 56;
    Chaplain 67.
Salford;  Denton.
[MEB, Crockfds]

Central Assn for Stopping Sale Intox Liquors on
    Sunday (F) 67-85, Exec.


CAINE, WILLIAM SPROSTON (1842-1903)

Metal Merchant 61.
Radical.  MP Scarborough 80-85, Barrow-In-Furness
    86-90, Bradford East 92-95, Camborne 00-03.
    Lord Admiralty 84-85, JP.
Liverpool;  Southwest London.
[DNB, WWW, Dods]

Central Assn for Stopping Sale Intox Liquors on
    Sunday 75-85, V-Pres.
Natl Assn for Repeal Contagious Diseases Acts
    81-81, V-Pres.


CAIRD, SIR JAMES (1816-1892)

Edinburgh High School;  U Edinburgh.
Farmer 41;  Author;  Sen. Enclosure Commissioner
    65;  Director, Board of Agriculture Land Dept
    89.
Liberal.  MP Dartmouth 57-59, Stirlingshire 59-65.
    DL, JP.
CB 69;  KCB 82;  PC 89.
Fellow Royal Society;  Fellow Royal Statistical
    Society.
Southwest London;  Scotland.
[DNB, MEB, Walfords, Dods, Direc Direcs]

Indian Reform Assn 84-84, Exec.


CAIRNES, JOHN ELLIOT (1823-1875)

Trin Col, Dublin.
Professor of Political Economy, U Col London 66;
    Barrister 57;  Political Economist.
West London;  Southeast London.
[DNB, MEB]

Jamaica Committee (F) 66-66.


CALDERON, PHILIP HERMOGENES (1833-1898)

Leigh's Art Sch.
Artist;  Keeper, Royal Academy 87.
Royal Academy.
Northwest London.
[DNB, Bryan's Painters]

Soc for Protection of Ancient Buildings (F) 78-78,
    Exec.


CALDICOTT, JOHN WILLIAM (1819-1895)

King Edward's School, Birm;  Jesus, Oxf.
School Head 60;  College Lecturer 52;  Ordained
    Priest<CE> 54;  Rector 83.
Bristol.
[MEB, Alum Oxon, Crockfds]

Natl Education League 71-71, Exec.


CALLENDER, WILLIAM ROMAINE ( -1872)

JP.
Manchester.

Central Assn for Stopping Sale Intox Liquors on
    Sunday 70-70, V-Pres.

CALLENDER, WILLIAM ROMAINE, JUN. (1825-1876)

    Cotton Manufacturer.
    Conservative. MP Manchester 74-76. DL, JP.
    Fellow Society of Antiquaries.
    Manchester.
    [MEB, Walfords, Dods]

    Central Assn for Stopping Sale Intox Liquors on
        Sunday 70-75, V-Pres.
    Natl Education Union (F) 69-71, Exec.


CAMERON, ANDREW

    Southwest London.

    London Municipal Reform League 82-85, Exec.


CAMERON, SIR CHARLES, 1ST BT. (1841-1924)

    Madras College, St Andrews; Trin Col, Dublin;
        Dublin(Medical).
    Newspaper Editor 64.
    Radical. MP Glasgow 74-85, Glasgow College 85-95,
        Glasgow Bridgeton 97-00. DL, JP.
    Baronet 93.
    Southwest London; Scotland.
    [WWW, BP, Dods, Direc Direcs]

    Intl Arbitration & Peace Assn 81-81, V-Pres.
    Central Assn for Stopping Sale Intox Liquors on
        Sunday 75-85, V-Pres.
    Free Land League 86-86, V-Pres.
    Natl Assn for Repeal Contagious Diseases Acts
        81-81, V-Pres.


CAMERON, DONALD (1835-1905)

    Harrow.
    Very Large Landowner 58; Attache, Dip Serv 52.
    Conservative. MP Inverness-Shire 68-85. Groom of
        the Robes 74-80, Lord Lieutenant, DL, JP.
    Scotland.
    [WWW, Walfords, Bateman, Dods, Direc Direcs]

    Natl Emigration League (F) 70-70, V-Pres.


CAMERON, JOHN MCDONALD (1847-1912)

    Royal School of Mines.
    Chemist, Inland Revenue 71; Instructor, Royal
        School of Mines 74; Master, Sydney Mint.
    Radical. MP Wick 85-92.
    West London.
    [Dods, Direc Direcs]

    Free Land League 86-86, V-Pres.


CAMPBELL, DAWSON

    Corpus Christi, Camb.
    Vicar 75; Curate 70; Ordained Priest<CE> 71.
    Ware.
    [Alum Cantab, Crockfds]

    Church Assn 75-78, Exec.


CAMPBELL, DUGALD JOHN PHILIP (1828-1885)

    Marshal, City of London 73; Sub-Lt., Army 46;
        Lieutenant, Army 49; Captain, Army 61; Major
        66.
    London.
    [MEB, Army List]

    Intl Arbitration & Peace Assn 81-81, V-Pres.


CAMPBELL, SIR GEORGE (1824-1892)

    Madras College, St Andrews; U St Andrews; Inner
        Temple.
    Author; India Civil Service 42; Judge, India 62;
        Lt Gov, Bengal 71.
    Liberal. MP Kirkcaldy 75-92. Council of India
        74-75, DL, JP.
    KCSI 73.
    Southwest London; Scotland.
    [DNB, MEB, BP, Alum Oxon, Fosters, Dods]

    Free Land League 86-86, V-Pres, Exec.
    Intl Arbitration & Peace Assn 81-81, V-Pres.


CAMPBELL, GEORGE DOUGLAS, 8TH DUKE OF ARGYLL (1823-1900)

    Very Large Landowner 47; Chancellor, U St Andrews
        51.
    Liberal(Unionist). Lord Privy Seal 52-55,
        Postmaster General 55-58, Lord Privy Seal
        59-66, Sec St India 68-74, Lord Privy Seal
        80-81, Lord Lieutenant 62-00.
    Duke 47; PC 53; KT 56; KG 84.
    Fellow Royal Society; Fellow Royal Society Edinb.
    West London; Scotland.
    [DNB, MEB, WWW, BP, Walfords, Bateman]

    Central Vigilance Comtee for Repression Immorality
        (F) 83-84, V-Pres.


CAMPBELL, JAMES COLQUHOUN (1813-1895)

    Trinity, Camb.
    Bishop Bangor 59; Curate 37; Ordained Priest<CE>
        38; Rector 39; Vicar 40; Prebendary 51;
        Archdeacon 57.
    Bangor.
    [MEB, Alum Cantab, Crockfds]

    Central Assn for Stopping Sale Intox Liquors on
        Sunday 70-85, V-Pres.


CAMPBELL, JAMES ROBERTSON (1814-1884)

    U Glasgow.
    Congregational Minister 35.
    Bradford.
    [MEB]

    Jamaica Committee (F) 66-66.

CAMPBELL, JOHN ALEXANDER GAVIN, 1ST MARQUIS OF
    BREADALBANE (1851-1922)

    U St Andrews.
    Very Large Landowner 71.
    Liberal.  Treas Royal Household 80-85, Lord Steward
        Royal Household 92-95, Lord Lieutenant 14-  ,
        DL, JP.
    Earl 71;  KG;  PC;  Marquis 85.
    West London;  Scotland.
    [WWW, BP, Bateman, Direc Direcs]

    Free Land League 86-86, V-Pres.


CAMPBELL, LEWIS (1830-1908)

    Edinburgh Academy;  Balliol, Oxf.
    Professor of Greek, St Andrews 63;  College Fellow
        55;  College Tutor 56;  Ordained Priest<CE> 57;
        Vicar 58.
    St Andrews.
    [DNB, Alum Oxon, Crockfds]

    Sunday Society 80-90, V-Pres.


CAMPE, CHARLES

    Perp. Curate 49;  Vicar 74;  Curate 46;  Ordained
        Priest<CE> 47.
    West London;  Torquay;  South London.
    [Crockfds]

    Church Assn 67-85, Exec.


CANNING, EMMELINE ROSABELLE ( -1898)

    [BP]

    Victoria Street Soc for Protection of Animals from
        Vivisection 80-82, Exec.


CAPARN, WILLIAM BARTON (1817- )

    Brasenose, Oxf.
    Vicar 46;  Ordained Priest<CE> 45.
    Taunton.
    [Alum Oxon, Crockfds]

    Soc for Promoting Increase of the Home Episcopate
        72-74, Exec.


CAPE, LAWSON (1807-1877)

    St Bartholomew's Hosp.
    Physician 33.
    Fellow Royal Col Physicians.
    West London.
    [MEB]

    Soc for Abolition of Vivisection 76-76, Exec.


CAPEL, BURY (1825-1815)

    Christ's, Camb.
    Vicar 63;  College Fellow 52;  Curate 52;  Ordained
        Priest<CE> 53;  Perp. Curate 60;  Prebendary
        77;  Rural Dean 95.
    Abergavenny.
    [Alum Cantab, Crockfds]

    Church Assn 70-75, Exec.


CAPEL, THOMAS JOHN (1836-1911)

    Rector, RC U Kensington 74;  Priest<RC> 60;
        Monsignor<RC> 68;  Domestic Prelate<RC> 73;
        School Head 73.
    London.
    [DNB, WWW]

    Sunday Society 76-80, V-Pres.


CAPELL, ARTHUR ALGERNON, 6TH EARL OF ESSEX (1803-1892)

    Eton.
    Very Large Landowner 39.
    JP.
    Earl 39.
    Southwest London;  Hertfordshire.
    [BP, Walfords, Bateman]

    Natl Soc for Preserving Memorials of Dead 84-84,
        Patron.


CAPELL, REGINALD ALGERNON (1830-1906)

    Harrow;  Trinity, Oxf.
    JP.
    West London;  Hertfordshire.
    [WWW, BP, Alum Oxon]

    Natl Assn for Promotion of State Colonization
        86-86, Exec.


CARBUTT, SIR EDWARD HAMER, 1ST BT.  (1838-1905)

    Manufacturing Engineer.
    Liberal.  MP Monmouthshire Dist 80-86.  DL.
    Baronet 92.
    West London;  Leeds;  Monmouthshire.
    [BP, Dods]

    Free Land League 86-86, V-Pres.


CARDELL, J. M.

    Salisbury.

    Assn for Promoting Extension of Contagious Diseases
        Act 68-70, V-Pres.


CAREY, FRANCIS E.

    Physician.
    Guernsey.

    Assn for Promoting Extension of Contagious Diseases
        Act 68-70, V-Pres.

CAREY, J. JAMES

    Fellow Royal Geograph Society.
    Brixham.

    Natl Soc for Preserving Memorials of Dead (F)
       81-81, Exec.


CARLETON, DUDLEY WILMOT, 4TH BARON DORCHESTER
    (1822-1897)

    Very Large Landowner 75; Sub-Lt., Army 40;
       Ensign, Army 41; Captain, Army 47; Lt.
       Colonel 54; Colonel 62.
    Liberal(Unionist).
    Baron 75.
    West London.
    [MEB, WWW, BP, Walfords, Bateman, Army List]

    Natl Assn for Promotion of State Colonization
       86-86, V-Pres, Exec.
    Metro Public Gardens Assn 84-90, V-Chairman.
    Sunday Society 79-90, V-Pres.
    Assn for Promoting Extension of Contagious Diseases
       Act 68-70, V-Pres.


CARLISLE, HENRY HERMANN

    Independent Minister.
    Southampton.

    Central Assn for Stopping Sale Intox Liquors on
       Sunday 85-85, Exec.


CARLYLE, THOMAS (1795-1881)

    U Edinburgh.
    Author; Literary Critic.
    Southwest London.
    [DNB, MEB]

    City Church & Churchyard Protection Soc (F) 80-80,
       V-Pres.
    Soc for Protection of Ancient Buildings (F) 78-80,
       Exec.
    Victoria Street Soc for Protection of Animals from
       Vivisection 80-80, V-Pres.


CARNEGIE, GEORGE JOHN, 9TH EARL OF NORTHESK (1843-1891)

    Large Landowner 78; Cornet, Army 62; Lieutenant,
       Army 62; Captain, Army 66; Lt. Colonel 73.
    DL.
    Earl 78.
    Angus.
    [BP, Walfords, Bateman, Army List]

    Natl Soc for Preserving Memorials of Dead (F)
       81-88, Exec.


CARPENTER, ALFRED (1825-1892)

    St Thomas´s Hospital Lond.
    Physician 59.
    Liberal. JP.
    Member Royal Col Physicians; Member Royal Col
       Surgeons; Br Medical Assn.
    Croydon.
    [DNB, MEB]

    Sanitary Institute 80-89, Chairman, V-Chairman.
    Smoke Abatement Committee 81-81.


CARPENTER, MARY (1807-1877)

    Reformatory School Head 52; Industrial School Head
       59.
    Bristol.
    [MEB]

    Sunday Society 76-77, V-Pres.


CARPENTER, WILLIAM

    London.

    Jamaica Committee (F) 66-66.


CARPENTER, WILLIAM BOYD (1841-1918)

    Royal Institution, Liverpool; St Catherine´s,
       Camb.
    Bishop Ripon 84; Ordained Priest<CE> 64; Curate
       64; Vicar 70; Canon 82.
    KCVO 12.
    Fellow Royal Society Literature.
    West London; Ripon.
    [DNB, WWW, Alum Cantab, Crockfds]

    Natl Assn for Promotion of State Colonization
       86-86, Patron.
    Central Assn for Stopping Sale Intox Liquors on
       Sunday 85-85, V-Pres.


CARR,

    Physician.

    Assn for Improvement of London Workhouse
       Infirmaries 66-66, Exec.


CARR, ISAAC

    Royston.

    Jamaica Committee (F) 66-66.


CARR, JOSEPH WILLIAM COMYNS (1849-1916)

    University Col London; Inner Temple.
    Barrister 72; Journal Editor 75; Literary Critic;
       Art Critic.
    Northwest London.
    [WWW, Fosters]

    Sunday Society 80-90, V-Pres.
    Soc for Protection of Ancient Buildings (F) 78-85,
       Exec.


CARREL, F. POINGDESTRE

    Kent.

    Natl Soc for Preserving Memorials of Dead (F)
       81-84, Exec.

CARRINGTON, CHARLES ROBERT WYNN-, 1ST MARQUIS OF
    LINCOLNSHIRE (1843-1928)

    Eton;  Trinity, Camb.
    Very Large Landowner;  Captain, Army 65;  Gov, New
        South Wales 85.
    Liberal.  MP Wycombe 65-68.  Chamberlain Royal
        Household 92-95, Pres Board of Agriculture
        05-11, Lord Privy Seal 11-12, DL, JP.
    Baron 68;  PC 81;  Viscount 95;  Earl 95;  KG 06;
        Marquis 12.
    Southwest London;  Buckinghamshire.
    [WWW, BP, Alum Cantab, Dods]

    Allotments & Small Holdings Assn 85-88, V-Pres.


CARSON, THOMAS

    Physician.
    Liverpool.

    Travelling Tax Abolition Committee 80-85, Exec.


CARTER, E.  HAROLD

    Allotments & Small Holdings Assn 85-85, Exec.


CARTER, JOHN (1804-1878)

    Watchmaker.
    Fellow Society of Antiquaries;  Fellow Royal
        Astronomical Society.
    East Central London.
    [MEB]

    Jamaica Committee (F) 66-66.


CARTER, JOHN MONEY

    Lt. Colonel 58;  Cornet, Army 32;  Lieutenant,
        Army 35;  Captain, Army 39.
    [Army List]

    Church Assn 85-85, Exec.


CARTER, ROBERT BRUDENELL (1828-1918)

    London Hospital.
    Surgeon.
    Fellow Royal Col Surgeons;  Medical Society of
        Lond.
    West London.
    [WWW]

    Sanitary Institute 78-89, Exec.
    Railway Passengers' Protection Assn 86-86, Exec.


CARTER, ROBERT MEEK (1814-1882)

    Coal Merchant;  Cloth Finisher.
    Radical.  MP Leeds 68-76.
    Southwest London;  Leeds;  Yorks, West Riding.
    [MEB, Walfords, Dods]

    Jamaica Committee (F) 66-66.
    Plimsoll and Seamen's Fund Committee (F) 73-73,
        Exec.


CASSAL, CHARLES EDWARD (1858-1921)

    Univ College School;  University Col London.
    College Laboratory Demonstrator 79;  Public Analyst
        85.
    Fellow Chemical Society;  Inst of Chemistry.
    Ealing.
    [WWW]

    Sanitary Institute 85-88, Exec.
    Sunday Society 79-89, Exec.


CASSIN, BURMAN (1835-1892)

    St Paul's, London;  Trinity, Camb.
    Rector 78;  Curate 58;  Ordained Priest<CE> 59;
        Vicar 60.
    Southeast London.
    [Alum Cantab, Crockfds]

    Church Assn 80-80, Exec.


CASSON, W.  A.

    North London.

    League for Defense of Constitutional Rights 84-84,
        Hon Sec.


CATCHPOOL, R.  D.

    Reading.

    Jamaica Committee (F) 66-66.


CATES, ARTHUR (1829-1901)

    King's College School.
    Architect.
    Fellow Royal Inst Br Architects;  Surveyors'
        Institute;  Br Archeol Assn;  Architectural
        Assn.
    Southwest London.
    [DNB, WWW]

    Sunday Society 80-90, V-Pres.


CATHCART, ALAN FREDERICK, 3RD EARL CATHCART (1828-1905)

    Scottish Nav and Mil Acad.
    Large Landowner 59;  Lieutenant, Army.
    Conservative.  DL, JP.
    Earl 59.
    Southwest London;  Yorks, North Riding.
    [WWW, BP, Walfords, Bateman, Alum Cantab]

    Church Assn 75-75, V-Pres.


CATHCART, EMILY ELIZA, LADY GORDON <MRS. J.  GORDON &
    LADY R.  CATHCART, nee PRINGLE>

    Surrey;  Scotland.
    [BP]

    Natl Assn for Promotion of State Colonization
        86-86, V-Pres.

CAVE, ALFRED THOMAS TOWNSHEND VERNEY-, 5TH BARON BRAYE
(1849-1928)

>Eton; Christ Church, Oxf.
Substantial Landowner 79; Poet.
Liberal(Unionist). DL, JP.
Baron 79.
West London; Warwickshire.
[WWW, BP, Bateman, Alum Oxon]

>Sanitary Institute 80-88, Treas.


CAVE, SIR STEPHEN (1820-1880)

>Harrow; Balliol, Oxf; Inner Temple.
Barrister 46.
Conservative. MP New Shoreham 59-80. Paymaster
    General 66-68, V-P Board of Trade 66-68, Judge
    Advocate General 74-75, Paymaster General
    74-80, DL, JP.
PC 66; GCB 80.
Fellow Society of Antiquaries; Fellow Zoological
    Society.
Southwest London; Bristol.
[DNB, MEB, Alum Oxon, Dods]

>Assn for Improvement of London Workhouse
    Infirmaries 66-66, Exec.


CAVENDISH, LORD GEORGE HENRY (1810-1880)

>Eton; Trinity, Camb.
Liberal. MP Derbyshire North 34-80. DL, JP.
Southwest London; Derbyshire.
[MEB, BP, Walfords, Dods]

>Plimsoll and Seamen's Fund Committee (F) 73-73,
    Exec.


CAVENDISH, SPENCER COMPTON, 8TH DUKE OF DEVONSHIRE
(1833-1908)

>Trinity, Camb.
Very Large Landowner 91.
Liberal(Unionist). MP Lancashire North 57-68,
    Radnor District 69-80, Lancashire NE 80-85,
    Rossendale, Lancs NE 85-91. Parl U-Sec War
    63-66, Sec St War 66-66, Postmaster General
    68-71, Chief Sec Ireland 71-74, Sec St India
    80-82, Sec St War 82-85, Lord Pres Council
    95-03, Pres Board of Education 00-02.
PC 66; Duke 91; KG 92; GCVO 07.
Fellow Royal Society.
West London; Derbyshire.
[DNB, BP, Walfords, Bateman, Alum Cantab, Alum
    Oxon, Dods, Direc Direcs]

>Natl Footpaths Preservation Soc 86-90, V-Pres.


CAWLEY, CHARLES EDWARD (1812-1877)

>Civil Engineer.
Conservative. MP Salford 68-77.
Member Inst Civ Engineers.
Southwest London; Salford.
[MEB, Walfords, Dods]

>Central Assn for Stopping Sale Intox Liquors on
    Sunday 70-75, V-Pres.
Natl Education Union 70-76, Exec.


CECIL, LORD EUSTACE HENRY BROWNLOW (1834-1921)

>Harrow; Royal Military College, Sandhurst.
Ensign, Army 51; Captain, Army 54; Lt. Colonel
    61.
Conservative. MP Essex South 65-68, Essex West
    68-85. Surveyor General Ordnance 74-80, JP.
Southwest London; Dorsetshire.
[WWW, BP, Walfords, Dods, Direc Direcs, Army List]

>Plimsoll and Seamen's Fund Committee (F) 73-73,
    Exec.


CECIL, ROBERT ARTHUR TALBOT GASCOYNE-, 3RD MARQUIS OF
SALISBURY (1830-1903)

>Eton; Christ Church, Oxf; Lincoln's Inn.
Very Large Landowner 68.
Conservative. MP Stamford 53-68. Sec St India
    66-67, Sec St India 74-78, Sec St Foreign Off
    78-80, Prime Minister 85-86, Prime Minister
    86-92, Prime Minister 95-02, Lord Warden Cinque
    Ports 96-02, DL.
PC 66; Marquis 68; KG 78; GCVO 02.
Southwest London; Hertfordshire; Dorsetshire.
[DNB, BP, Walfords, Bateman, Alum Oxon, Dods]

>Assn for Improvement of London Workhouse
    Infirmaries 66-66, Exec.


CECIL, WILLIAM ALLEYNE, 3RD MARQUIS OF EXETER
(1825-1895)

>Eton; St John's, Camb.
Very Large Landowner 67.
Conservative. MP Lincolnshire South 47-57,
    Northamptonshire N 57-67. Treas Royal
    Household 66-67, DL, JP.
PC 66; Marquis 67.
Lincolnshire.
[MEB, BP, Walfords, Bateman, Alum Cantab, Dods]

>Assn for Improvement of London Workhouse
    Infirmaries 66-66, Exec.
Plimsoll and Seamen's Fund Committee (F) 73-73,
    Exec.


CHADWICK, SIR EDWIN (1800-1890)

>Inner Temple.
Civil Servant; Barrister 30; Asst Poor Law Commnr
    32; Chief Poor Law Commnr 33; Sec, Poor Law
    Commn 34; General Board of Health 48.
CB 48; KCB 89.
Br Assn; Society of the Arts.
Southwest London.
[DNB, MEB, Fosters]

>Smoke Abatement Committee 81-81.
Sanitary Institute 78-89, V-Pres.


CHALKLEY, HENRY G.

>Howard Assn 78-84, Exec.

CHALMERS, FREDERICK WILLIAM MARSH (1836-1898)

Brighton College;  Gonville & Caius, Camb.
Merchant 69;  Ensign, Army 55;  Lieutenant, Army
58.
East Central London;  Kent.
[Alum Cantab, Direc Direcs, Army List]

Natl Assn for Promotion of State Colonization
86-86, V-Pres.

CHAMBERLAIN, JOHN HENRY (1831-1883)

Architect 56;  Manager, Midland Institute 68.
JP.
Fellow Royal Inst Br Architects;  Society of Br
Artists.
Birmingham.
[DNB]

Soc for Protection of Ancient Buildings 80-80,
Exec.
Natl Education League (F) 69-71, Exec.

CHAMBERLAIN, JOSEPH (1836-1914)

Univ College School.
Screw Manufacturer 54.
Liberal(Unionist).  MP Birmingham 76-85, Birmingham
West 85-06.  Pres Board of Trade 80-85, Pres
Local Govt Board 86-86, Sec St Colonial Off
95-03, JP.
PC 80.
Fellow Royal Society.
Southwest London;  Birmingham.
[DNB, WWW, Alum Cantab, Dods]

Allotments & Small Holdings Assn 85-85, V-Pres.
Sunday Society 76-90, V-Pres.
Free Land League 86-86, V-Pres.
Natl Education League (F) 69-71, Chairman,
V-Chairman.

CHAMBERLAIN, RICHARD (1840-1899)

Univ College School.
Brass Foundry Owner 63.
Liberal(Unionist).  MP Islington West 85-92.  JP.
West London;  Birmingham.
[MEB, Direc Direcs]

Sunday Society 86-90, V-Pres.

CHAMBERLAIN, THOMAS (1810-1892)

Westminster School;  Christ Church, Oxf.
Vicar 42;  Ordained Priest<CE> 33;  Perp.  Curate
37;  Rural Dean 44;  Hon. Canon 82.
Oxford.
[MEB, Alum Oxon, Crockfds]

Assn for Promoting Extension of Contagious Diseases
Act 68-70, V-Pres.

CHAMBERS, GEORGE FREDERICK (1841-1915)

Kings Col London;  Inner Temple.
Barrister 66;  Ensign, Army 60;  Asst Inspector,
LGB 73.
Conservative.
Fellow Royal Astronomical Society.
Southeast London;  Sussex.
[WWW, Walfords, Fosters, Army List]

Church Assn 67-67, Exec.

CHAMBERS, SIR THOMAS (1814-1891)

Clare, Camb;  Middle Temple.
Q.C.  61;  Barrister 40.
Liberal.  MP Hertford 52-57, Marylebone 65-85.
Kt 72.
West London;  Essex.
[DNB, MEB, BP, Walfords, Alum Cantab, Fosters,
Dods, Direc Direcs]

Commons Preservation Soc 69-86, Exec.
Church Assn 75-85, V-Pres.
Natl Emigration League (F) 70-70, V-Pres.

CHAMBERS, THOMAS KING (1818-1889)

Rugby;  Christ Church, Oxf;  St George's Hospital
Lond.
Physician 43.
Fellow Royal Col Physicians.
Northwest London.
[MEB, Alum Oxon]

Assn for Promoting Extension of Contagious Diseases
Act 68-68, Exec.

CHAMBRES, PHILIP HENRY (1822- )

Landowner.
DL, JP.
Rhyl;  Denbigh.
[Walfords, Direc Direcs]

Central Assn for Stopping Sale Intox Liquors on
Sunday 70-85, V-Pres.

CHAMEROVZOW, LOUIS ALEXIS

Author.
London.

Jamaica Committee (F) 66-66.

CHAMPION, HENRY HYDE (1859-1928)

Marlborough;  Royal Military Academy, Woolwich.
Journalist;  Publisher;  Lieutenant, RA 78.
Radical.
London.
[WWW, Army List, Aust Dict Biog]

English Land Restoration League (F) 83-84, Treas.

CHAMPNEYS, WILLIAM WELDON (1807-1875)

    Brasenose, Oxf.
    Canon 51;  Vicar 60;  Rural Dean 60;  Ordained
       Priest<CE> 31;  Curate 31;  Rector 37;  Dean
       68.
    East Central London;  Lichfield.
    [DNB, Alum Oxon, Crockfds]

    Church Assn 67-70, V-Pres.


CHANCE, ALEXANDER MACOMB ( -1917)

    Glass Manufacturer.
    Birmingham.

    Natl Assn for Promotion of State Colonization
       86-86, V-Pres.


CHANCE, R. L.

    Birmingham.

    Natl Education League (F) 69-69, Exec.


CHANNING, FRANCIS ALLSTON, 1ST BARON CHANNING
(1841-1926)

    Exeter, Oxf;  Lincoln's Inn.
    Landowner 69;  College Fellow 66;  Barrister 82.
    Radical.  MP Northamptonshire E 85-10.  JP.
    Baronet 06;  Baron 12.
    Southwest London;  Northamptonshire.
    [WWW, BP, Alum Oxon, Fosters, Dods]

    Commons Preservation Soc 86-86, Exec.
    Free Land League 86-86, V-Pres.


CHANNING, WILLIAM HENRY (1810-1884)

    Harvard.
    Unitarian Minister.
    Southwest London.
    [MEB]

    Intl Arbitration & Peace Assn 81-81, Exec.
    Victoria Street Soc for Protection of Animals from
       Vivisection 80-84, Exec.


CHANT, LAURA ORMISTON <MRS. THOMAS CHANT, nee DIBBIN>
(1848-1923)

    Undenominational Preacher;  Composer;  Asst
       Manager, Lunatic Asylum.
    Liberal.
    Worcestershire.
    [WWW]

    Natl Vigilance Assn (F) 85-85, Exec.


CHAPLIN, HENRY, 1ST VISCOUNT CHAPLIN (1840-1923)

    Harrow;  Christ Church, Oxf.
    Very Large Landowner 59.
    Conservative.  MP Lincolnshire Mid 68-85, Sleaford
       85-06, Wimbledon 07-16.  Chanc Duchy Lancaster
       85-86, Pres Board of Agriculture 89-92, Pres
       Local Govt Board 95-00, DL, JP.
    PC 85;  Viscount 16.

    Southwest London;  Lincolnshire.
    [DNB, BP, Walfords, Bateman, Alum Oxon, Dods]

    Natl Footpaths Preservation Soc 86-90, V-Pres.


CHAPMAN, HANNAH <MRS.>

    London.

    Sunday Society 76-90, V-Pres.


CHAPMAN, JOHN (1822-1894)

    St George's Hospital Lond.
    Journal Editor 51;  Physician 57;  Publisher 44.
    Member Royal Col Physicians;  Member Royal Col
       Surgeons.
    West London;  Paris.
    [DNB, MEB]

    Sunday Society (F) 75-90, V-Pres.


CHARLESWORTH, WILLIAM

    Leicester.

    Jamaica Committee (F) 66-66.


CHARLETON, ROBERT

    Gloucestershire.

    Natl Assn for Repeal Contagious Diseases Acts
       70-84, Treas.


CHARLEY, SIR WILLIAM THOMAS (1833-1904)

    Elstree House School, Lee, Kent;  St Johns, Oxf;
       Inner Temple.
    Barrister 65;  Police Court Magistrate 77;  Q.C.
       80.
    Conservative.  MP Salford 68-80.  DL.
    Kt 80.
    Southwest London;  Manchester.
    [DNB, WWW, BP, Alum Oxon, Fosters, Dods, Direc
       Direcs]

    Infant Life Protection Soc 71-71, Treas.
    Natl Emigration League (F) 70-70, V-Pres.


CHARLOTTE EUGENIE AUGUSTE AMALIE ALBERTINE, PRINCESS OF
SWEDEN (1830-1889)

    Sweden.

    Victoria Street Soc for Protection of Animals from
       Vivisection 84-85, V-Pres.


CHARLTON, GEORGE

    JP.
    Gateshead.

    Central Assn for Stopping Sale Intox Liquors on
       Sunday 75-80, V-Pres.

CHARRINGTON, FREDERICK NICHOLAS (1850-1936)

Brighton College.
East London.
[DNB, WWW]

Natl Vigilance Assn (F) 85-85, Exec.

CHEALES, HENRY JOHN (1830- )

Exeter, Oxf.
Vicar 69; Ordained Priest<CE> 61; Curate; Rural
    Dean 82.
Boston.
[Alum Oxon, Crockfds]

Natl Soc for Preserving Memorials of Dead 82-82,
    Exec.

CHEETHAM, JOHN (1802-1888)

Merchant; Manufacturer.
Liberal. MP Lancashire South 52-59, Salford 65-68.
DL, JP.
Stalybridge.
[MEB, Walfords, Dods]

Central Assn for Stopping Sale Intox Liquors on
    Sunday (F) 67-85, President, V-Pres.

CHEETHAM, JOHN FREDERICK (1835-1916)

University Col London.
Cotton Manufacturer.
Liberal. MP Derbyshire North 80-85, Stalybridge
    05-10. JP.
PC 11.
Stalybridge.
[WWW, Dods]

Commons Preservation Soc 81-86, Exec.

CHEETHAM, WILLIAM

Manchester.

Natl Education League 71-71, Exec.

CHESSON, FREDERICK WILLIAM (1833-1888)

Journalist 63.
Liberal.
Southwest London.
[MEB]

Anglo-Oriental Soc for Suppression Opium Trade (F)
    75-86, Exec.
Jamaica Committee (F) 66-66, Hon Sec.
Eastern Question Assn (F) 76-77, Hon Sec.

CHOLMONDELEY, LORD HENRY VERE (1834-1882)

Buckinghamshire.
[BP]

Church Assn 75-80, V-Pres.

CHOWDER, AUGUSTUS G.

Metro Free Libraries Assn 78-78, V-Pres.

CHOWN, JOSEPH PARBERY (1821-1886)

Horton College.
Baptist Minister 48.
Bradford; Northwest London.
[MEB]

Jamaica Committee (F) 66-66.

CHRISTIE, - <MISS>

Sunday Society (F) 75-75, Exec.

CHURCH, RICHARD WILLIAM (1815-1890)

Redland; Wadham, Oxf.
Dean 71; College Fellow 38; College Tutor 39;
    Ordained Priest<CE> 50; Rector 53; Author.
Liberal.
East Central London.
[DNB, MEB, Alum Oxon, Crockfds]

City Church & Churchyard Protection Soc (F) 80-83,
    V-Pres.

CHURCHILL, LORD ALFRED SPENCER (1824-1893)

Royal Military College, Sandhurst.
Cornet, Army 42; Lieutenant, Army 47.
Conservative. MP Woodstock 45-47, Woodstock 57-65.
    DL, JP.
Fellow Royal Geograph Society; Society of the
    Arts.
West London.
[MEB, BP, Walfords, Dods, Direc Direcs]

Natl Assn for Promotion of State Colonization
    86-86, V-Pres.
Metro Free Libraries Assn 68-68, V-Pres.
Jamaica Committee (F) 66-66.

CHURCHILL, JOHN WINSTON SPENCER, 7TH DUKE OF MARLBOROUGH
    (1822-1883)

Eton; Oriel, Oxf.
Very Large Landowner 57.
Conservative. MP Woodstock 40-45, Woodstock 47-57.
    Lord Steward Royal Household 66-67, Lord Pres
    Council 67-68, Lord Lt Ireland 76-80, Lord
    Lieutenant.
Duke 57; PC 66; KG 68.
Royal Agricultural Society.
Southwest London; Oxfordshire.
[DNB, MEB, BP, Walfords, Bateman, Alum Oxon, Dods]

Soc for Promoting Increase of the Home Episcopate
    72-74, V-Pres.

CHURCHILL, LORD RANDOLPH HENRY SPENCER (1849-1895)

Eton; Merton, Oxf.
Conservative. MP Woodstock 74-85, Paddington South
    85-95. Sec St India 85-86, Chancellor
    Exchequer 86-86, DL, JP.
PC 85.
West London; Oxfordshire.
[DNB, MEB, BP, Alum Cantab, Alum Oxon]

Commons Preservation Soc 80-86, Exec.
Natl Footpaths Preservation Soc 86-90, V-Pres.

CLAPHAM, JOHN

London.

Jamaica Committee (F) 66-66.

CLARK, C. W.

Sunday Society 78-78, Exec.

CLARK, GAVIN BROWN (1846-1930)

Kings Col London; Edinburgh(Medical).
Physician; Consul-General.
Radical. MP Caithness-Shire 85-00.
Fellow Royal Col Surgeons, Edinb.
Northwest London.
[WWW, Dods]

Indian Reform Assn 84-84, Chairman.
Land Nationalization Soc (F) 81-81, Exec.

CLARK, SIR JAMES, 1ST BT. (1788-1870)

Fordyce Grammar School; U Aberdeen; Edinb College
    Surgeons.
Physician 17; Med Service, RN 09.
Baronet 37; KCB 66.
Fellow Royal Society; Member Royal Col Surgeons.
Surrey.
[DNB, MEB, BP]

Commons Preservation Soc 69-69, Exec.

CLARK, SIR JOHN FORBES, 2ND BT. (1821-1910)

Eton; Trinity, Camb.
Small Landowner; Attache, Dip Serv 44.
DL, JP.
Baronet 70.
Southwest London; Aberdeen.
[BP, Walfords, Alum Cantab]

Sunday Society 76-90, V-Pres.

CLARK, ROBERT

Southwest London.

Howard Assn 72-80, Exec.
London Municipal Reform League 82-85, Exec.

CLARK, WILLIAM J.

Sunday Society 76-76, Exec.

CLARKE, SIR ANDREW (1824-1902)

King's School, Canterbury; Royal Military Academy,
    Woolwich.
Director of Works, Admiralty 64; 2nd Lt., RE 44;
    Lieutenant, RE 46; Captain, RE 54; Colonel,
    RE 77; Maj. General, RE 84; Lt. General, RE
    86.
Liberal.
CB 69; KCMG 73; CIE 77; GCMG 85.
West London.
[DNB, WWW, Direc Direcs, Army List, Aust Dict Biog]

Natl Emigration League (F) 70-70, V-Pres.

CLARKE, C.

Clergyman<Sect Unkn>.
Fellow Linnean Society.
Birmingham.

Natl Education League (F) 69-71, Exec.

CLARKE, CHARLES WILLIAM BARNETT ( -1916)

Worcester, Oxf.
Vicar 58; Curate 54; Ordained Priest<CE> 55;
    Perp. Curate 60; Dean 71; Rector 71.
Cadmore; Capetown.
[WWW, Alum Oxon, Crockfds]

Infant Life Protection Soc 71-71, Exec.

CLARKE, EBENEZER

East London.
[Direc Direcs]

Jamaica Committee (F) 66-66.

CLARKE, SIR EDWARD GEORGE (1841-1931)

Lincoln's Inn.
Q.C. 80; Civ Serv Clerk 59; Barrister 64.
Conservative. MP Southwark 80-80, Plymouth 80-00,
    City 06-06. Solicitor General 86-92.
Kt 86; PC 08.
West Central London.
[DNB, WWW, Fosters, Dods]

Commons Preservation Soc 80-86, Exec.
Proportional Representation Soc (F) 84-88, Exec.

CLARKE, JOHN CREEMER (1821-1895)

Merchant; Manufacturer.
Liberal. MP Abingdon 74-85. JP.
Abingdon.
[MEB, Dods, Direc Direcs]

Natl Assn for Repeal Contagious Diseases Acts
    81-81, V-Pres.
Intl Arbitration & Peace Assn 81-81, V-Pres.

CLARKE, JOHN HENRY (1852-1931)

> U Edinburgh.
> Physician 75.
> West London.
> [WWW]
>
> Victoria Street Soc for Protection of Animals from
>     Vivisection 84-85, Exec.

CLARKE, PERCY

> Allotments & Small Holdings Assn 85-85, Secretary.

CLARKE, THOMAS CHATFIELD (1829-1895)

> Architect;  Surveyor.
> JP.
> Fellow Royal Inst Br Architects;  Surveyors'
>     Institute.
> West London;  Isle of Wight.
> [MEB]
>
> Sunday Society 78-90, V-Pres.

CLARKE, WILLIAM FAIRLIE (1833-1884)

> Rugby;  Christ Church, Oxf;  Kings
>     College(Medical).
> Surgeon 63.
> Fellow Royal Col Surgeons.
> London;  Southborough.
> [DNB, MEB, Alum Oxon]
>
> Assn for Improvement of London Workhouse
>     Infirmaries 66-66, Exec.

CLAUGHTON, THOMAS LEGH (1808-1892)

> Rugby;  Trinity, Camb.
> Bishop Rochester 67;  Bishop St Alban's 77;
>     College Fellow 32;  Ordained Priest<CE> 36;
>     Vicar 41;  Hon. Canon 45;  Professor Poetry,
>     Oxford 52.
> Rochester;  St Albans.
> [DNB, MEB, Alum Oxon, Crockfds]
>
> Central Assn for Stopping Sale Intox Liquors on
>     Sunday 85-85, V-Pres.
> Soc for Promoting Increase of the Home Episcopate
>     72-74, V-Pres.

CLAYTON, -

> Canon.
>
> Church Assn 70-80, V-Pres.

CLAYTON, ELLEN CREATHORNE <MRS. JAMES HENRY NEEDHAM>
    (1834-1900)

> Artist;  Author.
> West London.
> [MEB]
>
> Sunday Society 78-78, Exec.

CLAYTON, F.  C.

> Birmingham.
>
> Anglo-Oriental Soc for Suppression Opium Trade (F)
>     75-75, Exec.

CLEEVE, FREDERICK

> Natl Assn for Promotion of State Colonization
>     86-86, Exec.

CLEGG, THOMAS

> Manchester;  Southport.
>
> Central Assn for Stopping Sale Intox Liquors on
>     Sunday (F) 67-75, V-Pres.
> Jamaica Committee (F) 66-66.

CLEGG, W.  W.

> English Land Restoration League 85-85, Exec.

CLEMENT, CHARLES GENT

> Oil and Seed Broker.
> Southwest London.
> [Direc Direcs]
>
> Soc for Protection of Ancient Buildings (F) 78-85,
>     Exec.

CLEMENT, WILLIAM JAMES (1804-1870)

> Shrewsbury School;  U Edinburgh.
> Surgeon.
> Liberal.  MP Shrewsbury 65-70.  DL, JP.
> Fellow Royal Col Surgeons;  Society of
>     Apothecaries.
> Shrewsbury.
> [MEB, Dods]
>
> Church Assn 67-67, V-Pres.

CLIFFORD, EDWARD C.  ( -1910)

> Artist.
> Society of Br Artists.
> West London.
> [WWW]
>
> Kyrle Soc 84-90, Exec.

CLIFFORD, JOHN (1836-1923)

> Midland Baptist College.
> Baptist Minister 58.
> Radical.
> CH 21.
> West London.
> [DNB, WWW]
>
> Natl Vigilance Assn (F) 85-85, Exec.

CLIVE, GEORGE HERBERT WINDSOR WINDSOR- (1835-1918)

    Eton.
    Lt. Colonel 68;  Ensign, Army 52;  Lieutenant,
       Army 54;  Captain, Army 59.
    Conservative.  MP Ludlow, Shropshire S 60-85.  DL,
       JP.
    West London;  Shropshire.
    [WWW, BP, Walfords, Dods, Direc Direcs, Army List]

    Natl Soc for Preserving Memorials of Dead 84-88,
       Exec.
    Assn for Promoting Extension of Contagious Diseases
       Act 68-70, V-Pres.


CLOSE, FRANCIS (1797-1882)

    Merchant Taylors;  St John's, Camb.
    Dean 56;  Curate 20;  Ordained Priest<CE> 21;
       Perp. Curate 26;  Rector 32;  Author.
    Carlisle.
    [DNB, MEB, Alum Cantab, Crockfds]

    Central Assn for Stopping Sale Intox Liquors on
       Sunday 70-80, V-Pres.
    Church Assn 67-80, V-Pres.


CLUTTON, W.  J.

    York.

    Church Assn 85-85, Exec.


COBB, HENRY PEYTON (1835-1910)

    University Col London.
    Solicitor 66;  Banker.
    Radical.  MP Rugby 85-95.
    West Central London;  Middlesex.
    [Dods]

    Free Land League 86-86, V-Pres.


COBBE, FRANCES POWER <MISS> (1822-1904)

    Journalist;  Author.
    North Wales.
    [WWW]

    Victoria Street Soc for Protection of Animals from
       Vivisection (F) 76-85, Hon Sec.


COBDEN, JANE E.  <MISS>

    West London.

    Sunday Society 81-90, V-Pres.


COBHAM, ALEXANDER WILLIAM (1832- )

    Captain, Army 57;  Ensign, Army 53;  Lieutenant,
       Army 54.
    JP.
    Berkshire.
    [Walfords, Army List]

    Church Assn 78-85, Chairman.


COCK, EDWARD

    Southeast London.

    Assn for Promoting Extension of Contagious Diseases
       Act 68-70, V-Pres.


COCKBURN, JAMES BALFOUR (1830- )

    Kings Col London;  Edinburgh(Medical).
    Surgeon, Army Medical Serv 64;  Asst Surgeon, Army
       Medical Serv 54;  Surgeon Major, Army Medical
       School 73;  Landowner 49.
    Kent.
    [Walfords, Army List]

    Assn for Promoting Extension of Contagious Diseases
       Act 68-70, V-Pres.


COCKS, HORROCKS (1818-1888)

    Congregational Minister 48;  Newspaper Editor 54.
    Liberal.
    Ingatestone;  Egham.
    [MEB]

    Natl Emigration League (F) 70-71, Secretary.


CODRINGTON, SIR GERALD WILLIAM HENRY, 6TH AND 1ST BT.
  (1850-1929)

    Eton.
    Large Landowner 64.
    Conservative.  JP.
    Baronet 64.
    Southwest London;  Gloucestershire.
    [WWW, BP, Walfords, Bateman]

    Victoria Street Soc for Protection of Animals from
       Vivisection 84-85, V-Pres.


COGHILL, DOUGLAS HARRY (1855-1928)

    Cheltenham College;  Corpus Christi, Oxf;  Inner
       Temple.
    Barrister 79.
    Liberal(Unionist).  MP Newcastle-under-Lyme 86-92,
       Stoke-on-Trent 95-06.
    Southwest London.
    [WWW, Alum Oxon, Fosters, Dods]

    Free Land League 86-86, V-Pres.


COHEN, ARTHUR JOSEPH (1830-1914)

    Magdalene, Camb;  Inner Temple.
    Q.C. 74;  Barrister 57;  India Office Counsel 93.
    Liberal.  MP Southwark 80-87.
    PC 05.
    Fellow British Assn.
    West London.
    [DNB, WWW, Alum Cantab, Fosters, Dods]

    Commons Preservation Soc 80-86, Exec.
    Free Land League 86-86, Exec, V-Pres.
    Proportional Representation Soc (F) 84-88, Exec.

COHEN, JAMES (1816-1891)

>    Christ´s Hospital; Pembroke, Camb.
>    Rector 60; Ordained Priest<CE> 43; Curate 43;
>        Chaplain 47; Vicar 75.
>    East London; West London.
>    [Alum Cantab, Crockfds]
>
>    Church Assn 70-78, Exec.

COLE, H. J.

>    Public Museums & Free Libraries Assn 68-68, Exec.

COLE, SIR HENRY (1808-1882)

>    Christ´s Hospital.
>    Sec, Science and Art Dept, South Kensington 52;
>        Civ Serv Clerk 24; Sen Asst, Keeper of Records
>        38; Artist.
>    CB 51; KCB 75.
>    Society of the Arts.
>    Northwest London.
>    [DNB, MEB, BP]
>
>    Sunday Society 76-82, V-Pres.

COLE, HENRY THOMAS (1816-1885)

>    Middle Temple.
>    Q.C. 67; Barrister 42.
>    Liberal. MP Penryn & Falmouth 74-80.
>    West London.
>    [MEB, Dods]
>
>    Howard Assn 75-79, Patron.

COLE, WILLIAM WILLOUGHBY, 3RD EARL OF ENNISKILLEN
    (1807-1886)

>    Harrow; Christ Church, Oxf.
>    Very Large Landowner 40.
>    Conservative. MP Fermanagh 31-40. DL, JP.
>    Earl 40.
>    Fellow Royal Society; Fellow Geological Society.
>    West London; Ireland.
>    [MEB, BP, Walfords, Bateman, Alum Oxon, Dods]
>
>    Church Assn 67-85, V-Pres.

COLERIDGE, BERNARD JOHN SEYMOUR, 2ND BARON COLERIDGE
    (1851-1927)

>    Eton; Trinity, Oxf; Middle Temple.
>    Barrister 77; Q.C. 92; Judge, King´s Bench 07.
>    Liberal. MP Sheffield Attercliffe 85-94. JP.
>    Baron 94.
>    Fellow Royal Society Literature.
>    West London; Ottery St Mary.
>    [DNB, WWW, BP, Alum Oxon, Dods]
>
>    Victoria Street Soc for Protection of Animals from
>        Vivisection 85-85, Secretary.

COLERIDGE, DERWENT (1800-1883)

>    St John´s, Camb.
>    Prebendary 46; Ordained Priest<CE> 27; School
>        Master 27; School Head 41; Rector 64.
>    West London.
>    [DNB, MEB, BP, Alum Cantab, Crockfds]
>
>    Natl Education Union 70-79, Exec.

COLERIDGE, JOHN DUKE, 1ST BARON COLERIDGE (1820-1894)

>    Eton; Balliol, Oxf; Middle Temple.
>    Lord Chief Justice 80; College Fellow 43;
>        Barrister 46; Q.C. 61; Sergeant at Law 73;
>        Judge, Common Pleas 75.
>    Liberal. MP Exeter 65-73. Solicitor General
>        68-71, Attorney General 71-73.
>    Kt 68; PC 73; Baron 74.
>    Fellow Royal Society.
>    West London; Ottery St Mary.
>    [DNB, MEB, BP, Walfords, Alum Oxon, Fosters, Dods]
>
>    Victoria Street Soc for Protection of Animals from
>        Vivisection 80-85, V-Pres.

COLERIDGE, SIR JOHN TAYLOR (1790-1876)

>    Eton; Exeter, Oxf; Middle Temple.
>    Judge, King´s Bench 35; College Fellow 12;
>        Barrister 19; Journal Editor 24; Sergeant at
>        Law 32.
>    Conservative. PC Judicial Committee 58- .
>    Kt 35; PC 58.
>    Ottery St Mary.
>    [DNB, MEB, BP, Walfords, Alum Oxon]
>
>    Soc for Promoting Increase of the Home Episcopate
>        72-74, Exec.

COLERIDGE, MILDRED MARY <LATER, MRS. CHARLES WARREN
    ADAMS> ( -1929)

>    [BP]
>
>    Victoria Street Soc for Protection of Animals from
>        Vivisection 80-82, Exec.

COLERIDGE, STEPHEN WILLIAM BUCHANAN (1854-1936)

>    Trinity, Camb; Middle Temple.
>    Author; Artist; Private Secretary 84; Barrister
>        86; Clerk of Assize 90.
>    London; Surrey.
>    [MEB, WWW, BP, Alum Cantab]
>
>    Victoria Street Soc for Protection of Animals from
>        Vivisection 84-85, Exec.

COLES, WILLIAM R. E.

>    Civil Engineer.
>    West London.
>
>    Smoke Abatement Committee 81-81, Hon Sec.
>    Sanitary Institute 81-86, Exec.

COLEY, JAMES (1816- )

    Christ Church, Oxf.
    Vicar 70;  Ordained Priest<CE> 42;  Chaplain 43;
        Curate 62;  Chaplain 84.
    West London.
    [Alum Oxon, Crockfds]

    Assn for Improvement of Public Morals 81-81, Exec.


COLLENETTE, BENJAMIN (1814-1884)

    St Thomas's Hospital Lond.
    Surgeon 36.
    Member Royal Col Surgeons.
    Guernsey.
    [MEB]

    Assn for Promoting Extension of Contagious Diseases
        Act 68-68, Exec.


COLLET, COLLET DOBSON (1812-1898)

    Chapel Music Director.
    North London.
    [MEB]

    Travelling Tax Abolition Committee (F) 77-85,
        Secretary.


COLLIER, W. F.

    Plymouth.

    Natl Education League 71-71, Exec.


COLLINGRIDGE, WILLIAM (1854-1927)

    Christ's, Camb; St Bartholomew's Hosp.
    Surgeon; Barrister 14.
    Med Off of Health 80-13, JP.
    Member Royal Col Surgeons.
    Greenwich.
    [WWW, Alum Cantab]

    Sanitary Institute 80-87, Exec.


COLLINGS, JESSE (1831-1920)

    Merchant 64;  Shop Clerk;  Commercial Traveller.
    Radical.  MP Ipswich 80-86, Birmingham Bordesley
        86-18.  Parl Sec Loc Govt Board 86-86, Parl
        U-Sec Home Off 95-02, JP.
    PC 92.
    Birmingham.
    [DNB, WWW, Dods]

    Allotments & Small Holdings Assn (F) 83-88,
        President.
    Natl Education League (F) 69-71, Hon Sec.


COLLINGWOOD, CHARLES EDWARD STUART (1831-1898)

    U Col, Durham.
    Rector 63;  College Fellow 53;  Curate 54;
        Ordained Priest<CE> 55.
    Southwick[Durham].
    [MEB, Crockfds]

    Assn for Improvement of Public Morals (F) 79-81,
        Exec.


COLLINS, EUGENE (1822-1895)

    Liberal.  MP Kinsale 74-85.
    West London; Kinsale.
    [MEB, Dods, Direc Direcs]

    Sunday Society 84-90, V-Pres.


COLLINS, H. H.

    Architect.
    Fellow Royal Inst Br Architects.
    West London.

    Sanitary Institute 80-87, Exec.


COLLINS, THOMAS (1825-1884)

    Charterhouse;  Wadham, Oxf;  Inner Temple.
    Barrister 49.
    Conservative.  MP Knaresborough 51-51,
        Knaresborough 57-65, Boston 68-74,
        Knaresborough 81-84.  DL, JP.
    London; Knaresborough.
    [MEB, Walfords, Alum Oxon, Dods]

    Natl Education Union 70-71, Exec.


COLLINS, W. J. ( -1884)

    Physician.
    Member Royal Col Surgeons.
    Northwest London; Bray.

    London Soc for Abolition of Compulsory Vaccination
        81-81, V-Pres, Exec.


COLLINS, SIR WILLIAM (1817-1895)

    Publisher 53.
    DL.
    Kt 81.
    Glasgow.
    [MEB, BP, Direc Direcs]

    Howard Assn 81-84, Patron.


COLMAN, JEREMIAH JAMES (1830-1898)

    Mustard Manufacturer;  Cattle Breeder.
    Liberal.  MP Norwich 71-95.  DL, JP.
    Norwich.
    [MEB, Dods]

    Howard Assn 72-84, Patron.
    Natl Assn for Repeal Contagious Diseases Acts
        81-81, V-Pres.

COLOMB, SIR JOHN CHARLES READY (1838-1909)

    Royal Naval College, Portsmouth.
    Landowner; 2nd Lieutenant, RM 54; Lieutenant, RM
       55; Captain, RM 67.
    Conservative. MP Tower Hamlets Bow&Bromley 86-92,
       Great Yarmouth 95-06. DL, JP.
    CMG 87; KCMG 88; PC 03.
    Fellow Royal Geograph Society.
    Southwest London; Co Kerry.
    [DNB, Walfords, Dods, Direc Direcs, Navy List]

    Natl Assn for Promotion of State Colonization
       86-86, V-Pres.
    Imperial Federation League (F) 84-84, V-Chairman.


COLQUHOUN, ARCHIBALD CAMPBELL CAMPBELL- (1829-1872)

    Eton; Christ Church, Oxf.
    Substantial Landowner 70.
    Conservative. JP.
    Southwest London; Scotland.
    [Walfords, Alum Oxon]

    Church Assn 70-70, V-Pres.


COLQUHOUN, JOHN CAMPBELL (1803-1870)

    Edinburgh High School; Oriel, Oxf.
    Landowner 20; Author.
    Conservative. MP Dumbartonshire 32-34, Kilmarnock
       37-41, Newcastle-under-Lyme 42-47. DL, JP.
    Southwest London; Scotland.
    [DNB, Dods]

    Church Assn 67-67, Chairman.


COLQUHOUN, JOHN ERSKINE CAMPBELL- (1831- )

    Rugby; Trinity, Oxf.
    Substantial Landowner 72; Ordained Priest<CE> 63;
       Perp. Curate 65; Vicar 70.
    DL, JP.
    Scotland.
    [Walfords, Bateman, Alum Oxon, Crockfds]

    Church Assn 75-80, V-Pres.


COLVIN, SIR SIDNEY (1845-1927)

    Trinity, Camb; Lincoln's Inn.
    Slade Professor of Fine Arts, Cambridge 73; Museum
       Director 76; Keeper Prints & Drawings, British
       Museum 84; College Fellow 68.
    Kt 11.
    West London.
    [DNB, WWW, Alum Cantab]

    Soc for Protection of Ancient Buildings (F) 78-85,
       Exec.


COMPTON, LORD ALWYNE (1825-1906)

    Eton; Trinity, Camb.
    Dean 79; Ordained Priest<CE> 51; Curate 51;
       Rector 52; Rural Dean 74; Archdeacon 75;
       Bishop Ely 86.
    Worcester; Ely.
    [DNB, WWW, BP, Alum Cantab, Crockfds]

    Natl Soc for Preserving Memorials of Dead (F)
       81-88, Exec.


COMPTON, WILLIAM GEORGE SPENCER SCOTT, 5TH MARQUIS
NORTHAMPTON (1851-1913)

    Eton; Trinity, Camb.
    Diplomatic Service 72; Private Secretary 80; Very
       Large Landowner 97.
    Liberal. MP Warwickshire SW 85-86, Barnsley, Yorks
       WR S 89-97. Lord Lieutenant 12-13, JP.
    Marquis 97; KG 08.
    Southwest London; Warwickshire; Northamptonshire.
    [WWW, BP, Alum Cantab, Dods]

    Natl Footpaths Preservation Soc 86-90, V-Pres.
    Allotments & Small Holdings Assn 85-88, V-Pres.


CONCANON, GEORGE BLAKE

    Trin Col, Dublin.
    Chaplain 65; Rector 56; Curate 73.
    Southwest London.
    [Crockfds]

    Church Assn 70-80, Secretary.


CONDER, G. W.

    Clergyman<Sect Unkn>.
    Manchester.

    Jamaica Committee (F) 66-66.


CONGREVE, RICHARD (1818-1899)

    Rugby; Wadham, Oxf.
    Positivist Leader 55; College Fellow 44; Asst
       School Master 45; College Lecturer 50;
       Physician 66; Author.
    Southwest London.
    [DNB, MEB, Alum Oxon]

    Jamaica Committee (F) 66-66.
    Anglo-French Intervention Committee (F) 70-70,
       President.


CONGREVE, WALTER

    Anglo-French Intervention Committee (F) 70-70,
       Exec.


CONNELL, J.

    English Land Restoration League 85-85, Exec.


CONOR, J. R.

    Wellington.

    Church Assn 78-78, Exec.

CONSTABLE, HENRY STRICKLAND- (1821-1909)

    Trinity, Camb.
    Large Landowner 65.
    Yorks, East Riding.
    [BP, Bateman, Alum Cantab]

    London Soc for Abolition of Compulsory Vaccination
       81-81, V-Pres.


CONWAY, MONCURE DANIEL (1832-1907)

    Dickenson Col, Pa.;  Harvard Divinity.
    Unitarian Minister 64;  Author.
    Chiswick.
    [WWW]

    League for Defense of Constitutional Rights 84-84,
       V-Pres.
    London Soc for Abolition of Compulsory Vaccination
       81-81, V-Pres.


CONWAY, WILLIAM (1815-1876)

    King's College School;  Trinity, Camb.
    Canon 64;  Curate 40;  Ordained Priest<CE> 41;
       Vicar 52;  Rector 64.
    Southwest London.
    [Alum Cantab, Crockfds]

    Church Assn 67-75, V-Pres, Exec.


CONYBEARE, CHARLES AUGUSTUS VANSITTART (1853-1919)

    Christ Church, Oxf;  Gray's Inn.
    Barrister 81.
    Radical.  MP Camborne 85-95.
    Southwest London;  Cornwall.
    [WWW, Alum Oxon, Fosters, Dods, Direc Direcs]

    Free Land League 86-86, V-Pres.


CONYNGHAM, GEORGE HENRY, 3RD MARQUIS OF CONYNGHAM
    (1825-1882)

    Eton.
    Very Large Landowner 76;  Cornet, Army 44;
       Captain, Army 54;  Lt. Colonel 61;  Colonel
       66;  Maj. General 77;  Lt. General 81.
    Conservative.  Equerry 70-82.
    Marquis 76.
    West London;  Kent;  Co Donegal.
    [MEB, BP, Walfords, Bateman, Army List]

    Sunday Society 79-82, V-Pres.


COODE, SIR JOHN (1816-1892)

    Civil Engineer 44;  Chief Engineer, Portland
       Harbour 56.
    Kt 72;  KCMG 86.
    Member Inst Civ Engineers.
    West London.
    [DNB, MEB, BP, Direc Direcs]

    Church Assn 80-85, Exec.


COOK, -

    Church of Scotland Minister.

    Natl Education Union 71-79, Exec.


COOK, BANCROFT

    Birkenhead.

    Natl Education League 71-71, Exec.


COOK, SIR WILLIAM THOMAS GUSTAVUS (1834-1908)

    Tack Manufacturer.
    Liberal.  MP Birmingham East 85-86.  JP.
    Kt 06.
    Birmingham.
    [WWW, Dods]

    Smoke Abatement Committee 81-81.


COOKE, -

    Physician.

    Assn for Improvement of London Workhouse
       Infirmaries 66-66, Exec.


COOKE, C. C.

    Litcham.

    Jamaica Committee (F) 66-66.


COOKE, GEORGE

    Liverpool.

    Jamaica Committee (F) 66-66.


COOKE, ISAAC B.

    Liverpool.

    Jamaica Committee (F) 66-66.


COOKESLEY, WILLIAM GIFFORD (1802-1880)

    Eton;  King's, Camb.
    Vicar 57;  College Fellow 24;  Asst School Master
       25;  Ordained Priest<CE> 35;  Curate 55;
       Rector 68.
    Hammersmith.
    [DNB, MEB, Alum Cantab, Crockfds]

    Church Assn 67-67, Exec.


COOPER, ANTHONY ASHLEY, 7TH EARL OF SHAFTESBURY
    (1801-1885)

    Harrow;  Christ Church, Oxf.
    Very Large Landowner 51.
    Conservative.  MP Woodstock 26-30, Dorchester
       30-31, Dorsetshire 31-46, Bath 47-51.
       Commissioner Board of Control 28-30, Lord
       Admiralty 34-35, Ecclesiastical Commissioner
       41-47, Lunacy Commissioner 28-85, Lord
       Lieutenant 56-  .

Earl 51;  KG 62.
West London;  Dorsetshire.
[DNB, MEB, BP, Walfords, Bateman, Alum Oxon, Dods]

Anglo-Oriental Soc for Suppression Opium Trade
    84-84, President.
Sanitary Institute (F) 76-85, V-Pres.
Natl Soc for Preserving Memorials of Dead 84-84,
    Patron.
Central Assn for Stopping Sale Intox Liquors on
    Sunday 75-80, V-Pres.
Central Vigilance Comtee for Repression Immorality
    (F) 83-84, President.
Intl Arbitration & Peace Assn 81-84, President,
    V-Pres.
Victoria Street Soc for Protection of Animals from
    Vivisection 80-85, President.
Natl Education Union 71-79, Exec.
Plimsoll and Seamen's Fund Committee (F) 73-73,
    Chairman.
Eastern Question Assn 77-77, V-Pres.


COOPER, CHARLES R.

    Norwich.

    Travelling Tax Abolition Committee 81-85, Exec.


COOPER, SIR DANIEL, 1ST BT.  (1821-1902)

    Univ College School.
    Australia Merchant 43;  Landowner.
    Liberal.  Col Agent-General, JP.
    Kt 57;  Baronet 63;  KCMG 80;  GCMG 88.
    West London;  New South Wales.
    [DNB, BP, Walfords, Direc Direcs, Aust Dict Biog,
        WWW]

    Imperial Federation League (F) 84-84, Exec.
    Natl Emigration League (F) 70-70, V-Pres.


COOPER, JOHN WILLIAM (1845- )

    Trinity, Camb;  Lincoln's Inn.
    Barrister 68.
    JP.
    Cambridge.
    [Alum Cantab, Fosters]

    Intl Arbitration & Peace Assn 81-81, V-Pres.


COOPER, JOSEPH (1800-1881)

    Author.
    London.
    [MEB]

    Howard Assn 67-81, Exec.
    Jamaica Committee (F) 66-66.


COOPER, R. A.

    Norwich.

    Natl Secular Soc 77-77, V-Pres.


COOTE, SIR ALGERNON CHARLES PLUMPTRE, 12TH BT.
    (1847-1920)

    Eton;  St John's, Camb.
    Very Large Landowner 99.
    Lord Lieutenant 00- , JP.
    Baronet 99.
    Fellow Royal Geograph Society.
    Ireland.
    [WWW, BP, Alum Cantab]

    Anglo-Oriental Soc for Suppression Opium Trade
        83-83, Exec.


COOTE, HOLMES (1817-1872)

    Westminster School;  St Bartholomew's Hosp.
    Surgeon 63;  Medical School Demonstrator 49;  Asst
        Surgeon 54.
    Fellow Royal Col Surgeons.
    West London.
    [DNB, MEB]

    Assn for Promoting Extension of Contagious Diseases
        Act 68-68, V-Pres.


COOTE, THOMAS (1850- )

    Colliery Agent.
    Liberal.  MP Huntingdon 85-86.
    Huntingdonshire.
    [Dods]

    Free Land League 86-86, V-Pres.


COOTE, WILLIAM ALEXANDER (1842-1919)

    Trade Union Leader;  Compositor.
    Radical.
    OBE 18.
    Southwest London.
    [WWW]

    Natl Assn for Promotion of State Colonization
        86-86, Exec.
    Natl Vigilance Assn (F) 85-85, Secretary.


CORBET, WILLIAM JOSEPH (1825-1909)

    Clerk, Irish Lunacy Office 47;  Chief Clerk, Irish
        Lunacy Office 53.
    Irish Nationalist.  MP Wicklow Co 80-85, Wicklow Co
        East 85-92, Wicklow Co East 95-00.
    Member Royal Irish Academy.
    Ireland.
    [WWW, Dods]

    Intl Arbitration & Peace Assn 81-81, V-Pres.


CORBETT, ARCHIBALD L.  CAMERON, 1ST BARON ROWALLAN
    (1856-1933)

    Landowner.
    Liberal(Unionist).  MP Glasgow Tradeston 85-11.
        JP.
    Baron 11.
    West London;  Scotland.
    [WWW, BP, Dods]

    Free Land League 86-86, V-Pres.

CORBETT, JOHN (1817-1901)

>   Salt Manufacturer; Civil Engineer; Substantial
>       Landowner.
>   Liberal(Unionist). MP Droitwich 74-85,
>       Worcestershire Mid 85-92. DL, JP.
>   Assoc Inst Civ Engineers.
>   West London; North Wales; Worcestershire.
>   [DNB, WWW, Bateman, Dods, Direc Direcs]
>
>   Howard Assn 75-84, Patron.
>   Intl Arbitration & Peace Assn 81-81, V-Pres.
>   Natl Assn for Repeal Contagious Diseases Acts
>       81-81, V-Pres.

CORBYN, M. A.

>   Guernsey.
>
>   Assn for Promoting Extension of Contagious Diseases
>       Act 68-70, V-Pres.

CORFIELD, WILLIAM HENRY (1843-1903)

>   Magdalen, Oxf; U College London(Medical).
>   Medical School Professor 69; College Fellow 65.
>   Med Off of Health 71-00.
>   Fellow Royal Col Physicians; Epidemiological
>       Society of London; Society Med Officers of
>       Health.
>   West London.
>   [DNB, WWW, Alum Oxon, Direc Direcs]
>
>   Sanitary Institute 78-89, Chairman, V-Chairman.
>   Sunday Society 76-90, Chairman, V-Pres.

CORKER, H. D.

>   Sunday Society 79-83, Exec.

CORNER, W. E.

>   Financial Reform Union (F) 68-69, Exec.

CORNISH, HENRY HUBERT (1812-1887)

>   Magdalen, Oxf.
>   College Head 66; Ordained Priest<CE> 43; Chaplain
>       45; College Tutor 58.
>   Oxford.
>   [MEB, Alum Oxon, Crockfds]
>
>   City Church & Churchyard Protection Soc (F) 80-83,
>       V-Pres.

CORRANCE, FREDERICK SNOWDON (1822-1906)

>   Harrow; Trinity, Camb.
>   Landowner; Captain, Army 42.
>   Conservative. MP Suffolk East 67-74. DL, JP.
>   Southwest London; Suffolk.
>   [Walfords, Alum Cantab, Dods, Army List]
>
>   Natl Education Union 70-71, Exec.

CORRIE, GEORGE ELWES (1793-1885)

>   St Catherine's, Camb.
>   College Head 49; College Fellow 17; Ordained
>       Priest<CE> 20; College Tutor 21; Norrisian
>       Professor Divinity, Cambridge 38; Rector 51;
>       Rural Dean 51.
>   Cambridge.
>   [DNB, MEB, Alum Cantab, Crockfds]
>
>   Assn for Promoting Extension of Contagious Diseases
>       Act 68-70, V-Pres.

CORRY, SIR JAMES PORTER, 1ST BT. (1826-1891)

>   Belfast Academy.
>   Shipowner; Merchant.
>   Conservative. MP Belfast 74-85, Armagh Co Mid
>       86-91. JP.
>   Baronet 85.
>   Southwest London; Belfast.
>   [MEB, Dods, Direc Direcs]
>
>   Howard Assn 74-76, Patron.

CORY, JOHN (1828-1910)

>   Coal Merchant; Shipowner; Colliery Owner 68.
>   Liberal. DL, JP.
>   West London; Cardiff.
>   [DNB, WWW, Direc Direcs]
>
>   Intl Arbitration & Peace Assn 81-81, V-Pres.

COSSHAM, HANDEL (1824-1890)

>   Colliery Owner 51; Colliery Manager 45.
>   MP Bristol East 85-90.
>   Fellow Geological Society.
>   Bristol; Bath.
>   [MEB, Dods]
>
>   English Land Restoration League 85-85, Exec.
>   Free Land League 86-86, V-Pres.
>   Jamaica Committee (F) 66-66.

COSSINS, JETHRO A.

>   Birmingham.
>
>   Natl Soc for Preserving Memorials of Dead (F)
>       81-82, Exec.

COSTELLOE, - <MRS. BENJAMIN FRANCIS CONN COSTELLOE>

>   Southwest London.
>
>   Natl Vigilance Assn (F) 85-85, Exec.

COSTELLOE, BENJAMIN FRANCIS CONN (1855-1899)

>   U Glasgow; Lincoln's Inn.
>   Barrister 81.
>   Southwest London.
>   [MEB, Alum Oxon, Fosters]
>
>   Natl Vigilance Assn (F) 85-85, Exec.

COTTERILL, HENRY (1812-1886)

St John's, Camb.
Bishop Edinburgh 72; College Fellow 35; Ordained
    Priest<CE> 36; Chaplain 36; School Asst Head
    46; School Head 51; Bishop Grahamstown 56.
Fellow Royal Society Edinb.
Edinburgh.
[MEB, Alum Cantab, Crockfds]

Natl Soc for Preserving Memorials of Dead 84-84,
    Patron.


COTTON, RICHARD LYNCH (1794-1880)

Charterhouse; Worcester, Oxf.
College Head 39; College Fellow 16; Ordained
    Priest<CE> 18; College Tutor 22; Vicar 23.
Oxford.
[DNB, MEB, Alum Oxon, Crockfds]

City Church & Churchyard Protection Soc (F) 80-80,
    V-Pres.


COURTENAY, WILLIAM REGINALD, 11TH EARL OF DEVON
(1807-1888)

Westminster School; Christ Church, Oxf; Lincoln's
    Inn.
Very Large Landowner 59; College Fellow 28;
    Inspector, Poor Law Board 47; Sec, Poor Law
    Board 51.
Conservative. MP Devonshire South 41-49. Chanc
    Duchy Lancaster 66-67, Pres Poor Law Board
    67-68, DL, JP.
Earl 59; PC 66.
Southwest London; Devonshire.
[DNB, MEB, BP, Walfords, Bateman, Alum Cantab, Alum
    Oxon, Dods]

City Church & Churchyard Protection Soc (F) 80-83,
    President.
Natl Soc for Preserving Memorials of Dead 84-84,
    Patron.
Natl Education Union 71-71, Exec.


COURTNEY, LEONARD HENRY, 1ST BARON COURTNEY OF PENWITH
(1832-1918)

St John's, Camb; Lincoln's Inn.
Journalist 65; College Fellow 56; Barrister 58;
    Professor of Political Economy, U Col London
    72.
Liberal(Unionist). MP Liskeard 75-85, Bodmin
    85-00. Parl U-Sec Home Off 80-81, Parl U-Sec
    Col Off 81-82, Sec Treasury 82-84, Deputy
    Speaker House of Commons 86-92, Chairman of
    Committees 86-92.
PC 89; Baron 06.
Fellow Royal Statistical Society.
Southwest London.
[DNB, WWW, Alum Cantab, Fosters, Dods, Direc
    Direcs]

City Church & Churchyard Protection Soc (F) 80-83,
    V-Pres.
Soc for Protection of Ancient Buildings (F) 78-85,
    Exec.
Proportional Representation Soc (F) 84-88, Exec.


COUTTS, ANGELA GEORGINA BURDETT-, BARONESS
BURDETT-COUTTS (1814-1906)

Banker 37; Landowner 37.
Baroness 71.
West London; Middlesex.
[DNB, WWW, BP, Walfords]

City Church & Churchyard Protection Soc 83-83,
    V-Pres.


COUTTS, FRANCIS BURDETT THOMAS MONEY- (1852-1923)

Eton; Trinity, Camb; Inner Temple.
Poet.
JP.
Surrey.
[Alum Cantab, Fosters]

Natl Assn for Promotion of State Colonization
    86-86, Exec, V-Pres.


COWAN, CHARLES (1806-1868)

Edinburgh(Medical).
Physician 35.
Reading.
[MEB]

Church Assn 67-67, Exec.


COWAN, JAMES (1816-1895)

Edinburgh High School; U Edinburgh.
Paper Manufacturer.
Liberal. MP Edinburgh 74-82.
Southwest London; Edinburgh.
[MEB, Dods, Direc Direcs]

Natl Assn for Promotion of State Colonization
    86-86, V-Pres.
Natl Assn for Repeal Contagious Diseases Acts
    81-81, V-Pres.


COWEN, SIR JOSEPH (1800-1873)

Coal Merchant; Brick Manufacturer.
Radical. MP Newcastle-upon-Tyne 65-73. JP.
Kt.
Southwest London; Newcastle-upon-Tyne.
[Walfords, Dods]

Assn for Promoting Extension of Contagious Diseases
    Act 68-70, V-Pres.


COWEN, JOSEPH (1831-1900)

U Edinburgh.
Brick Manufacturer 52; Newspaper Proprietor.
Radical. MP Newcastle-upon-Tyne 74-86.
Southwest London; Newcastle-upon-Tyne.
[DNB, MEB, WWW, Dods]

City Church & Churchyard Protection Soc 83-83,
    V-Pres.
Natl Education League 71-71, Exec.
Travelling Tax Abolition Committee (F) 77-85, Exec.
Natl Assn for Repeal Contagious Diseases Acts
    81-81, V-Pres.

COWIE, - <MISS>

Victoria Street Soc for Protection of Animals from Vivisection 80-80, Exec.

COWIE, BENJAMIN MORGAN (1816-1900)

St John's, Camb; Lincoln's Inn.
Dean 72; Ordained Priest<CE> 42; Curate 43;
    College Head 44; College Professor 54;
    Inspector of Schools 57; Vicar 57.
Fellow Society of Antiquaries.
Manchester; Exeter.
[DNB, MEB, WWW, Crockfds]

Natl Soc for Preserving Memorials of Dead (F)
    81-82, Exec.

COWPER, FRANCIS THOMAS DE GREY, 7TH EARL COWPER
(1834-1905)

Harrow; Christ Church, Oxf.
Very Large Landowner 56.
Liberal(Unionist). Lord Lt Ireland 80-82, Lord
    Lieutenant, DL, JP.
Earl 56; KG 65; PC 80.
West London; Hertfordshire.
[DNB, WWW, BP, Walfords, Bateman, Alum Oxon]

Soc for Protection of Ancient Buildings (F) 78-85,
    Exec.

COWPER, KATRINE CECILIA, COUNTESS COWPER <WIFE OF 7TH
EARL, nee COMPTON> (1845-1913)

West London; Hertfordshire.
[BP]

Central Vigilance Comtee for Repression Immorality
    (F) 83-84, V-Pres.

COWPER, T. A. <"COL.">

Land Tenure Reform Assn 73-73, Exec.

COX, J. C.

JP.

Land Tenure Reform Assn 73-73, Exec.

COXE, SIR JAMES (1811-1878)

Edinburgh(Medical).
Surgeon 35.
Lunacy Commissioner 57-78.
Kt 63.
Fellow Royal Col Surgeons; Fellow Royal Society
    Edinb.
Edinburgh.
[MEB, Walfords]

Sunday Society 76-78, V-Pres.

COYSH, T. S.

West London.

Church Assn 80-80, Exec.

CRAIES, WILLIAM FEILDEN (1854-1911)

Winchester College; New College, Oxf; Inner
    Temple.
Barrister 82; School Master.
West London.
[WWW, Alum Oxon, Fosters]

Natl Vigilance Assn (F) 85-85, Exec.

CRAIG, EDWARD THOMAS (1804-1894)

Journalist.
Radical.
Hammersmith.
[MEB, Dic Lab Biog]

Land Nationalization Soc 83-85, Exec.

CRAIGIE, PATRICK GEORGE (1843-1930)

St Catherine's, Camb.
Estate Agent 65; Captain, Army 61; Major 80;
    Asst Sec, Board of Agriculture 97.
CB 02.
Fellow Royal Statistical Society; Br Assn.
Northwest London; Devonshire.
[WWW, Alum Cantab, Direc Direcs, Army List]

Local Taxation Comtee [of Central Chamber of
    Agriculture] 71-89, Secretary.

CRAIK, DINAH MARIA <MRS. GEORGE LILLIE CRAIK, nee
MULOCK> (1826-1887)

Novelist; Poet; Translator.
Kent.
[DNB]

Sunday Society 80-87, V-Pres.

CRANE, ROBERT

Dartford.

Natl Soc for Preserving Memorials of Dead (F)
    81-82, Exec.

CRAWFORD, DONALD (1837-1919)

Edinburgh Academy; Balliol, Oxf.
Advocate 62; College Fellow 61; Chm, Scottish
    Fisheries Board 97; K.C. 03.
Liberal. MP Lanarkshire NE 85-95.
Southwest London.
[Dods, Alum Oxon]

Free Land League 86-86, V-Pres.

CRAWFORD, ROBERT FITZGERALD COPLAND- (1809-1895)

> General, RA 77; 2nd Lt., RA 28; Lieutenant, RA
>    29; Captain, RA 41; Colonel, RA 54; Maj.
>    General, RA 65; Lt. General, RA 72.
> Fellow Geological Society.
> Middlesex.
> [MEB, Army List]
>
> Church Assn 85-85, V-Pres.

CRAWFORD, SIR THOMAS (1824-1895)

> Edinburgh(Medical).
> Director General<India>, Army Medical Serv 82;
>    Asst Surgeon, Army Medical Serv 48; Surgeon,
>    Army Medical Serv 55; Surgeon Major, Army
>    Medical School 68; Deputy Inspector General,
>    Army Medical Serv 70; Surgeon General<India>,
>    Army Medical Serv 76.
> KCB 85.
> Fellow Royal Col Surgeons, Ire; Royal Col
>    Physicians, Ireland.
> Southeast London.
> [MEB, Army List]
>
> Sanitary Institute 84-89, Exec.

CRAWFORD, WILLIAM (1833-1890)

> Trade Union Leader; Miner 43.
> Liberal. MP Durham Co Mid 85-90.
> West Central London; Durham[County].
> [MEB, Dods, Dic Lab Biog]
>
> Free Land League 86-86, V-Pres.
> Land Law Reform League (F) 81-84, V-Pres.
> League for Defense of Constitutional Rights 84-84,
>    V-Pres.

CRAWSHAY, GEORGE (1821-1896)

> Trinity, Camb; Middle Temple.
> Large Builder/contractor.
> JP.
> Gateshead; Northumberland.
> [MEB, Alum Cantab]
>
> Travelling Tax Abolition Committee (F) 77-85, Exec.

CRAWSHAY, ROSE MARY <MRS. ROBERT THOMPSON CRAWSHAY, nee
YEATES

> Glamorganshire.
>
> Sunday Society (F) 75-90, V-Pres.

CREASY, SIR EDWARD SHEPHERD (1812-1878)

> Eton; King's, Camb; Lincoln's Inn.
> Chief Justice, Ceylon 60; College Fellow 34;
>    Barrister 37; Professor Ancient and Modern
>    History, U Col London 40.
> Kt 60.
> Ceylon; West Central London.
> [DNB, MEB, Alum Cantab]
>
> Intl Law Assn 74-74, V-Pres.

CREED, F. A.

> Southwest London.
>
> Free Land League 86-86, Secretary.

CREMER, SIR WILLIAM RANDAL (1828-1908)

> Trade Union Leader; Carpenter 43.
> Radical. MP Shoreditch Haggerstn 85-95, Shoreditch
>    Haggerstn 00-08.
> Kt 07.
> West Central London.
> [DNB, WWW, Dods]
>
> Land Tenure Reform Assn 73-73, Exec.
> Workmen's Peace Assn (F) 71-08, Secretary.

CRESSWELL, J.

> Alveley.
>
> Church Assn 85-85, Exec.

CRESSWELL, PEARSON ROBERT (1834-1905)

> Middlesex Hospital.
> Surgeon.
> JP.
> CB 98.
> Fellow Royal Col Surgeons.
> Merthyr Tydfil.
> [WWW]
>
> Assn for Promoting Extension of Contagious Diseases
>    Act 68-68, Exec.

CREWDSON, -

> Central Assn for Stopping Sale Intox Liquors on
>    Sunday (F) 67-67, V-Pres.

CROFTON, SIR WALTER FREDERICK (1815-1897)

> Commissioner of Prisons 66; 2nd Lt., RA 33;
>    Captain, RA 45; Chm, Directors of Prisons,
>    Ireland 54; Inspector Reformatory Schoools and
>    Debtors' Prisons.
> Liberal. JP.
> CB 57; Kt 62; PC Ireland 68.
> Winchester.
> [MEB, WWW, BP, Walfords, Army List]
>
> Assn for Promoting Extension of Contagious Diseases
>    Act 68-70, V-Pres.

CROFTS, W. C.

> West London.
>
> Liberty & Property Defense League (F) 82-84,
>    Secretary.
> State Resistance Union (F) 82-82, Hon Sec.

CROLL, ALEXANDER ANGUS (1811-1887)

    Civil Engineer.
    JP.
    North London; Surrey; Sussex.
    [MEB, Walfords]

    Howard Assn 76-84, Exec.
    Jamaica Committee (F) 66-66.


CROMPTON, ALBERT (1843-1908)

    Harrow; Trinity, Camb; Inner Temple.
    Steamship Co Manager.
    Liverpool.
    [Alum Cantab]

    Anglo-French Intervention Committee (F) 70-70,
        Exec.


CROMPTON, CHARLES (1833-1890)

    Univ College School; Trinity, Camb; Inner Temple.
    Q.C. 82; College Fellow 56; Barrister 64.
    Liberal. MP Staffordshire Leek 85-86.
    Southwest London.
    [MEB, Alum Cantab, Fosters, Dods]

    Free Land League 86-86, V-Pres.


CROMPTON, HENRY (1836-1904)

    Univ College School; Trinity, Camb; Inner Temple.
    Barrister 63; Clerk of Assize 58.
    Surrey.
    [DNB, Alum Cantab, Fosters]

    Anglo-French Intervention Committee (F) 70-70,
        Exec.


CROMWELL, JOHN GABRIEL

    Brasenose, Oxf.
    School Head 52; Ordained Priest<CE> 53; Hon.
       Canon 56; Rector 59; Rural Dean 71.
    Southwest London.
    [Alum Oxon, Crockfds, Direc Direcs]

    Natl Education Union (F) 69-71, Hon Sec.


CROOKES, SIR WILLIAM (1832-1919)

    Royal College Chemistry.
    Analytical Chemist; College Lecturer 55; Journal
       Editor 59.
    Kt 97; OM 10.
    Fellow Royal Society; Fellow Chemical Society; Br
       Assn; Inst of Elec Engineers; Pharmaceutical
       Society.
    Southeast London; West London.
    [DNB, WWW]

    Sanitary Institute 77-83, Exec.


CROPPER, JAMES (1823-1900)

    Royal Institution, Liverpool; U Edinburgh.
    Paper Manufacturer.
    Liberal(Unionist). MP Kendal 80-85. DL, JP.
    Kendal.
    [MEB, Walfords, Dods, Direc Direcs]

    Howard Assn 82-84, Patron.
    Jamaica Committee (F) 66-66.
    Proportional Representation Soc (F) 84-88, Exec.
    Natl Education Union (F) 69-76, Exec.


CROPPER, JOHN

    Liverpool.

    Jamaica Committee (F) 66-66.


CROSFIELD, JOHN

    Chemicals Manufacturer.
    JP.
    Warrington.
    [Direc Direcs]

    Jamaica Committee (F) 66-66.


CROSFIELD, WILLIAM

    Chemicals Manufacturer.
    JP.
    Liverpool.
    [Direc Direcs]

    Jamaica Committee (F) 66-66.


CROSS, RICHARD ASSHETON, 1ST VISCOUNT CROSS (1823-1914)

    Rugby; Trinity, Camb; Inner Temple.
    Banker 60; Barrister 49.
    Conservative. MP Preston 57-62, Lancashire SW
       68-85, Newton, Lancs SW 85-86. Sec St Home
       Office 74-80, Ecclesiastical Commissioner
       85- , Sec St Home Office 85-86, Sec St India
       86-92, Lord Privy Seal 95-00, DL, JP.
    PC 74; GCB 80; Viscount 86; GCSI 92.
    Fellow Royal Society.
    Southwest London; Warrington; Lancashire.
    [DNB, WWW, BP, Walfords, Alum Cantab, Alum Oxon,
       Fosters, Dods]

    Natl Footpaths Preservation Soc 86-90, V-Pres.
    Natl Soc for Preserving Memorials of Dead 84-84,
       Patron.


CROSSKEY, HENRY WILLIAM (1826-1893)

    New College, Manchester.
    Unitarian Minister 48.
    Fellow Geological Society.
    Birmingham.
    [MEB]

    Sunday Society (F) 75-90, V-Pres.
    Natl Education League (F) 69-71, Exec.

CROSSLEY, DAVID

    Bolton.

    Central Assn for Stopping Sale Intox Liquors on
       Sunday (F) 67-85, Exec.


CROSSLEY, EDWARD (1841-1905)

    Owens Col, Manch.
    Carpet Manufacturer.
    Liberal. MP Sowerby, Yorks WR N 85-92. JP.
    Fellow Royal Astronomical Society.
    Southwest London; Halifax.
    [Dods, Direc Direcs]

    Natl Assn for Repeal Contagious Diseases Acts
       84-84, V-Pres.


CROSSLEY, SIR FRANCIS, 1ST BT. (1817-1872)

    Carpet Manufacturer.
    Liberal. MP Halifax 52-59, Yorkshire W Riding
       59-65, Yorks W Riding North 65-72. DL, JP.
    Baronet 63.
    Halifax; Suffolk.
    [DNB, MEB, Walfords, Dods]

    Jamaica Committee (F) 66-66.


CROWE, W.

    Clergyman<Sect Unkn>.
    Hammersmith.

    Jamaica Committee (F) 66-66.


CRUIKSHANK, AUGUSTUS WALTER (1837- )

    Landowner 56.
    Forfarshire.
    [Walfords]

    Church Assn 67-67, Exec.


CUBITT, GEORGE, 1ST BARON ASHCOMBE (1828-1917)

    Trinity, Camb.
    Large Landowner 55.
    Conservative. MP Surrey West 60-85, Epsom 85-92.
       Church Estates Commissioner 74-79, DL, JP.
    PC 80; Baron 92.
    Southwest London; Surrey.
    [WWW, BP, Walfords, Alum Cantab, Dods, Bateman]

    Soc for Promoting Increase of the Home Episcopate
       72-74, Exec.


CUDWORTH, WILLIAM

    Darlington.

    Jamaica Committee (F) 66-66.


CUMBERLAND, CHARLES EDWARD (1830-1920)

    Royal Military Academy, Woolwich.
    Colonel, RE 84; 2nd Lt., RE 47; Lieutenant, RE
       51; Captain, RE 56; Major, RE 72; Lt.
       Colonel, RE 73; Maj. General, RE 87.
    JP.
    CB 81.
    Kent.
    [WWW, Army List]

    Natl Assn for Promotion of State Colonization
       86-86, V-Pres.


CUNDY, JAMES <"CAPT.">

    Kingston<?>.

    Church Assn 75-80, Exec.


CUNDY, THOMAS ( -1895)

    Eton.
    Architect; Surveyor 67.
    Fellow Royal Inst Br Architects.
    London.
    [MEB]

    Smoke Abatement Committee 81-81.


CUNLIFFE, SIR ROBERT ALFRED, 5TH BT. (1839-1905)

    Eton.
    Substantial Landowner 59; Lieutenant, Army 57;
       Captain, Army 62; Lt. Colonel 72.
    Liberal(Unionist). MP Flint District 72-74,
       Denbigh District 80-85. DL, JP.
    Baronet 59.
    Southwest London; Denbighshire.
    [WWW, BP, Walfords, Bateman, Dods, Army List]

    Commons Preservation Soc 80-86, Exec.


CUNNINGTON, JOHN

    Brentford.

    Sunday Society (F) 75-75, Exec.
    Jamaica Committee (F) 66-66.


CURGENVEN, JOHN BRENDON (1831- )

    Surgeon; Landowner 40.
    West London; Cornwall.
    [Walfords]

    Assn for Promoting Extension of Contagious Diseases
       Act 68-75, Hon Sec.
    Infant Life Protection Soc 71-71, Hon Sec.


CURLING, THOMAS BLIZARD (1811-1888)

    Surgeon 49.
    Fellow Royal Society; Fellow Royal Col Surgeons;
       Royal Med & Chir Society.
    West London.
    [MEB]

    Assn for Promoting Extension of Contagious Diseases
       Act 68-70, V-Pres.

CURRIE, BERTRAM WODEHOUSE (1827-1896)

    Eton.
    Banker 49.
    Council of India 80-95, JP.
    Southwest London;  Surrey;  Hampshire.
    [MEB, Alum Cantab, Direc Direcs]

    London Municipal Reform League 85-85, Treas.


CURRIE, SIR EDMUND HAY (1834-1913)

    Harrow.
    Distiller;  Chm, London Hospital;  Technical Col
       Head.
    Liberal.
    Kt 76.
    Southwest London;  Middlesex.
    [WWW, BP]

    Metro Free Libraries Assn 77-77, Exec.


CURZON, GEORGE HENRY ROPER-, 16TH BARON TEYNHAM
    (1798-1889)

    Westminster School;  Royal Military Academy,
       Woolwich.
    Landowner 42;  2nd Lt., RA 16.
    Liberal.
    Baron 42.
    Hertfordshire.
    [MEB, BP, Walfords, Army List]

    Natl Assn for Promotion of State Colonization
       86-86, V-Pres.


CURZON, ROBERT NATHANIEL CECIL GEORGE, 15TH BARON ZOUCHE
    (1851-1914)

    Eton;  Christ Church, Oxf.
    Large Landowner 73.
    Conservative.  DL, JP.
    Baron 73.
    Southwest London;  Sussex.
    [WWW, BP, Walfords, Bateman, Alum Oxon]

    Natl Assn for Promotion of State Colonization
       86-86, V-Pres.


CURZON, SIDNEY CAMPBELL HENRY ROPER (1810-1882)

    Worcester, Oxf.
    Surrey.
    [BP, Alum Oxon]

    Church Assn 67-80, V-Pres.


CUST, ARTHUR PERCEVAL PUREY (1828-1916)

    Brasenose, Oxf.
    Vicar 62;  Hon. Canon 74;  Archdeacon 75;  Dean
       80;  Curate 51;  Ordained Priest<CE> 52;
       Rector 53.
    JP.
    Fellow Society of Antiquaries.
    Reading;  Buckingham;  York.
    [WWW, Alum Oxon, Crockfds]

    Assn for Promoting Extension of Contagious Diseases
       Act 68-68, V-Pres.


    Natl Soc for Preserving Memorials of Dead (F)
       81-82, Exec.


CUTLER, THOMAS WILLIAM

    Architect.
    Fellow Royal Inst Br Architects.
    West Central London.

    Smoke Abatement Committee 81-81.
    Sanitary Institute 83-89, Exec.


CUTTS, EDWARD LEWES (1824-1901)

    Queens´, Camb.
    Vicar 71;  Ordained Priest<CE> 48;  Curate 48;
       Perp. Curate 59;  Antiquary.
    Northwest London.
    [DNB, Alum Cantab, Crockfds]

    Natl Soc for Preserving Memorials of Dead (F)
       81-82, Exec.


DAFFORNE, JAMES ( -1880)

    Art Critic 45;  Author.
    South London.
    [DNB, MEB]

    Church Assn 67-78, Exec.


DALDORPH, A.

    Sunday Society 79-90, Exec.


DALE, FREDERICK SPENCER (1827- )

    Trinity, Camb.
    Vicar 60;  Ordained Priest<CE> 51;  Curate 52.
    Birmingham;  Dartford.
    [Alum Cantab, Crockfds]

    Natl Education Union (F) 69-79, Exec.


DALE, ROBERT WILLIAM (1829-1895)

    Spring Hill College, Birm.
    Congregational Minister 59.
    Radical.
    Birmingham.
    [DNB, MEB]

    Natl Education League 71-71, Exec.


DALE, T. B.

    Warwick.

    Church Assn 70-85, Exec.

DALE, THOMAS (1797-1870)

Christ's Hospital; Corpus Christi, Camb.
Canon 43; Ordained Priest<CE> 22; Curate 22;
    College Professor 28; Vicar 35; Rector 61;
    Dean 70.
East Central London; Therfield.
[MEB, Alum Cantab, Crockfds]

Church Assn 67-67, V-Pres.


DALE, THOMAS

JP.
Manchester.

Natl Education Union 70-86, Treas.


DALLOW, -

Malthusian League (F) 77-77, Exec.


DALZIELL, JAMES

Intl Arbitration & Peace Assn 81-81, V-Pres.


DAMER, LIONEL SEYMOUR WILLIAM DAWSON-, 4TH EARL
    PORTARLINGTON (1832-1892)

Eton.
Substantial Landowner 56; Lieutenant, Army 49;
    Captain, Army 54; Very Large Landowner 89.
Conservative. MP Portarlington 57-65,
    Portarlington 68-80. DL, JP.
Earl 89.
West London; Dorsetshire.
[MEB, BP, Walfords, Bateman, Dods, Army List]

Natl Emigration League (F) 70-70, V-Pres.


DANDY, RICHARD

St. Bees.
Vicar 53; Ordained Priest<CE> 54.
Liverpool.
[Crockfds]

Church Assn 70-75, Exec.


DANSEY, G.

Devonport.

Assn for Promoting Extension of Contagious Diseases
    Act 68-68, Exec.


DARGENT, E. A.

Cheltenham.

Church Assn 78-80, Exec.


DARRAH, CHARLES

Central Assn for Stopping Sale Intox Liquors on
    Sunday (F) 67-67, Exec.


DARWIN, CHARLES ROBERT (1809-1882)

Shrewsbury School; Christ's, Camb.
Biologist; Author.
JP.
Fellow Royal Society; Fellow Geological Society.
Kent.
[DNB, MEB, Alum Cantab, Walfords]

Sunday Society 76-79, V-Pres.


DARWIN, ERASMUS ALVEY (1804-1881)

Shrewsbury School; Christ's, Camb.
West London.

Sunday Society 76-82, V-Pres.


DASENT, SIR GEORGE WEBBE (1817-1896)

Westminster School; Magdalen, Oxf; Middle Temple.
Civ Serv Commissioner 70; Journalist 45;
    Barrister 52; Professor of English Literature
    and History, Kings Col London 53; Historical
    Manuscripts Commissioner 69.
Kt 76.
Southwest London.
[DNB, MEB, BP, Alum Oxon, Fosters]

Soc for Protection of Ancient Buildings (F) 78-85,
    Exec.


DAVENPORT, EDWARD GERSHOM (1838-1874)

King's College School; Trinity, Camb.
Conservative. MP Cornwall W, St Ives 74-74.
West London; Cornwall.
[MEB, Alum Cantab, Dods]

Infant Life Protection Soc 71-71, Exec.


DAVENPORT, FRANCIS WILLIAM

Vicar 72; Curate 60; Ordained Priest<CE> 61.
Great Malvern.
[Crockfds]

Church Assn 75-75, Exec.


DAVENPORT, RICHARD

Natl Education Union 70-70, Exec.

DAVENPORT, WILLIAM BROMLEY- (1821-1884)

    Harrow; Christ Church, Oxf.
    Landowner 62.
    Conservative. MP Warwickshire North 64-84. DL.
    West London; Warwickshire.
    [MEB, Walfords, Alum Oxon, Dods]

    Assn for Improvement of London Workhouse
        Infirmaries 66-66, Exec.


DAVIDS, THOMAS WILLIAM RHYS (1843-1922)

    Breslau U.
    College Professor 82; Ceylon Civ Serv 66;
        Barrister 77; Orientalist.
    Liberal.
    British Academy; Royal Asiatic Society.
    London.
    [DNB, WWW, Fosters]

    Indian Reform Assn 84-84, Exec.
    Land Nationalization Soc 84-85, Exec.


DAVIDSON, JOHN MORRISON

    U Aberdeen; Middle Temple.
    Barrister 77.
    Southeast London.
    [Fosters]

    London Municipal Reform League 82-85, Exec.


DAVIE, JOHN

    Dunfermline.

    London Soc for Abolition of Compulsory Vaccination
        81-81, V-Pres.


DAVIES, CHARLES MAURICE

    U Col, Durham.
    School Head 61; College Fellow 50; Curate 51;
        Ordained Priest<CE> 52.
    London.
    [Crockfds]

    Sunday Society (F) 75-77, V-Pres.


DAVIES, DAVID (1818-1893)

    Railway Contractor; Colliery Owner.
    Liberal. MP Cardigan District 74-86. JP.
    Montgomeryshire.
    [MEB, Dods, Direc Direcs]

    Natl Assn for Repeal Contagious Diseases Acts
        81-81, V-Pres.


DAVIES, URIAH (1822-1893)

    St John's, Camb.
    Vicar 61; Curate 47; Ordained Priest<CE> 48;
        Chaplain 49.
    North London.
    [Alum Cantab, Crockfds]

    Church Assn 67-85, Exec, V-Pres.


DAVIS, F., JN.

    Enniscorthy.

    London Soc for Abolition of Compulsory Vaccination
        81-81, V-Pres.


DAVIS, FREDERICK WILLIAM (1843- )

    St Edmund Hall, Oxf.
    Perp. Curate 70; Curate 69; Ordained Priest<CE>
        71.
    Blairgowri.
    [Alum Oxon, Crockfds]

    Natl Soc for Preserving Memorials of Dead (F)
        81-82, Exec.


DAVIS, ISRAEL (1847-1927)

    City of London School; Christ's, Camb; Inner
        Temple.
    Barrister 73; Newspaper Proprietor 78.
    West London.
    [Alum Cantab, Fosters]

    Metro Free Libraries Assn 78-78, Exec.


DAVIS, JOSEPH

    Bristol.

    Jamaica Committee (F) 66-66.


DAVISON, R.

    West London.

    Natl Soc for Preserving Memorials of Dead (F)
        81-82, Exec.


DAWES, W. E.

    Camberwell.

    Jamaica Committee (F) 66-66.


DAWSON, EDWARD BOUSFIELD (1830- )

    London U; Inner Temple.
    Barrister 52.
    JP.
    Lancashire.
    [Fosters, Direc Direcs]

    Intl Arbitration & Peace Assn 81-81, V-Pres.


DAWSON, EDWARD STANLEY (1843-1919)

    Commander, RN 69; Sub-Lieutenant, RN 62; Captain,
        RN 81.
    JP.
    Southwest London; Berkshire.
    [WWW, BP, Navy List]

    Plimsoll and Seamen's Fund Committee (F) 73-73, Hon
        Sec.

DAWSON, GEORGE (1821-1876)

>U Glasgow.
>Baptist Minister 43; Newspaper Editor 71.
>Fellow Geological Society.
>Birmingham; Worcestershire.
>[DNB, MEB]

>Natl Education League (F) 69-71, Exec.


DAWSON, JOHN

>London.

>Jamaica Committee (F) 66-66.


DAWSON, RICHARD, 1ST EARL OF DARTREY (1817-1897)

>Eton; Christ Church, Oxf.
>Very Large Landowner 27.
>Lord Lieutenant, JP.
>Baron 27; KP 55; Earl 66.
>West London; Co Monaghan.
>[MEB, WWW, BP, Walfords, Bateman, Alum Oxon]

>Plimsoll and Seamen's Fund Committee (F) 73-73,
>    Exec.


DAWSON, WILLIAM (1831-1911)

>Royal Naval College, Portsmouth.
>Captain, RN 70; Cadet, RN 44; Mate, RN 50;
>    Lieutenant, RN 54; Commander, RN 62.
>West London.
>[WWW, Navy List]

>Plimsoll and Seamen's Fund Committee (F) 73-73,
>    Exec.


DAY, E. S.

>St Johns Wood.

>Natl Footpaths Preservation Soc (F) 85-86, Exec.


DEADMAN, GEORGE

>Sunday Society 77-90, Exec.


DE BATHE, HENRY PERCEVAL, 4TH BT. (1823-1907)

>Eton.
>Maj. General 68; Lieutenant, Army 39; Captain,
>    Army 45; Colonel 54; Lt. General 76;
>    General 79; Landowner 70.
>DL, JP.
>Baronet 70; KCB 05.
>Southwest London; Devonshire; Co Meath.
>[WWW, BP, Walfords, Army List]

>Assn for Promoting Extension of Contagious Diseases
>    Act 68-70, V-Pres.


DEBENHAM, FRANK

>Northwest London.

>London Municipal Reform League 82-85, Exec.


DE CHAUMONT, FRANCIS STEPHEN BENNETT FRANCOIS
(1833-1888)

>Edinburgh(Medical).
>Professor, Army Medical School 76; Army Medical
>    Service 54; Asst Professor, Army Medical
>    School 63; Surgeon, Army Medical Serv 65;
>    Surgeon Major, Army Medical School 76.
>Fellow Royal Society; Fellow Royal Col Surgeons,
>    Edinb.
>Hampshire.
>[MEB, Army List]

>Sanitary Institute 78-87, Chairman.
>Sunday Society 80-87, V-Pres.


DE GREY, THOMAS, 6TH BARON WALSINGHAM (1843-1919)

>Eton; Trinity, Camb.
>Very Large Landowner 70.
>Conservative. MP Norfolk West 65-70. Lord in
>    Waiting 74-75, DL, JP.
>Baron 70.
>Fellow Royal Society; Fellow Linnean Society;
>    Fellow Zoological Society; Entomological
>    Society.
>West London; Norfolk.
>[WWW, BP, Walfords, Bateman, Alum Cantab, Dods]

>Natl Soc for Preserving Memorials of Dead 84-84,
>    Patron.


DEIGHTON, JOHN

>Working Men's Comtee Promoting Separation Church
>    and State (F) 71-71, Exec.


DE LA RUE, WARREN (1815-1889)

>Stationer.
>Fellow Royal Society; Fellow Royal Astronomical
>    Society; Royal Institution.
>Northwest London.
>[DNB, Alum Oxon]

>Sunday Society 76-89, V-Pres.


DELAGARDE, PHILIP CHILWELL (1797-1871)

>Surgeon 18.
>Fellow Royal Col Surgeons.
>Exeter.
>[MEB]

>Assn for Promoting Extension of Contagious Diseases
>    Act 68-70, V-Pres.

D´ELBOUX, L.

    Southampton.

    Jamaica Committee (F) 66-66.

DELL, HENRY

    Intl Arbitration & Peace Assn 81-81, Exec.

DE LOUSADA, FRANCIS CLIFFORD, DUKE <SPANISH> DE LOUSADA
    Y LOUSADA (1842-1916)

    Commander, RN 72;  Lieutenant, RN 62.
    West London.
    [WWW, BP, Navy List]

    Natl Assn for Promotion of State Colonization
        86-86, V-Pres.

DEMERIC, VICTOR

    East Central London.

    Assn for Promoting Extension of Contagious Diseases
        Act 68-68, Exec.

DE MORGAN, WILLIAM FREND (1839-1917)

    Univ College School;  University Col London;  Royal
        Academy Sch.
    Artist;  Ceramics Craftsman.
    Southwest London;  Wimbledon.
    [DNB, WWW]

    Soc for Protection of Ancient Buildings (F) 78-85,
        Exec.

DENISON, GEORGE ANTHONY (1805-1896)

    Eton;  Christ Church, Oxf.
    Archdeacon 51;  College Fellow 28;  College Tutor
        30;  Ordained Priest<CE> 32;  Curate 32;  Vicar
        38;  Prebendary 41.
    Taunton.
    [DNB, Walfords, Crockfds]

    City Church & Churchyard Protection Soc (F) 80-83,
        V-Pres.
    Church and State Defense Society (F) 68-68, Exec.

DENISON, SIR WILLIAM THOMAS (1804-1871)

    Eton;  Royal Military Academy, Woolwich.
    Maj. General, RE 68;  Major, RE 41;  Lt Gov,
        Tasmania 47;  Gov, New South Wales 55;  Gov,
        Madras 61;  Colonel, RE 57;  Lt. General, RE
        70.
    Kt 46;  KCB 56.
    Fellow Royal Astronomical Society;  Assoc Inst Civ
        Engineers;  Fellow Royal Society.
    [DNB, MEB, Walfords, Army List]

    Central Assn for Stopping Sale Intox Liquors on
        Sunday 70-70, V-Pres.
    Natl Emigration League (F) 70-70, V-Pres.

DENMAN, GEORGE (1819-1896)

    Repton;  Trinity, Camb;  Lincoln´s Inn.
    Q.C. 61;  Sergeant at Law 72;  Judge, Common Pleas
        72;  Judge, Queen´s Bench 80;  College Fellow
        43;  Barrister 46.
    Liberal.  MP Tiverton 59-65, Tiverton 66-72.
    PC 93.
    Southwest London.
    [DNB, MEB, BP, Alum Cantab, Walfords, Fosters,
        Dods]

    Commons Preservation Soc 69-86, Exec.

DENT, JOHN DENT (1826-1894)

    Eton;  Trinity, Camb;  Lincoln´s Inn.
    Large Landowner 75.
    Liberal.  MP Knaresborough 52-57, Scarborough
        57-59, Scarborough 60-74.  DL, JP.
    West London;  Yorks, West Riding.
    [MEB, Walfords, Bateman, Alum Cantab, Fosters,
        Dods, Direc Direcs]

    Assn for Promoting Extension of Contagious Diseases
        Act 68-68, V-Pres.

DENTON, WILLIAM (1815-1888)

    Worcester, Oxf.
    Vicar 50;  Curate 44;  Ordained Priest<CE> 45;
        Author.
    West London.
    [DNB, MEB, Alum Cantab, Alum Oxon, Crockfds]

    Assn for Improvement of London Workhouse
        Infirmaries 66-66, Exec.

DE RICCI, JAMES HERMAN (1847-1900)

    Middle Temple.
    Barrister 72;  Attorney General, Fiji 75;  Advocate
        General, Mauritius 76;  Chief Justice, Bahama
        79.
    Conservative.
    Fellow Royal Geograph Society;  Fellow Royal Col
        Surgeons;  Fellow Society of Antiquaries.
    East Central London;  Twickenham.
    [MEB, Fosters]

    Natl Assn for Promotion of State Colonization
        86-86, V-Pres.

DEVENISH, MATTHEW

    Dorchester.

    Jamaica Committee (F) 66-66.

DEVERELL, JOHN (1798- )

    Wadham, Oxf.
    Landowner.
    JP.
    Hampshire.
    [Walfords]

    Assn for Promoting Extension of Contagious Diseases
        Act 68-70, V-Pres.

DE WINTON, CHARLOTTE A.   <MISS>

    Weymouth.

    Soc for Abolition of Vivisection 76-76, Exec.


DE WINTON, SIR FRANCIS WALTER (1835-1901)

    Royal Military Academy, Woolwich.
    Major 72;  Lieutenant, RA 54;  Captain, Army 60;
        Lt. Colonel 80;  Colonel 87;  Maj. General
        90;  Administrator-General, Belgian Congo 85.
    CMG 82;  KCMG 84;  CB 88;  GCMG 93.
    Fellow Royal Geograph Society.
    South London.
    [DNB, WWW, Army List]

    Intl Arbitration & Peace Assn 81-81, Exec.
    London Municipal Reform League 82-85, Exec.


DE WORMS, HENRY, 1ST BARON PIRBRIGHT (1840-1903)

    Kings Col London;  Inner Temple.
    Barrister 63;  College Fellow 63.
    Conservative.  MP Greenwich 80-85, Liverpool E
        Toxteth 85-95.  Parl Sec Board of Trade 85-86,
        Parl Sec Board of Trade 86-88, Parl U-Sec Col
        Off 88-92, DL, JP.
    PC 89;  Baron 95.
    Fellow Royal Society.
    Southwest London;  Surrey.
    [DNB, WWW, BP, Dods]

    Natl Footpaths Preservation Soc (F) 85-90, V-Pres.


DEXTER, J.  T.

    Public Museums & Free Libraries Assn 68-68,
        Secretary.


DICEY, EDWARD JAMES STEPHEN (1832-1911)

    King's College School;  Trinity, Camb;  Gray's Inn.
    Journalist;  Author;  Newspaper Editor 70.
    CB 86.
    Southwest London.
    [DNB, WWW, Alum Cantab, Fosters, Direc Direcs]

    Jamaica Committee (F) 66-66.


DICKENS, CHARLES (1812-1870)

    Novelist;  Journal Editor.
    Kent.
    [DNB, MEB]

    Assn for Improvement of London Workhouse
        Infirmaries 66-66, Exec.


DICKSEE, SIR FRANCIS BERNARD (1853-1928)

    Royal Academy Sch.
    Artist.
    Kt 25;  KCVO 27.
    Royal Academy.
    St Johns Wood.
    [DNB, WWW]

    Sunday Society 80-90, V-Pres.


DICKSON, JOSEPH

    Physician.
    Jersey.

    Assn for Promoting Extension of Contagious Diseases
        Act 68-70, V-Pres.


DICKSON, THOMAS ALEXANDER (1833-1909)

    Merchant;  Manufacturer.
    Liberal.  MP Dungannon 74-80, Tyrone 81-85, Dublin
        St Stephens G 88-92.  JP.
    PC Ireland 93.
    Dungannon;  Dublin.
    [WWW, Dods]

    Natl Assn for Repeal Contagious Diseases Acts
        81-81, V-Pres.


DIGBY, GEORGE DIGBY WINGFIELD (1798-1883)

    Westminster School;  Christ Church, Oxf;  Inner
        Temple.
    Very Large Landowner 56;  Barrister 21.
    DL, JP.
    West London;  Dorsetshire.
    [BP, Walfords, Bateman, Alum Oxon]

    Central Assn for Stopping Sale Intox Liquors on
        Sunday 70-80, V-Pres.
    Church Assn 70-80, V-Pres.


DIGBY, KENELM THOMAS JOSEPH (1843-1893)

    Liberal.  MP Queens Co 68-80.
    Southwest London.
    [MEB, Walfords, Dods]

    Plimsoll and Seamen's Fund Committee (F) 73-73,
        Exec.


DIGBY, WILLIAM (1849-1904)

    Journalist 68;  Newspaper Editor 77;  E India
        Merchant.
    Liberal.
    CIE 78.
    Northwest London.
    [DNB, WWW]

    Indian Reform Assn 84-84, Exec.


DILKE, ASHTON WENTWORTH (1850-1883)

    Trinity Hall, Camb.
    Newspaper Proprietor 75.
    Radical.  MP Newcastle-upon-Tyne 80-83.
    West London.
    [MEB, BP, Dods, Alum Cantab]

    Commons Preservation Soc 80-83, Exec.
    Land Law Reform League (F) 81-81, V-Pres.

DILKE, SIR CHARLES WENTWORTH, 2ND BT.  (1843-1911)

    Trinity Hall, Camb;  Middle Temple.
    Politician;  Barrister 66;  Journal Proprietor 69;
       Author.
    Radical.  MP Chelsea 68-86, Forest of Dean 92-11.
       Parl U-Sec For Off 80-82, Pres Local Govt Board
       82-85, JP.
    Baronet 69;  PC 82.
    Southwest London;  Surrey.
    [DNB, WWW, BP, Walfords, Alum Cantab, Fosters,
       Dods]

    Allotments & Small Holdings Assn 85-85, V-Pres.
    Commons Preservation Soc 69-85, Exec, V-Pres.
    Land Tenure Reform Assn 73-73, Exec.
    Natl Education League 71-71, Exec.


DILLON, FRANK (1823-1909)

    Bruce Castle School, Tottenham;  Royal Academy Sch.
    Artist.
    Liberal.
    Royal Institution;  Royal Inst Water Colour
       Painters.
    West London.
    [WWW]

    Soc for Protection of Ancient Buildings (F) 78-85,
       Exec.


DIMSDALE, ROBERT DIMSDALE (1828-1898)

    Eton;  Corpus Christi, Oxf;  Inner Temple.
    Substantial Landowner 72.
    Conservative.  MP Hertford 66-74, Hitchin 85-92.
       DL, JP.
    Southwest London;  Hertfordshire.
    [MEB, WWW, BP, Walfords, Bateman, Alum Oxon, Dods,
       Direc Direcs]

    Natl Emigration League (F) 70-70, V-Pres.


DITMAS, FREDERICK <"MAJ.">

    Church Assn 67-75, Secretary.


DIXON, GEORGE (1820-1898)

    Merchant.
    Radical.  MP Birmingham 67-76, Birmingham Edgbaston
       85-98.  JP.
    Southwest London;  Birmingham.
    [DNB, MEB, WWW, Walfords, Dods]

    Sunday Society 76-90, V-Pres.
    Natl Education League (F) 69-71, Chairman.


DOBBS, ARCHIBALD EDWARD (1838- )

    Balliol, Oxf;  Lincoln's Inn.
    Barrister 65.
    West London.
    [Alum Oxon, Fosters]

    Proportional Representation Soc (F) 84-88, Exec.


DOBELL, -

    Physician.

    Assn for Improvement of London Workhouse
       Infirmaries 66-66, Exec.


DOBELL, RICHARD REID (1837-1902)

    Liverpool College.
    Canada Merchant.
    PC 96.
    Quebec.
    [WWW]

    Imperial Federation League (F) 84-84, Exec.


DODD, JOHN THEODORE (1848- )

    Christ Church, Oxf;  Lincoln's Inn.
    Barrister 74.
    Northwest London;  Sheffield.
    [Alum Oxon, Fosters]

    City Church & Churchyard Protection Soc 80-83,
       Exec.
    Natl Soc for Preserving Memorials of Dead 82-88,
       Exec.


DODDS, JOSEPH (1819-1891)

    Solicitor.
    Liberal.  MP Stockton 68-88.  DL.
    Incorporated Law Society.
    Stockton-on-Tees.
    [MEB, Walfords, Dods]

    Natl Assn for Repeal Contagious Diseases Acts
       81-81, V-Pres.


DOMINIE, FRANK

    Sunday Society (F) 75-90, Exec.


DOMVILLE, HENRY JONES ( -1888)

    St Andrews(Medical).
    Dep Insp Gen, RN Medical Serv 64;  Asst Surgeon, RN
       Medical Serv 39;  Surgeon, RN Medical Serv 46;
       Insp Gen, RN Medical Serv 75.
    CB 67.
    Member Royal Col Surgeons.
    Plymouth.
    [MEB, Navy List]

    Assn for Promoting Extension of Contagious Diseases
       Act 68-68, V-Pres.


DOMVILLE, WILLIAM HENRY

    London.

    Sunday Society 76-90, V-Pres.

DONALDSON, J.  HUNTER

    West London.

    London Municipal Reform League 82-85, Exec.


DONALDSON, THOMAS LEVERTON (1795-1885)

    Royal Academy Sch.
    Architect;  Professor Architecture, U Col London
        41;  District Surveyor, South Kensington.
    Fellow Royal Inst Br Architects.
    West Central London;  Ayreshire.
    [DNB, MEB, Walfords]

    Church Assn 70-80, Exec.


DONISTHORPE, WORDSWORTH (1847- )

    Trinity, Camb;  Inner Temple.
    Barrister 79.
    West London.
    [Alum Cantab, Fosters]

    Liberty & Property Defense League (F) 82-84, Exec.


DOUGLAS, ARTHUR GASCOIGNE (1827-1905)

    U Col, Durham.
    Bishop Aberdeen and Orkney 83;  Curate 50;
        Ordained Priest<CE> 52;  Rector 55;  Vicar 72.
    Conservative.
    Aberdeen.
    [WWW, BP, Walfords, Crockfds]

    Natl Soc for Preserving Memorials of Dead 84-84,
        Patron.


DOUGLAS, FRANCIS RICHARD WEMYSS CHARTERIS, 10TH EARL OF
  WEMYSS (1818-1914)

    Eton;  Christ Church, Oxf.
    Very Large Landowner 83.
    Conservative.  MP Gloucestershire East 41-46,
        Haddingtonshire 47-83.  Junior Lord Treasury
        52-55, DL.
    Earl 83;  GCVO 09.
    Southwest London;  Perthshire.
    [DNB, WWW, BP, Walfords, Alum Oxon, Dods]

    Liberty & Property Defense League (F) 82-14,
        Chairman.
    Plimsoll and Seamen's Fund Committee (F) 73-73,
        Exec.


DOUGLAS, SIR ROBERT PERCY, 4TH BT.  (1805-1891)

    General 74;  Ensign, Army 20;  Lt. Colonel 42;  Lt
        Gov, Jersey 60;  Lt Gov, Cape of Good Hope 63;
        Colonel 64;  Maj. General 72.
    Baronet 61.
    Hampshire.
    [MEB, BP, Walfords, Army List]

    Victoria Street Soc for Protection of Animals from
        Vivisection 84-85, V-Pres.


DOUGLAS, SHOLTO DOUGLAS CAMPBELL

    Trinity, Camb.
    Rector 79;  Curate 65;  Ordained Priest<CE> 66;
        Vicar 71.
    West London.
    [Crockfds]

    Church Assn 78-80, Exec.


DOWNING, DAVID (1800-1888)

    Maj. General 57;  Ensign, Army 19;  Captain, Army
        32;  Major 39;  Colonel 55;  Lt. General 69;
        General 75.
    West London.
    [MEB, Army List]

    Assn for Promoting Extension of Contagious Diseases
        Act 68-70, V-Pres.


DOWNS, H.

    Basingstoke.

    Church Assn 70-75, Exec.


DOYLE, RICHARD (1824-1883)

    Artist;  Author.
    Southwest London.
    [DNB, MEB]

    Soc for Protection of Ancient Buildings (F) 78-80,
        Exec.


DRAPER, JOHN

    London Municipal Reform League 82-82, Exec.


DRAY, -

    Malthusian League (F) 77-78, Exec.


DRUITT, GEORGE

    Natl Emigration League (F) 70-70, Exec.


DRUITT, ROBERT (1814-1883)

    Kings College(Medical).
    Physician 37.
    Med Off of Health 56-67.
    Fellow Royal Col Physicians;  Fellow Royal Col
        Surgeons.
    West London.
    [DNB, MEB]

    Assn for Improvement of London Workhouse
        Infirmaries 66-66, Exec.

DRUMMOND, JAMES

    Bradford.

    Jamaica Committee (F) 66-66.

DRUMMOND, PETER

    JP.

    Intl Arbitration & Peace Assn 81-81, V-Pres.

DRUMMOND, ROBERT B.

    Clergyman<Sect Unkn>.

    Sunday Society 79-90, V-Pres.

DRYHURST, FREDERICK JOHN ( -1931)

    Civ Serv Clerk 82; Sen. Clerk, Civ Serv 96;
       Principal Clerk, Civ Serv 03; Convict Prisons
       Director 03; Prison Commissioner.
    CB 12.
    London.
    [WWW]

    Commons Preservation Soc 86-86, Exec.
    Kyrle Soc 85-90, Exec.

DRYSDALE, ALICE VICKERY (1844-1929)

    Paris(Medical).
    Physician 80.
    Royal Col Physicians, Ireland.
    Southeast London.

    Malthusian League (F) 77-84, Exec, V-Pres.

DRYSDALE, CHARLES ROBERT (1829-1907)

    Trinity, Camb; U College London(Medical).
    Physician.
    Fellow Royal Col Surgeons; Member Royal Col
       Physicians.
    West London.
    [Alum Cantab]

    Sunday Society (F) 75-80, V-Pres.
    Assn for Promoting Extension of Contagious Diseases
       Act 68-68, Exec.
    League for Defense of Constitutional Rights 84-84,
       V-Pres.
    Malthusian League (F) 77-07, President, Treas.

DU BOIS, CHARLES CONRAD ADOLPHUS, BARON<NETH.> DE
    FERRIERES (1823-1908)

    Liberal. MP Cheltenham 80-85. JP.
    Cheltenham.
    [WWW, Dods]

    Central Assn for Stopping Sale Intox Liquors on
       Sunday 75-85, V-Pres.
    Church Assn 67-75, Exec.
    Natl Assn for Repeal Contagious Diseases Acts
       81-81, V-Pres.

DUCKETT, SIR GEORGE FLOYD, 3RD BT. (1811-1902)

    Harrow; Christ Church, Oxf.
    Archaeologist; Author; Sub-Lt., Army 32;
       Lieutenant, Army 34; Captain, Army 39.
    DL, JP.
    Baronet 56.
    Fellow Society of Antiquaries.
    Suffolk; Oxfordshire.
    [DNB, WWW, BP, Walfords, Army List]

    Natl Soc for Preserving Memorials of Dead (F)
       81-84, Patron.
    Soc for Abolition of Vivisection (F) 75-76, Exec.

DUCKHAM, THOMAS (1816-1902)

    Farmer 49.
    Liberal. MP Herefordshire 80-85, Leominster 85-86.
    JP.
    Herefordshire.
    [Dods]

    Intl Arbitration & Peace Assn 81-81, V-Pres.

DUDDELL, G.

    Natl Emigration League (F) 70-70, Treas.

DUDFIELD, T. ORME

    Physician.
    Member Royal Col Surgeons.
    West London.

    Sanitary Institute 84-88, Exec.

DUFF, ALEXANDER WILLIAM GEORGE, 1ST DUKE OF FIFE
    (1849-1912)

    Eton.
    Very Large Landowner 79.
    Liberal(Unionist). MP Elgin & Nairn 74-79. Lord
       Lieutenant, DL.
    Earl 79; Duke 89; KG; KT; PC; GCVO.
    West London; Banffshire.
    [BP, Bateman, Dods, Direc Direcs]

    Natl Assn for Promotion of State Colonization
       86-86, Exec, V-Pres.
    Natl Footpaths Preservation Soc 86-90, V-Pres.

DUFF, MOUNTSTUART ELPHINSTONE GRANT- (1829-1906)

    Edinburgh Academy; Balliol, Oxf; Inner Temple.
    Barrister 54; Landowner 58; Gov, Madras 81;
       Author.
    Liberal. MP Elgin District 57-81. Parl U-Sec
       India 68-74, Parl U-Sec Col Off 80-81, DL, JP.
    CIE 81; GCSI 86; PC.
    Fellow Royal Society.
    West London; Middlesex; Banffshire.
    [DNB, WWW, Walfords, Fosters, Dods]

    Metro Free Libraries Assn 78-78, V-Pres.

**DUFF, ROBERT WILLIAM (1835-1895)**

Very Large Landowner 61;  Cadet, RN 48;
    Lieutenant, RN 56;  Commander, RN 70;  Gov, New
    South Wales 93.
Liberal.  MP Banffshire 61-93.  Junior Lord
    Treasury 82-85, Lord Admiralty 86-86, DL, JP.
PC 92;  GCMG 93.
West London;  Banffshire;  Kincardineshire.
[DNB, MEB, Walfords, Bateman, Dods, Navy List]

Plimsoll and Seamen's Fund Committee (F) 73-73,
    Exec.


**DUIGNAN, W. H.**

Solicitor.
Walsall.
[Direc Direcs]

Travelling Tax Abolition Committee 79-85, Exec.


**DUNBAR, SIR CHARLES GORDON CUMMING, 9TH BT.  (1844-1916)**

Winchester College;  U Jena.
Perp. Curate 78;  Chaplain 67;  Ordained
    Priest<CE> 68;  Vicar 75;  Bishop Pretoria 75;
    Archdeacon 75;  Vicar 87.
Baronet 10.
West Central London.
[WWW, BP, Crockfds]

Sunday Society 80-80, V-Pres.


**DUNDAS, LADY JANE <MRS. PHILIP DUNDAS, DAU.  8TH EARL OF WEMYSS> ( -1897)**

[BP]

Natl Assn for Promotion of State Colonization
    86-86, V-Pres.


**DUNDAS, JOHN CHARLES (1845-1892)**

Harrow;  Trinity, Camb;  Lincoln's Inn.
Barrister 69.
Liberal(Unionist).  MP Richmond, Yorks NR 73-85.
    Lord Lieutenant 72-92, DL, JP.
Yorks, North Riding.
[MEB, BP, Alum Cantab, Fosters, Dods]

Sunday Society 78-85, V-Pres.


**DUNDAS, JULIANA CAVENDISH, COUNTESS OF CAMPERDOWN <Wife of 2ND EARL, nee PHILIPS> ( -1898)**

[BP]

Victoria Street Soc for Protection of Animals from
    Vivisection 80-85, Exec.


**DUNLOP, -**

Physician.
Jersey.

Assn for Promoting Extension of Contagious Diseases
    Act 68-68, Exec.


**DUNN, ANDREW**

South London.

London Municipal Reform League 82-85, Exec.


**DUNN, R. W.**

West Central London.

Assn for Promoting Extension of Contagious Diseases
    Act 68-68, Exec.


**DU PRE, CALEDON GEORGE (1803-1886)**

Eton;  St Mary Hall, Oxf.
Large Landowner 70;  Cornet, Army.
Conservative.  MP Buckinghamshire 39-71.  DL, JP.
West London;  Buckinghamshire.
[MEB, Walfords, Bateman, Alum Oxon, Dods]

Assn for Promoting Extension of Contagious Diseases
    Act 68-70, V-Pres.


**DURANT, JOHN CHARLES (1846-1929)**

Printer.
Radical.  MP Twr Hmlts Stepney 85-86.
West Central London.
[Dods]

English Land Restoration League 85-85, Exec.
Land Nationalization Soc (F) 81-83, Exec.


**DURNFORD, RICHARD (1802-1895)**

Eton;  Magdalen, Oxf.
Bishop Chichester 70;  Ordained Priest<CE> 31;
    Rector 35;  Hon. Canon 54;  Rural Dean 54;
    Archdeacon 67;  Canon 68.
Chichester.
[DNB, MEB, Alum Oxon, Crockfds]

Soc for Promoting Increase of the Home Episcopate
    72-74, V-Pres.


**DYER, ALFRED STACE**

Publisher.
East Central London.

Assn for Improvement of Public Morals (F) 79-81,
    Exec.
London Comtee Exposure & Suppresn Traffic In Girls
    (F) 80-85, Exec.
Natl Vigilance Assn (F) 85-85, Exec.
Working Men's Natl League for Abolition State
    Regulation of Vice 81-81, Chairman.

DYMES, - <MISS>

    Kyrle Soc 85-90, Exec.

DYMOND, J.

    Bible Christian Minister.

    Central Assn for Stopping Sale Intox Liquors on
        Sunday 80-80, V-Pres.

DYMOND, J. J.

    Bradford.

    Jamaica Committee (F) 66-66.

EARLE, JOHN (1824-1903)

    Magdalen, Oxf.
    Rector 57; College Fellow 48; Professor
        Anglo-Saxon, Oxford 49; Ordained Priest<CE>
        57; Prebendary 71; Rural Dean 73.
    Bath; Oxford.
    [DNB, WWW, Alum Cantab, Alum Oxon, Crockfds]

    Assn for Promoting Extension of Contagious Diseases
        Act 68-70, V-Pres.

EARLE, RALPH ANSTRUTHER (1835-1879)

    Harrow; Trinity, Camb.
    Diplomatic Service 54.
    Conservative. MP Berwick-upon-Tweed 59-59, Maldon
        65-68. Parl Sec Poor Law Board 66-67.
    West London.
    [MEB, Walfords, Alum Cantab, Dods]

    Assn for Promoting Extension of Contagious Diseases
        Act 70-70, V-Pres.

EARP, THOMAS (1830- )

    Brewer.
    Liberal. MP Newark, Notts 74-85.
    Newark-on-Trent.
    [Dods]

    Intl Arbitration & Peace Assn 81-81, V-Pres.

EASSIE, WILLIAM (1832-1888)

    Civil Engineer.
    Fellow Linnean Society; Fellow Geological Society.
    West London.
    [MEB]

    Smoke Abatement Committee 81-81.
    Sanitary Institute 78-87, Exec.

EASTCOURT, R.

    English Land Restoration League 85-85, Exec.

EASTWICK, EDWARD BACKHOUSE (1814-1883)

    Charterhouse; Merton, Oxf; Middle Temple.
    Orientalist; Ensign, Army 36; India Civil
        Service; College Professor 45; Asst Pol Sec,
        India Office 59; Diplomatic Service 60.
    Conservative. MP Penryn & Falmouth 68-74.
    CB 66.
    Fellow Royal Society; Fellow Society of
        Antiquaries.
    Southwest London; Cornwall.
    [DNB, MEB, Walfords, Alum Oxon, Dods]

    Commons Preservation Soc 76-76, Exec.
    Natl Emigration League (F) 70-70, V-Pres.

EATON, -

    Workmen's Peace Assn 75-75, Exec.

ECROYD, WILLIAM FARRER (1827-1915)

    Worsted Manufacturer.
    Conservative. MP Preston 81-85. JP.
    Burnley; Herefordshire.
    [Dods]

    Howard Assn 81-84, Patron.
    Natl Education Union 75-79, Exec.

EDEN, ROBERT (1804-1886)

    Westminster School; Christ Church, Oxf.
    Bishop Moray and Ross 51; Ordained Priest<CE> 28;
        Rector 37; Landowner 39.
    JP.
    Inverness; Essex.
    [DNB, MEB, Walfords, Alum Oxon, Crockfds]

    Natl Soc for Preserving Memorials of Dead 84-84,
        Patron.
    Natl Education Union 71-79, Exec.

EDGAR, ANDREW

    West Central London.

    Infant Life Protection Soc 71-71, Exec.

EDGELL, EDGELL WYATT (1801-1888)

    Eton; Oriel, Oxf.
    Retired Clergyman 51; Ordained Priest<CE> 29;
        Rector 34.
    West London; Warwickshire.
    [Walfords, Alum Oxon, Crockfds]

    Natl Assn for Promotion of State Colonization
        86-86, Exec.
    Sanitary Institute 78-84, Treas.
    Assn for Promoting Extension of Contagious Diseases
        Act 68-68, Exec.
    Vigilance Assn for Defense of Personal Rights
        83-83, Exec.

EDWARDES, SIR HERBERT BENJAMIN (1819-1868)

    Kings Col London.
    Maj. General 66; Cadet, Army 41; Captain, Army
       50; Deputy Commissioner, Jalandhar 51;
       Commissioner, Peshawur 53; Colonel 60;
       Commissioner, Umballa 62.
    CB 49; KCB 60; KCSI 66.
    West London.
    [DNB, MEB, Alum Cantab, Alum Oxon, Army List]

    Church Assn 67-67, V-Pres.

EDWARDS, EDWIN (1823-1879)

    Artist 60; Solicitor 45.
    West London.
    [DNB, MEB, Bryan's Painters]

    Soc for Protection of Ancient Buildings (F) 78-78,
       Exec.

EDWARDS, JOHN PASSMORE (1824-1911)

    Newspaper Proprietor 76; Journal Proprietor 50.
    Liberal. MP Salisbury 80-85.
    West London.
    [DNB, WWW, Dods]

    Howard Assn 80-84, Patron.
    Intl Arbitration & Peace Assn 81-81, V-Pres.

EDWARDS, R. P.

    Bath.

    Jamaica Committee (F) 66-66.

EDWARDS, THOMAS DYER, JR.

    Clare, Camb.
    Banker.
    Southwest London.
    [Alum Cantab, Direc Direcs]

    Natl Assn for Promotion of State Colonization
       86-86, Exec.

EDWARDS, WILLIAM

    Southeast London.

    Jamaica Committee (F) 66-66.

EGERTON, ALGERNON FULKE (1825-1891)

    Harrow; Christ Church, Oxf; Inner Temple.
    Conservative. MP Lancashire South 59-68,
       Lancashire SE 68-80, Wigan 82-85. Parl Sec
       Admiralty 59-68, Parl Sec Admiralty 74-80, DL,
       JP.
    West London; Lancashire.
    [BP, Walfords, Alum Oxon, Dods]

    Assn for Promoting Extension of Contagious Diseases
       Act 68-70, V-Pres.
    Natl Education Union (F) 69-79, Exec.

EGERTON, FRANCIS (1824-1895)

    Harrow.
    Captain, RN 55; Cadet, RN 40; Lieutenant, RN 46;
       Commander, RN 50; Rear Admiral 73.
    Liberal. MP Derbyshire East 68-85, Derbyshire NE
       85-86. Lord Lieutenant 93-95.
    West London; Surrey.
    [MEB, BP, Walfords, Dods, Navy List]

    Natl Assn for Promotion of State Colonization
       86-86, V-Pres.
    Natl Education Union (F) 69-79, Exec.
    Plimsoll and Seamen's Fund Committee (F) 73-73,
       Exec.

EGERTON, WILBRAHAM, 1ST EARL EGERTON OF TATTON
    (1832-1909)

    Eton; Christ Church, Oxf.
    Very Large Landowner 83.
    Conservative. MP Cheshire North 58-68, Cheshire
       Mid 68-83. Ecclesiastical Commissioner 80-08,
       Lord Lieutenant 00-05, DL, JP.
    Baron 83; Earl 97.
    Southwest London; Cheshire.
    [WWW, BP, Walfords, Bateman, Alum Oxon, Dods, Direc
       Direcs]

    Natl Assn for Promotion of State Colonization
       86-86, Patron.
    Assn for Improvement of London Workhouse
       Infirmaries 66-66, Exec.
    Natl Education Union 70-79, Exec.

EGGLESTONE, W. M.

    Durham[County].

    Natl Soc for Preserving Memorials of Dead (F)
       81-82, Exec.

ELLERBY, W. P.

    Natl Education Union 70-71, Exec.

ELLICOTT, CHARLES JOHN (1819-1905)

    Oakham; St John's, Camb.
    Bishop Gloucester and Bristol 63; College Fellow
       45; Ordained Priest<CE> 47; Rector 48;
       Professor New Testament, Kings Col London 59;
       Dean 61.
    West London.
    [DNB, Alum Cantab, Crockfds]

    Natl Assn for Promotion of State Colonization
       86-86, Patron.
    Central Assn for Stopping Sale Intox Liquors on
       Sunday 75-85, V-Pres.
    Natl Education Union 79-79, Exec.

ELLIOT, SIR GEORGE AUGUSTUS (1813-1901)

    Admiral 70;  Cadet, RN 27;  Lieutenant, RN 34;
       Commander, RN 38;  Captain, RN 40;  Rear
       Admiral 58;  Vice-Admiral 65.
    Conservative.  MP Chatham 74-75.
    KCB 77.
    West London;  Wimbledon.
    [DNB, WWW, BP, Dods, Direc Direcs, Navy List]

    Plimsoll and Seamen's Fund Committee (F) 73-73,
       Exec.
    Liberty & Property Defense League (F) 82-82, Exec.

ELLIOT, GILBERT (1800-1891)

    St John's, Camb.
    Dean 50;  Ordained Priest<CE> 24;  Rector 24.
    JP.
    Bristol;  Berkshire.
    [MEB, Walfords, Alum Cantab, Crockfds]

    Church Assn 75-85, V-Pres.

ELLIOTT, ROWLAND A.

    Natl Education Union 71-71, Exec.

ELLIOTT, T. H.

    Land Nationalization Soc 83-85, Exec.

ELLIS, FREDERICK STARTRIDGE (1830-1901)

    Bookseller;  Author.
    West London.
    [DNB]

    Soc for Protection of Ancient Buildings (F) 78-85,
       Exec.

ELLIS, SIR JOHN WHITTAKER, 1ST BT.  (1829-1912)

    Merchant;  Estate Agent.
    Conservative.  MP Surrey Mid 84-85, Surrey Kingston
       85-92.  DL, JP.
    Baronet 82.
    West London;  Surrey.
    [WWW, Dods, Direc Direcs]

    Natl Assn for Promotion of State Colonization
       86-86, Patron.
    City Church & Churchyard Protection Soc (F) 80-83,
       V-Pres.

ELLIS, THOMAS

    Natl Secular Soc 70-70, V-Pres.

ELLIS, WILLIAM HORTON

    Stock Broker.
    Fellow Royal Meteorlog Society.
    Exeter.
    [Direc Direcs]

    Sanitary Institute 80-88, Exec.

ELMES, EDWARD

    Working Men's Natl League for Abolition State
       Regulation of Vice 81-81, V-Chairman.

ELMHIRST, WILLIAM (1827- )

    Winchester College;  Trinity, Oxf.
    Chaplain 62;  Curate 50;  Ordained Priest<CE> 51;
       Landowner 64.
    Yorks, West Riding.
    [Walfords, Alum Oxon, Crockfds]

    Church Assn 75-78, Exec.

ELMORE, ALFRED (1815-1881)

    Royal Academy Sch.
    Artist 34.
    Royal Academy.
    Southwest London.
    [DNB, MEB, Bryan's Painters]

    Sunday Society 80-80, V-Pres.

ELPHINSTONE, SIR JAMES DALRYMPLE HORN, 2ND BT.
    (1805-1886)

    Large Landowner 48;  Capt, HEIC Navy 35;  Director,
       East India Co.
    Conservative.  MP Portsmouth 57-65, Portsmouth
       68-80.  Junior Lord Treasury 74-80, DL, JP.
    Baronet 48.
    Southwest London;  Aberdeenshire.
    [MEB, BP, Walfords, Bateman, Dods]

    Natl Emigration League (F) 70-70, V-Pres.

ELT, CHARLES HENRY (1805-1882)

    Metropolitan Board of Works 66.
    North London.
    [MEB]

    Financial Reform Union (F) 68-69, Exec.
    Jamaica Committee (F) 66-66.

ELTON, SIR ARTHUR HALLAM, 7TH BT.  (1818-1883)

    Royal Military College, Sandhurst.
    Substantial Landowner 53;  Ensign, Army 36;
       Lieutenant, Army 40.
    Liberal.  MP Bath 57-59.  DL, JP.
    Baronet 53.
    Southwest London;  Somersetshire.
    [MEB, BP, Walfords, Bateman, Army List]

    Jamaica Committee (F) 66-66.

ELWIN, WHITWELL (1816-1900)

    Gonville & Caius, Camb.
    Rector 49;   Curate 39;   Ordained Priest<CE> 40;
       Journalist 43.
    Norfolk.
    [DNB, Alum Cantab, Crockfds]

    Soc for Protection of Ancient Buildings (F) 78-85,
       Exec.


EMANUEL, LEWIS

    West London.

    London Municipal Reform League 82-85, Exec.


EMBLETON, DENNIS (1810-1900)

    St Thomas's Hospital Lond.
    Physician 37;   Medical School Lecturer 39;   Medical
       School Professor 70.
    Fellow Royal Col Physicians;   Fellow Royal Col
       Surgeons.
    Newcastle-upon-Tyne.
    [MEB]

    Assn for Promoting Extension of Contagious Diseases
       Act 68-68, V-Pres.


EMERY, WILLIAM (1825-1910)

    City of London School;   Corpus Christi, Camb.
    Archdeacon 64;   College Fellow 47;   Ordained
       Priest<CE> 50;   College Dean 53;   College Tutor
       55;   Canon 70.
    Cambridge.
    [DNB, WWW, Alum Cantab, Crockfds, Direc Direcs]

    Natl Education Union 70-79, Exec.


EMPSON, CHARLES WILLIAM (1848-1919)

    Marlborough;   Trinity, Camb;   Lincoln's Inn.
    Barrister 76.
    JP.
    West London;   Yorkshire.
    [Alum Cantab, Fosters, Direc Direcs]

    Kyrle Soc 85-90, Exec.


ENDEAN, J. RUSSELL

    London Municipal Reform League 82-82, Exec.


EPPS, JOHN (1805-1869)

    Mill Hill School;   Edinburgh(Medical).
    Physician 27;   Medical School Lecturer 51.
    Radical.
    West Central London.
    [DNB, MEB]

    Jamaica Committee (F) 66-66.


ERICHSEN, SIR JOHN ERIC, 1ST BT.  (1818-1896)

    U College London(Medical).
    Surgeon 39;   Medical School Lecturer 44;   Medical
       School Professor 50;   Vivisection Inspector 77;
       Author.
    Liberal.
    Baronet 95.
    Fellow Royal Society;   Member Royal Col Physicians;
       Member Royal Col Surgeons.
    West London.
    [DNB, MEB]

    Assn for Promoting Extension of Contagious Diseases
       Act 68-70, V-Pres.


ERRINGTON, SIR GEORGE, 1ST BT.  (1839-1920)

    Roman Catholic U Ireland.
    Substantial Landowner.
    Liberal.  MP Longford Co 74-85.  JP.
    Baronet 85.
    West London;   Dublin;   Wexford.
    [WWW, Bateman, Dods]

    Sunday Society 80-90, V-Pres.


ERSKINE, JOHN ELPHINSTONE (1806-1887)

    Royal Naval College, Portsmouth.
    Admiral 69;   Cadet, RN 19;   Captain, RN 38;   Rear
       Admiral 57;   Vice-Admiral 64.
    Liberal.  MP Stirlingshire 65-74.
    West London;   Stirlingshire.
    [MEB, Walfords, Dods, Navy List]

    Plimsoll and Seamen's Fund Committee (F) 73-73,
       Exec.


ERSKINE, SHIPLEY GORDON STUART, 14TH EARL OF BUCHAN
    (1850-1934)

    Harrow.
    Substantial Landowner.
    DL, JP.
    Earl 99.
    Midlothian.
    [WWW, BP, Bateman]

    Victoria Street Soc for Protection of Animals from
       Vivisection 84-85, V-Pres.


ESCOMBE, - <MRS. FRANK ESCOMBE>

    London.

    Sunday Society (F) 75-77, Exec, V-Pres.


ESSLEMONT, PETER J.  (1834-1894)

    Draper;   Chm, Scottish Fisheries Board 92.
    Liberal.  MP Aberdeenshire East 85-92.  JP.
    Aberdeen;   Kincardine.
    [MEB, Dods, Direc Direcs]

    Free Land League 86-86, V-Pres.
    Intl Arbitration & Peace Assn 81-81, V-Pres.

ESTCOURT, J. H.

>   London.

>   Jamaica Committee (F) 66-66.

ESTLIN, MARY A.<OR E.>

>   Bristol.

>   Ladies' Natl Assn for Repeal of Contagious Diseases
>       Acts 70-72, Exec.

ETCHES, W. JEFFERY

>   Derby.

>   Jamaica Committee (F) 66-66.

EVANS, EVAN (1813-1891)

>   Pembroke, Oxf.
>   College Head 64;  Ordained Priest<CE> 38;  College
>       Tutor 41;  College Fellow 43;  Canon 64;
>       V-Chancellor, Oxford 78.
>   Oxford; Gloucester.
>   [MEB, Alum Oxon, Crockfds]

>   City Church & Churchyard Protection Soc (F) 80-83,
>       V-Pres.

EVANS, GEORGE M.

>   Bridport.

>   Assn for Promoting Extension of Contagious Diseases
>       Act 68-68, Exec.

EVANS, H. A.

>   Westward Ho!.

>   Natl Soc for Preserving Memorials of Dead 82-82,
>       Exec.

EVANS, HOWARD (1839-1915)

>   City of London School.
>   Newspaper Editor.
>   Radical.
>   Southwest London.
>   [WWW]

>   Land Tenure Reform Assn 73-73, Secretary.
>   Workmen's Peace Assn 78-82, Chairman, Treas.

EVANS, JOHN (1815-1891)

>   Trin Col, Dublin.
>   Archdeacon 66;  Curate 41;  Ordained Priest<CE> 42;
>       Perp. Curate 44;  Rector 57.
>   Bangor.
>   [MEB, Crockfds]

>   Central Assn for Stopping Sale Intox Liquors on
>       Sunday 70-80, V-Pres.

EVANS, THOMAS (1804-1880)

>   Edinburgh(Medical).
>   Physician 30.
>   Fellow Royal Col Physicians.
>   Gloucester.
>   [MEB]

>   Assn for Promoting Extension of Contagious Diseases
>       Act 68-70, V-Pres.

EVELYN, WILLIAM JOHN (1822-1908)

>   Rugby;  Balliol, Oxf.
>   Landowner 29.
>   Conservative.  MP Surrey West 49-57, Deptford
>       85-88. DL, JP.
>   Fellow Society of Antiquaries;  Fellow Royal
>       Geograph Society.
>   Surrey.
>   [WWW, Walfords, Alum Oxon, Dods]

>   City Church & Churchyard Protection Soc 83-83,
>       V-Pres.

EVEREST, R.

>   Clergyman<Sect Unkn>.
>   London.

>   Jamaica Committee (F) 66-66.

EVERSHED, SYDNEY (1825-1903)

>   Brewer 53;  Tax Commissioner.
>   Liberal.  MP Staffordshire South 86-00.  JP.
>   Burton-upon-Trent.
>   [WWW, Dods]

>   Free Land League 86-86, V-Pres.

EWART, WILLIAM (1798-1869)

>   Eton;  Christ Church, Oxf;  Middle Temple.
>   Barrister 27.
>   Radical.  MP Bletchingly 28-30, Liverpool 30-37,
>       Wigan 39-41, Dumfries District 41-68.  DL, JP.
>   Fellow Royal Geograph Society.
>   West London;  Devizes.
>   [DNB, MEB, Alum Oxon, Dods]

>   Public Museums & Free Libraries Assn 68-68, V-Pres.
>   Howard Assn 67-68, Patron.

EYNON, - <MRS.>

>   Bristol.

>   British Women's Temperance Assn 84-85, Exec.

EYRE, GEORGE EDWARD BRISCOE (1840- )

>   Balliol, Oxf;  Inner Temple.
>   Barrister 61.
>   JP.
>   Hampshire.
>   [Walfords, Alum Oxon]

>   Commons Preservation Soc 76-86, Exec.

FABER, GEORGE HENRY (1839-1910)

    Merchant Taylors.
    Insurance Underwriter.
    Liberal. MP Boston 06-10.
    London; Kent.
    [WWW, Dods]

    Railway Passengers' Protection Assn 86-86, Exec.


FAED, THOMAS (1826-1900)

    Edinburgh School of Design.
    Artist.
    Royal Academy.
    St Johns Wood.
    [DNB, MEB, WWW, Bryan's Painters]

    Sunday Society 86-90, V-Pres.


FAITHFULL, EMILY (1836-1895)

    Publisher 63.
    London.
    [MEB]

    Natl Assn for Promotion of State Colonization
       86-86, V-Pres.


FALCONER, RANDLE WILBRAHAM (1816-1881)

    Edinburgh(Medical).
    Physician 39.
    JP.
    Fellow Royal Col Physicians; Br Medical Assn.
    Bath.
    [DNB, MEB, Walfords]

    Assn for Promoting Extension of Contagious Diseases
       Act 68-70, V-Pres.


FANE, JOHN WILLIAM (1804-1875)

    Rugby; St John's, Camb.
    Landowner 50.
    Conservative. MP Oxfordshire 62-68. DL, JP.
    West London; Oxfordshire.
    [MEB, Walfords, Alum Cantab, Alum Oxon, Dods]

    Assn for Promoting Extension of Contagious Diseases
       Act 68-70, V-Pres.


FARISH, J.

    Church Assn 67-70, Exec.


FARMER, WILLIAM

    London.

    Jamaica Committee (F) 66-66.


FARQUHAR, HARVIE MORETON (1816-1887)

    Eton.
    Southwest London; Northamptonshire.
    [BP, Walfords]

    Plimsoll and Seamen's Fund Committee (F) 73-73,
       Exec.


FARQUHAR, SIR WALTER ROCKCLIFFE, 3RD BT. (1810-1900)

    Eton.
    Banker.
    DL, JP.
    Baronet 36.
    Southwest London; Middlesex; Surrey.
    [MEB, WWW, BP, Walfords]

    Assn for Improvement of London Workhouse
       Infirmaries 66-66, Exec.
    Liberty & Property Defense League 84-84, Treas.
    Plimsoll and Seamen's Fund Committee (F) 73-73,
       Treas.
    Soc for Promoting Increase of the Home Episcopate
       72-74, Exec.


FARQUHARSON, ROBERT (1836-1918)

    Edinburgh Academy; U Edinburgh; Paris(Medical).
    Physician 58; Asst Surgeon, Army Medical Serv 59;
       Medical School Lecturer; Very Large Landowner
       76; Author.
    Liberal. MP Aberdeenshire West 80-06. DL, JP.
    PC 06.
    Fellow Royal Col Physicians.
    West London; Aberdeenshire.
    [WWW, Bateman, Dods, Direc Direcs, Army List]

    Smoke Abatement Committee 81-81.


FARR, WILLIAM (1807-1883)

    Statistician 38; Physician 33; Asst Census
       Commissioner 51; Census Commissioner 71.
    CB 80.
    Fellow Royal Society; Fellow Royal Statistical
       Society.
    West London.
    [DNB, MEB, Alum Oxon]

    Sanitary Institute (F) 76-83, V-Pres.


FARRAR, JOHN (1802-1884)

    Woodhouse Grove School, Yorks.
    School Head 58; Wesleyan Minister 22; Asst School
       Master 22.
    Leeds.
    [DNB, MEB]

    Central Assn for Stopping Sale Intox Liquors on
       Sunday 70-70, V-Pres.

FARRE, ARTHUR (1811-1887)

Charterhouse; Gonville & Caius, Camb; St
    Bartholomew's Hosp.
Physician 41; Medical School Lecturer 36; Medical
    School Professor 41.
DL.
Fellow Royal Society; Fellow Royal Col Physicians;
    Obstetrical Society Lond; Royal Microscop
    Society.
Southwest London.
[DNB, MEB, Alum Cantab]

Assn for Improvement of London Workhouse
    Infirmaries 66-66, Exec.


FARRER, THOMAS HENRY, 1ST BARON FARRER OF ABINGER
(1819-1899)

Eton; Balliol, Oxf; Lincoln's Inn.
Sec, Board of Trade 65; Barrister 44; Asst Sec
    Maritime Dept, Board of Trade 50; Asst Sec,
    Board of Trade 64.
Liberal. DL, JP.
Baronet 83; Baron 93.
Fellow Linnean Society.
West London; Surrey.
[DNB, MEB, WWW, BP, Fosters, Direc Direcs]

Commons Preservation Soc 86-86, Exec.


FARRER, SIR WILLIAM JAMES (1822-1911)

Balliol, Oxf.
Solicitor.
DL, JP.
Kt 87.
West London; Berkshire.
[WWW, BP, Alum Oxon, Direc Direcs]

Commons Preservation Soc 69-69, Exec.


FARTHING, - <MRS. WILLIAM FARTHING>

Sunday Society 76-76, Exec.


FARTHING, WILLIAM

Sunday Society 76-76, Exec.


FAULCONER, ROBERT S.

Church Assn 67-75, Exec.


FAULKNER, CHARLES JOSEPH (1834-1892)

Pembroke, Oxf.
College Dean 70; College Fellow 56; College
    Lecturer 64; College Tutor 68.
Oxford.
[MEB, Alum Oxon]

Soc for Protection of Ancient Buildings (F) 78-85,
    Exec.


FAWCETT, HENRY (1833-1884)

King's College School; Trinity Hall, Camb;
    Lincoln's Inn.
Professor of Political Economy, Cambridge 63;
    College Fellow 56; Political Economist;
    Author; Ld Rector, U Glasgow 83.
Radical. MP Brighton 65-74, Hackney 74-84.
    Postmaster General 80-84.
PC 80.
Fellow Royal Society.
South London; Cambridge.
[DNB, MEB, Walfords, Alum Cantab, Dods]

Commons Preservation Soc 69-84, Exec, V-Pres.
Sunday Society 78-84, V-Pres.
Metro Free Libraries Assn 77-77, Exec.
Assn for Improvement of London Workhouse
    Infirmaries 66-66, Exec.
Natl Education League 71-71, Exec.


FAWCETT, MILLICENT GARRETT <MRS. HENRY FAWCETT, nee
GARRETT> (1847-1929)

Liberal(Unionist). JP.
GBE 25.
West Central London.
[DNB, WWW]

Commons Preservation Soc 85-86, Exec.
Natl Education League 71-71, Exec.
Natl Vigilance Assn (F) 85-85, Exec.


FEILDING, SIR PERCY ROBERT BASIL (1827-1904)

Rugby.
Colonel 65; Sub-Lt., Army 45; Captain, Army 51;
    Lt. Colonel 55; Maj. General 70; Lt.
    General 86; General 91.
CB; KCB 93.
West London; Surrey.
[WWW, BP, Army List]

Assn for Promoting Extension of Contagious Diseases
    Act 68-70, V-Pres.


FELL, - <MRS. W. T.>

Kyrle Soc 85-89, Exec.


FELL, W. T.

Kyrle Soc 84-89, Exec.


FELSHAW, JAMES

Edinburgh.

Jamaica Committee (F) 66-66.

FENN, W. W.

    Kyrle Soc 85-94, Exec.


FENWICK, CHARLES (1850-1918)

    Trade Union Leader 78;  Miner 60.
    Liberal.  MP Wansbeck, Northumb 85-18.
    PC 11.
    Southwest London;  Newcastle-upon-Tyne.
    [WWW, Dods, Dic Lab Biog]

    Free Land League 86-86, V-Pres.


FENWICK, PASCOE

    Southwest London.

    London Municipal Reform League 82-85, Exec.


FENWICK, RALPH

    Primitive Methodist Minister.

    Central Assn for Stopping Sale Intox Liquors on
        Sunday 85-85, V-Pres.


FERGUSON, ROBERT (1817-1898)

    Manufacturer.
    Liberal.  MP Carlisle 74-86.  JP.
    Fellow Society of Antiquaries.
    Southwest London;  Carlisle.
    [MEB, Walfords, Dods]

    Intl Arbitration & Peace Assn 81-81, V-Pres.
    Jamaica Committee (F) 66-66.


FERGUSSON, SIR JAMES, 6TH BT.  (1832-1907)

    Rugby;  University Col, Oxf.
    Very Large Landowner 49;  Lieutenant, Army 51;
        Captain, Army 54;  Gov, South Australia 68;
        Gov, New Zealand 73;  Gov, Bombay 80.
    Conservative.  MP Ayrshire 54-57, Ayrshire 59-68,
        Manchester Northeast 85-06.  Parl U-Sec India
        66-67, Parl U-Sec Home Off 67-68, Parl U-Sec
        For Off 86-91, Postmaster General 91-92.
    Baronet 49;  PC 68;  KCMG 75;  CIE 84;  GCSI 85.
    Southwest London;  Ayrshire.
    [DNB, WWW, BP, Walfords, Bateman, Alum Oxon, Dods,
        Direc Direcs]

    Assn for Improvement of London Workhouse
        Infirmaries 66-66, Exec.


FERGUSSON, SIR WILLIAM, 1ST BT.  (1808-1877)

    Edinburgh High School;  U Edinburgh.
    Surgeon 31;  Medical School Professor 40.
    Baronet 66.
    Fellow Royal Society;  Fellow Royal Col Surgeons;
        Pathological Society;  Br Medical Assn.
    West London.
    [DNB, MEB, BP, Walfords]

    Assn for Promoting Extension of Contagious Diseases
        Act 68-70, V-Pres.


    Assn for Improvement of London Workhouse
        Infirmaries 66-66, Exec.


FERREY, EDMUND B.  <OR B.  EDMUND>

    Architect.
    Fellow Royal Inst Br Architects;  Fellow Society of
        Antiquaries.
    Southwest London.

    City Church & Churchyard Protection Soc (F) 80-83,
        Exec.


FESTING, EDWARD ROBERT (1839-1912)

    Royal Military Academy, Woolwich.
    Lt.  Colonel, RE 80;  Lieutenant, RE 55;  Captain,
        RE 62;  Deputy General Superintendent, So Kens
        Museum 64;  Major, RE 72;  Colonel, RE 84;
        Director Science Dept, South Kensington Museum
        93.
    CB 00.
    Fellow Royal Society.
    Southwest London.
    [WWW, Army List]

    Smoke Abatement Committee 81-81, Exec.


FEW, ROBERT (1807-1887)

    Solicitor 28.
    London.
    [MEB]

    Soc for Promoting Increase of the Home Episcopate
        74-74, Exec.


FIELD, ALFRED

    Birmingham.

    Natl Education League (F) 69-71, Exec.


FIELD, EDWARD (1828-1912)

    Royal Naval College, Portsmouth.
    Rear Admiral 86;  Cadet, RN 45;  Lieutenant, RN 51;
        Commander, RN 59;  Captain, RN 69;  Admiral 97.
    Conservative.  MP Sussex South 85-00.  DL, JP.
    CB 97.
    Hampshire.
    [WWW, Dods, Direc Direcs, Navy List]

    Natl Assn for Promotion of State Colonization
        86-86, V-Pres.


FIELD, H.  J.

    Financial Reform Union (F) 68-69, Exec.

FIELD, ROGERS (1831-1900)

> London U.
> Drainage Engineer.
> Member Inst Civ Engineers.
> Southwest London.
> [MEB]
>
> Sanitary Institute 78-89, V-Chairman.

FIELDING, RUDOLPH WILLIAM BASIL, 8TH EARL OF DENBIGH
(1823-1892)

> Eton; Trinity, Camb.
> Substantial Landowner 65.
> Conservative. DL, JP.
> Earl 65.
> Southwest London; Flintshire; Leicestershire.
> [MEB, BP, Walfords, Bateman, Direc Direcs]
>
> Central Assn for Stopping Sale Intox Liquors on
> Sunday 75-85, V-Pres.

FIELDING, WILLIAM E.

> Southeast London.
>
> Sunday Society 76-86, Chairman.

FIENNES, FREDERICK BENJAMIN TWISELTON WYKEHAM, 16TH
BARON SAYE AND SELE (1799-1887)

> Winchester College; New College, Oxf.
> Archdeacon 63; Large Landowner 47; Ordained
> Priest<CE> 23; Rector 25; Prebendary 25;
> Canon 40; College Fellow.
> JP.
> Baron 47.
> Hereford; Oxfordshire.
> [MEB, BP, Walfords, Bateman, Alum Oxon, Crockfds]
>
> Natl Soc for Preserving Memorials of Dead 84-84,
> Patron.

FIRTH, JOSEPH FIRTH BOTTOMLEY (1842-1889)

> Middle Temple.
> Barrister 66.
> Liberal. MP Chelsea 80-85, Dundee 88-89.
> Southwest London.
> [MEB, Fosters, Dods]
>
> Sunday Society 80-89, V-Pres.
> London Municipal Reform League 82-85, Chairman.
> Victoria Street Soc for Protection of Animals from
> Vivisection 82-85, Exec.

FISHWICK, HENRY (1835-1914)

> Estate Agent; Antiquary.
> JP.
> Fellow Society of Antiquaries.
> Rochdale.
> [WWW]
>
> Natl Soc for Preserving Memorials of Dead (F)
> 81-82, Exec.

FITTON, SAMUEL

> Macclesfield.
>
> Jamaica Committee (F) 66-66.

FITZGERALD, DESMOND G.

> Land Nationalization Soc (F) 81-85, V-Pres, Exec.

FITZGERALD, GERALD STEPHEN

> Trin Col, Dublin.
> Rector 64; Curate 48; Ordained Priest<CE> 49;
> Perp. Curate 52.
> Wanstead.
> [Crockfds]
>
> Church Assn 70-70, Exec.

FITZGERALD, JOHN PURCELL (1803-1879)

> Trinity, Camb.
> Substantial Landowner.
> JP.
> Lancashire; Suffolk; Co Waterford.
> [Walfords, Alum Cantab]
>
> Central Assn for Stopping Sale Intox Liquors on
> Sunday (F) 67-75, V-Pres, Exec.

FITZGERALD, SIR ROBERT UNIAKE PENROSE, 1ST BT.
(1839-1919)

> Westminster School; Trinity Hall, Camb.
> Large Landowner 57.
> Conservative. MP Cambridge 85-06. DL, JP.
> Baronet 96.
> Southwest London; Co Cork.
> [WWW, Bateman, Alum Cantab, Dods, Direc Direcs]
>
> Natl Assn for Promotion of State Colonization
> 86-86, V-Pres.

FITZMAURICE, EDMOND GEORGE PETTY, 1ST BARON FITZMAURICE
OF LEIGH (1846-1935)

> Eton; Trinity, Camb; Lincoln's Inn.
> Liberal. MP Calne 68-85, Wilts N, Cricklade 98-05.
> Parl U-Sec For Off 83-85, Parl U-Sec For Off
> 05-08, Chanc Duchy Lancaster 08-09.
> Baron 06; PC 08.
> Fellow British Assn.
> Southwest London; Wiltshire.
> [DNB, WWW, BP, Alum Cantab, Fosters, Dods]
>
> Commons Preservation Soc 76-86, Exec.
> Metro Free Libraries Assn 77-77, V-Pres, Exec.

FITZROY, ERNEST JAMES AUGUSTUS

> Vicar 79; Ordained Priest<CE> 70; Curate 70;
> Chaplain 72; Perp. Curate 74; Rector 76.
> Liverpool.
> [Crockfds]
>
> Natl Soc for Preserving Memorials of Dead (F)
> 81-82, Exec.

FITZROY, LORD FREDERICK JOHN (1823-1919)

Eton.
Lt. Colonel 55;  Cadet, RN 36;  Ensign, Army 40;
    Lieutenant, Army 43;  Captain, Army 48.
Liberal.  MP Thetford 63-65.  JP.
West London;  Sussex.
[WWW, BP, Walfords, Dods, Army List]

Plimsoll and Seamen's Fund Committee (F) 73-73, Hon
    Sec.

FITZWILLIAM, CHARLES WILLIAM WENTWORTH (1826-1894)

Eton;  Trinity, Camb.
Attache, Dip Serv.
Liberal.  MP Malton 52-85.  JP.
Fellow Royal Geograph Society.
Southwest London;  Northamptonshire.
[BP, Walfords, Alum Cantab, Dods, Direc Direcs]

Natl Emigration League (F) 70-70, V-Pres.

FITZWILLIAM, W. S.

Plimsoll and Seamen's Fund Committee (F) 73-73,
    Exec.

FLEMING, ISAAC PLANT (1829-1887)

St Mary Hall, Oxf.
[Alum Oxon]

Church Assn 85-85, Secretary.

FLEMING, JOHN GIBSON (1809-1879)

Glasgow(Medical).
Surgeon 30.
Fellow Royal Society.
Glasgow.
[MEB]

Assn for Promoting Extension of Contagious Diseases
    Act 68-68, V-Pres.

FLETCHER, BANISTER (1833-1899)

Architect;  Surveyor.
Conservative.  MP Chippenham 85-86.  DL, JP.
Fellow Royal Inst Br Architects.
Northwest London.
[DNB, MEB, WWW, Dods]

Free Land League 86-86, V-Pres.

FLETCHER, LIONEL JOHN WILLIAM (1845-1911)

St Peter's College, Radley;  Jesus, Camb.
DL, JP.
Kent.
[Alum Cantab, Direc Direcs]

Public Museums & Free Libraries Assn 68-68, Exec.

FLINDT, GUSTAVUS K.

Kings Col London.
Perp. Curate 57;  Curate 53;  Ordained Priest<CE>
    56.
South London.
[Crockfds]

Church Assn 70-75, Exec.

FLOWER, CYRIL, 1ST BARON BATTERSEA (1843-1907)

Harrow;  Trinity, Camb;  Inner Temple.
Barrister 70.
Liberal.  MP Brecknock Borough 80-85, Bedfordshire
    South 86-92.  Junior Lord Treasury 86-86, DL.
Baronet 92.
West London;  Buckinghamshire;  Brecon.
[BP, Alum Cantab, Fosters, Dods, Direc Direcs]

Commons Preservation Soc 80-86, Exec.

FLOWER, WICKHAM

Southwest London.

Soc for Protection of Ancient Buildings (F) 78-85,
    Exec.

FLOWER, WILLIAM HENRY (1831-1899)

University Col London;  Middlesex Hospital.
Hunterian Professor Comparative Anatomy and
    Physiology, RCS 70;  Director South Kensington
    Museum 84;  Asst Surgeon, Army Medical Serv 54;
    Medical School Lecturer 58;  Asst Surgeon 58.
CB 87;  KCB 92.
Fellow Royal Society;  Fellow Royal Col Surgeons;
    Fellow Linnean Society;  Anthropological
    Institute;  British Academy;  Br Assn.
Southwest London.
[DNB, MEB, WWW, Alum Cantab]

Sunday Society 78-84, V-Pres.

FOGGO, GEORGE

Indian Reform Assn 84-84, Secretary.

FOLJAMBE, CECIL GEORGE SAVILE, 1ST EARL OF LIVERPOOL
    (1846-1907)

Eton.
Landowner;  Cadet, RN 60;  Lieutenant, RN 67.
Liberal.  MP Nottinghamshire N 80-85, Mansfield,
    Notts 85-92.  Lord in Waiting 94-95, Lord
    Steward Royal Household 05-07, DL, JP.
Baron 93;  Earl 05;  PC 06.
Fellow Society of Antiquaries.
Southwest London;  Nottinghamshire;  Yorks, East
    Riding.
[WWW, BP, Dods, Navy List]

City Church & Churchyard Protection Soc 83-83,
    V-Pres.
Natl Soc for Preserving Memorials of Dead (F)
    81-88, Exec.
Natl Assn for Repeal Contagious Diseases Acts
    81-81, V-Pres.

FOLLIOT, JAMES (1800-1876)

    Pembroke, Oxf.
    Landowner;  Ordained Priest<CE> 24.
    JP.
    Cheshire.
    [Walfords, Alum Oxon, Crockfds]

    Church Assn 67-67, Exec.


FOOTE, G. W.

    League for Defense of Constitutional Rights 84-84,
       V-Pres.
    Natl Secular Soc 84-84, V-Pres.


FORBES, EDWARD (1842-1910)

    Sidney Sussex, Camb.
    Vicar 67;  Curate 65;  Ordained Priest<CE> 66.
    Barnet.
    [Alum Cantab, Crockfds]

    Church Assn 75-75, Exec.


FORBES, HORACE COURTENAY GRAMMELL, 20TH BARON FORBES
    (1829-1914)

    Oriel, Oxf.
    Very Large Landowner 68.
    Conservative.  DL, JP.
    Baron 68.
    West London;  Aberdeenshire.
    [WWW, BP, Walfords, Bateman, Alum Oxon, Direc
       Direcs]

    City Church & Churchyard Protection Soc (F) 80-83,
       V-Pres.


FORD, FREDERICK A.

    Sunday Society (F) 75-75, Exec.


FORD, STEPHEN

    Civil Engineer.
    Southeast London.

    Assn for Improvement of Public Morals (F) 79-81,
       Exec.


FORDER, ROBERT

    Woolwich.

    Land Law Reform League (F) 81-84, Secretary.
    Natl Secular Soc 77-84, Secretary.
    Natl Assn for Repeal Blasphemy Laws (F) 84-84,
       Exec.


FORDHAM, EDWARD KING

    Brewer;  Farmer.
    JP.
    Hertfordshire.

    Intl Arbitration & Peace Assn 81-81, V-Pres.


FORDHAM, SIR GEORGE (1854-1929)

    University Col London;  Inner Temple.
    Brewer 75;  Barrister 85.
    Liberal.  JP.
    Kt 08.
    Fellow Royal Geograph Society;  Br Assn.
    Yorks, West Riding.
    [DNB, WWW, Fosters]

    Intl Arbitration & Peace Assn 81-81, Exec.


FORESTER, ORLANDO WATKIN WELD, 4TH BARON FORESTER
    (1813-1894)

    Westminster School;  Trinity, Camb.
    Canon 74;  Curate 36;  Ordained Priest<CE> 37;
       Rector 41;  Prebendary 47;  Rural Dean 74;
       Very Large Landowner 86.
    Baron 86.
    York.
    [MEB, BP, Walfords, Alum Cantab, Crockfds]

    Central Vigilance Comtee for Repression Immorality
       (F) 83-84, V-Pres.


FORREST, ROBERT WILLIAM ( -1908)

    Trin Col, Dublin.
    Chaplain 67;  Ordained Priest<CE> 56;  Curate 60;
       Perp. Curate 62;  Vicar 64;  Prebendary 87;
       Dean 91.
    West London.
    [WWW, Crockfds]

    Assn for Promoting Extension of Contagious Diseases
       Act 68-68, Exec.


FORSTER, HUGH OAKELEY ARNOLD- (1855-1909)

    Rugby;  University Col, Oxf;  Lincoln's Inn.
    Private Secretary 80;  Barrister 79;  Author;
       Publisher.
    Liberal(Unionist).  MP Belfast West 92-06, Croydon
       06-09.  Parl Sec Admiralty 00-03, Sec St War
       03-05.
    PC 03.
    Southwest London.
    [DNB, WWW, Alum Oxon, Fosters, Dods]

    Imperial Federation League (F) 84-84, Hon Sec.


FORSTER, JOSEPH

    Natl Assn for Repeal Blasphemy Laws (F) 84-84,
       Exec.

FORSTER, WILLIAM EDWARD (1818-1886)

    Friends' School, Tottenham.
    Woolen Manufacturer 42.
    Liberal. MP Bradford 61-85, Bradford Central
       85-86. Parl U-Sec Col Off 65-66, V-P Education
       Committee 68-74, Charity Commissioner 68-74,
       Chief Sec Ireland 80-82, DL, JP.
    PC 68.
    Fellow Royal Geograph Society; Fellow Royal
      Society.
    Southwest London; Yorks, West Riding.
    [DNB, MEB, Walfords, Alum Oxon, Dods, Friends]

    Imperial Federation League (F) 84-84, Chairman.


FORTESCUE, LADY CAMILLA ELEANOR <MRS. D.F. FORTESCUE,
    DAU. 4TH E. PORTSMOUTH> ( -1920)

    [BP]

    Kyrle Soc 84-90, Exec.


FORTESCUE, CHICHESTER SAMUEL PARKINSON, 1ST BARON
    CARLINGFORD (1823-1898)

    Eton; Christ Church, Oxf; Lincoln's Inn.
    Very Large Landowner; Colliery Owner.
    Liberal(Unionist). MP Louth Co 47-74. Junior Lord
      Treasury 54-55, Parl U-Sec Col Off 57-58, Parl
      U-Sec Col Off 59-65, Chief Sec Ireland 65-66,
      Chief Sec Ireland 68-70, Pres Board of Trade
      71-74, Lord Privy Seal 81-85, Lord Pres Council
      83-85.
    PC 64; Baron 74; KP 82.
    Southwest London; Somersetshire; Co Louth.
    [DNB, MEB, WWW, BP, Walfords, Bateman, Alum Oxon]

    Soc for Protection of Ancient Buildings (F) 78-85,
      Exec.


FORTESCUE, DUDLEY FRANCIS (1820-1909)

    Harrow; Trinity, Camb.
    Liberal. MP Andover 57-74. Lunacy Commissioner
      67-83, DL, JP.
    West London; Co Waterford.
    [WWW, BP, Walfords, Alum Cantab, Dods, Direc
      Direcs]

    Assn for Improvement of London Workhouse
      Infirmaries 66-66, Exec.
    Assn for Promoting Extension of Contagious Diseases
      Act 70-70, V-Pres.
    Plimsoll and Seamen's Fund Committee (F) 73-73,
      Exec.


FORTESCUE, HUGH, 3RD EARL FORTESCUE (1818-1905)

    Harrow; Trinity, Camb.
    Very Large Landowner 61; Author.
    Liberal(Unionist). MP Plymouth 41-52, Marylebone
      54-59. Junior Lord Treasury 46-47, Lord in
      Waiting 46- , Parl Sec Poor Law Board 47-51,
      DL, JP.
    Baron 59; Earl 61.
    Southwest London; Devonshire.
    [DNB, WWW, BP, Walfords, Bateman, Alum Cantab,
      Dods]

    Sanitary Institute 79-84, V-Pres.


    Assn for Improvement of London Workhouse
      Infirmaries 66-66, Exec.
    Liberty & Property Defense League 84-84, Exec.
    Natl Education Union 71-79, Exec.


FOSBERY,THOMAS VINCENT (1807-1875)

    Trin Col, Dublin.
    Vicar 57; Curate 31; Ordained Priest<CE> 32;
      Perp. Curate 47.
    Reading.
    [MEB, Crockfds]

    Assn for Promoting Extension of Contagious Diseases
      Act 68-70, V-Pres.


FOSTER, BALTHAZAR WALTER, 1ST BARON ILKESTON (1840-1913)

    Trin Col, Dublin.
    Physician; Medical School Professor 68.
    Radical. MP Chester 85-86, Ilkeston, Derbys 87-10.
      Lord Pres Council 84-87, Parl Sec Loc Govt
      Board 92-95, JP.
    Kt 86; PC 06; Baron 10.
    Fellow Royal Col Physicians; Br Medical Assn.
    Birmingham.
    [WWW, BP, Dods]

    Allotments & Small Holdings Assn 85-88, Chairman.
    Free Land League 86-86, V-Pres.


FOSTER, GEORGE T.

    Darlington.

    Natl Secular Soc 84-84, V-Pres.


FOSTER, W. H.

    Working Men's Comtee Promoting Separation Church
      and State (F) 71-71, Exec.


FOWLER, H. J.

    Smethwick.

    Church Assn 75-78, Exec.


FOWLER, HENRY HARTLEY, 1ST VISCOUNT WOLVERHAMPTON
    (1830-1911)

    Woodhouse Grove School, Yorks.
    Solicitor 52.
    Liberal. MP Wolverhampton 80-85, Wolverhampton
      East 85-08. Parl U-Sec Home Off 84-85, Sec
      Treasury 86-86, Pres Local Govt Board 92-94,
      Sec St India 94-95, Chanc Duchy Lancaster
      05-08, Lord Pres Council 08-10, DL, JP.
    PC 86; GCSI 95; Viscount 08.
    Wolverhampton.
    [DNB, WWW, BP, Dods, Direc Direcs]

    Free Land League 86-86, Exec, V-Pres.

FOWLER, SIR ROBERT NICHOLAS, 1ST BT.  (1828-1891)

    Grove House School, Tottenham;  University Col
       London.
    Banker 50.
    Conservative.  MP Penryn & Falmouth 68-74, City
       80-91.  JP.
    Baronet 85.
    West London;  Tottenham;  Wiltshire.
    [DNB, MEB, BP, Walfords, Dods]

    Natl Assn for Promotion of State Colonization
       86-86, Treas.
    Anglo-Oriental Soc for Suppression Opium Trade (F)
       75-75, Treas.
    Natl Footpaths Preservation Soc 86-90, V-Pres.
    Public Museums & Free Libraries Assn 68-68, V-Pres.
    City Church & Churchyard Protection Soc 81-83,
       V-Pres.
    Central Vigilance Comtee for Repression Immorality
       (F) 83-84, V-Pres.
    Howard Assn 67-84, Treas, Patron.


FOWLER, WILLIAM (1828-1905)

    University Col London;  Inner Temple.
    Banker 56;  Barrister 52;  College Fellow.
    Liberal.  MP Cambridge 68-74, Cambridge 80-85.  JP.
    West London;  Essex.
    [WWW, Walfords, Fosters, Dods, Direc Direcs]

    Howard Assn 69-73, Patron.


FOX, FRANCIS W.

    Natl Assn for Promotion of State Colonization
       86-86, V-Pres.


FOX, FRANKLIN <"CAPT.">

    Natl Footpaths Preservation Soc (F) 85-85, Exec.


FOX, JOSEPH JOHN

    Fellow Royal Statistical Society.

    Howard Assn 67-84, Exec.


FOX, SAMUEL

    Nottingham.

    Jamaica Committee (F) 66-66.


FOX, W. F.

    Dewsbury.

    London Soc for Abolition of Compulsory Vaccination
       81-81, V-Pres.


FOX, WILLIAM TILBURY (1836-1879)

    U College London(Medical).
    Physician 58.
    West London.
    [DNB, MEB]

    Assn for Promoting Extension of Contagious Diseases
       Act 68-68, Exec.


FRANCIS, FRANCIS (1822-1886)

    Journal Editor.
    Twickenham.
    [DNB, MEB]

    Travelling Tax Abolition Committee (F) 77-85, Exec.


FRANKLAND, SIR EDWARD (1825-1899)

    Marburg.
    Analytical Chemist;  College Professor 50.
    JP.
    KCB 97.
    Fellow Royal Society;  Fellow Chemical Society;
       Inst of Chemistry.
    Southwest London.
    [DNB, MEB, WWW, Alum Oxon]

    Smoke Abatement Committee 81-81, Exec.
    Sunday Society 76-90, V-Pres.


FRASER, - <"THE HON.  MRS.">

    Natl Vigilance Assn (F) 85-85, Exec.


FRASER, DONALD (1826-1892)

    U Aberdeen;  John Knox College, Toronto.
    Presbyterian Minister 70;  Free Church Minister 51.
    West London.
    [DNB, MEB]

    Central Assn for Stopping Sale Intox Liquors on
       Sunday 80-80, V-Pres.
    Intl Arbitration & Peace Assn 81-81, V-Pres.


FRASER, JAMES (1818-1885)

    Shrewsbury School;  Lincoln, Oxf.
    Bishop Manchester 70;  College Fellow 40;  College
       Tutor 42;  Ordained Priest<CE> 47;  Rector 47;
       Prebendary 61.
    Manchester.
    [DNB, MEB, Alum Oxon, Crockfds]

    Central Assn for Stopping Sale Intox Liquors on
       Sunday 70-80, V-Pres.
    Victoria Street Soc for Protection of Animals from
       Vivisection 80-80, V-Pres.

FRASER, JAMES (1842-1913)

    Marlborough; Corpus Christi, Camb.
    Chaplain 80; Curate 67; Ordained Priest<CE> 68;
       Rector 75; Prebendary 00.
    Chichester.
    [WWW, Alum Cantab, Crockfds]

    Natl Soc for Preserving Memorials of Dead (F)
       81-82, Exec.


FRECKLETON, J. W.

    Bradford.

    Jamaica Committee (F) 66-66.


FREEMAN, WILLIAM

    London.

    Jamaica Committee (F) 66-66.


FREESTON, J.

    Clergyman<Sect Unkn>.
    Stalybridge.

    Land Law Reform League 84-84, V-Pres.
    League for Defense of Constitutional Rights 84-84,
       V-Pres.


FREMANTLE, WILLIAM HENRY (1831-1916)

    Eton; Balliol, Oxf.
    Rector 66; College Fellow 54; Curate 55;
       Ordained Priest<CE> 56; Vicar 57; Canon 82;
       Dean 95.
    West London.
    [WWW, BP, Alum Oxon, Crockfds]

    Intl Arbitration & Peace Assn 81-81, V-Pres.


FREMANTLE, WILLIAM ROBERT (1807-1895)

    Westminster School; Christ Church, Oxf.
    Dean 76; College Fellow 31; Rector 32; Ordained
       Priest<CE> 34; Vicar 41; Rural Dean 41; Hon.
       Canon 69.
    Ripon.
    [MEB, Alum Oxon, Crockfds]

    Natl Soc for Preserving Memorials of Dead (F)
       81-84, Exec.
    Church Assn 75-85, V-Pres.


FRESHFIELD, EDWIN (1833-1918)

    Winchester College; Trinity, Camb.
    Solicitor 58; Antiquary.
    Fellow Society of Antiquaries.
    London.
    [Alum Cantab]

    City Church & Churchyard Protection Soc (F) 80-81,
       Exec.


FRETTON, WILLIAM GEORGE (1829-1900)

    School Master 47.
    Fellow Society of Antiquaries.
    Coventry.
    [MEB]

    Natl Soc for Preserving Memorials of Dead (F)
       81-82, Exec.


FREWER, J. R.

    Croydon.

    Church Assn 78-80, Exec.


FROBISHER, WILLIAM MARTIN

    Captain, Army 66; Ensign, Army 56; Lieutenant,
       Army 59.
    Plumstead.
    [Army List]

    Church Assn 75-75, Exec.


FROST, JOHN

    London.

    Jamaica Committee (F) 66-66.


FROST, R. P. B.

    English Land Restoration League 84-84, Hon Sec.


FROUDE, JAMES ANTHONY (1818-1894)

    Westminster School; Oriel, Oxf.
    Historian; College Fellow 42; Journal Editor 60;
       Regius Professor of Modern History, Oxford 92.
    Liberal(Unionist).
    Southwest London.
    [DNB, MEB, Alum Oxon]

    Natl Assn for Promotion of State Colonization
       86-86, V-Pres.


FRY, EDWARD

    Anglo-Oriental Soc for Suppression Opium Trade
       83-83, V-Pres.


FRY, LEWIS (1832-1921)

    Solicitor 54.
    Liberal(Unionist). MP Bristol 78-85, Bristol North
       85-92, Bristol North 95-00.
    PC 01.
    Southwest London; Bristol.
    [WWW, Dods, Direc Direcs]

    Howard Assn 79-84, Patron.

FRY, SIR THEODORE, 1ST BT. (1836-1912)

    Iron Manufacturer.
    Liberal. MP Darlington 80-95. DL, JP.
    Baronet 94.
    Fellow Society of Antiquaries.
    Southwest London; Darlington.
    [WWW, BP, Dods, Direc Direcs]

    Central Assn for Stopping Sale Intox Liquors on
        Sunday 85-85, V-Pres.
    Howard Assn 80-81, Patron.
    Natl Assn for Repeal Contagious Diseases Acts
        81-81, V-Pres.

FRYER, - <MISS>

    Blackpool.

    British Women's Temperance Assn 85-85, Exec.

FULCHER, E.

    "A working man".
    East London.

    Natl Assn for Promotion of State Colonization
        86-86, Exec.

FULFORD, HENRY CHARLES (1849-1897)

    Brewer 77; Maltster 61.
    Liberal. MP Lichfield, Staffs 95-95.
    Southwest London; Birmingham.
    [MEB, Dods, Direc Direcs]

    Allotments & Small Holdings Assn 84-84, Exec.

FURNIVALL, FREDERICK JAMES (1825-1910)

    Hanwell College; Trinity Hall, Camb; Gray's Inn.
    Barrister 49; Philologist.
    British Academy; Fellow British Assn;
        Philological Society.
    Northwest London.
    [DNB, WWW, Alum Cantab]

    Sunday Society (F) 75-90, V-Pres.

FYERS, WILLIAM AUGUSTUS (1815-1895)

    Lt. General 81; Ensign, Army 34; Captain, Army
        47; Major 55; Lt. Colonel 56; Colonel 64;
        Maj. General 69.
    CB 58; KCB 89.
    Southwest London.
    [MEB, Army List]

    Natl Assn for Promotion of State Colonization
        86-86, V-Pres.

FYFFE, CHARLES ALAN (1845-1892)

    Christ's Hospital; Balliol, Oxf; Inner Temple.
    Historian; College Fellow 70; College Tutor 70.
    Radical.
    Fellow Royal Historical Society.
    West London.
    [DNB, MEB, Alum Oxon, Fosters]

    Free Land League 86-86, Exec.

GALBRAITH, -

    Workmen's Peace Assn 75-75, Exec.

GALE, KNIGHT

    Kings Col London.
    Vicar 53; Curate 50; Ordained Priest<CE> 51.
    Bradford.
    [Crockfds]

    Church Assn 70-78, Exec.

GALLOWAY, J. C.

    Clergyman<Sect Unkn>.
    London.

    Jamaica Committee (F) 66-66.

GALTON, SIR DOUGLAS STRUTT (1822-1899)

    Rugby; Royal Military Academy, Woolwich.
    Chm, Public Works Loan Commission; 2nd Lt., RE 40;
        Lieutenant, RE 43; Captain, RE 51; Sec
        Railway Dept, Board of Trade 54; Asst U-Sec,
        War 62; Director, Public Works and Buildings
        69.
    CB 65; KCB 87.
    Br Assn; Fellow Geological Society; Fellow Royal
        Society; Fellow Linnean Society; Inst of Mech
        Engineers; Assoc Inst Civ Engineers.
    Southwest London; Worcestershire.
    [DNB, MEB, WWW, Alum Oxon, Direc Direcs, Army List]

    Smoke Abatement Committee 81-81, Exec.
    Sanitary Institute 78-89, V-Chairman, Chairman.

GAMLEN, R. H.

    Solicitor.
    London.

    Natl Assn for Promotion of State Colonization
        86-86, Exec.

GARBETT, EDWARD (1817-1887)

    Brasenose, Oxf.
    Vicar 63; Ordained Priest<CE> 42; Curate 42;
        Perp. Curate 54; Journal Editor 54; Rector
        77; Author.
    Kingston-upon-Thames.
    [DNB, MEB, Alum Oxon, Crockfds]

    Church Assn 70-70, Exec.

GARNHAM, JOHN WILLIAM

> Lt. Colonel, RA 85; Lieutenant, RA 64; Captain,
> RA 77; Major, RA 82.
> Chichester.
> [Army List]
>
> Railway Passengers´ Protection Assn 86-86, Exec.

GARRETT, CHARLES (1823-1900)

> Wesleyan Theological College, Richmond.
> Wesleyan Minister 50.
> Liverpool.
> [MEB, WWW, Direc Direcs, Wesl Min]
>
> Central Assn for Stopping Sale Intox Liquors on
> Sunday 85-85, V-Pres.

GARRETT, RHODA <MISS> (1841-1882)

> House Decorator.
> West Central London.
> [MEB]
>
> Soc for Protection of Ancient Buildings (F) 78-80,
> Exec.

GARSIDE, JOSEPH

> Methodist Free Church Minister.
>
> Central Assn for Stopping Sale Intox Liquors on
> Sunday 75-75, V-Pres.

GASCOYEN, G. G.

> West London.
>
> Assn for Promoting Extension of Contagious Diseases
> Act 68-68, Exec.

GASSIOTT, JOHN PETER (1797-1877)

> Electrical Scientist; Wine Merchant.
> DL, JP.
> Fellow Royal Society; Fellow Chemical Society.
> Clapham.
> [DNB, MEB, Walfords, Alum Cantab]
>
> Commons Preservation Soc 69-76, Exec.

GASTER, THOMAS JOSEPH

> Church Mission College, Islington.
> Perp. Curate 72; Church Missionary 56; Ordained
> Priest<CE> 57; Curate.
> Peckham.
> [Crockfds]
>
> Church Assn 80-80, Exec.

GAUNTLETT, PAUL E. I.

> Southwest London.
>
> Natl Footpaths Preservation Soc (F) 85-86, Exec.

GEDDES, J. C.

> Anglo-French Intervention Committee (F) 70-70,
> Exec.

GEDGE, SYDNEY (1829-1923)

> King Edward´s School, Birm; Corpus Christi, Camb.
> Solicitor 56.
> Conservative. MP Stockport 86-92, Walsall 95-00.
> West Central London.
> [WWW, Alum Cantab, Dods, Direc Direcs]
>
> Proportional Representation Soc (F) 84-88, Exec.

GELDART, EDMUND MARTIN (1844-1885)

> Merchant Taylors; Balliol, Oxf.
> Unitarian Minister 73; Asst School Master 67;
> Curate 69.
> Radical.
> Croydon.
> [DNB, MEB, Alum Oxon]
>
> Intl Arbitration & Peace Assn 81-81, Exec.
> Natl Assn for Repeal Blasphemy Laws (F) 84-84,
> Exec.

GIBB, THOMAS ECCLESTON (1838-1894)

> Kings Col London.
> Newspaper Proprietor.
> Liberal. MP St Pancras East 85-86.
> Northwest London; Hertfordshire.
> [MEB, Dods]
>
> Commons Preservation Soc 86-86, Exec.
> Free Land League 86-86, V-Pres.

GIBBON, SEPTIMUS (1822-1909)

> Oakham; Clare, Camb; St Bartholomew´s Hosp.
> Physician 51.
> Med Off of Health.
> Member Royal Col Physicians.
> West London.
> [Alum Cantab, Direc Direcs]
>
> Assn for Promoting Extension of Contagious Diseases
> Act 68-68, Exec.

GIBBONS, H. F.

> London Municipal Reform League 82-82, Exec.

GIBBS, FREDERIC WAYMOUTH (1821-1898)

    King's College School; Trinity, Camb; Lincoln's
        Inn.
    Barrister 48; College Fellow 45; Tutor, Prince of
        Wales 52; Q.C. 80; Author.
    CB 58.
    West London.
    [Alum Cantab, Fosters]

    Commons Preservation Soc 69-76, Exec.


GIBBS, G. S.

    Fellow Royal Statistical Society.
    Darlington.

    London Soc for Abolition of Compulsory Vaccination
        81-81, V-Pres.


GIBBS, HENRY HUCKS, 1ST BARON ALDENHAM (1819-1907)

    Rugby; Exeter, Oxf; Lincoln's Inn.
    Merchant 43; Newspaper Proprietor; Director, Bank
        of England 53; Governor, Bank of England 75;
        Substantial Landowner.
    Conservative. MP City 91-92. JP.
    Baron 96.
    Fellow Society of Antiquaries; Fellow Royal
        Geograph Society; Philological Society.
    Northwest London; Hertfordshire.
    [DNB, WWW, BP, Walfords, Bateman, Alum Oxon, Dods,
        Direc Direcs]

    Natl Assn for Promotion of State Colonization
        86-86, V-Pres.
    Natl Soc for Preserving Memorials of Dead 84-88,
        Exec.


GIBBS, MICHAEL (1812-1882)

    Gonville & Caius, Camb.
    Vicar 41; Curate 36; Ordained Priest<CE> 37;
        College Fellow 37; College Dean 38;
        Prebendary 56; Rural Dean 64.
    East Central London.
    [MEB, Alum Cantab, Crockfds]

    Soc for Promoting Increase of the Home Episcopate
        72-74, Exec.


GIBSON, CHARLES BERNARD (1807-1885)

    Workhouse Chaplain 74; Irish Evangelical Soc
        Minister 34; Ordained Priest<CE> 67; Curate
        67; Author.
    Member Royal Irish Academy.
    Northeast London.
    [MEB, Crockfds]

    Assn for Improvement of Public Morals (F) 79-79,
        Exec.


GIDLEY, B. G.

    Exeter.

    Natl Soc for Preserving Memorials of Dead 82-82,
        Exec.


GILBERT, SIR JOHN (1817-1894)

    Artist; Illustrator.
    Kt 71.
    Royal Academy; Royal Society Water Colour
        Painters.
    Southeast London.
    [DNB, MEB, BP, Bryan's Painters]

    Natl Soc for Preserving Memorials of Dead (F)
        81-82, Exec.


GILL, J.

    Clergyman<Sect Unkn>.
    Todmorden.

    Jamaica Committee (F) 66-66.


GILL, THOMAS HOWARD (1836-1894)

    King William's College; Trinity, Camb.
    Rector 65; Curate 59; Ordained Priest<CE> 60;
        Chaplain 63; Vicar 90.
    Manchester.
    [MEB, Alum Cantab, Crockfds]

    Church Assn 80-80, Exec.


GILLESPIE, J. D.

    Surgeon.
    Edinburgh.

    Assn for Promoting Extension of Contagious Diseases
        Act 68-68, Exec.


GILLETT, GEORGE

    Banker.
    London.

    Assn for Improvement of Public Morals (F) 79-81,
        Exec.
    London Comtee Exposure & Suppresn Traffic In Girls
        (F) 80-85, Treas.


GILLMAN, L.

    Workmen's Natl Assn for Abolition Sugar Bounties
        81-81, V-Chairman.

GILPIN, CHARLES (1815-1874)

    Publisher;  Bookseller.
    Liberal.  MP Northamptonshire 57-74.  Parl Sec Poor
       Law Board 59-65.
    West Central London.
    [MEB, Walfords, Dods]

    Howard Assn 69-73, Patron.
    Jamaica Committee (F) 66-66.


GIMSON, W.  GIMSON

    Physician.

    Victoria Street Soc for Protection of Animals from
       Vivisection 80-82, Exec.


GIRDLESTONE, EDWARD DEACON (1829-1892)

    Repton;  Wadham, Oxf.
    Author;  Curate 54.
    Radical.
    Weston-Super-Mare.
    [MEB, Alum Oxon, Crockfds]

    Land Nationalization Soc (F) 81-85, V-Pres.


GISBORNE, WILLIAM (1825-1898)

    Harrow.
    Landowner 77;  New Zealand Crown Lands Commissioner
       48;  New Zealand Insurance Commissioner 70.
    DL, JP.
    Derbyshire.
    [MEB, Dict New Zealand Biog]

    Imperial Federation League (F) 84-84, Exec.


GLADDISH, - <"COL.">

    Gravesend.

    Assn for Promoting Extension of Contagious Diseases
       Act 68-70, V-Pres.


GLADSTONE, HERBERT JOHN, 1ST VISCOUNT GLADSTONE
    (1854-1930)

    Eton;  University Col, Oxf.
    Politician;  Governor General, U South Africa 09.
    Liberal.  MP Leeds 80-85, Leeds West 85-10.  Junior
       Lord Treasury 81-85, Dep Commissioner Board of
       Works 85-85, Fin Sec War Office 86-86, Parl
       U-Sec Home Off 92-94, First Commissioner Works
       94-95, Sec St Home Office 05-09.
    PC 94;  Viscount 10;  GCMG 10;  GCB 14;  GBE 17.
    Southwest London.
    [DNB, WWW, BP, Alum Oxon, Dods]

    Free Land League 86-86, V-Pres.


GLADSTONE, JOHN HALL (1827-1902)

    University Col London;  Giessen.
    Analytical Chemist 47;  Author;  Professor, Royal
       Inst Chemistry 74.
    Liberal.
    Fellow Royal Society;  Fellow Chemical Society.
    West London.
    [DNB]

    Public Museums & Free Libraries Assn 68-68, V-Pres.
    Central Assn for Stopping Sale Intox Liquors on
       Sunday 75-85, V-Pres.
    Natl Emigration League (F) 70-70, V-Pres.


GLADSTONE, MURRAY (1816-1875)

    Merchant.
    Fellow Royal Astronomical Society.
    Manchester.
    [MEB]

    Natl Education Union (F) 69-69, Hon Sec.


GLADSTONE, R.

    Church Assn 70-70, V-Pres.


GLADSTONE, WILLIAM HENRY (1840-1891)

    Eton;  Christ Church, Oxf;  Lincoln's Inn.
    Politician;  Landowner 82.
    Liberal.  MP Flintshire 65-68, Whitby, Yorks NR
       68-80, Worcestershire East 80-85.  Junior Lord
       Treasury 69-74, DL, JP.
    West London;  Flintshire.
    [MEB, Alum Oxon, Dods]

    Assn for Improvement of London Workhouse
       Infirmaries 66-66, Exec.


GLASSCOCK, JOHN L., JUN.

    Bishop's Stortford.

    Natl Soc for Preserving Memorials of Dead (F)
       81-82, Exec.


GLASSE, JOHN (1848-1918)

    U St Andrews.
    Church of Scotland Minister 76.
    Radical.
    Edinburgh.
    [WWW]

    Sunday Society 81-90, V-Pres.


GLEDSTONE, J. P.

    Congregational Minister.

    Anglo-Oriental Soc for Suppression Opium Trade
       79-79, Exec.

GLEN, WILLIAM CUNNINGHAM

> Middle Temple.
> Barrister 44.
> West London;  Edinburgh.
> [Fosters]
>
> London Municipal Reform League 82-85, Exec.

GLOVER, - <MRS. R. R. GLOVER>

> Vigilance Assn for Defense of Personal Rights
>     83-83, Exec.

GLOVER, ROBERT R.

> JP.
>
> Howard Assn 82-84, Exec.

GLYDE, W. E.

> Bradford.
>
> Jamaica Committee (F) 66-66.

GODDARD, EUGENE

> Assn for Improvement of London Workhouse
>     Infirmaries 66-66, Exec.

GODSON, W.

> Croydon.
>
> Jamaica Committee (F) 66-66.

GODWIN, GEORGE (1815-1888)

> Architect;  Journalist.
> Fellow Royal Inst Br Architects;  Fellow Royal
>     Society;  Fellow Society of Antiquaries.
> Southwest London.
> [DNB, MEB]
>
> Smoke Abatement Committee 82-82.
> Sunday Society 79-87, V-Pres.
> Public Museums & Free Libraries Assn 68-68, V-Pres.

GODWIN, J. V.

> Bradford.
>
> Jamaica Committee (F) 66-66.

GOLDING, CHARLES

> Colchester.
>
> Natl Soc for Preserving Memorials of Dead (F)
>     81-82, Exec.

GOLDSMID, SIR JULIAN, 3RD BT.  (1838-1896)

> University Col London;  Lincoln's Inn.
> Barrister 64;  College Fellow 64;  Very Large
>     Landowner 78.
> Liberal(Unionist).  MP Honiton 66-68, Rochester
>     70-80, St Pancras South 85-96.  DL, JP.
> Baronet 78;  PC 95.
> West London;  Kent;  Gloucestershire.
> [MEB, BP, Walfords, Bateman, Fosters, Dods]
>
> Free Land League 86-86, V-Pres.
> Natl Footpaths Preservation Soc (F) 85-90, V-Pres.
> Plimsoll and Seamen's Fund Committee (F) 73-73,
>     Exec.

GOODENOUGH, JAMES GRAHAM (1830-1875)

> Westminster School;  Royal Naval College,
>     Portsmouth.
> Captain, RN 63;  Cadet, RN 44;  Lieutenant, RN 51;
>     Commander, RN 58.
> CB 75;  CMG 75.
> [DNB, MEB, Navy List]
>
> Plimsoll and Seamen's Fund Committee (F) 73-73,
>     Exec.

GOODEVE, HENRY IVES HARRY (1806-1884)

> Edinburgh(Medical).
> Physician 29;  Asst Surgeon, Army Medical Serv 31;
>     Surgeon, Army Medical Serv 48;  Medical School
>     Professor 41.
> Fellow Royal Col Physicians;  Fellow Royal Col
>     Surgeons.
> Gloucestershire.
> [MEB]
>
> Assn for Promoting Extension of Contagious Diseases
>     Act 68-70, V-Pres.

GOODWIN, HARVEY (1818-1891)

> Gonville & Caius, Camb.
> Bishop Carlisle 69;  Ordained Priest<CE> 44;
>     Curate 45;  Vicar 48;  Dean 58.
> Camden Society.
> Carlisle.
> [DNB, MEB, Alum Cantab, Crockfds]
>
> Natl Assn for Promotion of State Colonization
>     86-86, Patron.
> Central Assn for Stopping Sale Intox Liquors on
>     Sunday 85-85, V-Pres.
> Soc for Promoting Increase of the Home Episcopate
>     72-74, V-Pres.

GORDON, - <MISS>

> Victoria Street Soc for Protection of Animals from
>     Vivisection 80-82, Exec.

GORDON, JOHN CAMPBELL HAMILTON, 1ST MARQUIS OF ABERDEEN
    AND TEMAIR (1847-1934)

    Cheam;  University Col, Oxf.
    Very Large Landowner 70;  Governor General, Canada
        93.
    Liberal.  Lord Lt Ireland 86-86, Lord Lt Ireland
        06-15, Lord Lieutenant, JP.
    Earl 70;  PC 86;  GCMG 86;  KT 06;  GCVO 11;
        Marquis 16.
    West London;  Aberdeenshire.
    [DNB, WWW, BP, Walfords, Bateman, Alum Oxon, Direc
        Direcs]

    Central Vigilance Comtee for Repression Immorality
        (F) 83-84, V-Pres.


GOSSELIN <-GRIMSHAWE>, HELLIER ROBERT HADSLEY
    (1849-1924)

    JP.
    Hertfordshire.
    [WWW]

    Natl Soc for Preserving Memorials of Dead 82-88,
        Exec.


GOULBURN, EDWARD MEYRICK (1818-1897)

    Eton;  Balliol, Oxf.
    Dean 66;  Perp. Curate 41;  College Fellow 41;
        Ordained Priest<CE> 43;  School Head 50;
        Prebendary 58;  Vicar 59.
    Conservative.
    Fellow Society of Antiquaries.
    Norwich.
    [DNB, MEB, WWW, Alum Oxon, Crockfds]

    Natl Soc for Preserving Memorials of Dead 84-84,
        Exec.


GOULD, GEORGE (1818-1882)

    Bristol Baptist College.
    Baptist Minister 41.
    Norwich.
    [DNB, MEB]

    Central Assn for Stopping Sale Intox Liquors on
        Sunday 80-80, V-Pres.
    Jamaica Committee (F) 66-66.


GOULDEN, W.  W.

    Central Assn for Stopping Sale Intox Liquors on
        Sunday 70-70, Exec.


GOULT, SYDNEY <OR SIDNEY>

    London.

    London Comtee Exposure & Suppresn Traffic In Girls
        (F) 80-80, Exec.
    Working Men's Natl League for Abolition State
        Regulation of Vice 81-82, Secretary.


GOURLEY, SIR EDWARD TEMPERLEY (1828-1902)

    Shipowner;  Merchant.
    Radical.  MP Sunderland 68-00.  DL, JP.
    Kt 95.
    Sunderland.
    [WWW, Walfords, Dods, Direc Direcs]

    Natl Assn for Promotion of State Colonization
        86-86, V-Pres.
    Free Land League 86-86, V-Pres.
    Natl Assn for Repeal Contagious Diseases Acts
        81-81, V-Pres.
    Natl Emigration League (F) 70-70, V-Pres.


GOWER, ANNE SUTHERLAND LEVESON-, DUCHESS OF SUTHERLAND,
    COUNTESS OF CROMARTIE (1829-1888)

    Very Large Landowner.
    Liberal.  Mistress Robes 70-74.
    Countess 61;  VA.
    West London;  Staffordshire.
    [MEB, BP, Walfords]

    Victoria Street Soc for Protection of Animals from
        Vivisection 84-85, V-Pres.


GOWER, GEORGE GRANVILLE LEVESON- (1858-1951)

    Eton;  Balliol, Oxf.
    Politician;  Journal Editor 99;  Author.
    Liberal.  MP Staffordshire NW 85-86, Stoke-on-Trent
        90-95.  Junior Lord Treasury 86-86, Comptroller
        Royal Household 92-95, Woods & Forests
        Commissioner 08-24.
    KBE 21.
    West London;  Surrey.
    [WWW, BP, Alum Oxon, Dods, Direc Direcs]

    Free Land League 86-86, V-Pres.


GOWER, GRANVILLE GEORGE LEVESON-, 2ND EARL GRANVILLE
    (1815-1891)

    Eton;  Christ Church, Oxf.
    Politician;  Attache, Dip Serv 35.
    Liberal.  MP Morpeth 36-40, Lichfield, Staffs
        41-46.  Parl U-Sec For Off 40-41, V-P Board of
        Trade 48-51, Sec St Foreign Off 51-52, Chanc
        Duchy Lancaster 54-55, Sec St Colonial Off
        68-70, Sec St Foreign Off 70-74, Sec St Foreign
        Off 80-85, Sec St Colonial Off 86-86.
    Earl 46;  PC 46;  KG 57.
    Fellow Royal Society.
    West London;  Staffordshire.
    [DNB, MEB, BP, Walfords, Dods, Direc Direcs]

    Commons Preservation Soc 76-85, Exec.
    Natl Footpaths Preservation Soc 86-90, V-Pres.


GOWER, GRANVILLE WILLIAM GRESHAM LEVESON- (1838-1895)

    Eton;  Christ Church, Oxf.
    Large Landowner 60.
    Liberal.  MP Reigate 63-65.  DL, JP.
    Fellow Society of Antiquaries.
    West London;  Surrey.
    [MEB, BP, Walfords, Bateman, Alum Oxon, Dods]

    Natl Soc for Preserving Memorials of Dead 84-88,
        Exec.

GRAHAM, PETER

> Financial Reform Union (F) 68-69, Exec.

GRAMSHAW, J. H.

> Physician.
> Gravesend.
>
> Assn for Promoting Extension of Contagious Diseases
>     Act 68-68, Exec.

GRANE, WILLIAM JAMES

> Solicitor.
> West London.
>
> Church Assn 75-80, Exec.

GRANT, DANIEL (1826- )

> Engraver.
> Liberal. MP Marylebone 80-85.
> West London.
> [Dods]
>
> Proportional Representation Soc (F) 84-88, Exec.

GRANT, JAMES CORRIE BRIGHTON (1850-1924)

> City of London School;  Middle Temple.
> Barrister 77;  K.C.  06.
> Radical. MP Rugby 00-10.
> Chiswick.
> [WWW, Fosters, Dods]
>
> London Municipal Reform League 82-85, Exec.

GRANT, JAMES OGILVY, 9TH EARL OF SEAFIELD (1817-1888)

> Harrow.
> Very Large Landowner 84;  Ensign, Army 38;
>     Lieutenant, Army 40.
> MP Elgin & Nairn 68-74. DL, JP.
> Earl 84.
> Morayshire.
> [MEB, BP, Walfords, Dods]
>
> Natl Footpaths Preservation Soc 86-86, V-Pres.

GRANTHAM, RICHARD BOXALL (1805-1891)

> Civil Engineer;  Land Drainage Inspector 61.
> Member Inst Civ Engineers;  Surveyors' Institute;
>     Fellow Geological Society.
> Maida Vale.
> [MEB]
>
> Sanitary Institute 80-87, Exec.

GRANTHAM, SIR WILLIAM (1835-1911)

> King's College School;  Inner Temple.
> Barrister 63;  Q.C.  77;  Judge, Queen's Bench 86.
> Conservative.  MP Surrey East 74-85, Croydon 85-86.
>     JP.
> Kt 86.
> Southwest London;  Sussex.
> [DNB, WWW, Walfords, Fosters, Dods]
>
> City Church & Churchyard Protection Soc 81-83,
>     V-Pres.

GRAVE, JOHN

> Manchester.
>
> Central Assn for Stopping Sale Intox Liquors on
>     Sunday (F) 67-70, V-Pres.

GRAY, THOMAS

> Clergyman<Sect Unkn>.
>
> Central Assn for Stopping Sale Intox Liquors on
>     Sunday 80-85, Exec.

GRAY, WILLIAM (1814-1895)

> Conservative.  MP Bolton 57-74.  DL, JP.
> West London;  Lancashire.
> [Walfords, Dods]
>
> Assn for Promoting Extension of Contagious Diseases
>     Act 68-70, V-Pres.

GREAVES, TALBOT ADEN LEY (1826-1899)

> St John's, Camb.
> Rector 56;  Ordained Priest<CE> 50;  Curate 50;
>     Vicar 51;  Perp. Curate 91.
> Weymouth.
> [MEB, Alum Cantab, Crockfds]
>
> Church Assn 75-75, Exec.

GRECE, CLAIR J.

> Solicitor.
> Surrey.
> [Direc Direcs]
>
> Natl Assn for Repeal Blasphemy Laws (F) 84-84,
>     Exec.

GREEN, CHARLOTTE <MISS>

> Victoria Street Soc for Protection of Animals from
>     Vivisection 80-80, Exec.

GREEN, EDWARD F.

Intl Arbitration & Peace Assn 81-81, Exec.


GREEN, HENRY (1838-1900)

Cheam;  U Bonn.
Shipowner 57.
Liberal.  MP Tower Hamlets 85-86.  JP.
Southeast London.
[MEB, Dods]

Plimsoll and Seamen's Fund Committee (F) 73-73,
Exec.


GREEN, SIDNEY FAITHORN (1841-1916)

Trinity, Camb.
Rector 69;  Curate 65;  Ordained Priest<CE> 66.
Manchester.
[Alum Cantab, Crockfds]

Central Assn for Stopping Sale Intox Liquors on
Sunday 70-70, Exec.


GREENWELL, WILLIAM (1820-1918)

U Col, Durham;  Inner Temple.
Rector 65;  Ordained Priest<CE> 46;  Perp. Curate
47;  Curate 50;  College Head 52;  Canon 54;
Archaeologist.
JP.
Fellow Royal Society;  Fellow Society of
Antiquaries.
Durham[City].
[DNB, WWW, Walfords, Crockfds]

Soc for Protection of Ancient Buildings (F) 78-85,
Exec.


GREG, FRANCIS

Manchester.

Smoke Abatement Committee 81-81.


GREGORY, BENJAMIN (1820-1900)

Woodhouse Grove School, Yorks.
Wesleyan Minister 40;  Author.
[MEB, Wesl Min]

Central Assn for Stopping Sale Intox Liquors on
Sunday 80-80, V-Pres.


GREGORY, GEORGE BURROW (1813-1893)

Eton;  Trinity, Camb.
Solicitor 41.
Conservative.  MP Sussex East 68-85, East Grinstead
85-86.
Incorporated Law Society.
West Central London;  Sussex.
[MEB, Alum Cantab, Dods, Direc Direcs]

Natl Assn for Promotion of State Colonization
86-86, V-Pres.


GREIG, JAMES

Glasgow.

London Soc for Abolition of Compulsory Vaccination
81-81, V-Pres.


GREIG, JOHN

JP.

Natl Assn for Promotion of State Colonization
86-86, Exec.


GREVILLE, F.  <HON.>

London Municipal Reform League 82-82, Exec.


GREVILLE, FULKE SOUTHWELL, 1ST BARON GREVILLE
(1821-1883)

Very Large Landowner;  Sub-Lt., Army 38.
Liberal.  MP Longford Co 52-69.  Lord Lieutenant
71-83, DL, JP.
Baron 69.
Southwest London;  Co Westmeath;  Hertfordshire.
[MEB, BP, Walfords, Bateman, Dods, Direc Direcs,
Army List]

Plimsoll and Seamen's Fund Committee (F) 73-73,
Exec.


GREVILLE, GEORGE FREDERICK NUGENT (1842-1897)

Liberal.  MP Longford Co 70-74.  DL, JP.
West London.
[BP, Walfords, Dods]

Plimsoll and Seamen's Fund Committee (F) 73-73,
Exec.


GREY, ALBERT HENRY GEORGE, 4TH EARL GREY (1851-1917)

Harrow;  Trinity, Camb.
Very Large Landowner;  Governor General, Canada 04.
Liberal(Unionist).  MP Northumberland South 80-85,
Tyneside, Northumb 85-86.  Lord Lieutenant
99-04, JP.
Earl 94;  GCMG 04;  PC 08;  GCVO 11;  GCB 11.
West London;  Northumberland.
[DNB, WWW, BP, Alum Cantab, Dods, Direc Direcs]

Commons Preservation Soc 80-86, Exec.
Proportional Representation Soc (F) 84-88, Treas.


GREY, EDWARD, 1ST VISCOUNT GREY OF FALLODON (1862-1933)

Winchester College;  Balliol, Oxf.
Substantial Landowner 82.
Liberal.  MP Berwick-upon-Tweed 85-16.  Parl U-Sec
For Off 92-95, Sec St Foreign Off 05-16, DL,
JP.
Baronet 82;  PC 02;  KG 12;  Viscount 16.
Fellow Royal Society.
Southwest London;  Northumberland.
[DNB, WWW, BP, Alum Oxon, Dods]

Free Land League 86-86, V-Pres.

GREY, SIR GEORGE EDWARD (1812-1898)

>   Royal Military College, Sandhurst.
>   Colonial Statesman; Ensign, Army 29; Captain,
>       Army 39; Gov, South Australia 41; Gov, New
>       Zealand 46; Gov, Cape of Good Hope 54; Gov,
>       New Zealand 61.
>   Liberal.
>   KCB 48; PC 94.
>   Southwest London; New Zealand.
>   [DNB, MEB, WWW, BP, Walfords, Army List, Dict New
>       Zealand Biog]
>
>   Natl Emigration League (F) 70-70, Exec.

GREY, MARIA GEORGINA <MRS. WILLIAM THOMAS GREY, nee
SHIRREFF> (1816-1906)

>   Educator.
>   Southwest London.
>   [DNB, Women Rgn, Direc Direcs]
>
>   Sunday Society 76-90, V-Pres.

GRIFFITH, J.

>   St Johns Wood.
>
>   Church Assn 75-80, Exec.

GRIFFITH, JOHN (1817-1892)

>   St John's, Camb.
>   Vicar 72; Curate 43; Ordained Priest<CE> 44;
>       Perp. Curate 53; School Head 56.
>   St Albans.
>   [MEB, Alum Cantab, Crockfds]
>
>   Natl Soc for Preserving Memorials of Dead 82-82,
>       Exec.

GRIFFITHS, A. E.

>   Natl Soc for Preserving Memorials of Dead 84-88,
>       Exec.

GRIGG, J. COLLINGS

>   Exeter.
>
>   Assn for Promoting Extension of Contagious Diseases
>       Act 68-68, Exec.

GRIMSHAW, THOMAS WRIGLEY (1839-1900)

>   Trin Col, Dublin.
>   Surgeon 67; Medical School Lecturer;
>       Registrar-General, Ireland 79.
>   JP.
>   CB 97.
>   Royal Col Physicians, Ireland.
>   Dublin.
>   [MEB, WWW]
>
>   Sanitary Institute 80-84, Exec.

GROOM, JOHN

>   Howard Assn 78-84, Exec.

GROSVENOR, HUGH LUPUS, 1ST DUKE OF WESTMINSTER
(1825-1899)

>   Eton; Balliol, Oxf.
>   Very Large Landowner 69.
>   Liberal(Unionist). MP Chester 47-69. Master Horse
>       80-86, Lord Lieutenant 83-99.
>   Marquis 69; KG 70; Duke 74; PC 80.
>   West London; Cheshire.
>   [DNB, MEB, WWW, BP, Walfords, Bateman, Alum Oxon,
>       Dods]
>
>   Natl Footpaths Preservation Soc 86-90, Patron.
>   Smoke Abatement Committee 81-81, President.
>   Sunday Society 78-90, President, V-Pres.
>   City Church & Churchyard Protection Soc (F) 80-83,
>       V-Pres.
>   Central Vigilance Comtee for Repression Immorality
>       (F) 83-84, V-Pres.
>   Howard Assn 78-84, Patron.
>   Intl Arbitration & Peace Assn 81-81, V-Pres.
>   Plimsoll and Seamen's Fund Committee (F) 73-73,
>       Exec.
>   Eastern Question Assn 77-77, President.

GROSVENOR, NORMAN DE L'AIGLE (1845-1898)

>   Eton.
>   Ensign, Army 63; Captain, Army 67.
>   Liberal. MP Chester 69-74.
>   West London; Hertfordshire.
>   [MEB, BP, Walfords, Dods, Direc Direcs, Army List]
>
>   Soc for Protection of Ancient Buildings (F) 78-80,
>       Exec.

GROSVENOR, RICHARD, 2ND MARQUIS WESTMINSTER (1795-1869)

>   Westminster School; Christ Church, Oxf.
>   Very Large Landowner 45.
>   Liberal. MP Chester 18-20, Chester 26-30, Cheshire
>       31-32, Cheshire South 32-35. Lord Steward
>       Royal Household 50-52, Lord Lieutenant.
>   Marquis 45; PC 50; KG 57.
>   West London; Cheshire.
>   [DNB, MEB, BP, Alum Oxon, Dods]
>
>   Assn for Promoting Extension of Contagious Diseases
>       Act 68-70, V-Pres.

GROSVENOR, RICHARD CECIL (1848-1919)

>   Eton; Balliol, Oxf; Inner Temple.
>   Barrister 72.
>   West London.
>   [WWW, BP, Alum Oxon, Fosters]
>
>   Soc for Protection of Ancient Buildings (F) 78-85,
>       Hon Sec.

GROSVENOR, ROBERT, 1ST BARON EBURY (1801-1893)

    Westminster School;  Christ Church, Oxf;  Lincoln's
        Inn.
    Substantial Landowner.
    Liberal(Unionist).  MP Shaftesbury 22-26, Chester
        26-47, Middlesex 47-57.  Comptroller Royal
        Household 30-34, Treas Royal Household 46-47,
        DL, JP.
    PC 30;  Baron 57.
    West London;  Hertfordshire.
    [DNB, MEB, BP, Walfords, Bateman, Alum Oxon, Dods]

    Public Museums & Free Libraries Assn 68-68, V-Pres.


GROUT, -

    Malthusian League 78-79, Exec.


GROUT, - <MRS.>

    Malthusian League 79-79, Exec.


GRUBB, -

    Oxford.

    Jamaica Committee (F) 66-66.


GRUNDY, CHARLES SYDNEY

    Manchester.

    Sunday Society 80-90, V-Pres.


GUEST, MONTAGUE JOHN (1839-1909)

    Harrow.
    Liberal(Unionist).  MP Youghal 69-74, Wareham
        80-85.  DL, JP.
    Southwest London;  Dorsetshire.
    [WWW, BP, Walfords, Dods]

    City Church & Churchyard Protection Soc 81-83,
        V-Pres.


GUILE, DANIEL

    Ironworker;  Trade Union Leader.

    Working Men's Comtee Promoting Separation Church
        and State (F) 71-71, Treas.


GUINNESS, HENRY GRATTAN (1835-1910)

    New College, Hampstead.
    Undenominational Preacher 57.
    Fellow Royal Astronomical Society;  Fellow Royal
        Geograph Society.
    East London.
    [DNB, WWW]

    Anglo-Oriental Soc for Suppression Opium Trade (F)
        75-75, Exec.


GULLIVER, WILLIAM

    Birmingham.

    Working Men's Natl League for Abolition State
        Regulation of Vice 81-81, Hon Sec.


GULLY, WILLIAM COURT, 1ST VISCOUNT SELBY (1835-1909)

    Trinity, Camb;  Inner Temple.
    Q.C. 77;  Barrister 60.
    Liberal.  MP Carlisle 86-05.  Speaker House of
        Commons 95-05.
    PC 95;  Viscount 05.
    West London;  Sussex.
    [DNB, WWW, BP, Alum Cantab, Fosters, Dods]

    Free Land League 86-86, V-Pres.


GURNEY, J.

    JP.
    Northampton.

    Land Law Reform League (F) 81-84, V-Pres.
    League for Defense of Constitutional Rights 84-84,
        V-Pres.


GURNEY, SAMUEL (1816-1882)

    Banker.
    Liberal.  MP Penryn & Falmouth 57-65.  JP.
    Fellow Royal Geograph Society;  Fellow Linnean
        Society.
    West London;  Surrey.
    [MEB, Walfords, Dods]

    Anglo-Oriental Soc for Suppression Opium Trade (F)
        75-75, Exec.
    Public Museums & Free Libraries Assn 68-68, V-Pres.
    Howard Assn 70-81, Exec.
    Intl Arbitration & Peace Assn 81-81, V-Pres.


GUTHRIE, -

    Clergyman<Sect Unkn>.
    Edinburgh.

    Natl Assn for Repeal Contagious Diseases Acts
        84-84, V-Pres.


GUTHRIE, ELLEN E.  <MISS>

    Victoria Street Soc for Protection of Animals from
        Vivisection 82-82, Exec.


GUTHRIE, GEOFFREY DOMINICK AUGUSTUS FREDERICK BROWNE,
    2ND BARON ORANMORE (1819-1900)

    Harrow;  Trinity, Camb.
    Large Landowner 60.
    Conservative.  DL, JP.
    Baron 60.
    Southwest London;  Liverpool;  Co Mayo.
    [WWW, BP, Walfords, Bateman, Alum Cantab]

    Church Assn 67-80, Exec, V-Pres.

GUTHRIE, J.

London.

Jamaica Committee (F) 66-66.

HACKNEY, BERNARD BATIGAN

Middle Temple.
Barrister 81.
Birmingham.
[Fosters]

Allotments & Small Holdings Assn 85-85, Exec.

HADFIELD, GEORGE (1787-1879)

Retired 50; Solicitor 10.
Liberal. MP Sheffield 52-74.
Southwest London; Manchester.
[DNB, MEB, Walfords, Dods]

Howard Assn 69-73, Patron.

HADLEY, SYDNEY CHARLES

Ealing.

Assn for Improvement of Public Morals 81-81, Exec.
Working Men's Natl League for Abolition State
    Regulation of Vice 81-81, Treas.

HAGGARD, ALFRED HINUBER (1849- )

Lincoln's Inn.
Barrister 72; India Civil Service.
East London.
[Fosters]

Indian Reform Assn 84-84, Exec.

HALFORD, F. B.

West London.

London Municipal Reform League 82-85, Exec.

HALL, CHRISTOPHER NEWMAN (1816-1902)

London U; Highbury College.
Congregational Minister 42.
London.
[DNB, WWW]

Natl Assn for Promotion of State Colonization
    86-86, Patron.
Jamaica Committee (F) 66-66.

HALL, EDWARD HEPPLE-

Author.
Ventnor.

Natl Assn for Promotion of State Colonization
    86-86, Exec.

HALL, SAMUEL ROMILLY (1812-1876)

Hoxton Academy.
Wesleyan Minister 37; Author.
Manchester.
[MEB]

Central Assn for Stopping Sale Intox Liquors on
    Sunday (F) 67-70, V-Pres.

HALL, SPENCER TIMOTHY (1812-1885)

Homeopathic Doctor 52; Handloom Weaver 23;
    Bookseller 36; Postmaster 36.
Lytham.
[DNB, MEB]

London Soc for Abolition of Compulsory Vaccination
    81-81, V-Pres.

HALL, W. H.

Commons Preservation Soc 84-86, Exec.

HALL, WILLIAM JOHN (1830-1910)

Merchant Taylors; Trinity, Camb.
Rector 65; Curate 53; Ordained Priest<CE> 54;
    Perp. Curate 61; Canon 62.
East Central London.
[Alum Cantab, Crockfds]

City Church & Churchyard Protection Soc (F) 80-83,
    Exec.

HALL, SIR WILLIAM KING (1816-1886)

Captain, RN 53; Cadet, RN 29; Lieutenant, RN 41;
    Commander, RN 48; Rear Admiral 69;
    Vice-Admiral 75; Admiral 79.
CB 55; KCB 71.
Sheerness.
[DNB, MEB, BP, Navy List]

Assn for Promoting Extension of Contagious Diseases
    Act 68-70, V-Pres.

HAMBER, - <"CAPT.">

Liberty & Property Defense League 84-84, Exec.

HAMBRO, CHARLES JOSEPH THEOPHILUS (1834-1891)

Trinity, Camb; Inner Temple.
Barrister 60; Large Landowner 77.
Conservative. MP Weymouth 68-74, Dorsetshire South
    85-91. DL, JP.
West London; Dorsetshire.
[MEB, Walfords, Bateman, Alum Cantab, Fosters,
    Dods]

Plimsoll and Seamen's Fund Committee (F) 73-73,
    Exec.

HAMBRO, SIR EVERARD ALEXANDER (1842-1925)

    Trinity, Camb.
    Merchant;  Director, Bank of England.
    DL, JP.
    KCVO 08.
    Kent.
    [WWW, Alum Cantab, Direc Direcs]

    Natl Assn for Promotion of State Colonization
       86-86, V-Pres.


HAMILTON, ANDREW <"CAPT.">

    Natl Assn for Promotion of State Colonization
       86-86, Exec.


HAMILTON, SIR CHARLES EDWARD, 1ST BT.  (1845-1928)

    Conservative.  MP Southwark Rotherhithe 85-92.  DL,
       JP.
    Baronet 92.
    Southwest London;  Kent.
    [WWW, BP, Dods]

    Natl Assn for Promotion of State Colonization
       86-86, V-Pres.


HAMILTON, LORD CLAUD (1813-1884)

    Harrow;  Trinity, Camb.
    Conservative.  MP Tyrone 35-37, Tyrone 39-74.
       Treas Royal Household 52-52, Treas Royal
       Household 58-59, V-Chamberlain Royal Household
       66-68, DL, JP.
    PC 52.
    Southwest London;  Co Tyrone.
    [MEB, BP, Walfords, Alum Cantab, Dods]

    Central Assn for Stopping Sale Intox Liquors on
       Sunday 75-80, V-Pres.
    Plimsoll and Seamen's Fund Committee (F) 73-73,
       Exec.


HAMILTON, LORD CLAUD JOHN (1843-1925)

    Harrow.
    Lieutenant, Army 62;  Captain, Army 65;  Colonel
       67.
    Conservative.  MP Londonderry City 65-68, King's
       Lynn 69-80, Liverpool 80-85, Liverpool W Derby
       85-88, South Kensington 10-18.  Junior Lord
       Treasury 68-68.
    PC 17.
    West London;  Co Tyrone.
    [WWW, BP, Dods, Direc Direcs, Army List]

    Natl Footpaths Preservation Soc (F) 84-90, V-Pres.
    Assn for Promoting Extension of Contagious Diseases
       Act 68-68, V-Pres.
    Natl Emigration League (F) 70-70, V-Pres.
    Plimsoll and Seamen's Fund Committee (F) 73-73,
       Exec.


HAMILTON, LORD GEORGE FRANCIS (1845-1927)

    Harrow.
    Politician;  Ensign, Army 64;  Lieutenant, Army 68.
    Conservative.  MP Middlesex 68-85, Middlesex Ealing
       85-06.  Parl U-Sec India 74-78, V-P Education
       Committee 78-80, First Lord Admiralty 85-86,
       First Lord Admiralty 86-92, Sec St India 95-03,
       JP.
    PC 78;  GCSI 03.
    West London.
    [DNB, WWW, BP, Dods, Army List]

    Natl Emigration League (F) 70-70, V-Pres.
    Plimsoll and Seamen's Fund Committee (F) 73-73,
       Exec.
    Natl Education Union 71-76, Exec.


HAMILTON, JAMES, 2ND DUKE OF ABERCORN (1838-1913)

    Harrow;  Christ Church, Oxf.
    Very Large Landowner 85.
    Conservative.  MP Donegal 60-80.  Lord of the
       Bedchamber, P of W 66-86, Groom of the Stole, P
       of W 86-01, Lord Lieutenant 85- , JP.
    Duke 85;  KG 92;  PC;  CB.
    West London;  Co Tyrone;  Edinburgh.
    [DNB, WWW, BP, Walfords, Alum Oxon, Dods, Direc
       Direcs]

    City Church & Churchyard Protection Soc 81-83,
       V-Pres.
    Assn for Promoting Extension of Contagious Diseases
       Act 68-70, V-Pres.


HAMILTON, JOSEPH HARRIMAN (1799-1881)

    Rugby;  Trinity, Camb.
    Prebendary 59;  Chaplain 24;  Ordained Priest<CE>
       25;  Vicar 41;  Perp. Curate 48;  Rector 71;
       Canon 72.
    Southwest London.
    [MEB, Alum Cantab, Crockfds]

    Church Assn 67-67, Exec.


HAMMERSLEY, JOHN

    St Aidan's College, Birkenhead.
    Rector 71;  Curate 67;  Ordained Priest<CE> 68.
    Bury St Edmunds.
    [Crockfds]

    Church Assn 80-80, Exec.


HAMPSON, ROBERT

    Vigilance Assn for Defense of Personal Rights
       83-83, Exec.


HANBURY, SIR THOMAS (1832-1907)

    China Merchant 53.
    Liberal.
    KCVO 01.
    Italy.
    [WWW]

    Anglo-Oriental Soc for Suppression Opium Trade (F)
       75-75, Exec.

HANCOCK, -

    Workmen's Peace Assn 75-75, Exec.


HANCOCK, CHARLES FREDERICK (1848- )

    Merton, Oxf;  Middle Temple.
    Barrister 79.
    Middlesex.
    [Alum Oxon, Fosters]

    Sunday Society 76-90, V-Pres.


HANDYSIDE, VINOY ROBSON

    Kings Col London.
    Curate 80;  Ordained Priest<CE> 81;  Rector 86.
    Southeast London.
    [Crockfds]

    City Church & Churchyard Protection Soc (F) 80-83,
       Exec.


HANSARD, SEPTIMUS COX HOLMES (1823-1895)

    Rugby;  University Col, Oxf.
    Rector 64;  Curate 46;  Ordained Priest<CE> 47.
    East London.
    [MEB, Alum Oxon, Crockfds]

    Sunday Society 76-90, V-Pres.
    Metro Free Libraries Assn (F) 77-82, Exec.
    Assn for Improvement of London Workhouse
       Infirmaries 66-66, Exec.


HANSON, JAMES (1815-1895)

    Printer 50;  Newspaper Proprietor 58;  Educator.
    Bradford.
    [MEB]

    Jamaica Committee (F) 66-66.


HANSON, SIR REGINALD 1ST BT. (1840-1905)

    Rugby;  Trinity, Camb.
    Wholesale Grocer 61.
    Conservative. MP City 91-00. DL, JP.
    Kt 82;  Baronet 87.
    Fellow Society of Antiquaries.
    West London.
    [WWW, BP, Alum Cantab, Dods]

    City Church & Churchyard Protection Soc 83-83,
       V-Pres.


HARCOURT, SIR WILLIAM GEORGE GRANVILLE VENABLES VERNON
    (1827-1904)

    Trinity, Camb;  Inner Temple.
    Politician;  Barrister 54;  Q.C. 66;  Whewell
       Professor of International Law, Cambridge 69.
    Radical.  MP Oxford 68-80, Derby 80-95,
       Monmouthshire West 95-04.  Solicitor General
       73-74, Sec St Home Office 80-85, Chancellor
       Exchequer 86-86, Chancellor Exchequer 92-95,
       DL.
    Kt 73;  PC 80.

West London;  Hampshire.
[DNB, BP, Walfords, Alum Cantab, Fosters, Dods]

    Commons Preservation Soc 69-86, Exec.


HARDINGE, - <MRS.>

    Kyrle Soc 84-84, Exec.


HARDINGE, SIR ARTHUR EDWARD (1828-1892)

    Eton.
    Colonel 58;  Ensign, Army 44;  Major 54;  Maj.
       General 71;  Lt. General 77;  General 83;
       Gov, Gibralter 86.
    Equerry 61- .
    CB 57;  KCB 86;  CIE 86.
    [DNB, MEB, BP, Army List]

    Assn for Promoting Extension of Contagious Diseases
       Act 68-70, V-Pres.


HARDWICKE, HERBERT JUNIUS ( -1921)

    Surgeon.
    Fellow Royal Col Surgeons;  Member Royal Col
       Physicians.
    Sheffield.
    [WWW]

    Malthusian League 80-84, V-Pres.


HARDWICKE, WILLIAM

    Physician.
    West London;  Hendon.

    Assn for Promoting Extension of Contagious Diseases
       Act 68-68, Exec.


HARDY, ALFRED ERSKINE GATHORNE- (1845-1918)

    Eton;  Balliol, Oxf;  Inner Temple.
    Barrister 69;  Counsel to Woods and Forests 76;
       Counsel to Commissioner of Works;  Railway
       Commissioner 05.
    Conservative.  MP Canterbury 78-80, East Grinstead
       80-85, Sussex North 86-95.  DL, JP.
    West London;  Kent.
    [WWW, BP, Alum Oxon, Fosters, Dods, Direc Direcs]

    City Church & Churchyard Protection Soc (F) 80-83,
       V-Pres.


HARDY, HERBERT HARDY COZENS-, 1ST BARON COZENS-HARDY OF
    LETHERINGSETT (1838-1920)

    University Col London;  Lincoln's Inn.
    Q.C. 86;  Barrister 62;  Judge, Chancery 99;  Chm,
       Historical Manuscripts Commission 07;  College
       Fellow.
    Liberal.  MP Norfolk North 85-99.  Lord Justice of
       Appeal 01-07, Master of the Rolls 07-18.
    Kt 99;  PC 01;  Baron 14.
    West London;  Norfolk.
    [DNB, WWW, BP, Fosters, Dods]

    Commons Preservation Soc 86-86, Exec.

HARDY, JOHN STEWART GATHORNE-, 2ND EARL OF CRANBROOK
    (1839-1911)

    Eton;  Christ Church, Oxf.
    Large Landowner 06.
    Conservative.  MP Rye 68-80, Kent Mid 84-85, Medway
        85-92.  DL, JP.
    Earl 06.
    Southwest London;  Kent.
    [WWW, BP, Walfords, Alum Oxon, Dods]

    Natl Emigration League (F) 70-70, V-Pres.


HARE, THOMAS (1806-1891)

    Inner Temple.
    Barrister 33;  Charities Inspector 53.
    Asst Charity Commissioner 72-87.
    Southwest London;  Kingston-upon-Thames.
    [DNB, MEB, Fosters]

    Land Tenure Reform Assn 73-73, Exec.


HARE, WILLIAM IRVING (1821- )

    Gray's Inn.
    Barrister 52.
    Southwest London.
    [Fosters, Direc Direcs]

    Assn for Promoting Extension of Contagious Diseases
        Act 68-68, Exec.


HARGRAVE, WILLIAM (1795-1874)

    Dublin(Medical).
    Surgeon;  Author.
    Fellow Royal Col Surgeons.
    Dublin.
    [MEB]

    Assn for Promoting Extension of Contagious Diseases
        Act 68-70, V-Pres.


HARGREAVES, WILLIAM

    St John's, Camb;  Lincoln's Inn.
    JP.
    Surrey.
    [Alum Cantab]

    Jamaica Committee (F) 66-66.


HARINGTON, DALLAS OLDFIELD

    St Alban's, Oxf.
    Assoc Sec, Irish Church Mission 67;  Curate 60;
        Ordained Priest<CE> 61;  Perp. Curate 78;
        Rector 79.
    Cheltenham.
    [Alum Oxon, Crockfds]

    Church Assn 70-70, Exec.


HARMAN, J.

    City Church & Churchyard Protection Soc (F) 80-83,
        Treas.


HARRIS, ALFRED (1801- )

    DL, JP.
    Bradford;  Yorks, West Riding.
    [Walfords]

    Jamaica Committee (F) 66-66.


HARRIS, GEORGE (1809-1890)

    Rugby;  Middle Temple.
    Barrister 43;  County Court Judge 60.
    Anthropological Institute;  Fellow Society of
        Antiquaries.
    Southall.
    [DNB, MEB, Alum Cantab, Fosters]

    Railway Passengers' Protection Assn 86-86, Exec.


HARRIS, HENRY (1789- )

    Banker.
    Bradford;  Yorks, West Riding.
    [Walfords]

    Jamaica Committee (F) 66-66.


HARRIS, R.

    "Of the Gas, Light, and Coke Co".

    Smoke Abatement Committee 81-81.


HARRIS, WILLIAM

    Birmingham.

    Natl Education League (F) 69-71, Exec.


HARRISON, BENJAMIN (1808-1887)

    Christ Church, Oxf.
    Archdeacon 45;  Canon 45;  Ordained Priest<CE> 33;
        Chaplain 38.
    Fellow Society of Antiquaries.
    Canterbury.
    [DNB, MEB, Alum Cantab, Alum Oxon, Crockfds]

    Natl Soc for Preserving Memorials of Dead (F)
        81-84, Exec.


HARRISON, FREDERICK (1831-1923)

    King's College School;  Wadham, Oxf;  Lincoln's
        Inn.
    Barrister 58;  College Fellow 54;  Legal Scholar.
    Radical.  JP.
    Royal Historical Society.
    West London.
    [DNB, WWW, Alum Oxon, Fosters]

    Jamaica Committee (F) 66-66.

HARRISON, GILBERT

    Victoria Street Soc for Protection of Animals from
       Vivisection 84-85, Exec.

HARRISON, HARRIET <MISS>

    Kyrle Soc 84-89, Exec.

HARRISON, REGINALD (1837-1908)

    Rossall;  St Bartholomew's Hosp.
    Surgeon 60;  Medical School Demonstrator 64;
       Medical School Lecturer 65;  Quarantine
       Officer.
    Fellow Royal Col Surgeons;  Medical Society of
       Lond.
    Liverpool.
    [DNB, WWW]

    Assn for Promoting Extension of Contagious Diseases
       Act 68-68, Exec.

HARRISON, ROBERT (1820-1897)

    Librarian 55;  Private Tutor;  College Lecturer 44.
    Northwest London.
    [MEB]

    Metro Free Libraries Assn (F) 77-77, Exec.

HARRISON, W.

    Soc for Abolition of Vivisection (F) 75-76, Exec.

HART, ERNEST ABRAHAM (1835-1898)

    City of London School;  St George's Hospital Lond.
    Surgeon 59;  Journal Editor 63;  Medical School
       Head 63.
    Liberal.
    Member Royal Col Surgeons.
    West London.
    [DNB, MEB, WWW, Direc Direcs]

    Metro Public Gardens Assn (F) 83-90, V-Chairman.
    Smoke Abatement Committee 81-81, Chairman.
    Sanitary Institute 84-89, Exec.
    Assn for Promoting Extension of Contagious Diseases
       Act 68-68, Exec.
    Assn for Improvement of London Workhouse
       Infirmaries 66-66, Hon Sec.
    Infant Life Protection Soc 71-71, Exec.

HART, THOMAS DALE (1855-1896)

    Downing, Camb;  Middle Temple.
    Barrister 80.
    West London.
    [Alum Cantab, Fosters]

    Natl Footpaths Preservation Soc (F) 85-86, Exec.

HARTISHORNE, A.

    Natl Soc for Preserving Memorials of Dead (F)
       81-82, Exec.

HARTLEY, R.

    East London.

    Jamaica Committee (F) 66-66.

HARVEY, -

    Salford.

    Jamaica Committee (F) 66-66.

HARVEY, JAMES

    London.

    Jamaica Committee (F) 66-66.

HARVEY, W. C.

    London Municipal Reform League 82-82, Exec.

HASLAM, JAMES

    Central Assn for Stopping Sale Intox Liquors on
       Sunday (F) 67-67, Exec.

HASLEM, J.

    Clergyman<Sect Unkn>.
    Leeds.

    Natl Education League 71-71, Exec.

HASTINGS, GEORGE WOODYATT (1825-1917)

    Christ's, Camb;  Middle Temple.
    Barrister 50.
    Liberal(Unionist).  MP Worcestershire East 80-92.
    DL, JP.
    Worcestershire.
    [Alum Cantab, Fosters, Dods, Direc Direcs]

    Infant Life Protection Soc 71-71, Exec.

HASWELL, E. W.

    Braintree.

    British Women's Temperance Assn 85-85, Exec.

HATHAWAY, EDWARD PENROSE (1818- )

    Queen's, Oxf; Lincoln's Inn.
    Curate 66; Barrister 46; Ordained Priest<CE> 66;
       Rector 68; Vicar 82.
    Camberwell.
    [Alum Oxon, Fosters, Crockfds]

    Church Assn 67-67, Exec.


HATT, J.

    West London.

    League for Defense of Constitutional Rights 84-84,
       Hon Sec.


HATTON, HAROLD HENEAGE FINCH- (1856-1904)

    Eton; Balliol, Oxf.
    City Financier 83.
    Conservative. MP Newark, Notts 95-98.
    Southwest London.
    [WWW, BP, Alum Oxon, Dods]

    Natl Assn for Promotion of State Colonization
       86-86, V-Pres.
    Imperial Federation League (F) 84-84, Treas.


HATZFIELD, E.

    Land Nationalization Soc 85-85, Exec.


HAUGHTON, EDWARD

    Physician.
    Upper Norwood.

    London Soc for Abolition of Compulsory Vaccination
       81-81, V-Pres.


HAVILAND, A.

    Surgeon.
    Member Royal Col Surgeons.

    Sanitary Institute 79-84, Exec.


HAWEIS, HUGH REGINALD (1838-1901)

    Trinity, Camb.
    Perp. Curate 66; Journal Editor 68; Curate 61;
       Ordained Priest<CE> 62.
    West London.
    [DNB, WWW, Alum Cantab, Crockfds]

    Sunday Society 78-90, V-Pres.


HAWKES, HENRY (1815-1891)

    Solicitor 46.
    JP.
    Birmingham.
    [MEB, Direc Direcs]

    Natl Education League (F) 69-69, Exec.
    Natl Fair Trade League (F) 81-81, Exec.


HAWKINS, CAESAR HENRY (1798-1884)

    Christ's Hospital; St George's Hospital Lond.
    Surgeon; Author.
    Fellow Royal Society; Fellow Royal Col Surgeons.
    West London.
    [DNB, MEB]

    Assn for Promoting Extension of Contagious Diseases
       Act 68-70, V-Pres.


HAWKSWORTH, JOHN

    Church Assn 67-80, Exec.


HAWORTH, ABRAHAM

    St. Bees.
    Rector 59.
    Manchester.
    [Crockfds]

    Central Assn for Stopping Sale Intox Liquors on
       Sunday (F) 67-85, Exec.
    Jamaica Committee (F) 66-66.


HAWORTH, RICHARD

    JP.

    Central Assn for Stopping Sale Intox Liquors on
       Sunday (F) 67-80, Treas.


HAY, SIR JOHN CHARLES DALRYMPLE-, 3RD BT. (1821-1912)

    Rugby.
    Rear Admiral 66; Cadet, RN 34; Lieutenant, RN 45;
       Captain, RN 50; Vice-Admiral 72; Admiral 78;
       Landowner 61.
    Conservative. MP Wakefield 62-65, Stamford 66-80,
       Wigtown District 80-85. Lord Admiralty 66-68,
       DL, JP.
    Baronet 61; PC 74; CB; KCB; GCB.
    Fellow Royal Society; Fellow Royal Geograph
       Society.
    Southwest London; Wigtownshire.
    [WWW, BP, Walfords, Alum Oxon, Dods, Navy List]

    Plimsoll and Seamen's Fund Committee (F) 73-73,
       Exec.
    Natl Education Union 71-71, Exec.


HAY, WILLIAM MONTAGU, 10TH MARQUIS OF TWEEDDALE
(1826-1911)

    Haileybury College.
    Very Large Landowner 78; India Civil Service 45;
       Deputy Commissioner, Simla.
    Liberal. MP Taunton 65-68, Haddington District
       78-78. DL.
    Marquis 78; Baron 81; KT 98.
    West London; East Lothian.
    [BP, Walfords, Bateman, Dods, Direc Direcs]

    Natl Footpaths Preservation Soc 86-90, V-Pres.

HAYNE, CHARLES HAYNE SEALE (1833-1903)

>   Eton;  Lincoln's Inn.
>   Barrister 57;  Landowner 42;  Politician.
>   Liberal.  MP Devonshire Mid 85-03.  Paymaster
>       General 92-95, JP.
>   PC 92.
>   Southwest London;  Devonshire.
>   [DNB, Walfords, Fosters, Dods, Direc Direcs]
>
>   Free Land League 86-86, V-Pres.

HAYNES, WILLIAM B.  <"MAJ.">

>   JP.
>   West Central London;  Maidstone.
>   [Direc Direcs]
>
>   Sunday Society 80-90, V-Pres.

HAYWARD, JOHN CURTIS (1804-1895)

>   Winchester College;  Oriel, Oxf;  Lincoln's Inn.
>   Barrister 32;  Landowner 12.
>   DL, JP.
>   Gloucestershire.
>   [MEB, Walfords, Alum Oxon]
>
>   Assn for Promoting Extension of Contagious Diseases
>       Act 68-70, V-Pres.

HAYWARD, W.  H.

>   Oldbury.
>
>   Assn for Promoting Extension of Contagious Diseases
>       Act 68-68, Exec.

HEADLAM, STEWART DUCKWORTH (1847-1924)

>   Eton;  Trinity, Camb.
>   Curate 70;  Ordained Priest<CE> 72.
>   Radical.
>   East Central London.
>   [WWW, Alum Cantab, Crockfds, Dic Lab Biog]
>
>   English Land Restoration League 85-85, Exec.
>   Land Law Reform League (F) 81-84, V-Pres.
>   League for Defense of Constitutional Rights 84-84,
>       V-Pres.
>   Natl Assn for Repeal Blasphemy Laws (F) 84-84,
>       Exec.

HEADLAM, THOMAS EMERSON (1813-1875)

>   Shrewsbury School;  Trinity, Camb;  Inner Temple.
>   Q.C. 51;  Barrister 39.
>   Liberal.  MP Newcastle-upon-Tyne 47-74.  Judge
>       Advocate General 59-66, DL, JP.
>   PC 59.
>   Fellow Royal Geograph Society.
>   Southwest London;  Newcastle-upon-Tyne;
>       Durham[County].
>   [DNB, MEB, Walfords, Alum Cantab, Dods]
>
>   Assn for Promoting Extension of Contagious Diseases
>       Act 70-70, V-Pres.

HEALD, HENRY GEORGE (1822-1881)

>   Sec, Sunday School Institute 55.
>   Peckham.
>   [MEB]
>
>   Public Museums & Free Libraries Assn 68-68, Exec.

HEALES, ALFRED (1827-1898)

>   Proctor 49;  Antiquary.
>   Fellow Society of Antiquaries.
>   Streatham.
>   [MEB, Direc Direcs]
>
>   Natl Soc for Preserving Memorials of Dead (F)
>       81-88, Exec.
>   Soc for Protection of Ancient Buildings (F) 78-85,
>       Exec.

HEALEY, EDWARD CHARLES

>   Southwest London.
>
>   Natl Fair Trade League (F) 81-81, Exec.

HEANE, J.  P.

>   JP.
>   Gloucester.
>
>   Natl Secular Soc 70-70, V-Pres.

HEANE, WILLIAM CRAWSHAY

>   Physician.
>   Member Royal Col Surgeons.
>   Gloucestershire.
>
>   Natl Soc for Preserving Memorials of Dead (F)
>       81-82, Exec.

HEBB, JOHN

>   Architect, Metropolitan Board of Works.
>   Assoc Royal Inst Br Architects.
>   Southwest London.
>
>   City Church & Churchyard Protection Soc (F) 80-83,
>       Exec.
>   Soc for Protection of Ancient Buildings (F) 78-85,
>       Exec.

HEMBER, R.  G.

>   Malthusian League (F) 77-80, Exec.

HENDERSON, JAMES

>   Howard Assn 72-78, Exec.

HENDERSON, JOHN

> Banker.
> JP.
> Oxfordshire.
> [Direc Direcs]
>
> Natl Fair Trade League (F) 81-81, Exec.

HENEAGE, EDWARD, 1ST BARON HENEAGE (1840-1922)

> Eton.
> Very Large Landowner 64; Sub-Lt., Army 57;
>     Lieutenant, Army 62.
> Liberal(Unionist). MP Lincoln 65-68, Great Grimsby
>     80-92, Great Grimsby 93-95. Chanc Duchy
>     Lancaster 86-86, DL, JP.
> PC 86; Baron 96.
> Lincolnshire.
> [WWW, BP, Walfords, Bateman, Dods, Army List]
>
> Local Taxation Comtee [of Central Chamber of
>     Agriculture] 71-82, Exec.

HENNESSY, PATRICK

> Tailor.
> Radical.
> London.
>
> English Land Restoration League 85-85, Exec.
> Land Nationalization Soc (F) 81-81, Exec.

HENRIQUES, ALFRED GUTTEREZ

> Middle Temple.
> Barrister 53.
> DL, JP.
> West London; Brighton.
> [Fosters, Direc Direcs]
>
> Free Land League 86-86, Exec.

HENRY, MITCHELL (1826-1910)

> Univ College School; Pine Street School of
>     Medicine, Manchester.
> Merchant 62; Surgeon 48; Very Large Landowner.
> Liberal(Unionist). MP Galway Co 71-85, Glasgow
>     Blackfriars & Hutchesontown 85-86. DL, JP.
> Fellow Royal Col Surgeons.
> West London; Co Galway.
> [DNB, WWW, Dods]
>
> Howard Assn 79-81, Patron.

HEPBURN, HENRY POOLE (1822-1888)

> Maj. General 68; Lieutenant, Army 41; Captain,
>     Army 46; Lt. Colonel 54; Colonel 63; Lt.
>     General 81.
> CB 69.
> West London.
> [MEB, Army List]
>
> Assn for Promoting Extension of Contagious Diseases
>     Act 68-70, V-Pres.

HERBERT, AUBERON EDWARD WILLIAM MOLYNEUX (1838-1906)

> Eton; St Johns, Oxf.
> Author; College Fellow 55; Cornet, Army 58;
>     Lieutenant, Army 59; Journal Editor 90.
> Radical. MP Nottingham 70-74.
> Northwest London; Berkshire.
> [DNB, WWW, BP, Walfords, Alum Oxon, Dods, Army
>     List]
>
> Natl Education League 71-71, Exec.

HERBERT, EDWARD JAMES, 3RD EARL OF POWIS (1818-1891)

> Eton; St John's, Camb.
> Very Large Landowner 48.
> Conservative. MP Shropshire North 43-48. Lord
>     Lieutenant 77-  , DL, JP.
> Earl 48.
> West London; Shropshire; Montgomeryshire.
> [MEB, BP, Walfords, Bateman, Alum Cantab, Alum
>     Oxon, Dods, Direc Direcs]
>
> Natl Soc for Preserving Memorials of Dead 84-84,
>     Patron.
> Soc for Promoting Increase of the Home Episcopate
>     72-74, V-Pres.

HERBERT, GEORGE ROBERT CHARLES, 13TH EARL OF PEMBROKE
(1850-1895)

> Eton.
> Very Large Landowner 61; Author.
> Conservative. Parl U-Sec War 74-75.
> Baron 61; Earl 62.
> Southwest London; Wiltshire.
> [DNB, MEB, BP, Walfords, Bateman, Direc Direcs]
>
> Liberty & Property Defense League (F) 82-84, Exec.

HERBERT, H. V.

> Ordained Priest<CE>.
> Ipswich.
>
> Church Assn 75-78, Exec.

HERBERT, HENRY HOWARD MOLYNEUX, 4TH EARL CARNARVON
(1831-1890)

> Eton; Christ Church, Oxf.
> Very Large Landowner 49; Politician; Historical
>     Manuscripts Commissioner 82.
> Conservative. Parl U-Sec Col Off 58-59, Sec St
>     Colonial Off 66-67, Sec St Colonial Off 74-78,
>     Lord Lt Ireland 85-87, Lord Lieutenant, DL, JP.
> Earl 49; PC 66.
> Fellow Society of Antiquaries.
> West London; Berkshire.
> [DNB, MEB, BP, Walfords, Bateman, Alum Cantab, Alum
>     Oxon]
>
> Natl Soc for Preserving Memorials of Dead (F)
>     81-84, Patron.
> Assn for Improvement of London Workhouse
>     Infirmaries 66-66, Exec.

HERFORD, WILLIAM HENRY (1820-1908)

    Shrewsbury School;  Manchester College, York.
    Unitarian Minister 40;  Educator.
    Manchester.
    [DNB]

    Jamaica Committee (F) 66-66.


HERKOMER, SIR HUBERT VON (1849-1914)

    So Kens School of Art.
    Artist;  Art School Director 83;  Slade Professor
        of Fine Arts, Oxford 85.
    CVO 01;  Kt 07.
    Royal Academy;  Royal Inst Water Colour Painters.
    Hertfordshire.
    [DNB, WWW, Alum Oxon]

    Sunday Society 80-90, V-Pres.


HERRING, ARMINE STYLEMAN (1831-1896)

    Marlborough;  Corpus Christi, Camb.
    Vicar 65;  Curate 58;  Ordained Priest<CE> 59.
    North London.
    [Alum Cantab, Crockfds]

    Natl Emigration League (F) 70-70, Exec.


HERVEY, ARTHUR CHARLES (1808-1894)

    Eton;  Trinity, Camb.
    Bishop Bath and Wells 69;  Ordained Priest<CE> 32;
        Rector 32;  Archdeacon 62.
    Wells.
    [DNB, MEB, Alum Cantab]

    Victoria Street Soc for Protection of Animals from
        Vivisection 82-85, V-Pres.
    Central Assn for Stopping Sale Intox Liquors on
        Sunday 85-85, V-Pres.
    Soc for Promoting Increase of the Home Episcopate
        72-74, V-Pres.


HERVEY, LORD FRANCIS (1846-1931)

    Eton;  Balliol, Oxf;  Lincoln's Inn.
    Barrister 72;  College Fellow 74;  Second Civil
        Service Commissioner 92;  First Civil Service
        Commssioner 07.
    Conservative. MP Bury St Edmunds 74-80, Bury St
        Edmunds 85-86, Bury St Edmunds 86-92. JP.
    Southwest London;  Sussex.
    [WWW, BP, Alum Oxon, Fosters, Dods]

    Local Taxation Comtee [of Central Chamber of
        Agriculture] 75-85, Exec.


HERVEY, JAMES

    Manchester.

    Jamaica Committee (F) 66-66.


HESELTINE, JOHN POSTLE (1843-1929)

    Southwest London.
    [WWW]

    Soc for Protection of Ancient Buildings (F) 78-85,
        Exec.


HESLOP, THOMAS PRETIOUS (1823-1885)

    Edinburgh(Medical).
    Physician 48;  Medical School Lecturer 53.
    Birmingham.
    [DNB]

    Natl Education League (F) 69-69, Exec.


HESSEY, FRANCIS (1816-1882)

    Merchant Taylors;  St Johns, Oxf.
    Vicar 53;  College Fellow 34;  Curate 39;  Ordained
        Priest<CE> 40;  School Head 40.
    West London.
    [MEB, Alum Oxon, Crockfds]

    Soc for Promoting Increase of the Home Episcopate
        72-74, Exec.


HESTER, T.  J.

    London.

    Natl Assn for Promotion of State Colonization
        86-86, Exec.


HEWETT, SIR PRESCOTT GARDNER, 1ST BT.  (1812-1891)

    St George's Hospital Lond.
    Surgeon 61;  Medical School Demonstrator 36;
        Medical School Lecturer 45;  Asst Surgeon 48;
        Medical School Professor 67.
    Baronet 83.
    Fellow Royal Col Surgeons;  Fellow Royal Society;
        Pathological Society.
    West London.
    [DNB, MEB]

    Assn for Promoting Extension of Contagious Diseases
        Act 68-70, V-Pres.


HEWITT, FRANCIS (1832-1897)

    Newspaper Proprietor.
    Leicester.

    Jamaica Committee (F) 66-66.


HEWITT, GRAILY

    Physician.
    West London.

    Infant Life Protection Soc 71-71, Exec.

HEWITT, JAMES, 4TH VISCOUNT LIFFORD (1811-1887)

    Christ Church, Oxf.
    Landowner 55.
    Conservative. DL, JP.
    Viscount 55.
    Surrey; Co Donegal.
    [MEB, BP, Walfords, Alum Oxon]

    Assn for Promoting Extension of Contagious Diseases
        Act 68-75, Exec, V-Pres.


HEWLETT, EBENEZER

    Kings Col London.
    Rector 62; Ordained Priest<CE> 53; Curate 53.
    Manchester.
    [Crockfds]

    Central Assn for Stopping Sale Intox Liquors on
        Sunday 70-75, Exec.


HEY, WILLIAM (1796-1875)

    Surgeon 30; Medical School Lecturer 31.
    Fellow Royal Col Surgeons.
    Leeds.
    [DNB, MEB]

    Assn for Promoting Extension of Contagious Diseases
        Act 68-68, V-Pres.


HEYWOOD, ABEL (1810-1893)

    Bookseller 32; Publisher.
    Manchester.
    [MEB]

    Jamaica Committee (F) 66-66.


HEYWOOD, ARTHUR H.

    JP.
    Windemere.

    Central Assn for Stopping Sale Intox Liquors on
        Sunday 85-85, V-Pres.


HEYWOOD, JAMES (1810-1897)

    Trinity, Camb; Inner Temple.
    Barrister 38; College Fellow 56.
    Liberal. MP Lancashire North 47-57. DL, JP.
    Fellow Royal Society; Fellow Society of
        Antiquaries; Fellow Royal Geograph Society;
        Fellow Royal Statistical Society.
    West London; Lancashire.
    [MEB, Alum Cantab, Fosters, Dods]

    Sunday Society (F) 75-90, President, V-Pres.
    Metro Free Libraries Assn (F) 77-82, Exec.


HEYWOOD, ROBERT

    Bolton.

    Jamaica Committee (F) 66-66.


HIBBERD, -

    Sheffield.

    Natl Education League 71-71, Exec.


HIBBERT, SIR JOHN TOMLINSON (1824-1908)

    Shrewsbury School; St John's, Camb; Inner Temple.
    Barrister 49.
    Liberal. MP Oldham 62-74, Oldham 77-86, Oldham
        92-95. Parl Sec Loc Govt Board 72-74, Parl Sec
        Loc Govt Board 80-83, Parl U-Sec Home Off
        83-84, Sec Treasury 84-85, Parl Sec Admiralty
        86-86, Sec Treasury 92-95, DL, JP.
    PC 86; KCB 93.
    Southwest London; Lancashire.
    [DNB, WWW, BP, Walfords, Alum Cantab, Fosters,
        Dods]

    Howard Assn 67-73, Patron.


HICKMAN, WILLIAM

    Paymaster, RN 49; Paymaster-in-Chief, RN 70.
    Liverpool.
    [Navy List]

    Assn for Promoting Extension of Contagious Diseases
        Act 68-70, V-Pres.


HICKS, G. M.

    Assn for Improvement of London Workhouse
        Infirmaries 66-66, Exec.


HILL, ALEXANDER STAVELEY (1825-1905)

    King Edward's School, Birm; Exeter, Oxf; Inner
        Temple.
    Judge Advocate of the Fleet 75; Barrister 51;
        College Fellow 54; Q.C. 68; Landowner 81.
    Conservative. MP Coventry 68-74, Staffordshire
        West 74-85, Kingswinford, Staffs 85-00. DL,
        JP.
    PC 92.
    Southwest London; Staffordshire.
    [DNB, WWW, Alum Oxon, Fosters, Dods, Direc Direcs]

    Imperial Federation League (F) 84-84, Exec.


HILL, ALSAGER HAY (1839-1906)

    Brighton College; Trinity Hall, Camb; Inner
        Temple.
    Journal Editor 71; Barrister 64.
    London.
    [DNB, Alum Cantab, Fosters]

    League for Defense of Constitutional Rights 84-84,
        V-Pres.
    Liberty & Property Defense League (F) 82-84, Exec.

London Municipal Reform League 82-85, Exec.
Travelling Tax Abolition Committee 83-85, Exec.


HILL, ARTHUR GEORGE (1857-1923)

Westminster School; Jesus, Camb.
Organ Builder; Antiquary.
Fellow Society of Antiquaries.
Northwest London.
[WWW, Alum Cantab]

Natl Soc for Preserving Memorials of Dead (F)
    81-84, Exec.


HILL, CHARLES

Public Museums & Free Libraries Assn 68-68, Exec.


HILL, FERGUS

Trin Col, Dublin.
Vicar 78; Curate 69; Ordained Priest<CE> 71.
Manchester.
[Crockfds]

Central Assn for Stopping Sale Intox Liquors on
    Sunday 80-80, Exec.


HILL, MATTHEW BERKELEY (1834-1892)

Univ College School; University Col London.
Surgeon 62; Medical School Professor 75.
Fellow Royal Col Surgeons.
West London.
[MEB]

Assn for Improvement of London Workhouse
    Infirmaries 66-66, Exec.
Assn for Promoting Extension of Contagious Diseases
    Act 68-75, Hon Sec.


HILL, MATTHEW DAVENPORT (1792-1872)

Lincoln's Inn.
Q.C. 34; Barrister 19; Bankruptcy Commissioner
    51.
Radical. MP Hull 32-35. JP.
Gloucestershire.
[DNB, MEB, Walfords, Dods]

Assn for Promoting Extension of Contagious Diseases
    Act 68-70, V-Pres.


HILL, OCTAVIA (1838-1912)

Social Worker; Philanthropic Housing Manager.
Northwest London.
[DNB, WWW]

Commons Preservation Soc 76-86, Exec.
Kyrle Soc (F) 77-94, Treas.
Smoke Abatement Committee 81-81.


HILL, P. CARTERET- <"HON.">

Church Assn 85-85, Exec.


HILL, R. A.

London.

Smoke Abatement Committee 81-81.


HILL, ROWLAND, 2ND VISCOUNT HILL (1800-1875)

Oriel, Oxf.
Very Large Landowner 42; Cornet, Army 20.
Conservative. MP Shropshire 21-32, Shropshire
    North 32-42. Lord Lieutenant 45-75.
Baronet 24; Viscount 42.
West London; Shropshire.
[MEB, BP, Walfords, Alum Oxon, Dods, Army List]

Church Assn 67-70, V-Pres.


HILL, THOMAS ( -1875)

Trinity, Camb.
Archdeacon 47; Ordained Priest<CE> 12; Vicar 21;
    Canon 51; Prebendary 51; Curate 51.
Chesterfield.
[MEB, Alum Cantab, Crockfds]

Church Assn 67-70, V-Pres.


HILL, THOMAS ROWLEY (1816-1896)

University Col London.
Liberal. MP Worcester 74-85. DL, JP.
Worcester.
[MEB, Walfords, Dods]

Jamaica Committee (F) 66-66.


HILL, W.

Natl Vigilance Assn (F) 85-85, Exec.


HILLS, JOHN

Sunderland.

Jamaica Committee (F) 66-66.


HILTON, JOHN

Bromley.

Jamaica Committee (F) 66-66.

HILTON, JOHN

>   Anglo-Oriental Soc for Suppression Opium Trade (F)
>       75-75, Exec.

HILTON, JOHN

>   Intl Arbitration & Peace Assn 81-81, Exec.

HILTON, JOHN (1804-1878)

>   Guy's Hospital, Lond.
>   Surgeon 49;  Medical School Lecturer 27;  Asst
>       Surgeon 44;  Medical School Professor 59.
>   Fellow Royal Society;  Fellow Royal Col Surgeons.
>   Clapham.
>   [DNB, MEB]
>
>   Assn for Promoting Extension of Contagious Diseases
>       Act 68-70, V-Pres.

HINDEL, W.  R.

>   Leeds.
>
>   Jamaica Committee (F) 66-66.

HIPSLEY, HENRY

>   Anglo-Oriental Soc for Suppression Opium Trade (F)
>       75-75, Exec.

HITCHMAN, WILLIAM (1822-1888)

>   Guy's Hospital, Lond.
>   Physician 51.
>   Member Royal Col Surgeons.
>   Liverpool.
>   [MEB]
>
>   Malthusian League 81-84, V-Pres.

HOARE, EDWARD (1812-1894)

>   Trinity, Camb.
>   Vicar 47;  Ordained Priest<CE> 36;  Curate 36;
>       Perp. Curate 46;  Hon.  Canon 68.
>   Tunbridge Wells.
>   [Alum Cantab, Crockfds]
>
>   Church Assn 70-75, Exec.

HOARE, G.  H.

>   Ordained Priest<CE>.
>
>   Soc for Promoting Increase of the Home Episcopate
>       72-74, Exec.

HOARE, GURNEY

>   Commons Preservation Soc 69-69, Exec.

HOARE, H.  N.  HAMILTON

>   Banker.
>   London.
>
>   Public Museums & Free Libraries Assn 68-68, Treas.
>   Natl Assn for Promotion of State Colonization
>       83-86, V-Pres, Exec.

HOARE, HAMILTON A.

>   Assn for Improvement of London Workhouse
>       Infirmaries 66-66, Exec.

HOARE, HENRY

>   Soc for Promoting Increase of the Home Episcopate
>       72-74, Treas.

HOARE, JOSEPH

>   Church Assn 67-80, V-Pres, Chairman.

HOARE, RICHARD

>   St.  Bees.
>   Vicar 65;  Curate 57;  Ordained Priest<CE> 58;
>       Perp.  Curate 60.
>   North London.
>   [Crockfds]
>
>   Church Assn 75-75, Exec.

HOBHOUSE, ARTHUR, 1ST BARON HOBHOUSE (1819-1904)

>   Eton;  Balliol, Oxf;  Lincoln's Inn.
>   Law Member, India Council 72;  Barrister 45;  Q.C.
>       62;  Endowed Schools Commissioner 69.
>   Liberal.  Charity Commissioner 66-66, PC Judicial
>       Committee 81-01.
>   KCSI 77;  PC 81;  CIE;  Baron 85.
>   West London.
>   [DNB, WWW, BP, Alum Oxon, Fosters, Direc Direcs]
>
>   Sunday Society 79-90, V-Pres.

HOBHOUSE, HENRY (1854-1937)

>   Eton;  Balliol, Oxf;  Lincoln's Inn.
>   Barrister 80;  Substantial Landowner 62.
>   Liberal(Unionist).  MP Somersetshire East 85-06.
>       Ecclesiastical Commissioner 90-  , JP.
>   PC 02.
>   West London;  Somersetshire.
>   [DNB, WWW, Walfords, Alum Oxon, Fosters, Dods]
>
>   Commons Preservation Soc 86-86, Exec.
>   Free Land League 86-86, V-Pres.

HOBHOUSE, MARY, LADY <WIFE OF 1ST BARON HOBHOUSE, nee
    FARRER> ( -1905)

    West London.
    [BP]

    Natl Footpaths Preservation Soc 86-90, V-Pres.
    Kyrle Soc 84-90, Exec.


HODGE, - <MISS>

    Kyrle Soc 85-94, Exec.


HODGE, GEORGE WILLIAM

    Newcastle-upon-Tyne.

    Assn for Promoting Extension of Contagious Diseases
        Act 70-70, V-Pres.


HODGSON, JOHN EVAN (1831-1895)

    Rugby;  Royal Academy Sch.
    Artist 56.
    Royal Academy.
    St Johns Wood.
    [DNB, MEB, Bryan's Painters]

    Soc for Protection of Ancient Buildings (F) 78-80,
        Exec.


HODGSON, RICHARD (1855-1905)

    U Melbourne.
    College Lecturer 83.
    Cambridge.
    [Alum Cantab, Aust Dict Biog]

    London Soc for Abolition of Compulsory Vaccination
        81-81, V-Pres.


HOGG, JABEZ (1817-1899)

    Hunterian School of Medicine.
    Surgeon 50;  Journalist 43;  Author.
    Member Royal Col Surgeons;  Fellow Linnean Society;
        Royal Microscop Society;  Medical Society of
        Lond.
    West London.
    [DNB, MEB, WWW]

    Smoke Abatement Committee 81-81.


HOLCOMBE, F.  J.

    West Central London.

    Jamaica Committee (F) 66-66.


HOLDEN, ANGUS, 1ST BARON HOLDEN (1833-1912)

    Wesley College, Sheffield;  U Edinburgh.
    Manufacturer.
    Liberal.  MP Bradford East 85-86, Buckrose, Yorks
        ER 92-00.  JP.
    Baronet 97;  Baron 08.
    Bradford.
    [BP, Dods, Direc Direcs]

    Free Land League 86-86, V-Pres.


HOLDEN, FRANCES <MRS. LUTHER HOLDEN, nee STERRY>

    Ipswich.

    Victoria Street Soc for Protection of Animals from
        Vivisection 85-85, Exec.


HOLDEN, SIR ISAAC, 1ST BT.  (1807-1897)

    Woolen Manufacturer.
    Liberal.  MP Knaresborough 65-68, Yorks W Riding
        North 82-85, Keighley, Yorks WR N 85-95.  DL,
        JP.
    Baronet 93.
    Southwest London;  Yorks, West Riding.
    [DNB, MEB, WWW, BP, Walfords, Dods, Direc Direcs]

    Commons Preservation Soc 84-86, Exec.
    Free Land League 86-86, V-Pres.
    Jamaica Committee (F) 66-66.


HOLDEN, ROBERT (1805-1872)

    Christ Church, Oxf.
    Landowner 44.
    DL, JP.
    Nottinghamshire.
    [Walfords, Alum Oxon]

    Church Assn 70-70, Exec.


HOLE, JAMES (1820-1895)

    Educationalist;  Social Reformer.
    Radical.
    Southwest London.
    [MEB, Dic Lab Biog]

    Commons Preservation Soc 69-86, Hon Sec.


HOLL, FRANK (1845-1888)

    Univ College School;  Royal Academy Sch.
    Artist 62.
    Royal Academy;  Royal Society Water Colour
        Painters.
    Northwest London.
    [DNB, MEB, Bryan's Painters]

    Sunday Society 86-88, V-Pres.

HOLLAND, - <MISS>

    British Women´s Temperance Assn 84-84, Secretary.

HOLLAND, CHARLES

    Liverpool.

    Jamaica Committee (F) 66-66.

HOLLAND, H. W.

    Clergyman<Sect Unkn>.
    Leeds.

    Natl Education League 71-71, Exec.

HOLLAND, HENRY

    Birmingham.

    Natl Education League (F) 69-69, Exec.

HOLLAND, SAMUEL (1803-1892)

    Quarry Owner.
    Liberal. MP Merionethshire 70-85. DL, JP.
    Merionethshire.
    [MEB, Walfords, Dods, Direc Direcs]

    Sunday Society 80-90, V-Pres.
    Central Assn for Stopping Sale Intox Liquors on
        Sunday 70-85, V-Pres.
    Intl Arbitration & Peace Assn 81-81, V-Pres.
    Plimsoll and Seamen´s Fund Committee (F) 73-73,
        Exec.

HOLLIDAY, JAMES RICHARDSON (1840-1927)

    St John´s, Camb.
    Solicitor 67.
    Birmingham.
    [Alum Cantab]

    Soc for Protection of Ancient Buildings 80-85,
        Exec.

HOLLIDAY, WILLIAM

    JP.
    Birmingham.
    [Direc Direcs]

    Natl Education League (F) 69-69, Exec.

HOLLOND, EDMUND (1801-1884)

    Haileybury College; Queens´, Camb.
    Substantial Landowner 45; Ordained Priest<CE>.
    West London; Suffolk.
    [MEB, Walfords, Bateman, Alum Cantab, Crockfds]

    Church Assn 67-80, Exec, V-Pres.

HOLLOND, JOHN ROBERT (1843-1912)

    Harrow; Trinity, Camb; Inner Temple.
    Barrister 70; Landowner 84.
    Liberal. MP Brighton 80-85. DL, JP.
    West London; Middlesex.
    [Alum Cantab, Fosters, Dods]

    Commons Preservation Soc 81-86, Exec.

HOLMES, ARTHUR (1836-1875)

    Shrewsbury School; St John´s, Camb.
    College Lecturer 60; Author; College Fellow 60;
        Curate 60; Ordained Priest<CE> 61.
    Cambridge.
    [MEB, Alum Cantab, Crockfds]

    Natl Education Union 71-71, Exec.

HOLMES, G. B.

    East London.

    London Municipal Reform League 82-85, Exec.

HOLMS, JOHN (1830-1891)

    Cotton Manufacturer.
    Liberal. MP Hackney 68-85. Junior Lord Treasury
        80-82, Parl Sec Board of Trade 82-85, DL, JP.
    Fellow Royal Geograph Society.
    Southwest London; Glasgow.
    [MEB, Walfords, Dods, Direc Direcs]

    Commons Preservation Soc 76-86, Exec.
    Public Museums & Free Libraries Assn 68-68, V-Pres.
    Metro Free Libraries Assn 77-77, Exec.
    Natl Emigration League (F) 70-70, V-Pres.
    Natl Assn for Repeal Contagious Diseases Acts
        81-81, V-Pres.

HOLMS, WILLIAM (1827- )

    Cotton Manufacturer.
    Liberal. MP Paisley 74-83. JP.
    Edinburgh.
    [Dods, Direc Direcs]

    Natl Assn for Repeal Contagious Diseases Acts
        81-81, V-Pres.

HOLT, JAMES MADEN (1829-1911)

    Christ Church, Oxf.
    Conservative. MP Lancashire NE 68-80. JP.
    North London; Lancashire.
    [WWW, Alum Oxon, Dods]

    Church Assn 70-85, Chairman.
    Soc for Abolition of Vivisection (F) 75-76, Exec.

HOLT, ROBERT B.

    Land Nationalization Soc 85-85, Exec.


HOLYOAKE, AUSTIN (1826-1874)

    Printer 47;  Publisher.
    Radical.
    London.
    [Dic Lab Biog]

    Natl Secular Soc 70-70, V-Pres.


HOLYOAKE, GEORGE JACOB (1817-1906)

    Journal Editor.
    Radical.
    Southwest London.
    [DNB, WWW, Dic Lab Biog]

    Sunday Society 76-90, V-Pres.
    Natl Secular Soc 77-77, V-Pres.
    Travelling Tax Abolition Committee (F) 77-87,
       Chairman, President.


HOOD, SIR ALEXANDER BATEMAN PERIAM FULLER ACLAND-, 3RD
    BT. (1819-1892)

    Rugby;  Christ Church, Oxf.
    Very Large Landowner 51;  Cornet, Army 37;
       Lieutenant, Army 42;  Captain, Army 46.
    Conservative.  MP Somersetshire West 59-68.  DL,
       JP.
    Baronet 51.
    Somersetshire.
    [BP, Walfords, Bateman, Alum Oxon, Dods, Direc
       Direcs, Army List]

    Assn for Promoting Extension of Contagious Diseases
       Act 68-70, V-Pres.


HOOD, EDWIN PAXTON (1820-1885)

    Congregational Minister 52;  Journal Editor;
       Author.
    Liberal.
    Brighton.
    [DNB, MEB]

    Jamaica Committee (F) 66-66.


HOOLE, ELIJAH

    Smoke Abatement Committee 81-81.


HOOPELL, -

    Clergyman<Sect Unkn>.
    South Shields.

    Natl Assn for Repeal Contagious Diseases Acts
       70-84, Hon Sec.


HOOPER, JAMES

    Land Nationalization Soc (F) 81-84, Exec.


HOPE, - <MISS>

    West London.

    Assn for Improvement of Public Morals 81-81, Exec.


HOPE, ALEXANDER JAMES BERESFORD BERESFORD- (1820-1887)

    Harrow;  Trinity, Camb.
    Large Landowner 54;  Journal Proprietor 55;
       Author;  Art Patron.
    Conservative.  MP Maidstone 41-52, Maidstone 57-59,
       Stoke-on-Trent 65-68, Cambridge University
       68-87.
    PC 80.
    Fellow Royal Geograph Society;  Fellow Society of
       Antiquaries;  Fellow Royal Statistical Society.
    West London;  Kent.
    [DNB, MEB, Bateman, Alum Cantab, Dods]

    Commons Preservation Soc 76-86, Exec.
    City Church & Churchyard Protection Soc (F) 80-83,
       V-Pres.
    Natl Soc for Preserving Memorials of Dead (F)
       81-84, Patron.
    Assn for Improvement of London Workhouse
       Infirmaries 66-66, Exec.
    Soc for Promoting Increase of the Home Episcopate
       72-74, Exec.
    Natl Education Union 70-79, Exec.


HOPES, E.

    Sunday Society 77-77, Exec.


HOPGOOD, JAMES

    JP.
    Clapham.

    Sunday Society 76-90, V-Pres.


HOPKINS, ELICE <MISS>

    Natl Vigilance Assn (F) 85-85, Exec.


HOPPS, JOHN PAGE (1834-1911)

    Leicester Baptist College.
    Baptist Minister 55;  Unitarian Minister;  Journal
       Editor 63.
    Leicester.
    [WWW]

    Sunday Society 76-90, V-Pres.

HOPWOOD, CHARLES HENRY (1829-1904)

King´s College School; Kings Col London; Middle
    Temple.
Q.C. 74; Barrister 53.
Liberal. MP Stockport 74-85, Middleton,Lancs SE
    92-95.
St Johns Wood.
[DNB, Fosters, Dods]

Sunday Society 79-90, V-Pres.
Intl Arbitration & Peace Assn 81-81, V-Pres.


HORE, EDMUND CREEK

St. Bees.
Rector 60; Ordained Priest<CE> 55; Curate.
Manchester.
[Crockfds]

Central Assn for Stopping Sale Intox Liquors on
    Sunday (F) 67-75, Exec.


HORN, W. WILSON


Travelling Tax Abolition Committee 82-85, Exec.


HORNBY, EDWARD KENWORTHY (1839-1887)

Harrow.
Cotton Manufacturer.
Conservative. MP Blackburn 69-74. JP.
Southwest London; Blackburn; Cheshire.
[MEB, Walfords, Dods]

Natl Emigration League (F) 70-70, V-Pres.


HORNER, J. A.

Northwest London.

Jamaica Committee (F) 66-66.


HORNIMAN, JOHN (1803-1893)

Tea Merchant; Grocer.
Croydon.
[MEB]

Jamaica Committee (F) 66-66.


HORSFALL, THOMAS BERRY (1805-1878)

Merchant.
Conservative. MP Derby 52-53, Liverpool 53-68.
    DL, JP.
Liverpool; Staffordshire.
[MEB, Walfords, Dods]

Church Assn 67-75, V-Pres.


HORSFALL, THOMAS COGLAN (1841-1932)

Educationalist.
Manchester.
[WWW]

Sunday Society 79-90, V-Pres.


HORSLEY, JOHN WILLIAM (1845-1921)

King´s School, Canterbury; Pembroke, Oxf.
Prison Chaplain 76; Curate 70; Ordained
    Priest<CE> 72; Vicar 89; Rector 94; Hon.
    Canon 03.
East Central London.
[DNB, WWW, Alum Oxon, Crockfds]

Assn for Improvement of Public Morals 81-81, Exec.
Natl Vigilance Assn (F) 85-85, Exec.


HORSLEY, WILLIAM HENRY

Colonel, RE 62; 2nd Lt., RE 29; Lieutenant, RE
    38; Captain, RE 44; Major, RE 54; Lt.
    Colonel, RE 60.
Canterbury.
[Army List]

Church Assn 70-75, Exec.


HORTON, WILLIAM

Allotments & Small Holdings Assn 85-85, Exec.


HOULDER, A.

Natl Emigration League (F) 70-70, Exec.


HOULDSWORTH, JAMES

Church Assn 70-85, Exec.


HOULDSWORTH, SIR WILLIAM HENRY, 1ST BT. (1834-1917)

U St Andrews.
Cotton Manufacturer; Landowner.
Conservative. MP Manchester 83-85, Manchester
    Northwest 85-06. DL.
Baronet 87.
Southwest London; Manchester; Cheshire.
[WWW, BP, Dods, Direc Direcs]

Central Assn for Stopping Sale Intox Liquors on
    Sunday 85-85, V-Pres.


HOW, WILLIAM WALSHAM (1823-1897)

Shrewsbury School; Wadham, Oxf; Durham Theo.
Bishop Bedford<Suffragan> 79; Curate 46; Ordained
    Priest<CE> 47; Rector 51; Rural Dean 54;
    Hon. Canon 60; Bishop Wakefield 88.
East London.
[DNB, MEB, WWW, Alum Oxon, Crockfds]

Natl Assn for Promotion of State Colonization
    86-86, V-Pres.

Natl Soc for Preserving Memorials of Dead (F)
    81-84, Patron.
Natl Vigilance Assn (F) 85-85, Exec.


HOWARD, A.


English Land Restoration League 85-85, Exec.


HOWARD, EDWARD GEORGE FITZ-ALAN, 1ST BARON HOWARD OF
    GLOSSOP (1818-1883)

Eton;  Trinity, Camb.
Very Large Landowner 71.
Liberal.  MP Horsham 48-52, Arundel 52-68.
    V-Chamberlain Royal Household 46-52, DL, JP.
PC 46;  Baron 69.
Southwest London;  Inverness-shire;  Derbyshire.
[DNB, MEB, BP, Walfords, Bateman, Alum Cantab,
    Dods]

Natl Education Union (F) 69-79, Exec.


HOWARD, GEORGE JAMES, 9TH EARL OF CARLISLE (1843-1911)

Eton;  Trinity, Camb.
Very Large Landowner 89;  Artist.
Liberal(Unionist).  MP Cumberland East 79-80,
    Cumberland East 81-85.  JP.
Earl 89.
West London;  Yorks, West Riding;  Cumberland.
[DNB, WWW, BP, Alum Cantab, Dods]

Sunday Society 84-90, V-Pres, President.
Soc for Protection of Ancient Buildings (F) 78-85,
    Exec.
Eastern Question Assn (F) 76-77, Hon Sec.


HOWARD, HENRY FITZALAN, 15TH DUKE OF NORFOLK (1847-1917)

Very Large Landowner 60.
Conservative.  Postmaster General 95-00, Lord
    Lieutenant 05-  , JP.
Duke 60;  KG;  PC;  GCVO.
Southwest London;  Sussex;  Yorks, West Riding.
[DNB, WWW, BP, Walfords]

Natl Soc for Preserving Memorials of Dead 84-84,
    Patron.


HOWARD, JAMES (1821-1889)

Farmer 62;  Farm Equipment Manufacturer 51.
Liberal.  MP Bedford 68-74, Bedfordshire 80-85.
    DL, JP.
Royal Agricultural Society.
Bedfordshire.
[DNB, MEB, Walfords, Dods]

Free Land League 86-86, V-Pres, Exec.
Howard Assn 69-73, Patron.


HOWARD, MORGAN

East London.

Natl Education Union 70-79, Exec.


HOWE, - <MRS.>

Sunday Society 86-90, Exec.


HOWELL, GEORGE (1833-1910)

Labour Leader;  Journalist;  Bricklayer 53.
Radical.  MP Bethnal Green NE 85-95.
Fellow Royal Statistical Society.
Shepherds Bush.
[DNB, Dods, Direc Direcs, Dic Lab Biog]

Intl Arbitration & Peace Assn 81-81, Exec.
Plimsoll and Seamen's Fund Committee (F) 73-75,
    Secretary.
Travelling Tax Abolition Committee (F) 77-85, Exec.
Working Men's Comtee Promoting Separation Church
    and State (F) 71-72, Chairman.
Natl Education League 71-71, Exec.


HOWELL, W.  H.

Gloucester.

Travelling Tax Abolition Committee 80-85, Exec.


HOYLE, ISAAC (1828-1911)

Cotton Manufacturer.
Liberal.  MP Heywood, Lancs SE 85-92.  JP.
Heywood, Lancs;  Lancashire.
[Dods]

Central Assn for Stopping Sale Intox Liquors on
    Sunday 85-85, V-Pres.
Free Land League 86-86, V-Pres.


HOYLE, WILLIAM (1831-1886)

Cotton Manufacturer 51.
Tottington, Lancs.
[DNB, MEB]

Central Assn for Stopping Sale Intox Liquors on
    Sunday (F) 67-80, Exec.


HUBBARD, JOHN GELLIBRAND, 1ST BARON ADDINGTON
    (1805-1889)

Russia Merchant 21;  Substantial Landowner;
    Governor, Bank of England;  Chm, Public Works
    Loan Commission 53.
Conservative.  MP Buckingham 59-68, City 74-87.
    DL, JP.
PC 74;  Baron 87.
Fellow Royal Geograph Society.
West London;  Buckinghamshire.
[DNB, MEB, BP, Walfords, Bateman, Dods, Direc
    Direcs]

Soc for Promoting Increase of the Home Episcopate
    72-74, Exec.

HUGGINS, SAMUEL (1811-1885)

    Architect.
    Denbighshire.
    [DNB, MEB]

    Soc for Protection of Ancient Buildings (F) 78-80,
        Exec.


HUGHES, GEORGE

    JP.
    Deal.

    Sunday Society 76-77, V-Pres.


HUGHES, HUGH PRICE (1847-1902)

    University Col London;  Wesleyan Theological
        College, Richmond.
    Wesleyan Minister 69;  Journal Editor 85.
    Peckham.
    [DNB, WWW, Wesl Min]

    Assn for Improvement of Public Morals (F) 79-81,
        Exec.
    Natl Vigilance Assn (F) 85-85, Exec.


HUGHES, JOSHUA (1807-1889)

    St Davids Lampeter.
    Bishop St Asaph 70;  Curate 30;  Ordained
        Priest<CE> 31;  Vicar 39.
    St Asaph.
    [DNB, MEB, Crockfds]

    Central Assn for Stopping Sale Intox Liquors on
        Sunday 75-85, V-Pres.


HUGHES, THOMAS (1822-1896)

    Rugby;  Oriel, Oxf;  Inner Temple.
    Barrister 48;  Q.C. 69;  County Court Judge 82;
        Author.
    Liberal.  MP Lambeth 65-68, Somersetshire Frome
        68-74.
    Fellow Society of Antiquaries.
    West London.
    [DNB, MEB, Walfords, Alum Oxon, Fosters, Dods,
        Direc Direcs]

    Commons Preservation Soc (F) 65-86, Exec.
    Public Museums & Free Libraries Assn 68-68, V-Pres.
    Metro Free Libraries Assn 78-78, Exec.
    Anglo-Oriental Soc for Suppression Opium Trade (F)
        75-86, Exec.
    Assn for Improvement of London Workhouse
        Infirmaries 66-66, Exec.
    Jamaica Committee (F) 66-66.
    Plimsoll and Seamen's Fund Committee (F) 73-73,
        V-Chairman.


HULEATT, HUGH (1823- )

    Trin Col, Dublin.
    Vicar 79;  Curate 48;  Ordained Priest<CE> 49;
        Army Chaplain 54.
    East London;  Shalford, Surrey.
    [Crockfds, Army List]

    Natl Assn for Promotion of State Colonization
        86-86, Exec.


HULSE, SIR EDWARD, 5TH BT. (1809-1899)

    Eton;  Christ Church, Oxf.
    Large Landowner 54;  College Fellow 29.
    Conservative.  DL, JP.
    Baronet 54.
    West London;  Hampshire.
    [MEB, WWW, BP, Walfords, Bateman, Alum Oxon]

    Natl Emigration League (F) 70-70, V-Pres.


HUME, MARTIN ANDREW SHARP (1843-1910)

    Historian;  College Lecturer.
    Liberal.
    West London.
    [DNB, WWW]

    London Municipal Reform League 82-85, Exec.


HUMPHRY, GEORGE MURRAY (1820-1896)

    St Bartholomew's Hosp.
    Surgeon 42;  Professor of Human Anatomy, Cambridge
        66.
    Kt 93.
    Fellow Royal Society;  Fellow Royal Col Surgeons;
        Br Medical Assn;  Pathological Society.
    Cambridge.
    [DNB, Direc Direcs]

    Sanitary Institute 78-89, V-Pres.


HUNT, ALFRED WILLIAM (1830-1896)

    Liverpool College;  Corpus Christi, Oxf;  Royal
        Academy Sch.
    Artist 54;  College Fellow 53.
    Royal Society Water Colour Painters.
    West London.
    [DNB, MEB, Alum Oxon, Bryan's Painters]

    Soc for Protection of Ancient Buildings (F) 78-85,
        Exec.


HUNT, GEORGE WARD (1825-1877)

    Eton;  Christ Church, Oxf;  Inner Temple.
    Politician;  Barrister 51.
    Conservative.  MP Northamptonshire N 57-77.  Sec
        Treasury 66-68, Chancellor Exchequer 68-68,
        First Lord Admiralty 74-77, Education
        Committee, DL, JP.
    PC 68.
    Southwest London;  Northamptonshire.
    [DNB, MEB, Walfords, Alum Oxon, Dods]

    Soc for Promoting Increase of the Home Episcopate
        72-74, Exec.

HUNT, MARION EDITH HOLMAN <MRS. WILLIAM HOLMAN HUNT, nee
    WAUGH>

    West London.

    Sunday Society 80-90, V-Pres.


HUNT, WILFRED

    Sunday Society (F) 75-75, Exec.


HUNT, WILLIAM HOLMAN (1827-1910)

    Royal Academy Sch.
    Artist 46.
    OM 05.
    West London.
    [DNB, WWW]

    Sunday Society 80-90, V-Pres.
    City Church & Churchyard Protection Soc (F) 80-83,
        V-Pres.
    Soc for Protection of Ancient Buildings (F) 78-85,
        Exec.


HUNTER, JAMES (1817-1882)

    Church Mission College, Islington.
    Vicar 67;  Ordained Priest<CE> 44;   School Master;
        Archdeacon 54.
    West London.
    [MEB, Crockfds]

    Church Assn 75-80, Exec.


HUNTER, SIR ROBERT (1844-1913)

    London U.
    Solicitor 67;   General Post Office Solicitor 82.
    Liberal.  JP.
    Kt 94;  CB 09;  KCB 11.
    Haslemere.
    [DNB, WWW]

    Commons Preservation Soc 83-86, Exec.
    Kyrle Soc 84-94, Exec.


HUNTER, WILLIAM ALEXANDER (1844-1898)

    Aberdeen Grammar School;  U Aberdeen;  Middle
        Temple.
    Barrister 67;  Professor of Roman Law, U Col London
        69;  Professor of Jurisprudence, U Col London
        78.
    Liberal.  MP Aberdeen North 85-96.
    London;  Aberdeenshire.
    [DNB, WWW, Fosters, Dods, Direc Direcs]

    Land Tenure Reform Assn 73-73, Exec.
    Natl Assn for Repeal Blasphemy Laws (F) 84-84,
        Exec.


HUNTLEY, JOSEPH

    Reading.

    Jamaica Committee (F) 66-66.


HURST, GEORGE

    JP.

    Howard Assn 67-84, Exec.


HUSSEY, H.  S.  L.

    Commons Preservation Soc 69-76, Exec.


HUTCHINSON, EDWARD

    Anglo-Oriental Soc for Suppression Opium Trade (F)
        75-75, Exec.


HUTCHINSON, JOHN DYSON (1822-1882)

    Newspaper Proprietor.
    Radical.  MP Halifax 77-82.  JP.
    Yorks, West Riding.
    [MEB, Dods]

    Natl Education League 71-71, Exec.


HUTCHINSON, SIR JONATHAN (1828-1913)

    St Bartholomew's Hosp.
    Surgeon 56;   Medical School Lecturer 62;   Medical
        School Professor;   Small Landowner.
    Kt 08.
    Fellow Royal Col Surgeons;   Fellow Royal Society.
    East Central London;   Surrey.
    [DNB, WWW, Alum Cantab]

    Assn for Promoting Extension of Contagious Diseases
        Act 68-70, V-Pres.


HUTCHISON, G.  A.

    Fellow Royal Statistical Society.

    Public Museums & Free Libraries Assn 68-68, Exec.


HUTH, EDWARD

    Huddersfield.

    Natl Education League 71-71, Exec.


HUTT, SIR WILLIAM (1801-1882)

    Trinity, Camb.
    Landowner;  Colliery Owner;  RN<rank unknown>.
    Liberal.  MP Hull 32-41, Gateshead 41-74.  V-P
        Board of Trade 60-65, Paymaster General 60-65,
        JP.
    PC 60;  KCB 65.
    West London;  Isle of Wight;  Durham[County].
    [DNB, MEB, BP, Walfords, Alum Cantab, Alum Oxon,
        Dods]

Assn for Promoting Extension of Contagious Diseases
Act 70-70, V-Pres.


HUTTON, HENRY DIX

Anglo-French Intervention Committee (F) 70-70,
Exec.


HUTTON, J. E.

East Central London;  Sheffield.

Railway Passengers' Protection Assn 86-86, Hon Sec.


HUTTON, JAMES FREDERICK (1826-1890)

Kings Col London.
Africa Merchant;  Cotton Manufacturer.
Conservative.  MP Manchester North 85-86.  JP.
Fellow Royal Geograph Society.
Manchester.
[Dods, Direc Direcs]

Natl Assn for Promotion of State Colonization
86-86, V-Pres.


HUTTON, JOHN (1847-1921)

Eton;  Christ Church, Oxf.
Landowner 57.
Conservative.  MP Northallerton 68-74, Richmond,
Yorks NR 95-06.  DL, JP.
Yorks, North Riding.
[Walfords, Alum Oxon, Dods]

Natl Emigration League (F) 70-70, V-Pres.


HUTTON, WILLIAM

Trin Col, Dublin;  Durham Theo.
Rector 57;  Curate 50;  Ordained Priest<CE> 52;
Vicar 75.
Manchester;  Norwell.
[Crockfds]

Central Assn for Stopping Sale Intox Liquors on
Sunday (F).67-85, Exec.


HUXLEY, THOMAS HENRY (1825-1895)

Ealing School;  London U.
Biologist;  Author;  Asst Surgeon, RN Medical Serv
46;  Medical School Professor 63;  Ld Rector, U
Aberdeen 72;  Inspector Fisheries 81.
PC 92.
Fellow Royal Society;  Fellow Geological Society;
Ethnological Society;  Fellow Royal Col
Surgeons.
London.
[DNB, MEB, Alum Oxon, Navy List]

Sunday Society 76-90, V-Pres.


HUYSHE, WENTWORTH

Natl Soc for Preserving Memorials of Dead (F)
81-82, Exec.


HYDE, J. M.

West London.

Natl Fair Trade League (F) 81-81, Exec.


HYDE, JOSEPH

Travelling Tax Abolition Committee 82-84, Exec.


HYDE, T. RALPH

Sussex.

Natl Soc for Preserving Memorials of Dead (F)
81-82, Exec.


IBBETSON, HENRY JOHN SELWIN-, 1ST BARON ROOKWOOD
(1826-1902)

St John's, Camb.
Substantial Landowner 69.
Conservative.  MP Essex South 65-68, Essex West
68-85, Epping 85-92.  Parl U-Sec Home Off
74-78, Sec Treasury 78-80, Church Estates
Commissioner 85-86, Church Estates Commissioner
86-92, DL, JP.
Baronet 69;  PC 85;  Baron 92.
Southwest London;  Essex.
[DNB, WWW, BP, Walfords, Bateman, Alum Cantab,
Dods, Direc Direcs]

Natl Education Union 70-71, Exec.


ILBERT, SIR COURTENAY PEREGRINE (1841-1924)

Marlborough;  Balliol, Oxf;  Lincoln's Inn.
Barrister 69;  College Fellow 64;  Puisne Judge,
Bombay 79;  Law Member, India Council 82;  Asst
Counsel to Treasury 86;  Counsel to Treasury
99;  Clerk, House of Commons 02.
CIE 82;  CSI 85;  KCSI 95;  KCB 08;  GCB 11.
Southwest London;  Buckinghamshire.
[DNB, WWW, Alum Oxon, Fosters]

Commons Preservation Soc 80-86, Exec.


ILLINGWORTH, ALFRED (1827-1907)

Worsted Manufacturer;  Merchant.
Liberal.  MP Knaresborough 68-74, Bradford 80-85,
Bradford West 85-95.
Southwest London;  Bradford.
[WWW, Walfords, Dods, Direc Direcs]

Free Land League 86-86, V-Pres.
Howard Assn 69-73, Patron.
Jamaica Committee (F) 66-66.

IMPEY, FREDERIC

    Allotments & Small Holdings Assn 85-88, Hon Sec.

INGLIS, CORNELIUS

    Trinity, Camb;  Edinburgh(Medical).
    Surgeon 53.
    Member Royal Col Surgeons.
    West London.
    [Alum Cantab]

    Assn for Promoting Extension of Contagious Diseases
        Act 68-68, Exec.

INGRAM, GEORGE S.

    Richmond.

    Jamaica Committee (F) 66-66.

INGRAM, HENRY MANNING (1824-1911)

    Westminster School;  Trinity, Camb.
    School Master 61;  Curate 50;  Ordained Priest<CE>
        51;  Chaplain 52;  Rector 79.
    Southwest London.
    [Alum Cantab, Crockfds]

    Soc for Promoting Increase of the Home Episcopate
        72-74, Exec.

INGRAM, SIR WILLIAM JAMES, 1ST BT.  (1847-1924)

    Winchester College;  Trinity, Camb;  Inner Temple.
    Barrister 72;  Newspaper Manager;  Landowner 60.
    Liberal.  MP Boston 74-80, Boston 85-86, Boston
        92-95.  JP.
    Baronet 93.
    Southwest London;  Surrey.
    [WWW, BP, Walfords, Alum Cantab, Fosters, Dods,
        Direc Direcs]

    Free Land League 86-86, V-Pres.

INNS, RICHARD

    JP.
    Barnsley.
    [Direc Direcs]

    Church Assn 75-78, Exec.

INSKIP, JAMES

    Solicitor.
    Bristol.
    [Direc Direcs]

    Church Assn 85-85, Exec.

INSLEY, WILLIAM PIMBLETT (1840- )

    Wadham, Oxf.
    Rector 80;  Curate 63;  Ordained Priest<CE> 64;
        Vicar 71.
    East London.
    [Alum Oxon, Crockfds]

    Natl Assn for Promotion of State Colonization
        86-86, V-Pres, Exec.

INSULL, SAMUEL

    Proportional Representation Soc (F) 84-84,
        Secretary.

IRVING, SIR HENRY (1838-1905)

    Actor;  Theatre Manager 78.
    Kt 95.
    West London.
    [DNB, WWW, Alum Cantab]

    City Church & Churchyard Protection Soc (F) 80-83,
        V-Pres.
    Natl Soc for Preserving Memorials of Dead 84-88,
        Exec.

ISAACS, ALBERT AUGUSTUS ( -1903)

    Corpus Christi, Camb.
    Vicar 66;  Curate 50;  Ordained Priest<CE> 51;
        Prison Chaplain 75.
    Leicester.
    [Alum Cantab, Alum Oxon, Crockfds]

    Church Assn 70-85, Exec.

ISBISTER, ALEXANDER KENNEDY (1822-1883)

    U Edinburgh;  Middle Temple.
    School Head 55;  Asst School Master 49;  School
        Master 50;  Journal Editor 62;  Barrister 64.
    North London.
    [DNB, MEB]

    Jamaica Committee (F) 66-66.

JACKSON, -

    Canon.

    Intl Arbitration & Peace Assn 81-81, V-Pres.

JACKSON, - <MISS>

    Kyrle Soc 85-85, Exec.

JACKSON, EDWARD

    Central Assn for Stopping Sale Intox Liquors on
       Sunday 70-80, Exec.


JACKSON, SIR HENRY MATHER, 2ND BT. (1831-1881)

    St David's College School; Trinity, Camb;
       Lincoln's Inn.
    Q.C. 73; Barrister 55; Substantial Landowner.
    Liberal. MP Coventry 67-68, Coventry 74-81. DL.
    Baronet 76.
    West London.
    [MEB, BP, Alum Oxon, Dods]

    Howard Assn 78-80, Patron.


JACKSON, JOHN (1811-1885)

    Pembroke, Oxf.
    Bishop London 69; Ordained Priest<CE> 36; School
       Head 36; Rector 46; Canon 52; Bishop Lincoln
       53.
    PC 69.
    Southwest London.
    [DNB, MEB, Alum Oxon, Crockfds]

    Metro Free Libraries Assn 77-77, President.
    Central Assn for Stopping Sale Intox Liquors on
       Sunday 75-85, V-Pres.
    Natl Education Union 70-79, Exec.


JACOBSON, WILLIAM (1803-1884)

    Lincoln, Oxf.
    Bishop Chester 65; Private Tutor 27; College
       Fellow 29; Curate 30; Ordained Priest<CE> 31;
       Rector 48; Regius Professor of Divinity,
       Oxford 48.
    Liberal.
    Chester.
    [DNB, MEB, Alum Oxon]

    Central Assn for Stopping Sale Intox Liquors on
       Sunday 80-80, V-Pres.


JACOBY, SIR JAMES ALFRED (1852-1909)

    Lace Manufacturer.
    Liberal. MP Derbyshire Mid 85-09.
    Kt 06.
    Fellow Royal Statistical Society.
    Southwest London; Nottingham.
    [WWW, Dods]

    Free Land League 86-86, V-Pres.


JAFFRAY, SIR JOHN, 1ST BT. (1818-1901)

    Glasgow High School.
    Newspaper Proprietor; Banker.
    Liberal. DL, JP.
    Baronet 92.
    Birmingham; Warwickshire.
    [WWW, BP, Direc Direcs]

    Natl Education League (F) 69-71, Treas.


JAMES, HENRY, 1ST BARON HEREFORD (1828-1911)

    Cheltenham College; Middle Temple.
    Q.C. 69; Barrister 52.
    Liberal(Unionist). MP Taunton 68-85, Bury 85-86,
       Bury 86-95. Solicitor General 73-73, Attorney
       General 73-74, Attorney General 80-85, Chanc
       Duchy Lancaster 95-02, PC Judicial Committee
       96-  .
    Kt 73; PC 85; Baron 95; GCVO 02.
    Southwest London; Wiltshire.
    [DNB, WWW, BP, Walfords, Alum Cantab, Fosters,
       Dods]

    Natl Footpaths Preservation Soc 86-90, V-Pres.


JAMES, JOHN HUTCHISON (1816-1891)

    Wesleyan Minister 39; School Head 62.
    London.
    [WWW, Wesl Min]

    Central Assn for Stopping Sale Intox Liquors on
       Sunday 75-75, V-Pres.


JAMES, LILIAN <MISS>

    Kyrle Soc 85-94, Hon Sec.


JAMES, WALTER CHARLES, 1ST BARON NORTHBOURNE (1816-1893)

    Westminster School; Christ Church, Oxf.
    Large Landowner 29.
    Conservative. MP Hull 37-47. DL, JP.
    Baronet 29; Baron 84.
    Southwest London; Kent.
    [MEB, BP, Walfords, Bateman, Dods, Direc Direcs]

    Soc for Promoting Increase of the Home Episcopate
       72-74, Exec.
    Natl Education Union 71-79, Exec.


JAMES, WALTER HENRY, 2ND BARON NORTHBOURNE (1846-1923)

    St Peter's College, Radley; Christ Church, Oxf;
       Lincoln's Inn.
    Liberal. MP Gateshead 74-93. DL, JP.
    Baron 93.
    West London; Kent.
    [WWW, BP, Bateman, Alum Oxon, Dods]

    Commons Preservation Soc 80-86, Exec.
    Travelling Tax Abolition Committee 80-85, Exec.


JAMESON, WILLIAM

    English Land Restoration League 85-85, Exec.
    Land Nationalization Soc 85-85, Exec.

JARDINE, JOHN

    Church Assn 67-80, Exec.

JEFFERY, ALFRED

    West London.

    Jamaica Committee (F) 66-66.

JENCKEN, HENRY DIEDRICH (1828-1881)

    Lincoln's Inn.
    Barrister 61.
    West London.
    [MEB]

    Intl Law Assn (F) 73-81, Hon Sec.

JENKINS, -

    Canon.
    Welshpool.

    Central Assn for Stopping Sale Intox Liquors on
        Sunday 70-75, V-Pres.

JENKINS, DAVID JAMES (1824-1891)

    Shipowner;  Merchant.
    Liberal.  MP Penryn & Falmouth 74-86.
    North London.
    [MEB, Dods]

    Intl Arbitration & Peace Assn 81-81, V-Pres.

JENKINS, EBENEZER EVANS (1820-1905)

    Wesleyan Minister 45.
    London.
    [DNB, Wesl Min]

    Anglo-Oriental Soc for Suppression Opium Trade
        83-83, Exec.

JENKINS, JOHN EDWARD (1838-1910)

    McGill;  Lincoln's Inn.
    Barrister 64;  Novelist.
    Liberal, then Conservative.  MP Dundee 74-80.
    Southwest London.
    [DNB, WWW, Fosters, Dods]

    Howard Assn 74-76, Patron.
    Natl Emigration League (F) 70-70, Secretary.

JENNER, SIR WILLIAM, 1ST BT.  (1815-1898)

    University Col London.
    Physician 37;  Professor of Pathological Anatomy, U
        Col London 49.
    Baronet 68;  KCB 72;  GCB 89.
    Fellow Royal Society;  Fellow Royal Col Physicians;
        Epidemiological Society of London;
        Pathological Society.
    West London.
    [DNB, MEB, WWW, BP, Alum Oxon, Direc Direcs]

    Assn for Promoting Extension of Contagious Diseases
        Act 68-68, V-Pres.
    Assn for Improvement of London Workhouse
        Infirmaries 66-66, Exec.

JEPHSON, ARTHUR WILLIAM (1853-1935)

    Corpus Christi, Camb.
    Vicar 81;  Curate 76;  Ordained Priest<CE> 77;
        Rector 08.
    London.
    [WWW, Alum Cantab, Crockfds]

    Natl Vigilance Assn (F) 85-85, Exec.

JERVOISE, SIR JERVOISE CLARKE-, 2ND BT.  (1804-1889)

    Corpus Christi, Oxf.
    Landowner.
    Liberal.  MP Hampshire South 57-68.  DL.
    Baronet 52.
    West London;  Hampshire.
    [MEB, BP, Walfords, Alum Oxon, Dods]

    Assn for Promoting Extension of Contagious Diseases
        Act 68-70, V-Pres.
    London Soc for Abolition of Compulsory Vaccination
        81-81, V-Pres.

JESSE, GEORGE RICHARD (1820-1898)

    Civil Engineer.
    Henbury, Cheshire.
    [MEB]

    Soc for Abolition of Vivisection (F) 75-86, Hon
        Sec.

JEVONS, WILLIAM STANLEY (1835-1882)

    University Col London.
    Professor of Political Economy, U Col London 76;
        Political Economist;  Author;  College Tutor
        63;  College Fellow 64.
    Fellow Royal Society.
    Northwest London.
    [MEB]

    Metro Free Libraries Assn 77-82, Exec.

JOBSON, ROBERT

    London.

    Jamaica Committee (F) 66-66.

JOCELYN, ROBERT, 3RD EARL OF RODEN (1788-1870)

    Harrow.
    Very Large Landowner 20.
    Conservative.  MP Louth Co 10-20.  Treas Royal
        Household 12-12, V-Chamberlain Royal Household
        12-21, DL, JP.
    Earl 20;  KP 21;  PC.
    Edinburgh.
    [DNB, MEB, BP]

    Church Assn 67-70, V-Pres.

JODRELL, SIR EDWARD REPPS, 3RD BT. (1825-1882)

    Eton; New Inn Hall, Oxf.
    Large Landowner 61; Ordained Priest<CE> 51;
      Rector 55.
    JP.
    Baronet 61.
    West London; Norfolk.
    [MEB, BP, Walfords, Bateman, Alum Oxon, Crockfds]

    City Church & Churchyard Protection Soc 81-83,
      V-Pres.


JODRELL, LUCINDA EMMA MARIA, LADY <Wife of E.R.
    JODRELL, 3RD BT., nee GARDEN> (1825-1888)

    West London; Norfolk.
    [BP]

    City Church & Churchyard Protection Soc 83-83,
      V-Pres.


JOHNS, JASPER WILSON (1824-1891)

    Iron Merchant 54; Civil Engineer.
    Liberal. MP Warwickshire NE 85-86. DL, JP.
    Southwest London.
    [MEB, Dods, Direc Direcs]

    Natl Assn for Promotion of State Colonization
      86-86, V-Pres.
    Free Land League 86-86, V-Pres.


JOHNSON, - <MISS>

    Kyrle Soc 84-90, Exec.


JOHNSON, EDWARD

    Natl Education Union 70-86, Secretary.


JOHNSON, G. J.

    Birmingham.

    Natl Education League (F) 69-69, Exec.


JOHNSON, JOSEPH

    Clergyman<Sect Unkn>.

    Central Assn for Stopping Sale Intox Liquors on
      Sunday 85-85, Exec.


JOHNSON, JOSEPH WILLIAM (1832- )

    Trinity, Camb.
    Assoc Sec, Irish Church Mission 78; Curate 60;
      School Head 61; Ordained Priest<CE> 61; Vicar
      92; Rector 98.
    Leamington.
    [Alum Cantab, Crockfds]

    Church Assn 80-85, Exec.


JOHNSON, RICHARD

    Liverpool.

    Jamaica Committee (F) 66-66.


JOHNSON, WILLIAM

    Cambridge.

    Jamaica Committee (F) 66-66.


JOHNSTON, ANDREW (1835-1922)

    Rugby; University Col, Oxf.
    Iron Manufacturer; Landowner 62.
    Liberal. MP Essex South 68-74. DL, JP.
    West London; Essex; Suffolk.
    [WWW, Walfords, Alum Oxon, Dods, Direc Direcs]

    Commons Preservation Soc (F) 65-86, Chairman.


JOHNSTON, WILLIAM (1829-1902)

    Trin Col, Dublin.
    Barrister 72; Novelist; Landowner; Irish
      Fisheries Inspector 78.
    Conservative. MP Belfast 68-78, Belfast South
      85-02.
    Co Down.
    [DNB, WWW, Walfords, Dods]

    Plimsoll and Seamen's Fund Committee (F) 73-73,
      Exec.


JOHNSTONE, HARCOURT VANDEN BEMPDE, 1ST BARON DERWENT
    (1829-1916)

    Eton.
    Very Large Landowner 69; Sub-Lt., Army 46;
      Lieutenant, Army.
    Liberal. MP Scarborough 69-80. DL, JP.
    Baronet 69; Baron 81.
    West London; Yorks, North Riding.
    [WWW, BP, Walfords, Bateman, Dods, Army List]

    Sunday Society 78-90, V-Pres.


JOHNSTONE, HENRY ALEXANDER MUNRO BUTLER (1837-1902)

    Eton; Christ Church, Oxf.
    Very Large Landowner 79.
    Conservative. MP Canterbury 62-78. DL, JP.
    West London; Ross-shire.
    [Bateman, Alum Oxon, Dods]

    Assn for Promoting Extension of Contagious Diseases
      Act 68-70, V-Pres.


JOHNSTONE, J. D.

    Natl Education Union 70-71, Exec.

JOICEY, JAMES, 1ST BARON JOICEY (1846-1936)

>Partner, Mining Engineering Firm 67;  Colliery
>    Owner 96;  Landowner.
>Liberal.  MP Chester-le-Street, Durham 85-06.  DL,
>    JP.
>Baronet 93;  Baron 05.
>West London;  Northumberland.
>[DNB, WWW, BP, Dods, Direc Direcs]
>
>Free Land League 86-86, V-Pres.

JOINER, -

>Workmen's Peace Assn 75-75, Exec.

JONES, - <MISS>

>Natl Vigilance Assn (F) 85-85, Exec.

JONES, A. R.

>JP.
>Montgomery.
>
>Central Assn for Stopping Sale Intox Liquors on
>    Sunday 70-70, V-Pres.

JONES, ALFRED ( -1896)

>Kings Col London.
>School Head 64;  Curate 49;  Ordained Priest<CE>
>    50;  Chaplain 54;  Vicar 77.
>North London.
>[MEB, Crockfds]
>
>Public Museums & Free Libraries Assn 68-68, Exec.
>Soc for Promoting Increase of the Home Episcopate
>    66-75, Secretary.

JONES, ALFRED

>Methodist Free Church Minister.
>
>Central Assn for Stopping Sale Intox Liquors on
>    Sunday 85-85, V-Pres.

JONES, ALFRED STOWELL (1832-1920)

>Liverpool College;  Royal Military College,
>    Sandhurst.
>Sewerage Engineer;  Ensign, Army 52;  Lieutenant,
>    Army 55;  Captain, Army 58;  Major 60;  Lt.
>    Colonel 71;  Manager, Aldershot Sewerage Works
>    92.
>JP.
>VC 57.
>Assoc Inst Civ Engineers.
>Denbighshire.
>[WWW, Army List]
>
>Sanitary Institute 78-84, Exec.

JONES, EDMUND

>Working Men's Natl League for Abolition State
>    Regulation of Vice 82-82, President.

JONES, SIR EDWARD COLEY BURNE-, 1ST BT.  (1833-1898)

>King Edward's School, Birm;  Exeter, Oxf.
>Artist.
>Baronet 94.
>Royal Society Water Colour Painters;  Assoc Royal
>    Academy.
>Southwest London.
>[DNB, MEB, WWW, BP, Alum Oxon, Bryan's Painters]
>
>Soc for Protection of Ancient Buildings (F) 78-85,
>    Exec.

JONES, ELIJAH

>Hanley.
>
>Jamaica Committee (F) 66-66.

JONES, HARRY (1823-1900)

>St John's, Camb.
>Vicar 58;  Rector 73;  Ordained Priest<CE> 49;
>    Curate 50;  Prebendary 80;  Journal Editor 67.
>West London;  East London.
>[MEB, Walfords, Alum Cantab, Crockfds]
>
>Assn for Improvement of London Workhouse
>    Infirmaries 66-66, Exec.

JONES, JOHN JAMES

>East London.
>
>London Municipal Reform League 82-85, Exec.

JONES, LATIMER MAURICE (1833-1877)

>St Davids Lampeter.
>Vicar 63;  Curate 57;  Ordained Priest<CE> 58.
>Carmarthen.
>[MEB, Crockfds]
>
>Natl Education Union 71-76, Exec.

JONES, LLEWELLYN ARCHER ATHERLEY (1851-1929)

>Brasenose, Oxf;  Inner Temple.
>Barrister 75;  Q.C. 96;  Judge 06;  Author.
>Liberal.  MP Durham Co Northwest 85-14.  JP.
>West London;  Berkshire.
>[WWW, Alum Oxon, Fosters, Dods]
>
>Free Land League 86-86, V-Pres.

JONES, ROWLAND J.

Sunday Society 80-90, Exec.

JONES, T. B.

Central Assn for Stopping Sale Intox Liquors on
Sunday 70-70, Exec.

JONES, T. MASON

Financial Reform Union (F) 68-69, Exec.

JONES, THOMAS (1819-1882)

Congregational Minister 70; Independent Minister
44.
Swansea.
[DNB, MEB]

Central Assn for Stopping Sale Intox Liquors on
Sunday 70-70, V-Pres.

JONES, SIR THOMAS ALFRED (1823-1893)

Trin Col, Dublin; Royal Dublin Soc Sch.
Artist 49.
Kt 80.
Dublin.
[MEB, BP]

Sunday Society 81-90, V-Pres.

JONES, WILLIAM BASIL TICKELL (1822-1897)

Shrewsbury School; Trinity, Oxf.
Bishop St David´s 74; College Fellow 51; Ordained
Priest<CE> 53; College Lecturer 58; Vicar 65;
Archdeacon 67; Landowner 61.
JP.
Carmarthen; Cardiganshire.
[DNB, MEB, Walfords, Alum Oxon, Crockfds]

Central Assn for Stopping Sale Intox Liquors on
Sunday 75-85, V-Pres.

JORDAN, FURNEAUX

Physician.
Fellow Royal Col Surgeons, Edinb.
Birmingham.

Assn for Promoting Extension of Contagious Diseases
Act 68-68, V-Pres.

JOSELAND, GEORGE

Worcester.

Jamaica Committee (F) 66-66.

JOSEPH, ALEXANDER (1822- )

Brasenose, Oxf.
Rector 61; Ordained Priest<CE> 48; Curate 48;
Hon. Canon 77; Rural Dean.
Chatham.
[Alum Oxon, Crockfds]

Assn for Promoting Extension of Contagious Diseases
Act 68-68, V-Pres.

JOWITT, JOHN

JP.

Intl Arbitration & Peace Assn 81-81, V-Pres.

JOYCE, ELLEN <MRS. JAMES GERALD JOYCE, DAU. 5TH BARON
DYNEVOR> ( -1924)

CBE 20.
Winchester.
[BP]

Natl Assn for Promotion of State Colonization
86-86, V-Pres.

JOYCE, JOSEPH

East Central London.

London Comtee Exposure & Suppresn Traffic In Girls
(F) 80-80, Exec.
Working Men´s Natl League for Abolition State
Regulation of Vice 81-82, Secretary.

JOYNER, GEORGE

Sunday Society (F) 75-75, Exec.

JUDGE, EMILY <MRS. MARK HAYLER JUDGE, nee SIMPSON>

West London.

Sunday Society (F) 75-78, Exec.

JUDGE, MARK HAYLER (1847-1927)

Architect; Surveyor; Curator, Parkes Museum 78.
Assoc Royal Inst Br Architects.
West London.
[WWW]

Sunday Society (F) 75-90, Hon Sec.

JUPE, CHARLES

Mere.

Central Assn for Stopping Sale Intox Liquors on
Sunday 70-80, V-Pres.

KAY, HENRY CASSELS

>West London.
>[Direc Direcs]
>
>Soc for Protection of Ancient Buildings 85-85,
>    Exec.

KAY, JOHN ROBINSON

>JP.
>Summerseat.
>
>Natl Education Union (F) 69-70, Exec.

KEATINGE, RICHARD HARTE (1825-1904)

>Maj. General 84; Sub-Lt., Army 42; Lieutenant,
>    Army 45; Major 58; Lt. Colonel 66; Colonel
>    73; Lt. General 87.
>VC 58; CSI 66.
>West London; Sussex.
>[WWW, Direc Direcs, Army List]
>
>Kyrle Soc 84-90, Exec.

KEENE, CHARLES

>Southwest London.
>
>Soc for Protection of Ancient Buildings (F) 78-85,
>    Exec.

KELL, EDMUND (1799-1874)

>U Glasgow; Manchester College, York.
>Unitarian Minister 23.
>Fellow Society of Antiquaries.
>Southampton.
>[MEB]
>
>Jamaica Committee (F) 66-66.

KELL, ROBERT

>Bradford.
>
>Jamaica Committee (F) 66-66.

KELL, S. C.

>Bradford.
>
>Jamaica Committee (F) 66-66.

KELLY, CHARLES

>Physician.
>Fellow Royal Col Physicians.
>Worthing.
>
>Sanitary Institute 83-85, Exec.

KELLY, SIR FITZROY EDWARD (1796-1880)

>Lincoln's Inn.
>Lord Chief Baron 66; Judge, Supreme Court of
>    Judicature 75; Barrister 24; K.C. 34;
>    Sergeant at Law 66.
>Conservative. MP Ipswich 38-41, Cambridge 43-47,
>    Suffolk East 52-66. Solicitor General 45-46,
>    Solicitor General 52-52, Attorney General
>    58-59, DL.
>Kt 45; PC 66.
>West London; Suffolk.
>[DNB, MEB, Walfords, Dods]
>
>City Church & Churchyard Protection Soc (F) 80-80,
>    V-Pres.
>Intl Law Assn 78-79, President.
>Howard Assn 70-79, Patron.
>Victoria Street Soc for Protection of Animals from
>    Vivisection 80-80, V-Pres.

KELLY, THOMAS M.

>Workmen's Natl Assn for Abolition Sugar Bounties
>    81-81, Secretary.

KEMBALL, ANNA FRANCES, LADY <WIFE OF SIR A. B.
    KEMBALL, nee SHAW>

>West London.
>[BP]
>
>Victoria Street Soc for Protection of Animals from
>    Vivisection 82-85, Exec.

KEMBLE, CHARLES (1819-1874)

>Wadham, Oxf.
>Rector 59; Prebendary 66; Curate 42; Ordained
>    Priest<CE> 43; Perp. Curate 44; Landowner
>    69.
>Bath; Wiltshire.
>[MEB, Walfords, Alum Oxon, Crockfds]
>
>Assn for Promoting Extension of Contagious Diseases
>    Act 68-70, V-Pres.
>Church Assn 70-70, Exec.

KEMPE, JAMES CORY ( -1893)

>St John's, Camb.
>Rector 44; Prebendary 70; Curate 36; Ordained
>    Priest<CE> 38.
>Merton, Devon.
>[Alum Cantab, Crockfds]
>
>Soc for Promoting Increase of the Home Episcopate
>    72-74, Exec.

KEMPE, JOHN EDWARD (1810-1907)

>St Paul's, London; Clare, Camb.
>Rector 53; Prebendary 61; Curate 33; Ordained
>    Priest<CE> 34; College Fellow 36; School
>    Master 38; Curate 46.
>West London.
>[WWW, Alum Cantab, Crockfds, Direc Direcs]
>
>Natl Education Union 70-79, Exec.

KENNARD, EDMUND HEGAN (1835-1912)

St Peter´s College, Radley; Balliol, Oxf.
Cornet, Army 58; Lieutenant, Army 62; Captain,
    Army 66.
Conservative. MP Beverley 68-69, Lymington 74-85.
Fellow Royal Geograph Society.
West London; Surrey.
[WWW, Walfords, Alum Oxon, Dods, Direc Direcs, Army
    List]

Natl Assn for Promotion of State Colonization
    86-86, V-Pres.


KENNARD, STEPHEN P.

Natl Assn for Promotion of State Colonization
    86-86, V-Pres.


KENNAWAY, SIR JOHN, 2ND BT. (1797-1873)

Winchester College; Trinity, Camb; Lincoln´s Inn.
Substantial Landowner 36.
DL, JP.
Baronet 36.
Devonshire.
[MEB, BP, Walfords, Alum Cantab]

Church Assn 70-70, V-Pres.


KENNAWAY, SIR JOHN HENRY, 3RD BT. (1837-1919)

Harrow; Balliol, Oxf; Inner Temple.
Barrister 64; Substantial Landowner 73.
Conservative. MP Devonshire East 70-85, Honiton
    85-10. DL, JP.
Baronet 73; PC 97; CB 02.
West London; Devonshire.
[WWW, BP, Walfords, Bateman, Alum Oxon, Fosters,
    Dods, Direc Direcs]

Howard Assn 71-84, Exec, Patron.
Proportional Representation Soc (F) 84-88, Exec.
Natl Education Union 70-79, Exec.


KENNEDY, ARCHIBALD, 3RD MARQUIS OF AILSA (1847-1938)

Eton.
Very Large Landowner 70; Lieutenant, Army 66;
    Captain, Army 70.
Lord Lieutenant 19-  , DL, JP.
Marquis 70.
Ayreshire.
[WWW, BP, Walfords, Bateman, Army List]

Central Vigilance Comtee for Repression Immorality
    (F) 83-84, V-Pres.


KENNEDY, H. G.

Land Tenure Reform Assn 73-73, Exec.


KENNEDY, JOHN PITT (1796-1879)

Royal Military Academy, Woolwich.
Author; 2nd Lt., RE 15; Lieutenant, RE 21;
    Inspector-General Irish Education Dept 37;
    Estate Agent 43; Lieutenant, Army 53.
Member Inst Civ Engineers; Fellow Royal
    Statistical Society.
West London.
[DNB, MEB, Army List]

Natl Emigration League (F) 70-70, V-Pres.


KENNY, JOHN

London.

Jamaica Committee (F) 66-66.


KENRICK, JOHN ARTHUR (1829-1926)

Hollow Ware Manufacturer.
JP.
Birmingham.
[WWW, Direc Direcs]

Natl Education League (F) 69-69, Exec.


KENRICK, TIMOTHY (1807-1885)

Hollow Ware Manufacturer.
JP.
Birmingham.
[MEB]

Natl Education League (F) 69-69, Exec.


KENRICK, WILLIAM (1831-1919)

University Col London.
Hollow Ware Manufacturer.
Liberal(Unionist). MP Birmingham North 85-99. JP.
PC.
Birmingham.
[WWW, Dods, Direc Direcs]

Soc for Protection of Ancient Buildings 80-85,
    Exec.
Natl Education League (F) 69-71, Exec.


KENT, THOMAS RUSSEL

Solicitor.
London.
[Direc Direcs]

Railway Passengers´ Protection Assn 86-86, Exec.


KEPPEL, WILLIAM COUTTS, 7TH EARL OF ALBEMARLE
    (1832-1894)

Eton.
Author; Lieutenant, Army 49; Superintendent
    Indian Affairs, Canada 54; Large Landowner 91.
Liberal, then Conservative. MP Norwich 57-59, Wick
    60-65, Berwick-upon-Tweed 68-74. Treas Royal
    Household 59-66, Parl U-Sec War 78-80, Parl
    U-Sec War 85-86, JP.
PC 59; KCMG 70; Baron 76; Earl 91.

Fellow Royal Horticult Society.
Southwest London; Norfolk.
[DNB, MEB, BP, Walfords, Dods, Army List]

Plimsoll and Seamen's Fund Committee (F) 73-73,
    Exec.


KERR, SCHOMBERG HENRY, 9TH MARQUIS OF LOTHIAN
    (1833-1900)

Eton; New College, Oxf.
Very Large Landowner 70; Attache, Dip Serv 54;
    Second Secretary, Dip Serv 62.
Conservative. Lord Privy Seal Scotland 74-00, Sec
    St Scotland 87-92.
Marquis 70; KT 78; PC 86.
West London; Midlothian; Norfolk.
[DNB, MEB, WWW, BP, Walfords, Bateman, Alum Oxon,
    Direc Direcs]

Soc for Protection of Ancient Buildings 85-85,
    Exec.


KERSHAW, SAMUEL WAYLAND (1836-1914)

St John's, Camb.
Lambeth Palace Librarian 70.
Fellow Society of Antiquaries.
London.
[WWW, Alum Cantab]

City Church & Churchyard Protection Soc 83-88,
    Exec, V-Pres.
Soc for Protection of Ancient Buildings (F) 78-85,
    Exec.


KERWIN, EDWIN H.

Natl Vigilance Assn (F) 85-85, Exec.


KIBBLE, A. W.

Halstead.

Travelling Tax Abolition Committee 80-85, Exec.


KIDSTON, WILLIAM

Merchant.
Glasgow.

Natl Education Union 71-79, Exec.


KILLICK, RICHARD HENRY ( -1903)

Queens', Camb.
Rector 60; Curate 41; Ordained Priest<CE> 43;
    Vicar 45.
Southwest London.
[Alum Cantab, Crockfds]

Church Assn 67-67, Exec.


KIMBER, SIR HENRY, 1ST BT. (1834-1923)

University Col London.
Solicitor 58.
Conservative. MP Wandsworth 85-13.
Baronet 04.
Southwest London.
[WWW, BP, Dods, Direc Direcs]

Natl Assn for Promotion of State Colonization
    86-86, V-Pres.


KING, - <MRS. E. M. KING>

Vigilance Assn for Defense of Personal Rights
    83-83, Exec.


KING, EDWARD (1829-1887)

Jesus, Camb.
Vicar 79; Curate 54; Ordained Priest<CE> 55.
Werrington, Devon.
[Alum Cantab, Crockfds]

Natl Soc for Preserving Memorials of Dead (F)
    81-84, Exec.


KING, JOHN HYNDE ( -1870)

Colonel 63; Ensign, Army 44; Lieutenant, Army 46;
    Major 54; Lt. Colonel 55.
CB 69.
West London.
[MEB, Army List]

Assn for Promoting Extension of Contagious Diseases
    Act 68-68, V-Pres.


KING, R. L.

North London.

London Municipal Reform League 82-85, Exec.


KINGSFORD, ALGERNON GODFREY

Lichfield Theological College.
Rector 73; Curate 79; Vicar 82; Curate 70;
    Ordained Priest<CE> 71.
Shropshire.
[Crockfds]

Sunday Society (F) 75-90, V-Pres.


KINGSFORD, ANNA <MRS. ALGERNON GODFREY KINGSFORD, nee
    BONUS> (1846-1888)

Paris(Medical).
Physician 80; Journalist.
West London; Shropshire.
[DNB, MEB]

Sunday Society (F) 75-87, V-Pres.

KINGSLEY, HENRY

>    Plimsoll and Seamen´s Fund Committee (F) 73-73,
>        Exec.

KINGSTON, -

>    Workmen´s Peace Assn 75-75, Exec.

KINNAIRD, ARTHUR FITZGERALD, 10TH BARON KINNAIRD
    (1814-1887)

>    Eton.
>    Banker 37;  Very Large Landowner 78;  Attache, Dip
>        Serv 35.
>    Liberal.  MP Perth 37-39, Perth 52-78.  DL, JP.
>    Baron 78.
>    Fellow Royal Geograph Society.
>    Southwest London;  Perthshire.
>    [DNB, MEB, BP, Walfords, Bateman, Dods, Direc
>        Direcs]
>
>    Central Vigilance Comtee for Repression Immorality
>        (F) 83-84, Treas.
>    Plimsoll and Seamen´s Fund Committee (F) 73-73,
>        Exec.

KINNEAR, JOHN (1824-1894)

>    Royal College Belfast.
>    Presbyterian Minister 48.
>    Liberal.  MP Donegal 80-85.
>    Letterkenny, Donegal.
>    [MEB, Dods]
>
>    Intl Arbitration & Peace Assn 81-81, V-Pres.

KINNEAR, JOHN BOYD- (1828-1920)

>    U Edinburgh;  Inner Temple.
>    Small Landowner 82;  Advocate 50;  Pol Sec to Lord
>        Advocate 52;  Barrister 56;  Journalist 60.
>    Liberal(Unionist).  MP Fifeshire East 85-86.  JP.
>    West Central London;  Fifeshire.
>    [WWW, Walfords, Fosters, Dods]
>
>    Natl Assn for Promotion of State Colonization
>        86-86, V-Pres.

KIRK, JOHN (1813-1886)

>    Independent Minister;  Journal Editor 45;  Theology
>        Professor 59;  Author.
>    Edinburgh.
>    [MEB]
>
>    London Soc for Abolition of Compulsory Vaccination
>        81-81, V-Pres.

KITSON, JAMES, 1ST BARON AIREDALE (1835-1911)

>    University Col London.
>    Iron Manufacturer;  Engine Manufacturer.
>    Liberal.  MP Colne Valley,Yorks WR S 92-07.  JP.
>    Baronet 86;  PC 06;  Baron 07.
>    Member Inst Civ Engineers;  Inst of Mech Engineers.
>    Southwest London;  Yorks, North Riding.
>    [DNB, WWW, BP, Dods, Direc Direcs]
>
>    Free Land League 86-86, V-Pres.
>    Natl Education League 71-71, Exec.

KNELL, SAMUEL

>    Central Assn for Stopping Sale Intox Liquors on
>        Sunday 80-80, Exec.

KNIGHT, A. A.

>    Lewisham.
>
>    London Municipal Reform League 82-85, Exec.
>    Natl Vigilance Assn (F) 85-85, Exec.

KNIGHT, G. J., JUN.

>    Clapton.
>
>    London Municipal Reform League 82-85, Exec.

KNOWLES, MARK

>    Natl Vigilance Assn (F) 85-85, Exec.

KNOX, ROBERT BENT (1808-1893)

>    Trin Col, Dublin.
>    Bishop Down and Connor 49;  Ordained Priest<CI> 32;
>        Prebendary 41;  Archbishop Armagh 86.
>    Liberal.
>    Downpatrick.
>    [DNB, MEB, Alum Cantab]
>
>    Assn for Promoting Extension of Contagious Diseases
>        Act 68-70, V-Pres.

KNOX, THOMAS

>    JP.
>    Edinburgh.
>
>    Jamaica Committee (F) 66-66.

LABATT, HAMILTON

>    Surgeon.
>    Fellow Royal Col Surgeons, Ire.
>    Dublin.
>
>    Assn for Promoting Extension of Contagious Diseases
>        Act 68-68, Exec.

LABILLIERE, FRANCIS PETER

    Middle Temple.
    Barrister 63.
    Harrow-on-the-Hill.
    [Fosters]

    Church Assn 78-85, Exec, V-Pres.
    Imperial Federation League (F) 84-84, Hon Sec.
    Natl Emigration League (F) 70-70, Exec.


LAKE, BENJAMIN GREENE

    Solicitor.
    London.
    [Direc Direcs]

    City Church & Churchyard Protection Soc (F) 80-83,
        Exec.


LAKE, WILLIAM

    Sunday Society 79-90, Exec.


LAKE, WILLIAM CHARLES (1817-1897)

    Rugby;  Balliol, Oxf.
    Dean 69;  College Fellow 38;  College Tutor 42;
        Ordained Priest<CE> 44;  Rector 58;  Prebendary
        60.
    Durham[City].
    [MEB, Alum Oxon, Crockfds]

    Central Assn for Stopping Sale Intox Liquors on
        Sunday 80-85, V-Pres.
    Natl Education Union (F) 69-79, Exec.


LAMB, -

    JP.
    Manchester.

    Central Assn for Stopping Sale Intox Liquors on
        Sunday 70-85, V-Pres.


LAMB, ANDREW SIMON (1839- )

    U Edinburgh;  Inner Temple.
    Barrister 65.
    London;  Southampton.
    [Fosters]

    Church Assn 85-85, Exec.


LAMBART, FREDERICK JOHN WILLIAM, 8TH EARL OF CAVAN
    (1815-1887)

    Eton.
    Substantial Landowner 37;  Cornet, Army 31;
        Lieutenant, Army.
    DL, JP.
    Earl 37.
    Somersetshire.
    [MEB, BP, Walfords, Bateman, Army List]

    Church Assn 67-67, V-Pres.


LAMBERT, - <"COL.">

    Dorking.

    Church Assn 70-70, Exec.


LAMBERT, BROOKE (1834-1901)

    King's College School;  Brasenose, Oxf.
    Vicar 65;  Curate 58;  Ordained Priest<CE> 59.
    East London;  Greenwich.
    [DNB, WWW, Alum Oxon, Crockfds]

    Sunday Society 79-90, V-Pres.


LAMBERT, FREDERICK FOX ( -1920)

    Corpus Christi, Oxf.
    Rector 79;  Curate 66;  Ordained Priest<CE> 67;
        Vicar 68;  Chaplain 72;  Vicar 91;  Hon. Canon
        98.
    Clothall.
    [WWW, Crockfds]

    Natl Assn for Promotion of State Colonization
        86-86, Exec.


LAMPREY, J.  H.

    Natl Emigration League (F) 70-70, Exec.


LANCASTER, BENJAMIN

    Soc for Promoting Increase of the Home Episcopate
        72-74, Exec.


LANCASTER, G.

    North London.

    London Municipal Reform League 82-85, Exec.


LANE, JAMES R.

    West London.

    Assn for Promoting Extension of Contagious Diseases
        Act 68-68, Exec.


LANGLEY, J.  BAXTER

    London.

    Financial Reform Union (F) 68-69, Exec.
    Jamaica Committee (F) 66-66.


LANKESTER, EDWIN (1814-1874)

    London U;  Heidelberg(Medical).
    Coroner, Central Middlesex 59;  Physician 39;
        Professor of Natural History, New College
        London 50;  Medical School Lecturer 53;
        Journal Editor 53.
    Med Off of Health 56-74.
    Member Royal Col Surgeons;  Fellow Royal Society;
        Br Assn;  Ray Society;  Royal Microscop
        Society.

London.
[DNB, MEB]

Commons Preservation Soc 69-69, Exec.


LANKESTER, SIR EDWIN RAY (1847-1929)

St Paul's, London;  Christ Church, Oxf.
Professor of Zoology and Comparative Anatomy, U Col
    London 74;  College Fellow 72;  College Tutor
    72;  Regius Professor of Natural History,
    Edinburgh 82;  Dir Natural History, British
    Museum 98;  Journal Editor;  Author.
KCB 07.
Fellow Royal Society;  Br Assn.
Oxford.
[DNB, WWW, Alum Cantab, Alum Oxon]

Sunday Society 80-90, V-Pres.


LATHAM, GEORGE WILLIAM (1827-1886)

Brasenose, Oxf;  Inner Temple.
Barrister 52;  Landowner 53.
Radical.  MP Crewe, Cheshire 85-86.  JP.
Cheshire.
[MEB, Walfords, Alum Oxon, Fosters, Dods]

Intl Arbitration & Peace Assn 81-81, V-Pres.


LATHAM, R. MARSDEN

Working Men's Comtee Promoting Separation Church
    and State (F) 71-71, Exec.
Natl Emigration League (F) 70-70, Exec.


LA TOUCHE, JAMES DIGUES

Trin Col, Dublin.
Vicar 56;  Ordained Priest<CE> 51.
Stokesay.
[Crockfds]

Sunday Society 79-90, V-Pres.


LAW, HENRY

Civil Engineer.
Member Inst Civ Engineers.
Southwest London.

Sanitary Institute 78-89, Exec.


LAW, HENRY (1797-1884)

Eton;  St John's, Camb.
Dean 62;  College Tutor 20;  Ordained Priest<CE>
    21;  Vicar 22;  Archdeacon 24;  Canon 28;
    Rector 30.
Gloucester.
[DNB, MEB, Alum Cantab, Crockfds]

Assn for Promoting Extension of Contagious Diseases
    Act 68-70, V-Pres.
Church Assn 67-80, V-Pres.


LAWLEY, BEILBY, 3RD BARON WENLOCK (1849-1912)

Eton;  Trinity, Camb;  Inner Temple.
Very Large Landowner 80;  Gov, Madras 91.
Liberal(Unionist).  MP Chester 80-80.  Lord of the
    Bedchamber, P of W 01-10, V-Chamberlain Royal
    Household 10-12, JP.
Baron 80;  PC;  GCSI;  GCIE;  KCB.
West London;  Yorks, West Riding.
[BP, Bateman, Alum Cantab, Dods, Direc Direcs]

Natl Assn for Promotion of State Colonization
    86-86, V-Pres.


LAWRENCE, SIR ARTHUR JOHNSTONE (1809-1892)

Eton.
Maj. General 62;  Ensign, Army 27;  Captain, Army
    37;  Lt. Colonel 47;  Colonel 54;  Lt.
    General 71;  General 77.
CB 55;  KCB 69.
Surrey.
[MEB, BP, Walfords, Army List]

Church Assn 67-85, V-Pres.


LAWRENCE, F.

Natl Vigilance Assn (F) 85-85, Exec.


LAWRENCE, SIR JAMES CLARKE, 1ST BT. (1820-1897)

Large Builder/contractor.
Liberal.  MP Lambeth 65-65, Lambeth 68-85.  JP.
Baronet 69.
West London.
[MEB, WWW, BP, Walfords, Dods]

Commons Preservation Soc 69-86, Exec.
Public Museums & Free Libraries Assn 68-68, V-Pres.
Natl Emigration League (F) 70-70, V-Pres.


LAWRENCE, SIR JAMES JOHN TREVOR, 2ND BT. (1831-1913)

Winchester College;  St Bartholomew's Hosp.
Army Medical Service 53.
Conservative.  MP Surrey Mid 75-85, Reigate 85-92.
    JP.
Baronet 67;  KCVO 02.
Fellow Royal Geograph Society;  Fellow Royal
    Historical Society.
Southwest London;  Surrey.
[WWW, BP, Walfords, Dods]

Commons Preservation Soc 80-86, Exec.


LAWRENCE, PHILIP HENRY (1822-1895)

Lincoln's Inn.
Solicitor 48;  Barrister 72.
London.
[MEB, Fosters]

Commons Preservation Soc (F) 65-86, Exec.

LAWRENCE, SIR WILLIAM (1818-1897)

    Large Builder/contractor.
    Liberal. MP City 65-74, City 80-85. DL, JP.
    Kt 87.
    West London.
    [MEB, WWW, Walfords, Dods]

    Commons Preservation Soc 69-86, Exec.


LAWSON, HARRY LAWSON WEBSTER LEVY-, 1ST VISCOUNT BURNHAM
    (1862-1933)

    Eton; Balliol, Oxf; Inner Temple.
    Politician; Barrister 91; Newspaper Proprietor
       03; Large Landowner.
    Liberal(Unionist). MP St Pancras West 85-92,
       Gloucestershire East 93-95, Twr Hmlts Mile End
       05-06, Twr Hmlts Mile End 10-16. DL, JP.
    Baron 16; Viscount 19; CH 17; GCMG 27.
    West London.
    [DNB, WWW, BP, Alum Oxon, Dods]

    Natl Assn for Promotion of State Colonization
       86-86, V-Pres, Exec.
    Sunday Society 86-90, V-Pres.
    Free Land League 86-86, V-Pres, Treas.


LAWSON, HENRY

    Physician.
    London.

    Sunday Society 76-77, V-Pres.


LAWSON, MALCOLM

    Kyrle Soc 84-85, Exec.


LAWSON, SIR WILFRED, 2ND BT. (1829-1906)

    Large Landowner 67.
    Radical. MP Carlisle 59-65, Carlisle 68-85,
       Cockermouth, Cumb 86-00, Camborne 03-06,
       Cockermouth, Cumb 06-06. JP.
    Baronet 67.
    Southwest London; Cumberland.
    [DNB, WWW, BP, Walfords, Bateman, Dods, Direc
       Direcs]

    Central Assn for Stopping Sale Intox Liquors on
       Sunday (F) 67-85, V-Pres.
    Howard Assn 67-70, Patron.
    Jamaica Committee (F) 66-66.


LEACH, CHARLES (1847-1919)

    Ranmoor Theological College, Sheffield.
    Congregational Minister; Author.
    Liberal. MP Colne Valley,Yorks WR S 10-16.
    Kilburn, Derbys.
    [WWW, Dods, Direc Direcs]

    Allotments & Small Holdings Assn 85-85, Exec.


LEACH, JOHN

    Great Yarmouth.

    Travelling Tax Abolition Committee 80-85, Exec.


LEADER, NICHOLAS PHILPOT (1808-1880)

    Trin Col, Dublin.
    Landowner 36.
    Conservative. MP Cork Co 61-68. JP.
    Co Cork.
    [MEB, Walfords, Dods]

    Assn for Promoting Extension of Contagious Diseases
       Act 68-70, V-Pres.


LEAKE, ROBERT (1824-1901)

    Calico Printer.
    Liberal. MP Lancashire SE 80-85,
       Radcliffe-cum-Farnworth 85-95. JP.
    Lancashire.
    [Dods, Direc Direcs]

    Free Land League 86-86, V-Pres.


LEAN, WALTER

    Accountant.
    Inst of Chartered Accountants.

    Intl Arbitration & Peace Assn 81-81, Exec.


LEATHAM, WILLIAM HENRY (1815-1889)

    Bruce Castle School, Tottenham.
    Banker 34; Poet.
    Liberal. MP Wakefield 50-50, Wakefield 65-68,
       Yorks W Riding South 80-85. DL, JP.
    Southwest London; Yorks, West Riding.
    [DNB, MEB, Walfords, Dods]

    Intl Arbitration & Peace Assn 81-81, V-Pres.


LEAY, H.

    London Municipal Reform League 82-82, Exec.


LECHMERE, SIR EDMUND ANTHONY HARLEY, 3RD BT.
    (1826-1894)

    Charterhouse; St Mary Hall, Oxf.
    Banker; Large Landowner 56.
    Conservative. MP Tewkesbury 66-68, Worcestershire
       West 76-92, Evesham 92-94. DL, JP.
    Baronet 56.
    Fellow Society of Antiquaries.
    West London; Worcestershire.
    [MEB, BP, Walfords, Bateman, Alum Oxon, Dods]

    City Church & Churchyard Protection Soc (F) 80-83,
       V-Pres.
    Local Taxation Comtee [of Central Chamber of
       Agriculture] 79-85, Exec.

LECKY, WILLIAM EDWARD HARTPOLE (1838-1903)

    Cheltenham College;  Trin Col, Dublin.
    Historian;  Landowner 52.
    Liberal(Unionist).  MP Dublin University 95-03.
    PC 97;  OM 02.
    British Academy.
    Southwest London.
    [DNB, WWW, Alum Cantab, Dods]

    Sunday Society 76-90, V-Pres.


LEDSAM, DANIEL (1813-1904)

    St John's, Camb.
    Vicar 70;  Ordained Priest<CE> 37;  Curate 40;
       Perp. Curate 41.
    Hollington.
    [Alum Cantab, Crockfds]

    Church Assn 75-85, Exec.


LEE, C.

    Land Nationalization Soc (F) 81-84, Exec.


LEE, FREDERICK GEORGE (1832-1902)

    St Edmund Hall, Oxf;  Cuddesdon Theological
       College.
    Vicar 67;  Ordained Priest<CE> 56;  Curate 56.
    Fellow Society of Antiquaries.
    Southeast London.
    [DNB, WWW, Alum Oxon, Crockfds]

    Soc for Abolition of Vivisection 76-76, Exec.


LEE, HENRY (1817- )

    Merchant;  Manufacturer.
    Liberal.  MP Southampton 80-85.  JP.
    Prestwich.
    [Dods]

    Howard Assn 80-84, Patron.


LEE, JAMES PRINCE (1804-1869)

    St Paul's, London;  Trinity, Camb.
    Bishop Manchester 48;  College Fellow 29;  Ordained
       Priest<CE> 30;  Asst School Master 30;  School
       Head 38;  Hon. Canon 47.
    Manchester.
    [DNB, MEB, Alum Cantab, Crockfds]

    Central Assn for Stopping Sale Intox Liquors on
       Sunday (F) 67-69, V-Pres.


LEE, ROBERT

    Writer to the Signet.
    Edinburgh.

    Natl Education Union 71-79, Exec.


LEE, ROBERT JAMES (1841-1924)

    Brighton College;  Gonville & Caius, Camb;  St
       Thomas's Hospital Lond.
    Physician 69;  Medical School Lecturer.
    Fellow Royal Col Physicians.
    West London.
    [Alum Cantab]

    Sunday Society 80-89, Exec.


LEEMING, JAMES

    Natl Education Union 70-71, Exec.


LEES, JOHN

    Portobello.

    Natl Secular Soc 84-84, V-Pres.


LEES, JOHN

    Reigate.

    Railway Passengers' Protection Assn 86-86, Exec.


LEESE, JOSEPH

    Cotton Manufacturer.
    Altrincham.

    Jamaica Committee (F) 66-66.


LEFEVRE, EMILY OCTAVIA SHAW- <MISS>

    [BP]

    Kyrle Soc 84-90, Exec.
    Smoke Abatement Committee 81-81.


LEFEVRE, GEORGE JOHN SHAW-, 1ST BARON EVERSLEY
(1831-1928)

    Eton;  Trinity, Camb;  Inner Temple.
    Barrister 54;  Author.
    Liberal.  MP Reading 63-85, Bradford Central 86-95.
       Lord Admiralty 66-66, Parl Sec Board of Trade
       68-71, Parl U-Sec Home Off 71-71, Parl Sec
       Admiralty 71-74, First Commissioner Works
       80-83, Postmaster General 84-85, First
       Commissioner Works 92-94, Pres Local Govt Board
       94-95.
    PC 80;  Baron 06.
    West Central London;  Kent.
    [DNB, WWW, BP, Walfords, Alum Cantab, Fosters,
       Dods, Direc Direcs]

    Commons Preservation Soc (F) 65-86, Chairman,
       V-Pres.
    Jamaica Committee (F) 66-66.

LEFROY, ANTHONY (1800-1890)

Trin Col, Dublin.
Substantial Landowner 69.
Conservative. MP Longford Co 30-37, Longford Co
    42-47, Dublin University 58-70. DL, JP.
Southwest London; Co Longford.
[MEB, Walfords, Bateman, Dods]

Church Assn 67-85, V-Pres.


LEGARD, SIR CHARLES, 11TH BT. (1846-1901)

Eton.
Large Landowner 66; Ensign, Army.
Conservative. MP Scarborough 74-80. DL, JP.
Baronet 66.
West London; Scarborough.
[WWW, BP, Walfords, Bateman, Dods]

Victoria Street Soc for Protection of Animals from
    Vivisection 80-80, Exec.


LEGG, R. R.

Fellow Society of Antiquaries.
Southampton.

Assn for Promoting Extension of Contagious Diseases
    Act 68-68, Exec.


LEGGE, EDWARD HENRY (1834-1900)

Christ Church, Oxf.
Lt. Colonel 67; Lieutenant, Army 55; Captain,
    Army 59.
West London.
[BP, Alum Oxon, Direc Direcs, Army List]

Assn for Promoting Extension of Contagious Diseases
    Act 70-70, V-Pres.


LEGGE, JAMES (1815-1897)

Aberdeen Grammar School; U Aberdeen; Highbury
    College.
Professor of Chinese Language and Literature,
    Oxford 76; Congregational Missionary 39;
    Author.
Oxford.
[DNB, MEB, WWW, Alum Oxon]

Anglo-Oriental Soc for Suppression Opium Trade (F)
    75-75, Exec.


LEGGE, WILLIAM HENEAGE, 6TH EARL OF DARTMOUTH
    (1851-1936)

Eton; Christ Church, Oxf.
Politician 78; Very Large Landowner 91.
Conservative. MP Kent West 78-85, Lewisham 85-91.
    V-Chamberlain Royal Household 85-91, Lord
    Lieutenant 91-27, JP.
Earl 91; KCB 17; GCVO 28; PC.
West London; Yorks, West Riding.
[WWW, BP, Alum Oxon, Dods, Direc Direcs]

Natl Footpaths Preservation Soc (F) 85-90, V-Pres.


LEGGE, WILLIAM WALTER, 5TH EARL OF DARTMOUTH (1823-1891)

Eton; Christ Church, Oxf.
Very Large Landowner 53.
Conservative. MP Staffordshire South 49-53. Lord
    Lieutenant 87-91, DL, JP.
Earl 53.
West London; Staffordshire.
[MEB, BP, Walfords, Bateman, Alum Oxon, Dods]

Natl Assn for Promotion of State Colonization
    86-86, Patron.


LEGROS, ALPHONSE (1837-1911)

Ecole des Beaux Arts.
Artist; Slade Professor of Art, U Col London 70;
    Teacher, So Kens Sch of Art 63.
London.
[DNB, WWW]

Sunday Society 80-90, V-Pres.


LEHMANN, RUDOLPH (1819-1905)

Artist.
London; Hertfordshire.
[DNB, WWW]

Sunday Society 78-90, V-Pres.


LEHY, PATRICK

Archbishop Cashel<RC> 57.
Thurles.

Central Assn for Stopping Sale Intox Liquors on
    Sunday (F) 67-67, V-Pres.


LEICESTER, JOSEPH LYNN (1825-1903)

Glassblower 35; Labour Leader.
Radical. MP West Ham South 85-86.
South London.
[Dods, Dic Lab Biog]

Free Land League 86-86, V-Pres.


LEIGHTON, FRANCIS KNYVETT (1807-1881)

Rugby; Magdalen, Oxf.
Canon 68; College Head 58; V-Chancellor, Oxford
    66; Ordained Priest<CE> 32; Vicar 35; Rector
    41; Landowner 34.
Southwest London; Oxford; Montgomeryshire.
[MEB, Walfords, Alum Oxon, Crockfds]

City Church & Churchyard Protection Soc (F) 80-81,
    V-Pres.
Assn for Promoting Extension of Contagious Diseases
    Act 68-70, V-Pres.

LEIGHTON, FREDERICK, 1ST BARON LEIGHTON OF STRETTON
   (1830-1896)

   Artist.
   Kt 78; Baronet 86; Baron 96.
   Royal Academy;  Royal Society Water Colour
      Painters.
   West London.
   [DNB, MEB, BP, Alum Cantab, Alum Oxon, Bryan's
      Painters]

   Smoke Abatement Committee 81-81.
   Sunday Society 78-90, V-Pres.
   City Church & Churchyard Protection Soc (F) 80-83,
      V-Pres.


LEIGHTON, STANLEY (1837-1901)

   Harrow;  Balliol, Oxf;  Inner Temple.
   Landowner 71;  Barrister 61;  Antiquary.
   Conservative.  MP Shropshire North 76-85, Oswestry
      85-01.  DL, JP.
   Fellow Society of Antiquaries.
   Shropshire.
   [DNB, WWW, Alum Oxon, Fosters, Dods, Direc Direcs]

   Natl Assn for Promotion of State Colonization
      86-86, V-Pres.
   Natl Soc for Preserving Memorials of Dead (F)
      81-88, Exec.
   Local Taxation Comtee [of Central Chamber of
      Agriculture] 80-85, Exec.


LELAND, CHARLES GODFREY (1824-1903)

   Princeton.
   Fellow Royal Society Literature.
   Northwest London;  USA.

   Soc for Protection of Ancient Buildings (F) 78-85,
      Exec.


LE LUBEZ, P. A. V.

   East London.

   Land Law Reform League (F) 81-84, Treas.
   League for Defense of Constitutional Rights 84-84,
      V-Pres.
   Natl Secular Soc 70-84, V-Pres, Treas.


LE MARE, E. R.

   JP.
   Manchester;  Douglas.

   Central Assn for Stopping Sale Intox Liquors on
      Sunday (F) 67-80, V-Pres.


LEMON, SIR JAMES (1833-1923)

   Civil Engineer;  Asst, Metropolitan Board of Works.
   Liberal.  JP.
   Kt 09.
   Member Inst Civ Engineers;  Fellow Royal Inst Br
      Architects;  Surveyors' Institute.
   Southampton.
   [WWW]

   Sanitary Institute 78-84, Exec.


LENG, SIR JOHN (1828-1906)

   Newspaper Editor 47.
   Radical.  MP Dundee 89-06.  DL, JP.
   Kt 93.
   Dundee;  Fifeshire.
   [DNB, WWW, Dods, Direc Direcs]

   Free Land League 86-86, V-Pres.


LENNOX, LORD HENRY CHARLES GEORGE GORDON (1821-1886)

   Westminster School;  Christ Church, Oxf.
   Politician.
   Conservative.  MP Chichester 46-85.  Junior Lord
      Treasury 52-52, Junior Lord Treasury 58-59,
      Parl Sec Admiralty 66-68, First Commissioner
      Works 74-76.
   PC 74.
   Southwest London;  Sussex.
   [DNB, MEB, BP, Walfords, Alum Oxon, Dods]

   Assn for Improvement of London Workhouse
      Infirmaries 66-66, Exec.
   Howard Assn 69-76, Patron.


LENNOX, LORD WILLIAM PITT (1799-1881)

   Westminster School.
   Author;  Cornet, Army 13;  Captain, Army 22;
      Journal Editor 58;  Novelist.
   Liberal.  MP King's Lynn 31-35.  JP.
   West London.
   [DNB, MEB, BP, Walfords, Dods, Army List]

   Howard Assn 67-68, Patron.
   Natl Emigration League (F) 70-70, V-Pres.


LEON, GEORGE I.  <OR GEORGE J.>

   West London;  Hove.

   Sunday Society 79-79, Exec.


LEONARD, PETER (1801-1888)

   St Andrews(Medical).
   Insp Gen, RN Medical Serv 65;  Asst Surgeon, RN
      Medical Serv 23;  Surgeon, RN Medical Serv 29;
      Dep Insp Gen, RN Medical Serv.
   Member Royal Col Physicians.
   Upper Norwood.
   [MEB, Navy List]

   Assn for Promoting Extension of Contagious Diseases
      Act 68-70, V-Pres.


LEOPOLD GEORGE DUNCAN ALBERT, H.R.H.  PRINCE, DUKE OF
   ALBANY (1853-1884)

   Christ Church, Oxf.
   Colonel 82.
   KG 69;  KT 71;  PC 74;  GCSI 77;  GCMG 80;  Duke
      81.
   Society of the Arts.
   Surrey.
   [DNB, MEB, BP, Alum Oxon, Army List]

   Smoke Abatement Committee 81-81.

LEPPER, C. H.

    Natl Vigilance Assn (F) 85-85, Exec.


LETHBRIDGE, SIR JOHN HESKETH, 3RD BT. (1798-1873)

    Eton.
    Substantial Landowner 49.
    DL, JP.
    Baronet 49.
    Somersetshire.
    [MEB, BP, Walfords]

    Howard Assn 68-69, Patron.


LETHEBY, HENRY (1816-1876)

    Analytical Chemist; Physician 42; Medical School
        Lecturer.
    Med Off of Health 55-74.
    Fellow Linnean Society; Fellow Chemical Society.
    Northwest London.
    [DNB, MEB]

    Sunday Society (F) 75-75, V-Pres.


LEVEY, T. B. <OR LOVEY>

    Clergyman<Sect Unkn>.

    Jamaica Committee (F) 66-66.


LEVI, LEONE (1821-1888)

    Lincoln's Inn.
    Professor of Commerce, Kings Col London 52;
        Merchant 44; Barrister 59; Author.
    Fellow Royal Statistical Society; Fellow Society
        of Antiquaries; Society of the Arts.
    North London.
    [DNB, MEB, Fosters]

    Public Museums & Free Libraries Assn 68-68, V-Pres.
    Metro Free Libraries Assn (F) 77-77, Exec.


LEVY, JOSEPH HIAM (1838-1913)

    City of London School; City of London Col.
    Journalist 69; Board of Education Examiner 62;
        Professor of Logic and Economics, Birkbeck Col
        London.
    Liberal.
    Clapham.
    [WWW]

    League for Defense of Constitutional Rights 84-84,
        V-Pres.
    Vigilance Assn for Defense of Personal Rights
        75-83, Exec.


LEWIS, SIR CHARLES EDWARD, 1ST BT. (1825-1893)

    Solicitor 47; Author.
    Conservative. MP Londonderry City 72-86, Antrim
        North 87-92. JP.
    Baronet 87.
    Southwest London.
    [MEB, Dods, Direc Direcs]

    Howard Assn 74-84, Patron.


LEWIS, GEORGE PITT- (1845-1906)

    Middle Temple.
    Q.C. 85; Barrister 70.
    Liberal(Unionist). MP Barnstaple 85-92.
    West London.
    [WWW, Fosters, Dods]

    Free Land League 86-86, V-Pres.


LEWIS, RICHARD (1821-1905)

    Worcester, Oxf.
    Bishop Llandaff 83; Ordained Priest<CE> 46; Vicar
        47; Rector 51; Prebendary 67; Archdeacon 75;
        Substantial Landowner 86.
    Conservative.
    Llandaff.
    [DNB, Alum Cantab, Alum Oxon, Crockfds]

    Natl Soc for Preserving Memorials of Dead 84-84,
        Patron.


LEY, H. W.

    Land Nationalization Soc (F) 81-85, Hon Sec.


LEYCESTER, - <MISS>

    Kyrle Soc 84-94, Exec.


LIDDELL, HENRY GEORGE, 2ND EARL OF RAVENSWORTH
(1821-1903)

    Eton; Christ Church, Oxf.
    Very Large Landowner 78.
    Conservative. MP Northumberland South 52-78. DL,
        JP.
    Earl 78.
    West London; Durham[County].
    [WWW, BP, Walfords, Bateman, Alum Oxon, Dods]

    Assn for Promoting Extension of Contagious Diseases
        Act 70-70, V-Pres.


LIDDON, HENRY PARRY (1829-1890)

    King's College School; Christ Church, Oxf.
    Ireland Professor of Exegesis, Oxford 70; Canon
        70; Ordained Priest<CE> 53; College
        V-Principal 54; Prebendary 64.
    East Central London; Oxford.
    [DNB, MEB, Alum Cantab, Alum Oxon, Crockfds]

    City Church & Churchyard Protection Soc (F) 80-83,
        V-Pres.

LIDGETT, - <MISS>

    Natl Vigilance Assn (F) 85-85, Exec.


LIGHTFOOT, JOHN PRIDEAUX (1803-1887)

    Exeter, Oxf.
    Rector 33; College Fellow 24; College Tutor 27;
       Ordained Priest<CE> 32; Hon. Canon 53;
       V-Chancellor, Oxford 62.
    Oxford.
    [MEB, Alum Oxon, Crockfds]

    City Church & Churchyard Protection Soc (F) 80-83,
       V-Pres.


LIGHTFOOT, JOSEPH BARBER (1828-1889)

    King Edward's School, Birm; Trinity, Camb.
    Bishop Durham 79; Journal Editor 54; College
       Tutor 57; Ordained Priest<CE> 58; Hulsean
       Professor of Divinity, Cambridge 61; Canon 71;
       Lady Margaret Professor of Divinity, Cambridge
       75.
    Bishop Auckland.
    [DNB, MEB, Alum Cantab, Alum Oxon, Crockfds]

    Anglo-Oriental Soc for Suppression Opium Trade
       79-79, V-Pres.
    Central Assn for Stopping Sale Intox Liquors on
       Sunday 80-85, V-Pres.


LIGHTON, SIR CHRISTOPHER ROBERT, 6TH BT. (1819-1875)

    St John's, Camb.
    Vicar 48; Landowner 44; Curate 45; Ordained
       Priest<CE> 46.
    Baronet 44.
    Old Hill, Staffs; Herefordshire.
    [MEB, BP, Walfords, Alum Cantab, Crockfds]

    Church Assn 70-70, V-Pres.


LIGHTON, SIR CHRISTOPHER ROBERT, 7TH BT. (1848-1929)

    Repton; Trinity, Camb; Lincoln's Inn.
    Barrister 74; Landowner 75.
    DL, JP.
    Baronet 75.
    Herefordshire.
    [WWW, BP, Alum Cantab, Fosters]

    Church Assn 75-85, Exec.
    Soc for Abolition of Vivisection 76-76, Exec.


LINDSAY, CHARLES HUGH (1816-1889)

    Ensign, Army 35; Lieutenant, Army 40; Captain,
       Army 45; Lt. Colonel.
    Conservative. MP Abingdon 65-74.
    CB 81.
    Hampshire.
    [MEB, BP, Walfords, Dods, Army List]

    Assn for Promoting Extension of Contagious Diseases
       Act 68-70, V-Pres.


LINDSAY, SIR COUTTS, 2ND BT. (1824-1913)

    Large Landowner 37; Lieutenant, Army 41; Captain,
       Army 46.
    DL, JP.
    Baronet 37.
    Southwest London; Fifeshire.
    [WWW, BP, Walfords, Bateman, Direc Direcs, Army
       List]

    Sunday Society 83-90, V-Pres, President.


LINDSAY, WILLIAM ALEXANDER (1846-1926)

    Eton; Trinity, Camb; Middle Temple.
    Member Lloyds 68; Barrister 73; Q.C. 97.
    Conservative. DL, JP.
    CVO 24.
    Fellow Society of Antiquaries.
    Southwest London.
    [WWW, BP, Alum Cantab]

    Natl Education Union 71-79, Exec.


LINGARD, J. EDWARD

    Civil Engineer.
    Assoc Inst Civ Engineers.
    Derby.

    Sanitary Institute 80-86, Exec.


LINTON, SIR JAMES DROMGOLE (1840-1916)

    Newman Sreett School of Art.
    Artist.
    Kt 85.
    Inst Paintrs Oil; Royal Inst Water Colour
       Painters.
    Northwest London.
    [WWW]

    Sunday Society 86-90, V-Pres, President.


LINTON, SIR WILLIAM (1801-1880)

    U Edinburgh; Glasgow(Medical).
    Inspector General, Army Medical Serv 58; Asst
       Surgeon, Army Medical Serv 27; Surgeon, Army
       Medical Serv 41; Surgeon Major, Army Medical
       School 48; Deputy Inspector General, Army
       Medical Serv 54.
    CB 56; KCB 65.
    Cheltenham.
    [DNB, MEB, Walfords, Army List]

    Assn for Promoting Extension of Contagious Diseases
       Act 68-68, V-Pres.


LISTER, SAMUEL CUNLIFFE (1857- )

    St Johns, Oxf.
    Bradford; Yorks, West Riding.
    [Alum Oxon]

    Natl Fair Trade League (F) 81-81, Exec.

LISTER, THOMAS, 4TH BARON RIBBLESDALE (1854-1925)

> Harrow.
> Substantial Landowner 76;  Sub-Lt., Army 63;
>     Lieutenant, Army 73;  Captain, Army 81;  Major
>     86.
> Liberal.  Lord in Waiting 80-85, JP.
> Baron 76;  PC.
> Yorks, West Riding.
> [WWW, BP, Bateman, Direc Direcs, Army List]
>
> Natl Footpaths Preservation Soc 86-90, V-Pres,
>     President.

LITTLE, JAMES STANLEY (1856-1940)

> Kings Col London.
> Novelist;  Journal Editor 95.
> West London.
> [WWW]
>
> Natl Assn for Promotion of State Colonization
>     86-86, Exec.

LITTLETON, HENRY

> Travelling Tax Abolition Committee 79-85, Exec.

LIVESLEY, WILLIAM

> Manchester.
>
> Central Assn for Stopping Sale Intox Liquors on
>     Sunday 70-85, Exec.

LLOYD, - <MISS>

> Victoria Street Soc for Protection of Animals from
>     Vivisection 80-85, Exec.

LLOYD, EDWARD

> Intl Arbitration & Peace Assn 81-81, V-Pres.

LLOYD, GEORGE BRAITHWAITE

> Banker.
> JP.
> Birmingham.
> [Direc Direcs]
>
> Natl Education League (F) 69-69, Exec.

LLOYD, JOHN (1833- )

> St Johns, Oxf;  Middle Temple.
> Barrister 80.
> JP.
> West Central London;  Herefordshire.
> [Alum Oxon, Fosters]
>
> London Municipal Reform League 82-85, Hon Sec.

LLOYD, SAMPSON SAMUEL (1820-1889)

> Banker 40;  Manufacturer.
> Conservative.  MP Plymouth 74-80, Warwickshire
>     South 80-85.  JP.
> Southwest London;  Birmingham;  Warwickshire.
> [MEB, Dods, Direc Direcs]
>
> Natl Fair Trade League (F) 81-81, Chairman.

LLOYD, THOMAS (1814-1890)

> Grove House School, Tottenham.
> Banker 40;  Landowner 65.
> Liberal.  MP Barnstaple 63-64.  DL, JP.
> Birmingham;  Warwickshire.
> [MEB, Walfords, Dods, Direc Direcs]
>
> Assn for Promoting Extension of Contagious Diseases
>     Act 68-68, Exec.

LOCKE, JOHN (1805-1880)

> Dulwich College;  Trinity, Camb;  Inner Temple.
> Q.C. 57;  Barrister 33;  Author.
> Liberal.  MP Southwark 57-80.
> Southwest London.
> [DNB, MEB, Walfords, Alum Cantab, Dods]
>
> Commons Preservation Soc 69-76, V-Pres, Exec.

LOCKHART, WILLIAM (1811-1896)

> Guy's Hospital, Lond.
> Physician 38;  Director, London Missionary Soc 64.
> Fellow Royal Col Surgeons;  Fellow Royal Geograph
>     Society.
> Southeast London.
> [MEB]
>
> Anglo-Oriental Soc for Suppression Opium Trade (F)
>     75-75, Exec.

LOCKWOOD, SIR FRANK (1846-1897)

> Gonville & Caius, Camb;  Lincoln's Inn.
> Q.C. 82;  Barrister 72.
> Liberal.  MP York 85-97.  Solicitor General 94-95,
>     DL, JP.
> Kt 94.
> Southwest London;  Yorks, North Riding.
> [DNB, MEB, WWW, Alum Cantab, Fosters, Dods]
>
> Free Land League 86-86, V-Pres, Exec.

LOCKYER, SIR JOSEPH NORMAN (1836-1920)

> Sec, Science and Art Dept, South Kensington 75;
>     Civ Serv, War Office 57;  Director, Royal Col
>     of Science Observatory 90;  College Professor
>     90;  Author.
> CB 94;  KCB 97.
> Fellow Royal Society;  Fellow Royal Astronomical
>     Society.
> Southwest London;  Devonshire.
> [DNB, WWW]
>
> Smoke Abatement Committee 81-81.

LOFTIE, WILLIAM JOHN (1839-1911)

>
> Trin Col, Dublin.
> Journal Editor 72;  Curate 65;  Ordained Priest<CE>
>     66;  Asst Chaplain 71.
> Fellow Society of Antiquaries;  Fellow Zoological
>     Society.
> West London.
> [DNB, WWW, Crockfds]
>
> Soc for Protection of Ancient Buildings (F) 78-85,
>     Exec.

LOGAN, SIR THOMAS GALBRAITH (1808-1896)

>
> Glasgow(Medical).
> Director General, Army Medical Serv 67;  Asst
>     Surgeon, Army Medical Serv 30;  Surgeon, Army
>     Medical Serv 42;  Surgeon Major, Army Medical
>     School 52;  Deputy Inspector General, Army
>     Medical Serv 55;  Inspector General, Army
>     Medical Serv 59.
> CB 65;  KCB 69.
> Fellow Royal Col Physicians.
> West London.
> [MEB, BP, Army List]
>
> Assn for Promoting Extension of Contagious Diseases
>     Act 68-70, V-Pres.

LONG, FREDERICK

>
> Southeast London.
>
> Sunday Society 76-90, Treas.
> London Municipal Reform League 82-85, Exec.

LONG, GEORGE

>
> Clapham.
>
> Jamaica Committee (F) 66-66.

LONG, RICHARD PENRUDDOCKE (1825-1875)

>
> Harrow;  Trinity, Camb;  Inner Temple.
> Very Large Landowner 67.
> Conservative.  MP Chippenham 59-65, Wiltshire North
>     65-68.  DL, JP.
> West London;  Wiltshire;  Montgomeryshire.
> [MEB, Walfords, Alum Cantab, Dods]
>
> Church Assn 67-70, V-Pres.

LONGDEN, HENRY

>
> Financial Reform Union (F) 68-69, Exec.

LONGDON, -

>
> JP.
> Derby.
>
> Central Assn for Stopping Sale Intox Liquors on
>     Sunday 75-80, V-Pres.

LONGMAN, CHARLES JAMES (1852-1834)

>
> Harrow;  University Col, Oxf.
> Publisher 77;  Journal Editor 81.
> JP.
> West London;  Hertfordshire.
> [WWW, Alum Oxon]
>
> Commons Preservation Soc 80-86, Exec.

LONGMAN, WILLIAM (1813-1877)

>
> Publisher.
> Fellow Society of Antiquaries;  Fellow Geological
>     Society.
> Hertfordshire.
> [DNB, MEB]
>
> Commons Preservation Soc 69-76, Exec.

LOPES, HENRY CHARLES, 1ST BARON LUDLOW (1828-1899)

>
> Winchester College;  Balliol, Oxf;  Inner Temple.
> Judge, Queen's Bench 79;  Barrister 52;  Q.C. 69;
>     Judge, Common Pleas 76;  Judge, Court of Appeal
>     85.
> Conservative.  MP Launceston 68-74, Somersetshire
>     Frome 74-76.  DL, JP.
> Kt 76;  PC 85;  Baron 97.
> Southwest London;  Somersetshire.
> [DNB, WWW, BP, Walfords, Alum Oxon, Fosters, Dods,
>     Direc Direcs]
>
> Victoria Street Soc for Protection of Animals from
>     Vivisection 82-84, V-Pres.

LOPES, SIR MASSEY, 3RD BT.  (1818-1908)

>
> Winchester College;  Oriel, Oxf.
> Very Large Landowner 54.
> Conservative.  MP Westbury 57-68, Devonshire South
>     68-85.  Lord Admiralty 74-80, DL, JP.
> Baronet 54;  PC 85.
> West London;  Devonshire;  Wiltshire.
> [DNB, WWW, BP, Walfords, Bateman, Alum Oxon, Dods,
>     Direc Direcs]
>
> Local Taxation Comtee [of Central Chamber of
>     Agriculture] 71-85, Chairman.

LOUIS, ALFRED HYMAN (1829- )

>
> Trinity, Camb;  Lincoln's Inn.
> Barrister 55;  Journal Editor.
> West London.
> [Alum Cantab, Fosters]
>
> Commons Preservation Soc 69-69, Exec.

LOUISE CAROLINE ALBERTA, H.R.H.  PRINCESS <MARCHIONESS
OF LORNE> (1848-1939)

>
> VA;  CI;  GCVO;  GBE.
> West London;  Dumbartonshire.
> [DNB, BP]
>
> Kyrle Soc 84-94, V-Pres.

LOVELL, CHARLES H.

    North London.

    Church Assn 70-80, V-Chairman.


LOW, W.  F.

    West London.

    Assn for Promoting Extension of Contagious Diseases
       Act 68-68, Exec.


LOWE, - <MRS.>

    Malthusian League 78-78, V-Pres.


LOWE, - <MRS.>

    Land Nationalization Soc (F) 81-83, Exec.


LOWE, GEORGE (1788-1868)

    Gas Engineer.
    Fellow Royal Society;  Member Inst Civ Engineers;
       Fellow Geological Society.
    St Johns Wood.
    [MEB]

    Jamaica Committee (F) 66-66.


LOWE, L.  <MRS.>

    Sunday Society (F) 75-75, Exec.


LOWELL, JAMES RUSSELL (1819-1901)

    Harvard.
    Ambassador 77;  Professor of Modern Languages and
       Belles Lettres, Harvard 55;  Journal Editor 57;
       Poet.
    Southwest London;  Cambridge, Mass.
    [Alum Cantab, Alum Oxon]

    Soc for Protection of Ancient Buildings 85-85,
       Exec.


LOWTHER, SIR CHARLES HUGH, 3RD BT.  (1803-1894)

    Large Landowner 68.
    Baronet 68.
    West London;  Yorks, West Riding.
    [MEB, BP, Walfords, Bateman]

    Church Assn 70-85, V-Pres.


LOWTHER, WILLIAM (1821-1912)

    Magdalene, Camb.
    Attache, Dip Serv 41;  Sec Legation, Dip Serv 52;
       Minister Plenipotentiary 67.
    Conservative.  MP Westmorland 68-85, Westmorland
       North 85-92.  DL, JP.
    Southwest London;  Suffolk.
    [WWW, Walfords, Alum Cantab, Dods, Direc Direcs]

    Natl Assn for Promotion of State Colonization
       86-86, V-Pres, Exec.


LUBBOCK, JOHN, 1ST BARON AVEBURY (1834-1913)

    Eton.
    Banker;  Author.
    Liberal(Unionist).  MP Maidstone 70-80, London
       University 80-00.  DL, JP.
    Baronet 65;  PC 90;  Baron 00.
    Fellow Royal Society;  Fellow Society of
       Antiquaries;  Fellow Geological Society;
       Entomological Society;  Fellow Linnean Society;
       Ethnological Society.
    West London;  Kent.
    [DNB, WWW, BP, Walfords, Alum Cantab, Alum Oxon,
       Dods, Direc Direcs]

    Sanitary Institute 78-88, V-Pres.
    Public Museums & Free Libraries Assn 68-68, V-Pres.
    Metro Free Libraries Assn (F) 77-82, V-Pres, Exec.
    Soc for Protection of Ancient Buildings (F) 78-85,
       Exec.
    Intl Law Assn 74-74, Treas.
    Intl Arbitration & Peace Assn 81-81, V-Pres.
    Proportional Representation Soc (F) 84-88,
       President.


LUCAS, MARGARET <MRS. SAMUEL LUCAS, nee BRIGHT>
    (1818-1890)

    West Central London.
    [MEB]

    Ladies' Natl Assn for Repeal of Contagious Diseases
       Acts 70-72, Exec.
    British Women's Temperance Assn 84-85, President.


LUCRAFT, BENJAMIN (1810-1897)

    Labour Leader;  Cabinet Maker.
    Radical.
    London.
    [MEB]

    Public Museums & Free Libraries Assn 68-68, Exec.
    Working Men's Natl League for Abolition State
       Regulation of Vice 81-81, President.
    Workmen's Peace Assn 75-75, Exec.


LUDLOW, JOHN MALCOLM FORBES (1821-1911)

    Lincoln's Inn.
    Barrister 43;  Journal Editor 50;  Chief Registrar
       Friendly Societies 75.
    Radical.
    CB 87.
    Southwest London.
    [DNB, WWW, Fosters, Dic Lab Biog]

    Jamaica Committee (F) 66-66.

LUNN, WILLIAM JOSEPH

>   Physician.
>   Kingston-upon-Hull.
>
>   Church Assn 75-80, Exec.

LUSHINGTON, EDWARD HARBORD

>   JP.
>   Surrey.
>   [Direc Direcs]
>
>   City Church & Churchyard Protection Soc 81-83,
>       V-Pres.

LUSHINGTON, SIR GODFREY (1834-1907)

>   Rugby;  Balliol, Oxf;  Inner Temple.
>   Barrister 58;  Counsel to Home Office 69;  Asst
>       U-Sec, HO 76;  Perm U-Sec, HO 85;  College
>       Fellow 54.
>   KCB 92;  GCMG 99.
>   Southwest London;  Wiltshire.
>   [WWW, Alum Oxon, Fosters]
>
>   Commons Preservation Soc 69-69, Exec.
>   Jamaica Committee (F) 66-66.

LUSHINGTON, STEPHEN (1782-1873)

>   Eton;  Christ Church, Oxf;  Inner Temple.
>   Admiralty Judge 38;  Dean of Arches 58;  Barrister
>       06;  Judge, Consistory Court 28;  College
>       Fellow.
>   Liberal.  MP Great Yarmouth 06-08, Ilchester 20-26,
>       Tregony 26-30, Ilchester 31-31, Winchelsea
>       31-32, Tower Hamlets 32-41
>   PC 38.
>   Southwest London;  Hertfordshire.
>   [DNB, MEB, Walfords, Alum Oxon, Dods]
>
>   Howard Assn 67-72, Patron.

LUSHINGTON, VERNON (1832-1912)

>   Trinity, Camb;  Inner Temple.
>   County Court Judge 77;  Barrister 57;  Deputy Judge
>       Advocate General 64;  Q.C. 68;  Perm Sec,
>       Admiralty 69.
>   JP.
>   West London;  Surrey.
>   [WWW, Alum Cantab, Fosters]
>
>   Soc for Protection of Ancient Buildings (F) 78-85,
>       Exec.

LUSK, SIR ANDREW, 1ST BT.  (1810-1909)

>   Wholesale Grocer 35.
>   Liberal(Unionist).  MP Finsbury 65-85.  JP.
>   Baronet 74.
>   West London;  Hertfordshire.
>   [DNB, WWW, BP, Walfords, Dods, Direc Direcs]
>
>   Commons Preservation Soc 69-86, Exec.
>   Public Museums & Free Libraries Assn 69-69, V-Pres.
>   Howard Assn 71-84, Patron.
>   Natl Assn for Repeal Contagious Diseases Acts
>       81-81, V-Pres.

>   Financial Reform Union 69-69, Treas.
>   Plimsoll and Seamen's Fund Committee (F) 73-73,
>       Exec.

LYALL, MARY

>   Kyrle Soc 84-90, Exec.

LYCETT, SIR FRANCIS (1803-1880)

>   Glove Manufacturer;  Merchant.
>   JP.
>   Kt 67.
>   North London.
>   [MEB, Walfords]
>
>   Natl Emigration League (F) 70-70, V-Pres.

LYELL, LEONARD, 1ST BARON LYELL (1850-1926)

>   London U.
>   Large Landowner 76;  Professor of Natural Science,
>       U Col Wales.
>   Liberal.  MP Orkney&Shetland 85-00.  DL, JP.
>   Baronet 94;  Baron 14.
>   Southwest London;  Forfarshire.
>   [WWW, BP, Bateman, Dods, Direc Direcs]
>
>   Free Land League 86-86, V-Pres.

LYGON, FREDERICK, 6TH EARL BEAUCHAMP (1830-1891)

>   Eton;  Christ Church, Oxf;  Inner Temple.
>   Very Large Landowner 66;  College Fellow 52.
>   Conservative.  MP Tewkesbury 57-63, Worcestershire
>       West 63-66.  Lord Admiralty 59-59, Lord Steward
>       Royal Household 74-80, Paymaster General 85-86,
>       Paymaster General 86-87, Lord Lieutenant 76-91,
>       DL, JP.
>   Earl 66;  PC 74.
>   Fellow Society of Antiquaries.
>   Southwest London;  Worcestershire.
>   [DNB, MEB, BP, Walfords, Bateman, Alum Oxon, Dods]
>
>   Natl Soc for Preserving Memorials of Dead (F)
>       81-84, Patron.

LYNAM, C.

>   Architect.
>   Fellow Royal Inst Br Architects.
>   Stoke-upon-Trent.
>
>   Natl Soc for Preserving Memorials of Dead (F)
>       81-82, Exec.

LYNCH, - <MRS.>

>   Natl Vigilance Assn (F) 85-85, Exec.

LYNN, J. H.

Natl Assn for Repeal Contagious Diseases Acts
81-81, Exec.

LYON, SAMUEL EDMUND (1822- )

Wadham, Oxf.
Curate 59; Curate 45; Ordained Priest<CE> 46;
Perp. Curate 49.
East Stratton.
[Alum Oxon, Crockfds]

Church Assn 80-80, Exec.

LYON, WILLIAM

Plimsoll and Seamen's Fund Committee (F) 73-73,
Exec.

LYTE, FARNHAM MAXWELL (1827-1906)

Christ's, Camb.
Inventor of Photographic Processes 54.
Fellow Chemical Society; Inst of Chemistry; Assoc
Inst Civ Engineers; Photographic Society.
London.
[Alum Cantab]

Sanitary Institute 82-84, Exec.

LYTTLETON, - <"CAPT.">

Church Assn 70-70, Secretary.

LYTTLETON, GEORGE WILLIAM, 4TH BARON LYTTLETON
(1817-1876)

Eton; Trinity, Camb.
Large Landowner 37; College Head 45; Chief
Endowed Schools Commissioner 69.
Parl U-Sec Col Off 46-46, Lord Lieutenant 39-76,
JP.
Baron 37; PC 69; KCMG 69.
Fellow Royal Society.
West London; Worcestershire.
[DNB, MEB, BP, Walfords, Alum Cantab, Alum Oxon]

Soc for Promoting Increase of the Home Episcopate
72-74, Chairman, President.

LYTTLETON, WILLIAM HENRY (1820-1884)

Winchester College; Trinity, Camb.
Rector 47; Curate 43; Ordained Priest<CE> 44;
Perp. Curate 45; Hon. Canon 50; Canon 80;
Author.
Hagley.
[DNB, MEB, BP, Walfords, Alum Cantab, Crockfds]

Sunday Society (F) 75-75, V-Pres.

MABBS, GOODEVE

Clergyman<Sect Unkn>.

Anglo-Oriental Soc for Suppression Opium Trade
80-83, Exec.

MCARTHUR, ALEXANDER (1814-1909)

Australia Merchant.
Liberal. MP Leicester 74-92. DL, JP.
Br Assn; Fellow Royal Geograph Society.
Southwest London.
[WWW, Dods, Direc Direcs, Aust Dict Biog]

Free Land League 86-86, V-Pres.
Howard Assn 74-84, Patron.
Intl Arbitration & Peace Assn 81-81, V-Pres.
Jamaica Committee (F) 66-66.
Natl Assn for Repeal Contagious Diseases Acts
81-81, V-Pres.

MCARTHUR, WILLIAM ALEXANDER (1857-1923)

Australia Merchant.
Radical. MP Buckrose, Yorks ER 86-86, St Austell
87-08. Junior Lord Treasury 92-95, DL.
West London.
[Dods, Direc Direcs]

Free Land League 86-86, V-Pres.

MCARTHUR, SIR WILLIAM (1809-1887)

Australia Merchant; Accountant 25; Woolen Draper
31.
Liberal(Unionist). MP Lambeth 68-85. DL, JP.
KCMG 82.
Fellow Royal Geograph Society.
West London.
[DNB, MEB, Walfords, Dods, Direc Direcs]

Public Museums & Free Libraries Assn 68-68, V-Pres.
Anglo-Oriental Soc for Suppression Opium Trade (F)
75-79, V-Pres.
Central Assn for Stopping Sale Intox Liquors on
Sunday 85-85, V-Pres.
Free Land League 86-86, V-Pres.
Howard Assn 72-84, Patron.
Intl Arbitration & Peace Assn 81-81, V-Pres.
Jamaica Committee (F) 66-66.
Natl Emigration League (F) 70-70, V-Pres.
Natl Assn for Repeal Contagious Diseases Acts
81-81, V-Pres.

MCCARTHY, JUSTIN (1830-1912)

Journalist; Novelist.
Irish Nationalist. MP Longford Co 79-85, Longford
Co North 85-86, Londonderry City 86-92,
Longford Co North 92-00.
London.
[DNB, Dods]

Commons Preservation Soc 80-86, Exec.
Intl Arbitration & Peace Assn 81-81, V-Pres.

MCCAW, WILLIAM

    Presbyterian Minister 46;  Author.
    Manchester.
    [MEB]

    Central Assn for Stopping Sale Intox Liquors on
        Sunday (F) 67-85, Exec.


MCCLURE, THOMAS

    Working Men's Protestant League 82-82, Hon Sec.


MCCLURE, SIR THOMAS, 1ST BT.  (1806-1893)

    Belfast Academy.
    Merchant.
    Liberal.  MP Belfast 68-74, Londonderry Co 78-85.
        DL, JP.
    Baronet 74.
    Belfast.
    [MEB, BP, Walfords, Dods]

    Intl Arbitration & Peace Assn 81-81, V-Pres.


MACCOLL, NORMAN (1844-1904)

    Downing, Camb;  Lincoln's Inn.
    Journal Editor 71;  College Fellow 69;  Barrister
        75.
    West London.
    [DNB, WWW, Alum Cantab, Fosters]

    Soc for Protection of Ancient Buildings (F) 78-85,
        Exec.


MACCORMAC, SIR WILLIAM, 1ST BT.  (1836-1901)

    Belfast Academy;  Royal College Belfast.
    Physician 57;  Asst Surgeon 71;  Surgeon 73.
    Kt 81;  Baronet 97;  KCVO 98;  KCB 01.
    Fellow Royal Col Surgeons;  Fellow Royal Col
        Surgeons, Ire.
    Belfast.
    [DNB, WWW, BP]

    Assn for Promoting Extension of Contagious Diseases
        Act 68-68, Exec.


MCCOY, D.  <"MAJOR">

    DL, JP.

    Sanitary Institute 79-80, Secretary.


MCCRACKEN, J.

    JP.

    Intl Arbitration & Peace Assn 81-81, V-Pres.


MCCREE, GEORGE WILSON (1822-1892)

    Baptist Mission Worker 48;  Baptist Minister 73;
        Journal Editor 61.
    Southeast London.
    [MEB]

    Intl Arbitration & Peace Assn 81-81, Exec.


MCCULLOCH, JOHN (1842- )

    Farmer;  Land Valuator.
    Liberal.  MP Glasgow St Rollox 85-86.
    Wigtownshire.
    [Dods]

    Free Land League 86-86, V-Pres.


MCCURDY, ALEXANDER

    Methodist New Connection Minister.
    Loughborough.

    Central Assn for Stopping Sale Intox Liquors on
        Sunday 85-85, V-Pres.


MACDONALD, ALEXANDER (1821-1881)

    U Glasgow.
    Trade Union Leader 55;  Miner 31;  School Teacher
        51.
    Liberal.  MP Stafford 74-81.
    Lanarkshire.
    [MEB, Dods, Dic Lab Biog]

    Sunday Society 80-82, V-Pres.
    Land Law Reform League (F) 81-81, V-Pres.


MACDONALD, MACDONALD- <"COL.">

    Church Assn 78-85, Exec.


MACDONALD, RODERICK (1840-1894)

    U Glasgow.
    Surgeon 67.
    Radical.  MP Ross & Cromarty 85-92.  Med Off of
        Health.
    East London.
    [MEB, Dods, Direc Direcs, Dic Lab Biog]

    Free Land League 86-86, V-Pres.


MCDONNELL, A.

    Land Nationalization Soc 84-85, Hon Sec.


MCDOUGALL, SIR PATRICK LEONARD (1819-1894)

    Royal Military College, Sandhurst.
    General 83;  Ensign, Army 36;  Captain, Army 44;
        Major 49;  Colonel 58;  Maj. General 68;  Lt.
        General 77.
    KCMG 77.
    Southwest London;  Surrey.
    [DNB, MEB, BP, Army List]

Victoria Street Soc for Protection of Animals from
    Vivisection 84-85, Exec.

MACEVILLY, JOHN (1817-1902)

Maynooth Col.
Archbishop Tuam<RC> 81;  College Professor 42;
    Bishop Galway<RC> 57.
Tuam.
[WWW]

Victoria Street Soc for Protection of Animals from
    Vivisection 84-85, V-Pres.

MCFADYEN, J.

Central Assn for Stopping Sale Intox Liquors on
    Sunday (F) 67-67, Exec.

MACFARLANE, SIR DONALD HORNE (1830-1904)

E India Merchant.
Liberal.  MP Carlow Co 80-85, Argyllshire 85-86,
    Argyllshire 92-95.
Kt 94.
West London;  Norfolk.
[WWW, Dods]

Smoke Abatement Committee 81-81.
Free Land League 86-86, V-Pres.

MACFIE, M.

Fellow Royal Geograph Society.
Birmingham.

Natl Education League 71-71, Exec.

MACFIE, ROBERT ANDREW (1811-1893)

Edinburgh High School;  U Edinburgh.
Sugar Refiner 27.
Liberal.  MP Leith 68-74.  JP.
Fellow Royal Society Edinb.
Southwest London;  Cheshire;  Midlothian.
[DNB, MEB, Walfords, Dods]

Howard Assn 69-73, Patron.
Natl Emigration League (F) 70-70, V-Pres.

MCGAREL, CHARLES

Natl Emigration League (F) 70-70, V-Pres.

MCGILL, GEORGE HENRY (1818- )

Brasenose, Oxf.
Perp. Curate 54;  Ordained Priest<CE> 42;  Vicar
    46;  Rector 67.
East London.
[Alum Oxon, Crockfds]

Assn for Improvement of London Workhouse
    Infirmaries 66-66, Exec.

MCGRATH, HENRY WALTER (1803-1884)

Trin Col, Dublin.
Hon. Canon 58;  Ordained Priest<CE> 29;  Perp.
    Curate 32;  Rector 37.
Manchester;  Torquay.
[MEB, Crockfds]

Church Assn 70-78, Exec.

MACGREGOR, JOHN (1825-1892)

King's School, Canterbury;  Trinity, Camb;  Inner
    Temple.
Illustrator 45;  Barrister 51;  Author.
Southeast London.
[DNB, MEB, Alum Cantab, Fosters]

Plimsoll and Seamen's Fund Committee (F) 73-73,
    Exec.

MCIVER, SIR LEWIS, 1ST BT.  (1846-1920)

U Bonn;  Middle Temple.
India Civil Service 68.
Liberal(Unionist).  MP Torquay 85-86, Edinburgh
    West 95-09.
Baronet 96.
West London.
[WWW, BP, Fosters, Dods]

Free Land League 86-86, V-Pres.

MACKARNESS, GEORGE RICHARD (1823-1883)

Merton, Oxf.
Bishop Argyll and the Isles 74;  College Fellow 46;
    Curate 46;  Ordained Priest<CE> 48;  Vicar 54;
    Rural Dean 69.
Conservative.
Lochgilphead.
[MEB, Alum Oxon, Crockfds]

Natl Soc for Preserving Memorials of Dead (F)
    81-83, Patron.

MACKARNESS, JOHN FIELDER (1820-1889)

Eton;  Merton, Oxf.
Bishop Oxford 69;  Ordained Priest<CE> 45;  Vicar
    45;  Rector 55;  School Head 55;  Prebendary
    58;  Vicar 67.
Oxford.
[DNB, MEB, Alum Oxon, Crockfds]

Central Assn for Stopping Sale Intox Liquors on
    Sunday 80-85, V-Pres.
Victoria Street Soc for Protection of Animals from
    Vivisection 80-85, V-Pres.
Soc for Promoting Increase of the Home Episcopate
    72-74, V-Pres.

MACKENZIE, COLIN

    West London.

    Natl Assn for Promotion of State Colonization
       86-86, V-Pres.


MCKENZIE, COLIN (1806-1881)

    Lt. General 77;  Lieutenant, Army 27;  Captain,
       Army 41;  Major 56;  Lt. Colonel 61;  Maj.
       General 71.
    CB 68.
    Edinburgh.
    [DNB, MEB, Army List]

    Victoria Street Soc for Protection of Animals from
       Vivisection 80-80, Exec.


MACKENZIE, EDWARD MONTAGUE STUART GRANVILLE MONTAGU
    STUART WORTLEY, 1ST EARL OF WHARNCLIFFE (1827-1899)

    Eton.
    Very Large Landowner 55;  Colliery Owner;
       Lieutenant, Army 46.
    Conservative.  DL, JP.
    Baron 55;  Earl 76.
    Southwest London;  Yorks, West Riding.
    [MEB, WWW, BP, Walfords, Bateman, Direc Direcs,
       Army List]

    Soc for Protection of Ancient Buildings (F) 78-85,
       Exec.
    Plimsoll and Seamen's Fund Committee (F) 73-73,
       Exec.
    Soc for Promoting Increase of the Home Episcopate
       72-74, V-Pres.


MACKENZIE, J.

    Physician.
    Inverness.

    Jamaica Committee (F) 66-66.


MCKERROW, J. B.

    Central Assn for Stopping Sale Intox Liquors on
       Sunday (F) 67-67, Exec.


MACKIE, IVIE (1805-1873)

    Merchant;  Banker.
    JP.
    Manchester;  Kirkcudbrightshire.
    [MEB, Walfords]

    Assn for Promoting Extension of Contagious Diseases
       Act 68-70, V-Pres.


MACKONOCHIE, ALEXANDER HERIOT (1825-1887)

    Wadham, Oxf.
    Perp. Curate 62;  Curate 49;  Ordained Priest<CE>
       50.
    East Central London.
    [DNB, MEB, Alum Oxon, Crockfds]

    Church League for the Separation of Church and
       State (F) 77-77, President.


MACLAGAN, WILLIAM DALRYMPLE (1826-1910)

    Edinburgh High School;  Peterhouse, Camb.
    Rector 69;  Vicar 75;  Bishop Lichfield 78;
       Archbishop York 91;  Lieutenant, Army 47;
       Ordained Priest<CE> 57;  Curate 57.
    PC 91.
    South London;  West London;  Lichfield.
    [DNB, WWW, Crockfds]

    Natl Soc for Preserving Memorials of Dead (F)
       81-85, Patron.
    Natl Education Union 70-79, Exec.
    Soc for Promoting Increase of the Home Episcopate
       72-74, V-Pres.


MACLAREN, ALEXANDER (1826-1910)

    Glasgow High School;  U Glasgow;  Stepney College.
    Baptist Minister 46.
    Manchester.
    [DNB, WWW]

    Central Assn for Stopping Sale Intox Liquors on
       Sunday 85-85, V-Pres.


MCLAREN, CHARLES BENJAMIN BRIGHT, 1ST BARON ABERCONWAY
    (1850-1934)

    U Edinburgh;  Lincoln's Inn.
    Barrister 74;  Q.C. 97;  Landowner.
    Radical.  MP Stafford 80-86, Bosworth 92-10.  JP.
    Baronet 02;  PC 08;  Baron 11.
    Southwest London;  Denbighshire.
    [BP, Dods, Fosters]

    Free Land League 86-86, V-Pres.
    Intl Arbitration & Peace Assn 81-81, V-Pres.
    Natl Assn for Repeal Contagious Diseases Acts
       81-81, V-Pres.


MCLAREN, DAVID

    Anglo-Oriental Soc for Suppression Opium Trade (F)
       77-83, Exec.


MCLAREN, DUNCAN (1800-1886)

    Draper 24.
    Liberal.  MP Edinburgh 65-81.  DL, JP.
    Edinburgh.
    [DNB, MEB, Walfords, Dods, Direc Direcs]

    Intl Arbitration & Peace Assn 81-81, V-Pres.
    Jamaica Committee (F) 66-66.

MCLAREN, PRISCILLA <MRS. DUNCAN MCLAREN, nee BRIGHT>

    Glasgow.

    Ladies´ Natl Assn for Repeal of Contagious Diseases
       Acts 70-72, Exec.


MCLAREN, WALTER B.

    Vigilance Assn for Defense of Personal Rights
       83-83, Exec.


MCLEAN, ROBERT A.

    Accountant.
    Fellow Royal Geograph Society.
    London.
    [Direc Direcs]

    Intl Arbitration & Peace Assn 81-81, Exec.


MACMILLAN, SIR FREDERICK ORRIDGE (1851-1936)

    Uppingham.
    Publisher.
    DL, JP.
    Kt 09;  CVO 28.
    St Johns Wood.
    [DNB, WWW]

    Soc for Protection of Ancient Buildings (F) 78-85,
       Exec.


MCMINNIES, JOHN GORDON (1817-1890)

    Cotton Manufacturer.
    Liberal.  MP Warrington 80-85.  JP.
    Warrington.
    [MEB, Dods]

    Intl Arbitration & Peace Assn 81-81, V-Pres.
    Natl Assn for Repeal Contagious Diseases Acts
       81-81, V-Pres.


MCNEILE, HUGH (1795-1879)

    Trin Col, Dublin;  Lincoln´s Inn.
    Canon 60;  Dean 68;  Curate 20;  Ordained
       Priest<CE> 21;  Rector 22;  Perp. Curate 34;
       Hon.  Canon 45.
    Chester;  Ripon.
    [DNB, MEB, Alum Cantab, Crockfds]

    Church Assn 67-75, V-Pres.


MACRAE, CHARLES COLIN (1843-1922)

    Eton;  University Col, Oxf;  Lincoln´s Inn.
    Barrister 68;  Sec, Bengal Legislative Council;
       Counsel to India Office.
    JP.
    West London.
    [WWW, Alum Oxon, Fosters]

    Intl Arbitration & Peace Assn 81-81, Exec.


MADDISON, ARTHUR J.  S.

    Natl Vigilance Assn (F) 85-85, Exec.


MAGEE, WILLIAM CONNOR (1821-1891)

    Kilkenny College;  Trin Col, Dublin.
    Bishop Peterborough 68;  Curate 44;  Ordained
       Priest<CE> 45;  Prebendary 59;  Rector 61;
       Dean 61;  Archbishop York 91.
    Conservative.
    Peterborough.
    [DNB, MEB, Alum Oxon, Crockfds]

    Central Assn for Stopping Sale Intox Liquors on
       Sunday 75-85, V-Pres.
    Natl Education Union 70-79, Exec.


MAITLAND, EDWARD (1824-1897)

    Gonville & Caius, Camb.
    Journalist 57;  Author.
    London.
    [DNB, MEB, Alum Cantab]

    Sunday Society 76-90, V-Pres.


MAITLAND, ROBERT FULLER (1846- )

    Christ Church, Oxf.
    [Alum Oxon]

    Smoke Abatement Committee 81-81.


MAJENDIE, LEWIS ASHURST (1835-1885)

    Marlborough;  Christ Church, Oxf;  Lincoln´s Inn.
    Landowner 67.
    Conservative.  MP Canterbury 74-79.  DL, JP.
    West London;  Essex.
    [MEB, Walfords, Alum Oxon, Dods]

    Natl Soc for Preserving Memorials of Dead (F)
       81-82, Exec.


MAKINS, SIR WILLIAM THOMAS, 1ST BT.  (1840-1906)

    Harrow;  Trinity, Camb;  Middle Temple.
    Barrister 62.
    Conservative.  MP Essex South 74-85, Essex
       Southeast 85-86, Essex Southwest 86-92.  DL,
       JP.
    Baronet 03.
    Southwest London;  Henley-on-Thames.
    [BP, Alum Cantab, Fosters, Dods, Direc Direcs]

    Howard Assn 75-83, Patron.


MALET, SIR ALEXANDER, 2ND BT.  (1800-1886)

    Winchester College;  Christ Church, Oxf;  Middle
       Temple.
    Substantial Landowner 15;  Diplomatic Service 24;
       Sec Legation, Dip Serv 33;  Minister
       Plenipotentiary 49;  Author.
    DL, JP.
    Baronet 15;  KCB 66.
    Southwest London;  Wiltshire.

[DNB, MEB, BP, Walfords, Bateman, Alum Oxon]

Victoria Street Soc for Protection of Animals from
     Vivisection 84-85, V-Pres.


MALET, MARIAN DORA, LADY <WIFE OF SIR ALEXANDER MALET,
2ND BT., nee SPALDING> ( -1891)

Southwest London; Wiltshire.
[BP]

Soc for Abolition of Vivisection 76-76, Exec.


MALET, O. W.

Natl Soc for Preserving Memorials of Dead 84-84,
     Exec.


MALLESON, JOHN PHILIP (1796-1869)

U Glasgow.
Retired Clergyman 60;  School Head 22;  Unitarian
     Minister 29.
Croydon.
[DNB, MEB]

Jamaica Committee (F) 66-66.


MALLESON, WILLIAM TAYLOR

London.

Jamaica Committee (F) 66-66.
Vigilance Assn for Defense of Personal Rights
     83-83, Exec.
Natl Assn for Repeal Contagious Diseases Acts
     81-84, V-Chairman.


MALLET, - <MRS.>

Smoke Abatement Committee 81-81.


MALTBY, F. N.

Harrow-on-the-Hill.

Church Assn 70-75, Exec.


MANDER, S. S.

Wolverhampton.

Natl Education League 71-71, Exec.


MANEY, C.

North London.

Church Assn 75-75, Exec.


MANNING, HENRY EDWARD (1808-1892)

Harrow;  Balliol, Oxf.
Archbishop Westminster<RC> 65;  Cardinal<RC> 75;
     Ordained Priest<CE> 32;  Curate 32;  Rector 33;
     Archdeacon 40;  Priest<RC> 51.
Southwest London.
[DNB, MEB, Alum Oxon]

Natl Assn for Promotion of State Colonization
     86-86, Patron.
Central Assn for Stopping Sale Intox Liquors on
     Sunday (F) 67-85, V-Pres.
Howard Assn 82-84, Patron.
Natl Vigilance Assn (F) 85-85, Exec.
Victoria Street Soc for Protection of Animals from
     Vivisection 80-85, V-Pres.


MANNING, W. T.

Queen's Coroner.
Southwest London.

Howard Assn 73-77, Exec.
Infant Life Protection Soc 71-71, Exec.


MANSERGH, JAMES (1834-1905)

Sewerage Engineer.
JP.
Fellow Royal Society;  Member Inst Civ Engineers;
     Inst of Mech Engineers.
Southwest London.
[DNB, WWW]

Sanitary Institute 78-89, Exec.


MANSON, JAMES ALEXANDER (1851-1921)

Edinburgh High School;  U Edinburgh.
Publishing Company Editor 70;  Author.
Southeast London.
[WWW]

London Municipal Reform League 82-85, Exec.


MANT, NEWTON WILLIAM JOHN (1849-1911)

Sherborne;  St John's, Camb.
Vicar 78;  Curate 72;  Ordained Priest<CE> 73;
     Rector 07.
Fellow Society of Antiquaries.
Sledgmere.
[Alum Cantab, Crockfds]

Soc for Protection of Ancient Buildings (F) 78-85,
     Exec.


MAPOTHER, EDWARD DILLON (1835-1908)

Dublin(Medical).
Surgeon 57;  Medical School Professor 64.
Liberal.  Med Off of Health.
Royal Microscop Society;  Royal Med & Chir Society;
     Fellow Royal Col Surgeons, Ire.
Dublin.
[DNB, WWW]

Assn for Promoting Extension of Contagious Diseases
     Act 68-70, V-Pres.

MAPPIN, SIR FREDERICK THORPE, 1ST BT.  (1821-1910)

> Steel Manufacturer 59;  Cutlery Manufacturer 35.
> Liberal.  MP East Retford 80-85, Hallamshire,Yorks
>     WR S 85-06.  DL, JP.
> Baronet 86.
> Member Inst Civ Engineers;  Inst of Mech Engineers.
> Southwest London;  Sheffield.
> [DNB, WWW, BP, Dods, Direc Direcs]

> Free Land League 86-86, V-Pres.

MARCH, R. A.

> London Municipal Reform League 82-82, Exec.

MARKS, ALFRED

> London.

> Soc for Protection of Ancient Buildings (F) 78-85,
>     Treas.

MARKS, HENRY STACY (1829-1898)

> Leigh's Art Sch.
> Artist;  Illustrator.
> Assoc Royal Academy;  Royal Society Water Colour
>     Painters.
> St Johns Wood.
> [DNB, MEB, WWW, Bryan's Painters]

> Soc for Protection of Ancient Buildings (F) 78-85,
>     Exec.

MARKS, T. NEWMAN

> West London.

> Soc for Protection of Ancient Buildings 80-80,
>     Secretary.
> City Church & Churchyard Protection Soc (F) 80-81,
>     Exec.

MARLING, SIR SAMUEL STEPHENS, 1ST BT.  (1810-1883)

> Woolen Manufacturer;  Landowner.
> Liberal.  MP Gloucestershire West 68-73, Stroud
>     75-80.  DL, JP.
> Baronet 82.
> West London;  Stroud;  Gloucestershire.
> [MEB, BP, Walfords, Dods]

> Intl Arbitration & Peace Assn 81-81, V-Pres.

MARRIAGE, JOSEPH

> Howard Assn 83-83, Exec.

MARSDEN, MARK EAGLES

> West Central London.

> London Municipal Reform League 82-85, Exec.
> Travelling Tax Abolition Committee (F) 77-85,
>     V-Chairman.
> Vigilance Assn for Defense of Personal Rights
>     83-83, Exec.

MARSH, MATTHEW HENRY (1810-1881)

> Westminster School;  Christ Church, Oxf;  Inner
>     Temple.
> Very Large Landowner;  Barrister 36.
> Liberal.  MP Salisbury 57-68.  DL, JP.
> Fellow Royal Geograph Society.
> Hampshire;  New South Wales.
> [MEB, Walfords, Alum Oxon, Dods, Aust Dict Biog]

> Natl Emigration League (F) 70-70, V-Pres.

MARSHALL, - <MISS> ( -1884)

> British Women's Temperance Assn 84-84, Exec.

MARSHALL, GILBERT

> Commons Preservation Soc 69-69, Exec.

MARSON, J.

> Clergyman<Sect Unkn>.
> Birmingham.

> Assn for Promoting Extension of Contagious Diseases
>     Act 68-68, Exec.

MARSTON, - <MISS>

> London.

> Victoria Street Soc for Protection of Animals from
>     Vivisection 80-85, Exec.

MARSTON, CHARLES DALLAS (1824-1876)

> Eton;  Gonville & Caius, Camb.
> Vicar 73;  Ordained Priest<CE> 49;  Curate 49;
>     Perp. Curate 52;  Rector 62.
> Southwest London.
> [MEB, Alum Cantab, Crockfds]

> Church Assn 75-75, Exec.

MARTIN, SIR JAMES RANALD (1793-1874)

> St George's Hospital Lond.
> Surgeon;  Army Medical Service 18;  Sanitary
>     Commissioner, Eng 42;  Inspector General, Army
>     Medical Serv 64;  Author.
> CB 60;  Kt 60.
> Fellow Royal Society;  Fellow Royal Col Surgeons.
> West London.
> [DNB, MEB]

Assn for Improvement of London Workhouse
   Infirmaries 66-66, Exec.

MARTIN, JOHN

   Church Assn 67-78, Exec.

MARTIN, SAMUEL (1817-1878)

   Western College, Exeter.
   Congregational Minister 39.
   Southwest London.
   [DNB, MEB]

   Assn for Improvement of London Workhouse
      Infirmaries 66-66, Exec.

MARTIN, THOMAS H.

   Crawley<?>.

   Sunday Society (F) 75-75, Exec.

MARTIN, SIR WILLIAM FANSHAWE, 4TH BT.  (1801-1895)

   Admiral 63;  Cadet, RN 13;  Lieutenant, RN 20;
      Commander, RN 23;  Captain, RN 26;  Rear
      Admiral 53;  Vice-Admiral 58.
   Lord Admiralty 58-59.
   KCB 61;  Baronet 63;  GCB 73.
   Devonport.
   [DNB, MEB, BP, Walfords, Navy List]

   Assn for Promoting Extension of Contagious Diseases
      Act 70-70, V-Pres.

MARTINEAU, HARRIET (1802-1876)

   Author;  Journalist.
   Westmorland.
   [DNB, MEB]

   Ladies´ Natl Assn for Repeal of Contagious Diseases
      Acts 70-72, Exec.

MARTINEAU, JOHN

   Natl Emigration League (F) 70-70, Exec.

MARTINEAU, R.  F.

   Birmingham.

   London Comtee Exposure & Suppresn Traffic In Girls
      (F) 80-80, Exec.
   Natl Education League 71-71, Exec.

MASFEN, R.  H.

   Local Taxation Comtee [of Central Chamber of
      Agriculture] 71-79, Exec.

MASKELYNE, MERVYN HERBERT NEVIL STORY- (1823-1911)

   Wadham, Oxf;  Inner Temple.
   Professor of Mineralogy, Oxford 56;  College
      Lecturer 50;  Keeper of Minerals, British
      Museum 57;  Large Landowner 79;  Author.
   Liberal(Unionist).  MP Wilts N, Cricklade 80-85,
      Wiltshire North 85-92.  DL, JP.
   Fellow Royal Society;  Inst of Chemistry.
   Wiltshire.
   [DNB, WWW, Bateman, Alum Oxon, Dods, Direc Direcs]

   Commons Preservation Soc 81-86, Exec.

MASON, ARTHUR JAMES (1851-1928)

   Repton;  Trinity, Camb.
   Canon 77;  College Fellow 73;  Ordained Priest<CE>
      75;  Curate 75;  Vicar 84;  Lady Margaret
      Professor of Divinity, Cambridge 95;  College
      Head 03.
   Cambridge;  Truro.
   [DNB, WWW, Alum Cantab, Crockfds]

   City Church & Churchyard Protection Soc 83-83,
      Exec.

MASON, CHARLES A.  J.

   Natl Soc for Preserving Memorials of Dead 84-84,
      Exec.

MASON, HUGH (1820-1886)

   Cotton Manufacturer.
   Radical.  MP Ashton-Under-Lyne 80-85.  DL, JP.
   Ashton-Under-Lyne;  Lancashire.
   [MEB, Dods]

   Central Assn for Stopping Sale Intox Liquors on
      Sunday 70-75, V-Pres.
   Howard Assn 80-84, Patron.
   Jamaica Committee (F) 66-66.
   Natl Assn for Repeal Contagious Diseases Acts
      81-81, V-Pres.

MASSINGBERD, FRANCIS CHARLES (1800-1872)

   Rugby;  Magdalen, Oxf.
   Canon 62;  Ordained Priest<CE> 25;  Rector 25;
      Prebendary 47.
   Lincoln.
   [DNB, MEB, Walfords, Alum Oxon, Crockfds]

   Soc for Promoting Increase of the Home Episcopate
      72-72, Exec.

MATHER, SIR WILLIAM (1838-1920)

    Iron Manufacturer.
    Liberal.  MP Salford South 85-86, Gorton, Lancs SE
        89-95, Rossendale, Lancs NE 00-04.  JP.
    Kt 02;  PC.
    Member Inst Civ Engineers;  Inst of Mech Engineers.
    Manchester;  Salford.
    [WWW, Dods]

    Sunday Society 76-90, V-Pres.
    Free Land League 86-86, V-Pres.


MATHESON, DONALD

    Anglo-Oriental Soc for Suppression Opium Trade (F)
        75-80, Exec.


MATHIESON, JAMES E.

    Anglo-Oriental Soc for Suppression Opium Trade
        83-86, Exec.


MATKIN, C.

    Workmen's Peace Assn 75-75, Exec.


MATKIN, W.

    Workmen's Peace Assn 75-75, Exec.


MATTHEWS, C.  E.  <ALSO MATHEWS>

    Birmingham.

    Natl Education League (F) 69-71, Exec.


MATTHEWS, E.  <ALSO MATHEWS>

    Clergyman<Sect Unkn>.

    Central Assn for Stopping Sale Intox Liquors on
        Sunday (F) 67-70, Exec.


MATTHEWS, J.

    Clergyman<Sect Unkn>.

    Victoria Street Soc for Protection of Animals from
        Vivisection 84-85, Exec.


MATTHEWS, NORMAN H.

    Tickhill.

    Natl Soc for Preserving Memorials of Dead (F)
        81-82, Exec.


MATTINSON, JAMES

    Natl Education Union 70-71, Exec.


MAUDE, FRANCIS (1798-1886)

    Royal Naval College, Portsmouth.
    Cadet, RN 11;  Lieutenant, RN 20;  Commander, RN
        27;  Captain, RN 56.
    Southwest London.
    [MEB, BP, Walfords, Navy List]

    Church Assn 67-85, Exec.


MAUDE, FRANCIS CORNWALLIS (1828-1900)

    Royal Military Academy, Woolwich.
    Colonel, RA 66;  2nd Lt., RA 47;  Lieutenant, RA
        48;  Captain, RA 54;  Lt. Colonel, RA 58;
        Consul-General 76.
    CB 58;  VC 58.
    Windsor Castle.
    [MEB, WWW, Walfords, Army List]

    Natl Emigration League (F) 70-70, Exec.


MAUGHAN, JOHN

    Anglo-French Intervention Committee (F) 70-70,
        Exec.


MAUGHAN, VEARGITT WILLIAM (1863-1888)

    St Johns, Oxf.
    Oxford;  Surrey.
    [Alum Oxon]

    Natl Soc for Preserving Memorials of Dead (F)
        81-82, Exec.


MAURICE, CHARLES EDMUND (1843- )

    Christ Church, Oxf;  Inner Temple.
    Barrister 71.
    Northwest London.
    [Alum Oxon, Fosters]

    Commons Preservation Soc 83-86, Exec.
    Kyrle Soc 80-90, Exec.


MAURICE, EMILY SOUTHWOOD <MRS. CHARLES EDMUND MAURICE,
    nee HILL> (1840- )

    Kyrle Soc 79-90, Exec.


MAURICE, FREDERICK DENISON (1805-1872)

    Exeter, Oxf;  Inner Temple.
    Professor of Moral Theology, Cambridge 66;  Curate
        34;  Ordained Priest<CE> 35;  Professor of
        English Literature and History, Kings Col
        London 40;  College Head 57;  Perp. Curate 60;
        Vicar 71.
    Northwest London.
    [DNB, MEB, Alum Cantab, Alum Oxon, Crockfds]

Assn for Improvement of London Workhouse
    Infirmaries 66-66, Exec.


MAWER, WALTER

Natl Assn for Repeal Blasphemy Laws (F) 84-84,
    Exec.


MAXFIELD, MATTHEW (1809-1903)

Sunday School Worker.
Leicester.

Natl Education League 71-71, Exec.


MAXSE, FREDERICK AUGUSTUS (1833-1900)

Retired 67;  Cadet, RN 46;  Lieutenant, RN 52;
    Commander, RN 55;  Captain, RN 57;  Rear
    Admiral 75;  Admiral 85.
Radical.  JP.
West London;  Hampshire.
[DNB, MEB, WWW, Walfords, Navy List]

Sunday Society 76-90, V-Pres.
Land Tenure Reform Assn 73-73, Exec.
Natl Education League 71-71, Exec.


MAXWELL, SIR HERBERT EUSTACE, 7TH BT.  (1845-1937)

Eton;  Christ Church, Oxf.
Very Large Landowner 77;  Author.
Conservative.  MP Wigtonshire 80-06.  Junior Lord
    Treasury 86-92, Lord Lieutenant 03-35.
Baronet 77;  PC 97;  KT 33.
Fellow Royal Society.
Southwest London;  Wigtownshire.
[DNB, WWW, BP, Walfords, Bateman, Alum Oxon, Dods,
    Direc Direcs]

Natl Assn for Promotion of State Colonization
    86-86, V-Pres.


MAY, GEORGE

Reading.

Assn for Promoting Extension of Contagious Diseases
    Act 68-68, Exec, V-Pres.


MAYALL, J.  J.  E.

"In business".
Brighton.
[Direc Direcs]

Travelling Tax Abolition Committee (F) 77-85, Exec.


MAYNARD, H.  W.

Barnet.

Church Assn 70-70, Exec.


MAYNE, -

Clergyman<Sect Unkn>.
Reading.

Assn for Promoting Extension of Contagious Diseases
    Act 68-68, V-Pres.


MAYOR, JOHN EYTON BICKERSTETH (1825-1910)

Shrewsbury School;  St John's, Camb.
Professor of Latin, Cambridge 72;  College Fellow
    49;  Asst School Master 49;  College Lecturer
    53;  Ordained Priest<CE> 57;  College Head 02;
    Antiquary.
British Academy;  Philological Society.
Cambridge.
[DNB, WWW, Alum Cantab, Crockfds]

London Soc for Abolition of Compulsory Vaccination
    81-81, V-Pres.


MEAD, W.  H.

Sunday Society (F) 75-75, Exec.


MEADE, EDWARD R.  ( -1889)

West London.

Natl Assn for Promotion of State Colonization
    86-86, Exec.


MEARNS, ANDREW

Congregational Minister.
London.

Natl Vigilance Assn (F) 85-85, Exec.


MEDLAND, JOHN B.

Sunday Society 77-80, Exec.


MEDWIN, W.

Clapham.

Jamaica Committee (F) 66-66.


MELVILLE, ALEXANDER LESLIE-, 10TH EARL OF LEVEN AND 9TH
    EARL OF MELVILLE (1817-1889)

Eton;  Trinity, Camb.
Large Landowner 76;  Banker.
Conservative.
Earl 76.
Nairnshire.
[MEB, BP, Walfords, Bateman, Alum Cantab]

Victoria Street Soc for Protection of Animals from
    Vivisection 84-85, V-Pres.

MERRICK, GEORGE PURNELL (1842- )

    Exeter, Oxf.
    Prison Chaplain 77;  Curate 72;  Ordained
       Priest<CE> 74.
    Southwest London.
    [Alum Oxon, Crockfds]

    Natl Assn for Promotion of State Colonization
       86-86, Exec.

MERRIFIELD, JOHN (1834-1891)

    School Head 60;  Inventor of Navigational
       Equipment;  Author.
    Plymouth.
    [MEB]

    Natl Assn for Repeal Blasphemy Laws (F) 84-84, Hon
       Sec.

MERRYWEATHER, MARY <MISS>

    Liverpool.

    Ladies' Natl Assn for Repeal of Contagious Diseases
       Acts 70-72, Exec.

MEWBURN, WILLIAM

    Intl Arbitration & Peace Assn 81-81, V-Pres.

MIALL, EDWARD (1809-1881)

    Wymondley Theological Institute.
    Newspaper Editor 41;  Independent Minister 31.
    Radical.  MP Rochdale 52-57, Bradford 69-74.
    Southeast London.
    [DNB, MEB, Walfords, Dods]

    Jamaica Committee (F) 66-66.

MIALL, M.

    Clergyman<Sect Unkn>.

    League for Defense of Constitutional Rights 84-84,
       V-Pres.

MIDDLEMORE, WILLIAM (1802-1887)

    Leather Merchant.
    JP.
    Birmingham.
    [MEB]

    Natl Education League (F) 69-71, Exec.

MIDDLETON, JOHN HENRY (1846-1896)

    Cheltenham College;  Exeter, Oxf.
    Architect 77;  Slade Professor of Fine Arts,
       Cambridge 86;  College Fellow 88;  Director,
       Fitzwilliam Museum 89;  Dir Art, South
       Kensington 93;  Author.
    Fellow Society of Antiquaries.
    Southwest London.

    [DNB, MEB, Alum Oxon]

    Soc for Protection of Ancient Buildings 80-85, Hon
       Sec.

MIDWINTER, NATHANIEL (1816-1888)

    Magdalen Hall, Oxf.
    Rector 44;  Ordained Priest<CE> 43;  Vicar 74.
    Winchester.
    [Alum Oxon, Crockfds]

    Church Assn 70-70, Exec.

MILL, JOHN STUART (1806-1873)

    Political Economist;  Author;  Junior Clerk, India
       23;  Journal Editor 37;  Examiner, India House
       56.
    Radical.  MP Westminster 65-68.
    Southeast London.
    [DNB, MEB, Walfords, Dods]

    Commons Preservation Soc (F) 65-69, Exec.
    Jamaica Committee (F) 66-66, Chairman.
    Land Tenure Reform Assn (F) 70-73, Chairman.

MILLAIS, SIR JOHN EVERETT, 1ST BT.  (1829-1896)

    Royal Academy Sch.
    Artist.
    Baronet 85.
    Royal Academy.
    West London.
    [DNB, MEB, BP, Alum Oxon, Bryan's Painters]

    Sunday Society 80-90, V-Pres.

MILLER, SIR ALEXANDER EDWARD (1828-1903)

    Rugby;  Trin Col, Dublin;  Lincoln's Inn.
    Q.C. 72;  Barrister 54;  Railway Commissioner 77;
       Law Member, India Council 91.
    CSI 89.
    London;  Co Antrim.
    [WWW, Fosters]

    Intl Arbitration & Peace Assn 81-81, V-Pres.

MILLER, HENRY

    Church Assn 75-85, Exec.

MILLS, CHARLES HENRY, 1ST BARON HILLINGDON (1830-1898)

    Eton;  Christ Church, Oxf.
    Banker.
    Conservative.  MP Northallerton 65-66, Kent West
       68-85.  DL, JP.
    Baronet 72;  Baron 86.
    West London;  Kent.
    [MEB, WWW, BP, Walfords, Alum Oxon, Dods, Direc
       Direcs]

    Natl Footpaths Preservation Soc 86-90, V-Pres.

MILLS, FREDERICK C.

    Kyrle Soc 84-90, Exec.

MILLS, G. M. W.

    Jamaica Committee (F) 66-66.

MILLS, HALFORD L.

    Natl Vigilance Assn (F) 85-85, Exec.

MILLS, JOHN (1806-1892)

    Pembroke, Camb.
    Rector 37;  College Fellow 31;  Ordained Priest<CE>
      36.
    Peterborough.
    [MEB, Alum Cantab, Crockfds]

    Church Assn 70-78, Exec.

MILLSON, FRANK E.

    Clergyman<Sect Unkn>.
    Halifax.

    Sunday Society 79-90, V-Pres.

MILNE, WILLIAM

    Central Assn for Stopping Sale Intox Liquors on
      Sunday 75-80, Exec.

MILNER, SIR FREDERICK GEORGE, 7TH BT.  (1849-1931)

    Eton;  Christ Church, Oxf.
    Large Landowner 80.
    Conservative.  MP York 83-85, Bassetlaw, Notts
      90-06.  DL, JP.
    Baronet 80;  PC 00;  GCVO 30.
    Twickenham;  Yorks, West Riding.
    [WWW, BP, Bateman, Alum Oxon, Dods]

    Natl Footpaths Preservation Soc (F) 85-90, V-Pres.

MILNES, RICHARD MONCKTON, 1ST BARON HOUGHTON (1809-1885)

    Trinity, Camb.
    Large Landowner 58;  Author.
    Conservative, then Liberal.  MP Pontefract 37-63.
      DL, JP.
    Baron 63.
    Fellow Royal Society.
    West London;  Yorks, West Riding.
    [DNB, MEB, BP, Walfords, Bateman, Alum Cantab,
      Dods, Direc Direcs]

    Soc for Protection of Ancient Buildings (F) 78-85,
      Exec.

MITCHELL, - <MISS>

    Malthusian League (F) 77-79, Exec.

MITCHELL, - <MRS.>

    Natl Vigilance Assn (F) 85-85, Exec.

MITCHELL, ALEXANDER (1831-1873)

    Eton;  Christ Church, Oxf.
    Landowner 39;  Lieutenant, Army 50;  Captain, Army
      54.
    Liberal.  MP Berwick-upon-Tweed 65-68.  DL, JP.
    West London;  Kincardineshire.
    [MEB, Walfords, Alum Oxon, Dods, Army List]

    Assn for Improvement of London Workhouse
      Infirmaries 66-66, Exec.

MITCHELL, CHARLES T.

    Smoke Abatement Committee 81-81.

MITCHELL, SIR HENRY (1823-1898)

    Woolen Manufacturer 42.
    Conservative.
    Kt 87.
    Bradford.
    [MEB, WWW, Direc Direcs]

    Natl Fair Trade League (F) 81-81, Exec.

MITCHELL, JULIA

    Physician.
    Northwest London.

    Malthusian League 84-84, V-Pres.

MITCHELL, KATE

    Physician.
    Northwest London.

    Malthusian League 84-84, V-Pres.

MITCHINSON, HENRY CLARKE (1827- )

    Uppingham;  Clare, Camb.
    Vicar 64;  School Master 49;  School Head 50;
      Ordained Priest<CE> 51;  Curate 60.
    Southeast London.
    [Alum Cantab, Crockfds]

    Church Assn 75-85, Exec.

MITFORD, ALGERNON BERTRAM FREEMAN, 1ST BARON REDESDALE
(1837-1916)

    Eton;  Christ Church, Oxf.
    Sec Board of Works 74;  Diplomatic Service 58;
       Second Secretary, Dip Serv 63;  Very Large
       Landowner 86.
    Conservative.  MP Stratford-On-Avon 92-95.  DL, JP.
    CB 82;  Baron 02;  GCVO;  KCB.
    Southwest London.
    [DNB, BP, Alum Oxon, Dods]

    Soc for Protection of Ancient Buildings (F) 78-85,
       Exec.


MITFORD, WILLIAM TOWNLEY (1817-1889)

    Eton;  Oriel, Oxf.
    Substantial Landowner 31.
    Conservative.  MP Midhurst 59-74.  DL, JP.
    West London;  Sussex.
    [MEB, Walfords, Bateman, Alum Oxon, Dods]

    Assn for Promoting Extension of Contagious Diseases
       Act 68-70, Exec, V-Pres.


MOBERLY, GEORGE (1803-1885)

    Winchester College;  Balliol, Oxf.
    Bishop Salisbury 69;  College Fellow 26;  Ordained
       Priest<CE> 28;  School Head 35;  Rector 66;
       Canon 68;  Prebendary 69.
    Salisbury.
    [DNB, MEB, Alum Oxon, Crockfds]

    Anglo-Oriental Soc for Suppression Opium Trade
       79-79, V-Pres.
    Central Assn for Stopping Sale Intox Liquors on
       Sunday 80-80, V-Pres.


MOBERLY, H.  G.

    Land Nationalization Soc 83-85, Exec.


MOCATTA, FREDERICK DAVID (1828-1905)

    Bullion Broker 43.
    Fellow Society of Antiquaries.
    West London.
    [DNB, Direc Direcs]

    Natl Assn for Promotion of State Colonization
       86-86, V-Pres.
    Metro Public Gardens Assn (F) 83-90, V-Chairman.
    Sunday Society 79-90, V-Pres.


MOIR, JOHN MACRAE (1827-1881)

    U Aberdeen;  Middle Temple.
    Newspaper Editor 55;  Nonconformist Minister.
    Northwest London.
    [MEB]

    Assn for Improvement of London Workhouse
       Infirmaries 66-66, Exec.


MOLESWORTH, SAMUEL, 8TH VISCOUNT MOLESWORTH (1829-1906)

    Cheltenham College;  St John´s, Camb.
    Rector 76;  Curate 65;  Ordained Priest<CE> 66.
    Conservative.
    Viscount 75.
    Southwest London;  St Issey.
    [WWW, BP, Walfords, Alum Cantab, Crockfds]

    City Church & Churchyard Protection Soc 83-83,
       V-Pres.


MOLL, WILLIAM EDMUND (1856-1932)

    Worcester, Oxf.
    Curate 79;  Ordained Priest<CE> 80;  Vicar 93;
       Dean 24;  Rector 25.
    Radical.
    West London.
    [WWW, Alum Oxon, Crockfds]

    English Land Restoration League 85-85, Exec.


MOLYNEUX, CAPEL (1804-1877)

    Christ´s, Camb.
    Vicar 60;  Army<rank unknown>;  Ordained Priest<CE>
       29;  Curate 42.
    Southwest London.
    [MEB, Walfords, Alum Cantab, Crockfds]

    Church Assn 70-70, Exec.


MONCK, JOHN BLIGH (1811- )

    Eton;  New Inn Hall, Oxf;  Inner Temple.
    Landowner 34.
    JP.
    Berkshire.
    [Walfords, Alum Oxon]

    Assn for Promoting Extension of Contagious Diseases
       Act 70-70, V-Pres.


MONK, J.

    Bolton.

    Church Assn 80-80, Exec.


MONRO, - <MISS>

    Tunbridge Wells.

    Victoria Street Soc for Protection of Animals from
       Vivisection 80-82, Exec.


MONSELL, WILLIAM, 1ST BARON EMLY (1812-1894)

    Winchester College;  Oriel, Oxf.
    Substantial Landowner 22;  Clerk of the Ordnance
       53.
    Liberal.  MP Limerick Co 47-74.  Pres Board of
       Health 57-57, V-P Board of Trade 66-66,
       Paymaster General 66-66, Parl U-Sec Col Off
       68-70, Postmaster General 71-73, Lord
       Lieutenant 71-94, DL, JP.
    PC 55;  Baron 74.
    Member Royal Irish Academy.

West London;  Co Limerick.
[DNB, MEB, BP, Walfords, Bateman, Alum Oxon, Dods,
    Direc Direcs]

Proportional Representation Soc (F) 84-88, Exec.


MONTAGU, MONTAGU SAMUEL, 1ST BARON SWAYTHLING
    (1832-1911)

Banker;  Substantial Landowner.
Liberal.  MP Twr Hmlts Whitechapl 85-00.  DL, JP.
Baronet 94;  Baron 07.
Fellow Society of Antiquaries.
West London;  Hampshire.
[DNB, WWW, BP, Dods, Direc Direcs]

Free Land League 86-86, V-Pres.


MONTAGU, LORD ROBERT (1825-1902)

Trinity, Camb.
Politician;  Author.
Conservative.  MP Huntingdonshire 59-74, Westmeath
    74-80.  Pres Board of Health 67-67, Charity
    Commissioner 67-68, V-P Education Committee
    67-69, DL, JP.
PC 67.
Southwest London;  Folkstone.
[DNB, WWW, BP, Alum Cantab, Dods, Direc Direcs]

Church Assn 85-85, V-Pres.
Natl Education Union (F) 69-79, Exec.


MONTAGU, WILLIAM DROGO, 7TH DUKE OF MANCHESTER
    (1823-1890)

Royal Military College, Sandhurst.
Very Large Landowner 55;  Ensign, Army 41;
    Lieutenant, Army 42;  Captain, Army 46.
Conservative.  MP Bewdley 48-52, Huntingdonshire
    52-55.  DL, JP.
Duke 56;  KP 77.
West London;  Huntingdonshire.
[MEB, BP, Walfords, Bateman, Dods, Direc Direcs,
    Army List]

Natl Assn for Promotion of State Colonization
    86-86, Patron.
Natl Emigration League (F) 70-70, President.


MONTGOMERY, SIR GRAHAM GRAHAM, 3RD BT.  (1823-1901)

Christ Church, Oxf.
Very Large Landowner 39.
Conservative.  MP Peebles-Shire 52-68, Peebles &
    Selkirkshire 68-80.  Junior Lord Treasury
    66-68, Junior Lord Treasury 80-80, Lord
    Lieutenant 54-  , DL, JP.
Baronet 39.
Southwest London;  Peeblesshire.
[WWW, BP, Walfords, Bateman, Alum Oxon, Dods]

Natl Education Union 71-79, Exec.


MONTIETH, JOHN

Workmen's Natl Assn for Abolition Sugar Bounties
    81-81, Chairman.


MOODY, CLEMENT (1811-1871)

Magdalen, Oxf.
Vicar 53.
Newcastle-upon-Tyne.
[Alum Oxon, Crockfds]

Assn for Promoting Extension of Contagious Diseases
    Act 68-68, V-Pres.


MOODY, FRANCIS WOLLASTON (1824-1886)

Eton;  Trinity, Camb.
Teacher, So Kens Sch of Art;  Artist 50.
Southwest London.
[MEB, Alum Cantab, Bryan's Painters]

Soc for Protection of Ancient Buildings (F) 78-80,
    Exec.


MOOLA, N. J.

Indian Reform Assn 84-84, Exec.


MOORE, CECIL (1851-1885)

St Paul's, London;  Exeter, Oxf.
Curate 75;  Ordained Priest<CE> 76;  Poet.
West London.
[MEB, Alum Oxon, Crockfds]

Natl Soc for Preserving Memorials of Dead 84-84,
    Exec.


MOORE, GEORGE

Church Assn 67-75, V-Pres.


MOORE, JOHN

London.

Jamaica Committee (F) 66-66.


MOORE, JOHN HOWARD

Chm., London Road Car Co.
Surrey.
[Direc Direcs]

London Municipal Reform League 82-85, Exec.

MOORE, PONSONBY A.

    Church Assn 67-67, Exec.

MOORE, RICHARD (1810-1878)

    Woodcarver.
    Radical.
    West Central London.
    [DNB, MEB]

    Financial Reform Union (F) 68-69, Chairman.
    Jamaica Committee (F) 66-66.
    Travelling Tax Abolition Committee (F) 77-78, Exec.

MOORE, THOMAS

    Jamaica Committee (F) 66-66.

MORETON, HENRY HAUGHTON REYNOLDS- <STYLED LORD MORETON>
    (1857-1920)

    Trinity, Camb.
    Liberal. MP Gloucestershire West 80-85. DL, JP.
    West London.
    [WWW, BP, Dods]

    Commons Preservation Soc 80-86, Exec.

MORETON, HENRY JOHN REYNOLDS-, 3RD EARL OF DUCIE
    (1827-1921)

    Eton.
    Very Large Landowner 53.
    Liberal. MP Stroud 52-53. Lord Lieutenant 57-11,
        DL, JP.
    Earl 53; PC; GCVO.
    Fellow Royal Society.
    West London; Gloucestershire.
    [WWW, BP, Walfords, Bateman, Dods]

    Plimsoll and Seamen's Fund Committee (F) 73-73,
        Exec.
    Assn for Improvement of London Workhouse
        Infirmaries 66-66, Exec.

MORGAN, SIR GEORGE OSBORNE, 1ST BT. (1826-1897)

    Shrewsbury School; Worcester, Oxf; Lincoln's Inn.
    Q.C. 69; Barrister 53; Politician.
    Liberal. MP Denbighshire 68-85, Denbighshire East
        85-97. Judge Advocate General 80-85, Parl
        U-Sec Col Off 86-86, JP.
    PC 80; Baronet 92.
    Southwest London; Denbighshire.
    [DNB, MEB, WWW, BP, Walfords, Alum Oxon, Fosters,
        Dods]

    Central Assn for Stopping Sale Intox Liquors on
        Sunday 70-85, V-Pres.

MORGAN, OCTAVIUS VAUGHAN (1837-1896)

    Merchant 58; Crucible Manufacturer 67.
    Liberal. MP Battersey 85-92. JP.
    Fellow Royal Statistical Society.
    Southwest London.
    [MEB, Dods]

    Free Land League 86-86, V-Pres, Exec.

MORGAN, RICHARD COPE (1827-1908)

    Publisher; Journal Editor; Author.
    North London.
    [WWW]

    London Comtee Exposure & Suppresn Traffic In Girls
        (F) 80-85, Exec.
    Natl Vigilance Assn (F) 85-85, Exec.

MORGAN, SIR RICHARD FRANCIS (1821-1876)

    Lincoln's Inn.
    Chief Justice, Ceylon 74; Barrister 58; District
        Judge, Ceylon 56; Puisine Judge, Ceylon
        Supreme Court 57; Queen's Advocate, Ceylon 63.
    Kt 74.
    Colombo, Ceylon.
    [MEB]

    Intl Law Assn 74-74, V-Pres.

MORGAN, W.

    Anglo-Oriental Soc for Suppression Opium Trade (F)
        75-75, Exec.

MORGAN, WILLIAM

    Birmingham.

    Jamaica Committee (F) 66-66.

MORLEY, ARNOLD (1849-1916)

    Trinity, Camb; Inner Temple.
    Barrister 73; Counsel to Home Office 80;
        Patronage Sec, Treas 86; Politician.
    Liberal. MP Nottingham 80-85, Nottingham East
        85-95. Paymaster General 92-95.
    PC 92.
    Southwest London.
    [WWW, Fosters, Dods]

    Free Land League 86-86, V-Pres.

MORLEY, HENRY (1822-1894)

    Kings Col London.
    Professor of English Language and History, U Col
        London 65; School Master 48; Journalist 50;
        College Lecturer 57; Journal Editor; Author.
    Northwest London.
    [DNB, MEB]

    Sunday Society 78-90, V-Pres.
    Metro Free Libraries Assn (F) 77-77, Exec.

MORLEY, JOHN, 1ST VISCOUNT MORLEY OF BLACKBURN
   (1838-1923)

   Cheltenham College; Lincoln, Oxf; Lincoln´s Inn.
   Journal Editor 67; Politician.
   Radical. MP Newcastle-upon-Tyne 83-95, Montrose
      96-08. Chief Sec Ireland 86-86, Chief Sec
      Ireland 92-95, Sec St India 05-10, Lord Pres
      Council 10-14.
   PC 86; OM 02; Viscount 08.
   Fellow Royal Society; Royal Historical Society.
   Southwest London.
   [DNB, WWW, BP, Alum Cantab, Alum Oxon, Fosters,
      Dods]

   Free Land League 86-86, V-Pres.


MORLEY, SAMUEL (1809-1886)

   Bullers School, Southampton.
   Hosiery Manufacturer; Newspaper Proprietor;
      Director, Bank of England.
   Liberal. MP Nottingham 65-66, Bristol 68-85. DL,
      JP.
   West London; Kent.
   [DNB, MEB, Walfords, Dods, Direc Direcs]

   Anglo-Oriental Soc for Suppression Opium Trade
      83-83, V-Pres.
   Public Museums & Free Libraries Assn 68-68, V-Pres.
   Central Vigilance Comtee for Repression Immorality
      (F) 83-84, V-Pres.
   Financial Reform Union (F) 68-69, Exec.
   Howard Assn 69-84, Patron.
   Jamaica Committee (F) 66-66.
   Natl Vigilance Assn (F) 85-85, Treas.
   Natl Assn for Repeal Contagious Diseases Acts
      81-81, V-Pres.


MORLEY, SAMUEL HOPE, 1ST BARON HOLLENDEN (1845-1929)

   Trinity, Camb.
   Hosiery Manufacturer; Director, Bank of England;
      Governor, Bank of England 03.
   DL, JP.
   Baron 12.
   West London; Kent.
   [WWW, BP, Alum Cantab, Direc Direcs]

   Natl Footpaths Preservation Soc (F) 85-90, V-Pres.


MORRIS, H. A.

   English Land Restoration League 85-85, Exec.


MORRIS, J. T.

   JP.
   Reading.

   Assn for Promoting Extension of Contagious Diseases
      Act 68-68, V-Pres.


MORRIS, JOHN

   Intl Arbitration & Peace Assn 81-81, V-Pres.


MORRIS, SIR JOHN (1821-1889)

   Manufacturer.
   JP.
   Kt 66.
   Wolverhampton.
   [MEB, BP, Walfords]

   Church Assn 75-85, V-Pres.


MORRIS, WILLIAM (1834-1896)

   Marlborough; Exeter, Oxf.
   Artist; Poet; Novelist; House Decorator.
   Radical.
   Fellow Society of Antiquaries.
   Hammersmith; Gloucestershire.
   [DNB, MEB, WWW, Alum Oxon]

   Commons Preservation Soc 80-86, Exec.
   Soc for Protection of Ancient Buildings (F) 78-85,
      Hon Sec.
   Eastern Question Assn (F) 76-77, Treas.


MORRIS, WILLIAM

   Salford.

   Central Assn for Stopping Sale Intox Liquors on
      Sunday (F) 67-70, Exec.


MORRISON, - <MRS. FRANK MORRISON>

   Victoria Street Soc for Protection of Animals from
      Vivisection 82-85, Exec.


MORRISON, GEORGE

   Commons Preservation Soc 76-83, Exec.


MORRISON, JAMES

   Newcastle-upon-Tyne.

   Church Assn 70-70, V-Pres.


MORRISON, JOHN CHARLES DOWNIE

   Colonel, RM 65; Cornet, RM 42; Lieutenant, RM 47;
      Captain, RM 55; Major, RM 58; Lt. Colonel,
      RM 61.
   [Army List]

   Victoria Street Soc for Protection of Animals from
      Vivisection 80-82, Secretary.

MORRISON, WALTER (1836-1921)

Eton; Balliol, Oxf.
"In business"; Very Large Landowner.
Liberal(Unionist). MP Plymouth 61-74, Skipton,
    Yorks WR N 86-92, Skipton, Yorks WR N 95-00.
    JP.
Southwest London; Yorks, West Riding.
[DNB, WWW, Walfords, Bateman, Alum Oxon, Dods,
    Direc Direcs]

Proportional Representation Soc (F) 84-88, Exec.


MORTIMER, CHARLES (1837- )

Surrey.
[Walfords]

Church Assn 75-75, Exec.


MOSELY, BENJAMIN LEWIS

London U; Gray's Inn.
Barrister 74.
West Central London.
[Fosters]

Smoke Abatement Committee 81-81.


MOSLEY, SIR OSWALD, 2ND BT.  (1785-1871)

Rugby; Brasenose, Oxf.
Substantial Landowner 98.
MP Portarlington 06-07, Winchelsea 07-12, Midhurst
    17-18, Staffordshire North 32-37. DL, JP.
Baronet 98.
Fellow Geological Society.
West London; Staffordshire.
[MEB, BP, Walfords, Alum Oxon, Dods]

Church Assn 67-70, V-Pres.


MOSLEY, SIR TONMAN, 3RD BT.  (1813-1890)

Magdalene, Camb.
Substantial Landowner 71; Cornet, Army 32;
    Lieutenant, Army 35.
DL, JP.
Baronet 71.
Staffordshire.
[MEB, BP, Walfords, Bateman, Alum Cantab, Army
    List]

Church Assn 75-85, V-Pres.


MOSS, JOSEPH L.

Natl Assn for Repeal Blasphemy Laws (F) 84-84,
    Exec.


MOTTERSHEAD, THOMAS (1826-1884)

Silk Weaver.
Radical.
London.
[MEB]

Land Tenure Reform Assn 73-73, Exec.


MOUAT, SIR JAMES (1815-1899)

University Col London; Paris(Medical).
Surgeon General, Army Medical Serv 64; Asst
    Surgeon, Army Medical Serv 38; Surgeon, Army
    Medical Serv 48; Surgeon Major, Army Medical
    School 55; Deputy Inspector General, Army
    Medical Serv 58.
CB 56; VC 58; KCB 94.
Fellow Royal Col Surgeons; Fellow Chemical
    Society.
West London.
[MEB, WWW, Army List]

Assn for Promoting Extension of Contagious Diseases
    Act 68-70, V-Pres.


MOULD, J. CLARKE

West Central London.

City Church & Churchyard Protection Soc (F) 80-83,
    Exec.


MOULTON, JOHN FLETCHER, BARON MOULTON (1844-1921)

St John's, Camb; Middle Temple.
Barrister 74; Q.C. 85; College Fellow 68;
    College Lecturer 68; Judge, Court of Appeal
    06.
Liberal. MP Clapham Div, Battersea and Clapham
    85-86, Hackney South 94-95, Launceston 98-06.
    PC Judicial Committee 06-12.
PC 06; Kt 06; Baron 12; KCB 15; GBE 17.
Fellow Royal Society; Fellow Royal Astronomical
    Society.
Southwest London; Hampshire.
[DNB, WWW, BP, Alum Cantab, Fosters, Dods]

Commons Preservation Soc 86-86, Exec.
Smoke Abatement Committee 81-81.
Free Land League 86-86, V-Pres.


MOWBRAY, SIR JOHN ROBERT, 1ST BT.  (1815-1899)

Westminster School; Christ Church, Oxf; Inner
    Temple.
Barrister 41.
Conservative. MP Durham City 53-68, Oxford 68-99.
    Judge Advocate General 58-59, Judge Advocate
    General 66-68, Church Estates Commissioner
    71-92.
PC 58; Baronet 80.
Southwest London; Berkshire.
[DNB, MEB, WWW, BP, Walfords, Alum Oxon, Fosters,
    Dods]

Soc for Promoting Increase of the Home Episcopate
    72-72, Exec.

MUDALIAR, P. MURUGESA

Madras.

Natl Secular Soc 84-84, V-Pres.


MUELLER, FRIEDRICH MAX (1823-1900)

U Leipzig.
Corpus Professor of Comparative Philology, Oxford
    68;  Taylorian Professor of Modern Languages,
    Oxford 54;  College Fellow 58;  Author.
PC 96.
Oxford.
[DNB, MEB, WWW, Alum Cantab, Alum Oxon]

Sunday Society 79-90, V-Pres.


MUIR, SIR WILLIAM (1819-1905)

U Glasgow;  Haileybury.
Council of India 76;  India Civil Service 37;  Sec,
    Govt NWP India 47;  Sec, India Govt 58;
    Foreign Sec, India Govt 64;  Lt Gov, NWP India
    68;  Financial Minister, India Govt 74.
KCSI 67.
Royal Asiatic Society.
Southwest London.
[DNB, WWW, BP, Walfords, Alum Oxon, Direc Direcs]

Central Vigilance Comtee for Repression Immorality
    (F) 83-84, V-Pres.


MUJID, ABDUL

Indian Reform Assn 84-84, Exec.


MULLINER, FRANCIS

Church Assn 75-80, Exec.


MULLINS, J. A.

Liberty & Property Defense League 84-84, Exec.


MUNDELLA, ANTHONY JOHN (1825-1897)

Politician;  Hosiery Manufacturer.
Radical.  MP Sheffield 68-85, Sheffield Brightside
    85-97.  V-P Education Committee 80-85, Pres
    Board of Trade 86-86, Pres Board of Trade
    92-94, Charity Commissioner, JP.
PC 80.
Fellow Royal Geograph Society;  Fellow Royal
    Society;  Fellow Royal Statistical Society.
Southwest London;  Nottingham.
[DNB, MEB, WWW, Walfords, Dods, Direc Direcs]

City Church & Churchyard Protection Soc (F) 80-83,
    V-Pres.
Metro Free Libraries Assn 77-77, Exec.
Soc for Protection of Ancient Buildings (F) 78-85,
    Exec.
Victoria Street Soc for Protection of Animals from
    Vivisection 80-85, Exec, V-Pres.
Eastern Question Assn 77-77, Chairman.


MUNICH, C. J.

West London.

London Municipal Reform League 82-85, Exec.


MUNTZ, GEORGE FREDERICK (1822- )

Substantial Landowner 57.
JP.
Warwickshire.
[Walfords, Bateman]

Local Taxation Comtee [of Central Chamber of
    Agriculture] 71-75, Exec.


MURPHY, GEORGE

Clergyman<Sect Unkn>.

Natl Emigration League (F) 70-70, V-Pres.


MURPHY, GEORGE MOLLETT (1823-1887)

Undenominational Preacher 52;  Author.
Northwest London.
[MEB]

Travelling Tax Abolition Committee (F) 77-85, Exec.


MURPHY, GEORGE STORMONT ( -1893)

Hon Sec, Cabdrivers Benevolent Assn 70.
West London.
[MEB]

Assn for Improvement of Public Morals (F) 79-79,
    Secretary.


MURRAY, FREEMAN (1804-1885)

Maj. General 62;  Ensign, Army 25;  Captain, Army
    32;  Colonel 54;  Gov, Bermuda 54;  Lt.
    General 71;  General 77.
Chatham.
[MEB, Army List]

Assn for Promoting Extension of Contagious Diseases
    Act 68-70, V-Pres.


MURRAY, JOHN (1808-1892)

Charterhouse;  U Edinburgh.
Publisher.
Fellow Society of Antiquaries.
Wimbledon.
[DNB, MEB]

Commons Preservation Soc 69-86, Exec.

MURRAY, WILLIAM

JP.

Intl Arbitration & Peace Assn 81-81, V-Pres.

MUSPRATT, EDMUND K.  (1833-1923)

U Munich.
Alkali Manufacturer.
JP.
Fellow Chemical Society;  Inst of Chemistry.
Liverpool.
[WWW]

Free Land League 86-86, V-Pres.
Jamaica Committee (F) 66-66.

MYERS, ARTHUR BOWEN RICHARDS

Asst Surgeon, Army Medical Serv 59;  Surgeon, Army
    Medical Serv 73;  Surgeon Major, Army Medical
    School 83;  Brigade Surgeon 88.
Member Royal Col Surgeons.
[Army List]

Assn for Promoting Extension of Contagious Diseases
    Act 68-68, Exec.

NAE, W.

Intl Arbitration & Peace Assn 81-81, V-Pres.

NASMYTH, JAMES

Sunday Society 80-89, V-Pres.

NATHAN, WILLIAM

Chigwell.

Jamaica Committee (F) 66-66.

NATION, WILLIAM HAMILTON CODRINGTON (1843-1914)

Eton;  Oriel, Oxf.
Theatre Manager;  Journal Editor;  Author;  Poet;
    Substantial Landowner 61.
Southwest London;  Devonshire.
[WWW, Walfords, Bateman, Alum Oxon]

Sunday Society 79-90, V-Pres.

NATTALI, B.

Kyrle Soc 84-90, Treas.

NEATE, CHARLES (1806-1879)

Lincoln, Oxf;  Lincoln's Inn.
Political Economist;  College Fellow 28;  Barrister
    32;  College Lecturer 56;  Professor of
    Political Economy, Oxford 57.
Liberal.  MP Oxford 57-57, Oxford 63-68.
Oxford.
[DNB, MEB, Walfords, Alum Oxon, Dods]

Assn for Improvement of London Workhouse
    Infirmaries 66-66, Exec.

NEILD, EDWARD

Central Assn for Stopping Sale Intox Liquors on
    Sunday 80-85, Exec.

NELSON, SIR EDWARD MONTAGUE (1841-1919)

Frozen Meat Importer.
Conservative.  DL, JP.
KCMG 97.
Ealing;  Warwick.
[WWW, Direc Direcs]

Natl Fair Trade League (F) 81-81, Exec.

NELSON, HORATIO, 3RD EARL NELSON (1823-1913)

Eton;  Trinity, Camb.
Large Landowner 35.
Conservative.  DL, JP.
Earl 35.
West London;  Wiltshire.
[WWW, BP, Walfords, Bateman, Alum Cantab]

Soc for Promoting Increase of the Home Episcopate
    72-74, V-Pres.

NELSON, J.  E.

Manchester.

Jamaica Committee (F) 66-66.

NELSON, THOMAS (1822-1892)

Edinburgh High School.
Publisher 40.
Liberal.  JP.
Edinburgh.
[DNB, MEB, Direc Direcs]

Jamaica Committee (F) 66-66.

NEUMANN, GEORGE

JP.

Intl Arbitration & Peace Assn 81-81, V-Pres.

NEVILL, WILLIAM, 1ST MARQUIS OF ABERGAVENNY (1826-1915)

    Eton.
    Very Large Landowner 68;   Sub-Lt., Army 44.
    Conservative.  Lord Lieutenant 92-05, JP.
    Earl 68;   Marquis 76;   KG.
    West London;   Kent.
    [BP, Walfords, Bateman, Army List]

    Church Assn 67-85, V-Pres.


NEVILLE, F. SPOONER


    Allotments & Small Holdings Assn 85-88, Secretary.


NEWALL, ROBERT STIRLING (1812-1889)

    Mechanical Engineer;   Telegraph Cable Manufacturer
       40.
    JP.
    Fellow Royal Society;   Fellow Royal Astronomical
       Society;   Inst of Mech Engineers.
    Gateshead.
    [DNB, MEB]

    Assn for Promoting Extension of Contagious Diseases
       Act 70-70, V-Pres.


NEWCOMBE, C. P.


    Land Nationalization Soc 84-84, Exec.


NEWDEGATE, CHARLES NEWDIGATE (1816-1887)

    Eton;   Christ Church, Oxf.
    Large Landowner 32.
    Conservative.  MP Warwickshire North 43-85.  DL,
       JP.
    PC 86.
    Southwest London;   Warwickshire.
    [DNB, MEB, Walfords, Bateman, Alum Oxon, Dods]

    Church Assn 67÷85, V-Pres.


NEWELL, THOMAS

    Primitive Methodist Minister.

    Central Assn for Stopping Sale Intox Liquors on
       Sunday 80-80, V-Pres.


NEWMAN, FRANCIS WILLIAM (1805-1897)

    Ealing School;   Worcester, Oxf.
    Professor of Latin, U Col London 46;   College
       Fellow 26;   College Tutor 34;   College Head 38;
       Professor of Classical Literature, New Col
       Manch 40.
    London;   Weston-Super-Mare.
    [DNB, MEB, WWW]

    Jamaica Committee (F) 66-66.
    Land Nationalization Soc (F) 81-85, V-Pres.
    London Soc for Abolition of Compulsory Vaccination
       81-81, V-Pres.
    Natl Assn for Repeal Contagious Diseases Acts
       84-84, V-Pres.


NEWTON, C. E.

    Cheshire.

    Natl Soc for Preserving Memorials of Dead (F)
       81-82, Exec.


NEWTON, SIR HENRY WILLIAM (1842-1914)

    U Col, Durham.
    Surgeon.
    JP.
    Kt 09.
    Newcastle-upon-Tyne.
    [WWW]

    Natl Assn for Promotion of State Colonization
       86-86, V-Pres.


NICHOL, ELIZABETH PEASE <MRS. JOHN PRINGLE NICHOL, nee
    PEASE> (1807-1897)

    Journalist.
    Edinburgh.
    [MEB]

    Ladies' Natl Assn for Repeal of Contagious Diseases
       Acts 70-72, Exec.


NICHOLAY, JOHN AUGUSTUS ( -1873)

    Furrier;   Metropolitan Board of Works 56.
    West London.
    [MEB]

    Jamaica Committee (F) 66-66.
    Financial Reform Union (F) 68-69, Exec.


NICHOLLS, JAMES

    Physician.
    Chelmsford.

    Assn for Promoting Extension of Contagious Diseases
       Act 68-68, Exec.


NICHOLSON, -

    Clergyman<Sect Unkn>.
    Edinburgh.

    Natl Education Union 71-79, Exec.


NICHOLSON, SIR CHARLES, 1ST BT.  (1808-1903)

    U Edinburgh.
    Australian Landowner;   Physician 33;   Australian
       Businessman.
    Conservative.  JP.
    Kt 52;   Baronet 59.
    West London;   Essex;   New South Wales.
    [DNB, BP, Walfords, Alum Cantab, Alum Oxon, Direc
       Direcs, Aust Dict Biog]

    Natl Emigration League (F) 70-70, V-Pres.

NICHOLSON, EDWARD WILLIAMS BYRON (1849-1912)

    Trinity, Oxf.
    Librarian 73;  School Master 72.
    Radical.
    Oxford.
    [DNB, WWW, Alum Oxon]

    Metro Free Libraries Assn (F) 77-82, Hon Sec.

NICKALLS, SIR PATTESON (1836-1910)

    Stock Broker.
    Liberal. JP.
    Kt 93.
    Kent.
    [WWW]

    Natl Assn for Promotion of State Colonization
       86-86, V-Pres.

NICOL, JOHN

    JP.

    Intl Arbitration & Peace Assn 81-81, V-Pres.

NIEASS, J. D.

    League for Defense of Constitutional Rights 84-84,
       V-Pres.

NOAILLES, MARIE, COUNTESS DE

    London Soc for Abolition of Compulsory Vaccination
       81-81, V-Pres.

NOBLE, JOHN

    JP.
    Brighton.

    Jamaica Committee (F) 66-66.

NOBLE, JOHN

    Northwest London.

    Travelling Tax Abolition Committee (F) 77-82,
       V-Chairman.

NOBLE, JOHN (1827-1892)

    Railway Promoter;  Author.
    Radical.
    London.
    [DNB, MEB]

    Financial Reform Union (F) 68-69, Hon Sec.

NODAL, JOHN HOWARD (1831-1909)

    Newspaper Editor 71.
    Manchester.
    [DNB]

    Travelling Tax Abolition Committee 79-85, Exec.

NOEL, ERNEST (1831-1931)

    Stanmore, Middlesex;  Trinity, Camb.
    City Financier.
    Liberal. MP Dumfries District 74-86. DL, JP.
    West London;  Sussex.
    [WWW, BP, Walfords, Alum Cantab, Dods, Direc
       Direcs]

    Natl Assn for Repeal Contagious Diseases Acts
       81-81, V-Pres.

NOEL, ROBERT RALPH

    Magdalene, Camb.
    [Alum Cantab]

    Sunday Society 79-80, Exec.

NOLAN, THOMAS (1809-1882)

    Trin Col, Dublin.
    Vicar 41;  Ordained Priest<CE> 34;  Curate 37.
    West London.
    [MEB, Alum Cantab, Crockfds]

    Church Assn 70-80, Exec.

NORMAN, A.

    West Central London.

    London Municipal Reform League 82-85, Exec.

NORRIS, HENRY (1810- )

    Balliol, Oxf.
    DL, JP.
    Oxfordshire.
    [Walfords, Alum Oxon]

    City Church & Churchyard Protection Soc (F) 80-83,
       V-Pres.

NORRIS, JOHN PILKINGTON (1823-1891)

    Rugby;  Trinity, Camb.
    Canon 65;  Curate 49;  Inspector of Schools 49;
       Ordained Priest<CE> 50;  Perp. Curate 64;
       Vicar 70;  Archdeacon 81.
    Cobham, Surrey.
    [DNB, MEB, Alum Cantab, Crockfds]

    Natl Education Union (F) 69-70, Exec.

NORTH, JOHN SIDNEY (1804-1894)

> Royal Military College, Sandhurst.
> Large Landowner 35; Ensign, Army 21; Captain,
>     Army 25.
> Conservative. MP Oxfordshire 52-85. DL, JP.
> PC 86.
> West London; Oxfordshire; Cambridgeshire.
> [MEB, BP, Walfords, Bateman, Alum Oxon, Dods, Army
>     List]
>
> Assn for Promoting Extension of Contagious Diseases
>     Act 68-70, V-Pres.

NORTHCOTE, HENRY STAFFORD, 1ST BARON NORTHCOTE OF EXETER
(1846-1911)

> Eton; Merton, Oxf.
> Politician; Clerk, FO 68; Diplomatic Service 76;
>     Gov, Bombay 00; Governor General, Australia
>     03; Large Landowner 87.
> Conservative. MP Exeter 80-99. Fin Sec War Office
>     85-86, Surveyor General Ordnance 86-87, Charity
>     Commissioner 91-92.
> CB 80; Baronet 87; Baron 00; GCIE 04; GCMG 04;
>     PC 09.
> Southwest London.
> [DNB, MEB, WWW, BP, Alum Oxon, Dods]
>
> Natl Assn for Promotion of State Colonization
>     83-86, V-Pres.

NORTON, CECIL WILLIAM, 1ST BARON RATHCREEDAN (1850-1930)

> Trin Col, Dublin; Royal Military College,
>     Sandhurst.
> Major 81; Cornet, Army 70; Lieutenant, Army 71;
>     Captain, Army 76.
> Liberal. MP Newington West 92-16. Junior Lord
>     Treasury 05-10, Asst Postmaster General 10-15,
>     Parl Sec Munitions Ministry 19-21.
> Baron 16.
> Southwest London.
> [WWW, BP, Dods, Army List]
>
> Free Land League 86-86, Exec.

NORTON, JOHN <"CAPT.">

> Bray.
>
> Jamaica Committee (F) 66-66.

NORWOOD, THOMAS WILKINSON (1829-1908)

> Queens´, Camb.
> Vicar 78; Curate 51; Ordained Priest<CE> 52.
> Fellow Geological Society.
> Southwest London; Wrenbury.
> [Alum Cantab, Crockfds]
>
> Soc for Protection of Ancient Buildings (F) 78-85,
>     Exec.

NOVELLO, JOSEPH ALFRED (1810-1896)

> Music Publisher 29; Choir Master; Journal
>     Proprietor.
> London.
> [MEB]
>
> Travelling Tax Abolition Committee 81-85, Exec.

NUGENT, GEORGE THOMAS JOHN, 1ST MARQUIS OF WESTMEATH
(1785-1871)

> Rugby.
> Very Large Landowner 14.
> Lord Lieutenant 31-71, JP.
> Earl 14; Marquis 22.
> West London; Co Galway; Co Westmeath.
> [MEB, BP, Walfords]
>
> Church Assn 67-70, V-Pres.

NUGENT, RICHARD

> Church Assn 67-85, Exec.

NUNNELEY, JOSEPH

> Jamaica Committee (F) 66-66.

OAKES, JOHN WRIGHT (1820-1887)

> Artist.
> Assoc Royal Academy.
> West London.
> [DNB, MEB, Bryan´s Painters]
>
> Soc for Protection of Ancient Buildings (F) 78-80,
>     Exec.

OAKLEY, JOHN (1834-1890)

> Brasenose, Oxf.
> Dean 81; Curate 58; Ordained Priest<CE> 59;
>     Vicar 67.
> Liberal.
> Manchester.
> [DNB, MEB, Alum Oxon, Crockfds]
>
> Natl Assn for Promotion of State Colonization
>     86-86, Patron.

OATES, - <MRS. EDWARD OATES>

> Soc for Abolition of Vivisection 76-76, Exec.

OATES, EDWARD

> Soc for Abolition of Vivisection 76-76, Treas.

OATES, PARKINSON

    Physician.

    Indian Reform Assn 84-84, Exec.


O'BRIEN, SIR PATRICK 2ND BT.  (1823-1895)

    Trin Col, Dublin.
    Barrister 44.
    Liberal.  MP Kings Co 52-85.  DL, JP.
    Baronet 62.
    West London;  Queens Co.
    [MEB, BP, Walfords, Dods]

    Plimsoll and Seamen's Fund Committee (F) 73-73,
       Exec.


O'BRIEN, PHILIP STEPHEN

    Trin Col, Dublin.
    Vicar 74;  Curate 65;  Ordained Priest<CE> 66.
    Northwest London.
    [Crockfds]

    Church Assn 75-75, Exec.


O'CONNOR, THOMAS POWER (1848-1929)

    Queen's Col Galway.
    Journalist;  Author;  Newspaper Editor 87.
    Irish Nationalist.  MP Galway Borough 80-85,
       Liverpool Scotland 85-29.
    PC 24.
    Southwest London.
    [DNB, WWW, Dods]

    Intl Arbitration & Peace Assn 81-81, V-Pres.


OFFOR, GEORGE

    London.

    London Municipal Reform League 82-85, Exec.


OGILVY, DAVID GRAHAM DRUMMOND, 7TH EARL OF AIRLIE
    (1826-1881)

    Eton;  Christ Church, Oxf.
    Very Large Landowner 49.
    DL, JP.
    Earl 49;  KT 62.
    Fellow Royal Geograph Society.
    West London;  Forfarshire.
    [MEB, BP, Walfords, Alum Oxon]

    Assn for Improvement of London Workhouse
       Infirmaries 66-66, Exec.


OGLE, JOHN WILLIAM (1824-1905)

    Trinity, Oxf;  St George's Hospital Lond.
    Physician 50.
    Fellow Royal Col Physicians;  Fellow Society of
       Antiquaries.
    North London.
    [DNB, Alum Oxon]

    Assn for Improvement of London Workhouse
       Infirmaries 66-66, Exec.


OGLE, WILLIAM (1824-1905)

    Rugby;  St Catherine's, Camb;  St George's Hospital
       Lond.
    Physician 53;  Author.
    JP.
    Fellow Royal Col Physicians.
    West Central London;  Derby.
    [Alum Cantab]

    Sanitary Institute 77-83, Exec.


O'HAGAN, THOMAS, 1ST BARON O'HAGAN (1812-1885)

    Belfast Academy;  Gray's Inn.
    Judge, Common Pleas, Ire 65;  Barrister 34;  Q.C.
       49;  Sergeant at Law 59;  Large Landowner 78.
    Liberal.  MP Tralee 63-65.  Solicitor General, Ire
       61-61, Attorney General, Ire 61-65, Lord
       Chancellor, Ire 68-74, Lord Chancellor, Ire
       80-81.
    PC Ireland 61;  Baron 70;  KP 82.
    West London;  Dublin.
    [DNB, MEB, BP, Walfords, Bateman, Dods]

    Intl Law Assn 76-83, President.


OHREN, MAGNUS

    Civil Engineer.
    Assoc Inst Civ Engineers;  Fellow Chemical Society.
    Sydenham.

    Sanitary Institute 78-86, Exec.


OLIPHANT, LAURENCE (1829-1888)

    Lincoln's Inn.
    Journalist;  Barrister 55;  Sec Legation, Dip Serv
       57;  Author.
    Liberal.  MP Stirling District 65-67.
    London.
    [DNB, MEB, Walfords, Dods]

    Assn for Improvement of London Workhouse
       Infirmaries 66-66, Exec.


OLLARD, J.  F.

    Member Lloyds.
    London.

    Sanitary Institute 78-84, Exec.


O'NEILL, ARTHUR ALEXANDER

    Kings Col London.
    Curate 58;  Ordained Priest<CE> 59.
    Southeast London.
    [Crockfds]

    Assn for Improvement of Public Morals (F) 79-81,
       Exec.

O'NEILL, WILLIAM CHICHESTER, 1ST BARON O'NEILL
   (1813-1883)

   Trin Col, Dublin.
   Very Large Landowner 55;  Ordained Priest<CI> 37;
      Prebendary 48;  Composer;  Musician.
   Conservative.
   Baron 68.
   Southwest London;  Co Antrim.
   [DNB, BP, Walfords, Bateman]

   City Church & Churchyard Protection Soc (F) 80-83,
      V-Pres.


ONSLOW, WILLIAM HILLIER, 4TH EARL OF ONSLOW (1853-1911)

   Eton;  Exeter, Oxf.
   Very Large Landowner 70;  Gov, New Zealand 89.
   Conservative.  Lord in Waiting 80-80, Lord in
      Waiting 86-87, Parl U-Sec Col Off 87-88, Parl
      Sec Board of Trade 88-88, Parl U-Sec India
      95-00, Parl U-Sec Col Off 00-03, Pres Board of
      Agriculture 03-05.
   Earl 70;  KCMG 87;  GCMG 89;  PC 03.
   Surrey.
   [DNB, BP, Walfords, Bateman, Alum Oxon, Dict New
      Zealand Biog]

   Natl Footpaths Preservation Soc 86-90, V-Pres.


ORMAN, GEORGE

   Derby.

   Central Assn for Stopping Sale Intox Liquors on
      Sunday 85-85, Exec.


ORMEROD, OLIVER

   Rochdale.

   Jamaica Committee (F) 66-66.


ORMISTON, JAMES

   Kings Col London.
   Vicar 69;  Perp. Curate 75;  Curate 63;  Ordained
      Priest<CE> 64.
   East London;  Old Hill, Staffs.
   [Crockfds]

   Church Assn 70-78, Exec.


OSBORN, HENRY J.

   Central Assn for Stopping Sale Intox Liquors on
      Sunday 80-85, Exec.


OSBORNE, E.  C.

   Birmingham.

   Natl Education League (F) 69-69, Exec.


OSLER, ABRAHAM FOLLETT (1808-1903)

   Glass Manufacturer.
   Fellow Royal Society.
   Birmingham.
   [DNB]

   Natl Education League (F) 69-71, Exec.


OSWALD, EUGENE ( -1912)

   Goettingen.
   Journalist;  Translator;  Language Instructor.
   Northwest London.
   [WWW]

   Sunday Society (F) 75-75, Exec.


OTTAWAY, G.  J.

   Soc for Promoting Increase of the Home Episcopate
      72-74, Exec.


OTTER, FRANCIS (1832-1895)

   Rugby;  Corpus Christi, Oxf;  Lincoln's Inn.
   Barrister 67;  College Fellow 61;  College Tutor
      71.
   Radical.  MP Louth 85-86.  JP.
   Southwest London;  Lincolnshire.
   [MEB, Alum Oxon, Fosters, Dods]

   Commons Preservation Soc 86-86, Exec.
   Free Land League 86-86, V-Pres.
   Anglo-French Intervention Committee (F) 70-70,
      Exec.


OTTEY, GEORGE PHILIP (1824-1891)

   Rugby;  St John's, Camb.
   Curate 48;  Ordained Priest<CE> 50;  Diocesan
      Inspector of Schools 71;  Prebendary 76;
      Rector 86;  Author.
   East London.
   [MEB, Alum Cantab, Crockfds]

   Natl Emigration League (F) 70-70, Exec.


OULESS, WALTER WILLIAM (1848-1933)

   Royal Academy Sch.
   Artist.
   Royal Academy.
   West Central London.
   [DNB, WWW]

   Soc for Protection of Ancient Buildings (F) 78-85,
      Exec.


OUSELEY, SIR FREDERICK ARTHUR GORE, 2ND BT.  (1825-1889)

   Christ Church, Oxf.
   Professor of Music, Oxford 55;  Curate 49;
      Ordained Priest<CE> 55;  Vicar 56;  College
      Head 56;  Canon 86;  Composer.
   Baronet 44.
   Tenbury Wells.
   [DNB, MEB, BP, Walfords, Alum Cantab, Alum Oxon,
      Crockfds]

City Church & Churchyard Protection Soc (F) 80-83,
V-Pres.
Natl Soc for Preserving Memorials of Dead (F)
81-88, Exec.


OWEN, SIR FRANCIS PHILIP CUNLIFFE (1828-1894)

Director South Kensington Museum 73;  Cadet, RN 40;
Sec, Science and Art Dept, Marlborough House
54;  Deputy General Superintendent, So Kens
Museum 57;  Asst Director, South Kensington
Museum 60.
CB 75;  KCMG 78;  CIE 79;  KCB 86.
London.
[DNB, MEB, BP]

Natl Assn for Promotion of State Colonization
86-86, Patron.
Smoke Abatement Committee 81-81.
City Church & Churchyard Protection Soc 83-83,
V-Pres.


PAGE, -

Workmen's Peace Assn 75-75, Exec.


PAGE, - <MRS.>

Malthusian League 79-79, Exec.


PAGE, FLOOD <"MAJOR">

Natl Assn for Promotion of State Colonization
86-86, V-Pres.


PAGE, J.  K.

Malthusian League (F) 77-81, Exec.


PAGE, JAMES

Clergyman<Sect Unkn>.
Plymouth.

Assn for Promoting Extension of Contagious Diseases
Act 68-68, Exec.


PAGE, JOHN J.

Natl Education Union 70-70, Exec.


PAGE, P.  S.

Fring.

Natl Soc for Preserving Memorials of Dead (F)
81-82, Exec.


PAGET, SIR GEORGE EDWARD (1809-1892)

Charterhouse;  Gonville & Caius, Camb;  St
Bartholomew's Hosp.
Physician 39;  College Fellow 32;  Medical School
Lecturer 51;  Regius Professor of Physic,
Cambridge 72.
KCB 85.
Fellow Royal Society;  Fellow Royal Col Physicians.
Cambridge.
[DNB, MEB, Alum Cantab, Alum Oxon]

Assn for Promoting Extension of Contagious Diseases
Act 68-70, V-Pres.


PAGET, SIR JAMES, 1ST BT.  (1814-1899)

St Bartholomew's Hosp.
Surgeon 61.
Baronet 71.
Fellow Royal Society;  Fellow Royal Col Surgeons;
Fellow Linnean Society;  Royal Med & Chir
Society;  Pathological Society.
West London.
[DNB, MEB, WWW, BP, Alum Cantab, Alum Oxon, Direc
Direcs]

Assn for Promoting Extension of Contagious Diseases
Act 68-70, V-Pres.


PAGET, NINA <MISS>

Kyrle Soc 84-90, Exec.


PAGET, SIR RICHARD HORNER, 1ST BT.  (1832-1908)

Royal Military College, Sandhurst.
Large Landowner 66;  Ensign, Army 48;  Lieutenant,
Army 51;  Captain, Army 55.
Conservative.  MP Somersetshire East 65-68,
Somersetshire Mid 68-85, Somersetshire Wells
85-95.  DL, JP.
Baronet 86;  PC 95.
West London;  Somersetshire.
[WWW, BP, Walfords, Dods, Army List]

Local Taxation Comtee [of Central Chamber of
Agriculture] 71-85, Exec.


PAGET, WALPURGA EHRENGARDE HELENA DE HOHENTHAL, LADY
<Wife of SIR A.  B.  PAGET>

Victoria Street Soc for Protection of Animals from
Vivisection 84-85, Exec.


PAICE, BOWES A.

Architect.
Assoc Royal Inst Br Architects.
West London.

City Church & Churchyard Protection Soc (F) 80-81,
Exec.

PAKENHAM, WILLIAM LYGON, 4TH EARL OF LONGFORD
    (1819-1887)

    Winchester College;  Oriel, Oxf.
    Very Large Landowner 60;  Ensign, Army 37;
        Captain, Army 44;  Colonel 55;  Maj. General
        68;  Lt. General 77;  General 79.
    Conservative.  Parl U-Sec War 66-68, Lord
        Lieutenant 74-87, DL, JP.
    CB 55;  Earl 60;  KCB 61;  GCB 81.
    West London;  Co Westmeath.
    [MEB, BP, Walfords, Bateman, Alum Oxon, Army List]

    Natl Assn for Promotion of State Colonization
        86-86, V-Pres.


PALK, LAWRENCE, 1ST BARON HALDON (1818-1883)

    Eton.
    Very Large Landowner 60;  Lieutenant, Army 39.
    Conservative.  MP Devonshire South 54-68,
        Devonshire East 68-80.  DL, JP.
    Baronet 60;  Baron 80.
    Southwest London;  Devonshire.
    [BP, Walfords, Bateman, Dods, Army List]

    City Church & Churchyard Protection Soc (F) 80-82,
        V-Pres.


PALMER, SIR CHARLES JAMES, 9TH BT.  (1829-1895)

    Inner Temple.
    Barrister 63;  Landowner 65.
    DL, JP.
    Baronet 65.
    Fellow Society of Antiquaries.
    West London;  Buckinghamshire.
    [MEB, Walfords, Fosters]

    Assn for Improvement of Public Morals (F) 79-81,
        Exec.
    Church Assn 85-85, V-Pres.


PALMER, GEORGE (1818-1897)

    Friends' School, Sidcote.
    Biscuit Manufacturer 41;  Substantial Landowner.
    Liberal.  MP Reading 78-85.  JP.
    West London;  Reading.
    [DNB, MEB, Bateman, Dods, Direc Direcs]

    Natl Assn for Promotion of State Colonization
        86-86, V-Pres.
    Allotments & Small Holdings Assn 85-88, Treas.
    Sanitary Institute 79-80, Exec.
    Howard Assn 78-84, Patron.


PALMER, JOHN HINDE (1808-1884)

    Lincoln's Inn.
    Q.C. 59;  Barrister 32.
    Liberal.  MP Lincoln 68-74, Lincoln 80-84.  DL, JP.
    Southwest London.
    [MEB, Dods]

    Intl Law Assn 74-74, Exec.


PALMER, JORDAN ROQUETTE-PALMER- (1829-1885)

    Lincoln, Oxf.
    Chaplain 61;  Ordained Priest<CE> 53;  Curate 56.
    Fellow Society of Antiquaries;  Fellow Royal
        Geograph Society.
    Streatham.
    [Crockfds]

    Natl Education Union 70-71, Exec.


PALMER, JOSEPH

    Lewisham.

    Public Museums & Free Libraries Assn 68-68, Exec.


PALMER, W.  J.

    Reading.

    Jamaica Committee (F) 66-66.


PALMER, WILLIAM C.  <"CAPT.">

    Church Assn 70-80, Secretary.


PALMER, WILLIAM WALDEGRAVE, 2ND EARL OF SELBORNE
    (1859-1942)

    Winchester College;  University Col, Oxf.
    Politician;  Gov, Transvaal 05.
    Liberal(Unionist).  MP Hampshire East 85-92,
        Edinburgh West 92-95.  Parl U-Sec Col Off
        95-00, First Lord Admiralty 00-05, Pres Board
        of Agriculture 15-16, JP.
    Earl 95;  PC 00;  GCMG 05;  KG 09.
    West London;  Hampshire.
    [DNB, WWW, BP, Alum Oxon]

    Kyrle Soc 85-90, Exec.
    Free Land League 86-86, V-Pres.


PANKHURST, RICHARD MARSDEN (1836-1898)

    Owens Col, Manch;  Lincoln's Inn.
    Barrister 67.
    Radical.
    West Central London;  Manchester.
    [MEB, Fosters]

    Jamaica Committee (F) 66-66.


PARIS, CHARLES

    Dulwich.

    Railway Passengers' Protection Assn 86-86, Exec.

PARKER, - <MRS. EDWARD PARKER>

British Women's Temperance Assn 83-84, President.

PARKER, J.  A.

Land Nationalization Soc (F) 81-85, Hon Sec.

PARKER, JOSEPH (1830-1902)

University Col London.
Congregational Minister 53.
Liberal.
London.
[DNB, WWW]

Central Assn for Stopping Sale Intox Liquors on
Sunday 85-85, V-Pres.

PARKES, EDMUND ALEXANDER (1819-1876)

Christ's Hospital;  U College London(Medical).
Surgeon 45;  Asst Surgeon, Army Medical Serv 42;
Medical School Professor 49.
Fellow Royal Society;  Member Royal Col Surgeons.
Southampton.
[DNB, MEB]

Assn for Promoting Extension of Contagious Diseases
Act 68-68, V-Pres.

PARKES, LOUIS COLTMAN

Physician.
Southwest London.

Sanitary Institute 83-89, Exec.

PARKINSON, J.  C.

Commons Preservation Soc 69-86, Exec.
Assn for Improvement of London Workhouse
Infirmaries 66-66, Exec.

PARR, JOHN OWEN (1798-1877)

Charterhouse;  Brasenose, Oxf.
Vicar 24;  Ordained Priest<CE> 23;  Hon.  Canon 53;
Rural Dean.
JP.
Preston.
[Walfords, Alum Oxon, Crockfds]

Central Assn for Stopping Sale Intox Liquors on
Sunday 70-70, V-Pres.

PARRIS, - <MRS. TOUZEAU PARRIS>

West London.

Malthusian League (F) 77-79, Exec.

PARRIS, TOUZEAU

West London.

Malthusian League (F) 77-84, Exec, V-Pres.
Natl Secular Soc 81-81, V-Pres.

PARRY, J.  C.

Anglo-Oriental Soc for Suppression Opium Trade (F)
75-75, Exec.

PARSONS, ANNA F.  <MISS>

Shifnal.

Sunday Society 76-90, V-Pres.

PARTRIDGE, J.  ARTHUR

Castle Bromwich.

Jamaica Committee (F) 66-66.

PATERSON, J.  C.  <ALSO PATTERSON>

Clergyman<Sect Unkn>.

Central Assn for Stopping Sale Intox Liquors on
Sunday (F) 67-70, Exec.

PATERSON, THOMAS

Public Museums & Free Libraries Assn 68-68, Exec.

PATMORE, COVENTRY KERSEY DIGHTON (1823-1896)

Poet;  Assistant, British Museum 46.
Hastings.
[DNB, MEB]

Soc for Protection of Ancient Buildings (F) 78-85,
Exec.

PATON, J.  M.

Montrose.

Jamaica Committee (F) 66-66.

PATTERSON, JOHN

Corn Merchant.
JP.
Liverpool.
[Direc Direcs]

Central Assn for Stopping Sale Intox Liquors on
Sunday 85-85, V-Pres.
Jamaica Committee (F) 66-66.

PATTERSON, JOSEPH

    Central Assn for Stopping Sale Intox Liquors on
        Sunday 70-70, Exec.


PATTISON, H.  J.

    JP.

    Natl Assn for Promotion of State Colonization
        86-86, V-Pres.


PATTISON, MARK (1813-1884)

    Oriel, Oxf.
    Rector 61;  Author;  College Fellow 39;  College
        Tutor 43;  Ordained Priest<CE> 43;  Curator,
        Bodleian Library 69.
    Oxford.
    [DNB, MEB, Alum Oxon, Crockfds]

    Soc for Protection of Ancient Buildings (F) 78-80,
        Exec.


PAUL, CHARLES KEGAN (1828-1902)

    Eton;  Exeter, Oxf.
    Publisher 77;  Curate 51;  Ordained Priest<CE> 52;
        Asst School Master 53;  Vicar 62;  Journal
        Editor 73.
    West London.
    [DNB, WWW, Alum Oxon, Crockfds, Direc Direcs]

    Smoke Abatement Committee 81-81.
    Soc for Protection of Ancient Buildings 80-85,
        Exec.


PAULTON, ABRAHAM WALTER (1812-1876)

    Journalist.
    Radical.
    London.
    [DNB, MEB]

    Jamaica Committee (F) 66-66.


PAULTON, JAMES MELLOR (1857-1923)

    Trinity Hall, Camb;  Inner Temple.
    Politician.
    Liberal.  MP Bishop Aucklnd, Durham 85-10.
    West London;  Surrey.
    [MEB, Alum Cantab, Dods]

    Commons Preservation Soc 86-86, Exec.
    Free Land League 86-86, V-Pres.


PAYNE, RANDOLPH

    North London.

    Natl Soc for Preserving Memorials of Dead (F)
        81-82, Exec.


PAYNE, WILLIAM

    Southeast London.

    London Comtee Exposure & Suppresn Traffic In Girls
        (F) 80-82, Exec.


PEACH, W.  W.

    Sunday Society 76-76, Exec.


PEARCE, C.  T.

    Physician.

    Financial Reform Union (F) 68-69, Exec.


PEARCE, E.  R.

    London Municipal Reform League 82-82, Exec.


PEARCE, R.

    London Municipal Reform League 82-82, Exec.


PEARS, EDMUND WARD (1814-1878)

    Magdalen, Oxf.
    Rector 64;  Curate.
    Dorchester.
    [Alum Oxon, Crockfds]

    Church Assn 70-70, Exec.


PEARSE, GEORGE JOSEPH (1833-1903)

    King Edward's School, Birm;  Trinity, Camb.
    Asst School Master 55.
    Essex.
    [Alum Cantab]

    Railway Passengers' Protection Assn 86-86, Exec.


PEARSON, CORNELIUS (1809-1891)

    Artist.
    West Central London.
    [MEB, Bryan's Painters]

    London Soc for Abolition of Compulsory Vaccination
        81-81, Treas.


PEARSON, EDWARD

    Central Assn for Stopping Sale Intox Liquors on
        Sunday (F) 67-67, Exec.

PEARSON, JOHN LOUGHBOROUGH (1817-1897)

    Architect 43.
    Royal Academy;  Fellow Society of Antiquaries;
       Fellow Royal Inst Br Architects.
    West London.
    [DNB, MEB, WWW]

    City Church & Churchyard Protection Soc 83-83,
       V-Pres.


PEART, ROBERT S.

    Physician.
    North Shields.

    Assn for Promoting Extension of Contagious Diseases
       Act 68-68, Exec.


PEASE, ARTHUR (1837-1898)

    Grove House School, Tottenham.
    Banker 72;  Worsted Manufacturer;  Iron
       Manufacturer;  Colliery Owner.
    Liberal(Unionist).  MP Whitby, Yorks NR 80-85,
       Darlington 95-98.  DL, JP.
    Southwest London;  Darlington;  Yorks, North
       Riding.
    [MEB, WWW, Dods, Direc Direcs]

    Central Assn for Stopping Sale Intox Liquors on
       Sunday 75-85, President, V-Pres.
    Howard Assn 80-84, Patron.


PEASE, E. R.

    Kyrle Soc 84-85, Exec.


PEASE, EDWARD

    Birmingham.

    Anglo-Oriental Soc for Suppression Opium Trade (F)
       75-83, V-Pres, Exec.


PEASE, HENRY (1807-1881)

    Railway Promoter;  Merchant;  Woolen Manufacturer;
       Colliery Owner.
    Liberal.  MP Durham Co South 57-65.  JP.
    Southwest London;  Darlington;  Durham[County].
    [DNB, MEB, Walfords, Dods]

    Central Assn for Stopping Sale Intox Liquors on
       Sunday 75-80, V-Pres.


PEASE, JOSEPH (1799-1872)

    Railway Promoter;  Worsted Manufacturer.
    Liberal.  MP Durham Co South 32-41.
    West London;  Darlington;  Durham[County].
    [DNB, MEB, Walfords, Dods, Friends]

    Central Assn for Stopping Sale Intox Liquors on
       Sunday 70-70, V-Pres.


PEASE, JOSEPH WHITWELL, 1ST BT.  (1828-1903)

    Friends' School, York.
    Banker 45;  Woolen Manufacturer;  Colliery Owner;
       Substantial Landowner.
    Liberal.  MP Durham Co South 65-85, Barnard Castle,
       Durham 85-03.  DL, JP.
    Baronet 82.
    West London;  Yorks, North Riding.
    [DNB, WWW, BP, Walfords, Bateman, Dods, Direc
       Direcs]

    Central Assn for Stopping Sale Intox Liquors on
       Sunday 80-80, V-Pres.
    Howard Assn 73-84, Patron.
    Natl Education Union 70-70, Exec.


PEASE, THOMAS

    Westbury on Tyne.

    Natl Assn for Repeal Contagious Diseases Acts
       84-84, V-Pres.


PEATSON, J. CHADWICK

    Physician.
    Manchester.

    Assn for Promoting Extension of Contagious Diseases
       Act 68-68, Exec.


PEDDIE, JOHN DICK (1824-1891)

    U Edinburgh.
    Architect 48.
    Liberal.  MP Kilmarnock 80-85.
    Southwest London;  Edinburgh.
    [MEB, Dods, Direc Direcs]

    Intl Arbitration & Peace Assn 81-81, V-Pres.


PEDLEY, GEORGE

    London.

    Jamaica Committee (F) 66-66.


PEEK, FRANCIS (1834-1899)

    Tea Merchant 62;  Author.
    London.
    [MEB]

    Howard Assn 72-82, Exec.
    Infant Life Protection Soc 71-71, Exec.
    Commons Preservation Soc 76-86, Exec.


PEEK, SIR HENRY WILLIAM (1825-1898)

    Tea Merchant.
    Conservative.  MP Surrey Mid 68-84.  JP.
    Baronet 74.
    Southwest London;  Devonshire.
    [MEB, BP, Dods, Direc Direcs]

    Natl Education Union 71-79, Exec.

PEEK, RICHARD (1782-1867)

    Landowner 47.
    JP.
    Devonshire.
    [Walfords]

    Jamaica Committee (F) 66-66.


PEGGS, J. WALLACE

    Civil Engineer.
    Member Inst Civ Engineers.
    Southwest London.

    Sanitary Institute 79-89, Exec.


PELHAM, JOHN THOMAS (1811-1894)

    Westminster School;  Christ Church, Oxf.
    Bishop Norwich 57;  Curate 34;  Ordained Priest<CE>
        35;  Rector 37;  Hon. Canon 47;  Perp. Curate
        52;  Rector 55.
    Norwich.
    [DNB, MEB, Alum Oxon, Crockfds]

    Soc for Promoting Increase of the Home Episcopate
        72-74, V-Pres.


PELL, ALBERT (1820-1907)

    Rugby;  Trinity, Camb;  Inner Temple.
    Farmer;  Landowner.
    Conservative. MP Leicestershire South 68-85.  DL,
        JP.
    Royal Agricultural Society.
    Northamptonshire;  Cambridgeshire.
    [DNB, WWW, Walfords, Alum Cantab, Dods]

    Local Taxation Comtee [of Central Chamber of
        Agriculture] 71-85, Chairman.


PELLEW, H.

    Southwest London.

    Natl Education Union 70-71, Exec.


PENDER, - <MRS. JAMES PENDER>

    Victoria Street Soc for Protection of Animals from
        Vivisection 82-85, Exec.


PENNINGTON, FREDERICK (1819-1914)

    E India Merchant.
    Radical. MP Stockport 74-85.  JP.
    West London;  Surrey.
    [WWW, Dods, Direc Direcs]

    Sunday Society 78-85, V-Pres.
    Howard Assn 74-84, Patron.
    Land Tenure Reform Assn 73-73, Exec.
    Natl Education League 71-71, Exec.


PENROSE, SIR GEORGE DEVONSHIRE (1822- )

    Kt 76.
    Cork;  Kings Co.
    [BP, Direc Direcs]

    London Soc for Abolition of Compulsory Vaccination
        81-81, V-Pres.


PENROSE, THOMAS

    London.

    Jamaica Committee (F) 66-66.


PEPLOE, HANMER WILLIAM WEBB- (1837-1923)

    Cheltenham College;  Pembroke, Camb.
    Vicar 66;  Ordained Priest<CE> 63;  Curate 63;
        Prebendary 93.
    Southwest London.
    [WWW, Alum Cantab, Crockfds]

    Central Vigilance Comtee for Repression Immorality
        (F) 83-84, Chairman.
    Church Assn 80-80, Exec.


PERCY, ALGERNON GEORGE, 6TH DUKE OF NORTHUMBERLAND
    (1810-1899)

    Eton.
    Very Large Landowner 67;  Lieutenant, Army 31;
        Captain, Army 35.
    Conservative.  MP Bere Alston 31-32, Northumberland
        North 52-65.  Lord Admiralty 58-59, V-P Board
        of Trade 59-59, Lord Privy Seal 78-80, Lord
        Lieutenant 77-99, DL, JP.
    Duke 67;  PC;  KG.
    Royal Institution.
    West London;  Northumberland;  Surrey.
    [MEB, WWW, BP, Walfords, Bateman, Alum Oxon, Dods,
        Army List]

    Sanitary Institute (F) 76-89, President.


PERCY, HENRY GEORGE, 7TH DUKE OF NORTHUMBERLAND
    (1846-1918)

    Christ Church, Oxf.
    Very Large Landowner 99.
    Conservative.  MP Northumberland North 68-85.
        Treas Royal Household 74-75, Lord Lieutenant,
        DL, JP.
    Baron 87;  Duke 99;  KG;  PC.
    Fellow Royal Society.
    Southwest London;  Surrey;  Northumberland.
    [WWW, BP, Walfords, Alum Oxon, Dods]

    Central Vigilance Comtee for Repression Immorality
        (F) 83-84, V-Pres.


PERCY, LORD JOSCELINE WILLIAM (1811-1881)

    Eton;  St John's, Camb;  Inner Temple.
    Conservative.  MP Launceston 52-59.  DL, JP.
    Southwest London;  Berkshire.
    [MEB, BP, Walfords, Alum Cantab, Dods]

    Plimsoll and Seamen's Fund Committee (F) 73-73,
        Exec.

PERKINS, W. H.

Central Assn for Stopping Sale Intox Liquors on
Sunday 85-85, Secretary.

PERRIER, ANNA <MRS. JOHN PERRIER>

Sunday Society 79-89, Exec.

PERRY, -

Chelmsford.

Jamaica Committee (F) 66-66.

PERRY, FREDERIC J. (1832-1882)

Independent Minister;  Poet.
Manchester.
[MEB]

Central Assn for Stopping Sale Intox Liquors on
Sunday 73-82, Secretary.

PERY, WILLIAM HALE JOHN CHARLES, 3RD EARL OF LIMERICK
(1840-1896)

Large Landowner 66.
Conservative. Lord in Waiting 86-89, DL, JP.
Earl 66;  PC 89;  KP 92.
Southwest London;  Co Limerick.
[MEB, BP, Walfords, Bateman]

City Church & Churchyard Protection Soc (F) 80-83,
V-Pres.

PETERS, E.  J.

English Land Restoration League 85-85, Exec.

PETERS, SAMUEL

Workmen's Natl Assn for Abolition Sugar Bounties
81-81, Secretary.

PETHERICK, GEORGE WILLIAM

Trin Col, Dublin.
Rector 76;  Curate 63;  Ordained Priest<CE> 64;
Vicar 69.
Salford.
[Crockfds]

Central Assn for Stopping Sale Intox Liquors on
Sunday 80-80, Exec.

PETO, SIR SAMUEL MORTON, 1ST BT.  (1809-1889)

Large Builder/contractor.
Liberal.  MP Norwich 47-54, Finsbury 59-65, Bristol
65-68.  DL, JP.
Baronet 55.
Assoc Inst Civ Engineers.
West London;  Kent;  Perthshire.
[DNB, MEB, BP, Walfords, Dods]

Jamaica Committee (F) 66-66.

PETRIE, JOHN (1791-1883)

Iron Manufacturer 14.
Rochdale.
[MEB]

Jamaica Committee (F) 66-66.

PHILIPS, ROBERT

Manchester.

Central Assn for Stopping Sale Intox Liquors on
Sunday (F) 67-70, Exec.

PHILIPS, ROBERT NEEDHAM (1815-1890)

Rugby;  Manchester New College, Oxford.
Merchant;  Manufacturer;  Substantial Landowner.
Liberal.  MP Bury 57-59, Bury 65-85.  DL, JP.
West London;  Manchester;  Lancashire.
[MEB, Walfords, Bateman, Dods]

Free Land League 86-86, V-Pres.

PHILLIMORE, SIR ROBERT JOSEPH, 1ST BT.  (1810-1885)

Westminster School;  Christ Church, Oxf;  Middle
Temple.
Admiralty Judge 67;  Advocate, Doctors Commons 39;
Barrister 41;  Admiralty Advocate 55;  Judge,
Cinque Ports 55;  Q.C.  62;  Dean of Arches 67.
Liberal.  MP Tavistock 53-57.  Judge Advocate
General 62-67, Judge Advocate General 71-72.
Kt 62;  PC 67;  Baronet 81.
West London;  Oxfordshire.
[DNB, MEB, BP, Walfords, Alum Oxon, Fosters, Dods]

City Church & Churchyard Protection Soc (F) 80-83,
V-Pres.
Intl Law Assn 79-83, President.

PHILLIPPS, LUCY MARCH <MISS>

Cheltenham.

Ladies' Natl Assn for Repeal of Contagious Diseases
Acts 70-72, Exec.

PHILLIPS, EDWARD (1807-1885)

> Peterhouse, Camb.
> Retired Clergyman 70; Perp. Curate 45.
> West London.
> [Alum Cantab, Crockfds]
>
> Soc for Promoting Increase of the Home Episcopate
>     72-74, Exec.

PHILLIPS, R.

> Manchester.
>
> Church Assn 80-80, Exec.

PHILLIPS, WILLIAM

> "Of the Coal Exchange".
> London.
>
> London Municipal Reform League 82-85, V-Chairman,
>     Treas.

PHILLIPS, WILLIAM

> Intl Arbitration & Peace Assn (F) 80-84, Hon Sec.

PHILLPOTTS, WILLIAM JOHN

> Oriel, Oxf.
> Archdeacon 45; Curate 31; Ordained Priest<CE> 32;
>     Vicar 32; Prebendary 40.
> Penryn.
> [Alum Oxon, Crockfds]
>
> Central Assn for Stopping Sale Intox Liquors on
>     Sunday 80-85, V-Pres.

PHIPPS, PICKERING (1827-1890)

> Brewer; Landowner 87.
> Conservative. MP Northampton 74-80,
>     Northamptonshire S 81-85.
> West London; Northampton.
> [MEB, Dods, Direc Direcs]
>
> Local Taxation Comtee [of Central Chamber of
>     Agriculture] 75-85, Exec.

PICKARD, BENJAMIN (1842-1904)

> Trade Union Leader 73; Miner 54.
> Liberal. MP Normantn, Yorks WR S 85-04.
> Barnsley.
> [DNB, WWW, Dods, Dic Lab Biog]
>
> Free Land League 86-86, V-Pres.

PICKERSGILL, EDWARD HARE (1850-1911)

> London U; Inner Temple.
> Civil Servant; Barrister 84; Police Court
>     Magistrate 11.
> Liberal. MP Bethnal Green SW 85-00, Bethnal Green
>     SW 06-11.
> North London.
> [Fosters, Dods]
>
> Sunday Society (F) 75-75, Chairman.
> Free Land League 86-86, V-Pres.

PICKFORD, F.

> London Municipal Reform League 82-82, Exec.

PICKTON, - <MISS>

> Kyrle Soc 84-85, Exec.

PICTON, JAMES ALLANSON (1832-1910)

> Owens Col, Manch.
> Journalist 79; Independent Minister 56; Author.
> Radical. MP Leicester 84-94. JP.
> Northwest London.
> [DNB, WWW, Dods]
>
> Sunday Society 86-90, V-Pres.
> Free Land League 86-86, V-Pres.

PIERCY, GEORGE

> Clergyman<Sect Unkn>.
>
> Anglo-Oriental Soc for Suppression Opium Trade
>     83-83, Exec.

PILLANS, THOMAS D.

> Sunday Society (F) 75-83, Hon Sec.

PIM, JONATHAN (1806-1885)

> Textile Manufacturer; Merchant.
> Liberal. MP Dublin City 65-74.
> Dublin; Durham[County].
> [MEB, Walfords, Dods]
>
> Howard Assn 69-73, Patron.

PINNEY, WILLIAM (1806-1898)

> Eton; Trinity, Camb; Inner Temple.
> Landowner 45.
> Liberal. MP Lyme Regis 32-42, Somersetshire East
>     47-52, Lyme Regis 52-65. DL, JP.
> Royal Agricultural Society.
> West London; Somersetshire.
> [MEB, Walfords, Alum Cantab, Dods]
>
> Natl Assn for Promotion of State Colonization
>     86-86, V-Pres.

PIRKIS, FRED E.

>   Paymaster, RN 70;  Asst Paymaster, RN 60.
>   Fellow Royal Geograph Society.
>   Surrey.
>   [Direc Direcs, Navy List]
>
>   Victoria Street Soc for Protection of Animals from
>       Vivisection 82-85, Exec.

PITCAIRN, JAMES PELHAM (1821-1892)

>   Jesus, Camb.
>   Vicar 61;  Curate 46;  Ordained Priest<CE> 47;
>       Rector 50;  Rural Dean 70;  Hon. Canon 78.
>   Eccles.
>   [Alum Cantab, Crockfds]
>
>   Central Assn for Stopping Sale Intox Liquors on
>       Sunday (F) 67-67, V-Pres.

PITE, A. R.

>   Church Assn 70-70, Exec.

PITMAN, HENRY

>   Manchester.
>
>   London Soc for Abolition of Compulsory Vaccination
>       81-81, V-Pres.

PITMAN, SIR ISAAC (1813-1901)

>   British and Foreign School Society College.
>   Publisher 47;  School Master 32.
>   Kt 94.
>   Bath.
>   [DNB, MEB]
>
>   London Soc for Abolition of Compulsory Vaccination
>       81-81, V-Pres.

PLAYFAIR, LYON, 1ST BARON PLAYFAIR (1818-1898)

>   U St Andrews;  Giessen.
>   Analytical Chemist;  Sec, Science and Art Dept,
>       South Kensington 55;  Professor of Chemistry,
>       Edinburgh 58;  Author.
>   Liberal.  MP Edinb & St Ands Univ 68-85, Leeds
>       85-92.  Postmaster General 73-74, Deputy
>       Speaker House of Commons 80-83, V-P Education
>       Committee 86-86, Lord in Waiting 92-95.
>   CB 51;  PC 73;  KCB 83;  Baron 92;  GCB 95.
>   Fellow Royal Society;  Br Assn.
>   Southwest London.
>   [DNB, MEB, WWW, BP, Walfords, Dods, Direc Direcs]
>
>   Natl Footpaths Preservation Soc 86-90, V-Pres.
>   Smoke Abatement Committee 81-81.

PLOWDEN, SIR WILLIAM CHICHELE (1832-1915)

>   Harrow;  Haileybury.
>   India Civil Service 52;  Council of India.
>   Liberal.  MP Wolverhampton West 86-92.  JP.
>   KCSI 86.
>   Southwest London.
>   [WWW, Walfords, Dods, Direc Direcs]
>
>   Free Land League 86-86, V-Pres.

PLUMBE, ROWLAND

>   Architect.
>   Fellow Royal Inst Br Architects.
>   West London.
>
>   Sanitary Institute 83-85, Exec.

PLUMPTRE, CHARLES JOHN (1818-1887)

>   Kings Col London;  Gray's Inn.
>   Barrister 44;  College Lecturer 60;  Professor of
>       Elocution, King's Col London 66;  Substantial
>       Landowner.
>   St Johns Wood.
>   [DNB, MEB, Bateman, Fosters]
>
>   Sunday Society 76-87, V-Pres.

PLUNKETT, EDWARD, 16TH BARON DUNSANY (1808-1889)

>   Large Landowner 52;  Vice-Admiral 71;  Cadet, RN
>       23;  Captain, RN 46;  Rear Admiral 64.
>   Conservative.  JP.
>   Baron 52.
>   Southwest London;  Co Westmeath.
>   [MEB, BP, Walfords, Bateman, Navy List]
>
>   Natl Emigration League (F) 70-70, V-Pres.

POCHIN, HENRY DAVIS (1824-1895)

>   Analytical Chemist;  Iron Manufacturer;  Colliery
>       Owner.
>   Liberal.  MP Salford 68-69.  DL, JP.
>   Southwest London;  Salford;  Lancashire.
>   [MEB, Walfords, Dods, Direc Direcs]
>
>   Liberty & Property Defense League (F) 82-84, Exec.
>   Central Assn for Stopping Sale Intox Liquors on
>       Sunday (F) 67-68, V-Pres.

POLLARD, JAMES

>   Torquay.
>
>   Assn for Promoting Extension of Contagious Diseases
>       Act 68-68, Exec.

POLLOCK, CHARLES EDWARD (1823-1897)

>   St Paul's, London;  Inner Temple.
>   Barrister 47;  Q.C. 66;  Sergeant at Law 73;
>       Baron, Exchequer 73;  Judge, Exchequer 75;
>       Judge, Queen's Bench 79;  Author.
>   JP.
>   Kt 73.
>   Southeast London.

[DNB, MEB, WWW, BP, Fosters]

Commons Preservation Soc (F) 65-76, Exec.


POLLOCK, SIR FREDERICK, 3RD BT.  (1845-1937)

Eton;  Trinity, Camb;  Lincoln's Inn.
Corpus Professor of Jurisprudence, Oxford 83;
    College Fellow 68;  Barrister 71;  Journal
    Editor 85;  Judge, Cinque Ports 14;  K.C.  20;
    Author.
Baronet 88;  PC 11.
Fellow Society of Antiquaries;  British Academy.
West London.
[DNB, WWW, BP, Alum Cantab, Alum Oxon, Fosters]

Commons Preservation Soc 84-86, Exec.
Natl Footpaths Preservation Soc (F) 85-86, Exec.


POLLOCK, JAMES EDWARD (1819-1910)

Aberdeen(Medical).
Physician.
Fellow Royal Col Physicians.
West London.
[WWW, Direc Direcs]

Assn for Promoting Extension of Contagious Diseases
    Act 68-75, Exec, V-Pres.


POLLOCK, WILLIAM (1812-1873)

Trin Col, Dublin.
Archdeacon 67;  Curate 41;  Vicar 41;  Perp.
    Curate 46;  Vicar 56.
Bowdon.
[MEB, Crockfds]

Assn for Promoting Extension of Contagious Diseases
    Act 68-68, V-Pres.
Central Assn for Stopping Sale Intox Liquors on
    Sunday 70-70, V-Pres.


POLLOCK, SIR WILLIAM FREDERICK, 2ND BT.  (1815-1888)

St Paul's, London;  Trinity, Camb;  Inner Temple.
Supreme Court Master 74;  Barrister 38;  Exchequer
    Master 46.
Baronet 70.
West London.
[DNB, MEB, BP, Alum Cantab, Fosters, Direc Direcs]

Smoke Abatement Committee 81-81.
Metro Free Libraries Assn 77-77, Exec.


POMEROY, FLORENCE WALLACE, VISCOUNTESS HARBERTON <Wife
    of 6TH VISCOUNT, nee LEGGE> ( -1911)

Southwest London;  Surrey.
[WWW, BP]

Smoke Abatement Committee 81-81.


POMEROY, JAMES SPENCER, 6TH VISCOUNT HARBERTON
    (1836-1912)

Trinity Hall, Camb;  Lincoln's Inn.
Large Landowner 62.
JP.
Viscount 62.
Southwest London;  Surrey.
[WWW, BP, Walfords, Bateman, Alum Cantab]

Smoke Abatement Committee 81-81.
Sunday Society 80-90, V-Pres.


PONSONBY, HENRY FREDERICK (1825-1895)

Colonel 60;  Ensign, Army 42;  Lieutenant, Army 44;
    Major 49;  Lt. Colonel 55;  Maj.  General 68;
    Private Secretary to Queen 70.
CB 72;  KCB 79;  PC 80;  GCB 87.
West London.
[DNB, MEB, Army List]

Assn for Promoting Extension of Contagious Diseases
    Act 68-68, V-Pres.


PORT, H.

Birmingham.

London Soc for Abolition of Compulsory Vaccination
    81-81, V-Pres.


PORTAL, SIR WYNDHAM SPENCER, 1ST BT.  (1822-1905)

Harrow;  Royal Military College, Sandhurst.
Landowner.
DL, JP.
Baronet 01.
Southwest London;  Hampshire.
[WWW, BP, Walfords, Direc Direcs]

Intl Arbitration & Peace Assn 81-81, V-Pres.


PORTER, SIR GEORGE HORNIDGE, 1ST BT.  (1822-1895)

Trin Col, Dublin.
Surgeon 49;  Regius Professor of Surgery, U Dublin
    91.
Kt 83;  Baronet 89.
Fellow Royal Col Surgeons;  Fellow Royal Col
    Surgeons, Ire.
Dublin;  Co Wexford.
[DNB, MEB, BP]

Assn for Promoting Extension of Contagious Diseases
    Act 68-70, V-Pres.


PORTER, JAMES BIGGS (1843- )

Inner Temple.
Barrister 74.
West London.
[Fosters]

Assn for Improvement of Public Morals 81-81, Exec.
London Comtee Exposure & Suppresn Traffic In Girls
    85-85, Hon Sec.

PORTMAN, EDWIN BERKELEY (1830-1921)

    Rugby;  Balliol, Oxf;  Inner Temple.
    Barrister 52;  College Fellow 50.
    Liberal.  MP Dorsetshire North 85-92.
    West London.
    [WWW, BP, Alum Oxon, Fosters, Dods, Direc Direcs]

    Free Land League 86-86, V-Pres.


POTTER, - <MISS>

    Smoke Abatement Committee 81-81.


POTTER, GEORGE (1832-1893)

    Labour Leader;  Newspaper Editor 61;  Carpenter.
    Radical.
    London.
    [DNB, MEB]

    Working Men's Comtee Promoting Separation Church
      and State (F) 71-71, Secretary.
    Travelling Tax Abolition Committee (F) 77-85, Exec.
    Natl Emigration League (F) 70-70, Exec.


POTTER, THOMAS BAYLEY (1817-1898)

    Rugby;  University Col London.
    Wholesale Draper 37.
    Radical.  MP Rochdale 65-95.  DL, JP.
    Southwest London;  Manchester.
    [DNB, MEB, WWW, Walfords, Dods]

    Sunday Society 80-90, V-Pres.
    Jamaica Committee (F) 66-66.
    Natl Assn for Repeal Contagious Diseases Acts
      81-81, V-Pres.


POTTO, T.  C.

    East London.

    London Municipal Reform League 82-85, Exec.


POTTS, JOHN FAULKNER

    Clergyman<Sect Unkn>.
    Glasgow.

    London Soc for Abolition of Compulsory Vaccination
      81-81, V-Pres.


POULTER, R.  C.

    Northwest London.

    Natl Footpaths Preservation Soc (F) 85-86, Exec.
    Kyrle Soc 87-90, Exec.


POWELL, SIR FRANCIS SHARP, 1ST BT.  (1827-1911)

    Uppingham;  St John's, Camb;  Inner Temple.
    Barrister 53;  College Fellow 51.
    Conservative.  MP Wigan 57-59, Cambridge 63-68,
      Yorks W Riding North 72-74, Wigan 81-81, Wigan
      85-10.  DL, JP.
    Baronet 92.
    West London;  Yorks, West Riding.
    [WWW, Walfords, Alum Cantab, Alum Oxon, Fosters,
      Dods, Direc Direcs]

    Commons Preservation Soc 69-76, Exec.
    Natl Soc for Preserving Memorials of Dead 84-88,
      Exec.
    Natl Education Union (F) 69-86, Chairman, Hon Sec.


POWELL, RICHARD ASHMORE (1816-1892)

    Captain, RN 55;  Cadet, RN 31;  Commodore, RN 66;
      Rear Admiral 73;  Vice-Admiral 78.
    CB 55.
    Isle of Wight.
    [MEB, Navy List]

    Plimsoll and Seamen's Fund Committee (F) 73-73,
      Exec.


POWELL, WALTER RICE HOWELL (1819-1889)

    Christ Church, Oxf.
    Landowner 34.
    Liberal.  MP Carmarthenshire 80-85, Carmarthenshire
      West 85-89.  DL, JP.
    Carmarthenshire.
    [MEB, Walfords, Alum Oxon, Dods]

    Intl Arbitration & Peace Assn 81-81, V-Pres.


POWER, JOHN O'CONNOR (1846- )

    St Jarlath's Col, Tuam;  Middle Temple.
    Barrister 81.
    Liberal.  MP Mayo 74-85.
    London.
    [Fosters, Dods]

    Intl Arbitration & Peace Assn 81-81, V-Pres.


POYNDER, ROBERT

    Curate 83;  Ordained Priest<CE> 67.
    Reading.
    [Crockfds]

    Church Assn 85-85, Exec.


POYNTER, SIR EDWARD JOHN, 1ST BT.  (1836-1919)

    Westminster School;  Leigh's Art Sch.
    Artist;  Slade Professor of Art, U Col London 71;
      Dir Art, South Kensington;  Director, Natl
      Gallery 94.
    Kt 96;  Baronet 02;  KCVO 13;  GCVO 18.
    Royal Academy.
    Southwest London.
    [DNB, WWW, BP, Alum Cantab]

    City Church & Churchyard Protection Soc (F) 80-83,
      V-Pres.

Soc for Protection of Ancient Buildings (F) 78-85,
Exec.

PRAED, SIR HERBERT BULKLEY MACKWORTH, 1ST BT.
(1841-1921)

Harrow.
Banker; Ensign, Army 60.
Conservative. MP Colchester 74-80. DL, JP.
Baronet 05.
Southwest London; Newmarket.
[WWW, Dods, Direc Direcs, Army List]

Sunday Society 80-90, V-Pres.

PRATT, DANIEL

Natl Emigration League (F) 70-70, Exec.

PRATT, HODGSON (1824-1907)

Haileybury College; London U.
Cooperative Promoter; Author; India Civil Service
46; U-Sec, Bengal Govt.
Radical.
Fellow Royal Geograph Society.
Southwest London.
[DNB, Dic Lab Biog]

Natl Assn for Promotion of State Colonization
86-86, Exec, V-Pres.
Sunday Society 76-90, V-Pres.
Public Museums & Free Libraries Assn 68-68, Exec.
Intl Arbitration & Peace Assn (F) 80-84, Chairman.
Indian Reform Assn 84-84, Exec.
Workmen's Peace Assn 78-78, V-Chairman.
Travelling Tax Abolition Committee (F) 77-85, Exec.

PREST, EDWARD (1824-1882)

Uppingham; St John's, Camb.
Archdeacon 63; Ordained Priest<CE> 48; Chaplain
51; Hon. Canon 60; Rector 61; Canon 63.
Gateshead.
[MEB, Alum Cantab, Crockfds]

Assn for Promoting Extension of Contagious Diseases
Act 68-70, V-Pres.
Central Assn for Stopping Sale Intox Liquors on
Sunday 75-80, V-Pres.
Church Assn 67-78, V-Pres.

PREVOST, SIR GEORGE, 2ND BT. (1804-1893)

Oriel, Oxf.
Archdeacon 65; Curate 28; Ordained Priest<CE> 29;
Vicar 34; Rural Dean 52; Hon. Canon 59;
Landowner 16.
Baronet 16.
Stinchcombe.
[DNB, MEB, BP, Walfords, Alum Oxon, Crockfds]

Soc for Promoting Increase of the Home Episcopate
72-74, Exec.

PRICE, AUBREY CHARLES (1829-1897)

Winchester College; New College, Oxf.
Vicar 65; College Fellow 49; Ordained Priest<CE>
54; Curate 54; Rector 56.
Clapham.
[MEB, Alum Oxon, Crockfds]

Church Assn 67-67, Exec.

PRICE, BONAMY (1807-1888)

Worcester, Oxf.
Drummond Professor of Political Economy, Oxford 68;
School Master 30.
Oxford.
[DNB, MEB, Alum Oxon]

City Church & Churchyard Protection Soc (F) 80-83,
V-Pres.

PRICE, G.

Ordained Priest<CE>.
Cheltenham.

Church Assn 70-70, Exec.

PRICE, THOMAS

East Central London.

Jamaica Committee (F) 66-66.

PRICE, W. NICHOLSON

Leeds.

Assn for Promoting Extension of Contagious Diseases
Act 68-68, Exec.

PRICE, WILLIAM PHILIP (1817-1891)

Timber Merchant; Railway Commissioner 73.
Liberal. MP Gloucester 52-59, Gloucester 65-73.
DL, JP.
Southwest London; Gloucester.
[MEB, Walfords, Dods]

Assn for Promoting Extension of Contagious Diseases
Act 68-70, V-Pres.

PRIESTLEY, BRIGGS (1832-1907)

Worsted Manufacturer.
Liberal. MP Pudsey, Yorks WR E 85-00.
Southwest London; Bradford; Yorks, West Riding.
[WWW, Dods, Direc Direcs]

Free Land League 86-86, V-Pres.

PRIESTMAN, FREDERICK

>JP.
>Bradford.
>[Direc Direcs]
>
>Jamaica Committee (F) 66-66.

PRIESTMAN, J., JUN.

>Bradford.
>
>Jamaica Committee (F) 66-66.

PRIESTMAN, JOHN (1805-1866)

>Worsted Manufacturer.
>Liberal.
>Bradford.
>[DNB, MEB]
>
>Jamaica Committee (F) 66-66.

PRIESTMAN, MARY

>Ladies´ Natl Assn for Repeal of Contagious Diseases
>    Acts 70-72, Exec.

PRIMROSE, ARCHIBALD PHILIP, 5TH EARL OF ROSEBERY
(1847-1929)

>Eton;  Christ Church, Oxf.
>Very Large Landowner 68;  Politician.
>Liberal.  Parl U-Sec Home Off 81-83, First
>    Commissioner Works 85-85, Lord Privy Seal
>    85-85, Sec St Foreign Off 86-86, Sec St Foreign
>    Off 92-94, Prime Minister 94-95, Lord Pres
>    Council 94-95.
>Earl 68;  KG;  KT;  PC 85.
>Fellow Royal Society;  Fellow Society of
>    Antiquaries;  British Academy.
>West London;  West Lothian.
>[DNB, WWW, BP, Walfords, Bateman, Alum Oxon, Direc
>    Direcs]
>
>Sunday Society 78-90, President, V-Pres.
>Plimsoll and Seamen´s Fund Committee (F) 73-73,
>    Exec.

PRITCHARD, CHARLES (1808-1893)

>Christ´s Hospital;  St John´s, Camb.
>Savilian Professor of Astronomy, Oxford 70;
>    College Fellow 32;  School Head 33;  Ordained
>    Priest<CE> 34;  College Lecturer 67;  Author.
>Fellow Royal Astronomical Society;  Fellow Royal
>    Society;  Fellow Geological Society.
>Oxford.
>[DNB, MEB, Alum Cantab, Alum Oxon, Crockfds]
>
>City Church & Churchyard Protection Soc (F) 80-83,
>    V-Pres.

PROBYN, J.  W.

>Eastern Question Assn (F) 76-77, Hon Sec.

PROCTER, EDMUND

>Northumberland.
>
>London Soc for Abolition of Compulsory Vaccination
>    81-81, V-Pres.

PROCTOR, JAMES

>Manchester.
>
>Jamaica Committee (F) 66-66.

PROUDMAN, J.  W.

>Financial Reform Union (F) 68-69, Exec.

PROVAND, ANDREW DRYBURGH (1839-1915)

>Merchant.
>Liberal.  MP Glasgow Blackfriars & Hutchesontown
>    86-00.
>West London.
>[WWW, Dods]
>
>Free Land League 86-86, V-Pres.

PRYCE, EDWARD S.

>Eastern Question Assn (F) 76-77, Secretary.

PRYCE, R.  VAUGHAN (1834-1917)

>New College, Hampstead.
>Congregational Minister 62;  College Lecturer 77;
>    College Head 89;  Professor of Theology, New
>    Col London 89.
>Brighton.
>[WWW]
>
>Jamaica Committee (F) 66-66.

PRYOR, ARTHUR (1816- )

>Eton.
>Brewer;  Substantial Landowner 58.
>Conservative.  DL, JP.
>Essex.
>[Walfords, Bateman, Direc Direcs]
>
>Natl Fair Trade League (F) 81-81, Exec.

PRYOR, JOHN

> London.
>
> Jamaica Committee (F) 66-66.

PUCKLE, JOHN (1812-1894)

> Brasenose, Oxf.
> Vicar 42;  Ordained Priest<CE> 37;  Rural Dean 46;
>     Hon.  Canon 69.
> Dover.
> [MEB, Alum Oxon, Crockfds]
>
> Assn for Promoting Extension of Contagious Diseases
>     Act 68-68, V-Pres.

PULESTON, SIR JOHN HENRY (1830-1908)

> Kings Col London.
> Merchant.
> Conservative.  MP Devonport 74-92.  DL, JP.
> Kt 87.
> Southwest London;  Denbighshire.
> [WWW, Dods, Direc Direcs]
>
> Howard Assn 75-84, Patron.

PULLEY, SIR JOSEPH, 1ST BT.  (1822-1901)

> Stock Broker.
> Liberal.  MP Hereford [City] 80-86.  DL, JP.
> Baronet 93.
> West London;  Herefordshire.
> [WWW, Dods, Direc Direcs]
>
> Free Land League 86-86, V-Pres.

PUNSHON, WILLIAM MORLEY (1824-1881)

> Wesleyan Minister 45.
> Southwest London.
> [MEB]
>
> Central Assn for Stopping Sale Intox Liquors on
>     Sunday 75-75, V-Pres.

QUAIN, RICHARD (1800-1887)

> Aldersgate School Medicine, Lond.
> Surgeon 48;  Medical School Demonstrator 30;
>     Medical School Professor 32;  Asst Surgeon 34.
> Fellow Royal Society;  Fellow Royal Col Surgeons.
> West London.
> [DNB, MEB]
>
> Assn for Promoting Extension of Contagious Diseases
>     Act 68-70, V-Pres.

QUAIN, SIR RICHARD, 1ST BT.  (1816-1898)

> U College London(Medical).
> Physician 42;  College Fellow 43.
> Baronet 91.
> Fellow Royal Society;  Fellow Royal Col Physicians;
>     Royal Col Physicians, Ireland;  Pathological
>     Society.
> West London.
> [DNB, WWW, BP]

> Assn for Promoting Extension of Contagious Diseases
>     Act 68-70, V-Pres.

QUIN, WINDHAM THOMAS WYNDHAM, 4TH EARL OF DUNRAVEN
(1841-1926)

> Christ Church, Oxf.
> Very Large Landowner 71;  Cornet, Army 62;
>     Lieutenant, Army 65.
> Parl U-Sec Col Off 85-86, Parl U-Sec Col Off 86-87,
>     Lord Lieutenant 94-  .
> Earl 71;  PC Ireland 89;  CMG 02;  KP;  OBE.
> Southwest London;  Glamorganshire;  Co Limerick.
> [DNB, WWW, BP, Walfords, Bateman, Alum Oxon, Army
>     List]
>
> Sunday Society 79-90, V-Pres, President.

RADCLIFFE, CHARLES BLAND (1822-1889)

> Leeds School of Medicine.
> Physician 51;  Author.
> Fellow Royal Col Physicians.
> West London.
> [DNB, MEB]
>
> Assn for Improvement of London Workhouse
>     Infirmaries 66-66, Exec.

RADCLIFFE, JOHN NETTEN (1826-1884)

> Leeds School of Medicine.
> Surgeon 55;  Public Health Inspector 69;  Assistant
>     Medical Officer, LGB 71.
> Epidemiological Society of London.
> West London.
> [DNB, MEB]
>
> Assn for Improvement of London Workhouse
>     Infirmaries 66-66, Exec.

RAIKES, HENRY CECIL (1838-1891)

> Shrewsbury School;  Trinity, Camb;  Middle Temple.
> Politician;  Barrister 63.
> Conservative.  MP Chester 68-80, Preston 82-82,
>     Cambridge University 82-91.  Deputy Speaker
>     House of Commons 74-80, Postmaster General
>     86-91, DL, JP.
> PC 80.
> West London;  Flintshire.
> [DNB, MEB, Walfords, Alum Cantab, Fosters, Dods,
>     Direc Direcs]
>
> Soc for Promoting Increase of the Home Episcopate
>     72-74, Exec.
> Natl Education Union 70-79, Exec.

RAIMBACH, T. EMMERSON

> North London.
>
> Natl Footpaths Preservation Soc (F) 85-86, Exec.

RALEIGH, ALEXANDER (1817-1880)

    Lancashire College, Manchester.
    Congregational Minister 45.
    North London; West London.
    [DNB, MEB]

    Central Assn for Stopping Sale Intox Liquors on
        Sunday 70-80, V-Pres.
    Jamaica Committee (F) 66-66.

RAMSAY, SIR ALEXANDER, 3RD BT. (1813-1875)

    Substantial Landowner 52; Ensign, Army 30;
        Lieutenant, Army 34.
    Liberal. MP Rochdale 57-59. DL, JP.
    Baronet 52.
    Gloucestershire; Kincardineshire.
    [MEB, BP, Walfords, Dods, Army List]

    Assn for Promoting Extension of Contagious Diseases
        Act 68-68, V-Pres.

RAMSAY, JOHN WILLIAM, 13TH EARL OF DALHOUSIE (1847-1887)

    Balliol, Oxf.
    Very Large Landowner 80; Cadet, RN 61;
        Lieutenant, RN 67; Commodore, RN 74.
    Liberal. MP Liverpool 80-80. Lord in Waiting
        80-85, Sec St Scotland 86-86.
    Earl 80; KT 81; PC 86.
    West London; Angus.
    [DNB, MEB, BP, Alum Oxon, Dods, Navy List]

    Sunday Society 80-87, V-Pres.
    Free Land League 86-86, V-Pres, Exec.
    London Municipal Reform League 85-85, Chairman.

RAND, JOHN (1793- )

    Textile Manufacturer.
    DL, JP.
    Bradford; Yorks, West Riding.
    [Walfords]

    Church Assn 70-70, Exec.

RANDALL, JAMES S.

    Howard Assn 79-84, Exec.

RANDALL, LEWIS

    Financial Reform Union (F) 68-69, Exec.

RANKIN, JAMES H., 1ST BT. (1842-1915)

    Trinity, Camb.
    Substantial Landowner.
    Conservative. MP Leominster 80-85, Leominster
        86-06, Leominster 10-12. DL, JP.
    Baronet 98.
    Herefordshire.
    [WWW, BP, Walfords, Alum Cantab, Dods]

    Natl Assn for Promotion of State Colonization (F)
        83-86, V-Pres.

RANYARD, S.

    JP.
    Kingston<?>.

    Church Assn 80-85, Exec.

RAPER, ROBERT WILLIAM (1842-1915)

    Cheltenham College; Trinity, Oxf.
    College Dean 75; College Fellow 65; College
        Lecturer 65; College Tutor 69.
    Oxford; Herefordshire.
    [DNB, WWW, Alum Oxon]

    Commons Preservation Soc 80-86, Exec.

RATCLIFF, CHARLES (1822-1885)

    Downing, Camb; Lincoln's Inn.
    Banker; Barrister 58; Educationalist.
    DL, JP.
    Fellow Society of Antiquaries; Fellow Linnean
        Society.
    West London; Birmingham.
    [MEB, Alum Cantab, Fosters]

    Natl Education Union (F) 69-79, Hon Sec.

RATCLIFF, WALTER HENRY (1840-1925)

    King Edward's School, Birm; Trinity, Camb.
    Curate 65; Ordained Priest<CE> 65.
    [Alum Cantab, Crockfds]

    Land Nationalization Soc 84-85, Exec.

RATHBONE, BENSON

    Cotton Broker.
    Liverpool.
    [Direc Direcs]

    Intl Arbitration & Peace Assn 81-81, V-Pres.

RATHBONE, WILLIAM (1819-1902)

    Everton School.
    Merchant.
    Liberal. MP Liverpool 68-80, Carnarvon 80-85,
        Arfon Div, Carnarvon 85-95. DL, JP.
    Southwest London; Liverpool.
    [Walfords, Dods]

    Proportional Representation Soc (F) 84-88, Exec.

RAWLEY, WALTER J.

    Sunday Society 76-90, Exec.

RAWLINGS, CHARLES E., JUN.

    Liverpool.

    Jamaica Committee (F) 66-66.


RAWLINSON, SIR ROBERT (1810-1898)

    Civil Engineer;  Chief Engineering Inspector, LGB
       49;  Author.
    CB 65;  Kt 83;  KCB 88.
    Member Inst Civ Engineers;  Fellow Geological
       Society;  Society of the Arts.
    Southwest London.
    [DNB, MEB, WWW, Direc Direcs]

    Sanitary Institute 83-89, V-Pres.


RAWNSLEY, HARDWICKE DRUMMOND (1851-1920)

    Uppingham;  Balliol, Oxf.
    Vicar 78;  Ordained Priest<CE> 75;  Curate 75;
       Rural Dean 83.
    Keswick.
    [WWW, Alum Oxon, Crockfds]

    Natl Footpaths Preservation Soc (F) 85-86, Exec.


RAYNER, SIR THOMAS CROSSLEY (1860-1914)

    Owens Col, Manch;  Middle Temple.
    Barrister 82;  District Commissioner, Gold Coast
       87;  Magistrate, Trinidad 91;  Puisine Judge,
       Gold Coast 94;  Chief Justice, Lagos 95;
       Attorney General, British Guiana 02;  Chief
       Justice, British Guiana 12.
    Kt 99.
    Manchester.
    [WWW, Fosters]

    Central Assn for Stopping Sale Intox Liquors on
       Sunday 85-85, Exec.


READ, CLARE SEWELL (1826-1905)

    Farmer.
    Conservative.  MP Norfolk East 65-68, Norfolk South
       68-80, Norfolk West 84-85.  Parl Sec Loc Govt
       Board 74-75, JP.
    Royal Agricultural Society.
    Norfolk.
    [DNB, WWW, Walfords, Dods, Direc Direcs]

    Local Taxation Comtee [of Central Chamber of
       Agriculture] 71-85, Exec.


READE, CHARLES (1814-1884)

    Magdalen, Oxf;  Lincoln's Inn.
    Novelist;  College Fellow 35;  Barrister 43.
    West London.
    [DNB, MEB, Alum Cantab, Alum Oxon]

    Sunday Society (F) 75-83, V-Pres.


READE, CHARLES DARBY (1821- )

    Magdalen Hall, Oxf.
    Retired Clergyman;  Ordained Priest<CE> 48;  Rector
       50.
    JP.
    West London.
    [Alum Oxon, Crockfds]

    London Municipal Reform League 82-85, Exec.


READE, ESSEX E.

    Southwest London.
    [Direc Direcs]

    Soc for Protection of Ancient Buildings 85-85,
       Exec.


READWIN, T. A.

    Financial Reform Union (F) 68-69, Exec.


REANEY, - <MRS. GEORGE SALE REANEY>

    East London.

    British Women's Temperance Assn 84-84, Exec.


REANEY, GEORGE SALE

    Congregational Minister;  Curate 90;  Ordained
       Priest<CE> 91;  Vicar 93.
    East London.
    [Crockfds]

    Central Assn for Stopping Sale Intox Liquors on
       Sunday 75-75, Exec.


RECKITT, FRANCIS

    "In business".
    JP.
    North London.
    [Direc Direcs]

    Howard Assn 83-84, Exec.


REDFERN, THOMAS

    Birmingham.

    Jamaica Committee (F) 66-66.


REDFERN, WILLIAM

    London.

    Jamaica Committee (F) 66-66.

REDGRAVE, ALEXANDER (1818-1894)

    Factory Inspector 52;  Clerk, HO 34.
    CB 77.
    West London.
    [MEB]

    Natl Education Union (F) 69-70, Exec.


REDGRAVE, RICHARD (1804-1888)

    Royal Academy Sch.
    Artist;  Head, Govt School of Design 48;  Surveyor
      Crown Pictures 57.
    CB 80.
    Royal Academy.
    West London.
    [DNB, MEB, Bryan's Painters]

    Public Museums & Free Libraries Assn 68-68, V-Pres.


REED, CHARLES

    Financial Reform Union (F) 68-69, Exec.


REED, SIR CHARLES (1819-1881)

    London U.
    Typefounder 61;  Journal Editor 39;  Printer 42.
    Liberal.  MP Hackney 68-74, Cornwall W, St Ives
      80-81.  Thames Conserv Board 67÷ .
    Kt 74.
    Fellow Society of Antiquaries.
    East London.
    [DNB, MEB, Walfords, Dods]

    Natl Emigration League (F) 70-70, V-Pres.


REED, DANIEL M.

    Sunday Society 76-76, Exec.


REES, ELLEN ELCUM <MISS>

    Victoria Street Soc for Protection of Animals from
      Vivisection 84-85, Exec.
    Soc for Abolition of Vivisection 76-76, Exec.


REES, ROWLAND

    JP.
    Dover.

    London Soc for Abolition of Compulsory Vaccination
      81-81, V-Pres.


REEVES, W.

    Land Nationalization Soc 83-85, Exec.


REID, ANDREW

    Land Tenure Reform Assn (F) 70-73, Secretary.


REID, GEORGE WILLIAM (1819-1887)

    Keeper Prints & Drawings, British Museum 66.
    London.
    [DNB]

    Soc for Protection of Ancient Buildings (F) 78-80,
      Exec.


REID, HUGH GILZEAN (1836-1911)

    Newspaper Proprietor;  Newspaper Editor 56;
      Journalist;  Author.
    Liberal.  MP Aston Manor 85-86.  DL, JP.
    Kt 93.
    Middlesborough;  Warwickshire.
    [WWW, Dods]

    Allotments & Small Holdings Assn 85-88, Exec.


REID, JESSY <MRS.>

    Ladies' Natl Assn for Repeal of Contagious Diseases
      Acts 70-72, Exec.


REID, ROBERT THRESHIE, 1ST EARL LOREBURN (1846-1923)

    Cheltenham College;  Balliol, Oxf;  Inner Temple.
    Q.C. 82;  Barrister 71.
    Liberal.  MP Hereford [City] 80-85, Dumfries
      District 86-05.  Solicitor General 94-94,
      Attorney General 94-95, Lord Chancellor 05-12,
      JP.
    Kt 94;  GCMG 99;  PC 05;  Baron 06;  Earl 11.
    Southwest London;  Kent.
    [DNB, WWW, Alum Oxon, Fosters, Dods]

    Victoria Street Soc for Protection of Animals from
      Vivisection 82-85, Exec.


REID, W.

    East Central London.

    City Church & Churchyard Protection Soc (F) 80-81,
      Exec.


RENDEL, STUART, 1ST BARON RENDEL (1834-1913)

    Eton;  Oriel, Oxf;  Inner Temple.
    Barrister 61.
    Liberal.  MP Montgomeryshire 80-94.  JP.
    Baron 94.
    West London;  Surrey;  Montgomeryshire.
    [WWW, BP, Alum Oxon, Fosters, Dods, Direc Direcs]

    Free Land League 86-86, V-Pres.

RENNICK, - <MRS. CHARLES RENNICK>

    Malthusian League (F) 77-78, Exec.

RENNICK, CHARLES

    Sunday Society (F) 75-75, Chairman, Treas.
    Malthusian League 78-78, V-Pres.

REVELL, W. F.

    Clergyman<Sect Unkn>.
    London.

    Sunday Society (F) 75-76, V-Pres.

REYNOLDS, - <MRS.>

    Bridport.

    British Women's Temperance Assn 85-85, Exec.

REYNOLDS, W.

    Land Nationalization Soc 83-85, Exec.

REYNOLDS, W. J.

    Malthusian League 78-79, Exec.

REYNOLDS, WILLIAM HAMMOND

    Publisher.
    Southeast London.

    Sunday Society (F) 75-75, Exec.
    Malthusian League (F) 77-11, Hon Sec, Treas.
    Natl Secular Soc 81-84, V-Pres.

RHODES, A. A.

    Blackpool.

    British Women's Temperance Assn 85-85, Exec.

RHODES, JOHN

    Keighley.

    Natl Secular Soc 70-70, V-Pres, Exec.

RICE, ARTHUR DE CARDONNEL, 6TH BARON DYNEVOR (1836-1911)

    Christ Church, Oxf.
    Very Large Landowner 78.
    Conservative. DL, JP.
    Baron 78.
    Carmarthenshire.
    [WWW, BP, Walfords, Bateman, Alum Oxon]

    Natl Assn for Promotion of State Colonization
       86-86, Patron.

RICE, FRANCIS WILLIAM, 5TH BARON DYNEVOR (1804-1878)

    Westminster School;  Christ Church, Oxf.
    Vicar 28;  Rural Dean;  Ordained Priest<CE> 28;
       Very Large Landowner 69.
    Baron 69.
    Fairford;  Carmarthenshire.
    [MEB, BP, Walfords, Alum Oxon, Crockfds]

    Church Assn 75-75, V-Pres.

RICE, JOSEPH

    JP.
    Manchester.

    Central Assn for Stopping Sale Intox Liquors on
       Sunday 85-85, V-Pres.

RICHARD, HENRY (1812-1888)

    Highbury College.
    Newspaper Editor 55;  Congregational Minister 35.
    Liberal.  MP Merthyr-Tydvil 68-88.
    Southwest London.
    [DNB, MEB, Walfords, Dods]

    Metro Free Libraries Assn (F) 77-77, Exec.
    Intl Law Assn 74-74, Exec.
    Howard Assn 74-81, Patron.
    Jamaica Committee (F) 66-66.
    Natl Assn for Repeal Contagious Diseases Acts
       81-81, V-Pres.

RICHARDS, HENRY CHARLES (1851-1905)

    City of London School;  Gray's Inn.
    Barrister 81;  Counsel to Postmaster General 87;
       Q.C.  98.
    Conservative.  MP Finsbury East 95-05.
    Fellow Society of Antiquaries;  Fellow Royal
       Historical Society.
    West Central London;  St Leonards.
    [WWW, Fosters, Dods, Direc Direcs]

    City Church & Churchyard Protection Soc (F) 80-83,
       Chairman.

RICHARDSON, SIR BENJAMIN WARD (1828-1896)

    U St Andrews;  Andersonian U(Medical).
    Physician 54;  Medical School Lecturer 54;  Journal
       Proprietor 55;  Author.
    Liberal.
    Kt 93.
    Fellow Royal Col Physicians;  Fellow Royal Col
       Surgeons;  Medical Society of Lond;  Fellow
       Royal Society;  Fellow Society of Antiquaries.
    West London.
    [DNB, MEB, Direc Direcs]

    Sanitary Institute 78-89, Chairman, V-Pres.
    Sunday Society 78-90, V-Pres.
    Natl Emigration League (F) 70-70, V-Pres.

RICHARDSON, HENRY

    Intl Arbitration & Peace Assn 81-81, V-Pres.

RICHARDSON, JOHN

    London.

    Jamaica Committee (F) 66-66.

RICHARDSON, JOHN

    Ordained Priest<CE>.

    Church Assn 75-78, Exec.

RICHARDSON, MARY E.  <MISS>

    London.

    Sunday Society 80-90, V-Pres.

RICHARDSON, WILLIAM HENRY (1836- )

    St Mary Hall, Oxf.
    Asst School Master.
    Fellow Society of Antiquaries.
    West Central London;  Berkshire.
    [Alum Oxon]

    Natl Soc for Preserving Memorials of Dead (F)
       81-84, Exec.

RICHMOND, THOMAS KNYVETT (1834-1901)

    Charterhouse;  Exeter, Oxf;  Wells Theological
       College.
    Chaplain 63;  Curate 58;  Ordained Priest<CE> 59;
       Rector 68;  Vicar 74;  Rural Dean.
    London.
    [WWW, Alum Oxon, Crockfds]

    Assn for Improvement of London Workhouse
       Infirmaries 66-66, Exec.

RICHMOND, SIR WILLIAM BLAKE (1842-1921)

    Christ Church, Oxf;  Royal Academy Sch.
    Artist;  Slade Professor of Fine Arts, Oxford 78.
    KCB 97.
    Royal Academy.
    Hammersmith.
    [DNB, WWW, Alum Oxon]

    City Church & Churchyard Protection Soc (F) 80-83,
       V-Pres.
    Soc for Protection of Ancient Buildings (F) 78-85,
       Exec.

RIDDING, GEORGE (1828-1904)

    Winchester College;  Balliol, Oxf.
    Bishop Southwell 84;  College Fellow 52;  College
       Tutor 52;  Ordained Priest<CE> 56;  Asst School
       Master 63;  School Head 68.
    Liberal.
    Southwell.
    [DNB, WWW, Alum Oxon, Crockfds]

    Natl Vigilance Assn (F) 85-85, Exec.

RIDGWAY, N.  J.

    Manchester.

    Natl Secular Soc 70-77, V-Pres, Exec.

RIDLEY, MATTHEW WHITE, 1ST VISCOUNT RIDLEY (1842-1904)

    Harrow;  Balliol, Oxf;  Inner Temple.
    Very Large Landowner 77;  College Fellow 65.
    Conservative.  MP Northumberland North 68-85,
       Blackpool, Lancs N 86-00.  Parl U-Sec Home Off
       78-80, Parl U-Sec For Off 85-85, Sec Treasury
       85-86, Sec St Home Office 95-00, DL, JP.
    Baronet 77;  PC 92;  Viscount 00.
    Royal Agricultural Society.
    Southwest London;  Northumberland.
    [DNB, BP, Walfords, Bateman, Alum Oxon, Dods, Direc
       Direcs]

    Proportional Representation Soc (F) 84-88, Exec.

RIGAUD, GIBBES (1820-1885)

    Retired 73;  Ensign, Army 41;  Captain, Army 50;
       Major 58;  Lt. Colonel 61;  Colonel 68;  Maj.
       General 73.
    Oxford.
    [MEB, Alum Oxon, Army List]

    City Church & Churchyard Protection Soc (F) 80-83,
       V-Pres.

RIGAUD, JOHN (1821-1888)

    Magdalen, Oxf.
    College Dean 60;  College Fellow 47;  Ordained
       Priest<CE> 51.
    Oxford.
    [MEB, Alum Oxon, Crockfds]

    City Church & Churchyard Protection Soc (F) 80-83,
       V-Pres.

RIGG, JAMES HARRISON (1821-1909)

    Wesleyan Minister 49;  Asst School Master 39;
       School Master 43;  College Head 68;  Author.
    Southwest London.
    [DNB, WWW, Wesl Min]

    Natl Education Union (F) 69-70, Exec.
    Metro Free Libraries Assn 77-77, Exec.

RITCHIE, ANNE ISABELLA, LADY <WIFE OF SIR R. T. W.
    RITCHIE, nee THACKERAY> (1837-1919)

    Novelist.
    Southwest London.
    [DNB]

    Soc for Protection of Ancient Buildings (F) 78-85,
        Exec.


RITCHIE, J. J.

    Surgeon.
    Member Royal Col Surgeons.

    Malthusian League 80-80, V-Pres.


RIVERS, -

    Malthusian League (F) 77-79, Exec.


RIVIERE, BRITON (1840-1920)

    Cheltenham College; St Mary Hall, Oxf.
    Artist.
    Royal Academy.
    Northwest London.
    [DNB, WWW, Alum Oxon]

    Sunday Society 86-90, V-Pres.


ROBBERDS, JOHN (1814-1892)

    Unitarian Minister 40.
    Liverpool.

    Jamaica Committee (F) 66-66.


ROBERTS, EDWARD P.

    Central Assn for Stopping Sale Intox Liquors on
        Sunday 85-85, Exec.


ROBERTS, J.

    Assn of Revivers of British Industry (F) 69-69,
        Chairman.


ROBERTS, J. H. <OR J. G.>

    Clergyman<Sect Unkn>.
    West Central London.

    Assn for Improvement of Public Morals (F) 79-81,
        Exec.


ROBERTS, JOHN (1835-1894)

    Timber Merchant.
    Liberal. MP Flint District 78-92. JP.
    Denbighshire.
    [Dods]

    Free Land League 86-86, V-Pres.


ROBERTS, RICHARD

    Wesleyan Minister 45.
    London.
    [Wesl Min]

    Central Assn for Stopping Sale Intox Liquors on
        Sunday 85-85, V-Pres.


ROBERTS, THOMAS

    Manchester.

    Jamaica Committee (F) 66-66.


ROBERTS, WILLIAM CHANDLER <-AUSTEN AFTER 1885>
    (1843-1902)

    Royal School of Mines.
    Chemist of the Mint 70; Professor of Metallurgy,
        Royal School of Mines 80.
    CB 90; KCB 99.
    Fellow Royal Society; Fellow Chemical Society;
        Society of the Arts.
    Surrey.
    [DNB, WWW]

    Smoke Abatement Committee 81-81, Exec.


ROBINS, EDWARD COOKSWORTHY

    Architect.
    Fellow Royal Inst Br Architects; Fellow Society of
        Antiquaries.
    West Central London.

    Sanitary Institute 79-89, Exec.


ROBINSON, GEORGE FREDERICK SAMUEL, 1ST MARQUIS OF RIPON
    (1827-1909)

    Very Large Landowner 59; Attache, Dip Serv 49;
        Viceroy of India 80.
    Liberal. MP Hull 52-53, Huddersfield 53-57,
        Yorkshire W Riding 57-59. Parl U-Sec War
        59-61, Parl U-Sec India 61-61, Parl U-Sec War
        61-63, Sec St War 63-66, Sec St India 66-66,
        Lord Pres Council 68-73, First Lord Admiralty
        86-86, Sec St Colonial Off 92-95.
    Earl 59; PC 63; Marquis 71; KG; GCSI.
    Southwest London; Yorks, West Riding;
        Lincolnshire.
    [DNB, BP, Walfords, Bateman, Alum Oxon, Dods]

    Free Land League 86-86, V-Pres.

ROBINSON, H. W.

    Clergyman<Sect Unkn>.
    East London.

    Natl Assn for Promotion of State Colonization
       86-86, Exec.


ROBINSON, HENRY <"PROF.">

    Civil Engineer.
    Member Inst Civ Engineers.
    Southwest London.

    Sanitary Institute 79-89, Exec.


ROBINSON, HENRY CRABB (1775-1867)

    U Jena;  Middle Temple.
    Retired 28;  Solicitor 96;  Journalist 07;
       Barrister 13.
    Fellow Society of Antiquaries.
    West Central London.
    [DNB, MEB]

    Jamaica Committee (F) 66-66.


ROBINSON, JOSEPH

    Maryport.

    Central Assn for Stopping Sale Intox Liquors on
       Sunday 80-85, V-Pres.


ROBINSON, W. MOORE

    Croydon.

    Jamaica Committee (F) 66-66.


ROBINSON, WILLIAM

    Clergyman<Sect Unkn>.

    Central Assn for Stopping Sale Intox Liquors on
       Sunday 70-85, Exec.


ROBSON, EDWARD ROBERT (1835-1917)

    Architect.
    Fellow Royal Inst Br Architects;  Fellow Society of
       Antiquaries;  Surveyors' Institute.
    Southwest London.
    [WWW]

    Soc for Protection of Ancient Buildings (F) 78-80,
       Exec.


ROBSON, WILLIAM SNOWDON, BARON ROBSON (1852-1918)

    Gonville & Caius, Camb;  Inner Temple.
    Barrister 80;  Q.C. 92;  Judge, Court of Appeal
       10.
    Radical.  MP Tower Hamlets Bow&Bromley 85-86, South
       Shields 95-10.  Solicitor General 05-08,
       Attorney General 08-10.
    Kt 05;  PC 10;  Baron 10;  GCMG 11.
    Southwest London;  Newcastle-upon-Tyne.

    [DNB, WWW, Alum Cantab, Fosters, Dods]

    Commons Preservation Soc 86-86, Exec.
    Free Land League 86-86, V-Pres.


ROEBUCK, JOHN ARTHUR (1802-1879)

    Inner Temple.
    Q.C. 43;  Barrister 31;  Chm, Metropolitan Board
       of Works 55.
    Radical.  MP Bath 32-37, Bath 41-47, Sheffield
       49-68, Sheffield 74-79.
    PC 78.
    Southwest London;  Sheffield.
    [DNB, MEB, Walfords, Dods]

    Sunday Society (F) 75-79, V-Pres.


ROGERS, -

    Malthusian League (F) 77-78, Exec.


ROGERS, E. S.

    Central Assn for Stopping Sale Intox Liquors on
       Sunday (F) 67-67, Exec.


ROGERS, EDWARD DRESSER (1824-1890)

    Kings Col London.
    Architect;  Surveyor;  Metropolitan Board of Works
       68;  Newspaper Editor 72.
    Radical.
    Southeast London.
    [MEB]

    Free Land League 86-86, Exec.
    Financial Reform Union (F) 68-69, Exec.


ROGERS, JOSEPH (1821-1889)

    U St Andrews;  Middlesex Hospital.
    Surgeon 44.
    Med Off of Health 55-86.
    Member Royal Col Surgeons.
    West Central London.
    [DNB, MEB]

    Assn for Improvement of London Workhouse
       Infirmaries (F) 66-66, Hon Sec.


ROGERS, WILLIAM (1819-1896)

    Eton;  Balliol, Oxf;  Durham Theo.
    Rector 63;  Curate 43;  Ordained Priest<CE> 43;
       Perp. Curate 44;  Prebendary 62.
    East Central London.
    [DNB, MEB, Alum Oxon, Crockfds]

    Sunday Society 78-90, President, V-Pres.
    Metro Free Libraries Assn (F) 77-77, Exec.
    Assn for Promoting Extension of Contagious Diseases
       Act 68-70, V-Pres.
    Natl Emigration League (F) 70-70, V-Pres.

ROLPH, G.  F.

    West London.

    Soc for Protection of Ancient Buildings (F) 78-85,
      Exec.


ROMANES, GEORGE JOHN (1848-1894)

    Gonville & Caius, Camb;  University College,
      London.
    Physiologist;  Professor of Philosophy of Natural
      History, Edinburgh 86;  Author.
    Fellow Royal Society.
    Northwest London.
    [DNB, MEB, Alum Cantab]

    Sunday Society 83-90, V-Pres, President.


ROMILLY, WILLIAM, 2ND BARON ROMILLY (1835-1891)

    Univ College School;  Trinity, Camb;  Gray's Inn.
    Barrister 64;  Ensign, Army 55;  Lieutenant, Army
      57;  Substantial Landowner 74.
    Baron 74.
    Southwest London;  Glamorganshire.
    [MEB, BP, Alum Cantab, Fosters, Army List]

    Sunday Society 79-90, V-Pres.


RONNIGER, - <MADAME>

    West London.

    Sunday Society 76-90, V-Pres.


ROSCOE, HENRY ENFIELD (1833-1915)

    University Col London;  Heidelberg.
    Professor of Chemistry, Owens Col 57.
    Liberal.  MP Manchester South 85-95.
    Kt 84;  PC 09.
    Fellow Royal Society;  Fellow Chemical Society.
    Southwest London;  Surrey.
    [DNB, Alum Cantab, Alum Oxon, Dods, Direc Direcs]

    Sunday Society 86-90, V-Pres, President.
    Free Land League 86-86, V-Pres.


ROSE, HENRY

    West London.

    Church Assn 78-80, Exec.


ROSLING, SAMUEL

    Reading.

    Jamaica Committee (F) 66-66.


ROSS, CHARLES CAMPBELL (1849- )

    Brighton College;  Trinity, Camb.
    Banker.
    Conservative.  MP Cornwall W, St Ives 81-85.  JP.
    Penzance.
    [Alum Cantab, Dods]

    Central Assn for Stopping Sale Intox Liquors on
      Sunday 85-85, V-Pres.


ROSS, JOHN M.

    Clergyman<Sect Unkn>.
    London.

    Central Assn for Stopping Sale Intox Liquors on
      Sunday (F) 67-80, Exec.


ROSS, THOMAS

    Carlisle.

    Jamaica Committee (F) 66-66.


ROTHERA, G.  B.

    Nottingham.

    Natl Education League 71-71, Exec.


ROWDON, HUGH MARMADUKE

    Lichfield Theological College.
    Priest Vicar 77;  Ordained Priest<CE> 78;  Curate
      79.
    Lichfield.
    [Crockfds]

    Natl Soc for Preserving Memorials of Dead (F)
      81-82, Exec.


ROWE, W.  K.

    Southwest London.

    Jamaica Committee (F) 66-66.


ROWE, WILLIAM

    Primitive Methodist Minister.

    Central Assn for Stopping Sale Intox Liquors on
      Sunday 75-75, V-Pres.


ROWLANDS, JAMES (1851-1920)

    Goldsmith.
    Radical.  MP Finsbury East 86-95, Kent Northwest
      06-10, Kent Northwest 10-20.
    North London.
    [WWW, Dods]

    Sunday Society 76-77, Exec.
    Indian Reform Assn 84-84, Exec.

ROWLANDS, WILLIAM BOWEN (1837-1906)

Jesus, Oxf; Gray's Inn.
Q.C. 82; School Head 64; Barrister 71; County
Court Judge 00.
Liberal. MP Cardiganshire 86-95. JP.
Northwest London; Pembrokeshire.
[WWW, Alum Oxon, Fosters, Dods, Crockfds]

Free Land League 86-86, V-Pres.


ROWLANDSON, M. <"COL.">

Church Assn 67-85, V-Pres.


ROWNTREE, JOSHUA (1844-1915)

Friends' School, York.
Solicitor 65.
Liberal. MP Scarborough 86-92. JP.
Scarborough; York.
[Dods]

Free Land League 86-86, V-Pres.


ROXBURGH, - <"COL.">

Church Assn 75-75, Exec.


ROXBY, H. THORNHILL

Clapton.

Natl Soc for Preserving Memorials of Dead (F)
81-82, Exec.


ROY, THOMAS

Glasgow.

Natl Secular Soc 77-84, Exec, V-Pres.


RULE, WILLIAM HARRIS (1802-1890)

Wesleyan Minister 26; School Master 22.
Croydon.
[DNB, MEB, Wesl Min]

Natl Assn for Repeal Contagious Diseases Acts
84-84, V-Pres.


RUMNEY, -

JP.
Manchester.

Central Assn for Stopping Sale Intox Liquors on
Sunday (F) 67-70, V-Pres.
Natl Education League 71-71, Exec.


RUMSEY, HENRY WYLDBORE (1809-1876)

Trin Col, Dublin; St George's Hospital Lond.
Surgeon 31.
Fellow Royal Col Surgeons; Fellow Royal Society.
Cheltenham.
[MEB]

Assn for Promoting Extension of Contagious Diseases
Act 68-68, V-Pres.


RUSKIN, JOHN (1819-1900)

Christ Church, Oxf.
Art Critic; College Lecturer 53; Slade Professor
of Fine Arts, Oxford 70; Author; Artist.
Fellow Geological Society; Fellow Zoological
Society; Fellow Royal Inst Br Architects.
Oxford; Coniston, Lancs.
[DNB, MEB, WWW, Alum Cantab, Alum Oxon]

Soc for Protection of Ancient Buildings (F) 78-85,
Exec.


RUSSELL, LORD ARTHUR JOHN EDWARD (1825-1892)

Liberal. MP Tavistock 57-85.
West London.
[MEB, BP, Dods]

Commons Preservation Soc 83-86, Exec.


RUSSELL, SIR CHARLES, 3RD BT. (1826-1883)

Eton.
Substantial Landowner 52; Ensign, RA 43;
Lieutenant, Army 46; Captain, Army 53; Major
55; Lt. Colonel 58; Lt. General 68.
Conservative. MP Berkshire 65-68, Westminster
74-82. DL, JP.
Baronet 52; VC 57.
Southwest London; Berkshire.
[DNB, MEB, BP, Walfords, Bateman, Dods, Army List]

Assn for Promoting Extension of Contagious Diseases
Act 70-70, V-Pres.


RUSSELL, CHARLES ARTHUR, BARON RUSSELL OF KILLOWEN
(1833-1900)

Trin Col, Dublin; Lincoln's Inn.
Q.C. 72; Solicitor 54; Barrister 59; Judge,
Court of Appeal 94; Lord Chief Justice 94.
Liberal. MP Dundalk 80-85, Hackney South 85-94.
Attorney General 86-86, Attorney General 92-94,
JP.
Kt 86; GCMG 93; PC 94; Baron 94.
West London; Surrey.
[DNB, MEB, WWW, BP, Fosters, Dods, Direc Direcs]

Free Land League 86-86, V-Pres.

RUSSELL, EDWARD RICHARD (1834-1920)

Newspaper Editor 69.
Liberal. MP Glasgow Bridgeton 85-87.
Kt 93; Baron 19.
Liverpool.
[WWW, BP, Dods]

Free Land League 86-86, V-Pres.

RUSSELL, FRANCIS ALBERT ROLLO (1849-1914)

Harrow; Christ Church, Oxf.
Author.
Fellow Royal Meteorlog Society.
Southwest London; Surrey.
[WWW, BP, Alum Oxon, Direc Direcs]

Sanitary Institute 79-89, Exec.
Smoke Abatement Committee 81-81.
Intl Arbitration & Peace Assn 81-81, V-Pres.

RUSSELL, GEORGE WILLIAM ERSKINE (1853-1919)

Harrow; University Col, Oxf; Inner Temple.
Politician; Author.
Radical. MP Aylesbury 80-85, Bedfordshire North
    92-95. Parl Sec Loc Govt Board 83-85, Parl
    U-Sec India 92-94, Parl U-Sec Home Off 94-95.
PC 07.
Southwest London.
[WWW, Alum Oxon, Dods]

Intl Arbitration & Peace Assn 81-81, V-Pres.
Natl Vigilance Assn (F) 85-85, Chairman.

RUSSELL, SIR JAMES ALEXANDER (1846-1918)

Edinburgh(Medical).
Physician; Anatomy Inspector, Scotland.
Liberal. Lord Lieutenant 91-94, DL, JP.
Kt 94.
Fellow Royal Society Edinb; Fellow Royal Col
    Physicians, Edinb.
Edinburgh.
[WWW, Direc Direcs]

Sanitary Institute 78-84, Exec.

RUSSELL, JOHN, 1ST EARL RUSSELL (1792-1878)

Westminster School; U Edinburgh.
Politician.
Liberal. MP Tavistock 13-19, Huntingdonshire
    20-26, Bandon 26-30, Devonshire South 31-35,
    Stroud 35-41, City 41-61
    Sec St Home Office 35-39, Sec St Colonial Off
    39-41, Prime Minister 46-52, Sec St Foreign Off
    52-53, Lord Pres Council 54-55, Sec St Colonial
    Off 55-55, Sec St Foreign Off 59-65, Prime
    Minister 65-66.
PC 30; Earl 61; KG 62; GCMG 69.
Fellow Royal Society; Royal Historical Society.
Southwest London; Devonshire.
[DNB, MEB, BP, Walfords, Dods]

Assn for Promoting Extension of Contagious Diseases
    Act 70-70, V-Pres.
Howard Assn 68-77, Patron.

RUSSELL, RICHARD

Travelling Tax Abolition Committee (F) 77-85, Exec.

RUSSELL, LORD WRIOTHESLEY (1804-1886)

Westminster School; Trinity, Camb.
Rector 29; Canon 40; Prebendary.
Amersham.
[MEB, BP, Alum Cantab, Crockfds]

Church Assn 78-80, V-Pres.

RUSSON, JOSEPH

Local Taxation Comtee [of Central Chamber of
    Agriculture] 82-85, Exec.

RUTHERFURD, HENRY (1831- )

U Edinburgh; Middle Temple.
Barrister 55; Landowner 63.
JP.
Ealing; Roxburghshire.
[Walfords, Fosters]

Sunday Society 78-90, Exec.

RUTLAND, J.

Buckinghamshire.

Natl Soc for Preserving Memorials of Dead 82-82,
    Exec.

RYAN, SIR EDWARD (1793-1875)

Trinity, Camb; Lincoln's Inn.
First Civil Service Commssioner 62; Barrister 17;
    Puisne Judge, Calcutta Supreme Court 26; Chief
    Justice, Bengal 33; Railway Commissioner 46;
    Asst Controller, Exchequer 51; Civil Service
    Commissioner 55.
PC Judicial Committee 43-62.
PC 43; Kt 26.
Fellow Royal Astronomical Society; Fellow Royal
    Society; Fellow Geological Society.
West London.
[DNB, MEB, Alum Cantab]

Commons Preservation Soc 69-69, Exec.

RYDER, DUDLEY, 2ND EARL OF HARROWBY (1798-1882)

Christ Church, Oxf.
Very Large Landowner 47; Sec, India Board 30.
Conservative. MP Tiverton 19-31, Liverpool 31-47.
    Lord Admiralty 27-28, Ecclesiastical
    Commissioner 47-55, Chanc Duchy Lancaster
    55-55, Lord Privy Seal 55-57, DL, JP.
Earl 47; PC 55; KG 59.
Fellow Royal Society; Br Assn.
West London; Staffordshire.
[DNB, MEB, BP, Walfords, Bateman, Alum Oxon, Dods]

Central Assn for Stopping Sale Intox Liquors on
    Sunday 75-80, V-Pres.

Natl Education Union (F) 69-79, Exec.
Soc for Promoting Increase of the Home Episcopate
    72-74, V-Pres.


RYDER, DUDLEY FRANCIS STUART, 3RD EARL OF HARROWBY
    (1831-1900)

Harrow;  Christ Church, Oxf.
Politician;  Very Large Landowner 82.
Liberal, then Conservative.  MP Lichfield, Staffs
    56-60, Liverpool 68-82.  Education Committee
    74-78, Pres Board of Trade 78-80, Lord Privy
    Seal 85-86.
PC 74;  Earl 82.
West London;  Staffordshire.
[DNB, MEB, WWW, BP, Walfords, Alum Oxon, Dods]

Assn for Improvement of London Workhouse
    Infirmaries 66-66, Exec.
Natl Education Union 70-71, Exec.


RYE, MARIA SUSAN <MISS> (1829-1903)

Social Reformer.
London.
[DNB]

Natl Assn for Promotion of State Colonization
    86-86, V-Pres.


RYE, WALTER (1843-1929)

Solicitor.
Norwich.
[WWW]

Natl Soc for Preserving Memorials of Dead 84-84,
    Exec.


RYLAND, ARTHUR (1807-1877)

Solicitor 28.
Birmingham.
[MEB]

Natl Education League (F) 69-71, Exec.


RYLAND, WILLIAM

Birmingham.

Natl Education League (F) 69-69, Exec.


RYLANDS, PETER (1820-1887)

Steel Manufacturer 64;  Merchant.
Radical.  MP Warrington 68-74, Burnley 76-87.  JP.
West London;  Burnley;  Cheshire.
[DNB, MEB, Walfords, Dods]

Central Assn for Stopping Sale Intox Liquors on
    Sunday 70-85, V-Pres.
Natl Assn for Repeal Contagious Diseases Acts
    81-81, V-Pres.


RYLE, JOHN CHARLES (1816-1900)

Eton;  Christ Church, Oxf.
Vicar 61;  Bishop Liverpool 80;  Curate 41;
    Ordained Priest<CE> 42;  Rector 43;  Rural Dean
    70;  Hon. Canon 72.
Stradbrooke;  Liverpool.
[DNB, MEB, WWW, Alum Oxon, Crockfds]

Anglo-Oriental Soc for Suppression Opium Trade
    83-83, V-Pres.
Central Assn for Stopping Sale Intox Liquors on
    Sunday 85-85, V-Pres.
Church Assn 70-78, V-Pres.
Victoria Street Soc for Protection of Animals from
    Vivisection 85-85, V-Pres.


RYLETT, HAROLD (1851-1936)

New College, Manchester;  Owens Col, Manch.
Unitarian Minister 77;  Journal Editor 99.
Radical.
Maidstone.
[WWW]

English Land Restoration League 85-85, Exec.


RYLEY, T. C.

Wigan.

Jamaica Committee (F) 66-66.


SAINSBURY, - <MRS. SAMUEL SAINSBURY>

Clapham.

Sunday Society 76-90, V-Pres.


SAINSBURY, ALAN FOX

Sunday Society 77-77, Exec.


SAINSBURY, SAMUEL

Clapham.

Sunday Society 76-83, V-Pres.


ST. JOHN, AUBREY BEAUCLERC LENNOX (1846- )

[BP]

Intl Arbitration & Peace Assn 81-81, Treas.


SALT, J. C.

London.

City Church & Churchyard Protection Soc (F) 80-83,
    Treas.

SALT, SIR THOMAS, 1ST BT. (1830-1904)

    Rugby; Balliol, Oxf.
Banker 54; Public Works Loan Commissioner 75.
Conservative. MP Stafford 59-65, Stafford 69-80,
    Stafford 81-85, Stafford 86-92. Parl Sec Loc
    Govt Board 75-80, Church Estates Commissioner
    79-80, Ecclesiastical Commissioner 80-04,
    Lunacy Commissioner 86-92, DL, JP.
Baronet 99.
Southwest London; Staffordshire.
[WWW, BP, Walfords, Alum Oxon, Dods, Direc Direcs]

    Sanitary Institute 78-88, Exec.


SALT, SIR TITUS, 1ST BT. (1803-1876)

    Woolen Manufacturer 36; Woolstapler 24.
Liberal. MP Bradford 59-61. DL, JP.
Baronet 69.
Bradford; Yorks, West Riding.
[DNB, MEB, BP, Walfords, Dods]

    Central Assn for Stopping Sale Intox Liquors on
    Sunday 75-75, V-Pres.
Howard Assn 72-76, Patron.
Jamaica Committee (F) 66-66.


SALTER, SAMUEL JAMES AUGUSTUS (1825-1897)

    London U(Medical).
Dental Surgeon.
Fellow Royal Society; Member Royal Col Surgeons;
    Fellow Linnean Society; Fellow Geological
    Society.
London.
[MEB]

    Natl Soc for Preserving Memorials of Dead 84-84,
    Exec.


SALWEY, HENRY (1794-1874)

    Eton.
Retired; Ensign, Army 11; Captain, Army 15; Lt.
    Colonel 26; Colonel 41.
Liberal. MP Ludlow, Shropshire S 37-41, Ludlow,
    Shropshire S 47-52. JP.
Southwest London; Surrey.
[MEB, Walfords, Dods, Army List]

    Jamaica Committee (F) 66-66.


SAMUELSON, SIR HENRY BERNHARD, 2ND BT. (1845-1937)

    Rugby; Trinity, Oxf.
Liberal. MP Cheltenham 68-74, Somersetshire Frome
    76-85. JP.
Baronet 05.
West London; Torquay.
[WWW, BP, Walfords, Alum Oxon, Dods, Army List]

    Intl Arbitration & Peace Assn 81-81, V-Pres.


SANDERS, H. W.

    Southeast London.

    Church Assn 78-80, Exec.


SANDERSON, THOMAS JAMES COBDEN- (1840-1922)

    Trinity, Camb; Inner Temple.
Bookbinder 82; Publisher; Barrister 71.
Northwest London.
[DNB, Alum Cantab, Fosters]

    Soc for Protection of Ancient Buildings 85-85,
    Exec.


SANDFORD, GEORGE MONTAGU WARREN <FORMERLY PEACOCK>
(1821-1879)

    Eton; New Inn Hall, Oxf; Inner Temple.
Barrister 46.
Conservative. MP Hawick 52-53, Maldon 54-57,
    Maldon 59-68, Maldon 74-78. DL, JP.
West London; Essex.
[MEB, Walfords, Alum Oxon, Dods]

    Commons Preservation Soc 76-76, Exec.


SANDWITH, HUMPHREY (1822-1881)

    U College London(Medical).
Surgeon 46.
CB 56.
Member Royal Col Surgeons.
Wimbledon.
[DNB, MEB]

    Sunday Society (F) 75-82, V-Pres.
Jamaica Committee (F) 66-66.


SARGOOD, AUGUSTINE (1815-1880)

    Gray's Inn.
Barrister 46; Sergeant at Law 68.
London.
[MEB]

    Assn for Improvement of London Workhouse
    Infirmaries 66-66, Exec.


SARSON, GEORGE ( -1902)

    St Catherine's, Camb.
Rector 78; Curate 71; Ordained Priest<CE> 73;
    Vicar 86.
Ashford.
[Alum Cantab, Crockfds]

    Land Law Reform League 84-84, V-Pres.


SAUNDERS, R.

    Croydon.

    Church Assn 75-75, Exec.

SAUNDERS, SEDGWICK <"DR.">

Fellow Society of Antiquaries.

Metro Free Libraries Assn (F) 77-77, Exec.


SAUNDERS, WILLIAM (1823-1895)

Quarry Owner 44;  Newspaper Proprietor 60.
Radical.  MP Hull East 85-86, Newington Walworth
    92-95.
Streatham;  Kingston-upon-Hull.
[DNB, MEB, Dods]

Central Assn for Stopping Sale Intox Liquors on
    Sunday 70-85, V-Pres.
English Land Restoration League 85-85, Treas.
Land Nationalization Soc (F) 81-81, Exec.


SAVAGE, -

Workmen's Peace Assn 75-75, Exec.


SAVAGE, G.  F.

Public Museums & Free Libraries Assn 68-68, Exec.


SAVILE, HENRY BOURCHIER OSBORNE (1819-1917)

Royal Military Academy, Woolwich.
Captain, RA 46;  2nd Lt., RA 37;  Lieutenant, RA
    40.
JP.
CB 02.
Bristol.
[WWW, Direc Direcs, Army List]

Church Assn 67-78, Exec.


SAVORY, SIR JOSEPH, 1ST BT.  (1843-1921)

Harrow.
"Of the Goldsmiths Alliance Co".
Conservative.  MP Westmorland 92-00.  DL, JP.
Baronet 91.
Southwest London;  Berkshire.
[WWW, BP, Dods, Direc Direcs]

City Church & Churchyard Protection Soc 83-83,
    V-Pres.


SAWYER, ROBERT

Anglo-Oriental Soc for Suppression Opium Trade (F)
    75-75, Exec.


SCARLETT, HELEN, LADY ABINGER <WIFE OF 3RD BARON
    ABINGER, nee MAGRUDER> ( -1915)

West London;  Inverness-shire.
[BP]

Victoria Street Soc for Protection of Animals from
    Vivisection 82-85, Exec.


SCHNADHORST, FRANCIS (1840-1900)

King Edward's School, Birm.
Politician;  Sec, National Liberal Federation 87.
Liberal.
London.
[MEB, WWW]

Free Land League 86-86, V-Pres.


SCHWANN, CHARLES E.

Intl Arbitration & Peace Assn 81-81, V-Pres.


SCLATER, PHILIP LUTLEY (1829-1913)

Winchester College;  Corpus Christi, Oxf;
    Lincoln's Inn.
Barrister 55;  College Fellow 53;  Journal Editor.
Fellow Royal Society;  Fellow Zoological Society.
Southwest London;  Hampshire.
[WWW, Alum Oxon, Fosters]

Assn for Promoting Extension of Contagious Diseases
    Act 68-70, V-Pres.


SCOTT, ARCHIBALD (1837-1909)

Glasgow High School;  U Glasgow.
Church of Scotland Minister 60.
Edinburgh.
[DNB, WWW]

Natl Education Union 71-79, Exec.


SCOTT, BENJAMIN (1814-1892)

Chamberlain of London 58;  Junior Clerk,
    Chamberlain of London 27;  Chief Clerk,
    Chamberlain of London 41.
Fellow Royal Astronomical Society.
West London.
[DNB, MEB]

Intl Arbitration & Peace Assn 81-81, V-Pres.
Jamaica Committee (F) 66-66.
London Comtee Exposure & Suppresn Traffic In Girls
    (F) 80-85, Chairman.


SCOTT, CHARLES BRODERICK (1825-1894)

Eton;  Trinity, Camb;  Inner Temple.
School Head 55;  College Fellow 49;  Ordained
    Priest<CE> 55;  Prebendary 73.
Southwest London;  Bury.
[MEB, Alum Cantab, Crockfds]

Natl Education Union 70-79, Exec.


SCOTT, CHARLES PRESTWICH (1846-1932)

Corpus Christi, Oxf.
Newspaper Editor 72;  Newspaper Proprietor 05.
Liberal.  MP Leigh, Lancs SW 95-06.  JP.
Manchester.
[DNB, WWW, Alum Oxon, Dods]

Proportional Representation Soc (F) 84-88, Exec.

SCOTT, GEORGE GILBERT (1839-1897)

Eton;  Jesus, Camb.
Architect;  College Fellow 71.
Fellow Society of Antiquaries.
Southwest London.
[Alum Cantab]

City Church & Churchyard Protection Soc (F) 80-83,
    V-Pres.


SCOTT, HENRY JOHN MONTAGU DOUGLAS, 1ST BARON MONTAGU OF
    BEAULIEU (1832-1905)

Eton.
Large Landowner.
Conservative.  MP Selkirkshire 61-68, Hampshire
    South 68-84.  DL, JP.
Baron 85.
West London;  Hampshire.
[WWW, BP, Walfords, Bateman, Dods]

Commons Preservation Soc 76-86, Exec.
Assn for Improvement of London Workhouse
    Infirmaries 66-66, Exec.
Natl Emigration League (F) 70-70, V-Pres.
Plimsoll and Seamen's Fund Committee (F) 73-73,
    Exec.


SCOTT, HENRY YOUNG DARRACOTT (1822-1883)

Royal Military Academy, Woolwich.
Retired 71;  2nd Lt., RE 40;  Lieutenant, RE 43;
    Captain, RE 51;  Lt. Colonel, RE 63;  Maj.
    General, RE 71.
CB 71.
Fellow Royal Society;  Assoc Inst Civ Engineers.
Ealing.
[DNB, MEB, Army List]

Smoke Abatement Committee 81-81.
Sanitary Institute 78-83, Exec.


SCOTT, ROBSON J.

Sunday Society 81-90, Exec.


SCOTT, SEPTIMUS RICHARD ( -1895)

Stock Broker.
Bromley.
[MEB, Direc Direcs]

London Comtee Exposure & Suppresn Traffic In Girls
    (F) 80-85, Exec.


SCOTT, WALTER FRANCIS MONTAGU DOUGLAS, 5TH DUKE OF
    BUCCLEUCH (1806-1884)

Eton;  St John's, Camb.
Very Large Landowner 19.
Conservative.  Lord Privy Seal 42-46, Lord Pres
    Council 46-46, Lord Lieutenant 28-84.
Duke 19;  KT 30;  KG 35;  PC 42.
Br Assn;  Fellow Royal Society.
Southwest London;  Buckinghamshire;  Edinburgh.
[DNB, MEB, BP, Walfords, Bateman, Alum Cantab, Alum
    Oxon]


Soc for Promoting Increase of the Home Episcopate
    72-74, V-Pres.


SCOTT, WILLIAM BELL (1811-1890)

Edinburgh High School.
Artist;  Poet;  Author.
Southwest London.
[DNB, MEB, Bryan's Painters]

Soc for Protection of Ancient Buildings (F) 78-85,
    Exec.


SEAGER, JAMES

Clergyman<Sect Unkn>.

Central Assn for Stopping Sale Intox Liquors on
    Sunday 85-85, Exec.


SEEBOHM, FREDERICK (1833-1912)

Middle Temple.
Banker 57;  Barrister 56;  Historian.
Liberal(Unionist).  JP.
Hitchin.
[DNB, WWW, Fosters, Direc Direcs]

Proportional Representation Soc (F) 84-88, Exec.


SEELEY, SIR JOHN ROBERT (1834-1895)

City of London School;  Christ's, Camb.
Professor of Modern History, Cambridge 69;  College
    Fellow 58;  Professor of Latin, U Col London
    63;  Author.
Liberal(Unionist).
KCMG 94.
Cambridge.
[DNB, MEB, Alum Cantab]

Sunday Society 76-90, V-Pres.


SELIGMAN, ISAAC

Merchant.
London.
[Direc Direcs]

Intl Arbitration & Peace Assn 81-81, Exec.


SELLAR, ALEXANDER CRAIG (1835-1890)

Rugby;  Balliol, Oxf.
Barrister 62;  Asst, Scot Education Commission 64;
    Legal Sec to Lord Advocate 70;  Politician.
Liberal(Unionist).  MP Haddington District 82-85,
    Partick, Lanarkshire 85-90.  DL, JP.
Southwest London.
[DNB, MEB, Dods]

Commons Preservation Soc 83-86, Exec.

SELWYN, WILLIAM (1806-1875)

    Eton;  St John's, Camb.
    Lady Margaret Professor of Divinity, Cambridge 55;
       College Fellow 29;  Ordained Priest<CE> 31;
       Rector 31;  Canon 33;  Vicar 46.
    Cambridge;  Ely.
    [DNB, MEB, Walfords, Alum Cantab, Alum Oxon,
       Crockfds]

    Assn for Promoting Extension of Contagious Diseases
       Act 68-70, V-Pres.


SERGEANT, LEWIS (1841-1902)

    St Catherine's, Camb;  Middle Temple.
    Journalist;  Asst School Master 65;  Journal
       Editor.
    Liberal.
    West London.
    [DNB, WWW, Alum Cantab]

    Intl Arbitration & Peace Assn 81-81, Exec.


SETTNA, A.  K.

    Indian Reform Assn 81-81, Exec.


SEYLER, -

    Malthusian League (F) 77-78, Exec.


SEYMOUR, HENRY DANBY (1820-1877)

    Eton;  Christ Church, Oxf;  Gray's Inn.
    Landowner 49;  Barrister 62.
    Liberal.  MP Poole 50-68.  DL, JP.
    West London;  Wiltshire.
    [MEB, Walfords, Alum Oxon, Dods]

    Assn for Improvement of London Workhouse
       Infirmaries 66-66, Exec.


SEYMOUR, HUGH DE GREY, 6TH MARQUIS OF HERTFORD
    (1843-1912)

    Royal Military College, Sandhurst.
    Very Large Landowner 84;  Lieutenant, Army 62;
       Captain, Army 65.
    Conservative.  MP Antrim 69-74, Warwickshire South
       74-80.  Comptroller Royal Household 79-80, Lord
       Lieutenant, JP.
    Marquis 84;  PC;  CB.
    London;  Warwickshire.
    [BP, Walfords, Dods, Army List]

    Victoria Street Soc for Protection of Animals from
       Vivisection 85-85, V-Pres.


SEYMOUR, SIR MICHAEL (1802-1887)

    Royal Naval College, Portsmouth.
    Admiral 64;  Cadet, RN 18;  Lieutenant, RN 22;
       Captain, RN 26;  Commodore, RN 51;  Rear
       Admiral 54;  Vice-Admiral 60.
    Liberal.  MP Devonport 59-63.  JP.
    KCB 55;  GCB 64.
    Southwest London;  Hampshire.
    [DNB, MEB, BP, Walfords, Dods, Navy List]

    Assn for Promoting Extension of Contagious Diseases
       Act 68-70, V-Pres.


SHAEN, WILLIAM (1821-1887)

    University Col London.
    Solicitor 48;  College Fellow 46.
    West Central London.
    [MEB]

    Jamaica Committee (F) 66-66.
    London Comtee Exposure & Suppresn Traffic In Girls
       (F) 80-80, Exec.
    Vigilance Assn for Defense of Personal Rights
       83-83, Exec.
    Natl Assn for Repeal Contagious Diseases Acts
       81-84, Chairman.
    Natl Vigilance Assn (F) 85-85, Exec.


SHANN, GEORGE (1809-1882)

    Repton;  Trinity, Camb.
    Physician.
    Fellow Royal Col Physicians.
    York.
    [Alum Cantab]

    Church Assn 67-80, Exec.


SHARLAND, HENRY

    Hampshire.

    Jamaica Committee (F) 66-66.


SHARMAN, WILLIAM (1841-1889)

    Unitarian Minister 69.
    Plymouth;  Preston.
    [MEB]

    English Land Restoration League 85-85, Exec.
    Land Law Reform League 84-84, V-Pres.
    League for Defense of Constitutional Rights 84-84,
       V-Pres.
    Natl Assn for Repeal Blasphemy Laws (F) 84-84, Hon
       Sec.
    Travelling Tax Abolition Committee 80-85, Exec.


SHARPE, HENRY

    St Aidan's College, Birkenhead.
    Vicar 72;  Curate 56;  Ordained Priest<CE> 66.
    Northwest London.
    [Crockfds]

    Church Assn 75-80, Exec.

SHARPE, JOSEPH (1827-1880)

    City of London School; Jesus, Camb; Inner Temple.
    Barrister 52; Professor of Jurisprudence, U Col
       London 60.
    West London.
    [MEB, Alum Cantab]

    Assn for Improvement of London Workhouse
       Infirmaries 66-66, Exec.


SHARPEY, WILLIAM (1802-1880)

    U Edinburgh.
    Surgeon 23; Professor of Anatomy and Physiology,
       London U 36.
    Fellow Royal Society; Fellow Royal Society Edinb;
       Fellow Royal Col Surgeons, Edinb.
    Northwest London.
    [DNB, MEB]

    Assn for Promoting Extension of Contagious Diseases
       Act 68-70, V-Pres.


SHAW, JOSEPH

    Leighton<?>.

    Jamaica Committee (F) 66-66.


SHAW, THOMAS (1823-1893)

    Woolen Manufacturer; Merchant.
    Radical. MP Halifax 82-93. DL, JP.
    Southwest London; Halifax; Yorks, West Riding.
    [MEB, Dods, Direc Direcs]

    Free Land League 86-86, V-Pres.


SHEARER, - <MRS.>

    Vigilance Assn for Defense of Personal Rights
       83-83, Exec.


SHEARER, J. R.

    Malthusian League (F) 77-79, Exec.


SHEPPARD, J. G.

    Church Assn 67-80, Exec, V-Pres.


SHERIDAN, HENRY BRINSLEY (1820-1906)

    Inner Temple.
    Barrister 56.
    Liberal. MP Dudley 57-86. JP.
    Fellow Royal Geograph Society.
    West London; Kent.
    [Walfords, Fosters, Dods]

    Intl Arbitration & Peace Assn 81-81, V-Pres.


SHERIFF, ALEXANDER CLUNES (1816-1877)

    Deputy Chairman, Metropolitan District Railway.
    Liberal. MP Worcester 65-77. JP.
    West London; Worcestershire.
    [Dods]

    Assn for Promoting Extension of Contagious Diseases
       Act 70-70, V-Pres.


SHERWOOD, JOSEPH

    Natl Education Union 70-70, Exec.


SHIELD, HUGH (1831-1903)

    King Edward's School, Birm; Jesus, Camb; Gray's
       Inn.
    Q.C. 81; Barrister 60.
    Liberal. MP Cambridge 80-85.
    West Central London; Cambridge.
    [WWW, Alum Cantab, Fosters, Dods, Direc Direcs]

    Intl Arbitration & Peace Assn 81-81, V-Pres.


SHIPMAN, JAMES

    Clergyman<Sect Unkn>.
    Hulme<?>.

    Central Assn for Stopping Sale Intox Liquors on
       Sunday 70-85, Exec.


SHIPTON, GEORGE (1839-1911)

    Gen Sec, London House Painters 66; Labour Leader.
    London.

    Travelling Tax Abolition Committee (F) 77-85, Exec.
    Natl Emigration League (F) 70-70, Exec.


SHIPTON, W. EDWYN

    Public Museums & Free Libraries Assn 68-68, Exec.
    Church Assn 67-85, Exec.


SHIRLEY, WALTER SHIRLEY (1851-1888)

    Rugby; Balliol, Oxf; Inner Temple.
    Barrister 76; Author.
    Liberal. MP Doncaster, Yorks WR S 85-88.
    London; Scarborough.
    [MEB, Alum Oxon, Fosters, Dods]

    Free Land League 86-86, V-Pres.


SHORE, CHARLES JOHN, 2ND BARON TEIGNMOUTH (1796-1885)

    Trinity, Camb.
    Conservative. MP Marylebone 38-41. DL, JP.
    Baron 34.
    Fellow Royal Society.
    West London; Somersetshire.
    [MEB, BP, Walfords, Alum Cantab, Alum Oxon, Dods]

    Church Assn 75-80, V-Pres.

SHORE, THOMAS

    English Land Restoration League 85-85, Exec.


SHUTTLEWORTH, HENRY CARY (1850-1900)

    Forest Leytonstone School;  St Mary Hall, Oxf.
    Canon 76;  Curate 73;  Ordained Priest<CE> 74;
        Rector 83;  College Lecturer 83.
    Liberal.
    East Central London.
    [MEB, WWW, Alum Oxon, Crockfds]

    Sunday Society 80-90, V-Pres.
    City Church & Churchyard Protection Soc (F) 80-83,
        Exec.
    English Land Restoration League 85-85, Exec.


SHUTTLEWORTH, SIR JAMES PHILLIPS KAY-, 1ST BT.
(1804-1877)

    Edinburgh(Medical).
    Educator;  Physician 27;  Asst Poor Law Commnr 35;
        Sec, PC Education Committee 39;  Substantial
        Landowner.
    Liberal. DL, JP.
    Baronet 49.
    Southwest London;  Lancashire.
    [DNB, MEB, BP, Walfords, Alum Oxon]

    Assn for Improvement of London Workhouse
        Infirmaries 66-66, Exec.


SHUTTLEWORTH, UGHTRED JAMES KAY-, 1ST BARON SHUTTLEWORTH
(1844-1939)

    Harrow;  London U;  Inner Temple.
    Substantial Landowner 77.
    Liberal.  MP Hastings 69-80, Clitheroe, Lancs NE
        85-02.  Parl U-Sec India 86-86, Chanc Duchy
        Lancaster 86-86, Parl Sec Admiralty 92-95, Lord
        Lieutenant 08-  , JP.
    Baronet 77;  PC 86;  Baron 02.
    West London;  Lancashire;  Westmorland.
    [WWW, BP, Bateman, Dods]

    Smoke Abatement Committee 81-81, Exec.


SIBSON, FRANCIS (1814-1876)

    London U;  Guy's Hospital, Lond.
    Surgeon 35.
    Fellow Royal Society;  Fellow Royal Col Physicians;
        Br Medical Assn;  Member Royal Col Surgeons,
        Edinb.
    West London.
    [DNB, MEB]

    Assn for Improvement of London Workhouse
        Infirmaries 66-66, Exec.


SIEMENS, <CHARLES> SIR WILLIAM (1823-1883)

    Goettingen.
    Electrical Scientist.
    Kt 83.
    Fellow Royal Society;  Br Assn;  Member Inst Civ
        Engineers.
    London.
    [DNB, MEB, Alum Oxon]

    Smoke Abatement Committee 81-81, Exec.
    Sunday Society 80-83, V-Pres.


SIMEON, SIR JOHN, 3RD BT.  (1815-1870)

    Christ Church, Oxf;  Lincoln's Inn.
    Large Landowner 54.
    Liberal.  MP Isle Of Wight 47-51, Isle Of Wight
        65-70.
    Baronet 54.
    Southwest London;  Isle of Wight.
    [MEB, BP, Alum Oxon, Dods]

    Assn for Promoting Extension of Contagious Diseases
        Act 68-70, V-Pres.


SIMMONS, ALFRED

    Journalist;  Sec, Kent and Sussex Labourers' Union.
    Maidstone.

    Natl Assn for Promotion of State Colonization (F)
        83-86, Secretary.
    Working Men's Natl League for Abolition State
        Regulation of Vice 81-81, Hon Sec.


SIMON, SIR JOHN (1818-1897)

    University Col London;  Middle Temple.
    Sergeant at Law 64;  Barrister 42.
    Liberal.  MP Dewsbury 68-88.
    Kt 86.
    West Central London.
    [DNB, MEB, WWW, Walfords, Fosters, Dods]

    Howard Assn 76-84, Patron.


SIMPSON, SIR ALEXANDER RUSSELL (1835-1916)

    U Edinburgh.
    Physician.
    Kt 06.
    Royal Microscop Society.
    Glasgow.
    [WWW]

    Assn for Promoting Extension of Contagious Diseases
        Act 68-68, Exec.


SIMPSON, E. MARSH

    Civil Engineer.

    Sunday Society 85-86, Exec.

SIMPSON, G.

Mottram.

Travelling Tax Abolition Committee (F) 77-79, Exec.

SIMPSON, HENRY T.

Sunday Society 77-78, Exec.

SIMPSON, SIR JAMES YOUNG, 1ST BT.  (1811-1870)

U Edinburgh.
Physician 32;  Professor of Midwifery, Edinburgh
    40.
Baronet 66.
Edinburgh.
[DNB, MEB, BP]

Assn for Promoting Extension of Contagious Diseases
    Act 68-70, V-Pres.

SIMPSON, JANE H.  <MRS.>

Stockwell.

Sunday Society (F) 75-90, V-Pres.

SIMPSON, JOHN H.

Sunday Society (F) 75-78, Exec.

SIMPSON, LIGHTLY

JP.

Howard Assn 75-82, Exec.

SIMPSON, ROBERT JAMES

Trin Col, Dublin.
Rector 72;  Curate 54;  Ordained Priest<CE> 55.
Felbrig.
[Crockfds]

Natl Soc for Preserving Memorials of Dead (F)
    81-82, Exec.
Plimsoll and Seamen's Fund Committee (F) 73-73,
    Exec.

SIMPSON, THOMAS BOURNE (1829-1879)

Lincoln, Oxf.
Vicar 56;  Curate 51;  Perp. Curate 55.
Thetford.
[Alum Oxon, Crockfds]

Central Assn for Stopping Sale Intox Liquors on
    Sunday 75-75, Exec.

SIMS, F. MANLEY

Surgeon.
Fellow Royal Col Surgeons.

Sunday Society 78-78, Exec.

SINCLAIR, SIR JOHN GEORGE TOLLEMACHE, 3RD BT.
    (1825-1912)

Very Large Landowner 68;  Lieutenant, Army 40.
Liberal.  MP Caithness-Shire 69-85.  DL, JP.
Baronet 68.
Southeast London;  Caithness.
[WWW, BP, Walfords, Bateman, Dods, Army List]

Natl Assn for Promotion of State Colonization
    86-86, V-Pres.
Intl Arbitration & Peace Assn 81-81, V-Pres.

SINDEN, R. H.

Victoria Street Soc for Protection of Animals from
    Vivisection 84-85, Exec.

SINGH, RAMPAL, RAJAH OF KALAKANKAR (1848-1909)

Journal Editor;  Journal Proprietor 83.
Rajah 85.
London.
[Indian Dict Nat Biog]

Indian Reform Assn 81-81, Exec.

SKETCHLEY, RICHARD FORSTER (1827- )

Exeter, Oxf.
[Alum Oxon]

Natl Soc for Preserving Memorials of Dead (F)
    81-84, Exec.

SKEY, FREDERICK CARPENTER (1798-1872)

St Bartholomew's Hosp.
Surgeon;  Medical School Demonstrator 26;  Asst
    Surgeon 27;  Medical School Lecturer 43;
    Medical School Professor 52.
CB 68.
Fellow Royal Society;  Fellow Royal Col Surgeons;
    Royal Med & Chir Society.
West London.
[DNB, MEB]

Assn for Promoting Extension of Contagious Diseases
    Act 68-70, V-Pres.

SKILLICORNE, WILLIAM NASH (1807- )

Worcester, Oxf.
Landowner 34.
DL, JP.
Gloucestershire.
[Walfords, Alum Oxon]

Intl Arbitration & Peace Assn 81-81, V-Pres.

SKIPWORTH, GEORGE BORMAN (1820- )

    Middle Temple.
    Large Landowner 60;  Barrister 45.
    DL.
    Lincolnshire.
    [Walfords, Bateman, Fosters]

    London Soc for Abolition of Compulsory Vaccination
        81-81, V-Pres.

SLACK, HENRY JAMES (1818-1896)

    Middle Temple.
    Barrister 53;  Journal Editor 62.
    Liberal.
    Fellow Geological Society;  Fellow Royal Meteorlog
        Society;  Royal Microscop Society.
    London.
    [DNB, MEB, Fosters]

    Jamaica Committee (F) 66-66.

SLATER, JOHN

    Clergyman<Sect Unkn>.

    Central Assn for Stopping Sale Intox Liquors on
        Sunday 75-85, Exec.

SLATER, THOMAS

    Bury.

    Natl Secular Soc 70-84, V-Pres.

SMELT, THOMAS

    Manchester.

    Church Assn 80-85, Exec.

SMITH, A.  M.

    Travelling Tax Abolition Committee 79-85, Exec.

SMITH, BENJAMIN

    Clergyman<Sect Unkn>.

    Central Assn for Stopping Sale Intox Liquors on
        Sunday 75-75, Exec.

SMITH, BENJAMIN LEIGH (1828-1913)

    Bruce Castle School, Tottenham;  Jesus, Camb;
        Inner Temple.
    Oceanographer;  Explorer;  Barrister 56.
    West Central London;  Sussex.
    [Walfords, Alum Cantab, Fosters]

    Commons Preservation Soc 76-86, Exec.

SMITH, BROOKES

    Birmingham.

    Jamaica Committee (F) 66-66.

SMITH, C.

    Clergyman<Sect Unkn>.
    Edinburgh.

    Natl Education Union 71-79, Exec.

SMITH, CHARLES

    London;  Coggeshall.

    Howard Assn 67-84, Exec.

SMITH, D.

    Writer to the Signet.
    Glasgow.

    Natl Education Union 71-79, Exec.

SMITH, F.  W.

    Church Assn 85-85, Exec.

SMITH, GEORGE (1815-1871)

    Magdalen Hall, Oxf.
    Retired Clergyman 66;  Curate 39;  Ordained
        Priest<CE> 40;  Perp. Curate 41;  Bishop
        Victoria 49.
    Southeast London.
    [DNB, MEB, Crockfds]

    Assn for Promoting Extension of Contagious Diseases
        Act 70-70, V-Pres.

SMITH, GEORGE JAMES PHILIP (1805-1886)

    Harrow;  Trinity, Camb;  Inner Temple.
    Barrister 30;  Master, Queens Bench 71;  Supreme
        Court Master 79.
    West London.
    [MEB, Alum Cantab, Fosters]

    Church Assn 67-85, V-Pres, Exec.

SMITH, GEORGE VANCE (1816-1902)

    Manchester College, York.
    Unitarian Minister 41;  College V-Principal 46;
        College Head 50.
    Sheffield;  Carmarthen.
    [DNB]

    Sunday Society (F) 75-90, V-Pres.

SMITH, GOLDWIN (1823-1910)

    Eton; Magdalen, Oxf; Lincoln's Inn.
    Regius Professor of Modern History, Oxford 58;
       College Fellow 46; College Tutor 50;
       Barrister 50; Journalist 71.
    Radical.
    Oxford.
    [DNB, WWW, Fosters]

    Jamaica Committee (F) 66-66.


SMITH, HELY HUTCHINSON AUGUSTUS

    Worcester, Oxf.
    Rector 67; Ordained Priest<CE> 53; Curate 54.
    Market Rasen.
    [Crockfds]

    Church Assn 85-85, Exec.


SMITH, HENRY SPENCER (1812-1901)

    St Bartholomew's Hosp.
    Surgeon 41; Medical School Head 54.
    Fellow Royal Col Surgeons; Royal Med & Chir
       Society.
    West London.
    [DNB]

    Assn for Promoting Extension of Contagious Diseases
       Act 68-75, Treas.


SMITH, J.

    Methodist New Connection Minister.

    Central Assn for Stopping Sale Intox Liquors on
       Sunday 70-70, V-Pres.


SMITH, JAMES PARKER (1854-1929)

    Winchester College; Trinity, Camb; Lincoln's Inn.
    Barrister 81; College Fellow 79; College Head 15.
    Liberal(Unionist). MP Partick, Lanarkshire 90-06.
       DL, JP.
    PC 04.
    Southwest London; Edinburgh.
    [WWW, Alum Cantab, Fosters, Dods]

    Proportional Representation Soc (F) 84-88, Exec.


SMITH, JOHN

    Bradford.

    Jamaica Committee (F) 66-66.


SMITH, JOHN ABEL (1801-1871)

    Eton; Christ's, Camb.
    Banker.
    Liberal. MP Midhurst 30-31, Chichester 31-59,
       Chichester 63-68. JP.
    Southwest London.
    [DNB, MEB, Alum Cantab, Dods]

    Assn for Promoting Extension of Contagious Diseases
       Act 68-70, V-Pres.


SMITH, JOHN WILLIAM SIDNEY (1814-1900)

    Royal Military College, Sandhurst.
    Colonel 58; Ensign, Army 32; Captain, Army 40;
       Major 51; Lt. Colonel 55; Maj. General 68;
       Lt. General 77.
    CB.
    Chatham.
    [MEB, Army List]

    Assn for Promoting Extension of Contagious Diseases
       Act 68-70, V-Pres.


SMITH, JOSEPH

    Maidenhead.

    Jamaica Committee (F) 66-66.


SMITH, KENELM HENRY (1837-1917)

    St John's, Camb.
    Curate 60; Ordained Priest<CE> 64; Prison
       Chaplain 68; Antiquary.
    Ely.
    [Alum Cantab, Crockfds]

    Natl Soc for Preserving Memorials of Dead (F)
       81-82, Exec.


SMITH, MANSFIELD GEORGE

    Lieutenant, RN 81; Sub-Lieutenant, RN 78.
    [Navy List]

    Natl Assn for Promotion of State Colonization
       86-86, Exec.


SMITH, ROBERT OWEN

    East Central London.

    Natl Secular Soc 84-84, V-Pres.


SMITH, ROBERT PAYNE- (1819-1895)

    Pembroke, Oxf.
    Dean 71; Ordained Priest<CE> 44; School Master
       47; Vicar 48; Rector 65; Canon 65; Regius
       Professor of Divinity, Oxford 65.
    Canterbury.
    [DNB, MEB, Alum Oxon, Crockfds]

    Natl Soc for Preserving Memorials of Dead 82-84,
       Exec.
    Central Assn for Stopping Sale Intox Liquors on
       Sunday 80-85, V-Pres.


SMITH, ROWLAND (1826- )

    Brasenose, Oxf.
    Conservative. MP Derbyshire South 68-74. JP.
    Derbyshire.
    [Walfords, Alum Oxon, Dods]

    Church Assn 70-80, Exec.

SMITH, SAMUEL (1836-1906)

    U Edinburgh.
    Cotton Broker;  Cotton Manufacturer.
    Liberal.  MP Liverpool 82-85, Flintshire 86-06.
       JP.
    Liverpool.
    [DNB, WWW, Dods]

    Commons Preservation Soc 84-86, Exec.
    Natl Assn for Promotion of State Colonization
       86-86, Patron.
    Howard Assn 83-84, Patron.
    Intl Arbitration & Peace Assn 81-81, V-Pres.

SMITH, T.

    Gen Sec, Amalg Cab-drivers' Assoc, London.
    London.

    Natl Assn for Promotion of State Colonization
       86-86, Exec.

SMITH, THOMAS EUSTACE (1831- )

    Shipowner;  Merchant.
    Liberal.  MP Tynemouth 68-85.  JP.
    West London;  Newcastle-upon-Tyne;  Northumberland.
    [Walfords, Dods]

    Assn for Promoting Extension of Contagious Diseases
       Act 68-70, V-Pres.

SMITH, W. H.

    Natl Footpaths Preservation Soc 86-86, V-Pres.

SMITH, W. H.

    Assn for Improvement of London Workhouse
       Infirmaries 66-66, Exec.

SMITH, W. HICKMAN

    Clergyman<Sect Unkn>.
    Penge.

    Jamaica Committee (F) 66-66.

SMITH, WALTER F.

    Insurance Underwriter;  Member Lloyds.
    London.
    [Direc Direcs]

    Natl Assn for Promotion of State Colonization
       86-86, V-Pres.

SMITH, WILLIAM HENRY (1825-1891)

    Bookseller;  Large Landowner 65.
    Conservative.  MP Westminster 68-85, Strand 85-91.
       Sec Treasury 74-77, First Lord Admiralty 77-80,
       Sec St War 85-86, Sec St War 86-86, Chief Sec
       Ireland 86-86, First Lord Treasury 87-91, Lord
       Warden Cinque Ports 91-91, DL.
    PC 77.
    West London;  Oxfordshire.
    [DNB, MEB, Walfords, Bateman, Dods]

    Natl Education Union 70-70, Hon Sec.

SMITHIES, THOMAS BYWATER (1815-1883)

    Journal Editor.
    London.
    [MEB, Direc Direcs]

    Anglo-Oriental Soc for Suppression Opium Trade (F)
       75-75, Exec.

SMITHSON, EDWARD

    Sunday Society 79-79, Exec.

SMYTH, J. D. HIRST

    West London.

    Sunday Society 77-77, Chairman.

SMYTH, RICHARD (1826-1878)

    U Glasgow.
    Theology Professor 70;  Presbyterian Minister.
    Liberal.  MP Londonderry Co 74-78.
    Londonderry.
    [DNB, MEB, Dods]

    Howard Assn 74-76, Patron.

SMYTHE, EMILY ANNE, LADY STRANGFORD <Wife of 8TH
    VISCOUNT STRANGFORD, nee BEAUFORT> ( -1887)

    Author.
    West London;  Kent.
    [DNB, MEB, Walfords]

    Natl Assn for Promotion of State Colonization (F)
       83-86, V-Pres.

SMYTHE, WILLIAM BARLOW (1809-1886)

    Winchester College;  Corpus Christi, Oxf.
    Large Landowner 15.
    Conservative.  JP, DL.
    Dublin;  Co Westmeath.
    [Walfords, Bateman, Alum Oxon]

    Church Assn 70-78, Exec.

SNELL, H.  SAXON

    Architect.
    Fellow Royal Inst Br Architects.
    West Central London.

    Smoke Abatement Committee 81-81.
    Sanitary Institute 79-89, Exec.


SOANES, TEMPLE

    Kent.

    Soc for Protection of Ancient Buildings (F) 78-85,
       Exec.


SOLLY, HENRY (1813-1903)

    London U.
    Unitarian Minister 40.
    Radical.
    Northwest London.

    Sunday Society (F) 75-90, V-Pres.
    Jamaica Committee (F) 66-66.


SOMERSET, HENRY ADELBERT WELLINGTON FITZROY, 9TH DUKE OF
BEAUFORT (1847-1924)

    Cornet, Army 65;  Lieutenant, Army 68;  Captain,
       Army 69;  Very Large Landowner 99.
    DL, JP.
    Duke 99.
    Gloucestershire.
    [WWW, BP, Army List]

    Victoria Street Soc for Protection of Animals from
       Vivisection 84-85, V-Pres.


SOMERSET, LORD HENRY RICHARD CHARLES (1849-1932)

    Conservative.  MP Monmouthshire 71-80.  Comptroller
       Royal Household 74-79, DL, JP.
    PC.
    West London;  Monmouthshire.
    [WWW, BP, Dods]

    City Church & Churchyard Protection Soc 83-83,
       V-Pres.


SOMERVILLE, ROBERT

    Intl Arbitration & Peace Assn 81-81, V-Pres.


SOMES, GEORGE (1828- )

    Worcester, Oxf;  Lincoln's Inn.
    Barrister 71.
    JP.
    Roehampton.
    [Alum Oxon, Fosters, Direc Direcs]

    Natl Assn for Promotion of State Colonization
       86-86, V-Pres.


SOMES, JOSEPH

    London.

    Central Assn for Stopping Sale Intox Liquors on
       Sunday 70-70, V-Pres.


SOMMERVILLE, WILLIAM

    Bristol.

    Jamaica Committee (F) 66-66.


SOUTHEY, - <MRS.>

    Intl Arbitration & Peace Assn 81-81, Exec.


SOUTHWARD, JOHN

    Central Vigilance Comtee for Repression Immorality
       (F) 83-84, Exec.


SOUTTER, FRANCIS WILLIAM (1844-1932)

    Saw Mill Worker 67;  Carpenter 56;  Professional
       Agitator.
    Radical.
    Southeast London.
    [WWW]

    Sunday Society 76-78, Exec.
    English Land Restoration League 85-85, Exec.


SPAFFORD, EDWARD JAMES

    Central Assn for Stopping Sale Intox Liquors on
       Sunday 85-85, Exec.


SPEARS, ROBERT (1825-1899)

    Unitarian Minister 52;  School Master 46;  Journal
       Editor 56.
    Southeast London.
    [DNB, MEB]

    Jamaica Committee (F) 66-66.


SPENCER, HERBERT (1820-1903)

    Philosopher;  Author;  Civil Engineer 37;
       Sub-Editor 44.
    West London.
    [DNB, WWW]

    Sunday Society 76-90, V-Pres.
    Jamaica Committee 66-66.

SPENSLEY, HOWARD (1834-1902)

    Middle Temple.
    Barrister 64; Journalist; Solicitor General,
        Victoria 71.
    Liberal. MP Finsbury Central 85-86.
    Fellow Royal Geograph Society; Fellow Royal
        Statistical Society.
    Southwest London.
    [Fosters, Dods, Direc Direcs]

    Free Land League 86-86, Exec, V-Pres.


SPENSLEY, WILLIAM

    Congregational Minister.
    Stoke Newington.

    Natl Assn for Promotion of State Colonization
        86-86, V-Pres.


SPONG, JAMES

    Clergyman<Sect Unkn>.
    London.

    Jamaica Committee (F) 66-66.


SPOTTISWOODE, WILLIAM (1825-1883)

    Harrow; Balliol, Oxf.
    Printer 46; Mathematician.
    Fellow Royal Society; Br Assn; Fellow Royal
        Astronomical Society; Fellow Royal Geograph
        Society.
    West London.
    [DNB, Alum Cantab, Alum Oxon]

    Sunday Society 80-83, V-Pres.


SPRENGEL, HERMANN JOHANN PHILIPP (1834-1906)

    Goettingen; Heidelberg.
    Analytical Chemist.
    Fellow Royal Society; Fellow Chemical Society.
    Southwest London.
    [DNB]

    Smoke Abatement Committee 81-81.


SPURGEON, CHARLES HADDON (1834-1892)

    Baptist Minister 52.
    London.
    [DNB, MEB]

    Natl Assn for Promotion of State Colonization
        86-86, Patron.
    Anglo-Oriental Soc for Suppression Opium Trade (F)
        75-86, V-Pres.


SQUARE, ELLIOT

    Plymouth.

    Assn for Promoting Extension of Contagious Diseases
        Act 68-68, Exec.


SQUARE, W. J.

    Plymouth.

    Assn for Promoting Extension of Contagious Diseases
        Act 68-70, V-Pres.


SQUARE, WILLIAM

    Plymouth.

    Assn for Promoting Extension of Contagious Diseases
        Act 68-68, Exec.


SQUIRE, JAMES

    Working Men's Comtee Promoting Separation Church
        and State (F) 71-71, Exec.


STAFFORD, WILLIAM

    Sunday Society 76-78, Exec.


STAINER, SIR JOHN (1840-1901)

    Magdalen, Oxf.
    Organist 54; Professor of Music, Oxford 89.
    Kt 88.
    East Central London.
    [DNB, WWW, Alum Oxon]

    City Church & Churchyard Protection Soc (F) 80-83,
        V-Pres.


STALLARD, -

    Physician.

    Assn for Improvement of London Workhouse
        Infirmaries 66-66, Exec.


STAMER, SIR LOVELACE TOMLINSON, 3RD BT. (1829-1908)

    Rugby; Trinity, Camb.
    Rector 58; Ordained Priest<CE> 53; Curate 53;
        Rural Dean 58; Prebendary 75; Archdeacon 77;
        Bishop Shrewsbury(Suffragen) 88.
    Baronet 60.
    Stoke-upon-Trent.
    [DNB, WWW, BP, Walfords, Alum Cantab, Crockfds]

    Central Assn for Stopping Sale Intox Liquors on
        Sunday 75-85, V-Pres.

STANDRING, GEORGE

Newspaper Editor.
Radical.
North London.

League for Defense of Constitutional Rights 84-84,
    V-Pres.
Malthusian League (F) 77-79, Exec.
Natl Secular Soc 75-84, Hon Sec, V-Pres.


STANGER, W. HARRY

Civil Engineer.
Southwest London.

Railway Passengers' Protection Assn 86-86, Exec.


STANHOPE, ARTHUR PHILIP, 6TH EARL STANHOPE (1838-1905)

Harrow.
Very Large Landowner 75; Lieutenant, Army 58;
    Captain, Army 62.
Conservative. MP Leominster 68-68, Suffolk East
    70-75. Junior Lord Treasury 74-75, Church
    Estates Commissioner 78-05, Lord Lieutenant
    90-05, DL, JP.
Earl 75.
Fellow Society of Antiquaries.
West London; Kent.
[WWW, BP, Walfords, Bateman, Dods, Direc Direcs,
    Army List]

Central Vigilance Comtee for Repression Immorality
    (F) 83-84, V-Pres.
Natl Emigration League (F) 70-70, V-Pres.


STANHOPE, PHILIP JAMES, 1ST BARON WEARDALE (1847-1923)

Politician; Lieutenant, RN 62.
Liberal. MP Wednesbury 86-92, Burnley 93-00,
    Harborough 04-05. JP.
Baron 06.
West London; Kent.
[WWW, BP, Dods, Direc Direcs]

Free Land League 86-86, V-Pres.


STANHOPE, SIR WALTER THOMAS WILLIAM SPENCER (1827-1911)

Eton; Christ Church, Oxf.
Landowner.
Conservative. MP Yorks W Riding South 72-80. DL,
    JP.
CB 87; KCB 04.
West London; Yorks, West Riding.
[WWW, Alum Oxon, Dods]

Local Taxation Comtee [of Central Chamber of
    Agriculture] 75-85, Exec.
Natl Education Union 75-79, Exec.


STANLEY, ARTHUR PENRHYN (1815-1881)

Rugby; Balliol, Oxf.
Dean 64; College Fellow 38; Ordained Priest<CE>
    41; College Dean 48; Canon 51; Regius
    Professor of Ecclesiastical History, Oxford 56;
    Rector 74.
Fellow Royal Society.
Southwest London.
[DNB, MEB, Alum Cantab, Alum Oxon, Crockfds]

Sunday Society 77-80, President, V-Pres.
Assn for Promoting Extension of Contagious Diseases
    Act 68-70, V-Pres.
Victoria Street Soc for Protection of Animals from
    Vivisection 80-80, V-Pres.


STANLEY, EDWARD HENRY, 15TH EARL OF DERBY (1826-1893)

Rugby; Trinity, Camb.
Very Large Landowner 69.
Conservative, then Liberal. MP King's Lynn 48-69.
    Parl U-Sec For Off 52-52, Sec St Colonial Off
    58-58, Sec St India 58-59, Sec St Foreign Off
    66-68, Sec St Foreign Off 74-78, Sec St
    Colonial Off 82-85, DL, JP.
PC 58; Earl 69; KG 84.
Fellow Royal Society.
Southwest London; Lancashire.
[DNB, MEB, BP, Walfords, Bateman, Alum Cantab, Alum
    Oxon, Dods]

Sanitary Institute 83-89, V-Pres.
Sunday Society 80-90, V-Pres.
Howard Assn 82-84, Patron.
Intl Arbitration & Peace Assn 81-81, V-Pres.


STANLEY, EDWARD LYULPH, 4TH BARON STANLEY OF ALDERLEY
AND 4TH BARON SHEFFIELD (1839-1925)

Eton; Balliol, Oxf; Inner Temple.
Barrister 65; College Fellow 62; Very Large
    Landowner 03.
Liberal. MP Oldham 80-85.
Baronet 03.
West London; Yorks, North Riding; Cheshire.
[DNB, BP, Alum Oxon, Fosters, Dods]

Metro Free Libraries Assn 77-77, Exec.
Land Tenure Reform Assn 73-73, Exec.


STANLEY, HENRY EDWARD JOHN, 3RD BARON STANLEY OF
ALDERLEY (1827-1903)

Eton; Trinity, Camb.
Very Large Landowner 69; Clerk, FO 47; Attache,
    Dip Serv 51; Sec Legation, Dip Serv 54;
    Orientalist.
Independent.
Baron 69.
Royal Asiatic Society; Hakluyt Society.
Southwest London; Cheshire.
[DNB, WWW, BP, Walfords, Bateman, Alum Cantab]

Natl Education Union 71-79, Exec.

STANNUS, BEAUCHAMP WALTER

    Trin Col, Dublin.
    Rector 63;  Curate 45;  Ordained Priest<CE> 46;
       Perp.  Curate 46.
    Arrow, Warwicks.
    [Walfords, Crockfds]

    Church Assn 70-78, Exec.


STANSFELD, SIR JAMES (1820-1898)

    University Col London;  Middle Temple.
    Politician;  Brewer;  Barrister 49.
    Radical.  MP Halifax 59-95.  Lord Admiralty 63-64,
       Parl U-Sec India 66-66, Junior Lord Treasury
       68-69, Sec Treasury 69-71, Pres Poor Law Board
       71-71, Pres Local Govt Board 71-74, Pres Local
       Govt Board 86-86.
    PC 69;  GCB 95.
    Southwest London;  Sussex.
    [DNB, WWW, Walfords, Fosters, Dods]

    Natl Vigilance Assn (F) 85-85, Exec.
    Natl Assn for Repeal Contagious Diseases Acts
       81-81, V-Pres.
    Victoria Street Soc for Protection of Animals from
       Vivisection 80-85, V-Pres.


STANTON, CHARLES HOLBROW (1825- )

    Rugby;  Balliol, Oxf;  Lincoln's Inn.
    Barrister 51;  Asst Commissioner of Endowed Schools
       71.
    Asst Charity Commissioner 76-  , JP.
    Southwest London.
    [Alum Oxon, Fosters]

    Sunday Society 78-90, Exec.


STANYER, WILLIAM

    Ordained Priest<CE> 66;  Curate 76.
    Manchester;  Cheadle, Cheshire.
    [Crockfds]

    Central Assn for Stopping Sale Intox Liquors on
       Sunday (F) 67-67, Exec.
    Natl Education Union (F) 69-76, Secretary.


STAPLES, SIR JOHN (1815-1888)

    Merchant;  Tavern Owner;  Metropolitan Board of
       Works 84.
    KCMG 86.
    Fellow Society of Antiquaries.
    Northwest London.
    [MEB]

    City Church & Churchyard Protection Soc 83-83,
       V-Pres.


STARTIN, ARTHUR

    Local Taxation Comtee [of Central Chamber of
       Agriculture] 71-82, Exec.


STATHAM, E.

    Smoke Abatement Committee 81-81.


STEAD, S.  A.

    Church Assn 85-85, Exec.


STEAD, WILLIAM THOMAS (1849-1912)

    Newspaper Editor 71;  Journal Editor 90.
    Southwest London.
    [DNB, WWW]

    Natl Vigilance Assn (F) 85-85, Exec.


STEBBING, J.  R.

    Fellow Royal Astronomical Society.
    Southampton.

    Assn for Promoting Extension of Contagious Diseases
       Act 68-68, V-Pres.


STEELE, STEPHEN

    JP.

    Sunday Society 85-85, Exec.


STEER, - <MISS>

    Natl Vigilance Assn (F) 85-85, Exec.


STEER, W.

    English Land Restoration League 85-85, Exec.


STEINTHAL, S.  ALFRED

    Clergyman<Sect Unkn>.
    Manchester.

    Central Assn for Stopping Sale Intox Liquors on
       Sunday (F) 67-85, Exec.
    Jamaica Committee (F) 66-66.
    Natl Education League 71-71, Exec.

STEPHEN, SIR LESLIE (1832-1904)

    Eton;  Trinity Hall, Camb;  Inner Temple.
    Literary Critic;  Author;  College Fellow 54;
       Ordained Priest<CE> 59;  Relinquished Orders
       75;  Journal Editor 71;  College Lecturer 83.
    KCB 02.
    Southwest London.
    [DNB, WWW, Alum Cantab]

    Commons Preservation Soc 69-86, Exec.
    Soc for Protection of Ancient Buildings (F) 78-85,
       Exec.


STEPHENS, FREDERICK

    Clergyman<Sect Unkn>.
    Croydon.

    Jamaica Committee (F) 66-66.


STEPHENS, FREDERICK GEORGE (1828-1907)

    Royal Academy Sch.
    Art Critic.
    Hammersmith.
    [DNB]

    Soc for Protection of Ancient Buildings (F) 78-85,
       Exec.


STEPHENS, HENRY CHARLES (1841-1918)

    University Col London.
    Writing Ink Manufacturer.
    Conservative.  MP Middlesex Hornsey 87-00.  JP.
    Fellow Chemical Society;  Fellow Linnean Society;
       Fellow Royal Geograph Society.
    Southwest London.
    [Dods]

    Sanitary Institute 78-84, Exec.
    Liberty & Property Defense League (F) 82-84, Exec.


STEPHENS, W. D.

    JP.

    Intl Arbitration & Peace Assn 81-81, V-Pres.


STEPHENS, W. F. D.

    Croydon.

    Jamaica Committee (F) 66-66.


STEPHENSON, SIR FREDERICK CHARLES ARTHUR (1821-1911)

    Colonel 61;  Lieutenant, Army 37;  Captain, Army
       43;  Lt. Colonel 54;  Maj. General 68;  Lt.
       General 78;  General 86.
    CB 58;  KCB 84;  GCB 86.
    Southwest London.
    [DNB, WWW, Army List]

    Assn for Promoting Extension of Contagious Diseases
       Act 68-70, V-Pres.


STEPHENSON, T. BOWMAN (1839-1912)

    London U.
    Wesleyan Minister 60;  Children's Home Manager 73.
    North London.
    [WWW, Wesl Min]

    Central Assn for Stopping Sale Intox Liquors on
       Sunday (F) 67-85, Exec.
    Natl Vigilance Assn (F) 85-85, Exec.


STEPHENSON, T. S.

    English Land Restoration League 85-85, Exec.


STERN, SYDNEY JAMES, 1ST BARON WANDSWORTH (1845-1912)

    Magdalene, Camb;  Inner Temple.
    City Financier;  Landowner.
    Liberal.  MP Stowmarket 91-95.  JP.
    Baron 95.
    West London;  Suffolk.
    [WWW, BP, Walfords, Alum Cantab, Dods]

    Natl Assn for Promotion of State Colonization
       86-86, V-Pres.


STEVENS, D. M.

    Guildford.

    Jamaica Committee (F) 66-66.


STEVENS, DE GRASS <MISS>

    Kyrle Soc 84-90, Exec.


STEVENSON, FRANCIS SEYMOUR (1862-1938)

    Harrow;  Balliol, Oxf;  Lincoln's Inn.
    Railway Promoter;  Author.
    Liberal.  MP Eye 85-06.  Charity Commissioner
       94-95, DL, JP.
    West London;  Suffolk.
    [WWW, Alum Oxon, Dods]

    Free Land League 86-86, V-Pres.


STEVENSON, JAMES COCHRAN (1825-1905)

    Glasgow High School;  U Glasgow.
    Chemicals Manufacturer 44.
    Liberal.  MP South Shields 68-95.  JP.
    Inst of Chemistry.
    Northwest London;  South Shields.
    [WWW, Walfords, Dods]

    Central Assn for Stopping Sale Intox Liquors on
       Sunday 85-85, V-Pres.

STEVENSON, JOHN JAMES (1831-1908)

>Glasgow High School;  U Glasgow.
Architect 60.
Fellow Society of Antiquaries;  Fellow Royal Inst
    Br Architects.
West London.
[DNB]

>Soc for Protection of Ancient Buildings (F) 78-85,
    Exec.

STEWARD, MARY <MRS.>

>Ongar, Essex.

>London Comtee Exposure & Suppresn Traffic In Girls
    (F) 80-85, Exec.

STEWART, - <MRS.>

>British Women's Temperance Assn 85-85, Treas.

STEWART, ALAN PLANTAGENET, 10TH EARL OF GALLOWAY
    (1835-1901)

>Harrow;  Christ Church, Oxf.
Captain, Army 61;  Cornet, Army 55;  Lieutenant,
    Army 57;  Very Large Landowner 73.
Conservative.  MP Wigtonshire 68-73.  DL, JP.
Earl 73;  KT.
West London;  Wigtownshire.
[WWW, BP, Walfords, Bateman, Alum Oxon, Dods, Direc
    Direcs, Army List]

>Natl Emigration League (F) 70-70, V-Pres.

STEWART, DAVID JAMES (1814-1898)

>Trinity, Camb.
Inspector of Schools 51;  Ordained Priest<CE> 40;
    Curate 43;  Vicar 49;  Hon. Canon 93.
West London.
[Alum Cantab, Crockfds]

>Soc for Protection of Ancient Buildings (F) 78-80,
    Exec.

STEWART, SIR HALLEY (1838-1937)

>Vegetable Oil Refiner 70;  Independent Minister 63;
    Journal Editor 77.
Liberal.  MP Spaulding 87-95, Greenock 06-10.  JP.
Kt 32.
St Leonards;  Hertfordshire.
[DNB, WWW, Dods]

>Free Land League 86-86, Exec, V-Pres.

STEWART, JAMES (1827-1895)

>Edinburgh Academy.
Shipowner;  Merchant.
Liberal.  MP Greenock 78-84.  DL, JP.
Greenock;  Ayreshire.
[MEB, Dods]

>Natl Assn for Repeal Contagious Diseases Acts
    81-81, V-Pres.

STEWART, JOHN ARCHIBALD SHAW (1828-1900)

>Eton;  Christ Church, Oxf.
DL, JP.
[MEB, BP, Alum Oxon]

>Assn for Improvement of London Workhouse
    Infirmaries 66-66, Exec.

STEWART, JOHN LORNE (1800- )

>Landowner.
DL, JP.
Dumfriesshire;  Argyllshire.
[Walfords]

>Intl Arbitration & Peace Assn 81-81, V-Pres.

STIDSTONE, CONWAY

>Southeast London.

>Central Assn for Stopping Sale Intox Liquors on
    Sunday 85-85, Exec.

STIRLING, CHARLES (1828- )

>Exeter, Oxf.
Vicar 67;  Curate 51;  Ordained Priest<CE> 52;
    School Master 55.
New Malden.
[Alum Oxon, Crockfds]

>Church Assn 67-78, Exec.

STITT, JOHN J.

>Liverpool.

>Jamaica Committee (F) 66-66.

STONE, DAVID HENRY (1812-1890)

>Solicitor 39.
JP.
Fellow Royal Geograph Society.
East Central London;  St Leonards.
[MEB, Direc Direcs]

>City Church & Churchyard Protection Soc (F) 80-83,
    V-Pres.

STONE, WILLIAM HENRY (1834-1896)

>Harrow;  Trinity, Camb.
E India Merchant;  Landowner;  College Fellow 59.
Liberal.  MP Portsmouth 65-74.  DL, JP.
Dulwich;  Hampshire.
[MEB, Walfords, Alum Cantab, Dods, Direc Direcs]

>Assn for Promoting Extension of Contagious Diseases
    Act 68-70, V-Pres.

STONOR, THOMAS, 3RD BARON CAMOYS (1797-1881)

    Large Landowner.
    Liberal. MP Oxford 32-33. Lord in Waiting 46-52,
        Lord in Waiting 53-58, Lord in Waiting 59-66,
        Lord in Waiting 68-74, DL, JP.
    Baron 39.
    Oxfordshire.
    [MEB, BP, Walfords, Bateman, Dods]

    Eastern Question Assn 77-77, V-Pres.


STOREY, SAMUEL (1840-1925)

    Manufacturer; Newspaper Proprietor.
    Radical. MP Sunderland 81-95, Sunderland 10-10.
        DL, JP.
    Durham[County].
    [WWW, Dods]

    Intl Arbitration & Peace Assn 81-81, V-Pres.


STORR, JOHN STEPHENS (1829-1895)

    Auction Mart Proprietor 64.
    Radical.
    West Central London; Edenbridge.
    [MEB]

    Assn for Improvement of London Workhouse
        Infirmaries 66-66, Treas.


STORRAR, JOHN (1811-1886)

    Physician 39.
    Northwest London.
    [MEB]

    Assn for Promoting Extension of Contagious Diseases
        Act 68-70, V-Pres.


STOVEL, CHARLES (1799-1883)

    Baptist Minister.
    East London.
    [MEB]

    Central Assn for Stopping Sale Intox Liquors on
        Sunday 75-75, V-Pres.
    Jamaica Committee (F) 66-66.


STOW, EDWARD

    London.

    Jamaica Committee (F) 66-66.


STOWELL, THOMAS ALFRED (1831-1916)

    Queen's, Oxf.
    Rector 65; Curate 57; Ordained Priest<CE> 58;
        Perp. Curate 60; Rural Dean 76; Hon. Canon
        79.
    Salford.
    [WWW, Alum Oxon, Crockfds]

    Central Assn for Stopping Sale Intox Liquors on
        Sunday (F) 67-85, Hon Sec.


STRANGE, W.

    Banbury.

    Church Assn 75-78, Exec.


STRANGWAYS, HENRY EDWARD FOX-, 5TH EARL OF ILCHESTER
(1847-1905)

    Eton; Christ Church, Oxf.
    Very Large Landowner 65.
    Lord Lieutenant, JP.
    Earl 65; PC.
    Somersetshire; Dorsetshire.
    [BP, Walfords, Bateman, Alum Oxon]

    Sunday Society 80-90, V-Pres.


STRAWSON, G. W.

    Kent.

    Natl Soc for Preserving Memorials of Dead (F)
        81-88, Exec.


STREET, GEORGE EDMUND (1824-1881)

    Camberwell Grammar School.
    Architect 49.
    Royal Academy; Fellow Society of Antiquaries.
    West London; Surrey.
    [DNB, MEB]

    City Church & Churchyard Protection Soc (F) 80-81,
        V-Pres.


STREETER, E. W.

    West London.

    London Municipal Reform League 82-85, Exec.


STRICKLAND, JOHN CAMPBELL (1823-1907)

    Queens', Camb.
    Perp. Curate 64; Ordained Priest<CE> 54; Vicar
        61.
    North London.
    [Alum Cantab, Crockfds]

    Church Assn 80-85, Exec.


STRONG, RICHARD (1833- )

    Liberal. MP Camberwell North 85-86. JP.
    Southwest London.
    [Dods]

    Free Land League 86-86, V-Pres.

STRUTT, CLARA ELIZABETH LA TOUCHE, LADY RAYLEIGH <Wife
    of 2ND BARON, nee VICARS> ( -1900)

    Essex.
    [BP]

    Victoria Street Soc for Protection of Animals from
        Vivisection 85-85, Exec.


STRUTT, EDWARD, 1ST BARON BELPER (1801-1880)

    Trinity, Camb;  Inner Temple.
    Cotton Manufacturer;  Large Landowner;  Railway
        Commissioner 46.
    Liberal.  MP Derby 30-47, Arundel 51-52, Nottingham
        52-56.  Chanc Duchy Lancaster 52-54, Lord
        Lieutenant 64-  , DL, JP.
    PC 46;  Baron 56.
    Fellow Royal Society;  Fellow Geological Society;
        Fellow Zoological Society.
    Southwest London;  Derbyshire.
    [DNB, MEB, BP, Walfords, Alum Cantab, Dods]

    Sunday Society 79-80, V-Pres.


STUART, JAMES (1843-1913)

    Madras College, St Andrews;  U St Andrews.
    Professor of Applied Mechanics, Cambridge 75;
        College Fellow 67;  Ld Rector, U St Andrews 98.
    Liberal.  MP Hackney 84-85, Shoreditch Hoxton
        85-00, Sunderland 06-10.
    PC 09.
    Assoc Inst Civ Engineers.
    Southwest London;  Cambridge;  Norfolk.
    [WWW, Alum Cantab, Dods]

    Assn for Improvement of Public Morals (F) 79-81,
        Exec.
    London Comtee Exposure & Suppresn Traffic In Girls
        (F) 80-80, Exec.
    Natl Vigilance Assn (F) 85-85, Exec.
    Vigilance Assn for Defense of Personal Rights (F)
        71-83, Exec.


STUART, JAMES FREDERICK DUDLEY CRICHTON- (1824-1891)

    Eton;  Trinity, Camb.
    Landowner 59;  Lieutenant, Army 42;  Captain, Army
        47;  Lt. Colonel 55.
    Liberal.  MP Cardiff 57-80.  Lord Lieutenant 59- ,
        JP.
    Southwest London.
    [BP, Walfords, Alum Cantab, Dods, Army List]

    Natl Emigration League (F) 70-70, V-Pres.


STUART, JOHN

    Manchester.

    Central Assn for Stopping Sale Intox Liquors on
        Sunday 75-75, V-Pres.


STUART, JOHN PATRICK CRICHTON, 3RD MARQUIS OF BUTE
    (1847-1900)

    Harrow;  Christ Church, Oxf.
    Very Large Landowner 48.
    Conservative.  Lord Lieutenant 92-00, DL.
    Marquis 48;  KT.
    Southwest London;  Glamorganshire;  Ayreshire.
    [DNB, MEB, WWW, BP, Walfords, Bateman, Alum Oxon,
        Direc Direcs]

    Victoria Street Soc for Protection of Animals from
        Vivisection 80-85, V-Pres.


STUART, P.

    Liverpool.

    Jamaica Committee (F) 66-66.


STUART, R.  <OR W.>

    Physician.
    Woolwich.

    Assn for Promoting Extension of Contagious Diseases
        Act 68-70, V-Pres, Exec.


STUART, SIR ROBERT (1816-1896)

    U Edinburgh;  Lincoln's Inn.
    Chief Justice, Northwest Province India 71;
        Barrister 56;  Q.C. 68.
    Kt 71.
    Allahabad, Bengal.
    [MEB, BP]

    Intl Law Assn 74-74, V-Pres.


STURGE, CHARLES DICKINSON (1833-1915)

    Allotments & Small Holdings Assn 82-88, Secretary.


STURGE, EDMUND (1808-1893)

    Charlbury.
    [MEB, Direc Direcs]

    Anglo-Oriental Soc for Suppression Opium Trade (F)
        75-75, Exec.
    Howard Assn 70-84, Exec.


STURGE, JOSEPH

    Liberal.

    Anglo-Oriental Soc for Suppression Opium Trade (F)
        75-75, Exec.

STURT, CHARLES NAPIER (1832-1886)

Harrow.
Lt. Colonel 60; Lieutenant, Army 51; Captain,
     Army 54.
Conservative. MP Dorchester 56-74. JP.
Southwest London; Dorsetshire.
[Walfords, Dods, Army List]

Assn for Promoting Extension of Contagious Diseases
     Act 68-70, V-Pres.


SULIVAN, SIR BARTHOLOMEW JAMES (1810-1890)

Royal Naval College, Portsmouth.
Rear Admiral 63; Lieutenant, RN 30; Commander, RN
     41; Captain, RN 45; Naval Officer, Board of
     Trade 56; Vice-Admiral 70; Admiral 77.
CB 55; KCB 69.
Bournemouth.
[DNB, MEB, BP, Walfords, Navy List]

Church Assn 67-85, V-Pres.


SULLIVAN, SIR EDWARD, 1ST BT. (1822-1885)

Trin Col, Dublin.
Master of the Rolls, Ireland 70; Barrister 48;
     Q.C. 58; Sergeant at Law 60.
Liberal. MP Mallow 65-70. Solicitor General, Ire
     65-66, Attorney General, Ire 68-70, Lord
     Chancellor, Ire 83-85.
PC 69; Baronet 81.
Dublin.
[DNB, MEB, BP, Walfords, Dods]

Sunday Society 79-85, V-Pres.


SUMMERS, WILLIAM (1853-1893)

University Col London; Lincoln's Inn.
Barrister 81.
Liberal. MP Stalybridge 80-85, Huddersfield 86-93.
Fellow Royal Statistical Society.
London; Lancashire.
[MEB, Alum Oxon, Fosters, Dods]

Free Land League 86-86, V-Pres, Exec.


SURR, JOSEPH

North London.

Church Assn 70-75, Exec.


SUTHERST, THOMAS (1852-1915)

Pembroke, Oxf; Inner Temple.
Barrister 77; Labour Leader.
Radical.
London.
[Alum Cantab, Fosters]

Natl Assn for Promotion of State Colonization
     86-86, Exec.


SUTTON, MARTIN HOPE

Seed Merchant.
Reading.

Jamaica Committee (F) 66-66.


SWAAGMAN, - <MRS. JOANNES SWAAGMAN>

St Johns Wood.

Malthusian League (F) 77-78, Exec.


SWAAGMAN, JOANNES

St Johns Wood.

League for Defense of Constitutional Rights 84-84,
     V-Pres.
Malthusian League 78-84, Treas.
Natl Secular Soc 81-84, V-Pres.


SWANWICK, ANNA <MISS> (1813-1899)

Translator; Educator.
Northwest London.
[DNB, MEB, WWW]

Natl Assn for Promotion of State Colonization
     86-86, V-Pres, Exec.
Sunday Society (F) 75-90, V-Pres.
Assn for Improvement of Public Morals (F) 79-81,
     Exec.


SWEETNAM, MATTHEW

St Aidan's College, Birkenhead.
Vicar 84; Curate 77; Ordained Priest<CE> 78.
West Central London.
[Crockfds]

Church Assn 85-85, Exec.


SWIFT, F. <"BARON">

Venice.

Natl Secular Soc 84-84, V-Pres.


SWINTON, A. C.

Upper Norwood.

Land Nationalization Soc (F) 81-85, Treas, Hon Sec.
London Soc for Abolition of Compulsory Vaccination
     81-81, Exec.


SYKES, JOHN FREDERICK JOSEPH ( -1913)

University Col London; Guy's Hospital, Lond.
Physician; Medical School Lecturer.
Med Off of Health.
Member Royal Col Surgeons; Fellow Royal
     Statistical Society; Epidemiological Society
     of London.
West London.
[WWW, Direc Direcs]

Sanitary Institute 80-89, Exec.

SYMES, JOHN ELLIOTSON (1847-1921)

Downing, Camb.
Professor of English Lit, U Col Nottingham 81;
    Asst School Master 72;  Ordained Priest<CE> 75;
    School Master 80;  College Head 90.
Nottingham.
[Alum Cantab, Crockfds]

English Land Restoration League 85-85, Exec.
Land Law Reform League 84-84, V-Pres.


SYMES, JOSEPH

Birmingham.

Natl Secular Soc 81-84, V-Pres.


SYMONDS, ARTHUR GIBB (1844- )

Corpus Christi, Oxf.
Manchester.
[Alum Oxon]

League for Defense of Constitutional Rights 84-84,
    V-Pres.


SYMONDS, JOHN ADDINGTON (1807-1871)

Edinburgh(Medical).
Physician 28;  Medical School Lecturer.
Fellow Royal Col Physicians;  Fellow Royal Society
    Edinb.
Bristol.
[DNB, MEB]

Assn for Promoting Extension of Contagious Diseases
    Act 68-70, V-Pres.


SYMONS, GEORGE JAMES (1838-1900)

St Peter's College, Westminster;  Royal School of
    Mines.
Meteorologist.
Fellow Royal Society;  Royal Botanical Society;
    Fellow Royal Meteorlog Society.
[DNB, MEB]

Sanitary Institute 79-95, Exec.


TADEMA, SIR LAWRENCE ALMA- (1836-1912)

Royal Academy, Antwerp.
Artist.
Kt 99;  OM 05.
Royal Academy;  Royal Society Water Colour
    Painters;  Fellow Society of Antiquaries.
Northwest London.
[DNB, WWW]

Sunday Society 78-90, V-Pres.
Soc for Protection of Ancient Buildings (F) 78-85,
    Exec.


TAIT, ARCHIBALD CAMPBELL (1811-1882)

Edinburgh High School;  Balliol, Oxf.
Archbishop Canterbury 69;  College Fellow 34;
    College Tutor 35;  Ordained Priest<CE> 36;
    School Head 42;  Dean 49;  Bishop London 56.
PC 56.
Fellow Royal Society.
Southeast London.
[DNB, MEB, Walfords, Alum Oxon, Crockfds]

Metro Free Libraries Assn 77-82, Exec, V-Pres.
Natl Soc for Preserving Memorials of Dead (F)
    81-82, Patron.
Central Assn for Stopping Sale Intox Liquors on
    Sunday 75-82, V-Pres.


TALBOT, JAMES, 4TH BARON TALBOT DE MALAHIDE (1805-1883)

Trinity, Camb.
Substantial Landowner 50.
Liberal.  MP Athlone 32-34.  Lord in Waiting 63-66,
    DL, JP.
Baron 50.
Fellow Royal Society;  Fellow Society of
    Antiquaries;  Fellow Geological Society;
    Fellow Royal Geograph Society.
Southwest London;  Co Dublin.
[BP, Walfords, Bateman, Alum Cantab, Dods]

City Church & Churchyard Protection Soc (F) 80-81,
    V-Pres.
Natl Soc for Preserving Memorials of Dead (F)
    81-82, Patron.
Soc for Protection of Ancient Buildings (F) 78-80,
    Exec.


TALBOT, JOHN GILBERT (1835-1910)

Charterhouse;  Christ Church, Oxf.
Small Landowner.
Conservative.  MP Kent West 68-78, Oxford
    University 78-10.  Parl Sec Board of Trade
    78-80, Ecclesiastical Commissioner, DL, JP.
PC 97.
Southwest London;  Kent.
[WWW, Walfords, Alum Oxon, Dods, Direc Direcs]

Natl Education Union 71-79, Exec.
Soc for Promoting Increase of the Home Episcopate
    74-74, Exec.


TALBOT, SIR WELLINGTON PATRICK MANVERS CHETWYND
(1817-1898)

Eton;  Royal Military College, Sandhurst.
Ensign, Army 34;  Lieutenant, Army 37;  Captain,
    Army 42.
Conservative.  JP.
Sergeant-at-Arms, House of Lords 58;  KCB 97.
Southwest London;  Surrey;  Worcestershire.
[MEB, WWW, BP, Walfords, Direc Direcs, Army List]

City Church & Churchyard Protection Soc 83-83,
    V-Pres.

TALLACK, WILLIAM (1831-1908)

Friends´ School, Sidcote;  Founders´ College,
    Yorks.
School Teacher 45.
East Central London.
[DNB]

Howard Assn 66-01, Secretary.


TANGYE, SIR RICHARD (1833-1906)

Friends´ School, Sidcote.
Hardware Manufacturer 55.
Liberal.  JP.
Kt 94.
Fellow Royal Geograph Society.
Birmingham.
[DNB, WWW, Direc Direcs]

Allotments & Small Holdings Assn 85-88, V-Pres.


TANNER, - <MRS. T. SLINGSBY TANNER>

Kyrle Soc 84-90, Exec.


TANNER, JAMES GOSSET (1832- )

Magdalen Hall, Oxf.
Vicar 73;  Ordained Priest<CE> 56;  Curate 71.
West London.
[Alum Oxon, Crockfds]

Church Assn 78-85, Exec.


TANNER, M. A. <MRS. ARTHUR TANNER>

Somersetshire.

Ladies´ Natl Assn for Repeal of Contagious Diseases
    Acts 71-81, Treas.


TANNER, T. SLINGSBY

Kyrle Soc 84-94, Hon Sec.


TANNER, WILLIAM (1835-1927)

Peterhouse, Camb.
Vicar 71;  Ordained Priest<CE> 60;  Perp. Curate
    66.
Horton, Northants.
[Alum Cantab, Crockfds]

Natl Soc for Preserving Memorials of Dead (F)
    81-82, Exec.


TARRING, SIR CHARLES JAMES (1845-1923)

City of London School;  Trinity, Camb;  Inner
    Temple.
Consular Judge, Constantinople 83;  Barrister 71;
    Professor of Law, Japan Imperial U 78;  Chief
    Justice, Grenada 97.
Liberal.  JP.
Kt 06.

East Central London;  Constantinople.
[WWW, Alum Cantab, Fosters]

London Comtee Exposure & Suppresn Traffic In Girls
    82-83, Hon Sec.
Vigilance Assn for Defense of Personal Rights
    83-83, Exec.


TATE, HENRY CARR

Lt. General, RM 70;  General, RM 75;  Cornet, RM
    29;  Lieutenant, RM 37;  Captain, RM 47;
    Colonel, RM 62;  Maj. General, RM 65.
Portsmouth.
[Army List]

Church Assn 70-78, Exec.


TATHAM, GEORGE

Chairman, Colliery Company.
JP.
Leeds.
[Direc Direcs]

London Soc for Abolition of Compulsory Vaccination
    81-81, V-Pres.


TAYLER, JOHN JAMES (1797-1869)

U Glasgow.
Professor of Theology, Manchester New College 52;
    Unitarian Minister 20;  College Professor 40;
    College Head 53.
West Central London;  Oxford.
[DNB, MEB]

Jamaica Committee (F) 66-66.


TAYLOR, CLEMENTIA <MRS. PETER ALFRED TAYLOR, nee
DOUGHTY> ( -1908)

Southwest London.

Vigilance Assn for Defense of Personal Rights (F)
    71-83, Treas.


TAYLOR, FRANCIS

Manchester.

Jamaica Committee (F) 66-66.


TAYLOR, GEORGE G.

Sunday Society 76-76, Exec.


TAYLOR, HARRY

London.

Jamaica Committee (F) 66-66.

TAYLOR, HELEN <MISS> (1831-1907)

>   Radical.
>   Southwest London.
>   [DNB]
>
>   Sunday Society (F) 75-83, V-Pres.
>   English Land Restoration League 85-85, Exec.
>   Land Nationalization Soc (F) 81-85, V-Pres, Exec.

TAYLOR, J.

>   Sheffield.
>
>   Natl Education League 71-71, Exec.

TAYLOR, JAMES

>   Natl Education Union 70-70, Exec.

TAYLOR, JAMES, JUN.

>   Birmingham.
>
>   Jamaica Committee (F) 66-66.

TAYLOR, JOHN

>   London.
>
>   Jamaica Committee (F) 66-66.

TAYLOR, JONATHAN

>   Sheffield.
>
>   Land Nationalization Soc 83-84, Exec.

TAYLOR, PETER ALFRED (1819-1891)

>   Silk Merchant; Newspaper Proprietor 73.
>   Radical. MP Leicester 62-84.
>   Southwest London.
>   [DNB, MEB, Walfords, Dods]
>
>   Commons Preservation Soc 76-86, Exec.
>   Sunday Society 76-90, V-Pres.
>   Howard Assn 73-84, Patron.
>   Jamaica Committee (F) 66-66, Treas.
>   Land Tenure Reform Assn (F) 70-73, Treas.
>   Land Law Reform League (F) 81-84, V-Pres.
>   London Soc for Abolition of Compulsory Vaccination
>       81-81, President.
>   Vigilance Assn for Defense of Personal Rights
>       83-83, Exec.
>   Natl Assn for Repeal Contagious Diseases Acts
>       81-81, V-Pres.

TAYLOR, ROBERT

>   Presbyterian Minister.
>
>   Central Assn for Stopping Sale Intox Liquors on
>       Sunday 85-85, V-Pres.

TAYLOR, SHERBROOKE

>   London.
>
>   Jamaica Committee (F) 66-66.

TAYLOR, THOMAS <STYLED EARL OF BECTIVE, HEIR OF 3RD
MARQUIS OF HEADFORT> (1844-1893)

>   Eton;  Christ Church, Oxf.
>   Very Large Landowner;  Cattle Breeder.
>   Conservative.  MP Westmorland 71-85, Westmorland
>       South 85-92.  DL, JP.
>   West London;  Westmorland.
>   [MEB, BP, Walfords, Bateman, Alum Oxon, Dods]
>
>   Natl Footpaths Preservation Soc (F) 85-86,
>       President.
>   Soc for Protection of Ancient Buildings (F) 78-85,
>       Exec.

TEBB, WILLIAM (1830-1918)

>   Fellow Royal Geograph Society.
>   Surrey.
>   [WWW]
>
>   London Soc for Abolition of Compulsory Vaccination
>       81-81, Chairman.

TEBBS, H.  VIRTUE

>   West London.
>
>   Soc for Protection of Ancient Buildings (F) 78-80,
>       Exec.

TEDDER, HENRY RICHARD (1850-1924)

>   Librarian 73.
>   Fellow Society of Antiquaries;  Royal Historical
>       Society.
>   London.
>   [WWW]
>
>   Metro Free Libraries Assn (F) 77-82, Secretary,
>       Treas.

TEMPLE, FREDERICK (1821-1902)

>   Balliol, Oxf.
>   Bishop Exeter 69;  Ordained Priest<CE> 47;  School
>       Head 48;  Inspector of Schools 55;  Bishop
>       London 85;  Archbishop Canterbury 96.
>   PC 96.
>   Exeter;  London.
>   [DNB, Walfords, Alum Cantab, Alum Oxon, Crockfds]
>
>   Sanitary Institute 80-84, Exec.
>   Central Assn for Stopping Sale Intox Liquors on
>       Sunday 70-80, V-Pres.
>   Natl Vigilance Assn (F) 85-85, Exec.
>   Soc for Promoting Increase of the Home Episcopate
>       72-74, V-Pres.

TEMPLE, GEORGIANA COWPER-,LADY MOUNT-TEMPLE <Wife of 1ST
    BARON, nee TOLLEMACHE> ( -1901)

    West London; Hampshire.
    [BP]

    Victoria Street Soc for Protection of Animals from
        Vivisection 80-85, Exec.


TEMPLE, SIR RICHARD, 1ST BT. (1826-1902)

    Rugby; Haileybury.
    Landowner; India Civil Service 46; Chief
        Commissioner, Central Provinces India 65;
        Foreign Sec, India Govt 68; Lt Gov, Bengal 74;
        Gov, Bombay 77; Author.
    Conservative. MP Evesham 85-92, Surrey Kingston
        92-95. JP.
    CSI 66; KCSI 67; Baronet 76; GCSI 78; CIE 78;
        PC 96.
    Fellow Royal Society; Br Assn.
    Northwest London; Worcestershire.
    [DNB, BP, Walfords, Alum Cantab, Alum Oxon, Dods]

    Liberty & Property Defense League (F) 82-82, Exec.


TEMPLE, WILLIAM FRANCIS COWPER-, 1ST BARON MOUNT-TEMPLE
    (1811-1888)

    Eton.
    Large Landowner 65; Cornet, Army 27; Lieutenant,
        Army 32; Captain, Army 35; Major 52.
    Liberal. MP Hertford 35-68, Hampshire South 68-80.
        Junior Lord Treasury 41- , Lord Admiralty
        46-55, Parl U-Sec Home Off 55-55, Pres Board of
        Health 55-58, Pres Board of Trade 59-60,
        Paymaster General 59-60, First Commissioner
        Works 60-66, JP.
    PC 55; Baron 80.
    West London; Hampshire; Devonshire.
    [DNB, MEB, BP, Walfords, Bateman, Dods, Army List]

    Commons Preservation Soc (F) 65-86, President.
    Central Assn for Stopping Sale Intox Liquors on
        Sunday 85-85, V-Pres.
    Victoria Street Soc for Protection of Animals from
        Vivisection 80-85, V-Pres.


TEMPLER, WILLIAM CHRISTOPHER (1823-1885)

    Westminster School; Trinity, Camb.
    Rector 60; Curate 46; Ordained Priest<CE> 47;
        Vicar 49.
    Burton Bradstock.
    [Alum Cantab, Crockfds]

    Church Assn 70-78, Exec.


TENNANT, SIR CHARLES, 1ST BT. (1823-1906)

    Glasgow High School.
    Chemicals Manufacturer; Merchant; Large
        Landowner.
    Liberal. MP Glasgow 79-80, Peebles & Selkirkshire
        80-86. DL, JP.
    Baronet 85.
    West London; Glasgow; Peeblesshire.
    [DNB, WWW, BP, Walfords, Bateman, Dods, Direc
        Direcs]

    Natl Footpaths Preservation Soc 86-90, V-Pres.


TENNYSON, ALFRED, 1ST BARON TENNYSON (1809-1892)

    Trinity, Camb.
    Poet; Small Landowner 56.
    Poet Laureat 50; Baron 84.
    Fellow Royal Society.
    Surrey; Isle of Wight.
    [DNB, MEB, BP, Walfords, Alum Cantab, Alum Oxon]

    Natl Footpaths Preservation Soc 86-90, V-Pres.
    City Church & Churchyard Protection Soc (F) 80-83,
        V-Pres.
    Victoria Street Soc for Protection of Animals from
        Vivisection 80-85, V-Pres.


TEULON, WILLIAM MILFORD

    Architect.
    Fellow Royal Inst Br Architects.
    West Central London.

    City Church & Churchyard Protection Soc (F) 80-83,
        Chairman, V-Pres.


THICKNESSE, RALPH (1856- )

    Christ Church, Oxf; Lincoln's Inn.
    Barrister 81.
    Liberal.
    West Central London.
    [Alum Oxon, Fosters]

    Natl Vigilance Assn (F) 85-85, Hon Sec.


THISTLETHWAITE, J.

    Bradford.

    Jamaica Committee (F) 66-66.


THOMAS, EDWIN

    Manchester.

    Central Assn for Stopping Sale Intox Liquors on
        Sunday 75-85, Exec.
    Natl Education Union 70-70, Exec.


THOMAS, FRANK R.

    Sunday Society 77-78, Exec.


THOMAS, J. H.

    Physician.
    Merthyr Tydfil.

    Sunday Society (F) 75-90, V-Pres.

THOMAS, JOHN FRYER (1797-1877)

>India Civil Service 16;  Sec, Govt Madras 44.
>London.
>[DNB]
>
>Anglo-Oriental Soc for Suppression Opium Trade (F)
>    75-75, Exec.

THOMAS, W. CAVE

>Fellow Royal Statistical Society.
>West London.
>
>Sunday Society 80-90, V-Pres.

THOMAS, WILLIAM LUSON (1830-1900)

>Newspaper Proprietor 69;  Artist;  Engraver.
>Royal Society Water Colour Painters;  Inst Paintrs
>    Oil;  Royal Inst Water Colour Painters.
>Southwest London;  Surrey.
>[DNB, MEB, Bryan's Painters]
>
>Sunday Society 79-90, V-Pres.

THOMASSON, JOHN PENNINGTON (1841-1904)

>Univ College School.
>Cotton Manufacturer.
>Liberal.  MP Bolton 80-85.
>Bolton.
>[WWW, Dods]
>
>Howard Assn 80-84, Patron.
>Natl Assn for Repeal Contagious Diseases Acts
>    81-81, V-Pres.

THOMASSON, THOMAS (1808-1876)

>Cotton Manufacturer.
>Radical.
>Bolton;  Lancashire.
>[MEB]
>
>Jamaica Committee (F) 66-66.

THOMPSON, GEORGE IVAN

>Captain, Army 71;  Cornet, Army 61;  Lieutenant,
>    Army 63.
>[Army List]
>
>Metro Public Gardens Assn (F) 83-85, Secretary.

THOMPSON, HENRY (1797-1878)

>St John's, Camb.
>Vicar 53;  Curate 24;  Ordained Priest<CE> 27.
>Chard.
>[DNB, MEB, Alum Cantab, Crockfds]
>
>Church Assn 67-67, Exec.

THOMPSON, SIR HENRY, 1ST BT.  (1820-1904)

>U College London(Medical).
>Surgeon;  Medical School Professor 66;  Artist;
>    Novelist.
>Kt 67;  Baronet 99.
>Fellow Royal Col Surgeons.
>West London.
>[DNB, WWW, BP]
>
>Sunday Society 76-90, President, V-Pres.
>Assn for Promoting Extension of Contagious Diseases
>    Act 68-70, V-Pres.

THOMPSON, JOHN

>South London.
>
>Church Assn 80-80, Exec.

THOMPSON, JOSEPH

>Manchester.
>
>Travelling Tax Abolition Committee (F) 77-85, Exec.

THOMPSON, JOSEPH WILLIAM

>University Col London;  Middle Temple.
>Barrister 79.
>West Central London;  Glamorganshire.
>[Alum Cantab, Fosters]
>
>Sunday Society 79-81, Exec.

THOMPSON, THOMAS CHARLES (1821-1892)

>Harrow;  U Col, Durham;  Middle Temple.
>Barrister 44;  Landowner 36;  College Fellow 41.
>Liberal.  MP Durham City 74-74, Durham City 80-85.
>    JP.
>Southwest London;  Sussex.
>[MEB, Walfords, Fosters, Dods]
>
>Intl Arbitration & Peace Assn 81-81, V-Pres.

THOMPSON, W. ALLIN

>Oxford.
>
>Assn for Promoting Extension of Contagious Diseases
>    Act 68-68, Exec.

THOMPSON, WILLIAM HEPWORTH (1810-1886)

>Trinity, Camb.
>College Head 66;  V-Chancellor, Cambridge 67;
>    College Fellow 34;  School Head 36;  Ordained
>    Priest<CE> 38;  Canon 53;  Regius Professor of
>    Greek, Cambridge 53.
>Cambridge.
>[DNB, MEB, BP, Alum Cantab, Crockfds]
>
>Assn for Promoting Extension of Contagious Diseases
>    Act 68-70, V-Pres.

THOMSON, ALEXANDER (1815-1895)

    U Aberdeen.
    Congregational Minister;  College Professor.
    Manchester.
    [MEB]

    Central Assn for Stopping Sale Intox Liquors on
        Sunday 75-75, V-Pres.


THOMSON, JOHN

    Central Assn for Stopping Sale Intox Liquors on
        Sunday 80-80, Exec.


THOMSON, WILLIAM (1819-1890)

    Shrewsbury School;  Queen's, Oxf.
    Archbishop York 62;  Ordained Priest<CE> 43;
        Curate 44;  College Tutor 47;  College Provost
        55;  Rector 55;  Bishop Gloucester and Bristol
        61.
    PC 63.
    Fellow Royal Society;  Fellow Royal Geograph
        Society.
    West London;  York.
    [DNB, MEB, Walfords, Alum Cantab, Alum Oxon,
        Crockfds]

    Natl Soc for Preserving Memorials of Dead 82-82,
        Patron.
    Central Assn for Stopping Sale Intox Liquors on
        Sunday 75-85, V-Pres.
    Natl Education Union 70-76, Exec.


THOMSON, WILLIAM, 1ST BARON KELVIN (1824-1907)

    U Glasgow.
    Professor of Natural Philosophy, Glasgow 46;
        College Fellow 45;  College Lecturer 45;
        Electrical Scientist.
    Liberal(Unionist).  DL.
    Kt 66;  Baron 92;  OM 02;  PC 02;  GCVO.
    Fellow Royal Society;  Br Assn.
    Southwest London;  Glasgow;  Ayrshire.
    [DNB, WWW, BP, Alum Cantab, Alum Oxon, Direc
        Direcs]

    Victoria Street Soc for Protection of Animals from
        Vivisection 80-84, V-Pres.


THORNE, EDWIN

    Intl Arbitration & Peace Assn 81-81, Exec.


THOROLD, ANTHONY WILSON (1825-1895)

    Stanmore, Middlesex;  Queen's, Oxf.
    Bishop Rochester 77;  Ordained Priest<CE> 50;
        Curate 50;  Rector 57;  Rural Dean 69;  Canon
        74;  Bishop Winchester 90.
    Rochester;  Surrey.
    [DNB, MEB, Alum Oxon, Crockfds]

    Central Assn for Stopping Sale Intox Liquors on
        Sunday 85-85, V-Pres.


THORP, JOSEPH <ALSO THORPE>

    JP.
    Halifax.

    Central Assn for Stopping Sale Intox Liquors on
        Sunday (F) 67-70, V-Pres.


THORPE, RICHARD OSCAR TUGWELL (1828-1906)

    Christ's, Camb.
    Vicar 69;  College Fellow 53;  Ordained Priest<CE>
        54;  Vicar 54;  Chaplain 60;  Curate 64;
        Rector 94.
    Southeast London.
    [Alum Cantab, Crockfds]

    Infant Life Protection Soc 71-71, Hon Sec.


THYNNE, HARRIET, MARCHIONESS<DOWAGER> OF BATH <Wife of
3RD MARQUIS, nee BARING> ( -1892)

    [BP]

    City Church & Churchyard Protection Soc 83-83,
        V-Pres.


THYNNE, JOHN ALEXANDER, 4TH MARQUIS OF BATH (1831-1896)

    Eton;  Christ Church, Oxf.
    Very Large Landowner 37;  Ambassador 58.
    Lord Steward Royal Household 66-67, Lord Lieutenant
        89-96, DL, JP.
    Marquis 37.
    Southwest London;  Wiltshire.
    [DNB, MEB, BP, Walfords, Bateman, Alum Oxon]

    Eastern Question Assn 77-77, V-Pres.


TIBBITS, R. W.

    Bristol.

    Assn for Promoting Extension of Contagious Diseases
        Act 68-68, Exec.


TIMMINS, SAMUEL ( -1903)

    "In business";  Author.
    JP.
    Fellow Society of Antiquaries;  Fellow Royal
        Society Literature.
    Birmingham;  Warwickshire.
    [WWW]

    Intl Arbitration & Peace Assn 81-81, V-Pres.
    Natl Education League (F) 69-71, Exec.


TINLING, EDWARD DOUGLAS (1815-1898)

    Christ Church, Oxf.
    Canon 67;  Ordained Priest<CE> 39;  Rector 44;
        Prebendary 63;  Dean 86;  Inspector of Schools
        47.
    Southwest London;  Gloucester.
    [MEB, WWW, Alum Oxon, Crockfds]

    Assn for Promoting Extension of Contagious Diseases
        Act 68-70, V-Pres.

TIPPING, WILLIAM (1816-1897)

Conservative. MP Stockport 68-74, Stockport 85-86.
JP.
Fellow Society of Antiquaries.
Kent.
[MEB, Walfords, Dods, Direc Direcs]

Natl Soc for Preserving Memorials of Dead (F)
81-88, Exec.


TITCOMB, JONATHAN HOLT (1819-1887)

King's College School; Peterhouse, Camb.
Vicar 61; Curate 42; Ordained Priest<CE> 43;
Perp. Curate 45; Rural Dean 70; Hon. Canon
74; Bishop Rangoon 77.
Southeast London.
[DNB, MEB, Alum Cantab, Crockfds]

Church Assn 70-70, Exec.


TODD, ISABELLA<MISS>

Belfast.

Assn for Improvement of Public Morals (F) 79-81,
Exec.
Vigilance Assn for Defense of Personal Rights (F)
71-71, Exec.


TOLLEMACHE, HAMILTON JAMES (1852-1893)

Inner Temple.
Barrister 78.
West London.
[BP, Fosters]

Church Assn 80-80, Exec.


TOLME, JULIEN H.

Civil Engineer.
Southwest London.

Assn for Promoting Extension of Contagious Diseases
Act 70-70, V-Pres.


TOMKINS, J. SIDNEY

East Central London.

City Church & Churchyard Protection Soc (F) 80-83,
Exec.


TOMLINSON, SIR WILLIAM EDWARD MURRAY, 1ST BT.
(1838-1912)

Westminster School; Christ Church, Oxf; Inner
Temple.
Barrister 65.
Conservative. MP Preston 82-06. DL, JP.
Baronet 02.
Fellow Royal Geograph Society.
Southwest London; Lancashire.
[WWW, Alum Oxon, Fosters, Dods, Direc Direcs]

Liberty & Property Defense League (F) 82-82, Exec.


TONGE, RICHARD (1826-1895)

St John's, Camb.
Rector 67; Curate 55; Ordained Priest<CE> 56;
Hon. Canon 75.
Manchester.
[Alum Cantab, Crockfds]

Natl Education Union (F) 69-69, Hon Sec.


TOOLE, -

Canon<RC>.
Manchester.

Central Assn for Stopping Sale Intox Liquors on
Sunday (F) 67-80, Exec.


TORR, JAMES FENNING (1846-1915)

King William's College; Pembroke, Oxf; Middle
Temple.
Barrister 73.
Liberal.
Fellow Society of Antiquaries.
Southwest London.
[WWW, Alum Oxon, Fosters]

Natl Footpaths Preservation Soc (F) 85-86, Exec.
London Municipal Reform League (F) 82-85, Exec.


TORR, JOHN BERRY (1817-1878)

Middle Temple.
Barrister 50; Q.C. 72.
Manchester.
[MEB]

Jamaica Committee (F) 66-66.


TORRENS, SIR ROBERT RICHARD (1814-1884)

Trin Col, Dublin.
Customs Collector, South Australia 51;
Registrar-General, South Australia 52.
Liberal. MP Cambridge 68-74. JP.
KCMG 72; GCMG 84.
West London; Devonshire.
[DNB, MEB, BP, Walfords, Dods, Aust Dict Biog]

Natl Emigration League (F) 70-70, V-Pres.


TORRENS, WILLIAM TORRENS MCCULLAGH (1813-1894)

Trin Col, Dublin; Lincoln's Inn.
Barrister 36; Asst Commissioner, Irish Poor Relief
35.
Liberal. MP Dundalk 47-52, Great Yarmouth 57-57,
Finsbury 65-85.
West London.
[DNB, MEB, Walfords, Fosters, Dods]

City Church & Churchyard Protection Soc 83-83,
V-Pres.
Natl Emigration League (F) 70-70, V-Pres.
Liberty & Property Defense League (F) 82-84, Exec.
Assn for Improvement of London Workhouse
Infirmaries 66-66, Exec.
Jamaica Committee (F) 66-66.
Travelling Tax Abolition Committee (F) 77-85, Exec.

Natl Assn for Repeal Contagious Diseases Acts
    81-81, V-Pres.

TOTTENHAM, CHARLES GEORGE (1838-1918)

    Eton;  Trinity, Camb.
    Lt. Colonel 60;  Lieutenant, Army 54;  Captain,
        Army 55;  Very Large Landowner 86.
    Conservative.  MP New Ross 66-68, New Ross 79-80.
    DL, JP.
    Southwest London;  Co Wicklow.
    [WWW, Walfords, Alum Cantab, Dods, Direc Direcs,
        Army List]

    Assn for Promoting Extension of Contagious Diseases
        Act 68-70, V-Pres.

TOWNEND, T.  W.

    Methodist Free Church Minister.

    Central Assn for Stopping Sale Intox Liquors on
        Sunday 80-80, V-Pres.

TOWNSEND, C.  HARRISON

    Kyrle Soc 84-94, Exec.

TOWNSHEND, JOHN VILLIERS STUART, 5TH MARQUIS TOWNSHEND
    (1831-1899)

    Eton.
    Very Large Landowner 63;  Clerk, FO 50.
    Liberal.  MP Tamworth 56-63.  DL, JP.
    Marquis 63.
    Fellow Society of Antiquaries.
    West London;  Norfolk;  Hertfordshire.
    [MEB, WWW, BP, Walfords, Bateman, Dods, Direc
        Direcs]

    Commons Preservation Soc 69-69, Exec.
    Assn for Improvement of Public Morals (F) 79-81,
        Treas.

TOYN, JOSEPH (1838-1924)

    Pres, Cleveland Miners' Association 75;  Miner.
    Radical.  JP.
    Cleveland.
    [Dic Lab Biog]

    Land Law Reform League (F) 81-84, V-Pres.
    League for Defense of Constitutional Rights 84-84,
        V-Pres.

TRANT, W.

    Land Nationalization Soc 84-85, Exec.

TREHERNE, GEORGE GILBERT TREHERNE (1838- )

    Balliol, Oxf.
    [Alum Oxon]

    Commons Preservation Soc 84-86, Exec.

TREMENHEERE, CHARLES WILLIAM (1813-1898)

    Lt. General, RE 74;  2nd Lt., RE 29;  Captain, RE
        44;  Major, RE 54;  Lt. Colonel, RE 58;
        Colonel, RE 61;  Maj. General, RE 67.
    CB 61.
    West London.
    [MEB, Army List]

    Anglo-Oriental Soc for Suppression Opium Trade
        79-83, Chairman.

TRENCH, W.

    Physician.
    Liverpool.

    Assn for Promoting Extension of Contagious Diseases
        Act 68-70, V-Pres.

TRESTRAIL, FREDERICK (1803-1890)

    Bristol Baptist College.
    Baptist Minister 32.
    London;  Cork.
    [MEB]

    Jamaica Committee (F) 66-66.

TREVELYAN, ARTHUR (1802-1878)

    Harrow.
    JP.
    Edinburgh;  Haddingtonshire.
    [MEB, BP]

    Sunday Society (F) 75-77, V-Pres.
    Jamaica Committee (F) 66-66.
    Malthusian League 78-78, V-Pres.
    Natl Secular Soc 70-77, V-Pres.

TREVELYAN, SIR CHARLES EDWARD, 1ST BT.  (1807-1886)

    Charterhouse;  Haileybury.
    Very Large Landowner 79;  India Civil Service 26;
        Asst Sec, Treas 40;  Gov, Madras 59;  Financial
        Minister, India Govt 62.
    Liberal.
    KCB 48;  Baronet 74.
    Southwest London;  Northumberland.
    [DNB, MEB, BP, Walfords, Bateman]

    Howard Assn 79-84, Patron.

TREVELYAN, SIR GEORGE OTTO, 2ND BT.  (1838-1928)

    Harrow;  Trinity, Camb;  Lincoln's Inn.
    Historian;  Politician;  Very Large Landowner 86.
    Liberal.  MP Tynemouth 65-68, Hawick 68-86, Glasgow
        Bridgeton 87-97.  Lord Admiralty 68-70, Parl
        Sec Admiralty 81-82, Chief Sec Ireland 82-84,
        Chanc Duchy Lancaster 84-85, Sec St Scotland
        86-86, Sec St Scotland 92-95, DL.
    PC 82;  Baronet 86;  OM 11.
    Southwest London;  Hawick;  Northumberland.
    [DNB, WWW, BP, Walfords, Alum Cantab, Alum Oxon,
        Dods]

    Central Assn for Stopping Sale Intox Liquors on
        Sunday 75-85, V-Pres.
    Free Land League 86-86, V-Pres.


TREVELYAN, SIR WALTER CALVERLEY, 6TH BT.  (1797-1879)

    Harrow;  University Col, Oxf.
    Very Large Landowner 46.
    DL, JP.
    Baronet 46.
    Fellow Geological Society;  Fellow Society of
        Antiquaries;  Fellow Royal Society Edinb.
    Northumberland.
    [DNB, MEB, BP, Walfords, Alum Oxon]

    Howard Assn 67-78, Patron.


TRIMBLE, ROBERT

    Liverpool.

    Jamaica Committee (F) 66-66.


TRIPE, JOHN WILLIAM (1820-1892)

    St Andrews(Medical).
    Physician 46.
    Med Off of Health 56-92.
    Fellow Royal Col Physicians;  Member Royal Col
        Surgeons.
    East London.
    [MEB, Direc Direcs]

    Smoke Abatement Committee 81-81.


TRIST, JOHN

    Clergyman<Sect Unkn>.

    Sunday Society 81-84, V-Pres.


TROLLOPE, ANTHONY (1815-1882)

    Harrow.
    Novelist;  General Post Office Clerk 34;  Journal
        Editor 67.
    West London;  Sussex.
    [DNB, MEB]

    Metro Free Libraries Assn 82-82, Exec.


TROLLOPE, EDWARD (1817-1893)

    Eton;  Christ Church, Oxf.
    Bishop Nottingham<Suffragan> 77;  Curate 40;
        Ordained Priest<CE> 41;  Vicar 41;  Rector 43;
        Prebendary 60;  Archdeacon 67.
    JP.
    Fellow Society of Antiquaries.
    Nottingham;  Leasingham.
    [DNB, MEB, BP, Walfords, Alum Oxon]

    City Church & Churchyard Protection Soc (F) 80-83,
        V-Pres.
    Natl Soc for Preserving Memorials of Dead (F)
        81-84, President, Patron.


TROWER, ARTHUR (1819- )

    Lincoln, Oxf.
    Rector 74;  Curate 43;  Ordained Priest<CE> 44;
        Perp.  Curate 47.
    East Central London.
    [Alum Oxon, Crockfds]

    City Church & Churchyard Protection Soc (F) 80-83,
        Exec.


TROWER, G.

    West Central London.

    City Church & Churchyard Protection Soc (F) 80-81,
        Hon Sec.


TROWER, H. SEYMOUR

    West London.

    Natl Assn for Promotion of State Colonization
        86-86, Exec.


TRUELOVE, EDWARD (1809-1897)

    Bookseller.
    Radical.
    North London.
    [MEB]

    Malthusian League (F) 77-79, Exec.
    Natl Secular Soc 81-84, V-Pres.
    Anglo-French Intervention Committee (F) 70-70,
        Exec.


TRUSCOTT, SIR FRANCIS WYATT (1824-1895)

    Kings Col London.
    Stationer;  Printer;  Metropolitan Board of Works
        72.
    Conservative.  DL.
    Kt 72.
    Northwest London.
    [MEB, BP]

    City Church & Churchyard Protection Soc 80-83,
        V-Pres.

TUCK, WILLIAM

>    Bath.

>    Jamaica Committee (F) 66-66.

TUCKER, JOSEPH

>    Merchant;  Substantial Landowner.
>    JP.
>    London;  Bedfordshire.
>    [Walfords, Bateman]

>    Central Assn for Stopping Sale Intox Liquors on
>        Sunday 70-75, V-Pres.

TUCKER, STEPHEN ISAACSON (1835-1887)

>    Heraldist.
>    West London.
>    [MEB]

>    Soc for Protection of Ancient Buildings (F) 78-85,
>        Exec.

TUCKETT, FREDERICK

>    London.

>    Jamaica Committee (F) 66-66.

TUFNELL, THOMAS R.

>    JP.
>    Surrey.
>    [Direc Direcs]

>    Church Assn 70-80, Exec.

TUGWELL, LEWEN

>    New Inn Hall, Oxf.
>    Hon. Canon 77;  Curate 51;  Ordained Priest<CE>
>        52;  Chaplain 54;  Vicar 58;  Rector 65.
>    West Central London.
>    [Alum Oxon, Crockfds]

>    Church Assn 80-80, Exec.

TULLEDGE, H. E.

>    Natl Education Union 70-70, Exec.

TURBY, J. H. <"MAJ.">

>    Bristol.

>    Church Assn 70-78, Exec.

TURLE, HENRY FREDERIC (1835-1883)

>    Westminster School.
>    Journal Editor 78;  Civ Serv, War Office 56.
>    West Central London.
>    [DNB]

>    Soc for Protection of Ancient Buildings 78-80,
>        Exec.

TURNER, ERNEST

>    Architect.
>    Fellow Royal Inst Br Architects.
>    West London.

>    Sanitary Institute 78-89, Exec.
>    Smoke Abatement Committee 81-81.

TURNER, F. S.

>    Anglo-Oriental Soc for Suppression Opium Trade (F)
>        75-75, Secretary.

TURNER, SIR LLEWELYN (1823-1903)

>    DL.
>    Kt 70.
>    Carnarvonshire.
>    [WWW, BP, Walfords, Direc Direcs]

>    Central Assn for Stopping Sale Intox Liquors on
>        Sunday 85-85, V-Pres.

TURNER, THACKERAY

>    West Central London.

>    Soc for Protection of Ancient Buildings 85-85,
>        Secretary.

TURNER, WILLIAM (1800-1872)

>    English College, Rome.
>    Bishop Salford<RC> 51;  Priest<RC> 25.
>    Salford.
>    [MEB]

>    Central Assn for Stopping Sale Intox Liquors on
>        Sunday (F) 67-70, V-Pres.

TWISS, SIR TRAVERS (1809-1897)

>    University Col, Oxf;  Lincoln´s Inn.
>    Q.C. 58;  Barrister 40;  Advocate, Doctors Commons
>        41;  Drummond Professor of Political Economy,
>        Oxford 42;  Regius Professor of Law, Oxford 55;
>        Judge Advocate of the Fleet 62;  Judge Advocate
>        General 67.
>    Kt 67.
>    Fellow Royal Society.
>    Northwest London.
>    [DNB, MEB, BP, Walfords, Alum Oxon, Fosters]

>    Intl Law Assn (F) 73-76, V-Pres.

TYNDALL, JOHN (1820-1893)

    Marburg.
    Thermodynamic Scientist;  College Lecturer 47;
       Professor of Natural Philosophy, Royal Inst 53.
    Liberal(Unionist).
    Fellow Royal Society.
    Surrey.
    [DNB, MEB, Alum Cantab, Alum Oxon]

    Sunday Society 78-90, V-Pres.


TYSE, CAREY

    Wallington.

    Jamaica Committee (F) 66-66.


URE, J.

    Sanitary Institute 84-84, Exec.


VALPY, LEONARD R.

    Church Assn 67-80, Exec.


VANDERBYL, PHILIP (1827-1892)

    Edinburgh(Medical).
    Australia Merchant 58;  Banker;  Physician 49.
    Liberal.  MP Somersetshire Bridgewater 66-68,
       Portsmouth 85-86.
    Member Royal Col Physicians;  Member Royal Col
       Surgeons.
    West London;  Hampshire.
    [MEB, Walfords, Dods, Direc Direcs]

    Free Land League 86-86, V-Pres.


VARLEY, CROMWELL FLEETWOOD (1828-1883)

    Electrical Engineer 46.
    Fellow Royal Society;  Member Inst Civ Engineers.
    Bexley Heath.
    [DNB, MEB]

    Intl Arbitration & Peace Assn 81-81, Exec.


VATCHER, JOHN SIDNEY ADOLPHUS (1848-1926)

    St John's, Camb.
    Vicar 83;  Curate 71;  Ordained Priest<CE> 72.
    East London.
    [Alum Cantab, Crockfds]

    Metro Public Gardens Assn (F) 83-90, Hon Sec.


VAUDIN, CHARLES

    Jersey.

    Assn for Promoting Extension of Contagious Diseases
       Act 68-70, V-Pres.


VAUGHAN, CHARLES JOHN (1816-1897)

    Rugby;  Trinity, Camb;  Lincoln's Inn.
    Dean 79;  College Fellow 39;  Ordained Priest<CE>
       41;  Vicar 41;  School Head 44;  Substantial
       Landowner.
    East Central London;  Llandaff.
    [DNB, MEB, WWW, Bateman, Alum Cantab, Alum Oxon,
       Crockfds]

    Howard Assn 80-84, Patron.
    Victoria Street Soc for Protection of Animals from
       Vivisection 80-85, V-Pres.


VAUGHAN, HERBERT ALFRED (1832-1903)

    Bishop Salford<RC> 72;  Priest<RC> 54;  Archbishop
       Westminster<RC> 92;  Cardinal<RC> 93.
    Salford.
    [DNB, WWW]

    Central Assn for Stopping Sale Intox Liquors on
       Sunday 75-85, V-Pres.


VAVASSEUR, J.

    Financial Reform Union (F) 68-69, Exec.


VENABLES, EDMUND (1819-1895)

    Merchant Taylors;  Pembroke, Camb.
    Canon 67;  Ordained Priest<CE> 46;  Curate 46;
       Prebendary 65;  Antiquary.
    Camden Society.
    Lincoln.
    [DNB, MEB, Crockfds]

    Soc for Protection of Ancient Buildings (F) 78-85,
       Exec.


VENN, HENRY (1796-1873)

    Queens', Camb.
    Prebendary 46;  College Fellow 19;  Curate 20;
       Ordained Priest<CE> 21;  College Lecturer 24;
       Perp. Curate 26.
    Surrey.
    [DNB, MEB, Crockfds]

    Church Assn 70-70, V-Pres.


VENTURI, EMILIE <MRS. G. A. VENTURI, nee ASHURST>
( -1893)

    Author.
    Southwest London.
    [MEB]

    Sunday Society 81-90, V-Pres.
    Vigilance Assn for Defense of Personal Rights (F)
       71-83, Secretary.
    Ladies' Natl Assn for Repeal of Contagious Diseases
       Acts 70-72, Exec.

VERINDER, FREDERICK

English Land Restoration League 85-85, Secretary.
Natl Assn for Repeal Blasphemy Laws (F) 84-84,
    Exec.


VERNEY, SIR EDMOND HOPE, 3RD BT. (1838-1910)

Harrow.
Captain, RN 77; Cadet, RN 51; Lieutenant, RN 58;
    Commander, RN 66; Very Large Landowner 94;
    Author.
Liberal. MP Buckinghamshire N 85-86,
    Buckinghamshire N 89-91. DL, JP.
Baronet 94.
Fellow Royal Geograph Society; Fellow Royal
    Meteorlog Society; Fellow Royal Historical
    Society.
Southwest London; Buckinghamshire; Anglesey.
[WWW, BP, Dods, Navy List]

Natl Assn for Promotion of State Colonization
    86-86, V-Pres, Exec.
Free Land League 86-86, V-Pres.


VERNEY, GEORGE HOPE LLOYD- (1842-1896)

Surrey.
[BP]

Railway Passengers' Protection Assn 86-86, Treas.


VERNEY, SIR HARRY, 2ND BT. (1801-1894)

Harrow; Downing, Camb; Royal Military College,
    Sandhurst.
Very Large Landowner; Ensign, Army 19; Captain,
    Army 22; Major 27.
Liberal. MP Buckingham 32-41, Bedford 47-52,
    Buckingham 57-74, Buckingham 80-85. DL, JP.
Baronet 26; PC 85.
Fellow Royal Geograph Society; Royal Agricultural
    Society.
West London; Buckinghamshire.
[DNB, MEB, BP, Walfords, Bateman, Alum Cantab,
    Dods, Army List]

Public Museums & Free Libraries Assn 68-68, V-Pres.
Church Assn 75-85, V-Pres.


VERNON, -

East Central London.

Jamaica Committee (F) 66-66.


VERNON, AUGUSTUS HENRY VENABLES-, 6TH BARON VERNON
    (1829-1883)

Eton; Magdalene, Camb.
Large Landowner 66; Lieutenant, Army 48; Captain,
    Army 50.
DL, JP.
Baron 66.
Royal Agricultural Society.
Southwest London; Cheshire; Northumberland.
[DNB, MEB, BP, Walfords, Bateman, Alum Cantab, Army
    List]

Plimsoll and Seamen's Fund Committee (F) 73-73,
    Exec.


VERNON, GEORGE WILLIAM HENRY VENABLES-, 7TH BARON VERNON
    (1854-1898)

Eton.
Large Landowner 83; Sub-Lt., Army 73; Lieutenant,
    Army 75; Captain, Army 83.
Baron 83.
West London; Cheshire; Derbyshire.
[MEB, WWW, BP, Army List]

Free Land League 86-86, V-Pres.


VERSCHOYLE, JOHN STUART (1853-1915)

Uppingham; Pembroke, Camb.
Curate 81; Ordained Priest<CE> 82; Rector 91.
West London.
[Alum Cantab, Crockfds]

Victoria Street Soc for Protection of Animals from
    Vivisection 84-85, Exec.


VESEY, JOHN ROBERT WILLIAM, 4TH VISCOUNT DE VESCI
    (1844-1903)

Eton.
Very Large Landowner 75; Lieutenant, Army 63;
    Captain, Army 66; Lt. Colonel 74.
Liberal(Unionist). Lord Lieutenant 83-00, JP.
Viscount 75; Baron 84.
Southwest London; Queens Co.
[BP, Walfords, Bateman, Direc Direcs, Army List]

Natl Assn for Promotion of State Colonization
    86-86, Patron.
Metro Public Gardens Assn 84-90, V-Chairman.


VICARS, GEORGE R.

Howard Assn 83-83, Exec.


VIGERS, EDWARD

Architect.
Assoc Royal Inst Br Architects; Surveyors'
    Institute.
Southwest London.

Sanitary Institute 82-85, Exec.


VILLIERS, CHARLES PELHAM (1802-1898)

Haileybury College; St John's, Camb; Lincoln's
    Inn.
Barrister 27; Asst Poor Law Commnr 32; Judge
    Advocate General 52; Substantial Landowner.
Liberal(Unionist). MP Wolverhampton 35-85,
    Wolverhampton South 85-98. Pres Poor Law Board
    59-66, DL, JP.
PC 53.
Fellow Royal Society.
Southwest London; Surrey.
[DNB, MEB, WWW, BP, Walfords, Bateman, Alum Cantab,
    Dods]

Intl Arbitration & Peace Assn 81-81, V-Pres.

VINALL, C. G.

West Central London.

Soc for Protection of Ancient Buildings (F) 78-85,
Hon Sec.

VINCE, CHARLES (1824-1874)

Stepney College.
Baptist Minister 52.
Birmingham.
[MEB]

Natl Education League (F) 69-71, Exec.

VINCE, W. B.

Allotments & Small Holdings Assn 85-88, Exec.

VINCENT, - <MRS.>

Malthusian League 79-79, Exec.

VINCENT, J. E. M.

Land Nationalization Soc (F) 81-81, Exec.

VINCENT, WILLIAM

Norwich.

Natl Soc for Preserving Memorials of Dead (F)
81-88, Secretary.

VINCENT, SIR WILLIAM, 12TH BT. (1834-1914)

Christ Church, Oxf.
Rector 64; Ordained Priest<CE> 59; Curate 59;
Diocesan Inspector of Schools 72; Landowner
83.
DL, JP.
Baronet 83.
Norwich; Surrey.
[BP, Alum Oxon, Crockfds, Direc Direcs]

Metro Public Gardens Assn 84-90, V-Chairman.

VINTRAS, ACHILLE

Physician.
West London.

Assn for Promoting Extension of Contagious Diseases
Act 68-68, Exec.

VIVIAN, HENRY HUSSEY, 1ST BARON SWANSEA (1821-1894)

Eton; Trinity, Camb.
Smelting Works Owner 42.
Liberal. MP Cornwall Truro 52-57, Glamorganshire
57-85, Swansea District 85-93. DL, JP.
Baronet 82; Baron 93.
Fellow Geological Society.
Southwest London; Glamorganshire.
[DNB, MEB, BP, Alum Cantab, Dods, Direc Direcs]

Smoke Abatement Committee 81-81.

VOILE, THOMAS

Cheltenham.

Church Assn 78-80, Exec.

VOSE, JAMES

Physician.
Liverpool.

Assn for Promoting Extension of Contagious Diseases
Act 68-70, V-Pres.

VOYSEY, CHARLES (1828-1912)

Stockwell Grammar; St Edmund Hall, Oxf.
Head, Theistic Church 71; Ordained Priest<CE> 51;
Curate 51; Vicar 64.
Dulwich.
[DNB, WWW, Alum Oxon]

Sunday Society 76-90, V-Pres.

VYVYAN, C. <MISS>

Kyrle Soc 84-90, Exec.

WADDINGTON, F. S.

Chiswick.

Natl Footpaths Preservation Soc (F) 85-86, Exec.

WADDINGTON, JOHN BARTON

St. Bees.
Vicar 66; Curate 63; Ordained Priest<CE> 64.
Low Moor.
[Crockfds]

Church Assn 75-78, Exec.

WADDY, SAMUEL DANKS (1830-1902)

Wesley College, Sheffield; London U; Inner
Temple.
Q.C. 74; Barrister 58; County Court Judge 96.
Liberal. MP Barnstaple 74-79, Sheffield 79-80,
Edinburgh 82-85, Lindsey North, Lincs 86-94.
Northwest London; Barnstaple.
[WWW, Fosters, Dods, Direc Direcs]

Central Assn for Stopping Sale Intox Liquors on
Sunday 75-85, V-Pres.

Free Land League 86-86, V-Pres.

WADE, J. A.

JP.
Kingston-upon-Hull.

Central Assn for Stopping Sale Intox Liquors on
Sunday (F) 67-85, V-Pres.

WAGNER, HENRY (1840- )

Merton, Oxf;  Inner Temple.
Barrister 71.
Fellow Society of Antiquaries.
West London.
[Alum Oxon, Fosters]

Natl Soc for Preserving Memorials of Dead (F)
81-84, Exec.
Natl Assn for Promotion of State Colonization
86-86, V-Pres.

WAINWRIGHT, FREDERICK ( -1921)

Trinity, Camb.
Vicar 66;  Curate 61;  Ordained Priest<CE> 62;
Hon. Canon 08.
Altrincham.
[WWW, Alum Cantab, Crockfds]

Central Assn for Stopping Sale Intox Liquors on
Sunday 85-85, Exec.

WAINWRIGHT, SIR JAMES GADESDEN (1837-1929)

Kings Col London.
Conservative. JP.
Kt 19.
Southwest London.
[WWW]

Church Assn 75-75, Exec.

WAINWRIGHT, R. E.

London.

Jamaica Committee (F) 66-66.

WAINWRIGHT, SAMUEL ( -1899)

St. Bees.
Sec, Protestant Institute, Islington 72;  Ordained
Priest<CE>;  Vicar 60;  Curate 70;  Perp.
Curate 86;  Author.
Stoke Newington.
[MEB, Crockfds]

Church Assn 75-85, V-Pres, Exec.

WAKEFIELD, WILLIAM HENRY (1828-1889)

Banker;  Gunpowder Manufacturer;  Large Landowner
66.
Liberal. JP.
Royal Agricultural Society.
Milnthorpe.
[MEB, Walfords, Bateman]

Central Assn for Stopping Sale Intox Liquors on
Sunday 75-85, V-Pres.

WAKELING, C.

West London.

Assn for Promoting Extension of Contagious Diseases
Act 68-68, Exec.

WALDEGRAVE, WILLIAM FREDERICK, 9TH EARL WALDEGRAVE
(1851-1930)

Eton;  Trinity, Camb.
Landowner 59.
Conservative. Lord in Waiting 86-92, Lord in
Waiting 95-96, DL, JP.
Earl 59;  PC.
West London;  Somersetshire;  Surrey.
[WWW, BP, Walfords, Alum Cantab]

Central Vigilance Comtee for Repression Immorality
(F) 83-84, V-Pres.

WALFORD, EDWARD (1823-1897)

Charterhouse;  Balliol, Oxf.
Journal Editor 58;  Asst School Master 46;
Ordained Priest<CE> 47;  Antiquary;  Compiler.
Br Archeol Assn.
London.
[DNB, MEB, Alum Oxon]

Natl Soc for Preserving Memorials of Dead (F)
81-88, Exec.

WALHOUSE, - <"CAPT.">

London.

Jamaica Committee (F) 66-66.

WALHOUSE, EDWARD

Travelling Tax Abolition Committee (F) 77-82, Exec.

WALKER, -

Workmen's Peace Assn 75-75, Exec.

WALKER, ALFRED

    Financial Reform Union (F) 68-69, Secretary.

WALKER, THOMAS FERDINAND

    Arms Manufacturer.
    Birmingham.
    [Direc Direcs]

    English Land Restoration League (F) 83-85, Exec.

WALKER, WILLIAM

    Natl Education Union 70-70, Exec.

WALLACE, - <MRS.>

    West London.

    London Soc for Abolition of Compulsory Vaccination
       81-81, V-Pres.

WALLACE, ALFRED RUSSELL (1823-1913)

    Naturalist;  Surveyor 38;  School Master 44;
       Architect;  Author.
    Radical.
    OM 10.
    Fellow Royal Geograph Society;  Fellow Royal
       Society.
    Godalming.
    [DNB, WWW]

    Land Nationalization Soc (F) 81-85, Chairman,
       President.

WALLIS, E.  WHITE

    Fellow Royal Meteorlog Society;  Fellow Royal
       Statistical Society.

    Sanitary Institute 80-89, Secretary.

WALLIS, H.

    Northwest London.

    Soc for Protection of Ancient Buildings (F) 78-78,
       Exec.

WALLIS, MARRIAGE

    Brighton.

    Jamaica Committee (F) 66-66.

WALLOP, LADY EVELINE ALICIA JULIANA, COUNTESS OF
    PORTSMOUTH <Wife of 5TH EARL> ( -1906)

    Southwest London;  Hampshire.
    [BP]

    Victoria Street Soc for Protection of Animals from
       Vivisection 80-85, Exec.

WALLOP, ISAAC NEWTON, 5TH EARL OF PORTSMOUTH (1825-1891)

    Rugby;  Trinity, Camb.
    Very Large Landowner 54;  Cornet, Army 46.
    DL, JP.
    Earl 54.
    Southwest London;  Hampshire.
    [MEB, BP, Walfords, Bateman, Army List]

    Victoria Street Soc for Protection of Animals from
       Vivisection 80-80, V-Pres.

WALLOP, NEWTON, 6TH EARL PORTSMOUTH (1856-1917)

    Eton;  Balliol, Oxf.
    Very Large Landowner 91.
    Liberal(Unionist).  MP Barnstaple 80-85, Devonshire
       North 85-91.  Parl U-Sec War 05-08, DL, JP.
    Earl 91.
    Fellow Society of Antiquaries;  Fellow Zoological
       Society.
    West London;  Hampshire;  Devonshire.
    [WWW, BP, Alum Oxon, Dods, Direc Direcs]

    Commons Preservation Soc 84-86, Exec.

WALLS, J.  G.

    Jamaica Committee 66-66, Exec.

WALTER, JAMES

    JP.
    Swansea.

    Sunday Society 77-90, V-Pres.

WALTERS, W.

    Clergyman<Sect Unkn>.
    Newcastle-upon-Tyne.

    Jamaica Committee (F) 66-66.

WARD, FREDERICK P.

    Church Assn 67-80, Exec.

WARD, W.  GIBSON

    Fellow Royal Historical Society.
    Ross-shire.

    London Soc for Abolition of Compulsory Vaccination
       81-81, V-Pres.

WARDLE, GEORGE Y.

West Central London.

Soc for Protection of Ancient Buildings (F) 78-85,
    Exec.


WARDLE, HENRY (1832-1892)

Brewer.
Liberal. MP Derbyshire South 85-92. DL, JP.
Burton-upon-Trent.
[MEB, Dods, Direc Direcs]

Free Land League 86-86, V-Pres.
Church Assn 67-78, Exec.


WARDLE, SIR THOMAS (1831-1909)

Silk Manufacturer.
JP.
Kt 97.
Fellow Geological Society;  Fellow Chemical
    Society.
Leek.
[DNB, WWW]

Soc for Protection of Ancient Buildings (F) 78-85,
    Exec.


WARING, CHARLES ( -1887)

Large Builder/contractor.
Liberal. MP Poole 65-68, Poole 74-74.
West Central London.
[MEB, Walfords, Dods]

Assn for Promoting Extension of Contagious Diseases
    Act 68-75, V-Pres, Exec.
Assn for Improvement of London Workhouse
    Infirmaries 66-66, Exec.
Natl Emigration League (F) 70-70, V-Pres.


WARR, GEORGE CHARLES WINTER (1845-1901)

Royal Institution, Liverpool;  Trinity, Camb.
Professor of Classical Lit, Kings Col London 81;
    Asst School Master 69;  College Lecturer 74.
Northwest London.
[WWW, Alum Cantab]

Central Vigilance Comtee for Repression Immorality
    83-83, Exec.


WARREN, GEORGE FLEMING, 2ND BARON DE TABLEY (1811-1887)

Eton;  Christ Church, Oxf.
Large Landowner 27.
Conservative. Lord in Waiting 53-66, Treas Royal
    Household 68-72, DL, JP.
Baron 27;  PC.
West London;  Cheshire.
[MEB, BP, Walfords, Bateman, Alum Oxon]

City Church & Churchyard Protection Soc (F) 80-83,
    V-Pres.


WASHBURN, EMORY

Intl Law Assn 74-74, Exec.


WASON, EUGENE (1846-1927)

Rugby;  Wadham, Oxf;  Middle Temple.
Barrister 85;  Solicitor 76.
Liberal. MP Ayreshire South 85-86, Ayreshire South
    92-95, Clackmannan & Kinross 99-18. DL, JP.
PC 07.
Northwest London;  Ayreshire.
[WWW, Alum Oxon, Dods]

Free Land League 86-86, V-Pres.


WATERHOUSE, SAMUEL (1815-1881)

Conservative. MP Pontefract 63-80. DL, JP.
Halifax.
[MEB, Dods]

Assn for Promoting Extension of Contagious Diseases
    Act 68-70, V-Pres.


WATERLOW, SIR SYDNEY HEDLEY, 1ST BT.  (1822-1906)

Stationer 44.
Liberal. MP Dumfrieshire 68-69, Maidstone 74-80,
    Gravesend 80-85. JP.
Kt 67;  Baronet 73;  KCVO 02.
Southwest London;  Kent.
[DNB, WWW, Walfords, Dods, Direc Direcs]

Howard Assn 70-78, Patron.


WATERMAN, -

Workmen's Peace Assn 75-75, Exec.


WATHERSTON, EDWARD J.

Metro Free Libraries Assn 77-77, Exec.


WATKIN, SIR EDWARD WILLIAM, 1ST BT.  (1819-1901)

Cotton Merchant;  Railway Promoter 45.
Liberal(Unionist).  MP Great Yarmouth 57-57,
    Stockport 64-68, Hythe 74-95. DL, JP.
Kt 68;  Baronet 80.
Southwest London;  Cheshire.
[DNB, WWW, BP, Walfords, Dods, Direc Direcs]

Liberty & Property Defense League (F) 82-84, Exec.


WATKINS, HENRY GEORGE, JUN.  (1849- )

Christ Church, Oxf.
Curate 74;  Ordained Priest<CE> 77.
Wimbledon.
[Alum Oxon, Crockfds]

Natl Assn for Promotion of State Colonization
    86-86, Exec.

WATSON, CHRISTOPHER KNIGHT (1824-1901)

> Trinity, Camb.
> Sec, Soc of Antiquaries 60.
> Fellow Society of Antiquaries.
> West London.
> [Alum Cantab]
>
> City Church & Churchyard Protection Soc (F) 80-83,
>     Exec.

WATSON, ROBERT SPENCE (1837-1911)

> Friends' School, York;  University Col London.
> Solicitor.
> Liberal.
> PC 06.
> Newcastle-upon-Tyne.
> [DNB, WWW]
>
> Travelling Tax Abolition Committee 80-85, Exec.

WATSON, SAMUEL

> Intl Arbitration & Peace Assn 81-81, Exec.

WATSON, SIR THOMAS, 1ST BT.  (1792-1882)

> St John's, Camb;  St Bartholomew's Hosp.
> Physician 27;  College Fellow 16;  Medical School
>     Professor 28;  Author.
> Baronet 66.
> Fellow Royal Society;  Fellow Royal Col Physicians;
>     Pathological Society.
> West London.
> [DNB, MEB, BP, Walfords, Alum Cantab, Alum Oxon]
>
> Assn for Promoting Extension of Contagious Diseases
>     Act 68-70, V-Pres.
> Assn for Improvement of London Workhouse
>     Infirmaries 66-66, Exec.

WATSON, THOMAS HENRY (1839- )

> Architect.
> Fellow Royal Inst Br Architects.
>
> Sunday Society 80-90, V-Pres.

WATT, HUGH (1848-1921)

> U Geneva.
> Merchant.
> Liberal.  MP Glasgow Camlachie 85-92.
> Southwest London.
> [Dods, Direc Direcs]
>
> Free Land League 86-86, V-Pres.

WATT, JOHN BROWN (1826-1897)

> U Edinburgh.
> Australia Merchant.
> New South Wales.
> [Aust Dict Biog]
>
> Imperial Federation League (F) 84-84, Exec.

WATTENBACH, AUGUSTUS

> Plimsoll and Seamen's Fund Committee (F) 73-73,
>     Exec.

WATTS, CHARLES

> London.
>
> Natl Secular Soc 70-77, Secretary, V-Pres.

WATTS, EDWARD HENRY

> Travelling Tax Abolition Committee (F) 77-85, Exec.

WATTS, GEORGE FREDERICK (1817-1904)

> Artist.
> OM 02.
> Royal Academy.
> West London;  Isle of Wight.
> [DNB, WWW, Alum Cantab, Alum Oxon, Bryan's
>     Painters]
>
> Sunday Society 78-90, V-Pres.

WATTS, J. C.

> Methodist New Connection Minister.
>
> Central Assn for Stopping Sale Intox Liquors on
>     Sunday 80-80, V-Pres.

WATTS, SIR JAMES (1804-1878)

> Merchant 30.
> JP.
> Kt 57.
> Manchester;  Cheshire.
> [MEB, BP, Walfords]
>
> Howard Assn 67-76, Patron.
> Jamaica Committee (F) 66-66.

WATTS, JOHN (1818-1887)

> Giessen.
> Cooperative Promoter;  Educationalist;  Insurance
>     Co Manager 57.
> Radical.
> Manchester.
> [DNB, MEB, Dic Lab Biog]
>
> Travelling Tax Abolition Committee (F) 77-85,
>     Treas.

WATTS, SAMUEL

> Manchester.
>
> Jamaica Committee (F) 66-66.

WAUGH, BENJAMIN (1839-1908)

    Airdale College, Bradford.
    Congregational Minister 65;  "In business" 53;
       Journal Editor 74.
    Greenwich.
    [DNB, WWW]

    Natl Vigilance Assn (F) 85-85, Exec.


WAY, ROBERT E.

    Sunday Society (F) 75-75, Exec.


WAYMAN, THOMAS (1833-1901)

    Woolstapler 57.
    Liberal.  MP Elland, Yorks WR 85-99.  JP.
    Halifax.
    [WWW, Dods]

    Free Land League 86-86, V-Pres.


WEBB, SIR ASTON (1849-1930)

    Architect 73.
    Conservative.
    Kt 04;  CB 09;  CVO 11;  KCVO 14;  GCVO 25.
    Royal Academy;  Fellow Royal Inst Br Architects;
       Fellow Society of Antiquaries.
    Southwest London.
    [DNB, MEB]

    Natl Soc for Preserving Memorials of Dead 84-84,
       Exec.


WEBB, PHILIP SPEAKMAN (1831-1915)

    Architect.
    West Central London.
    [DNB]

    Soc for Protection of Ancient Buildings (F) 78-85,
       Exec.


WEBB, R.  D.

    Dublin.

    Jamaica Committee (F) 66-66.


WEBB, WILLIAM

    London.

    Jamaica Committee (F) 66-66.


WEBBER, WILLIAM THOMAS THORNHILL (1837-1903)

    Pembroke, Oxf.
    Bishop Brisbane 85;  Curate 60;  Ordained
       Priest<CE> 61;  Vicar 65.
    West Central London;  Brisbane.
    [WWW, Alum Oxon, Crockfds]

    Natl Assn for Promotion of State Colonization
       86-86, Exec, V-Pres.


WEBSTER, ALEXANDER RHIND (1816-1889)

    St Mary Hall, Oxf.
    Rector 63;  Curate 41;  Ordained Priest<CE> 42;
       Perp. Curate 43;  Rural Dean 49;  Diocesan
       Inspector of Schools 64.
    Chatham.
    [MEB, Alum Oxon, Crockfds]

    Assn for Promoting Extension of Contagious Diseases
       Act 68-70, V-Pres.


WEBSTER, JOHN (1810-1891)

    Marischal College;  U Aberdeen.
    Advocate 31.
    Liberal(Unionist).  MP Aberdeen 80-85.
    Br Assn.
    Aberdeen.
    [MEB, Dods, Direc Direcs]

    Victoria Street Soc for Protection of Animals from
       Vivisection 82-85, Exec.


WEBSTER, THOMAS (1810-1875)

    Charterhouse;  Trinity, Camb;  Lincoln's Inn.
    Q.C. 65;  Barrister 41.
    Fellow Royal Society;  Society of the Arts.
    West London.
    [DNB, MEB, Alum Cantab]

    Intl Law Assn (F) 73-74, Exec.


WEDDERBURN, SIR DAVID, 3RD BT.  (1835-1882)

    Trinity, Camb.
    Advocate 61.
    Liberal.  MP Ayrshire South 68-74, Haddington
       District 79-82.  JP.
    Baronet 62.
    Midlothian;  Gloucestershire.
    [MEB, BP, Walfords, Alum Cantab, Dods]

    Central Assn for Stopping Sale Intox Liquors on
       Sunday 75-80, V-Pres.


WEDGWOOD, FRANCIS (1800-1888)

    Rugby;  Peterhouse, Camb.
    Pottery Manufacturer.
    JP.
    Stoke-upon-Trent.
    [BP, Alum Cantab]

    Sunday Society 76-76, V-Pres.


WELDON, GEORGE WARBURTON (1825-1889)

    Trinity, Camb.
    Vicar 62;  Ordained Priest<CE> 51;  Curate 52;
       Author.
    Southwest London.
    [MEB, Alum Cantab, Crockfds]

    Church Assn 70-80, Exec.

WELLESLEY, LADY VICTORIA CATHERINE MARY
    POLE-TYLNEY-LONG- (1818-1897)

    Landowner 64.
    Sussex.
    [BP, Walfords]

    Natl Assn for Promotion of State Colonization
        86-86, V-Pres.


WELLS, -

    Chelmsford.

    Jamaica Committee (F) 66-66.


WELLS, JAMES

    Northampton.

    Jamaica Committee (F) 66-66.


WELLS, THOMAS

    West London.

    Soc for Protection of Ancient Buildings (F) 78-85,
        Exec.


WELLS, WILLIAM (1818-1889)

    Harrow; Balliol, Oxf.
    Large Landowner 26; Sub-Lt., Army 37; Farmer.
    Liberal. MP Beverley 52-57, Peterborough 68-74.
        DL, JP.
    Royal Agricultural Society.
    West London; Huntingdonshire; Kent.
    [DNB, MEB, Walfords, Bateman, Alum Oxon, Dods,
        Direc Direcs, Army List]

    Plimsoll and Seamen's Fund Committee (F) 73-73,
        Exec.
    Liberty & Property Defense League 84-84, Exec.


WENTNER, JOSEPH

    Clapton.

    Jamaica Committee (F) 66-66.


WEST, JAMES GRAHAM

    Croydon.

    Jamaica Committee (F) 66-66.


WEST, JOSEPH ROBERT ORR

    St. Bees.
    Rector 74; Curate 69; Ordained Priest<CE> 70;
        Vicar 70.
    Manchester.
    [Crockfds]

    Central Assn for Stopping Sale Intox Liquors on
        Sunday 75-75, Exec.


WEST, WILLIAM NOWELL

    Church Assn 67-85, Exec.


WESTGARTH, WILLIAM (1815-1889)

    Edinburgh High School.
    Australia Merchant; Colonial Speculator; Stock
        Broker.
    Radical.
    Southwest London.
    [DNB, MEB, Aust Dict Biog]

    Natl Assn for Promotion of State Colonization
        86-86, V-Pres, Exec.


WESTLAKE, JOHN (1828-1913)

    Lostwithiel School; Trinity, Camb; Lincoln's Inn.
    Q.C. 74; College Fellow 51; Barrister 54;
        Whewell Professor of International Law,
        Cambridge 88.
    Liberal(Unionist). MP Romford 85-86. Asst Charity
        Commissioner.
    Southwest London; Cornwall.
    [DNB, WWW, Alum Cantab, Fosters, Dods]

    Commons Preservation Soc 86-86, Exec.
    Sunday Society 76-90, V-Pres.
    Proportional Representation Soc (F) 84-88, Exec.


WESTROPP, SIR MICHAEL ROBERTS (1817-1890)

    Trin Col, Dublin.
    Chief Justice, Bombay 70; Barrister 40; Advocate
        General, Bombay 56; 63.
    Kt 70.
    Bombay.
    [MEB, BP, Walfords]

    Intl Law Assn 74-74, V-Pres.


WESTWOOD, JOHN OBADIAH (1805-1893)

    Hope Professor of Zoology, Oxford 61; Author.
    Fellow Linnean Society; Entomological Society.
    Oxford.
    [DNB, MEB, Alum Oxon]

    City Church & Churchyard Protection Soc (F) 80-83,
        V-Pres.


WHALLEY, GEORGE HAMMOND (1813-1878)

    University Col London; Gray's Inn.
    Barrister 39; Asst Tithe Commissioner 36;
        Substantial Landowner 41.
    Liberal. MP Peterborough 53-53, Peterborough
        59-78. DL, JP.
    Southwest London; Brighton; Denbighshire.
    [DNB, MEB, Walfords, Dods]

    Natl Emigration League (F) 70-70, V-Pres.

WHALLEY, GEORGE HAMMOND (1851- )

    Substantial Landowner 78;  Cadet, RN.
    Liberal.  MP Peterborough 80-83.  JP.
    West London;  Denbighshire.
    [Bateman, Dods]

    Land Law Reform League (F) 81-81, V-Pres.
    London Municipal Reform League 82-82, Exec.


WHEELER, ALEXANDER

    Darlington.

    London Soc for Abolition of Compulsory Vaccination
        81-81, V-Pres.


WHEELER, FREDERIC

    Rochester.

    Assn for Improvement of Public Morals (F) 79-81,
        Exec.


WHEELER, THOMAS WHITTENBURY (1839-1923)

    Westminster School;  Trinity Hall, Camb;  Inner
        Temple.
    Barrister 65;  Q.C.  86;  County Court Judge 05.
    Liberal(Unionist).  JP.
    Southwest London.
    [WWW, Alum Cantab, Fosters]

    Infant Life Protection Soc 71-71, Exec.


WHETSTONE, F.  J.

    Working Men's Comtee Promoting Separation Church
        and State (F) 71-71, Exec.


WHITBREAD, SAMUEL (1830-1915)

    Rugby;  Trinity, Camb.
    Very Large Landowner 79.
    Liberal.  MP Bedford 52-95.  Lord Admiralty 59-63,
        DL, JP.
    West London;  Bedfordshire.
    [Walfords, Bateman, Alum Cantab, Dods]

    Howard Assn 72-72, Patron.


WHITE, ALFRED CROMWELL

    Christ Church, Oxf;  Middle Temple.
    Barrister 75.
    Wandsworth.
    [Alum Oxon, Fosters, Direc Direcs]

    Proportional Representation Soc (F) 84-88, Exec.


WHITE, ARNOLD (1848-1925)

    Author.
    Farnham Common.
    [WWW]

    Natl Assn for Promotion of State Colonization
        86-86, Exec, V-Pres.


WHITE, EDWARD (1819-1898)

    Glasgow Theological Hall.
    Congregational Minister 41;  Journal Editor 59;
        Professor of Homiletics, New Col London 86.
    Northwest London.
    [MEB]

    Central Assn for Stopping Sale Intox Liquors on
        Sunday 85-85, V-Pres.


WHITE, F.  A.

    "Lloyds".
    London.

    Plimsoll and Seamen's Fund Committee (F) 73-73,
        Exec.


WHITE, F.  A.

    Northwest London.

    Soc for Protection of Ancient Buildings (F) 78-85,
        Exec.


WHITE, GEORGE

    London.

    Jamaica Committee (F) 66-66.


WHITE, HENRY (1836-1890)

    King's College School;  Worcester, Oxf.
    Chaplain 60;  Curate 58;  Ordained Priest<CE> 59.
    West Central London.
    [MEB, Alum Oxon, Crockfds]

    City Church & Churchyard Protection Soc (F) 80-83,
        V-Pres.


WHITE, JAMES (1809-1883)

    China Merchant.
    Liberal.  MP Plymouth 57-59, Brighton 60-74.
    London;  Brighton.
    [MEB, Walfords, Dods]

    Jamaica Committee (F) 66-66.

WHITE, VERNER M.

>   Clergyman<Sect Unkn>.
>   London; Liverpool.
>
>   Central Assn for Stopping Sale Intox Liquors on
>       Sunday 70-85, V-Pres.

WHITE, WILLIAM

>   London Soc for Abolition of Compulsory Vaccination
>       81-81, Exec.

WHITE, WILLIAM O.

>   Sunday Society 77-77, Exec.

WHITEHEAD, -

>   Bradford.
>
>   Jamaica Committee (F) 66-66.

WHITEHEAD, - <MISS>

>   Natl Vigilance Assn (F) 85-85, Exec.

WHITEHEAD, SIR JAMES, 1ST BT.  (1834-1917)

>   Merchant 60.
>   Liberal. MP Leicester 92-94.  DL, JP.
>   Baronet 89.
>   Fellow Society of Antiquaries;  Fellow Royal
>       Historical Society;  Fellow Royal Statistical
>       Society.
>   Northwest London;  Kent.
>   [WWW, BP, Dods, Direc Direcs]
>
>   Intl Arbitration & Peace Assn 81-81, V-Pres.

WHITELAW, ALEXANDER (1823-1879)

>   Iron Manufacturer.
>   Conservative. MP Glasgow 74-79.
>   Southwest London;  Glasgow;  Lanarkshire.
>   [MEB, Dods]
>
>   Natl Education Union 75-79, Exec.

WHITING, JOHN BRADFORD (1828-1914)

>   Gonville & Caius, Camb.
>   Vicar 61;  Curate 51;  Ordained Priest<CE> 52;
>       Assoc Sec, Church Missionary Society 56.
>   Ramsgate.
>   [Alum Cantab, Crockfds]
>
>   Church Assn 67-70, Exec.

WHITMORE, C.  J.

>   Clergyman<Sect Unkn>.
>
>   Public Museums & Free Libraries Assn 68-68, Exec.

WHITMORE, CHARLES ALGERNON (1851-1908)

>   Eton;  Balliol, Oxf;  Inner Temple.
>   Barrister 76;  College Fellow 74.
>   Conservative.  MP Chelsea 86-06.  Church Estates
>       Commissioner, JP.
>   Southwest London;  Gloucestershire.
>   [WWW, Alum Oxon, Fosters, Dods, Direc Direcs]
>
>   Kyrle Soc 84-90, Exec.

WHITTAKER, W.

>   London.
>
>   Jamaica Committee (F) 66-66.

WHITTINGTON, RICHARD (1825-1900)

>   St Paul's, London;  Trinity, Camb.
>   Rector 67;  Asst School Master 47;  Curate 48;
>       Ordained Priest<CE> 49;  College Head 61;
>       Prebendary 81;  Rural Dean 00.
>   West Central London.
>   [MEB, WWW, Alum Cantab, Alum Oxon, Crockfds, Direc
>       Direcs]
>
>   City Church & Churchyard Protection Soc 83-83,
>       Exec.

WHITTLE, JAMES LOWRY (1840- )

>   Trin Col, Dublin;  Inner Temple.
>   Registrar in Lunacy 80;  Asst Clerk, Great Seal
>       Patent Office 83;  Asst Registrar, Patent
>       Office 76.
>   London.
>   [Fosters]
>
>   Smoke Abatement Committee 81-81, Exec.

WHITWELL, EDWARD

>   Central Assn for Stopping Sale Intox Liquors on
>       Sunday (F) 67-85, Hon Sec.

WHITWELL, JOHN (1812-1880)

>   Manufacturer.
>   Liberal. MP Kendal 68-80.  JP.
>   Southwest London;  Kendal.
>   [MEB, Walfords, Dods]
>
>   Howard Assn 72-80, Patron.

WHITWORTH, BENJAMIN (1816-1893)

    Cotton Merchant 38;  Cotton Manufacturer.
    Liberal.  MP Drogheda 65-69, Kilkenny City 75-80,
       Drogheda 80-85.  JP.
    West London;  Manchester;  Drogheda.
    [MEB, Walfords, Dods, Direc Direcs]

    Sunday Society 79-90, V-Pres.
    Central Assn for Stopping Sale Intox Liquors on
       Sunday (F) 67-85, V-Pres.
    Howard Assn 78-84, Patron.

WHITWORTH, ROBERT

    Cotton Manufacturer.
    Manchester.
    [Direc Direcs]

    Jamaica Committee (F) 66-66.
    Central Assn for Stopping Sale Intox Liquors on
       Sunday (F) 67-85, Hon Sec.

WHITWORTH, THOMAS (1844- )

    Cotton Merchant.
    Liberal.  MP Drogheda 69-74.
    Manchester;  Lancashire.
    [Dods]

    Central Assn for Stopping Sale Intox Liquors on
       Sunday 70-85, V-Pres.

WIBLIN, JOHN (1814-1900)

    University Col London;  Paris(Medical).
    Physician;  Sanitary Surveyor, Board of Trade 37.
    Fellow Royal Col Surgeons.
    Southampton.
    [MEB]

    Assn for Promoting Extension of Contagious Diseases
       Act 68-68, V-Pres.

WIGGIN, SIR HENRY, 1ST BT.  (1824-1905)

    Nickel and Cobalt Refiner.
    Liberal(Unionist).  MP Staffordshire East 80-85,
       Handsworth, Staffs 85-93.  DL, JP.
    Baronet 92.
    Birmingham;  Staffordshire.
    [WWW, BP, Dods, Direc Direcs]

    Natl Education League (F) 69-69, Exec.

WIGHAM, JANE <MISS>

    Edinburgh.

    Ladies' Natl Assn for Repeal of Contagious Diseases
       Acts 70-72, Exec.

WIGHTMAN, CHARLES EDWARD LEOPOLD (1816-1896)

    Lincoln, Oxf.
    Vicar 41;  Curate 39;  Ordained Priest<CE> 40;
       Prebendary 92.
    Shrewsbury.
    [MEB, Alum Oxon, Crockfds]

    Church Assn 70-70, Exec.

WIGLESWORTH, PARKIN

    Boston.

    Jamaica Committee (F) 66-66.

WILBERFORCE, ALBERT BASIL ORME (1841-1916)

    Eton;  Exeter, Oxf.
    Rector 71;  Curate 66;  Ordained Priest<CE> 67;
       Hon. Canon 76;  Dean;  Archdeacon 00.
    Southampton.
    [WWW, Alum Oxon, Crockfds]

    Assn for Improvement of Public Morals (F) 79-81,
       Exec.

WILBERFORCE, ERNEST ROLAND (1840-1907)

    Harrow;  Exeter, Oxf.
    Bishop Newcastle 82;  Curate 64;  Ordained
       Priest<CE> 65;  Rector 66;  Vicar 73;  Canon
       78;  Bishop Chichester 95.
    Liberal(Unionist).
    Newcastle-upon-Tyne.
    [DNB, WWW, Alum Oxon, Crockfds]

    Natl Assn for Promotion of State Colonization
       86-86, Patron.
    Anglo-Oriental Soc for Suppression Opium Trade
       83-83, V-Pres.
    Central Assn for Stopping Sale Intox Liquors on
       Sunday 85-85, V-Pres.

WILBERFORCE, HENRY WILLIAM (1807-1873)

    Oriel, Oxf;  Lincoln's Inn.
    Journalist;  Author;  Perp. Curate 34;  Vicar 41.
    Worcestershire.
    [DNB, MEB, Alum Oxon]

    Jamaica Committee (F) 66-66.

WILBRAHAM, EDWARD BOOTLE-, 1ST EARL OF LATHOM
(1837-1898)

    Eton;  Christ Church, Oxf.
    Very Large Landowner 53.
    Conservative.  Lord in Waiting 66-68, Chamberlain
       Royal Household 85-86, Chamberlain Royal
       Household 86-92, Chamberlain Royal Household
       95-98, DL, JP.
    Baron 53;  PC 74;  Earl 80;  GCB 92.
    West London;  Lancashire.
    [MEB, WWW, BP, Bateman, Alum Oxon, Dods, Direc
       Direcs]

    City Church & Churchyard Protection Soc (F) 80-83,
       V-Pres.

WILDE, JAMES PLAISTED, 1ST BARON PENZANCE (1816-1899)

>Winchester College; Trinity, Camb; Inner Temple.
>Judge, Provincial Courts of Canterbury and York 75;
>    Barrister 39; Q.C. 55; Counsel to Duchy of
>    Lancaster 59; Baron, Exchequer 60; Judge,
>    Probate and Divorce Court 63.
>Liberal.
>Kt 60; PC 64; Baron 69.
>West London; Surrey.
>[DNB, MEB, WWW, BP, Walfords, Alum Cantab, Fosters]

>Liberty & Property Defense League (F) 82-84, Exec.

WILDES, J. ST. S.

>Surgeon.
>Member Royal Col Surgeons.
>Birmingham.

>Assn for Promoting Extension of Contagious Diseases
>    Act 68-68, Exec.

WILKINS, W.  C.

>"A working man".

>Assn of Revivers of British Industry (F) 69-69,
>    Secretary.

WILKINSON, F.  R.  <MISS>

>Kyrle Soc 84-94, Exec.

WILKINSON, GEORGE HOWARD (1833-1907)

>Oriel, Oxf.
>Bishop Truro 83; Curate 57; Ordained Priest<CE>
>    58; Perp. Curate 59; Vicar 70; Hon. Canon
>    78.
>West London; Truro.
>[DNB, WWW, Alum Oxon, Crockfds]

>Natl Assn for Promotion of State Colonization
>    86-86, Patron.
>Soc for Protection of Ancient Buildings 83-84,
>    Patron.

WILKINSON, JAMES JOHN GARTH (1812-1899)

>Homeopathic Doctor 37; Author.
>Member Royal Col Surgeons.
>West London.
>[DNB, MEB]

>London Soc for Abolition of Compulsory Vaccination
>    81-81, V-Pres.

WILKINSON, N.  M.

>London.

>Jamaica Committee (F) 66-66.

WILKINSON, R.

>North London.

>Jamaica Committee (F) 66-66.

WILKINSON, WILLIAM (1816- )

>Trin Col, Dublin.
>Rector 66; Curate 40; Ordained Priest<CE> 41;
>    Perp. Curate 51; Hon. Canon 71; Rural Dean
>    74.
>Birmingham.
>[Alum Cantab, Crockfds]

>Central Assn for Stopping Sale Intox Liquors on
>    Sunday 70-85, V-Pres.
>Church Assn 70-78, Exec.

WILKS, JOHN MARK (1830-1894)

>New College, Hampstead.
>Congregational Minister 58.
>North London.
>[MEB]

>Sunday Society 76-90, V-Pres.
>Jamaica Committee (F) 66-66.

WILKS, SIR SAMUEL, 1ST BT.  (1824-1911)

>Univ College School; Guy's Hospital, Lond.
>Physician 50.
>Baronet 97.
>Fellow Royal Society; Fellow Royal Col Physicians;
>    Pathological Society; Member Royal Col
>    Surgeons.
>West London.
>[DNB, BP]

>Assn for Promoting Extension of Contagious Diseases
>    Act 68-70, V-Pres.

WILL, JOHN SHIRESS (1840-1910)

>Kings Col London; Middle Temple.
>Q.C. 83; Barrister 64; County Court Judge 06.
>Liberal. MP Montrose 85-96.
>Southwest London; Angus.
>[DNB, WWW, Fosters, Dods]

>Free Land League 86-86, V-Pres.

WILLIAMS, CHARLES

>Baptist Minister.
>Southampton.

>Central Assn for Stopping Sale Intox Liquors on
>    Sunday 85-85, V-Pres.
>Jamaica Committee (F) 66-66.

WILLIAMS, CHARLES WILLIAM <ALSO WILLIAM CHARLES
    WILLIAMS> (1820-1889)

>    Trinity, Camb.
>    Rector 66;  Ordained Priest<CE> 46;  School Head
>        57.
>    Fellow Royal Astronomical Society.
>    Northwest London.
>    [Alum Cantab, Crockfds]
>
>    Patrons Defense Assn (F) 76-76, Hon Sec, Treas.

WILLIAMS, H.  M.

>    Lincolns Inn.
>
>    Jamaica Committee (F) 66-66.

WILLIAMS, J.

>    Clergyman<Sect Unkn>.
>
>    Assn for Improvement of London Workhouse
>        Infirmaries 66-66, Exec.

WILLIAMS, JOHN

>    Grays Inn.
>
>    Jamaica Committee (F) 66-66.

WILLIAMS, JOSHUA (1813-1881)

>    University Col London;  Lincoln's Inn.
>    Q.C.  65;  Barrister 38;  Author.
>    West London.
>    [DNB, MEB]
>
>    Intl Law Assn 74-74, Exec.

WILLIAMS, MORGAN B.

>    Banker.
>    JP.
>    Swansea.
>    [Direc Direcs]
>
>    Intl Arbitration & Peace Assn 81-81, V-Pres.

WILLIAMS, OWEN LEWIS COPE (1836-1904)

>    Eton.
>    Lt.  Colonel 66;  Lieutenant, Army 56;  Captain,
>        Army 58;  Colonel 71;  Maj. General 82;  Lt.
>        General 86;  Very Large Landowner 75.
>    Conservative.  MP Marlow 80-85.  JP.
>    West London;  Anglesey;  Buckinghamshire.
>    [WWW, Bateman, Dods, Army List]
>
>    Assn for Promoting Extension of Contagious Diseases
>        Act 68-70, V-Pres.

WILLIAMS, R.

>    London.
>
>    Natl Education League 71-71, Exec.

WILLIAMS, S.  D.

>    London.
>
>    Jamaica Committee (F) 66-66.

WILLIAMS, T.  A.  <MRS.>

>    Kyrle Soc 85-90, Exec.

WILLIAMSON, J.  W.

>    Church Assn 78-85, Exec.

WILLIAMSON, JAMES, 1ST BARON ASHTON (1842-1930)

>    Manufacturer.
>    Liberal.  MP Lancaster, Lancs N 86-95.  DL, JP.
>    Baron 95.
>    Southwest London;  Lancaster;  Lancashire.
>    [WWW, BP, Dods]
>
>    Free Land League 86-86, V-Pres.

WILLIS, THOMAS

>    Clergyman<Sect Unkn>.
>
>    Central Assn for Stopping Sale Intox Liquors on
>        Sunday 70-75, Exec.

WILLS, WILLIAM HENRY (1810-1880)

>    Journal Editor.
>    JP.
>    London;  Welwyn.
>    [DNB, MEB]
>
>    Jamaica Committee (F) 66-66.

WILLS, WILLIAM HENRY, 1ST BARON WINTERSTOKE (1830-1911)

>    Mill Hill School;  University Col London.
>    Tobacco Manufacturer.
>    Liberal.  MP Coventry 80-85, Bristol East 95-00.
>        DL, JP.
>    Baronet 93;  Baron 06.
>    Fellow Royal Geograph Society.
>    West London;  Somersetshire.
>    [DNB, WWW, BP, Dods]
>
>    Free Land League 86-86, V-Pres.

WILLSON, T.  J.

>    West Central London.
>
>    Soc for Protection of Ancient Buildings 80-85,
>       Exec.

WILMOT, EDWARD REVELL EARDLEY- (1812-1899)

>    Trinity Hall, Camb.
>    Rector 55;  Cadet, Army 29;  Lieutenant, Army 35;
>       Ordained Priest<CE> 41;  Vicar 45.
>    London.
>    [MEB, BP, Crockfds]
>
>    Church Assn 67-70, Exec.

WILMOT, SIR JOHN EARDLEY EARDLEY-, 2ND BT.  (1810-1892)

>    Winchester College;  Balliol, Oxf;  Lincoln's Inn.
>    County Court Judge 54;  Barrister 42.
>    Conservative.  MP Warwickshire South 74-85.  DL,
>       JP.
>    Baronet 47.
>    West London;  Warwickshire.
>    [DNB, MEB, BP, Walfords, Alum Oxon, Fosters, Dods,
>       Direc Direcs]
>
>    Howard Assn 75-84, Patron.
>    Natl Education Union 70-70, Exec.
>    Victoria Street Soc for Protection of Animals from
>       Vivisection 80-85, Exec.
>    Natl Fair Trade League (F) 81-81, President.

WILSHAW, WILLIAM

>    Methodist New Connection Minister.
>
>    Central Assn for Stopping Sale Intox Liquors on
>       Sunday 75-75, V-Pres.

WILSON, CHARLES HENRY, 1ST BARON NUNBURNHOLME
    (1833-1907)

>    Shipowner;  Merchant;  Large Landowner.
>    Liberal.  MP Hull 74-85, Hull West 85-05.  DL, JP.
>    Baron 05.
>    West London;  Kingston-upon-Hull.
>    [DNB, WWW, BP, Bateman, Dods]
>
>    Central Assn for Stopping Sale Intox Liquors on
>       Sunday 75-85, V-Pres.

WILSON, DANIEL (1805-1886)

>    Wadham, Oxf.
>    Vicar 32;  Ordained Priest<CE> 29;  Rector 29;
>       Rural Dean 60;  Prebendary 72.
>    North London.
>    [MEB, Alum Oxon, Crockfds]
>
>    Church Assn 67-78, Exec.

WILSON, EDWARD (1813-1878)

>    Newspaper Proprietor 48;  Landowner.
>    Radical.
>    Kent;  Melbourne.
>    [DNB, MEB, Aust Dict Biog]
>
>    Natl Emigration League (F) 70-70, V-Pres.

WILSON, GEORGE

>    Physician.
>    Leamington.
>
>    Sanitary Institute 79-84, Exec.

WILSON, HENRY JOSEPH (1833-1914)

>    University Col London.
>    Smelting Works Owner.
>    Liberal.  MP Holmfirth,Yorks WR S 85-12.  JP.
>    Sheffield.
>    [WWW, Dods]
>
>    London Comtee Exposure & Suppresn Traffic In Girls
>       (F) 80-80, Exec.

WILSON, HENRY WILLIAM, 11TH BARON BERNERS (1797-1871)

>    Eton;  Emmanuel, Camb.
>    Landowner 51;  Sheep Breeder.
>    Conservative.  DL, JP.
>    Baron 51.
>    Royal Agricultural Society.
>    Leicestershire;  Norfolk.
>    [MEB, BP, Walfords, Alum Cantab]
>
>    Church Assn 67-70, V-Pres.

WILSON, ISAAC (1822-1899)

>    Iron Manufacturer;  Earthenware Manufacturer.
>    Liberal.  MP Middlesborough 78-92.  DL, JP.
>    Middlesborough;  Yorks, North Riding.
>    [MEB, Dods, Direc Direcs]
>
>    Intl Arbitration & Peace Assn 81-81, V-Pres.

WILSON, JOHN (1837-1915)

>    Treasurer, Durham Miners' Association 82;  Miner
>       47;  Labour Leader.
>    Radical.  MP Houghton-le-Spring, Durham 85-86,
>       Durham Co Mid 90-15.
>    Southwest London;  Durham[City].
>    [WWW, Dods, Dic Lab Biog]
>
>    English Land Restoration League 85-85, Exec.

WILSON, JOHN (1812-1888)

>    University Col London.
>    Professor of Agriculture and Rural Economy,
>       Edinburgh 54;  College Head 46.
>    Fellow Royal Society Edinb.
>    Edinburgh.
>    [DNB, MEB]
>
>    Natl Assn for Promotion of State Colonization
>       86-86, V-Pres.

WILSON, JOSEPH EDWARD MAITLAND

> Captain, RN 72; Lieutenant, RN 55; Commander, RN
>     65.
> [Navy List]
>
> Plimsoll and Seamen's Fund Committee (F) 73-73,
>     Exec.


WILSON, LUCY <MISS>

> Central Vigilance Comtee for Repression Immorality
>     83-83, Exec.


WILSON, SIR SAMUEL (1832-1895)

> Australian Landowner; Sheep Farmer; Politician.
> Conservative. MP Portsmouth 86-92. DL.
> Kt 75.
> Fellow Royal Geograph Society; Fellow Linnean
>     Society.
> West London; Buckinghamshire; Victoria.
> [MEB, BP, Dods, Aust Dict Biog]
>
> Imperial Federation League (F) 84-84, Exec.


WILSON, SIR WILLIAM JAMES ERASMUS (1809-1884)

> St Bartholomew's Hosp.
> Surgeon 31; Medical School Lecturer 40; Medical
>     School Professor 69.
> Kt 81.
> Fellow Royal Society; Fellow Royal Col Surgeons.
> West Central London.
> [DNB, MEB, BP]
>
> Assn for Promoting Extension of Contagious Diseases
>     Act 68-70, V-Pres.


WINDER, F. A.

> Land Nationalization Soc 83-85, Exec.


WINDUST, C. A.

> Land Nationalization Soc 84-85, Exec.


WINGFIELD, MERVYN EDWARD, 7TH VISCOUNT POWERSCOURT
    (1836-1904)

> Eton.
> Very Large Landowner 44; Sub-Lt., Army 54;
>     Lieutenant, Army 56.
> Liberal(Unionist). DL, JP.
> Viscount 44; Baron 85; KP; PC.
> Member Royal Irish Academy.
> West London; Co Wicklow.
> [WWW, BP, Walfords, Bateman, Army List]
>
> Sunday Society 80-90, V-Pres, President.


WINKS, A. F.

> Land Nationalization Soc 83-84, Exec.


WINKWORTH, STEPHEN

> Manchester; Bolton.
>
> Commons Preservation Soc 83-85, Exec.
> Jamaica Committee (F) 66-66.
> Natl Education League 71-71, Exec.


WINN, ROWLAND, 1ST BARON ST. OSWALD (1820-1893)

> Trinity, Camb.
> Large Landowner 74.
> Conservative. MP Lincolnshire North 68-85. Junior
>     Lord Treasury 74-80, DL, JP.
> Baron 85.
> West London; Lincolnshire; Yorks, West Riding.
> [BP, Bateman, Alum Cantab, Dods]
>
> Local Taxation Comtee [of Central Chamber of
>     Agriculture] 71-82, Exec.


WINTERBOTHAM, ARTHUR BREND (1838-1892)

> Woolen Manufacturer.
> Liberal. MP Cirencester 85-92. JP.
> Dursley.
> [MEB, Dods]
>
> Free Land League 86-86, V-Pres.


WINTERBOTHAM, L.

> Cheltenham.
>
> Assn for Promoting Extension of Contagious Diseases
>     Act 68-68, Exec.


WITHINGTON, J. S.

> Methodist Free Church Minister.
>
> Central Assn for Stopping Sale Intox Liquors on
>     Sunday 75-75, V-Pres.


WOAKES, EDWARD

> Surgeon.
> West London.
>
> Malthusian League 80-84, V-Pres.


WOLFF, SIR HENRY DRUMMOND CHARLES (1830-1908)

> Rugby.
> Politician; Clerk, FO 46; Diplomatic Service 52;
>     Ambassador 87.
> Conservative. MP Christchurch 74-80, Portsmouth
>     80-85.
> CMG 59; KCMG 62; GCMG 78; KCB 79; PC 85; GCB
>     89.
> Southwest London; Bournemouth.
> [DNB, WWW, BP, Walfords, Dods]

Natl Emigration League (F) 70-70, V-Pres.

WOLSELEY, GARNET JOSEPH, 1ST VISCOUNT WOLSELEY
     (1833-1913)

     General 82;  Cornet, Army 52;  Captain, Army 55;
          Lt. Colonel 59;  Colonel 65;  Lt. General 78;
          Field Marshal 94.
     Liberal(Unionist).
     CB 70;  KCMG 70;  KCB 74;  GCMG 74;  GCB 80;  Baron
          84;  Viscount 85.
     Surrey.
     [DNB, WWW, BP, Walfords, Alum Cantab, Alum Oxon,
          Army List]

     Natl Assn for Promotion of State Colonization
          86-86, Patron.

WOLSTENCROFT, THOMAS

     St. Bees.
     Rector 66;  Curate 51;  Ordained Priest<CE> 52.
     Lancashire.
     [Crockfds]

     Central Assn for Stopping Sale Intox Liquors on
          Sunday 75-75, Exec.

WOLSTENHOLME, ELIZABETH C.

     Vigilance Assn for Defense of Personal Rights (F)
          71-71, Exec.
     Ladies' Natl Assn for Repeal of Contagious Diseases
          Acts 70-72, Exec.

WOOD, ALEXANDER (1817-1884)

     Edinburgh Academy;  Edinburgh(Medical).
     Physician 39;  Journal Editor.
     Fellow Royal Col Physicians, Edinb.
     Edinburgh.
     [DNB, MEB]

     Assn for Promoting Extension of Contagious Diseases
          Act 68-70, V-Pres.

WOOD, ANDREW (1810-1881)

     Edinburgh(Medical).
     Surgeon 31;  Anatomy Inspector, Scotland;  Author.
     Fellow Royal Society Edinb;  Fellow Royal Col
          Surgeons, Edinb.
     Edinburgh.
     [MEB, Alum Cantab]

     Assn for Promoting Extension of Contagious Diseases
          Act 68-70, V-Pres.

WOOD, JOHN DENNISTOUN (1829-1914)

     Edinburgh Academy;  U Edinburgh;  Middle Temple.
     Barrister 52;  Australian Landowner;  Solicitor
          General, Victoria 57;  Attorney General,
          Victoria 59;  Minister of Justice, Victoria 61.
     West London.
     [Fosters, Aust Dict Biog]

     Sunday Society (F) 75-75, V-Pres.

Imperial Federation League (F) 84-86, Treas.

WOOD, R. H.

     Fellow Society of Antiquaries.

     Natl Soc for Preserving Memorials of Dead 68-68,
          Exec.

WOOD, RICHARD (1811-1880)

     St Johns, Oxf.
     Vicar 55;  College Fellow 28;  Ordained Priest<CE>
          34;  Rector 79.
     West London.
     [Alum Oxon, Crockfds]

     Infant Life Protection Soc 71-71, Exec.

WOOD, RICHARD

     Heywood, Lancs.

     Church Assn 78-78, Exec.

WOOD, ROBERT

     Clergyman<Sect Unkn>.
     West Central London.

     Infant Life Protection Soc 71-71, Exec.

WOOD, W. MARTIN

     West London.
     [Direc Direcs]

     Indian Reform Assn 84-84, Exec.
     Intl Arbitration & Peace Assn 81-81, Exec.

WOOD, WILLIAM PAGE, 1ST BARON HATHERLEY (1801-1881)

     Winchester College;  Trinity, Camb;  Lincoln's Inn.
     Barrister 27;  Q.C. 45;  Judge, Court of Appeal
          68.
     Liberal.  MP Oxford 47-53.  V-Chanc Duchy Lancaster
          49-51, Solicitor General 51-53, V-Chanc Duchy
          Lancaster 53-68, Lord High Chancellor 68-72.
     Kt 51;  PC 68;  Baron 68.
     Fellow Royal Society.
     Southwest London.
     [DNB, MEB, BP, Walfords, Alum Oxon, Dods]

     Soc for Promoting Increase of the Home Episcopate
          74-74, V-Pres.

WOODALL, WILLIAM (1832-1901)

     Earthenware Manufacturer.
     Liberal.  MP Stoke-on-Trent 80-85, Hanley 85-00.
          Surveyor General Ordnance 86-86, Fin Sec War
          Office 92-95, JP.
     Southwest London;  Burslem.
     [DNB, WWW, Dods, Direc Direcs]

     Intl Arbitration & Peace Assn 81-81, V-Pres.

WOODFORD, JAMES RUSSELL (1820-1885)

    Merchant Taylors;  Pembroke, Camb.
    Bishop Ely 73;  Curate 43;  Ordained Priest<CE> 45;
        Vicar 45;  Hon. Canon 66.
    Ely.
    [DNB, MEB, Alum Cantab, Crockfds]

    Natl Soc for Preserving Memorials of Dead (F)
        81-84, Patron.


WOODROOFE, THOMAS <ALSO WOODROOFFE AND WOODROFFE>
(1789-1878)

    Merchant Taylors;  St Johns, Oxf.
    Canon 45;  Professor of Classics, Sandhurst 14;
        Ordained Priest<CE>;  Perp. Curate 30;  Rector
        31;  Vicar 54;  Rector 62.
    Godalming.
    [MEB, Alum Oxon, Crockfds]

    Natl Education Union 71-78, Exec.


WOODS, SIR ALBERT WILLIAM (1816-1904)

    Heraldist 38.
    KCMG 90;  KCB 97;  GCVO 03.
    Fellow Society of Antiquaries.
    Southwest London.
    [DNB, WWW, BP, Walfords]

    Natl Soc for Preserving Memorials of Dead 84-84,
        Patron.


WOOLACOTT, JOHN EVANS (1862-1936)

    Journalist.
    [WWW]

    English Land Restoration League 85-85, Exec.


WOOLLCOMBE, HENRY <ALSO WOOLCOMBE> (1813-1885)

    Westminster School;  Christ Church, Oxf;  Lincoln's
        Inn.
    Archdeacon 65;  Curate 38;  Ordained Priest<CE> 39;
        Prebendary 43;  Vicar 44;  Canon 61;  Large
        Landowner 66.
    Barnstaple;  Ashbury.
    [MEB, Walfords, Bateman, Alum Oxon, Crockfds]

    Central Assn for Stopping Sale Intox Liquors on
        Sunday 80-80, V-Pres.


WOOLLCOMBE, THOMAS (1800-1876)

    Solicitor 23.
    Devonport.
    [MEB]

    Assn for Promoting Extension of Contagious Diseases
        Act 68-75, Exec, V-Pres.


WOOLLEY, GEORGE B.

    London.

    Jamaica Committee (F) 66-66.


WOOLNER, THOMAS (1825-1892)

    Ipswich Grammar School;  Royal Academy Sch.
    Sculptor;  Poet.
    Royal Academy.
    West London.
    [DNB, MEB, Aust Dict Biog]

    Sunday Society 78-90, V-Pres.


WORBY, JOSHUA

    Sunday Society 76-76, Exec.


WORDSWORTH, CHRISTOPHER (1807-1885)

    Winchester College;  Trinity, Camb.
    Bishop Lincoln 69;  College Fellow 30;  Ordained
        Priest<CE> 35;  School Head 36;  Canon 44;
        Vicar 50;  Archdeacon 65.
    Lincoln.
    [DNB, MEB, Alum Cantab, Alum Oxon, Crockfds]

    Central Assn for Stopping Sale Intox Liquors on
        Sunday 70-80, V-Pres.
    Soc for Promoting Increase of the Home Episcopate
        72-74, V-Pres.


WORLEY, W. C.

    Workmen's Peace Assn 75-78, Chairman, Hon Sec.


WORSFOLD, JOHN NAPPER

    St. Bees.
    Vicar 68;  Curate 53;  Ordained Priest<CE> 54;
        Vicar 59;  Perp. Curate 60;  Rector 74.
    North London;  Staffordshire.
    [Crockfds]

    Church Assn 70-70, Exec.


WORTLEY, ARCHIBALD HENRY PLANTAGENET STUART- (1832-1890)

    Lt. Colonel 62;  Lieutenant, Army 48;  Captain,
        Army 52;  Major 54;  Curator, Patent Office
        Museum.
    Conservative.  MP Honiton 57-59.
    Southwest London.
    [BP, Walfords, Dods, Army List]

    Smoke Abatement Committee 81-81.
    Soc for Protection of Ancient Buildings (F) 78-85,
        Exec.

WORTLEY, CHARLES BEILBY STUART-, 1ST BARON STUART OF
    WORTLEY (1851-1926)

    Rugby;  Balliol, Oxf;  Inner Temple.
    Barrister 76;  Q.C. 92.
    Conservative.  MP Sheffield 80-85, Sheffield Hallam
        85-16.  Parl U-Sec Home Off 85-86, Parl U-Sec
        Home Off 86-92, Church Estates Commissioner
        95- , Ecclesiastical Commissioner 95- .
    PC 96;  Baron 17.
    Southwest London.
    [WWW, BP, Alum Oxon, Fosters, Dods, Direc Direcs]

    Proportional Representation Soc (F) 84-88, Exec.


WREN, WALTER (1834-1898)

    Christ's, Camb.
    Private Tutor 67.
    Radical.  MP Wallingford 80-80.
    Fellow Royal Statistical Society;  Fellow Royal
        Historical Society.
    West London.
    [MEB, WWW, Alum Cantab, Dods]

    Intl Arbitration & Peace Assn 81-81, V-Pres, Exec.
    Land Nationalization Soc (F) 81-81, Exec.


WRIGHT, CALEB (1810-1898)

    Cotton Manufacturer 45;  Textile Worker 19.
    Liberal.  MP Leigh, Lancs SW 85-95.  JP.
    Southwest London;  Lancashire.
    [MEB, Dods]

    Free Land League 86-86, V-Pres.


WRIGHT, FRANCIS

    Church Assn 70-70, V-Pres.


WRIGHT, HENRY

    London.

    City Church & Churchyard Protection Soc (F) 80-83,
        Hon Sec.
    Natl Soc for Preserving Memorials of Dead (F)
        81-82, Exec.


WRIGHT, JOHN SKIRROW (1822-1880)

    Button Manufacturer;  Merchant.
    Liberal.  MP Nottingham 80-80.  JP.
    Birmingham.
    [MEB, Dods]

    Central Assn for Stopping Sale Intox Liquors on
        Sunday 75-75, V-Pres.
    Natl Education League (F) 69-71, Exec.


WRIGHT, JOSEPH COLEMAN HORNSBY (1831-1897)

    Surgeon, Army Medical Serv 62;  Asst Surgeon, Army
        Medical Serv 52;  Surgeon Major, Army Medical
        School 72;  Deputy Surgeon General, Army
        Medical Serv 80.
    Member Royal Col Surgeons.
    Northwest London.
    [MEB, Army List]

    Church Assn 70-80, Exec.


WRIGHT, THEODORE

    Travelling Tax Abolition Committee 80-85, Exec.


WRIGHT, WILLIAM ALDIS (1831-1914)

    Trinity, Camb.
    Philologist;  School Teacher 55;  Librarian 63;
        Journal Editor 68;  College Fellow 78.
    Cambridge.
    [DNB, WWW, Alum Cantab, Alum Oxon]

    Soc for Protection of Ancient Buildings (F) 78-85,
        Exec.


WYATT, JOHN (1825-1874)

    Surgeon Major, Army Medical School 63;  Asst
        Surgeon, Army Medical Serv 51;  Surgeon, Army
        Medical Serv 57.
    CB 73.
    Fellow Royal Col Surgeons.
    Southwest London.
    [DNB, MEB, Army List]

    Assn for Promoting Extension of Contagious Diseases
        Act 68-70, V-Pres.


WYLD, GEORGE

    Edinburgh(Medical).
    Physician 51.
    Southwest London.
    [Direc Direcs]

    Smoke Abatement Committee 81-81.


WYLIE, ALEXANDER (1815-1887)

    Shanghai Press Superintendent, London Missionary
        Society 47.
    Northwest London.
    [DNB, MEB]

    Anglo-Oriental Soc for Suppression Opium Trade
        79-79, Exec.


WYNDHAM, GEORGE, 1ST BARON LECONFIELD (1787-1869)

    Very Large Landowner 37;  Cornet, Army 03;
        Captain, Army 05;  Major 11.
    Baron 59.
    Sussex.
    [MEB, BP, Army List]

    Church Assn 67-67, V-Pres.

WYNDHAM, PERCY SCAWEN (1835-1911)

    Eton.
    Substantial Landowner 60;  Lieutenant, Army;
       Captain, Army.
    Conservative.  MP Cumberland West 60-85.  DL, JP.
    Southwest London;  Wiltshire.
    [WWW, BP, Walfords, Bateman, Dods]

    City Church & Churchyard Protection Soc 81-83,
       V-Pres.
    Soc for Protection of Ancient Buildings (F) 78-85,
       Exec.
    Assn for Promoting Extension of Contagious Diseases
       Act 68-70, V-Pres.

YATES, HOLT <DR.>

    Church Assn 67-67, Exec.

YATES, JAMES (1789-1871)

    U Glasgow;  Manchester College, York.
    Antiquary;  Unitarian Minister 12.
    Fellow Royal Society;  Br Assn;  Fellow Geological
       Society;  Fellow Linnean Society;  Philological
       Society.
    North London.
    [DNB, MEB]

    Jamaica Committee (F) 66-66.

YEAMES, WILLIAM FREDERICK (1835-1918)

    Artist 60.
    Royal Academy.
    Devonshire.
    [WWW]

    Sunday Society 86-90, V-Pres.

YEO, FRANK ASH (1832-1888)

    Colliery Owner.
    Liberal.  MP Glamorganshire 85-88.  JP.
    Glamorganshire.
    [MEB, Dods]

    Intl Arbitration & Peace Assn 81-81, V-Pres.

YORKE, HARRIOT <MISS>

    "Private Means".
    West London;  Kent.

    Smoke Abatement Committee 81-81.
    Kyrle Soc 84-90, Exec.

YORKE, JOHN REGINALD (1836-1912)

    Eton;  Balliol, Oxf.
    Landowner.
    Conservative.  MP Tewkesbury 64-68, Gloucestershire
       East 72-85, Tewkesbury 85-86.  DL, JP.
    Fellow Royal Geograph Society.
    West London;  Gloucestershire.
    [WWW, Alum Oxon, Dods]

    Local Taxation Comtee [of Central Chamber of
       Agriculture] 75-85, Exec.

YOUNG, -

    Malthusian League (F) 77-79, Exec.

YOUNG, B.  C.

    Staffordshire.

    Jamaica Committee (F) 66-66.

YOUNG, SIR FREDERICK (1817-1913)

    Merchant.
    DL, JP.
    KCMG 88.
    Southwest London.
    [WWW, Direc Direcs]

    Natl Assn for Promotion of State Colonization
       86-86, V-Pres.
    Imperial Federation League (F) 84-84, V-Chairman.
    Natl Emigration League (F) 70-70, Chairman.
    Natl Fair Trade League (F) 81-81, Exec.

YOUNG, GEORGE H.

    Sunday Society (F) 75-75, Exec.

YOUNG, WILLIAM

    Southwest London.

    London Soc for Abolition of Compulsory Vaccination
       81-81, Secretary.

ZINCKE, FOSTER BARHAM (1817-1893)

    Bedford Grammar;  Wadham, Oxf.
    Vicar 47;  Curate 40;  Ordained Priest<CE> 41.
    Radical.
    Wherstead.
    [DNB, MEB, Alum Oxon, Crockfds]

    Natl Education League 71-71, Exec.

# A P P E N D I X

Allotments & Small Holdings Assn

ALBRIGHT, ARTHUR
ARCH, JOSEPH
BRUNNER, SIR JOHN TOMLINSON, 1ST BT.
CARRINGTON, CHARLES ROBERT WYNN-, 1ST MARQUIS OF
   LINCOLNSHIRE
CARTER, E. HAROLD
CHAMBERLAIN, JOSEPH
CLARKE, PERCY
COLLINGS, JESSE
COMPTON, WILLIAM GEORGE SPENCER SCOTT, 5TH MARQUIS
   NORTHAMPTON
DILKE, SIR CHARLES WENTWORTH, 2ND BT.
FOSTER, BALTHAZAR WALTER, 1ST BARON ILKESTON
FULFORD, HENRY CHARLES
HACKNEY, BERNARD BATIGAN
HORTON, WILLIAM
IMPEY, FREDERIC
LEACH, CHARLES
NEVILLE, F. SPOONER
PALMER, GEORGE
REID, HUGH GILZEAN
STURGE, CHARLES DICKINSON
TANGYE, SIR RICHARD
VINCE, W. B.


Anglo-Armenian Assn

BRYCE, JAMES, 1ST VISCOUNT BRYCE


Anglo-French Intervention Committee

BARTON, F. B.
BEESLY, EDWARD SPENCER
BRIDGES, JOHN HENRY
CONGREVE, RICHARD
CONGREVE, WALTER
CROMPTON, ALBERT
CROMPTON, HENRY
GEDDES, J. C.
HUTTON, HENRY DIX
MAUGHAN, JOHN
OTTER, FRANCIS
TRUELOVE, EDWARD


Anglo-Oriental Soc for Suppression Opium Trade

ALBRIGHT, ARTHUR
ALEXANDER, JOSEPH GUNDRY
ALEXANDER, ROBERT
AMOS, SHELDON
BAXTER, ROBERT
BENNETT, JAMES RISDON
BICKERSTETH, ROBERT
BROOMHALL, B.
BURT, THOMAS
CAINE, WILLIAM SPROSTON
CAMERON, SIR CHARLES, 1ST BT.
CHESSON, FREDERICK WILLIAM
CHURCHILL, LORD ALFRED SPENCER
CLARKE, SIR EDWARD GEORGE
CLAYTON, F. C.
COLMAN, JEREMIAH JAMES
COOPER, ANTHONY ASHLEY, 7TH EARL OF SHAFTESBURY
COOTE, SIR ALGERNON CHARLES PLUMPTRE, 12TH BT.

COWAN, JAMES
COWEN, JOSEPH
COWIE, BENJAMIN MORGAN
FOWLER, SIR ROBERT NICHOLAS, 1ST BT.
FRY, EDWARD
GLEDSTONE, J. P.
GUINNESS, HENRY GRATTAN
GURNEY, SAMUEL
HANBURY, SIR THOMAS
HILTON, JOHN
HIPSLEY, HENRY
HUGHES, THOMAS
HUTCHINSON, EDWARD
JAMES, WALTER HENRY, 2ND BARON NORTHBOURNE
JENKINS, EBENEZER EVANS
LEGGE, JAMES
LEVI, LEONE
LIDDON, HENRY PARRY
LIGHTFOOT, JOSEPH BARBER
LOCKHART, WILLIAM
MABBS, GOODEVE
MCARTHUR, ALEXANDER
MCARTHUR, SIR WILLIAM
MCCARTHY, JUSTIN
MCLAREN, DAVID
MATHESON, DONALD
MATHIESON, JAMES E.
MOBERLY, GEORGE
MORGAN, W.
MORLEY, ARNOLD
MORLEY, SAMUEL
NOEL, ERNEST
PALMER, GEORGE
PARRY, J. C.
PEASE, EDWARD
PIERCY, GEORGE
RICHARD, HENRY
RICHARDSON, SIR BENJAMIN WARD
RYLE, JOHN CHARLES
SAWYER, ROBERT
SMITHIES, THOMAS BYWATER
SPURGEON, CHARLES HADDON
STURGE, EDMUND
STURGE, JOSEPH
THOMAS, JOHN FRYER
TREMENHEERE, CHARLES WILLIAM
TURNER, F. S.
VERNEY, SIR HARRY, 2ND BT.
WHITWORTH, BENJAMIN
WILBERFORCE, ERNEST ROLAND
WYLIE, ALEXANDER


Assn for Improvement of London Workhouse Infirmaries

ACLAND, SIR THOMAS DYKE, 11TH BT.
ALLEN, HUGH
ANSTIE, FRANCIS EDMUND
ASHBURNHAM, THOMAS
ASHURST, WILLIAM
BAGEHOT, WALTER
BARCLAY, A. C.
BIGG, HENRY HEATHER
BRODRICK, GEORGE CHARLES
BRUCE, LORD CHARLES WILLIAM BRUDENELL
CARR, -
CAVE, SIR STEPHEN
CECIL, ROBERT ARTHUR TALBOT GASCOYNE-, 3RD MARQUIS OF
   SALISBURY

CECIL, WILLIAM ALLEYNE, 3RD MARQUIS OF EXETER
CLARKE, WILLIAM FAIRLIE
COOKE, -
DAVENPORT, WILLIAM BROMLEY-
DENTON, WILLIAM
DICKENS, CHARLES
DOBELL, -
DRUITT, ROBERT
EGERTON, WILBRAHAM, 1ST EARL EGERTON OF TATTON
FARQUHAR, SIR WALTER ROCKCLIFFE, 3RD BT.
FARRE, ARTHUR
FAWCETT, HENRY
FERGUSSON, SIR JAMES, 3TH BT.
FERGUSSON, SIR WILLIAM, 1ST BT.
FORTESCUE, DUDLEY FRANCIS
FORTESCUE, HUGH, 3RD EARL FORTESCUE
GLADSTONE, WILLIAM HENRY
GODDARD, EUGENE
HANSARD, SEPTIMUS COX HOLMES
HART, ERNEST ABRAHAM
HERBERT, HENRY HOWARD MOLYNEUX, 4TH EARL CARNARVON
HICKS, G. M.
HILL, MATTHEW BERKELEY
HOARE, HAMILTON A.
HOPE, ALEXANDER JAMES BERESFORD BERESFORD-
HUGHES, THOMAS
JENNER, SIR WILLIAM, 1ST BT.
JONES, HARRY
LENNOX, LORD HENRY CHARLES GEORGE GORDON
MCGILL, GEORGE HENRY
MARTIN, SIR JAMES RANALD
MARTIN, SAMUEL
MAURICE, FREDERICK DENISON
MITCHELL, ALEXANDER
MOIR, JOHN MACRAE
MORETON, HENRY JOHN REYNOLDS-, 3RD EARL OF DUCIE
NEATE, CHARLES
OGILVY, DAVID GRAHAM DRUMMOND, 7TH EARL OF AIRLIE
OGLE, JOHN WILLIAM
OLIPHANT, LAURENCE
PARKINSON, J. C.
RADCLIFFE, CHARLES BLAND
RADCLIFFE, JOHN NETTEN
RICHMOND, THOMAS KNYVETT
ROGERS, JOSEPH
RYDER, DUDLEY FRANCIS STUART, 3RD EARL OF HARROWBY
SARGOOD, AUGUSTINE
SCOTT, HENRY JOHN MONTAGU DOUGLAS, 1ST BARON MONTAGU
    OF BEAULIEU
SEYMOUR, HENRY DANBY
SHARPE, JOSEPH
SHUTTLEWORTH, SIR JAMES PHILLIPS KAY-, 1ST BT.
SIBSON, FRANCIS
SMITH, W. H.
STALLARD, -
STEWART, JOHN ARCHIBALD SHAW
STORR, JOHN STEPHENS
TORRENS, WILLIAM TORRENS MCCULLAGH
WARING, CHARLES
WATSON, SIR THOMAS, 1ST BT.
WILLIAMS, J.

Assn for Improvement of Public Morals

BACKHOUSE, EDWARD
BACKHOUSE, KATHERINE E. <MRS. EDWARD BACKHOUSE, nee
    MOUNSEY>
BEWICKE, ALICIA E. N. <MISS>
BRADLEY, - <MRS. J. W. BRADLEY>
BRADLEY, J. W.
BUTLER, GEORGE
BUTLER, JOSEPHINE E. <MRS. GEORGE BUTLER, nee GREY>
COLEY, JAMES
COLLINGWOOD, CHARLES EDWARD STUART
DYER, ALFRED STACE
FORD, STEPHEN

GIBSON, CHARLES BERNARD
GILLETT, GEORGE
HADLEY, SYDNEY CHARLES
HOPE, - <MISS>
HORSLEY, JOHN WILLIAM
HUGHES, HUGH PRICE
MURPHY, GEORGE STORMONT
O'NEILL, ARTHUR ALEXANDER
PALMER, SIR CHARLES JAMES, 9TH BT.
PORTER, JAMES BIGGS
ROBERTS, J. H. <OR J. G.>
STUART, JAMES
SWANWICK, ANNA <MISS>
TODD, ISABELLA<MISS>
TOWNSHEND, JOHN VILLIERS STUART, 5TH MARQUIS
    TOWNSHEND
WHEELER, FREDERIC
WILBERFORCE, ALBERT BASIL ORME

Assn for Promoting Extension of Contagious Diseases Act

ACLAND, SIR HENRY WENTWORTH, 1ST BT.
ADAMSON, JOSEPH SAMUEL
ALDRIDGE, JOHN H.
ANCRUM, W. R.
ANDERSON, DAVID
ANDERSON, SIR HENRY LACON
ANGUS, H.
ANNESLEY, HUGH, 5TH EARL ANNESLEY
ARMITAGE, SIR ELKANAH
ARMSTRONG, SIR ALEXANDER
ARMSTRONG, JOHN
ARNISON, WILLIAM CHRISTOPHER
BAGGE, SIR WILLIAM, 1ST BT.
BAILEY, JOSEPH GREENOAK
BANKS, SIR JOHN THOMAS
BARNETT, HENRY
BARR, WILLIAM ALEXANDER
BARRY, ALFRED
BATTEN, JOHN WINTERBOTHAM
BATTEN, RAYNER W.
BEDDOE, JOHN
BENNETT, JAMES RISDON
BENTINCK, GEORGE AUGUSTUS FREDERICK CAVENDISH
BLANDY, -
BLIGH, JOHN STUART, 6TH EARL OF DARNLEY
BLISSARD, JOHN CHARLES
BOUVERIE, EDWARD PLEYDELL
BOWLES, THOMAS GIBSON
BOWRING, SIR JOHN
BRACEY, CHARLES J.
BRADY, JOHN
BRIDGEMAN, GEORGE CECIL ORLANDO, 4TH EARL OF BRADFORD
BRUCE, LORD CHARLES WILLIAM BRUDENELL
BRUCE, JOHN COLLINGWOOD
BRUCE, MICHAEL
BRYSON, ALEXANDER
BUCHANAN, GEORGE
BURROWS, SIR GEORGE, 1ST BT.
BUXTON, CHARLES
BYRNE, THOMAS
CARDELL, J. M.
CAREY, FRANCIS E.
CARLETON, DUDLEY WILMOT, 4TH BARON DORCHESTER
CHAMBERLAIN, THOMAS
CHAMBERS, THOMAS KING
CLIVE, GEORGE HERBERT WINDSOR WINDSOR-
COCK, EDWARD
COCKBURN, JAMES BALFOUR
COLLENETTE, BENJAMIN
COOTE, HOLMES
CORBYN, M. A.
CORRIE, GEORGE ELWES
COWEN, SIR JOSEPH
CRESSWELL, PEARSON ROBERT
CROFTON, SIR WALTER FREDERICK

CURGENVEN, JOHN BRENDON
CURLING, THOMAS BLIZARD
CUST, ARTHUR PERCEVAL PUREY
DANSEY, G.
DE BATHE, HENRY PERCEVAL, 4TH BT.
DELAGARDE, PHILIP CHILWELL
DEMERIC, VICTOR
DENT, JOHN DENT
DEVERELL, JOHN
DICKSON, JOSEPH
DOMVILLE, HENRY JONES
DOWNING, DAVID
DRYSDALE CHARLES ROBERT
DUNLOP, -
DUNN, R. W.
DU PRE, CALEDON GEORGE
EARLE, JOHN
EARLE, RALPH ANSTRUTHER
EDGELL, EDGELL WYATT
EGERTON, ALGERNON FULKE
EMBLETON, DENNIS
ERICHSEN, SIR JOHN ERIC, 1ST BT.
EVANS, GEORGE M.
EVANS, THOMAS
FALCONER, RANDLE WILBRAHAM
FANE, JOHN WILLIAM
FEILDING, SIR PERCY ROBERT BASIL
FERGUSSON, SIR WILLIAM, 1ST BT.
FLEMING, JOHN GIBSON
FORREST, ROBERT WILLIAM
FORTESCUE, DUDLEY FRANCIS
FOSBERY,THOMAS VINCENT
FOX, WILLIAM TILBURY
GASCOYEN, G. G.
GIBBON, SEPTIMUS
GILLESPIE, J. D.
GLADDISH, - <"COL.">
GOODEVE, HENRY IVES HARRY
GRAMSHAW, J. H.
GRAY, WILLIAM
GRIGG, J. COLLINGS
GROSVENOR, RICHARD, 2ND MARQUIS WESTMINSTER
HALL, SIR WILLIAM KING
HAMILTON, LORD CLAUD JOHN
HAMILTON, JAMES, 2ND DUKE OF ABERCORN
HARDINGE, SIR ARTHUR EDWARD
HARDWICKE, WILLIAM
HARE, WILLIAM IRVING
HARGRAVE, WILLIAM
HARRISON, REGINALD
HART, ERNEST ABRAHAM
HAWKINS, CAESAR HENRY
HAYWARD, JOHN CURTIS
HAYWARD, W. H.
HEADLAM, THOMAS EMERSON
HEPBURN, HENRY POOLE
HEWETT, SIR PRESCOTT GARDNER, 1ST BT.
HEWITT, JAMES, 4TH VISCOUNT LIFFORD
HEY, WILLIAM
HICKMAN, WILLIAM
HILL, MATTHEW BERKELEY
HILL, MATTHEW DAVENPORT
HILTON, JOHN
HODGE, GEORGE WILLIAM
HOOD, SIR ALEXANDER BATEMAN PERIAM FULLER ACLAND-,
    3RD BT.
HUTCHINSON, SIR JONATHAN
HUTT, SIR WILLIAM
INGLIS, CORNELIUS
JENNER, SIR WILLIAM, 1ST BT.
JERVOISE, SIR JERVOISE CLARKE-, 2ND BT.
JOHNSTONE, HENRY ALEXANDER MUNRO BUTLER
JORDAN, FURNEAUX
JOSEPH, ALEXANDER
KEMBLE, CHARLES
KING, JOHN HYNDE
KNOX, ROBERT BENT

LABATT, HAMILTON
LANE, JAMES R.
LAW, HENRY
LEADER, NICHOLAS PHILPOT
LEGG, R. R.
LEGGE, EDWARD HENRY
LEIGHTON, FRANCIS KNYVETT
LEONARD, PETER
LIDDELL, HENRY GEORGE, 2ND EARL OF RAVENSWORTH
LINDSAY, CHARLES HUGH
LINTON, SIR WILLIAM
LLOYD, THOMAS
LOGAN, SIR THOMAS GALBRAITH
LOW, W. F.
MACCORMAC, SIR WILLIAM, 1ST BT.
MACKIE, IVIE
MAPOTHER, EDWARD DILLON
MARSON, J.
MARTIN, SIR WILLIAM FANSHAWE, 4TH BT.
MAY, GEORGE
MAYNE, -
MITFORD, WILLIAM TOWNLEY
MONCK, JOHN BLIGH
MOODY, CLEMENT
MORRIS, J. T.
MOUAT, SIR JAMES
MURRAY, FREEMAN
MYERS, ARTHUR BOWEN RICHARDS
NEWALL, ROBERT STIRLING
NICHOLLS, JAMES
NORTH, JOHN SIDNEY
PAGE, JAMES
PAGET, SIR GEORGE EDWARD
PAGET, SIR JAMES, 1ST BT.
PARKES, EDMUND ALEXANDER
PEART, ROBERT S.
PEATSON, J. CHADWICK
POLLARD, JAMES
POLLOCK, JAMES EDWARD
POLLOCK, WILLIAM
PONSONBY, HENRY FREDERICK
PORTER, SIR GEORGE HORNIDGE, 1ST BT.
PREST, EDWARD
PRICE, W. NICHOLSON
PRICE, WILLIAM PHILIP
PUCKLE, JOHN
QUAIN, RICHARD
QUAIN, SIR RICHARD, 1ST BT.
RAMSAY, SIR ALEXANDER, 3RD BT.
ROGERS, WILLIAM
RUMSEY, HENRY WYLDBORE
RUSSELL, SIR CHARLES, 3RD BT.
RUSSELL, JOHN, 1ST EARL RUSSELL
SCLATER, PHILIP LUTLEY
SELWYN, WILLIAM
SEYMOUR, SIR MICHAEL
SHARPEY, WILLIAM
SHERIFF, ALEXANDER CLUNES
SIMEON, SIR JOHN, 3RD BT.
SIMPSON, SIR ALEXANDER RUSSELL
SIMPSON, SIR JAMES YOUNG, 1ST BT.
SKEY, FREDERICK CARPENTER
SMITH, GEORGE
SMITH, HENRY SPENCER
SMITH, JOHN ABEL
SMITH, JOHN WILLIAM SIDNEY
SMITH, THOMAS EUSTACE
SQUARE, ELLIOT
SQUARE, W. J.
SQUARE, WILLIAM
STANLEY, ARTHUR PENRHYN
STEBBING, J. R.
STEPHENSON, SIR FREDERICK CHARLES ARTHUR
STONE, WILLIAM HENRY
STORRAR, JOHN
STUART, R. <OR W.>
STURT, CHARLES NAPIER

SYMONDS, JOHN ADDINGTON
THOMPSON, SIR HENRY, 1ST BT.
THOMPSON, W. ALLIN
THOMPSON, WILLIAM HEPWORTH
TIBBITS, R. W.
TINLING, EDWARD DOUGLAS
TOLME, JULIEN H.
TOTTENHAM, CHARLES GEORGE
TRENCH, W.
VAUDIN, CHARLES
VINTRAS, ACHILLE
VOSE, JAMES
WAKELING, C.
WARING, CHARLES
WATERHOUSE, SAMUEL
WATSON, SIR THOMAS, 1ST BT.
WEBSTER, ALEXANDER RHIND
WIBLIN, JOHN
WILDES, J. ST. S.
WILKS, SIR SAMUEL, 1ST BT.
WILLIAMS, OWEN LEWIS COPE
WILSON, SIR WILLIAM JAMES ERASMUS
WINTERBOTHAM, L.
WOOD, ALEXANDER
WOOD, ANDREW
WOOLLCOMBE, THOMAS
WYATT, JOHN
WYNDHAM, PERCY SCAWEN


Assn of Revivers of British Industry

ROBERTS, J.
WILKINS, W. C.


British Women's Temperance Assn

ADAMS, ANNIE
BOOCOCK, - <MRS. S. G. BOOCOCK>
EYNON, - <MRS.>
FRYER, - <MISS>
HASWELL, E. W.
HOLLAND, - <MISS>
LUCAS, MARGARET <MRS. SAMUEL LUCAS, nee BRIGHT>
MARSHALL, - <MISS>
PARKER, - <MRS. EDWARD PARKER>
REANEY, - <MRS. GEORGE SALE REANEY>
REYNOLDS, - <MRS.>
RHODES, A. A.
STEWART, - <MRS.>


Central Assn for Stopping Sale Intox Liquors on Sunday

ALLEN, WILLIAM SHEPHERD
ANSON, THOMAS GEORGE, 2ND EARL OF LICHFIELD
ANTROBUS, W. D. B.
ARNOLD, A. J.
ATLAY, JAMES
BACKHOUSE, EDWARD
BAINES, SIR EDWARD
BALFOUR, ALEXANDER
BALLANTINE, ROBERT FREDERICK
BANCROFT, GEORGE
BARBOUR, ROBERT
BARLOW, JAMES
BARNES, ROBERT
BARTON, EDWARD
BAXTER, ROBERT
BAZLEY, SIR THOMAS, 1ST BT.
BENSON, EDWARD WHITE
BIRCH, HENRY MILDRED
BIRLEY, HUGH
BIRLEY, ROBERT
BISHOP, EDWARD
BLACKLOCK, WILLIAM THOMAS

BLAKE, THOMAS
BLINKHORN, OCTAVIUS
BLUNT, RICHARD FREDERICK LEFEVRE
BOWLY, SAMUEL
BOYD, ARCHIBALD
BOYD, JAMES
BRAITHWAITE, G. F.
BRAY, W.
BRIGHT, JACOB
BROWNE, EDWARD HAROLD
CAINE, WILLIAM
CAINE, WILLIAM SPROSTON
CALLENDER, WILLIAM ROMAINE
CALLENDER, WILLIAM ROMAINE, JUN.
CAMERON, SIR CHARLES, 1ST BT.
CAMPBELL, JAMES COLQUHOUN
CARLISLE, HENRY HERMANN
CARPENTER, WILLIAM BOYD
CAWLEY, CHARLES EDWARD
CHAMBRES, PHILIP HENRY
CHARLTON, GEORGE
CHEETHAM, JOHN
CLAUGHTON, THOMAS LEGH
CLEGG, THOMAS
CLOSE, FRANCIS
COOPER, ANTHONY ASHLEY, 7TH EARL OF SHAFTESBURY
CREWDSON, -
CROSSLEY, DAVID
DARRAH, CHARLES
DENISON, SIR WILLIAM THOMAS
DIGBY, GEORGE DIGBY WINGFIELD
DU BOIS, CHARLES CONRAD ADOLPHUS, BARON<NETH.> DE
    FERRIERES
DYMOND, J.
ELLICOTT, CHARLES JOHN
EVANS, JOHN
FARRAR, JOHN
FENWICK, RALPH
FIELDING, RUDOLPH WILLIAM BASIL, 8TH EARL OF DENBIGH
FITZGERALD, JOHN PURCELL
FRASER, DONALD
FRASER, JAMES
FRY, SIR THEODORE, 1ST BT.
GARRETT, CHARLES
GARSIDE, JOSEPH
GLADSTONE, JOHN HALL
GOODWIN, HARVEY
GOULD, GEORGE
GOULDEN, W. W.
GRAVE, JOHN
GRAY, THOMAS
GREEN, SIDNEY FAITHORN
GREGORY, BENJAMIN
HALL, SAMUEL ROMILLY
HAMILTON, LORD CLAUD
HASLAM, JAMES
HAWORTH, ABRAHAM
HAWORTH, RICHARD
HERVEY, ARTHUR CHARLES
HEWLETT, EBENEZER
HEYWOOD, ARTHUR H.
HILL, FERGUS
HOLLAND, SAMUEL
HORE, EDMUND CREEK
HOULDSWORTH, SIR WILLIAM HENRY, 1ST BT.
HOYLE, ISAAC
HOYLE, WILLIAM
HUGHES, JOSHUA
HUTTON, WILLIAM
JACKSON, EDWARD
JACKSON, JOHN
JACOBSON, WILLIAM
JAMES, JOHN HUTCHISON
JENKINS, -
JOHNSON, JOSEPH
JONES, A. R.
JONES, ALFRED

JONES, T. B.
JONES, THOMAS
JONES, WILLIAM BASIL TICKELL
JUPE, CHARLES
KNELL, SAMUEL
LAKE, WILLIAM CHARLES
LAMB, -
LAWSON, SIR WILFRED, 2ND BT.
LEE, JAMES PRINCE
LEHY, PATRICK
LE MARE, E. R.
LIGHTFOOT, JOSEPH BARBER
LIVESLEY, WILLIAM
LONGDON, -
MCARTHUR, SIR WILLIAM
MCCAW, WILLIAM
MCCURDY, ALEXANDER
MCFADYEN, J.
MACKARNESS, JOHN FIELDER
MCKERROW, J. B.
MACLAREN, ALEXANDER
MAGEE, WILLIAM CONNOR
MANNING, HENRY EDWARD
MASON, HUGH
MATTHEWS, E. <ALSO MATHEWS>
MILNE, WILLIAM
MOBERLY, GEORGE
MORGAN, SIR GEORGE OSBORNE, 1ST BT.
MORRIS, WILLIAM
NEILD, EDWARD
NEWELL, THOMAS
ORMAN, GEORGE
OSBORN, HENRY J.
PARKER, JOSEPH
PARR, JOHN OWEN
PATERSON, J. C. <ALSO PATTERSON>
PATTERSON, JOHN
PATTERSON, JOSEPH
PEARSON, EDWARD
PEASE, ARTHUR
PEASE, HENRY
PEASE, JOSEPH
PEASE, JOSEPH WHITWELL, 1ST BT.
PERKINS, W. H.
PERRY, FREDERIC J.
PETHERICK, GEORGE WILLIAM
PHILIPS, ROBERT
PHILLPOTTS, WILLIAM JOHN
PITCAIRN, JAMES PELHAM
POCHIN, HENRY DAVIS
POLLOCK, WILLIAM
PREST, EDWARD
PUNSHON, WILLIAM MORLEY
RALEIGH, ALEXANDER
RAYNER, SIR THOMAS CROSSLEY
REANEY, GEORGE SALE
RICE, JOSEPH
ROBERTS, EDWARD P.
ROBERTS, RICHARD
ROBINSON, JOSEPH
ROBINSON, WILLIAM
ROGERS, E. S.
ROSS, CHARLES CAMPBELL
ROSS, JOHN M.
ROWE, WILLIAM
RUMNEY, -
RYDER, DUDLEY, 2ND EARL OF HARROWBY
RYLANDS, PETER
RYLE, JOHN CHARLES
SALT, SIR TITUS, 1ST BT.
SAUNDERS, WILLIAM
SEAGER, JAMES
SHIPMAN, JAMES
SIMPSON, THOMAS BOURNE
SLATER, JOHN
SMITH, BENJAMIN
SMITH, J.

SMITH, ROBERT PAYNE-
SOMES, JOSEPH
SPAFFORD, EDWARD JAMES
STAMER, SIR LOVELACE TOMLINSON, 3RD BT.
STANYER, WILLIAM
STEINTHAL, S. ALFRED
STEPHENSON, T. BOWMAN
STEVENSON, JAMES COCHRAN
STIDSTONE, CONWAY
STOVEL, CHARLES
STOWELL, THOMAS ALFRED
STUART, JOHN
TAIT, ARCHIBALD CAMPBELL
TAYLOR, ROBERT
TEMPLE, FREDERICK
TEMPLE, WILLIAM FRANCIS COWPER-, 1ST BARON
    MOUNT-TEMPLE
THOMAS, EDWIN
THOMSON, ALEXANDER
THOMSON, JOHN
THOMSON, WILLIAM
THOROLD, ANTHONY WILSON
THORP, JOSEPH <ALSO THORPE>
TOOLE, -
TOWNEND, T. W.
TREVELYAN, SIR GEORGE OTTO, 2ND BT.
TUCKER, JOSEPH
TURNER, SIR LLEWELYN
TURNER, WILLIAM
VAUGHAN, HERBERT ALFRED
WADDY, SAMUEL DANKS
WADE, J. A.
WAINWRIGHT, FREDERICK
WAKEFIELD, WILLIAM HENRY
WATTS, J. C.
WEDDERBURN, SIR DAVID, 3RD BT.
WEST, JOSEPH ROBERT ORR
WHITE, EDWARD
WHITE, VERNER M.
WHITWELL, EDWARD
WHITWORTH, BENJAMIN
WHITWORTH, ROBERT
WHITWORTH, THOMAS
WILBERFORCE, ERNEST ROLAND
WILKINSON, WILLIAM
WILLIAMS, CHARLES
WILLIS, THOMAS
WILSHAW, WILLIAM
WILSON, CHARLES HENRY, 1ST BARON NUNBURNHOLME
WITHINGTON, J. S.
WOLSTENCROFT, THOMAS
WOOLLCOMBE, HENRY <ALSO WOOLCOMBE>
WORDSWORTH, CHRISTOPHER
WRIGHT, JOHN SKIRROW


Central Brewers' License Repeal Assn

    PRYOR, ARTHUR


Central Vigilance Comtee for Repression Immorality

    ADDERLEY, CHARLES BOWYER, 1ST BARON NORTON
    ANSON, THOMAS GEORGE, 2ND EARL OF LICHFIELD
    ASHBY, RICHARD C.
    BRABAZON, REGINALD, 12TH EARL OF MEATH
    CAMPBELL, GEORGE DOUGLAS, 8TH DUKE OF ARGYLL
    COOPER, ANTHONY ASHLEY, 7TH EARL OF SHAFTESBURY
    COWPER, KATRINE CECILIA, COUNTESS COWPER <WIFE OF 7TH
        EARL, nee COMPTON>
    FORESTER, ORLANDO WATKIN WELD, 4TH BARON FORESTER
    FOWLER, SIR ROBERT NICHOLAS, 1ST BT.
    GORDON, JOHN CAMPBELL HAMILTON, 1ST MARQUIS OF
        ABERDEEN AND TEMAIR
    GROSVENOR, HUGH LUPUS, 1ST DUKE OF WESTMINSTER
    KENNEDY, ARCHIBALD, 3RD MARQUIS OF AILSA

KINNAIRD, ARTHUR FITZGERALD, 10TH BARON KINNAIRD
MORLEY, SAMUEL
MUIR, SIR WILLIAM
PEPLOE, HANMER WILLIAM WEBB-
PERCY, HENRY GEORGE, 7TH DUKE OF NORTHUMBERLAND
SOUTHWARD, JOHN
STANHOPE, ARTHUR PHILIP, 6TH EARL STANHOPE
WALDEGRAVE, WILLIAM FREDERICK, 9TH EARL WALDEGRAVE
WARR, GEORGE CHARLES WINTER
WILSON, LUCY <MISS>


Church Assn

ABBOTT, SIR FREDERICK
ADAMSON, WILLIAM
ALFORD, CHARLES RICHARD
ALLAN, WILLIAM
ALLCROFT, JOHN DERBY
ANDERSON, DAVID
ANDREWS, THOMAS R.
ASHLEY, ANTHONY WILLIAM
ASTON, JOHN WALTER
AURIOL, EDWARD
AUSTIN, JOHN SOUTHGATE
AYLMER, HENRY
BANNISTER, EDWARD
BASSANO, W.
BATE, S. S.
BATEMAN, JAMES
BATEMAN, JOHN
BAXTER, R.
BAZETT, - <"COL.">
BENNETT, JOHN
BERGUER, HENRY JOHN
BERNARD, FRANCIS, 3RD EARL OF BANDON
BERNARD, JAMES FRANCIS, 4TH EARL OF BANDON
BEVAN, FRANCIS AUGUSTUS
BEVAN, ROBERT COOPER LEE
BIGGS, -
BILLING, ROBERT CLAUDIUS
BINGHAM, CHARLES WILLIAM
BIRKS, THOMAS RAWSON
BLAKENEY, RICHARD PAUL
BLEAZBY, WILLIAM
BONAR, A.
BOSANQUET, HORACE JAMES SMITH-
BOULTBEE, THOMAS POWNALL
BOURDILLON, JAMES DEWAR
BOUSFIELD, C. H.
BOVILLE, E. C.
BOWKER, HENRY F.
BRIDGES, SIR BROOK WILLIAM, 5TH BT. AND 1ST BARON
    FITZWALTER
BROWNE, PHILIP
BUCKE, BENJAMIN WALTER
BULLER, SPENCER <"CAPT.">
BURBIDGE, JOHN
BURNLEY, W. F.
CAMPBELL, DAWSON
CAMPE, CHARLES
CAPEL, BURY
CARTER, JOHN MONEY
CASSIN, BURMAN
CATHCART, ALAN FREDERICK, 3RD EARL CATHCART
CHAMBERS, GEORGE FREDERICK
CHAMBERS, SIR THOMAS
CHAMPNEYS, WILLIAM WELDON
CHOLMONDELEY, LORD HENRY VERE
CLAYTON, -
CLEMENT, WILLIAM JAMES
CLOSE, FRANCIS
CLUTTON, W. J.
COBHAM, ALEXANDER WILLIAM
COHEN, JAMES
COLE, WILLIAM WILLOUGHBY, 3RD EARL OF ENNISKILLEN
COLQUHOUN, ARCHIBALD CAMPBELL CAMPBELL-

COLQUHOUN, JOHN CAMPBELL
COLQUHOUN, JOHN ERSKINE CAMPBELL-
CONCANON, GEORGE BLAKE
CONOR, J. R.
CONWAY, WILLIAM
COODE, SIR JOHN
COOKESLEY, WILLIAM GIFFORD
COWAN, CHARLES
COYSH, T. S.
CRAWFORD, ROBERT FITZGERALD COPLAND-
CRESSWELL, J.
CRUIKSHANK, AUGUSTUS WALTER
CUNDY, JAMES <"CAPT.">
CURZON, SIDNEY CAMPBELL HENRY ROPER
DAFFORNE, JAMES
DALE, T. B.
DALE, THOMAS
DANDY, RICHARD
DARGENT, E. A.
DAVENPORT, FRANCIS WILLIAM
DAVIES, URIAH
DIGBY, GEORGE DIGBY WINGFIELD
DITMAS, FREDERICK <"MAJ.">
DONALDSON, THOMAS LEVERTON
DOUGLAS, SHOLTO DOUGLAS CAMPBELL
DOWNS, H.
DU BOIS, CHARLES CONRAD ADOLPHUS, BARON<NETH.> DE
    FERRIERES
EDWARDES, SIR HERBERT BENJAMIN
ELLIOT, GILBERT
ELMHIRST, WILLIAM
FARISH, J.
FAULCONER, ROBERT S.
FITZGERALD, GERALD STEPHEN
FLEMING, ISAAC PLANT
FLINDT, GUSTAVUS K.
FOLLIOT, JAMES
FORBES, EDWARD
FOWLER, H. J.
FREMANTLE, WILLIAM ROBERT
FREWER, J. R.
FROBISHER, WILLIAM MARTIN
GALE, KNIGHT
GARBETT, EDWARD
GASTER, THOMAS JOSEPH
GILL, THOMAS HOWARD
GLADSTONE, R.
GRANE, WILLIAM JAMES
GREAVES, TALBOT ADEN LEY
GRIFFITH, J.
GUTHRIE, GEOFFREY DOMINICK AUGUSTUS FREDERICK BROWNE,
    2ND BARON ORANMORE
HAMILTON, JOSEPH HARRIMAN
HAMMERSLEY, JOHN
HARINGTON, DALLAS OLDFIELD
HATHAWAY, EDWARD PENROSE
HAWKSWORTH, JOHN
HERBERT, H. V.
HILL, P. CARTERET- <"HON.">
HILL, ROWLAND, 2ND VISCOUNT HILL
HILL, THOMAS
HOARE, EDWARD
HOARE, JOSEPH
HOARE, RICHARD
HOLDEN, ROBERT
HOLLOND, EDMUND
HOLT, JAMES MADEN
HORSFALL, THOMAS BERRY
HORSLEY, WILLIAM HENRY
HOULDSWORTH, JAMES
HUNTER, JAMES
INNS, RICHARD
INSKIP, JAMES
ISAACS, ALBERT AUGUSTUS
JARDINE, JOHN
JOCELYN, ROBERT, 3RD EARL OF RODEN
JOHNSON, JOSEPH WILLIAM

KEMBLE, CHARLES
KENNAWAY, SIR JOHN, 2ND BT.
KILLICK, RICHARD HENRY
LABILLIERE, FRANCIS PETER
LAMB, ANDREW SIMON
LAMBART, FREDERICK JOHN WILLIAM, 8TH EARL OF CAVAN
LAMBERT, - <"COL.">
LAW, HENRY
LAWRENCE, SIR ARTHUR JOHNSTONE
LEDSAM, DANIEL
LEFROY, ANTHONY
LIGHTON, SIR CHRISTOPHER ROBERT, 6TH BT.
LIGHTON, SIR CHRISTOPHER ROBERT, 7TH BT.
LONG, RICHARD PENRUDDOCKE
LOVELL, CHARLES H.
LOWTHER, SIR CHARLES HUGH, 3RD BT.
LUNN, WILLIAM JOSEPH
LYON, SAMUEL EDMUND
LYTTLETON, - <"CAPT.">
MACDONALD, MACDONALD- <"COL.">
MCGRATH, HENRY WALTER
MCNEILE, HUGH
MALTBY, F. N.
MANEY, C.
MARSTON, CHARLES DALLAS
MARTIN, JOHN
MAUDE, FRANCIS
MAYNARD, H. W.
MIDWINTER, NATHANIEL
MILLER, HENRY
MILLS, JOHN
MITCHINSON, HENRY CLARKE
MOLYNEUX, CAPEL
MONK, J.
MONTAGU, LORD ROBERT
MOORE, GEORGE
MOORE, PONSONBY A.
MORRIS, SIR JOHN
MORRISON, JAMES
MORTIMER, CHARLES
MOSLEY, SIR OSWALD, 2ND BT.
MOSLEY, SIR TONMAN, 3RD BT.
MULLINER, FRANCIS
NEVILL, WILLIAM, 1ST MARQUIS OF ABERGAVENNY
NEWDEGATE, CHARLES NEWDIGATE
NOLAN, THOMAS
NUGENT, GEORGE THOMAS JOHN, 1ST MARQUIS OF WESTMEATH
NUGENT, RICHARD
O'BRIEN, PHILIP STEPHEN
ORMISTON, JAMES
PALMER, SIR CHARLES JAMES, 9TH BT.
PALMER, WILLIAM C. <"CAPT.">
PEARS, EDMUND WARD
PEPLOE, HANMER WILLIAM WEBB-
PHILLIPS, R.
PITE, A. R.
POYNDER, ROBERT
PREST, EDWARD
PRICE, AUBREY CHARLES
PRICE, G.
RAND, JOHN
RANYARD, S.
RICE, FRANCIS WILLIAM, 5TH BARON DYNEVOR
RICHARDSON, JOHN
ROSE, HENRY
ROWLANDSON, M. <"COL.">
ROXBURGH, - <"COL.">
RUSSELL, LORD WRIOTHESLEY
RYLE, JOHN CHARLES
SANDERS, H. W.
SAUNDERS, R.
SAVILE, HENRY BOURCHIER OSBORNE
SHANN, GEORGE
SHARPE, HENRY
SHEPPARD, J. G.
SHIPTON, W. EDWYN
SHORE, CHARLES JOHN, 2ND BARON TEIGNMOUTH

SMELT, THOMAS
SMITH, F. W.
SMITH, GEORGE JAMES PHILIP
SMITH, HELY HUTCHINSON AUGUSTUS
SMITH, ROWLAND
SMYTHE, WILLIAM BARLOW
STANNUS, BEAUCHAMP WALTER
STEAD, S. A.
STIRLING, CHARLES
STRANGE, W.
STRICKLAND, JOHN CAMPBELL
SULIVAN, SIR BARTHOLOMEW JAMES
SURR, JOSEPH
SWEETNAM, MATTHEW
TANNER, JAMES GOSSET
TATE, HENRY CARR
TEMPLER, WILLIAM CHRISTOPHER
THOMPSON, HENRY
THOMPSON, JOHN
TITCOMB, JONATHAN HOLT
TOLLEMACHE, HAMILTON JAMES
TUFNELL, THOMAS R.
TUGWELL, LEWEN
TURBY, J. H. <"MAJ.">
VALPY, LEONARD R.
VENN, HENRY
VERNEY, SIR HARRY, 2ND BT.
VOILE, THOMAS
WADDINGTON, JOHN BARTON
WAINWRIGHT, SIR JAMES GADESDEN
WAINWRIGHT, SAMUEL
WARD, FREDERICK P.
WARDLE, HENRY
WELDON, GEORGE WARBURTON
WEST, WILLIAM NOWELL
WHITING, JOHN BRADFORD
WIGHTMAN, CHARLES EDWARD LEOPOLD
WILKINSON, WILLIAM
WILLIAMSON, J. W.
WILMOT, EDWARD REVELL EARDLEY-
WILSON, DANIEL
WILSON, HENRY WILLIAM, 11TH BARON BERNERS
WOOD, RICHARD
WORSFOLD, JOHN NAPPER
WRIGHT, FRANCIS
WRIGHT, JOSEPH COLEMAN HORNSBY
WYNDHAM, GEORGE, 1ST BARON LECONFIELD
YATES, HOLT <DR.>


Church League for the Separation of Church and State

    MACKONOCHIE, ALEXANDER HERIOT


Church and State Defense Society

    DENISON, GEORGE ANTHONY


City Church & Churchyard Protection Soc

    BARRY, CHARLES
    BENHAM, WILLIAM
    BENTINCK, GEORGE AUGUSTUS FREDERICK CAVENDISH
    BIRCH, GEORGE HENRY
    BOYLE, GEORGE FREDERICK, 6TH EARL OF GLASGOW
    BREWER, H. W.
    BULLEY, FREDERIC
    CARLYLE, THOMAS
    CHURCH, RICHARD WILLIAM
    CORNISH, HENRY HUBERT
    COTTON, RICHARD LYNCH
    COURTENAY, WILLIAM REGINALD, 11TH EARL OF DEVON
    COURTNEY, LEONARD HENRY, 1ST BARON COURTNEY OF
        PENWITH
    COUTTS, ANGELA GEORGINA BURDETT-, BARONESS

BURDETT-COUTTS
COWEN, JOSEPH
DENISON, GEORGE ANTHONY
DODD, JOHN THEODORE
ELLIS, SIR JOHN WHITTAKER, 1ST BT.
EVANS, EVAN
EVELYN, WILLIAM JOHN
FERREY, EDMUND B. <OR B. EDMUND>
FOLJAMBE, CECIL GEORGE SAVILE, 1ST EARL OF LIVERPOOL
FORBES, HORACE COURTENAY GRAMMELL, 20TH BARON FORBES
FOWLER, SIR ROBERT NICHOLAS, 1ST BT.
FRESHFIELD, EDWIN
GRANTHAM, SIR WILLIAM
GROSVENOR, HUGH LUPUS, 1ST DUKE OF WESTMINSTER
GUEST, MONTAGUE JOHN
HALL, WILLIAM JOHN
HAMILTON, JAMES, 2ND DUKE OF ABERCORN
HANDYSIDE, VINOY ROBSON
HANSON, SIR REGINALD 1ST BT.
HARDY, ALFRED ERSKINE GATHORNE-
HARMAN, J.
HEALES, ALFRED
HEBB, JOHN
HOPE, ALEXANDER JAMES BERESFORD BERESFORD-
HUNT, WILLIAM HOLMAN
IRVING, SIR HENRY
JODRELL, SIR EDWARD REPPS, 3RD BT.
JODRELL, LUCINDA EMMA MARIA, LADY <wife of Sir E. R.
    JODRELL, 3RD BT., nee GARDEN>
KELLY, SIR FITZROY EDWARD
KERSHAW, SAMUEL WAYLAND
LAKE, BENJAMIN GREENE
LECHMERE, SIR EDMUND ANTHONY HARLEY, 3RD BT.
LEIGHTON, FRANCIS KNYVETT
LEIGHTON, FREDERICK, 1ST BARON LEIGHTON OF STRETTON
LIDDON, HENRY PARRY
LIGHTFOOT, JOHN PRIDEAUX
LUSHINGTON, EDWARD HARBORD
MARKS, ALFRED
MARKS, T. NEWMAN
MASON, ARTHUR JAMES
MOLESWORTH, SAMUEL, 8TH VISCOUNT MOLESWORTH
MORRIS, WILLIAM
MOULD, J. CLARKE
MUNDELLA, ANTHONY JOHN
NORRIS, HENRY
O'NEILL, WILLIAM CHICHESTER, 1ST BARON O'NEILL
OUSELEY, SIR FREDERICK ARTHUR GORE, 2ND BT.
OWEN, SIR FRANCIS PHILIP CUNLIFFE
PAICE, BOWES A.
PALK, LAWRENCE, 1ST BARON HALDON
PAYNE, RANDOLPH
PEARSON, JOHN LOUGHBOROUGH
PERY, WILLIAM HALE JOHN CHARLES, 3RD EARL OF LIMERICK
PHILLIMORE, SIR ROBERT JOSEPH, 1ST BT.
POYNTER, SIR EDWARD JOHN, 1ST BT.
PRICE, BONAMY
PRITCHARD, CHARLES
REID, W.
RICHARDS, HENRY CHARLES
RICHMOND, SIR WILLIAM BLAKE
RIGAUD, GIBBES
RIGAUD, JOHN
ROXBY, H. THORNHILL
SALT, J. C.
SAVORY, SIR JOSEPH, 1ST BT.
SCOTT, GEORGE GILBERT
SHUTTLEWORTH, HENRY CARY
SOMERSET, LORD HENRY RICHARD CHARLES
STAINER, SIR JOHN
STAPLES, SIR JOHN
STONE, DAVID HENRY
STREET, GEORGE EDMUND
TALBOT, JAMES, 4TH BARON TALBOT DE MALAHIDE
TALBOT, SIR WELLINGTON PATRICK MANVERS CHETWYND
TENNYSON, ALFRED, 1ST BARON TENNYSON
TEULON, WILLIAM MILFORD

THYNNE, HARRIET, MARCHIONESS<DOWAGER> OF BATH <wife
    of 3RD MARQ., nee BARING>
TOMKINS, J. SIDNEY
TORRENS, WILLIAM TORRENS MCCULLAGH
TROLLOPE, EDWARD
TROWER, ARTHUR
TROWER, G.
TRUSCOTT, SIR FRANCIS WYATT
VENABLES, EDMUND
VINALL, C. G.
WARDLE, GEORGE Y.
WARREN, GEORGE FLEMING, 2ND BARON DE TABLEY
WATSON, CHRISTOPHER KNIGHT
WESTWOOD, JOHN OBADIAH
WHITE, HENRY
WHITTINGTON, RICHARD
WILBRAHAM, EDWARD BOOTLE-, 1ST EARL OF LATHOM
WORDSWORTH, CHRISTOPHER
WRIGHT, HENRY
WYNDHAM, PERCY SCAWEN

Commons Preservation Soc

ALCOCK, THOMAS ST. LEGER
BENSON, EDWARD WHITE
BLENNERHASSETT, ROWLAND PONSONBY
BOND, EDWARD
BROWN, SIR ALEXANDER HARGREAVES, 1ST BT.
BRYCE, JAMES, 1ST VISCOUNT BRYCE
BURNEY, GEORGE
BUXTON, CHARLES
BUXTON, EDWARD NORTH
BUXTON, FRANCIS WILLIAM
BUXTON, GERALD
BUXTON, SAMUEL GURNEY
BUXTON, SYDNEY CHARLES, 1ST EARL BUXTON
BUXTON, SIR THOMAS FOWELL, 3RD BT.
CHAMBERS, SIR THOMAS
CHANNING, FRANCIS ALLSTON, 1ST BN.CHANNING
CHEETHAM, JOHN FREDERICK
CHURCHILL, LORD RANDOLPH HENRY SPENCER
CLARK, SIR JAMES, 1ST BT.
CLARKE, SIR EDWARD GEORGE
COHEN, ARTHUR JOSEPH
CUNLIFFE, SIR ROBERT ALFRED, 5TH BT.
DENMAN, GEORGE
DILKE, ASHTON WENTWORTH
DILKE, SIR CHARLES WENTWORTH, 2ND BT.
DRYHURST, FREDERICK JOHN
EASTWICK, EDWARD BACKHOUSE
EYRE, GEORGE EDWARD BRISCOE
FARRER, THOMAS HENRY, 1ST BARON FARRER OF ABINGER
FARRER, SIR WILLIAM JAMES
FAWCETT, HENRY
FAWCETT, MILLICENT GARRETT <MRS. HENRY FAWCETT, nee
    GARRETT>
FITZMAURICE, EDMOND GEORGE PETTY, 1ST BARON
    FITZMAURICE OF LEIGH
FLOWER, CYRIL, 1ST BARON BATTERSEA
GASSIOTT, JOHN PETER
GIBB, THOMAS ECCLESTON
GIBBS, FREDERIC WAYMOUTH
GOWER, GRANVILLE GEORGE LEVESON-, 2ND EARL GRANVILLE
GREY, ALBERT HENRY GEORGE, 4TH EARL GREY
GROSVENOR, HUGH LUPUS, 1ST DUKE OF WESTMINSTER
HALL, W. H.
HARCOURT, SIR WILLIAM GEORGE GRANVILLE VENABLES
    VERNON
HARDY, HERBERT HARDY COZENS-, 1ST BARON COZENS-HARDY
    OF LETHERINGSETT
HILL, OCTAVIA
HOARE, GURNEY
HOBHOUSE, HENRY
HOLDEN, SIR ISAAC, 1ST BT.
HOLE, JAMES
HOLLOND, JOHN ROBERT

HOLMS, JOHN
HOPE, ALEXANDER JAMES BERESFORD BERESFORD-
HUGHES, THOMAS
HUNTER, SIR ROBERT
HUSSEY, H. S. L.
HUXLEY, THOMAS HENRY
ILBERT, SIR COURTENAY PEREGRINE
JAMES, WALTER HENRY, 2ND BARON NORTHBOURNE
JOHNSTON, ANDREW
LANKESTER, EDWIN
LAWRENCE, SIR JAMES CLARKE, 1ST BT.
LAWRENCE, SIR JAMES JOHN TREVOR, 2ND BT.
LAWRENCE, PHILIP HENRY
LAWRENCE, SIR WILLIAM
LEFEVRE, GEORGE JOHN SHAW-, 1ST BARON EVERSLEY
LOCKE, JOHN
LONGMAN, CHARLES JAMES
LONGMAN, WILLIAM
LOUIS, ALFRED HYMAN
LUSHINGTON, SIR GODFREY
LUSK, SIR ANDREW, 1ST BT.
MCCARTHY, JUSTIN
MARSHALL, GILBERT
MASKELYNE, MERVYN HERBERT NEVIL STORY-
MAURICE, CHARLES EDMUND
MILL, JOHN STUART
MORETON, HENRY HAUGHTON REYNOLDS- <STYLED LORD
    MORETON>
MORRIS, WILLIAM
MORRISON, GEORGE
MOULTON, JOHN FLETCHER, BARON MOULTON
MURRAY, JOHN
OTTER, FRANCIS
PARKINSON, J. C.
PAULTON, JAMES MELLOR
PEEK, FRANCIS
POLLOCK, CHARLES EDWARD
POLLOCK, SIR FREDERICK, 3RD BT.
POWELL, SIR FRANCIS SHARP, 1ST BT.
RAPER, ROBERT WILLIAM
ROBSON, WILLIAM SNOWDON, BARON ROBSON
ROGERS, WILLIAM
RUSSELL, LORD ARTHUR JOHN EDWARD
RYAN, SIR EDWARD
SANDFORD, GEORGE MONTAGU WARREN <FORMERLY PEACOCK>
SCOTT, HENRY JOHN MONTAGU DOUGLAS, 1ST BARON MONTAGU
    OF BEAULIEU
SELLAR, ALEXANDER CRAIG
SMITH, BENJAMIN LEIGH
SMITH, SAMUEL
STEPHEN, SIR LESLIE
TAIT, ARCHIBALD CAMPBELL
TAYLOR, PETER ALFRED
TEMPLE, WILLIAM FRANCIS COWPER-, 1ST BARON
    MOUNT-TEMPLE
TOWNSHEND, JOHN VILLIERS STUART, 5TH MARQUIS
    TOWNSHEND
TREHERNE, GEORGE GILBERT TREHERNE
WALLOP, NEWTON, 6TH EARL PORTSMOUTH
WESTLAKE, JOHN
WINKWORTH, STEPHEN


Eastern Question Assn

    BRYCE, JAMES, 1ST VISCOUNT BRYCE
    CHESSON, FREDERICK WILLIAM
    COOPER, ANTHONY ASHLEY, 7TH EARL OF SHAFTESBURY
    GROSVENOR, HUGH LUPUS, 1ST DUKE OF WESTMINSTER
    HOWARD, GEORGE JAMES, 9TH EARL OF CARLISLE
    MORRIS, WILLIAM
    MUNDELLA, ANTHONY JOHN
    PROBYN, J. W.
    PRYCE, EDWARD S.
    STONOR, THOMAS, 3RD BARON CAMOYS
    THYNNE, JOHN ALEXANDER, 4TH MARQUIS OF BATH


English Land Restoration League

    BRIGGS, THOMAS
    BURROUGHS, S. M.
    CHAMPION, HENRY HYDE
    CLEGG, W. W.
    CONNELL, J.
    COSSHAM, HANDEL
    DURANT, JOHN CHARLES
    EASTCOURT, R.
    FROST, R. P. B.
    HEADLAM, STEWART DUCKWORTH
    HENNESSY, PATRICK
    HOWARD, A.
    JAMESON, WILLIAM
    MOLL, WILLIAM EDMUND
    MORRIS, H. A.
    PETERS, E. J.
    RYLETT, HAROLD
    SAUNDERS, WILLIAM
    SHARMAN, WILLIAM
    SHORE, THOMAS
    SHUTTLEWORTH, HENRY CARY
    SOUTTER, FRANCIS WILLIAM
    STEER, W.
    STEPHENSON, T. S.
    SYMES, JOHN ELLIOTSON
    TAYLOR, HELEN <MISS>
    VERINDER, FREDERICK
    WALKER, THOMAS FERDINAND
    WILSON, JOHN
    WOOLACOTT, JOHN EVANS


Financial Reform Union

    BEAL, JAMES
    BOLTON, THOMAS HENRY
    CORNER, W. E.
    ELT, CHARLES HENRY
    FIELD, H. J.
    GRAHAM, PETER
    JONES, T. MASON
    LANGLEY, J. BAXTER
    LONGDEN, HENRY
    LUSK, SIR ANDREW, 1ST BT.
    MOORE, RICHARD
    MORLEY, SAMUEL
    NICHOLAY, JOHN AUGUSTUS
    NOBLE, JOHN
    PEARCE, C. T.
    PROUDMAN, J. W.
    RANDALL, LEWIS
    READWIN, T. A.
    REED, CHARLES
    ROGERS, EDWARD DRESSER
    TORRENS, WILLIAM TORRENS MCCULLAGH
    VAVASSEUR, J.
    WALKER, ALFRED


Free Land League

    AGNEW, WILLIAM
    ALLEN, H. G.
    ALLISON, SIR ROBERT ANDREW
    ANDERSON, CHARLES HENRY
    ARCH, JOSEPH
    ARMITAGE, BENJAMIN
    ARNOLD, SIR ARTHUR
    BAKER, LAWRENCE JAMES
    BARBOUR, WILLIAM BOYLE
    BASS, HAMAR ALFRED
    BASS, MICHAEL ARTHUR, 1ST BARON BURTON
    BEITH, GILBERT
    BENNETT, JOSEPH
    BLADES, JOHN HORTON

BLAKE, THOMAS
BOLTON, JOSEPH CHENEY
BOLTON, THOMAS DOLLING
BOLTON, THOMAS HENRY
BRADLAUGH, CHARLES
BRASSEY, THOMAS, 1ST EARL BRASSEY
BRINTON, JOHN
BROADHURST, HENRY
BROWN, ALEXANDER LAING
BRUCE, THOMAS JOHN HOVELL THURLOW-CUMMING-, 5TH BARON
   THURLOW
BRUNNER, SIR JOHN TOMLINSON, 1ST BT.
BURT, THOMAS
BUXTON, SYDNEY CHARLES, 1ST EARL BUXTON
CAMERON, SIR CHARLES, 1ST BT.
CAMERON, JOHN MCDONALD
CAMPBELL, SIR GEORGE
CAMPBELL, JOHN ALEXANDER GAVIN, 1ST MARQUIS OF
   BREADALBANE
CARBUTT, SIR EDWARD HAMER, 1ST BT.
CHAMBERLAIN, JOSEPH
CHANNING, FRANCIS ALLSTON, 1ST BN.CHANNING
COBB, HENRY PEYTON
COGHILL, DOUGLAS HARRY
COHEN, ARTHUR JOSEPH
CONYBEARE, CHARLES AUGUSTUS VANSITTART
COOTE, THOMAS
CORBETT, ARCHIBALD L. CAMERON, 1ST BARON ROWALLAN
COSSHAM, HANDEL
CRAWFORD, DONALD
CRAWFORD, WILLIAM
CREED, F. A.
CROMPTON, CHARLES
ESSLEMONT, PETER J.
EVERSHED, SYDNEY
FENWICK, CHARLES
FLETCHER, BANISTER
FOSTER, BALTHAZAR WALTER, 1ST BARON ILKESTON
FOWLER, HENRY HARTLEY, 1ST VISCOUNT WOLVERHAMPTON
FYFFE, CHARLES ALAN
GIBB, THOMAS ECCLESTON
GLADSTONE, HERBERT JOHN, 1ST VISCOUNT GLADSTONE
GOLDSMID, SIR JULIAN, 3RD BT.
GOURLEY, SIR EDWARD TEMPERLEY
GOWER, GEORGE GRANVILLE LEVESON-
GREY, EDWARD, 1ST VISCOUNT GREY OF FALLODON
GULLY, WILLIAM COURT, 1ST VISCOUNT SELBY
HAYNE, CHARLES HAYNE SEALE
HENRIQUES, ALFRED GUTTEREZ
HOBHOUSE, HENRY
HOLDEN, ANGUS, 1ST BARON HOLDEN
HOLDEN, SIR ISAAC, 1ST BT.
HOWARD, JAMES
HOYLE, ISAAC
ILLINGWORTH, ALFRED
INGRAM, SIR WILLIAM JAMES, 1ST BT.
JACOBY, SIR JAMES ALFRED
JOHNS, JASPER WILSON
JOICEY, JAMES, 1ST BARON JOICEY
JONES, LLEWELLYN ARCHER ATHERLEY
KITSON, JAMES, 1ST BARON AIREDALE
LAWSON, HARRY LAWSON WEBSTER LEVY-, 1ST VISCOUNT
   BURNHAM
LEAKE, ROBERT
LEICESTER, JOSEPH LYNN
LENG, SIR JOHN
LEWIS, GEORGE PITT-
LOCKWOOD, SIR FRANK
LYELL, LEONARD, 1ST BARON LYELL
MCARTHUR, ALEXANDER
MCARTHUR, WILLIAM ALEXANDER
MCARTHUR, SIR WILLIAM
MCCULLOCH, JOHN
MACDONALD, RODERICK
MACFARLANE, SIR DONALD HORNE
MCIVER, SIR LEWIS, 1ST BT.
MCLAREN, CHARLES BENJAMIN BRIGHT, 1ST BARON

ABERCONWAY
MAPPIN, SIR FREDERICK THORPE, 1ST BT.
MATHER, SIR WILLIAM
MONTAGU, MONTAGU SAMUEL, 1ST BARON SWAYTHLING
MORGAN, OCTAVIUS VAUGHAN
MORLEY, ARNOLD
MORLEY, JOHN, 1ST VISCOUNT MORLEY OF BLACKBURN
MOULTON,JOHN FLETCHER, BARON MOULTON
MUSPRATT, EDMUND K.
NORTON, CECIL WILLIAM, 1ST BARON RATHCREEDAN
OTTER, FRANCIS
PALMER, WILLIAM WALDEGRAVE, 2ND EARL OF SELBORNE
PAULTON, JAMES MELLOR
PHILIPS, ROBERT NEEDHAM
PICKARD, BENJAMIN
PICKERSGILL, EDWARD HARE
PICTON, JAMES ALLANSON
PLOWDEN, SIR WILLIAM CHICHELE
PORTMAN, EDWIN BERKELEY
PRIESTLEY, BRIGGS
PROVAND, ANDREW DRYBURGH
PULLEY, SIR JOSEPH, 1ST BT.
RAMSAY, JOHN WILLIAM, 13TH EARL OF DALHOUSIE
RENDEL, STUART, 1ST BARON RENDEL
ROBERTS, JOHN
ROBINSON, GEORGE FREDERICK SAMUEL, 1ST MARQUIS OF
   RIPON
ROBSON, WILLIAM SNOWDON, BARON ROBSON
ROGERS, EDWARD DRESSER
ROSCOE, HENRY ENFIELD
ROWLANDS, WILLIAM BOWEN
ROWNTREE, JOSHUA
RUSSELL, CHARLES ARTHUR, BARON RUSSELL OF KILLOWEN
RUSSELL, EDWARD RICHARD
SCHNADHORST, FRANCIS
SHAW, THOMAS
SHIRLEY, WALTER SHIRLEY
SPENSLEY, HOWARD
STANHOPE, PHILIP JAMES, 1ST BARON WEARDALE
STEVENSON, FRANCIS SEYMOUR
STEWART, SIR HALLEY
STRONG, RICHARD
SUMMERS, WILLIAM
TREVELYAN, SIR GEORGE OTTO, 2ND BT.
VANDERBYL, PHILIP
VERNEY, SIR EDMOND HOPE, 3RD BT.
VERNON, GEORGE WILLIAM HENRY VENABLES-, 7TH BARON
   VERNON
WADDY, SAMUEL DANKS
WARDLE, HENRY
WASON, EUGENE
WATT, HUGH
WAYMAN, THOMAS
WILL, JOHN SHIRESS
WILLIAMSON, JAMES, 1ST BARON ASHTON
WILLS, WILLIAM HENRY, 1ST BARON WINTERSTOKE
WINTERBOTHAM, ARTHUR BREND
WRIGHT, CALEB


Howard Assn

ALLEN, RICHARD
ALLEN, STAFFORD
ALSOP, ROBERT
ANSON, THOMAS GEORGE, 2ND EARL OF LICHFIELD
ARNEY, SIR GEORGE ALFRED
BACKHOUSE, EDMUND
BARRAN, SIR JOHN, 1ST BT.
BARRETT, RICHARD
BASSETT, FRANCIS
BAYNES, W. W.
BIRLEY, HUGH
BLAKE, THOMAS
BOWRING, SIR JOHN
BRIGHT, JACOB
BRIGHT, JOHN

BROUGHAM, HENRY PETER, 1ST BARON BROUGHAM AND VAUX
BUXTON, CHARLES
BUXTON, SIR THOMAS FOWELL, 3RD BT.
CHALKLEY, HENRY G.
CLARK, ROBERT
COLE, HENRY THOMAS
COLLINS, SIR WILLIAM
COLMAN, JEREMIAH JAMES
COOPER, JOSEPH
CORBETT, JOHN
CORRY, SIR JAMES PORTER, 1ST BT.
CROLL, ALEXANDER ANGUS
CROPPER, JAMES
ECROYD, WILLIAM FARRER
EDWARDS, JOHN PASSMORE
EWART, WILLIAM
FOWLER, SIR ROBERT NICHOLAS, 1ST BT.
FOWLER, WILLIAM
FOX, JOSEPH JOHN
FRY, LEWIS
FRY, SIR THEODORE, 1ST BT.
GILPIN, CHARLES
GLOVER, ROBERT R.
GROOM, JOHN
GROSVENOR, HUGH LUPUS, 1ST DUKE OF WESTMINSTER
GURNEY, SAMUEL
HADFIELD, GEORGE
HENDERSON, JAMES
HENRY, MITCHELL
HIBBERT, SIR JOHN TOMLINSON
HOWARD, JAMES
HURST, GEORGE
ILLINGWORTH, ALFRED
JACKSON, SIR HENRY MATHER, 2ND BT.
JENKINS, JOHN EDWARD
KELLY, SIR FITZROY EDWARD
KENNAWAY, SIR JOHN HENRY, 3RD BT.
LAWSON, SIR WILFRED, 2ND BT.
LEE, HENRY
LENNOX, LORD HENRY CHARLES GEORGE GORDON
LENNOX, LORD WILLIAM PITT
LETHBRIDGE, SIR JOHN HESKETH, 3RD BT.
LEWIS, SIR CHARLES EDWARD, 1ST BT.
LUSHINGTON, STEPHEN
LUSK, SIR ANDREW, 1ST BT.
MCARTHUR, ALEXANDER
MCARTHUR, SIR WILLIAM
MACFIE, ROBERT ANDREW
MAKINS, SIR WILLIAM THOMAS, 1ST BT.
MANNING, HENRY EDWARD
MANNING, W. T.
MARRIAGE, JOSEPH
MASON, HUGH
MORLEY, SAMUEL
PALMER, GEORGE
PEASE, ARTHUR
PEASE, JOSEPH WHITWELL, 1ST BT.
PEEK, FRANCIS
PENNINGTON, FREDERICK
PIM, JONATHAN
PULESTON, SIR JOHN HENRY
RANDALL, JAMES S.
RECKITT, FRANCIS
RICHARD, HENRY
RUSSELL, JOHN, 1ST EARL RUSSELL
SALT, SIR TITUS, 1ST BT.
SIMON, SIR JOHN
SIMPSON, LIGHTLY
SMITH, CHARLES
SMITH, SAMUEL
SMYTH, RICHARD
STANLEY, EDWARD HENRY, 15TH EARL OF DERBY
STURGE, EDMUND
TALLACK, WILLIAM
TAYLOR, PETER ALFRED
THOMASSON, JOHN PENNINGTON
TREVELYAN, SIR CHARLES EDWARD, 1ST BT.

TREVELYAN, SIR WALTER CALVERLEY, 6TH BT.
VAUGHAN, CHARLES JOHN
VICARS, GEORGE R.
WATERLOW, SIR SYDNEY HEDLEY, 1ST BT.
WATTS, SIR JAMES
WHITBREAD, SAMUEL
WHITWELL, JOHN
WHITWORTH, BENJAMIN
WILMOT, SIR JOHN EARDLEY EARDLEY-, 2ND BT.

Imperial Federation League

BEACH, MICHAEL EDWARD HICKS-, 1ST EARL ST. ALDWYN
BELL, HENRY THOMAS MACKENZIE
BORLASE, WILLIAM COPELAND
BOUVERIE, WILLIAM PLEYDELL, 5TH EARL OF RADNOR
BRYCE, JAMES, 1ST VISCOUNT BRYCE
CAINE, WILLIAM SPROSTON
COHEN, ARTHUR JOSEPH
COLOMB, SIR JOHN CHARLES READY
COOPER, ANTHONY ASHLEY, 7TH EARL OF SHAFTESBURY
COOPER, SIR DANIEL, 1ST BT.
COWEN, JOSEPH
CROPPER, JAMES
DOBELL, RICHARD REID
DOUGLAS, FRANCIS RICHARD WEMYSS CHARTERIS, 10TH EARL
    OF WEMYSS
FORSTER, HUGH OAKELEY ARNOLD-
FORSTER, WILLIAM EDWARD
FOWLER, SIR ROBERT NICHOLAS, 1ST BT.
GISBORNE, WILLIAM
GOURLEY, SIR EDWARD TEMPERLEY
HATTON, HAROLD HENEAGE FINCH-
HAY, SIR JOHN CHARLES DALRYMPLE-, 3RD BT.
HENEAGE, EDWARD, 1ST BARON HENEAGE
HILL, ALEXANDER STAVELEY
LABILLIERE, FRANCIS PETER
LEGGE, WILLIAM HENEAGE, 6TH EARL OF DARTMOUTH
LLOYD, SAMPSON SAMUEL
LUBBOCK, JOHN, 1ST BARON AVEBURY
MCARTHUR, ALEXANDER
MCARTHUR, SIR WILLIAM
MASKELYNE, MERVYN HERBERT NEVIL STORY-
MAXWELL, SIR HERBERT EUSTACE, 7TH BT.
MONSELL, WILLIAM, 1ST BARON EMLY
MORLEY, SAMUEL
PLAYFAIR, LYON, 1ST BARON PLAYFAIR
PRIMROSE, ARCHIBALD PHILIP, 5TH EARL OF ROSEBERY
QUIN, WINDHAM THOMAS WYNDHAM, 4TH EARL OF DUNRAVEN
SEELEY, SIR JOHN ROBERT
SIMMONS, ALFRED
SIMON, SIR JOHN
SMITH, SAMUEL
SMITH, WILLIAM HENRY
SUMMERS, WILLIAM
TENNYSON, ALFRED, 1ST BARON TENNYSON
WATT, JOHN BROWN
WESTGARTH, WILLIAM
WILSON, SIR SAMUEL
WOOD, JOHN DENNISTOUN
YOUNG, SIR FREDERICK

Indian Reform Assn

BELL, THOMAS EVANS
BHOWNAGGREE, SIR MANCHERJEE MERWANJEE
BORLASE, WILLIAM COPELAND
CAIRD, SIR JAMES
CLARK, GAVIN BROWN
DAVIDS, THOMAS WILLIAM RHYS
DIGBY, WILLIAM
FOGGO, GEORGE
HAGGARD, ALFRED HINUBER
MOOLA, N. J.
MUJID, ABDUL

OATES, PARKINSON
PRATT, HODGSON
ROWLANDS, JAMES
SETTNA, A. K.
SINGH, RAMPAL, RAJAH OF KALAKANKAR
WOOD, W. MARTIN

Infant Life Protection Soc

ASHURST, WILLIAM
CHARLEY, SIR WILLIAM THOMAS
CLARKE, CHARLES WILLIAM BARNETT
CURGENVEN, JOHN BRENDON
DAVENPORT, EDWARD GERSHOM
EDGAR, ANDREW
HART, ERNEST ABRAHAM
HASTINGS, GEORGE WOODYATT
HEWITT, GRAILY
MANNING, W. T.
PEEK, FRANCIS
THORPE, RICHARD OSCAR TUGWELL
WHEELER, THOMAS WHITTENBURY
WOOD, RICHARD
WOOD, ROBERT

Intl Arbitration & Peace Assn

AGNEW, WILLIAM
ANDERSON, GEORGE
APPLETON, LEWIS
ARNOLD, SIR ARTHUR
BAYLY, JOHN
BENDIX, PAUL
BENNETT, SAMUEL R.
BIGG, LOUISA <MISS>
BLAKE, THOMAS
BORLASE, WILLIAM COPELAND
BRINTON, JOHN
BROADHURST, HENRY
BROUGH, JOSHUA
BROWN, JOHN
BUCHANAN, GEORGE
BURT, THOMAS
CAMERON, SIR CHARLES, 1ST BT.
CAMPBELL, DUGALD JOHN PHILIP
CAMPBELL, SIR GEORGE
CHANNING, WILLIAM HENRY
CLARKE, JOHN CREEMER
COOPER, ANTHONY ASHLEY, 7TH EARL OF SHAFTESBURY
COOPER, JOHN WILLIAM
CORBET, WILLIAM JOSEPH
CORBETT, JOHN
CORY, JOHN
DALZIELL, JAMES
DAWSON, EDWARD BOUSFIELD
DELL, HENRY
DE WINTON, SIR FRANCIS WALTER
DRUMMOND, PETER
DUCKHAM, THOMAS
EARP, THOMAS
EDWARDS, JOHN PASSMORE
ESSLEMONT, PETER J.
FERGUSON, ROBERT
FORDHAM, EDWARD KING
FORDHAM, SIR GEORGE
FRASER, DONALD
FREMANTLE, WILLIAM HENRY
GELDART, EDMUND MARTIN
GREEN, EDWARD F.
GROSVENOR, HUGH LUPUS, 1ST DUKE OF WESTMINSTER
GURNEY, SAMUEL
HILTON, JOHN
HOLLAND, SAMUEL
HOPWOOD, CHARLES HENRY
HOWELL, GEORGE

JACKSON, -
JENKINS, DAVID JAMES
JOWITT, JOHN
KINNEAR, JOHN
LATHAM, GEORGE WILLIAM
LEAN, WALTER
LEATHAM, WILLIAM HENRY
LLOYD, EDWARD
LUBBOCK, JOHN, 1ST BARON AVEBURY
MCARTHUR, ALEXANDER
MCARTHUR, SIR WILLIAM
MCCARTHY, JUSTIN
MCCLURE, SIR THOMAS 1ST BT.
MCCRACKEN, J.
MCCREE, GEORGE WILSON
MCLAREN, CHARLES BENJAMIN BRIGHT, 1ST BARON
    ABERCONWAY
MCLAREN, DUNCAN
MCLEAN, ROBERT A.
MCMINNIES, JOHN GORDON
MACRAE, CHARLES COLIN
MARLING, SIR SAMUEL STEPHENS, 1ST BT.
MEWBURN, WILLIAM
MILLER, SIR ALEXANDER EDWARD
MORRIS, JOHN
MURRAY, WILLIAM
NAE, W.
NEUMANN, GEORGE
NICOL, JOHN
O'CONNOR, THOMAS POWER
PEDDIE, JOHN DICK
PHILLIPS, WILLIAM
PORTAL, SIR WYNDHAM SPENCER, 1ST BT.
POWELL, WALTER RICE HOWELL
POWER, JOHN O'CONNOR
PRATT, HODGSON
RATHBONE, BENSON
RICHARDSON, HENRY
RUSSELL, FRANCIS ALBERT ROLLO
RUSSELL, GEORGE WILLIAM ERSKINE
ST. JOHN, AUBREY BEAUCLERC LENNOX
SAMUELSON, SIR HENRY BERNHARD, 2ND BT.
SCHWANN, CHARLES E.
SCOTT, BENJAMIN
SELIGMAN, ISAAC
SERGEANT, LEWIS
SHERIDAN, HENRY BRINSLEY
SHIELD, HUGH
SINCLAIR, SIR JOHN GEORGE TOLLEMACHE, 3RD BT.
SKILLICORNE, WILLIAM NASH
SMITH, SAMUEL
SOMERVILLE, ROBERT
SOUTHEY, - <MRS.>
STANLEY, EDWARD HENRY, 15TH EARL OF DERBY
STEPHENS, W. D.
STEWART, JOHN LORNE
STOREY, SAMUEL
THOMPSON, THOMAS CHARLES
THORNE, EDWIN
TIMMINS, SAMUEL
VARLEY, CROMWELL FLEETWOOD
VILLIERS, CHARLES PELHAM
WATSON, SAMUEL
WHITEHEAD, SIR JAMES, 1ST BT.
WILLIAMS, MORGAN B.
WILSON, ISAAC
WOOD, W. MARTIN
WOODALL, WILLIAM
WREN, WALTER
YEO, FRANK ASH

Int1 Law Assn

ALEXANDER, JOSEPH GUNDRY
AMOS, SHELDON
BERNARD, MONTAGUE
BROWN, JOSEPH
CREASY, SIR EDWARD SHEPHERD
JENCKEN, HENRY DIEDRICH
KELLY, SIR FITZROY EDWARD
LUBBOCK, JOHN, 1ST BARON AVEBURY
MORGAN, SIR RICHARD FRANCIS
O'HAGAN, THOMAS, 1ST BARON O'HAGAN
PALMER, JOHN HINDE
PHILLIMORE, SIR ROBERT JOSEPH, 1ST BT.
RICHARD, HENRY
STUART, SIR ROBERT
TWISS, SIR TRAVERS
WASHBURN, EMORY
WEBSTER, THOMAS
WESTROPP, SIR MICHAEL ROBERTS
WILLIAMS, JOSHUA


Jamaica Committee

ABLEY, EDWARD
ACTON, ROGER
AITKEN, D.
ALDER, THOMAS P.
ALDIS, WILLIAM STEADMAN
ALEXANDER, EDWARD, JUN.
ALEXANDER, J.
ALLEN, RICHARD
ALLEN, STAFFORD
ANDERSON, A.
ANDERSON, WILLIAM
ARTHUR, WILLIAM
ASHBY, THOMAS, JUN.
ASHWORTH, EDMUND
ATTENBOROUGH, GEORGE
BACKHOUSE, EDWARD
BACKHOUSE, JAMES
BACKHOUSE, JAMES, JUN.
BACON, J. P.
BAILHACHE, CLEMENT
BAINES, SIR EDWARD
BAINES, FREDERICK
BALL, GEORGE V.
BARNARD, J. E.
BARNARD, JABEZ
BARNARD, W.
BARNES, THOMAS
BARROW, C.
BARTLETT, G. D.
BATCHELOR, HENRY
BAXTER, WILLIAM EDWARD
BEALES, EDMOND
BEECHAM, JOHN
BEESLY, EDWARD SPENCER
BENNETT, ALFRED WILLIAM
BIGGS, R. W.
BOARDMAN, C.
BOORNE, JAMES
BOSHER, W.
BRABY, ALFRED
BRIGGS, E. A.
BRIGGS, N.
BRIGHT, JACOB
BRIGHT, JOHN
BROWN, HENRY
BROWNE, H. D.
BROWNE, SAMUEL W.
BUCKLEY, J. W.
BURNEY, GEORGE
BURNS, DAWSON
BUTTERWORTH, EDWIN
BUXTON, CHARLES

BUXTON, THOMAS FOWELL
BUXTON, SIR THOMAS FOWELL, 3RD BT.
CAIRNES, JOHN ELLIOT
CAMPBELL, JAMES ROBERTSON
CARPENTER, WILLIAM
CARR, ISAAC
CARTER, JOHN
CARTER, ROBERT MEEK
CATCHPOOL, R. D.
CHAMEROVZOW, LOUIS ALEXIS
CHARLESWORTH, WILLIAM
CHESSON, FREDERICK WILLIAM
CHOWN, JOSEPH PARBERY
CHURCHILL, LORD ALFRED SPENCER
CLAPHAM, JOHN
CLARKE, EBENEZER
CLEGG, THOMAS
CONDER, G. W.
CONGREVE, RICHARD
COOKE, C. C.
COOKE, GEORGE
COOKE, ISAAC B.
COOPER, JOSEPH
COSSHAM, HANDEL
CROLL, ALEXANDER ANGUS
CROPPER, JAMES
CROPPER, JOHN
CROSFIELD, JOHN
CROSFIELD, WILLIAM
CROSSLEY, SIR FRANCIS, 1ST BT.
CROWE, W.
CUDWORTH, WILLIAM
CUNNINGTON, JOHN
DAVIS, JOSEPH
DAWES, W. E.
DAWSON, JOHN
D'ELBOUX, L.
DEVENISH, MATTHEW
DICEY, EDWARD JAMES STEPHEN
DRUMMOND, JAMES
DYMOND, J. J.
EDWARDS, R. P.
EDWARDS, WILLIAM
ELT, CHARLES HENRY
ELTON, SIR ARTHUR HALLAM, 7TH BT.
EPPS, JOHN
ESTCOURT, J. H.
ETCHES, W. JEFFERY
EVEREST, R.
FARMER, WILLIAM
FELSHAW, JAMES
FERGUSON, ROBERT
FITTON, SAMUEL
FOX, SAMUEL
FRECKLETON, J. W.
FREEMAN, WILLIAM
FROST, JOHN
GALLOWAY, J. C.
GILL, J.
GILPIN, CHARLES
GLYDE, W. E.
GODSON, W.
GODWIN, J. V.
GOULD, GEORGE
GRUBB, -
GUTHRIE, J.
HALL, CHRISTOPHER NEWMAN
HANSON, JAMES
HARGREAVES, WILLIAM
HARRIS, ALFRED
HARRIS, HENRY
HARRISON, FREDERICK
HARTLEY, R.
HARVEY, -
HARVEY, JAMES
HAWORTH, ABRAHAM
HERFORD, WILLIAM HENRY

HERVEY, JAMES
HEWITT, FRANCIS
HEYWOOD, ABEL
HEYWOOD, ROBERT
HILL, THOMAS ROWLEY
HILLS, JOHN
HILTON, JOHN
HINDEL, W. R.
HOLCOMBE, F. J.
HOLDEN, SIR ISAAC, 1ST BT.
HOLLAND, CHARLES
HOOD, EDWIN PAXTON
HORNER, J. A.
HORNIMAN, JOHN
HUGHES, THOMAS
HUNTLEY, JOSEPH
ILLINGWORTH, ALFRED
INGRAM, GEORGE S.
ISBISTER, ALEXANDER KENNEDY
JEFFERY, ALFRED
JOBSON, ROBERT
JOHNSON, RICHARD
JOHNSON, WILLIAM
JONES, ELIJAH
JOSELAND, GEORGE
KELL, EDMUND
KELL, ROBERT
KELL, S. C.
KENNY, JOHN
KNOX, THOMAS
LANGLEY, J. BAXTER
LAWSON, SIR WILFRED, 2ND BT.
LEESE, JOSEPH
LEFEVRE, GEORGE JOHN SHAW-, 1ST BARON EVERSLEY
LEVEY, T. B. <OR LOVEY>
LONG, GEORGE
LOWE, GEORGE
LUDLOW, JOHN MALCOLM FORBES
LUSHINGTON, SIR GODFREY
MCARTHUR, ALEXANDER
MCARTHUR, SIR WILLIAM
MACKENZIE, J.
MCLAREN, DUNCAN
MALLESON, JOHN PHILIP
MALLESON, WILLIAM TAYLOR
MASON, HUGH
MEDWIN, W.
MIALL, EDWARD
MILL, JOHN STUART
MILLS, G. M. W.
MOORE, JOHN
MOORE, RICHARD
MOORE, THOMAS
MORGAN, WILLIAM
MORLEY, SAMUEL
MUSPRATT, EDMUND K.
NATHAN, WILLIAM
NELSON, J. E.
NELSON, THOMAS
NEWMAN, FRANCIS WILLIAM
NICHOLAY, JOHN AUGUSTUS
NOBLE, JOHN
NORTON, JOHN <"CAPT.">
NUNNELEY, JOSEPH
ORMEROD, OLIVER
PALMER, W. J.
PANKHURST, RICHARD MARSDEN
PARTRIDGE, J. ARTHUR
PATON, J. M.
PATTERSON, JOHN
PAULTON, ABRAHAM WALTER
PEDLEY, GEORGE
PEEK, RICHARD
PENROSE, THOMAS
PERRY, -
PETO, SIR SAMUEL MORTON, 1ST BT.
PETRIE, JOHN

POTTER, THOMAS BAYLEY
PRICE, THOMAS
PRIESTMAN, FREDERICK
PRIESTMAN, J., JUN.
PRIESTMAN, JOHN
PROCTOR, JAMES
PRYCE, R. VAUGHAN
PRYOR, JOHN
RALEIGH, ALEXANDER
RAWLINGS, CHARLES E., JUN.
REDFERN, THOMAS
REDFERN, WILLIAM
RICHARD, HENRY
RICHARDSON, JOHN
ROBBERDS, JOHN
ROBERTS, THOMAS
ROBINSON, HENRY CRABB
ROBINSON, W. MOORE
ROSLING, SAMUEL
ROSS, THOMAS
ROWE, W. K.
RYLEY, T. C.
SALT, SIR TITUS, 1ST BT.
SALWEY, HENRY
SANDWITH, HUMPHREY
SCOTT, BENJAMIN
SHAEN, WILLIAM
SHARLAND, HENRY
SHAW, JOSEPH
SMITH, BROOKES
SMITH, GOLDWIN
SMITH, JOHN
SMITH, JOSEPH
SMITH, W. HICKMAN
SOLLY, HENRY
SOMMERVILLE, WILLIAM
SPEARS, ROBERT
SPENCER, HERBERT
SPONG, JAMES
STEINTHAL, S. ALFRED
STEPHENS, FREDERICK
STEPHENS, W. F. D.
STEVENS, D. M.
STITT, JOHN J.
STOVEL, CHARLES
STOW, EDWARD
STUART, P.
SUTTON, MARTIN HOPE
TAYLER, JOHN JAMES
TAYLOR, FRANCIS
TAYLOR, HARRY
TAYLOR, JAMES, JUN.
TAYLOR, JOHN
TAYLOR, PETER ALFRED
TAYLOR, SHERBROOKE
THISTLETHWAITE, J.
THOMASSON, THOMAS
TORR, JOHN BERRY
TORRENS, WILLIAM TORRENS MCCULLAGH
TRESTRAIL, FREDERICK
TREVELYAN, ARTHUR
TRIMBLE, ROBERT
TUCK, WILLIAM
TUCKETT, FREDERICK
TYSE, CAREY
VERNON, -
WAINWRIGHT, R. E.
WALHOUSE, - <"CAPT.">
WALLIS, MARRIAGE
WALLS, J. G.
WALTERS, W.
WATTS, SIR JAMES
WATTS, SAMUEL
WEBB, R. D.
WEBB, WILLIAM
WELLS, -
WELLS, JAMES

WENTNER, JOSEPH
WEST, JAMES GRAHAM
WHITE, GEORGE
WHITE, JAMES
WHITEHEAD, -
WHITTAKER, W.
WHITWORTH, ROBERT
WIGLESWORTH, PARKIN
WILBERFORCE, HENRY WILLIAM
WILKINSON, N. M.
WILKINSON, R.
WILKS, JOHN MARK
WILLIAMS, CHARLES
WILLIAMS, H. M.
WILLIAMS, JOHN
WILLIAMS, S. D.
WILLS, WILLIAM HENRY
WINKWORTH, STEPHEN
WOOLLEY, GEORGE B.
YATES, JAMES
YOUNG, B. C.

## Kyrle Soc

ADAMS, COLE A.
ALFRED ERNEST ALBERT, DUKE OF EDINBURGH AND OF
    SAXE-COBURG AND GOTHA
ATKINSON, - <MRS. BEAVINGTON ATKINSON>
BOSTOCK, - <MISS>
BRABAZON, REGINALD, 12TH EARL OF MEATH
BUSK, E. S. <MISS>
CLIFFORD, EDWARD C.
DRYHURST, FREDERICK JOHN
DYMES, - <MISS>
EMPSON, CHARLES WILLIAM
FELL, - <MRS. W. T.>
FELL, W. T.
FENN, W. W.
FORTESCUE, LADY CAMILLA ELEANOR <MRS. D.F. FORTESCUE,
    DAU. 4TH E. PORTSMOUTH>
GROSVENOR, HUGH LUPUS, 1ST DUKE OF WESTMINSTER
HARDINGE, - <MRS.>
HARRISON, HARRIET <MISS>
HILL, OCTAVIA
HOBHOUSE, MARY, LADY <WIFE OF 1ST BARON HOBHOUSE, nee
    FARRER>
HODGE, - <MISS>
HUNTER, SIR ROBERT
JACKSON, - <MISS>
JAMES, LILIAN <MISS>
JOHNSON, - <MISS>
KEATINGE, RICHARD HARTE
LAMBERT, BROOKE
LAWSON, MALCOLM
LEFEVRE, EMILY OCTAVIA SHAW- <MISS>
LEYCESTER, - <MISS>
LOUISE CAROLINE ALBERTA, H.R.H. PRINCESS <MARCHIONESS
    OF LORNE>
LYALL, MARY
MAURICE, CHARLES EDMUND
MAURICE, EMILY SOUTHWOOD <MRS. CHARLES EDMUND
    MAURICE, nee HILL>
MILLS, FREDERICK C.
MORRIS, WILLIAM
NATTALI, B.
PAGET, NINA <MISS>
PALMER, WILLIAM WALDEGRAVE, 2ND EARL OF SELBORNE
PEASE, E. R.
PICKTON, - <MISS>
POULTER, R. C.
ROBERTS, WILLIAM CHANDLER <-AUSTEN after 1885>
STEVENS, DE GRASS <MISS>
TANNER, - <MRS. T. SLINGSBY TANNER>
TANNER, T. SLINGSBY
TOWNSEND, C. HARRISON
VYVYAN, C. <MISS>

WATTS, GEORGE FREDERICK
WHITMORE, CHARLES ALGERNON
WILKINSON, F. R. <MISS>
WILLIAMS, T. A. <MRS.>
YORKE, HARRIOT <MISS>

## Ladies´ Natl Assn for Repeal of Contagious Diseases Acts

BACKHOUSE, KATHERINE E. <MRS. EDWARD BACKHOUSE, nee
    MOUNSEY>
BECKER, LYDIA ERNESTINE
BLACKBURN, CATHERINE <MRS.>
BRIGHT, URSULA M. <MRS. JACOB BRIGHT, nee MELLOR>
BUTLER, JOSEPHINE E. <MRS. GEORGE BUTLER, nee GREY>
ESTLIN, MARY A.<OR E.>
LUCAS, MARGARET <MRS. SAMUEL LUCAS, nee BRIGHT>
MCLAREN, PRISCILLA <MRS. DUNCAN MCLAREN, nee BRIGHT>
MARTINEAU, HARRIET
MERRYWEATHER, MARY <MISS>
NICHOL, ELIZABETH PEASE <MRS. JOHN PRINGLE NICHOL,
    nee PEASE>
PHILLIPPS, LUCY MARCH <MISS>
PRIESTMAN, MARY
REID, JESSY <MRS.>
TANNER, M. A. <MRS. ARTHUR TANNER>
VENTURI, EMILIE <MRS. G. A. VENTURI, nee ASHURST>
WIGHAM, JANE <MISS>
WOLSTENHOLME, ELIZABETH C.

## Land Law Reform League

ARCH, JOSEPH
AVELING, EDWARD BIBBONS
BESANT, ANNIE
BRADLAUGH, CHARLES
BRYSON, JOHN
BURT, THOMAS
CRAWFORD, WILLIAM
DILKE, ASHTON WENTWORTH
FORDER, ROBERT
FREESTON, J.
GURNEY, J.
HEADLAM, STEWART DUCKWORTH
LE LUBEZ, P. A. V.
MACDONALD, ALEXANDER
SARSON, GEORGE
SHARMAN, WILLIAM
SYMES, JOHN ELLIOTSON
TAYLOR, PETER ALFRED
TOYN, JOSEPH
WHALLEY, GEORGE HAMMOND

## Land Nationalization Soc

BRIGGS, THOMAS
BURROWS, HERBERT
BUTTIFANT, A. G.
CLARK, GAVIN BROWN
CRAIG, EDWARD THOMAS
DAVIDS, THOMAS WILLIAM RHYS
DURANT, JOHN CHARLES
ELLIOTT, T. H.
FITZGERALD, DESMOND G.
GIRDLESTONE, EDWARD DEACON
HATZFIELD, E.
HENNESSY, PATRICK
HOLT, ROBERT B.
HOOPER, JAMES
JAMESON, WILLIAM
LEE, C.
LEY, H. W.
LOWE, - <MRS.>
LUCRAFT, BENJAMIN
MCDONNELL, A.

MOBERLY, H. G.
NEWCOMBE, C. P.
NEWMAN, FRANCIS WILLIAM
PARKER, J. A.
RATCLIFF, WALTER HENRY
REEVES, W.
REYNOLDS, W.
SAUNDERS, WILLIAM
SWINTON, A. C.
TAYLOR, HELEN <MISS>
TAYLOR, JONATHAN
TRANT, W.
VINCENT, J. E. M.
WALKER, THOMAS FERDINAND
WALLACE, ALFRED RUSSELL
WINDER, F. A.
WINDUST, C. A.
WINKS, A. F.
WREN, WALTER

Land Tenure Reform Assn

BOURNE, HENRY RICHARD FOX
COWPER, T. A. <"COL.">
COX, J. C.
CREMER, SIR WILLIAM RANDAL
DILKE, SIR CHARLES WENTWORTH, 2ND BT.
EVANS, HOWARD
HARE, THOMAS
HUNTER, WILLIAM ALEXANDER
KENNEDY, H. G.
MAXSE, FREDERICK AUGUSTUS
MILL, JOHN STUART
MOTTERSHEAD, THOMAS
PENNINGTON, FREDERICK
REID, ANDREW
STANLEY, EDWARD LYULPH, 4TH BN. STANLEY OF ALDERLEY
    AND 4TH BN. SHEFFIELD
TAYLOR, PETER ALFRED

League for Defense of Constitutional Rights

ADAMS, -
ARCH, JOSEPH
AVELING, EDWARD BIBBONS
BELL, THOMAS EVANS
BESANT, ANNIE
CASSON, W. A.
CONWAY, MONCURE DANIEL
CRAWFORD, WILLIAM
DRYSDALE CHARLES ROBERT
FOOTE, G. W.
FREESTON, J.
GURNEY, J.
HATT, J.
HEADLAM, STEWART DUCKWORTH
HILL, ALSAGER HAY
LE LUBEZ, P. A. V.
LEVY, JOSEPH HIAM
MIALL, M.
NIEASS, J. D.
SHARMAN, WILLIAM
STANDRING, GEORGE
SWAAGMAN, JOANNES
SYMONDS, ARTHUR GIBB
TOYN, JOSEPH

Liberty & Property Defense League

BRAMWELL, GEORGE WILLIAM WILSHERE, 1ST BARON BRAMWELL
CROFTS, W. C.
DONISTHORPE, WORDSWORTH
DOUGLAS, FRANCIS RICHARD WEMYSS CHARTERIS, 10TH EARL
    OF WEMYSS
ELLIOT, SIR GEORGE AUGUSTUS
FARQUHAR, SIR WALTER ROCKCLIFFE, 3RD BT.
FORTESCUE, HUGH, 3RD EARL FORTESCUE
HAMBER, - <"CAPT.">
HERBERT, GEORGE ROBERT CHARLES, 13TH EARL OF PEMBROKE
HILL, ALSAGER HAY
MULLINS, J. A.
POCHIN, HENRY DAVIS
STEPHENS, HENRY CHARLES
TEMPLE, SIR RICHARD, 1ST BT.
TOMLINSON, SIR WILLIAM EDWARD MURRAY, 1ST BT.
TORRENS, WILLIAM TORRENS MCCULLAGH
WATKIN, SIR EDWARD WILLIAM, 1ST BT.
WELLS, WILLIAM
WILDE, JAMES PLAISTED, 1ST BARON PENZANCE

Local Taxation Comtee [of Central Chamber of
Agriculture]

ANDREWS, H. GENGE
BACKHOUSE, EDMUND
BEACH, MICHAEL EDWARD HICKS-, 1ST EARL ST. ALDWYN
CRAIGIE, PATRICK GEORGE
HENEAGE, EDWARD, 1ST BARON HENEAGE
HERVEY, LORD FRANCIS
LECHMERE, SIR EDMUND ANTHONY HARLEY, 3RD BT.
LEIGHTON, STANLEY
LOPES, SIR MASSEY, 3RD BT.
MASFEN, R. H.
MUNTZ, GEORGE FREDERICK
PAGET, SIR RICHARD HORNER, 1ST BT.
PELL, ALBERT
PHIPPS, PICKERING
READ, CLARE SEWELL
RUSSON, JOSEPH
STANHOPE, SIR WALTER THOMAS WILLIAM SPENCER
STARTIN, ARTHUR
WINN, ROWLAND, 1ST BARON ST. OSWALD
YORKE, JOHN REGINALD

London Comtee Exposure & Suppresn Traffic In Girls

BASTIN, EDWARD PHILIP
BOYD, THOMAS LUNHAM
BUNTING, MARY HYETT <MRS. PERCY BUNTING, nee LIDGETT>
BUTLER, GEORGE GREY
BUTLER, JOSEPHINE E. <MRS. GEORGE BUTLER, nee GREY>
DYER, ALFRED STACE
GILLETT, GEORGE
GOULT, SYDNEY <OR SIDNEY>
JOYCE, JOSEPH
MARTINEAU, R. F.
MORGAN, RICHARD COPE
PAYNE, WILLIAM
PORTER, JAMES BIGGS
SCOTT, BENJAMIN
SCOTT, SEPTIMUS RICHARD
SHAEN, WILLIAM
STEWARD, MARY <MRS.>
STUART, JAMES
TARRING, SIR CHARLES JAMES
WILSON, HENRY JOSEPH

London Municipal Reform League

BARNES, F. W.
BAYLEY, EDWARD HODSON
BUXTON, SYDNEY CHARLES, 1ST EARL BUXTON
CAMERON, ANDREW
CLARK, ROBERT
CURRIE, BERTRAM WODEHOUSE
DAVIDSON, JOHN MORRISON
DEBENHAM, FRANK
DE WINTON, SIR FRANCIS WALTER
DONALDSON, J. HUNTER
DRAPER, JOHN
DUNN, ANDREW
EMANUEL, LEWIS
ENDEAN, J. RUSSELL
FENWICK, PASCOE
FIRTH, JOSEPH FIRTH BOTTOMLEY
GIBBONS, H. F.
GLEN, WILLIAM CUNNINGHAM
GRANT, JAMES CORRIE BRIGHTON
GREVILLE, F. <HON.>
HALFORD, F. B.
HARVEY, W. C.
HILL, ALSAGER HAY
HOLMES, G. B.
HUME, MARTIN ANDREW SHARP
JONES, JOHN JAMES
KING, R. L.
KNIGHT, A. A.
KNIGHT, G. J., JUN.
LANCASTER, G.
LEAY, H.
LLOYD, JOHN
LONG, FREDERICK
MANSON, JAMES ALEXANDER
MARCH, R. A.
MARSDEN, MARK EAGLES
MOORE, JOHN HOWARD
MUNICH, C. J.
NORMAN, A.
OFFOR, GEORGE
PEARCE, E. R.
PEARCE, R.
PHILLIPS, WILLIAM
PICKFORD, F.
POTTO, T. C.
RAMSAY, JOHN WILLIAM, 13TH EARL OF DALHOUSIE
READE, CHARLES DARBY
STREETER, E. W.
TORR, JAMES FENNING
WHALLEY, GEORGE HAMMOND


London Soc for Abolition of Compulsory Vaccination

AYTON, WILLIAM ALEXANDER
BAKER, THOMAS
BEALE, GEORGE C.
BLENNERHASSETT, ROWLAND PONSONBY
BLIGH, EDWARD HENRY STUART, 7TH EARL OF DARNLEY
BURT, THOMAS
BUTLER, JOSEPHINE E. <MRS. GEORGE BUTLER, nee GREY>
COLLINS, W. J.
CONSTABLE, HENRY STRICKLAND-
CONWAY, MONCURE DANIEL
DAVIE, JOHN
DAVIS, F., JN.
FOX, W. F.
GIBBS, G. S.
GREIG, JAMES
HALL, SPENCER TIMOTHY
HAUGHTON, EDWARD
HODGSON, RICHARD
JERVOISE, SIR JERVOISE CLARKE-, 2ND BT.
KIRK, JOHN
MAYOR, JOHN EYTON BICKERSTETH

NEWMAN, FRANCIS WILLIAM
NOAILLES, MARIE, COUNTESS DE
PEARSON, CORNELIUS
PENROSE, SIR GEORGE DEVONSHIRE
PITMAN, HENRY
PITMAN, SIR ISAAC
PORT, H.
POTTS, JOHN FAULKNER
PROCTER, EDMUND
REES, ROWLAND
SKIPWORTH, GEORGE BORMAN
SWINTON, A. C.
TATHAM, GEORGE
TAYLOR, PETER ALFRED
TEBB, WILLIAM
WALLACE, - <MRS.>
WARD, W. GIBSON
WHEELER, ALEXANDER
WHITE, WILLIAM
WILKINSON, JAMES JOHN GARTH
YOUNG, WILLIAM


Malthusian League

ALLBUTT, H. ARTHUR
ANDERSEN, GEORGE
BELL, -
BESANT, ANNIE
BIRCH, WILLIAM JOHN
BOND, C. R.
BRADLAUGH, CHARLES
BROWN, -
BRYSON, JOHN
DALLOW, -
DRAY, -
DRYSDALE, ALICE VICKERY
DRYSDALE CHARLES ROBERT
GROUT, -
GROUT, - <MRS.>
HARDWICKE, HERBERT JUNIUS
HEMBER, R. G.
HITCHMAN, WILLIAM
LOWE, - <MRS.>
MITCHELL, - <MISS>
MITCHELL, JULIA
MITCHELL, KATE
PAGE, - <MRS.>
PAGE, J. K.
PARRIS, - <MRS. TOUZEAU PARRIS>
PARRIS, TOUZEAU
RENNICK, - <MRS. CHARLES RENNICK>
RENNICK, CHARLES
REYNOLDS, W. J.
REYNOLDS, WILLIAM HAMMOND
RITCHIE, J. J.
RIVERS, -
ROGERS, -
SEYLER, -
SHEARER, J. R.
STANDRING, GEORGE
SWAAGMAN, - <MRS. JOANNES SWAAGMAN>
SWAAGMAN, JOANNES
TREVELYAN, ARTHUR
TRUELOVE, EDWARD
VINCENT, - <MRS.>
WOAKES, EDWARD
YOUNG, -

Metro Free Libraries Assn

BENNETT, SIR JOHN
BRUCE, HENRY AUSTIN, 1ST BARON ABERDARE
CHOWDER, AUGUSTUS G.
CHURCHILL, LORD ALFRED SPENCER
CURRIE, SIR EDMUND HAY
DAVIS, ISRAEL
DUFF, MOUNTSTUART ELPHINSTONE GRANT-
FAWCETT, HENRY
FITZMAURICE, EDMOND GEORGE PETTY, 1ST BARON
    FITZMAURICE OF LEIGH
HANSARD, SEPTIMUS COX HOLMES
HARRISON, ROBERT
HEYWOOD, JAMES
HOLMS, JOHN
HUGHES, THOMAS
JACKSON, JOHN
JEVONS, WILLIAM STANLEY
LEVI, LEONE
LUBBOCK, JOHN, 1ST BARON AVEBURY
MORLEY, HENRY
MUNDELLA, ANTHONY JOHN
NICHOLSON, EDWARD WILLIAMS BYRON
POLLOCK, SIR WILLIAM FREDERICK, 2ND BT.
RICHARD, HENRY
RIGG, JAMES HARRISON
ROGERS, WILLIAM
SAUNDERS, SEDGWICK <"DR.">
STANLEY, EDWARD LYULPH, 4TH BN. STANLEY OF ALDERLEY
    AND 4TH BN. SHEFFIELD
TAIT, ARCHIBALD CAMPBELL
TEDDER, HENRY RICHARD
TROLLOPE, ANTHONY
WATHERSTON, EDWARD J.


Metro Public Gardens Assn

BEDFORD, JOHN THOMAS
BILLING, ROBERT CLAUDIUS
BIRKETT, PERCIVAL
BOND, EDWARD
BRABAZON, REGINALD, 12TH EARL OF MEATH
BRYCE, JAMES, 1ST VISCOUNT BRYCE
BURGES, YNYR HENRY
BUXTON, EDWARD NORTH
CAINE, WILLIAM SPROSTON
CARLETON, DUDLEY WILMOT, 4TH BARON DORCHESTER
CARPENTER, WILLIAM BOYD
CASSIN, BURMAN
CATES, ARTHUR
CECIL, ROBERT ARTHUR TALBOT GASCOYNE-, 3RD MARQUIS OF
    SALISBURY
CHAMBERS, SIR THOMAS
COUTTS, FRANCIS BURDETT THOMAS MONEY-
COWPER, FRANCIS THOMAS DE GREY, 7TH EARL COWPER
COWPER, KATRINE CECILIA, COUNTESS COWPER <WIFE OF 7TH
    EARL, nee COMPTON>
EGERTON, WILBRAHAM, 1ST EARL EGERTON OF TATTON
ELLIS, SIR JOHN WHITTAKER, 1ST BT.
FAWCETT, HENRY
FIRTH, JOSEPH FIRTH BOTTOMLEY
FLOWER, CYRIL, 1ST BARON BATTERSEA
GORDON, JOHN CAMPBELL HAMILTON, 1ST MARQUIS OF
    ABERDEEN AND TEMAIR
GROSVENOR, HUGH LUPUS, 1ST DUKE OF WESTMINSTER
GROSVENOR, RICHARD CECIL
GROSVENOR, ROBERT, 1ST BARON EBURY
HAMILTON, LORD CLAUD JOHN
HAMILTON, LORD GEORGE FRANCIS
HANSARD, SEPTIMUS COX HOLMES
HART, ERNEST ABRAHAM
HAWEIS, HUGH REGINALD
HAY, WILLIAM MONTAGU, 10TH MARQUIS OF TWEEDDALE
HOLLOND, JOHN ROBERT
HOLMS, JOHN

HOW, WILLIAM WALSHAM
HUBBARD, JOHN GELLIBRAND, 1ST BARON ADDINGTON
HULEATT, HUGH
JAMES, WALTER HENRY, 2ND BARON NORTHBOURNE
JEPHSON, ARTHUR WILLIAM
JONES, HARRY
KENNEDY, ARCHIBALD, 3RD MARQUIS OF AILSA
LLOYD, JOHN
LOWTHER, WILLIAM
MEADE, EDWARD R.
MOCATTA, FREDERICK DAVID
MOORE, CECIL
MORLEY, SAMUEL
NATION, WILLIAM HAMILTON CODRINGTON
NOEL, ERNEST
PLUNKETT, EDWARD, 16TH BARON DUNSANY
PRATT, HODGSON
RICE, ARTHUR DE CARDONNEL, 6TH BARON DYNEVOR
ROGERS, WILLIAM
RUSSELL, FRANCIS ALBERT ROLLO
SHUTTLEWORTH, HENRY CARY
STANHOPE, ARTHUR PHILIP, 6TH EARL STANHOPE
THOMPSON, GEORGE IVAN
THOROLD, ANTHONY WILSON
TYNDALL, JOHN
VATCHER, JOHN SIDNEY ADOLPHUS
VESEY, JOHN ROBERT WILLIAM, 4TH VISCOUNT DE VESCI
VINCENT, SIR WILLIAM, 12TH BT.
WEBBER, WILLIAM THOMAS THORNHILL
WESTGARTH, WILLIAM
WESTLAKE, JOHN
WHITE, HENRY
WILBRAHAM, EDWARD BOOTLE-, 1ST EARL OF LATHOM
WRIGHT, HENRY


Natl Assn for Promotion of State Colonization

ACHESON, ARCHIBALD BRABAZON SPARROW, 4TH EARL OF
    GOSFORD
BAILLIE, ALEXANDER DUNDAS ROSS COCHRANE-WISHEART-,
    1ST BARON LAMINGTON
BARCLAY, JAMES WILLIAM
BELL, HENRY THOMAS MACKENZIE
BILLING, ROBERT CLAUDIUS
BLANCHARD, - <MRS. EDWARD LITT LEMAN BLANCHARD>
BOUVERIE, WILLIAM PLEYDELL, 5TH EARL OF RADNOR
BRABAZON, REGINALD, 12TH EARL OF MEATH
BRASSEY, THOMAS, 1ST EARL BRASSEY
BRIDGER, JOHN
BROOKE, SIR RICHARD, 7TH BT.
BUXTON, EDWARD NORTH
BYRON, GEORGE FREDERICK WILLIAM, 9TH BARON BYRON
CAPELL, REGINALD ALGERNON
CARLETON, DUDLEY WILMOT, 4TH BARON DORCHESTER
CARPENTER, WILLIAM BOYD
CATHCART, EMILY ELIZA, LADY GORDON <MRS. J. GORDON &
    LADY R. CATHCART, nee PR
CAVE, ALFRED THOMAS TOWNSHEND VERNEY-, 5TH BARON
    BRAYE
CHALMERS, FREDERICK WILLIAM MARSH
CHANCE, ALEXANDER MACOMB
CHURCHILL, LORD ALFRED SPENCER
CLEEVE, FREDERICK
COLOMB, SIR JOHN CHARLES READY
COOTE, WILLIAM ALEXANDER
COUTTS, FRANCIS BURDETT THOMAS MONEY-
COWAN, JAMES
CUMBERLAND, CHARLES EDWARD
CURZON, GEORGE HENRY ROPER-, 16TH BARON TEYNHAM
CURZON, ROBERT NATHANIEL CECIL GEORGE, 15TH BARON
    ZOUCHE
DE LOUSADA, FRANCIS CLIFFORD, DUKE <SPANISH> DE
    LOUSADA Y LOUSADA
DE RICCI, JAMES HERMAN
DUFF, ALEXANDER WILLIAM GEORGE, 1ST DUKE OF FIFE
DUNDAS, LADY JANE <MRS. PHILIP DUNDAS, DAU. 8TH EARL

OF WEMYSS>
EDGELL, EDGELL WYATT
EDWARDS, THOMAS DYER, JR.
EGERTON, FRANCIS
EGERTON, WILBRAHAM, 1ST EARL EGERTON OF TATTON
ELLICOTT, CHARLES JOHN
ELLIS, SIR JOHN WHITTAKER, 1ST BT.
FAITHFULL, EMILY
FIELD, EDWARD
FITZGERALD, SIR ROBERT UNIAKE PENROSE, 1ST BT.
FOWLER, SIR ROBERT NICHOLAS, 1ST BT.
FOX, FRANCIS W.
FROUDE, JAMES ANTHONY
FULCHER, E.
FYERS, WILLIAM AUGUSTUS
GAMLEN, R. H.
GIBBS, HENRY HUCKS, 1ST BARON ALDENHAM
GOODWIN, HARVEY
GOURLEY, SIR EDWARD TEMPERLEY
GREGORY, GEORGE BURROW
GREIG, JOHN
HALL, CHRISTOPHER NEWMAN
HALL, EDWARD HEPPLE-
HAMBRO, SIR EVERARD ALEXANDER
HAMILTON, ANDREW <"CAPT.">
HAMILTON, SIR CHARLES EDWARD, 1ST BT.
HATTON, HAROLD HENEAGE FINCH-
HESTER, T. J.
HOARE, H. N. HAMILTON
HOW, WILLIAM WALSHAM
HULEATT, HUGH
HUTTON, JAMES FREDERICK
INSLEY, WILLIAM PIMBLETT
JOHNS, JASPER WILSON
JOYCE, ELLEN <MRS. JAMES GERALD JOYCE, DAU. 5TH BARON
    DYNEVOR>
KENNARD, EDMUND HEGAN
KENNARD, STEPHEN P.
KIMBER, SIR HENRY, 1ST BT.
KINNEAR, JOHN BOYD-
LAMBERT, FREDERICK FOX
LAWLEY, BEILBY, 3RD BARON WENLOCK
LAWSON, HARRY LAWSON WEBSTER LEVY-, 1ST VISCOUNT
    BURNHAM
LEGGE, WILLIAM WALTER, 5TH EARL OF DARTMOUTH
LEIGHTON, STANLEY
LITTLE, JAMES STANLEY
LOWTHER, WILLIAM
MACKENZIE, COLIN
MANNING, HENRY EDWARD
MAXWELL, SIR HERBERT EUSTACE, 7TH BT.
MEADE, EDWARD R.
MERRICK, GEORGE PURNELL
MOCATTA, FREDERICK DAVID
MONTAGU, WILLIAM DROGO, 7TH DUKE OF MANCHESTER
NEWTON, SIR HENRY WILLIAM
NICKALLS, SIR PATTESON
NORTHCOTE, HENRY STAFFORD, 1ST BARON NORTHCOTE OF
    EXETER
OAKLEY, JOHN
OWEN, SIR FRANCIS PHILIP CUNLIFFE
PAGE, FLOOD <"MAJOR">
PAKENHAM, WILLIAM LYGON, 4TH EARL OF LONGFORD
PALMER, GEORGE
PATTISON, H. J.
PINNEY, WILLIAM
PRATT, HODGSON
PULESTON, SIR JOHN HENRY
RANKIN, JAMES H., 1ST BT.
REANEY, GEORGE SALE
RICE, ARTHUR DE CARDONNEL, 6TH BARON DYNEVOR
ROBINSON, H. W.
RYE, MARIA SUSAN <MISS>
SALT, SIR THOMAS, 1ST BT.
SIMMONS, ALFRED
SINCLAIR, SIR JOHN GEORGE TOLLEMACHE, 3RD BT.
SMITH, MANSFIELD GEORGE

SMITH, SAMUEL
SMITH, T.
SMITH, WALTER F.
SMYTHE, EMILY ANNE, LADY STRANGFORD <wife of 8TH
    VISCOUNT STRANGFORD, nee BEAUFORT>
SOMES, GEORGE
SPENSLEY, WILLIAM
SPURGEON, CHARLES HADDON
STERN, SYDNEY JAMES, 1ST BARON WANDSWORTH
SUTHERST, THOMAS
SWANWICK, ANNA <MISS>
TENNYSON, ALFRED, 1ST BARON TENNYSON
TROWER, H. SEYMOUR
TYNDALL, JOHN
VERNEY, SIR EDMOND HOPE, 3RD BT.
VESEY, JOHN ROBERT WILLIAM, 4TH VISCOUNT DE VESCI
WAGNER, HENRY
WATKINS, HENRY GEORGE, JUN.
WEBBER, WILLIAM THOMAS THORNHILL
WELLESLEY, LADY VICTORIA CATHERINE MARY
    POLE-TYLNEY-LONG-
WESTGARTH, WILLIAM
WHITE, ARNOLD
WILBERFORCE, ERNEST ROLAND
WILKINSON, GEORGE HOWARD
WILSON, JOHN
WOLSELEY, GARNET JOSEPH, 1ST VISCOUNT WOLSELEY
YOUNG, SIR FREDERICK


Natl Assn for Repeal Blasphemy Laws

    BURROWS, HERBERT
    FORDER, ROBERT
    FORSTER, JOSEPH
    GELDART, EDMUND MARTIN
    GRECE, CLAIR J.
    HEADLAM, STEWART DUCKWORTH
    HUNTER, WILLIAM ALEXANDER
    MAWER, WALTER
    MERRIFIELD, JOHN
    MOSS, JOSEPH L.
    SHARMAN, WILLIAM
    VERINDER, FREDERICK


Natl Assn for Repeal Contagious Diseases Acts

    ARMITSTEAD, GEORGE, 1ST BARON ARMITSTEAD
    ARNOLD, SIR ARTHUR
    ARTHUR, WILLIAM
    BANKS, - <MRS. FREDERICK CHARLES BANKS>
    BANKS, FREDERICK CHARLES
    BRIGHT, JACOB
    BROGDEN, ALEXANDER
    BROWN, SIR ALEXANDER HARGREAVES, 1ST BT.
    BUDGETT, JAMES S.
    BUDGETT, SAMUEL
    BURT, THOMAS
    CAINE, WILLIAM SPROSTON
    CAMERON, SIR CHARLES, 1ST BT.
    CHARLETON, ROBERT
    CLARKE, JOHN CREEMER
    COLMAN, JEREMIAH JAMES
    CORBETT, JOHN
    COWAN, JAMES
    COWEN, JOSEPH
    CROSSLEY, EDWARD
    DAVIES, DAVID
    DICKSON, THOMAS ALEXANDER
    DODDS, JOSEPH
    DU BOIS, CHARLES CONRAD ADOLPHUS, BARON<NETH.> DE
        FERRIERES
    FOLJAMBE, CECIL GEORGE SAVILE, 1ST EARL OF LIVERPOOL
    FRY, SIR THEODORE, 1ST BT.
    GOURLEY, SIR EDWARD TEMPERLEY
    GUTHRIE, -

HOLMS, JOHN
HOLMS, WILLIAM
HOOPELL, -
LUSK, SIR ANDREW, 1ST BT.
LYNN, J. H.
MCARTHUR, ALEXANDER
MCARTHUR, SIR WILLIAM
MCLAREN, CHARLES BENJAMIN BRIGHT, 1ST BARON
    ABERCONWAY
MCMINNIES, JOHN GORDON
MALLESON, WILLIAM TAYLOR
MASON, HUGH
MORLEY, SAMUEL
NEWMAN, FRANCIS WILLIAM
NOEL, ERNEST
PEASE, THOMAS
POTTER, THOMAS BAYLEY
RICHARD, HENRY
RULE, WILLIAM HARRIS
RYLANDS, PETER
SHAEN, WILLIAM
STANSFELD, SIR JAMES
STEWART, JAMES
TAYLOR, PETER ALFRED
THOMASSON, JOHN PENNINGTON
TORRENS, WILLIAM TORRENS MCCULLAGH


Natl Education League

ADAMS, FRANCIS
APPLEGARTH, ROBERT
BAZLEY, C. H.
BEALE, WILLIAM JOHN
BROWN, J. JENKYN
BUNCE, JOHN THACKRAY
CALDICOTT, JOHN WILLIAM
CHAMBERLAIN, JOHN HENRY
CHAMBERLAIN, JOSEPH
CHANCE, R. L.
CHEETHAM, WILLIAM
CLARKE, C.
COLLIER, W. F.
COLLINGS, JESSE
COOK, BANCROFT
COWEN, JOSEPH
CROSSKEY, HENRY WILLIAM
DALE, ROBERT WILLIAM
DAWSON, GEORGE
DILKE, SIR CHARLES WENTWORTH, 2ND BT.
DIXON, GEORGE
FAWCETT, HENRY
FAWCETT, MILLICENT GARRETT <MRS. HENRY FAWCETT, nee
    GARRETT>
FIELD, ALFRED
HARRIS, WILLIAM
HASLEM, J.
HAWKES, HENRY
HERBERT, AUBERON EDWARD WILLIAM MOLYNEUX
HESLOP, THOMAS PRETIOUS
HIBBERD, -
HOLLAND, H. W.
HOLLAND, HENRY
HOLLIDAY, WILLIAM
HOWELL, GEORGE
HUTCHINSON, JOHN DYSON
HUTH, EDWARD
JAFFRAY, SIR JOHN, 1ST BT.
JOHNSON, G. J.
KENRICK, JOHN ARTHUR
KENRICK, TIMOTHY
KENRICK, WILLIAM
KITSON, JAMES, 1ST BARON AIREDALE
LLOYD, GEORGE BRAITHWAITE
MACFIE, M.
MANDER, S. S.
MARTINEAU, R. F.

MATTHEWS, C. E. <ALSO MATHEWS>
MAXFIELD, MATTHEW
MAXSE, FREDERICK AUGUSTUS
MIDDLEMORE, WILLIAM
OSBORNE, E. C.
OSLER, ABRAHAM FOLLETT
PENNINGTON, FREDERICK
ROTHERA, G. B.
RUMNEY, -
RYLAND, ARTHUR
RYLAND, WILLIAM
STEINTHAL, S. ALFRED
TAYLOR, J.
TIMMINS, SAMUEL
VINCE, CHARLES
WIGGIN, SIR HENRY, 1ST BT.
WILLIAMS, R.
WINKWORTH, STEPHEN
WRIGHT, JOHN SKIRROW
ZINCKE, FOSTER BARHAM


Natl Education Union

ABBOT, REGINALD CHARLES EDWARD, 3RD BARON COLCHESTER
ADDINGTON, WILLIAM WELLS, 3RD VISCOUNT SIDMOUTH
AKROYD, EDWARD HALIFAX
ALLEN, GEORGE
ALLIES, THOMAS WILLIAM
ARKWRIGHT, AUGUSTUS PETER
BAINES, SIR EDWARD
BAIRD, JAMES
BAKER, ROBERT
BARRY, ALFRED
BEGG, JAMES
BIRCH, HENRY MILDRED
BIRLEY, HUGH
BUTLER, GEORGE
BUXTON, CHARLES
CALLENDER, WILLIAM ROMAINE, JUN.
CAWLEY, CHARLES EDWARD
COLERIDGE, DERWENT
COLLINS, THOMAS
COOK, -
COOPER, ANTHONY ASHLEY, 7TH EARL OF SHAFTESBURY
CORRANCE, FREDERICK SNOWDON
COURTENAY, WILLIAM REGINALD, 11TH EARL OF DEVON
CROMWELL, JOHN GABRIEL
CROPPER, JAMES
DALE, FREDERICK SPENCER
DALE, THOMAS
DAVENPORT, RICHARD
EASTWICK, EDWARD BACKHOUSE
ECROYD, WILLIAM FARRER
EDEN, ROBERT
EGERTON, ALGERNON FULKE
EGERTON, FRANCIS
EGERTON, WILBRAHAM, 1ST EARL EGERTON OF TATTON
ELLERBY, W. P.
ELLICOTT, CHARLES JOHN
ELLIOTT, ROWLAND A.
EMERY, WILLIAM
FORTESCUE, HUGH, 3RD EARL FORTESCUE
GLADSTONE, MURRAY
HAMILTON, LORD GEORGE FRANCIS
HAY, SIR JOHN CHARLES DALRYMPLE-, 3RD BT.
HOLMES, ARTHUR
HOPE, ALEXANDER JAMES BERESFORD BERESFORD-
HOWARD, EDWARD GEORGE FITZ-ALAN, 1ST BARON HOWARD OF
    GLOSSOP
HOWARD, MORGAN
IBBETSON, HENRY JOHN SELWIN-, 1ST BARON ROOKWOOD
JACKSON, JOHN
JAMES, WALTER CHARLES, 1ST BARON NORTHBOURNE
JOHNSON, EDWARD
JOHNSTONE, J. D.
JONES, LATIMER MAURICE

KAY, JOHN ROBINSON
KEMPE, JOHN EDWARD
KENNAWAY, SIR JOHN HENRY, 3RD BT.
KIDSTON, WILLIAM
LAKE, WILLIAM CHARLES
LEE, ROBERT
LEEMING, JAMES
LINDSAY, WILLIAM ALEXANDER
MACLAGAN, WILLIAM DALRYMPLE
MAGEE, WILLIAM CONNOR
MATTINSON, JAMES
MONTAGU, LORD ROBERT
MONTGOMERY, SIR GRAHAM GRAHAM, 3RD BT.
NICHOLSON, -
NORRIS, JOHN PILKINGTON
PAGE, JOHN J.
PALMER, JORDAN ROQUETTE-PALMER-
PEASE, JOSEPH WHITWELL, 1ST BT.
PEEK, SIR HENRY WILLIAM
PELLEW, H.
PITCAIRN, JAMES PELHAM
POWELL, SIR FRANCIS SHARP, 1ST BT.
RAIKES, HENRY CECIL
RATCLIFF, CHARLES
REDGRAVE, ALEXANDER
RIGG, JAMES HARRISON
RYDER, DUDLEY, 2ND EARL OF HARROWBY
RYDER, DUDLEY FRANCIS STUART, 3RD EARL OF HARROWBY
SCOTT, ARCHIBALD
SCOTT, CHARLES BRODERICK
SHERWOOD, JOSEPH
SMITH, C.
SMITH, D.
SMITH, WILLIAM HENRY
STANHOPE, SIR WALTER THOMAS WILLIAM SPENCER
STANLEY, HENRY EDWARD JOHN, 3RD BARON STANLEY OF
    ALDERLEY
STANYER, WILLIAM
TALBOT, JOHN GILBERT
TAYLOR, JAMES
TEMPLE, WILLIAM FRANCIS COWPER-, 1ST BARON
    MOUNT-TEMPLE
THOMAS, EDWIN
THOMSON, WILLIAM
TONGE, RICHARD
TOOLE, -
TULLEDGE, H. E.
WALKER, WILLIAM
WHITELAW, ALEXANDER
WILMOT, SIR JOHN EARDLEY EARDLEY-, 2ND BT.
WOODROOFE, THOMAS <ALSO WOODROOFFE AND WOODROFFE>

Natl Emigration League

ABBOT, REGINALD CHARLES EDWARD, 3RD BARON COLCHESTER
ALLEN, HUGH
APPLEGARTH, ROBERT
BAKER, GEORGE
BATE, JOHN
BAYLEY, JONATHAN
BEALES, EDMOND
BOWRING, EDGAR ALFRED
BOWRING, SIR JOHN
BRASSEY, HENRY ARTHUR
BRASSEY, THOMAS
BRASSEY, THOMAS, 1ST EARL BRASSEY
CAMERON, DONALD
CHAMBERS, SIR THOMAS
CHARLEY, SIR WILLIAM THOMAS
CLARKE, SIR ANDREW
COCKS, HORROCKS
COOPER, SIR DANIEL, 1ST BT.
DAMER, LIONEL SEYMOUR WILLIAM DAWSON-, 4TH EARL
    PORTARLINGTON
DENISON, SIR WILLIAM THOMAS
DIMSDALE, ROBERT DIMSDALE

DRUITT, GEORGE
DUDDELL, G.
EASTWICK, EDWARD BACKHOUSE
ELPHINSTONE, SIR JAMES DALRYMPLE HORN, 2ND BT.
FITZWILLIAM, CHARLES WILLIAM WENTWORTH
GLADSTONE, JOHN HALL
GOURLEY, SIR EDWARD TEMPERLEY
GREY, SIR GEORGE EDWARD
HAMILTON, LORD CLAUD JOHN
HAMILTON, LORD GEORGE FRANCIS
HARDY, JOHN STEWART GATHORNE-, 2ND EARL OF CRANBROOK
HERRING, ARMINE STYLEMAN
HOARE, H. N. HAMILTON
HOLMS, JOHN
HORNBY, EDWARD KENWORTHY
HOULDER, A.
HULSE, SIR EDWARD, 5TH BT.
HUTTON, JOHN
JENKINS, JOHN EDWARD
KENNEDY, JOHN PITT
LABILLIERE, FRANCIS PETER
LAMPREY, J. H.
LATHAM, R. MARSDEN
LAWRENCE, SIR JAMES CLARKE, 1ST BT.
LENNOX, LORD WILLIAM PITT
LYCETT, SIR FRANCIS
MCARTHUR, SIR WILLIAM
MACFIE, ROBERT ANDREW
MCGAREL, CHARLES
MARSH, MATTHEW HENRY
MARTINEAU, JOHN
MAUDE, FRANCIS CORNWALLIS
MONTAGU, WILLIAM DROGO, 7TH DUKE OF MANCHESTER
MURPHY, GEORGE
NICHOLSON, SIR CHARLES, 1ST BT.
OTTEY, GEORGE PHILIP
PLUNKETT, EDWARD, 16TH BARON DUNSANY
POTTER, GEORGE
PRATT, DANIEL
REED, SIR CHARLES
RICHARDSON, SIR BENJAMIN WARD
ROGERS, WILLIAM
SCOTT, HENRY JOHN MONTAGU DOUGLAS, 1ST BARON MONTAGU
    OF BEAULIEU
SHIPTON, GEORGE
STANHOPE, ARTHUR PHILIP, 6TH EARL STANHOPE
STEWART, ALAN PLANTAGENET, 10TH EARL OF GALLOWAY
STUART, JAMES FREDERICK DUDLEY CRICHTON-
TORRENS, SIR ROBERT RICHARD
TORRENS, WILLIAM TORRENS MCCULLAGH
WARING, CHARLES
WHALLEY, GEORGE HAMMOND
WILSON, EDWARD
WOLFF, SIR HENRY DRUMMOND CHARLES
YOUNG, SIR FREDERICK

Natl Fair Trade League

BROWNE, HAROLD CARLYON GORE
HAWKES, HENRY
HEALEY, EDWARD CHARLES
HENDERSON, JOHN
HYDE, J. M.
LISTER, SAMUEL CUNLIFFE
LLOYD, SAMPSON SAMUEL
MITCHELL, SIR HENRY
NELSON, SIR EDWARD MONTAGUE
PRYOR, ARTHUR
WILMOT, SIR JOHN EARDLEY EARDLEY-, 2ND BT.
YOUNG, SIR FREDERICK

Natl Footpaths Preservation Soc

ALLNUTT, HENRY
BALL, GEORGE V.
BLAIR, ROBERT
BONE, J. W.
BRASSEY, THOMAS, 1ST EARL BRASSEY
BRYCE, JAMES, 1ST VISCOUNT BRYCE
BUXTON, EDWARD NORTH
BUXTON, SYDNEY CHARLES, 1ST EARL BUXTON
BYNG, GEORGE HENRY CHARLES, 3RD EARL OF STRAFFORD
CAVENDISH, SPENCER COMPTON, 8TH DUKE OF DEVONSHIRE
CHAPLIN, HENRY, 1ST VISCOUNT CHAPLIN
CHURCHILL, LORD RANDOLPH HENRY SPENCER
CLARKE, THOMAS CHATFIELD
COMPTON, WILLIAM GEORGE SPENCER SCOTT, 5TH MARQUIS
    NORTHAMPTON
CONYBEARE, CHARLES AUGUSTUS VANSITTART
CORBETT, JOHN
CROSS, RICHARD ASSHETON, 1ST VISCOUNT CROSS
DAY, E. S.
DE WORMS, HENRY. 1ST BN. PIRBRIGHT
DILKE, SIR CHARLES WENTWORTH, 2ND BT.
DODD, JOHN THEODORE
DUFF, ALEXANDER WILLIAM GEORGE, 1ST DUKE OF FIFE
FIRTH, JOSEPH FIRTH BOTTOMLEY
FLOWER, CYRIL, 1ST BARON BATTERSEA
FORDHAM, SIR GEORGE
FORTESCUE, DUDLEY FRANCIS
FOWLER, SIR ROBERT NICHOLAS, 1ST BT.
FOX, FRANKLIN <"CAPT.">
FYFFE, CHARLES ALAN
GAUNTLETT, PAUL E. I.
GLADSTONE, JOHN HALL
GOLDSMID, SIR JULIAN, 3RD BT.
GOWER, GRANVILLE GEORGE LEVESON-, 2ND EARL GRANVILLE
GRANT, JAMES OGILVY, 9TH EARL OF SEAFIELD
GROSVENOR, HUGH LUPUS, 1ST DUKE OF WESTMINSTER
HAMILTON, LORD CLAUD JOHN
HAMILTON, LORD GEORGE FRANCIS
HART, THOMAS DALE
HAY, WILLIAM MONTAGU, 10TH MARQUIS OF TWEEDDALE
HOBHOUSE, HENRY
HOBHOUSE, MARY, LADY <WIFE OF 1ST BARON HOBHOUSE, nee
    FARRER>
HOLE, JAMES
JAMES, HENRY, 1ST BARON HEREFORD
JAMES, WALTER HENRY, 2ND BARON NORTHBOURNE
KNIGHT, G. J., JUN.
LAWSON, HARRY LAWSON WEBSTER LEVY-, 1ST VISCOUNT
    BURNHAM
LEGGE, WILLIAM HENEAGE, 6TH EARL OF DARTMOUTH
LISTER, THOMAS, 4TH BARON RIBBLESDALE
LUSHINGTON, VERNON
MASKELYNE, MERVYN HERBERT NEVIL STORY-
MILLS, CHARLES HENRY, 1ST BARON HILLINGDON
MILNER, SIR FREDERICK GEORGE, 7TH BT.
MOCATTA, FREDERICK DAVID
MORLEY, ARNOLD
MORLEY, JOHN, 1ST VISCOUNT MORLEY OF BLACKBURN
MORLEY, SAMUEL HOPE, 1ST BARON HOLLENDEN
NATION, WILLIAM HAMILTON CODRINGTON
ONSLOW, WILLIAM HILLIER, 4TH EARL OF ONSLOW
PICTON, JAMES ALLANSON
PLAYFAIR, LYON, 1ST BARON PLAYFAIR
POLLOCK, SIR FREDERICK, 3RD BT.
POULTER, R. C.
PROVAND, ANDREW DRYBURGH
PULESTON, SIR JOHN HENRY
RAIMBACH, T. EMMERSON
RAWNSLEY, HARDWICKE DRUMMOND
RUSKIN, JOHN
SMITH, W. H.
TAYLOR, THOMAS <STYLED EARL OF BECTIVE, HEIR OF 3RD
    MARQUIS OF HEADFORT>
TENNANT, SIR CHARLES, 1ST BT.
TENNYSON, ALFRED, 1ST BARON TENNYSON

TORR, JAMES FENNING
TROWER, H. SEYMOUR
VERNEY, SIR HARRY, 2ND BT.
WADDINGTON, F. S.
WESTGARTH, WILLIAM
WINTERBOTHAM, ARTHUR BREND

Natl Secular Soc

ANDERSON, GEORGE
AVELING, EDWARD BIBBONS
BESANT, ANNIE
BILLCLIFFE, J.
BRADLAUGH, ALICE
BRADLAUGH, CHARLES
BRADLAUGH, HYPATIA
COOPER, R. A.
ELLIS, THOMAS
FOOTE, G. W.
FORDER, ROBERT
FOSTER, GEORGE T.
HEANE, J. P.
HOLYOAKE, AUSTIN
HOLYOAKE, GEORGE JACOB
LEES, JOHN
LE LUBEZ, P. A. V.
MUDALIAR, P. MURUGESA
PARRIS, TOUZEAU
REYNOLDS, WILLIAM HAMMOND
RHODES, JOHN
RIDGWAY, N. J.
ROY, THOMAS
SLATER, THOMAS
SMITH, ROBERT OWEN
STANDRING, GEORGE
SWAAGMAN, JOANNES
SWIFT, F. <"BARON">
SYMES, JOSEPH
TREVELYAN, ARTHUR
TRUELOVE, EDWARD
WATTS, CHARLES

Natl Soc for Preserving Memorials of the Dead

ASTLEY, JOHN
ATHILL, CHARLES HAROLD
BACON, HENRY F.
BAXTER, THOMAS PRESTON NOWELL
BENSON, EDWARD WHITE
BENTLY, SEYMOUR
BICKERSTETH, EDWARD
BIGNOLD, CHARLES EDWARD <"COL.">
BLACK, WILLIAM GEORGE
BLACKMORE, JOHN CHANTER
BLAIR, ROBERT
BLAYDES, F. A.
BOLINGBROKE, NATHANIEL
BOWKER, CHARLES E. B.
BOYLE, GEORGE FREDERICK, 6TH EARL OF GLASGOW
BRABAZON, REGINALD, 12TH EARL OF MEATH
BRIDGES, ALEXANDER HENRY
BROOKES, W. M.
BROWNE, EDWARD HAROLD
BUCKLER, C. A.
BURT, JAMES
CAPELL, ARTHUR ALGERNON, 6TH EARL OF ESSEX
CAREY, J. JAMES
CARNEGIE, GEORGE JOHN, 9TH EARL OF NORTHESK
CARREL, F. POINGDESTRE
CHEALES, HENRY JOHN
CLIVE, GEORGE HERBERT WINDSOR WINDSOR-
COMPTON, LORD ALWYNE
COOPER, ANTHONY ASHLEY, 7TH EARL OF SHAFTESBURY
COSSINS, JETHRO A.
COTTERILL, HENRY

COURTENAY, WILLIAM REGINALD, 11TH EARL OF DEVON
COWIE, BENJAMIN MORGAN
CRANE, ROBERT
CROSS, RICHARD ASSHETON, 1ST VISCOUNT CROSS
CUST, ARTHUR PERCEVAL PUREY
CUTTS, EDWARD LEWES
DAVIS, FREDERICK WILLIAM
DAVISON, R.
DE GREY, THOMAS, 6TH BN. WALSINGHAM
DODD, JOHN THEODORE
DOUGLAS, ARTHUR GASCOIGNE
DUCKETT, SIR GEORGE FLOYD, 3RD BT.
EDEN, ROBERT
EGGLESTONE, W. M.
EVANS, H. A.
FIENNES, FREDERICK BENJAMIN TWISELTON WYKEHAM, 16TH
  BARON SAYE AND SELE
FISHWICK, HENRY
FITZROY, ERNEST JAMES AUGUSTUS
FOLJAMBE, CECIL GEORGE SAVILE, 1ST EARL OF LIVERPOOL
FRASER, JAMES
FREMANTLE, WILLIAM ROBERT
FRETTON, WILLIAM GEORGE
GIBBS, HENRY HUCKS, 1ST BARON ALDENHAM
GIDLEY, B. G.
GILBERT, SIR JOHN
GLASSCOCK, JOHN L., JUN.
GOLDING, CHARLES
GOSSELIN <-GRIMSHAWE>, HELLIER ROBERT HADSLEY
GOULBURN, EDWARD MEYRICK
GOWER, GRANVILLE WILLIAM GRESHAM LEVESON-
GRIFFITH, JOHN
GRIFFITHS, A. E.
HARRISON, BENJAMIN
HARTISHORNE, A.
HEALES, ALFRED
HEANE, WILLIAM CRAWSHAY
HERBERT, EDWARD JAMES, 3RD EARL OF POWIS
HERBERT, HENRY HOWARD MOLYNEUX, 4TH EARL CARNARVON
HILL, ARTHUR GEORGE
HOPE, ALEXANDER JAMES BERESFORD BERESFORD-
HOW, WILLIAM WALSHAM
HOWARD, HENRY FITZALAN, 15TH DUKE OF NORFOLK
HUYSHE, WENTWORTH
HYDE, T. RALPH
IRVING, SIR HENRY
KING, EDWARD
LEIGHTON, STANLEY
LEWIS, RICHARD
LYGON, FREDERICK, 6TH EARL BEAUCHAMP
LYNAM, C.
MACKARNESS, GEORGE RICHARD
MACLAGAN, WILLIAM DALRYMPLE
MAJENDIE, LEWIS ASHURST
MALET, O. W.
MASON, CHARLES A. J.
MATTHEWS, NORMAN H.
MAUGHAN, VEARGITT WILLIAM
MOORE, CECIL
NEWTON, C. E.
OUSELEY, SIR FREDERICK ARTHUR GORE, 2ND BT.
PAGE, P. S.
PAYNE, RANDOLPH
POWELL, SIR FRANCIS SHARP, 1ST BT.
RICHARDSON, WILLIAM HENRY
ROWDON, HUGH MARMADUKE
ROXBY, H. THORNHILL
RUTLAND, J.
RYE, WALTER
SALTER, SAMUEL JAMES AUGUSTUS
SIMPSON, ROBERT JAMES
SKETCHLEY, RICHARD FORSTER
SMITH, KENELM HENRY
SMITH, ROBERT PAYNE-
STRAWSON, G. W.
TAIT, ARCHIBALD CAMPBELL
TALBOT, JAMES, 4TH BARON TALBOT DE MALAHIDE

TANNER, WILLIAM
THOMSON, WILLIAM
TIPPING, WILLIAM
TROLLOPE, EDWARD
VINCENT, WILLIAM
WAGNER, HENRY
WALFORD, EDWARD
WEBB, SIR ASTON
WOOD, R. H.
WOODFORD, JAMES RUSSELL
WOODS, SIR ALBERT WILLIAM
WRIGHT, HENRY


Natl Vigilance Assn

BAKER, - (MISS)
BEWICKE, ALICIA E. N. <MISS>
BOOTH, WILLIAM BRAMWELL
BRADLEY, - <MRS. J. W. BRADLEY>
BRITTEN, J.
BUNTING, - <MRS.>
BUNTING, MARY HYETT <MRS. PERCY BUNTING, nee LIDGETT>
BUNTING, SIR PERCY WILLIAM
BUTLER, GEORGE
BUTLER, JOSEPHINE E. <MRS. GEORGE BUTLER, nee GREY>
CHANT, LAURA ORMISTON <MRS. THOMAS CHANT, nee DIBBIN>
CHARRINGTON, FREDERICK NICHOLAS
CLIFFORD, JOHN
COOTE, WILLIAM ALEXANDER
COSTELLOE, - <MRS. BENJAMIN FRANCIS CONN COSTELLOE>
COSTELLOE, BENJAMIN FRANCIS CONN
CRAIES, WILLIAM FEILDEN
DYER, ALFRED STACE
FAWCETT, MILLICENT GARRETT <MRS. HENRY FAWCETT, nee
  GARRETT>
FRASER, - <"THE HON. MRS.">
HILL, W.
HOPKINS, ELICE <MISS>
HORSLEY, JOHN WILLIAM
HOW, WILLIAM WALSHAM
HUGHES, HUGH PRICE
JEPHSON, ARTHUR WILLIAM
JONES, - <MISS>
KERWIN, EDWIN H.
KNIGHT, A. A.
KNOWLES, MARK
LAWRENCE, F.
LEPPER, C. H.
LIDGETT, - <MISS>
LYNCH, - <MRS.>
MADDISON, ARTHUR J. S.
MANNING, HENRY EDWARD
MEARNS, ANDREW
MILLS, HALFORD L.
MITCHELL, - <MRS.>
MORGAN, RICHARD COPE
MORLEY, SAMUEL
RIDDING, GEORGE
RUSSELL, GEORGE WILLIAM ERSKINE
SHAEN, WILLIAM
STANSFELD, SIR JAMES
STEAD, WILLIAM THOMAS
STEER, - <MISS>
STEPHENSON, T. BOWMAN
STUART, JAMES
TEMPLE, FREDERICK
THICKNESSE, RALPH
WAUGH, BENJAMIN
WHITEHEAD, - <MISS>

Patrons Defense Assn

WILLIAMS, CHARLES WILLIAM <ALSO WILLIAM CHARLES
  WILLIAMS>


Plimsoll and Seamen's Fund Committee

ALCOCK, SIR RUTHERFORD
ANSON, THOMAS GEORGE, 2ND EARL OF LICHFIELD
ARNOLD, SIR ARTHUR
BALFOUR, ALEXANDER
BEAUCHAMP, SIR THOMAS WILLIAM BROGRAVE PROCTOR-, 4TH
  BT.
BENTINCK, GEORGE AUGUSTUS FREDERICK CAVENDISH
BERESFORD, MARCUS
BRAND, HENRY ROBERT, 2ND VISCOUNT HAMPDEN AND 24TH
  BARON DACRE
BURNS, JOHN
BUTLER, HENRY MONTAGUE
CARTER, ROBERT MEEK
CAVENDISH, LORD GEORGE HENRY
CECIL, LORD EUSTACE HENRY BROWNLOW
CECIL, WILLIAM ALLEYNE, 3RD MARQUIS OF EXETER
COOPER, ANTHONY ASHLEY, 7TH EARL OF SHAFTESBURY
DAWSON, EDWARD STANLEY
DAWSON, RICHARD, 1ST EARL OF DARTREY
DAWSON, WILLIAM
DIGBY, KENELM THOMAS JOSEPH
DOUGLAS, FRANCIS RICHARD WEMYSS CHARTERIS, 10TH EARL
  OF WEMYSS
DUFF, ROBERT WILLIAM
EGERTON, FRANCIS
ELLIOT, SIR GEORGE AUGUSTUS
ERSKINE, JOHN ELPHINSTONE
FARQUHAR, HARVIE MORETON
FARQUHAR, SIR WALTER ROCKCLIFFE, 3RD BT.
FITZROY, LORD FREDERICK JOHN
FITZWILLIAM, W. S.
FORTESCUE, DUDLEY FRANCIS
GOLDSMID, SIR JULIAN, 3RD BT.
GOODENOUGH, JAMES GRAHAM
GREEN, HENRY
GREVILLE, FULKE SOUTHWELL, 1ST BARON GREVILLE
GREVILLE, GEORGE FREDERICK NUGENT
GROSVENOR, HUGH LUPUS, 1ST DUKE OF WESTMINSTER
HAMBRO, CHARLES JOSEPH THEOPHILUS
HAMILTON, LORD CLAUD
HAMILTON, LORD CLAUD JOHN
HAMILTON, LORD GEORGE FRANCIS
HAY, SIR JOHN CHARLES DALRYMPLE-, 3RD BT.
HOLLAND, SAMUEL
HOWELL, GEORGE
HUGHES, THOMAS
JOHNSTON, WILLIAM
KEPPEL, WILLIAM COUTTS, 7TH EARL OF ALBEMARLE
KINGSLEY, HENRY
KINNAIRD, ARTHUR FITZGERALD, 10TH BARON KINNAIRD
LUSK, SIR ANDREW, 1ST BT.
LYON, WILLIAM
MACGREGOR, JOHN
MACKENZIE, EDWARD M. S. G. MONTAGU STUART WORTLEY,
  1ST EARL OF WHARNCLIFFE
MORETON, HENRY JOHN REYNOLDS-, 3RD EARL OF DUCIE
O'BRIEN, SIR PATRICK 2ND BT.
PERCY, LORD JOSCELINE WILLIAM
POWELL, RICHARD ASHMORE
PRIMROSE, ARCHIBALD PHILIP, 5TH EARL OF ROSEBERY
SCOTT, HENRY JOHN MONTAGU DOUGLAS, 1ST BARON MONTAGU
  OF BEAULIEU
SIMPSON, ROBERT JAMES
VERNON, AUGUSTUS HENRY VENABLES-, 6TH BARON VERNON
WATTENBACH, AUGUSTUS
WELLS, WILLIAM
WHITE, F. A.
WILSON, JOSEPH EDWARD MAITLAND

Proportional Representation Soc

BIDDULPH, MICHAEL, 1ST BARON BIDDULPH
BLENNERHASSETT, ROWLAND PONSONBY
BOUVERIE, WILLIAM PLEYDELL, 5TH EARL OF RADNOR
CLARKE, SIR EDWARD GEORGE
COHEN, ARTHUR JOSEPH
COURTNEY, LEONARD HENRY, 1ST BARON COURTNEY OF
  PENWITH
CROPPER, JAMES
DOBBS, ARCHIBALD EDWARD
GEDGE, SYDNEY
GRANT, DANIEL
GREY, ALBERT HENRY GEORGE, 4TH EARL GREY
INSULL, SAMUEL
KENNAWAY, SIR JOHN HENRY, 3RD BT.
LUBBOCK, JOHN, 1ST BARON AVEBURY
MONSELL, WILLIAM, 1ST BARON EMLY
MORRISON, WALTER
RATHBONE, WILLIAM
RIDLEY, MATTHEW WHITE, 1ST VISCOUNT RIDLEY
SCOTT, CHARLES PRESTWICH
SEEBOHM, FREDERICK
SMITH, JAMES PARKER
WESTLAKE, JOHN
WHITE, ALFRED CROMWELL
WORTLEY, CHARLES BEILBY STUART-, 1ST BARON STUART OF
  WORTLEY


Public Museums & Free Libraries Assn

ALLEN, HUGH
ANSON, THOMAS GEORGE, 2ND EARL OF LICHFIELD
BEALES, EDMOND
BUCKMASTER, J. C.
BURNS, DAWSON
BUXTON, CHARLES
COLE, H. J.
DEXTER, J. T.
EWART, WILLIAM
FLETCHER, LIONEL JOHN WILLIAM
FOWLER, SIR ROBERT NICHOLAS, 1ST BT.
GLADSTONE, JOHN HALL
GODWIN, GEORGE
GROSVENOR, ROBERT, 1ST BARON EBURY
GURNEY, SAMUEL
HANSARD, SEPTIMUS COX HOLMES
HEALD, HENRY GEORGE
HERBERT, AUBERON EDWARD WILLIAM MOLYNEUX
HILL, CHARLES
HOARE, H. N. HAMILTON
HOLMS, JOHN
HUGHES, THOMAS
HUTCHISON, G. A.
JONES, ALFRED
JONES, HARRY
LAWRENCE, SIR JAMES CLARKE, 1ST BT.
LEVI, LEONE
LUBBOCK, JOHN, 1ST BARON AVEBURY
LUCRAFT, BENJAMIN
LUSK, SIR ANDREW, 1ST BT.
MCARTHUR, SIR WILLIAM
MCCREE, GEORGE WILSON
MARTIN, SAMUEL
MIALL, EDWARD
MORLEY, SAMUEL
PALMER, JOSEPH
PATERSON, THOMAS
POTTER, GEORGE
PRATT, HODGSON
PROBYN, J. W.
REDGRAVE, RICHARD
ROGERS, EDWARD DRESSER
SAVAGE, G. F.
SCOTT, BENJAMIN
SHIPTON, W. EDWYN

SWANWICK, ANNA <MISS>
VERNEY, SIR HARRY, 2ND BT.
WHITMORE, C. J.
WOODALL, WILLIAM


Railway Passengers' Protection Assn

ACWORTH, SIR WILLIAM MITCHELL
BALLISTON. W. H. T.
BRADY, SIR ANTONIO
BRANTHWAITE, HARRISON
CARTER, ROBERT BRUDENELL
FABER, GEORGE HENRY
GARNHAM, JOHN WILLIAM
HARRIS, GEORGE
HUTTON, J. E.
KENT, THOMAS RUSSEL
LEES, JOHN
PARIS, CHARLES
PEARSE, GEORGE JOSEPH
STANGER, W. HARRY
VERNEY, GEORGE HOPE LLOYD-


Sanitary Institute

ADAMS, G. E. D'ARCY
ANNINGSON, BUSHELL
BARR, WILLIAM ALEXANDER
BARTLETT, H. CRITCHETT
BASS, HAMAR ALFRED
BELL, CHARLES W.
BLYTH, ALEXANDER WYNTER
BOULNOIS, H. PERCY
BRABAZON, REGINALD, 12TH EARL OF MEATH
BRADY, SIR ANTONIO
BRANTHWAITE, HARRISON
BROWNING, BENJAMIN
BURDETT, HENRY C.
CARPENTER, ALFRED
CARTER, ROBERT BRUDENELL
CASSAL, CHARLES EDWARD
CAVE, ALFRED THOMAS TOWNSHEND VERNEY-, 5TH BARON
    BRAYE
CHADWICK, SIR EDWIN
COLES, WILLIAM R. E.
COLLINGRIDGE, WILLIAM
COLLINS, H. H.
COLLINS, W. J.
COLLINS, SIR WILLIAM
COLMAN, JEREMIAH JAMES
COOPER, ANTHONY ASHLEY, 7TH EARL OF SHAFTESBURY
CORFIELD, WILLIAM HENRY
CRAWFORD, SIR THOMAS
CROOKES, SIR WILLIAM
CUTLER, THOMAS WILLIAM
DE CHAUMONT, FRANCIS STEPHEN BENNETT FRANCOIS
DENISON, GEORGE ANTHONY
DUDFIELD, T. ORME
EASSIE, WILLIAM
EDGELL, EDGELL WYATT
ELLIS, WILLIAM HORTON
EMBLETON, DENNIS
FARR, WILLIAM
FIELD, ROGERS
FORD, STEPHEN
FORTESCUE, HUGH, 3RD EARL FORTESCUE
FOSTER, BALTHAZAR WALTER, 1ST BARON ILKESTON
GALTON, SIR DOUGLAS STRUTT
GRANTHAM, RICHARD BOXALL
GRIMSHAW, THOMAS WRIGLEY
GROSVENOR, ROBERT, 1ST BARON EBURY
HARDWICKE, WILLIAM
HART, ERNEST ABRAHAM
HAVILAND, A.
HOWARD, JAMES

HUMPHRY, GEORGE MURRAY
JONES, ALFRED STOWELL
KELLY, CHARLES
LAW, HENRY
LEE, ROBERT JAMES
LEMON, SIR JAMES
LEON, GEORGE I. <OR GEORGE J.>
LINGARD, J. EDWARD
LUBBOCK, JOHN, 1ST BARON AVEBURY
LYTE, FARNHAM MAXWELL
MCARTHUR, ALEXANDER
MCARTHUR, SIR WILLIAM
MCCOY, D. <"MAJOR">
MANSERGH, JAMES
NELSON, SIR EDWARD MONTAGUE
OGLE, WILLIAM
OHREN, MAGNUS
OLLARD, J. F.
PALMER, GEORGE
PARKES, LOUIS COLTMAN
PEGGS, J. WALLACE
PERCY, ALGERNON GEORGE, 6TH DUKE OF NORTHUMBERLAND
PLUMBE, ROWLAND
RAWLINSON, SIR ROBERT
RICHARDSON, SIR BENJAMIN WARD
ROBINS, EDWARD COOKSWORTHY
ROBINSON, HENRY <"PROF.">
RUSSELL, FRANCIS ALBERT ROLLO
RUSSELL, SIR JAMES ALEXANDER
SALT, SIR THOMAS, 1ST BT.
SCOTT, HENRY YOUNG DARRACOTT
SNELL, H. SAXON
STANLEY, EDWARD HENRY, 15TH EARL OF DERBY
STEPHENS, HENRY CHARLES
SYKES, JOHN FREDERICK JOSEPH
SYMONS, GEORGE JAMES
TEMPLE, FREDERICK
THOMAS, W. CAVE
TURNER, ERNEST
URE, J.
VARLEY, CROMWELL FLEETWOOD
VIGERS, EDWARD
WALLIS, E. WHITE
WEBB, PHILIP SPEAKMAN
WILSON, GEORGE


Smoke Abatement Committee

ABEL, SIR FREDERICK AUGUSTUS, 1ST BT.
ATCHISON, ARTHUR TURNOUR
BLYTH, ALEXANDER WYNTER
BORTHWICK, ALICE BEATRICE <MRS. A. BORTHWICK, LATER
    LADY GLENESK, nee LISTER>
BRADY, SIR ANTONIO
BRAMWELL, SIR FREDERICK JOSEPH, 1ST BT.
BRUCE, HENRY AUSTIN, 1ST BARON ABERDARE
CARPENTER, ALFRED
CHADWICK, SIR EDWIN
COLES, WILLIAM R. E.
COOK, SIR WILLIAM THOMAS GUSTAVUS
CUNDY, THOMAS
CUTLER, THOMAS WILLIAM
EASSIE, WILLIAM
FARQUHARSON, ROBERT
FESTING, EDWARD ROBERT
FRANKLAND, SIR EDWARD
GALTON, SIR DOUGLAS STRUTT
GODWIN, GEORGE
GREG, FRANCIS
GROSVENOR, HUGH LUPUS, 1ST DUKE OF WESTMINSTER
HARRIS, R.
HART, ERNEST ABRAHAM
HILL, OCTAVIA
HILL, R. A.
HOGG, JABEZ
HOOLE, ELIJAH

LEFEVRE, EMILY OCTAVIA SHAW- <MISS>
LEIGHTON, FREDERICK, 1ST BARON LEIGHTON OF STRETTON
LEOPOLD GEORGE DUNCAN ALBERT, H.R.H. PRINCE, DUKE OF
    ALBANY
LOCKYER, SIR JOSEPH NORMAN
MACFARLANE, SIR DONALD HORNE
MAITLAND, ROBERT FULLER
MALLET, - <MRS.>
MITCHELL, CHARLES T.
MOSELY, BENJAMIN LEWIS
MOULTON,JOHN FLETCHER, BARON MOULTON
OWEN, SIR FRANCIS PHILIP CUNLIFFE
PAUL, CHARLES KEGAN
PLAYFAIR, LYON, 1ST BARON PLAYFAIR
POLLOCK, SIR WILLIAM FREDERICK, 2ND BT.
POMEROY, FLORENCE WALLACE, VISCOUNTESS HARBERTON
    <WIFE 6TH VISCOUNT, nee LEGGE>
POMEROY, JAMES SPENCER, 6TH VISCOUNT HARBERTON
POTTER, - <MISS>
ROBERTS, WILLIAM CHANDLER <-AUSTEN after 1885>
RUSSELL, FRANCIS ALBERT ROLLO
SCOTT, HENRY YOUNG DARRACOTT
SHUTTLEWORTH, UGHTRED JAMES KAY-, 1ST BARON
    SHUTTLEWORTH
SIEMENS, <CHARLES> SIR WILLIAM
SNELL, H. SAXON
SPRENGEL, HERMANN JOHANN PHILIPP
STATHAM, E.
TRIPE, JOHN WILLIAM
TURNER, ERNEST
VIVIAN, HENRY HUSSEY, 1ST BARON SWANSEA
WHITTLE, JAMES LOWRY
WORTLEY, ARCHIBALD HENRY PLANTAGENET STUART-
WYLD, GEORGE
YORKE, HARRIOT <MISS>

Soc for Abolition of Vivisection

BAGSHAWE, WILLIAM HENRY GUNNING
BRADLEY, FRANCIS JOHN
CAPE, LAWSON
DE WINTON, CHARLOTTE A. <MISS>
DUCKETT, SIR GEORGE FLOYD, 3RD BT.
HARRISON, W.
HOLT, JAMES MADEN
JESSE, GEORGE RICHARD
LEE, FREDERICK GEORGE
LIGHTON, SIR CHRISTOPHER ROBERT, 7TH BT.
MALET, MARIAN DORA, LADY <WIFE OF SIR ALEXANDER
    MALET, 2ND BT., nee SPALDING>
OATES, - <MRS. EDWARD OATES>
OATES, EDWARD
REES, ELLEN ELCUM <MISS>

Soc for Promoting Increase of the Home Episcopate

ATLAY, JAMES
BEACH, MICHAEL EDWARD HICKS-, 1ST EARL ST. ALDWYN
BELCHER, BRYMER
BICKERSTETH, EDWARD
BROWNE, EDWARD HAROLD
CAPARN, WILLIAM BARTON
CHURCHILL, JOHN WINSTON SPENCER, 7TH DUKE OF
    MARLBOROUGH
CLAUGHTON, THOMAS LEGH
COLERIDGE, SIR JOHN TAYLOR
CUBITT, GEORGE, 1ST BARON ASHCOMBE
DURNFORD, RICHARD
FARQUHAR, SIR WALTER ROCKCLIFFE, 3RD BT.
FEW, ROBERT
GIBBS, MICHAEL
GOODWIN, HARVEY
HERBERT, EDWARD JAMES, 3RD EARL OF POWIS
HERVEY, ARTHUR CHARLES
HESSEY, FRANCIS

HOARE, G. H.
HOARE, HENRY
HOPE, ALEXANDER JAMES BERESFORD BERESFORD-
HUBBARD, JOHN GELLIBRAND, 1ST BARON ADDINGTON
HUNT, GEORGE WARD
INGRAM, HENRY MANNING
JAMES, WALTER CHARLES, 1ST BARON NORTHBOURNE
JONES, ALFRED
KEMPE, JAMES CORY
LANCASTER, BENJAMIN
LYTTLETON, GEORGE WILLIAM, 4TH BARON LYTTLETON
MACKARNESS, JOHN FIELDER
MACKENZIE, EDWARD M. S. G. MONTAGU STUART WORTLEY,
    1ST EARL OF WHARNCLIFFE
MACLAGAN, WILLIAM DALRYMPLE
MASSINGBERD, FRANCIS CHARLES
MOWBRAY, SIR JOHN ROBERT, 1ST BT.
NELSON, HORATIO, 3RD EARL NELSON
OTTAWAY, G. J.
PELHAM, JOHN THOMAS
PHILLIPS, EDWARD
PREVOST, SIR GEORGE, 2ND BT.
RAIKES, HENRY CECIL
RYDER, DUDLEY, 2ND EARL OF HARROWBY
SCOTT, WALTER FRANCIS MONTAGU DOUGLAS, 5TH DUKE OF
    BUCCLEUCH
TALBOT, JOHN GILBERT
TEMPLE, FREDERICK
WOOD, WILLIAM PAGE, 1ST BARON HATHERLEY
WORDSWORTH, CHRISTOPHER

Soc for Protection of Ancient Buildings

AITCHISON, GEORGE
ALEXANDER, WILLIAM CLEVERLY
ARMSTRONG, THOMAS
BACON, HENRY F.
BALFOUR, EUSTACE JAMES ANTHONY
BARNES, J. W.
BENSON, EDWARD WHITE
BENTINCK, GEORGE AUGUSTUS FREDERICK CAVENDISH
BENTLEY, JOHN FRANCIS
BIRDWOOD, SIR GEORGE CHRISTOPHER MOLESWORTH
BOWES, JAMES LORD
BOYCE, GEORGE PRICE
BREWER, H. W.
BREWER, JOHN SHERREN
BROOKE, STOPFORD AUGUSTUS
BRYCE, JAMES, 1ST VISCOUNT BRYCE
BURTON, SIR FREDERIC WILLIAM
BYWATER, INGRAM
CALDERON, PHILIP HERMOGENES
CARLYLE, THOMAS
CARR, JOSEPH WILLIAM COMYNS
CHAMBERLAIN, JOHN HENRY
CLEMENT, CHARLES GENT
COBDEN, JANE E. <MISS>
COLVIN, SIR SIDNEY
COSSINS, JETHRO A.
COURTNEY, LEONARD HENRY, 1ST BARON COURTNEY OF
    PENWITH
COUTTS, ANGELA GEORGINA BURDETT-, BARONESS
    BURDETT-COUTTS
COWPER, FRANCIS THOMAS DE GREY, 7TH EARL COWPER
DASENT, SIR GEORGE WEBBE
DE MORGAN, WILLIAM FREND
DILKE, SIR CHARLES WENTWORTH, 2ND BT.
DILLON, FRANK
DOYLE, RICHARD
EDWARDS, EDWIN
ELLIS, FREDERICK STARTRIDGE
ELWIN, WHITWELL
FAULKNER, CHARLES JOSEPH
FAWCETT, MILLICENT GARRETT <MRS. HENRY FAWCETT, nee
    GARRETT>
FLOWER, WICKHAM

FORTESCUE, CHICHESTER SAMUEL PARKINSON, 1ST BARON
   CARLINGFORD
FURNIVALL, FREDERICK JAMES
GARRETT, RHODA <MISS>
GREENWELL, WILLIAM
GROSVENOR, NORMAN DE L'AIGLE
GROSVENOR, RICHARD CECIL
HEALES, ALFRED
HEBB, JOHN
HESELTINE, JOHN POSTLE
HILL, ARTHUR GEORGE
HODGSON, JOHN EVAN
HOLLIDAY, JAMES RICHARDSON
HOLLOND, JOHN ROBERT
HOWARD, GEORGE JAMES, 9TH EARL OF CARLISLE
HUGGINS, SAMUEL
HUNT, ALFRED WILLIAM
HUNT, WILLIAM HOLMAN
HUTCHINSON, JOHN DYSON
JONES, SIR EDWARD COLEY BURNE-, 1ST BT.
KAY, HENRY CASSELS
KEENE, CHARLES
KENRICK, WILLIAM
KERR, SCHOMBERG HENRY, 9TH MARQUIS OF LOTHIAN
KERSHAW, SAMUEL WAYLAND
LANKESTER, SIR EDWIN RAY
LECKY, WILLIAM EDWARD HARTPOLE
LEIGHTON, STANLEY
LELAND, CHARLES GODFREY
LOFTIE, WILLIAM JOHN
LOWELL, JAMES RUSSELL
LUBBOCK, JOHN, 1ST BARON AVEBURY
LUSHINGTON, SIR GODFREY
LUSHINGTON, VERNON
MACCOLL, NORMAN
MACKENZIE, EDWARD M. S. G. MONTAGU STUART WORTLEY,
   1ST EARL OF WHARNCLIFFE
MCLAREN, CHARLES BENJAMIN BRIGHT, 1ST BARON
   ABERCONWAY
MACMILLAN, SIR FREDERICK ORRIDGE
MANT, NEWTON WILLIAM JOHN
MARKS, ALFRED
MARKS, HENRY STACY
MARKS, T. NEWMAN
MATTHEWS, C. E. <ALSO MATHEWS>
MIDDLETON, JOHN HENRY
MILLAIS, SIR JOHN EVERETT, 1ST BT.
MILNES, RICHARD MONCKTON, 1ST BARON HOUGHTON
MITFORD, ALGERNON BERTRAM FREEMAN, 1ST BARON
   REDESDALE
MOCATTA, FREDERICK DAVID
MOODY, FRANCIS WOLLASTON
MORRIS, WILLIAM
MORRISON, WALTER
MUNDELLA, ANTHONY JOHN
NORWOOD, THOMAS WILKINSON
OAKES, JOHN WRIGHT
OULESS, WALTER WILLIAM
OWEN, SIR FRANCIS PHILIP CUNLIFFE
PATMORE, COVENTRY KERSEY DIGHTON
PATTISON, MARK
PAUL, CHARLES KEGAN
POYNTER, SIR EDWARD JOHN, 1ST BT.
RAPER, ROBERT WILLIAM
READE, ESSEX E.
REID, GEORGE WILLIAM
RICHMOND, SIR WILLIAM BLAKE
RITCHIE, ANNE ISABELLA, LADY <WIFE OF SIR R. T. W.
   RITCHIE, nee THACKERAY>
ROBSON, EDWARD ROBERT
ROLPH, G. F.
RUSKIN, JOHN
SANDERSON, THOMAS JAMES COBDEN-
SCOTT, WILLIAM BELL
SOANES, TEMPLE
STEPHEN, SIR LESLIE
STEPHENS, FREDERICK GEORGE

STEVENSON, JAMES COCHRAN
STEVENSON, JOHN JAMES
STEWART, DAVID JAMES
TADEMA, SIR LAWRENCE ALMA-
TALBOT, JAMES, 4TH BARON TALBOT DE MALAHIDE
TAYLOR, HELEN <MISS>
TAYLOR, THOMAS <STYLED EARL OF BECTIVE, HEIR OF 3RD
   MARQUIS OF HEADFORT>
TEBBS, H. VIRTUE
TEULON, WILLIAM MILFORD
TIMMINS, SAMUEL
TROWER, ARTHUR
TUCKER, STEPHEN ISAACSON
TURLE, HENRY FREDERIC
TURNER, THACKERAY
VENABLES, EDMUND
VERNEY, SIR HARRY, 2ND BT.
VINALL, C. G.
WALLIS, H.
WARDLE, GEORGE Y.
WARDLE, SIR THOMAS
WARR, GEORGE CHARLES WINTER
WATTS, GEORGE FREDERICK
WEBB, PHILIP SPEAKMAN
WELLS, THOMAS
WESTLAKE, JOHN
WHITE, F. A.
WHITTLE, JAMES LOWRY
WHITWELL, JOHN
WILKINSON, GEORGE HOWARD
WILLSON, T. J.
WORTLEY, ARCHIBALD HENRY PLANTAGENET STUART-
WRIGHT, WILLIAM ALDIS
WYNDHAM, PERCY SCAWEN


State Resistance Union

   CROFTS, W. C.
   DONISTHORPE, WORDSWORTH


Sunday Society

   ALDER, WILLIAM S.
   AMOS, SHELDON
   ARMITAGE, BENJAMIN
   ARMITAGE, EDWARD
   ATCHISON, ARTHUR TURNOUR
   AXON, WILLIAM EDWARD ARMYTAGE
   BAIN, ALEXANDER
   BARFOOT, WILLIAM
   BEAL, JAMES
   BEALE, SOPHIA
   BICKNELL, HENRY S.
   BINNS, WILLIAM
   BOOTH, JAMES
   BOWES, JAMES LORD
   BOWRING, - <LADY>
   BOYDEN, KATE <MISS>
   BRAMWELL, GEORGE WILLIAM WILSHERE, 1ST BARON BRAMWELL
   BRAY, - <MRS. CHARLES BRAY>
   BRIGHT, JACOB
   BROOKE, STOPFORD AUGUSTUS
   BROWNING, G.
   BRUCE, THOMAS JOHN HOVELL THURLOW-CUMMING-, 5TH BARON
      THURLOW
   BRUNNER, SIR JOHN TOMLINSON, 1ST BT.
   BUCKMASTER, J. C.
   BUDWORTH, PHILIP JOHN
   BURBURY, - <MRS. WILLIAM BURBURY>
   BURN, HENRY W.
   BURROWS, SIR JOHN CORDY
   BURT, THOMAS
   BUSZARD, MARSTON CLARKE
   CAMPBELL, LEWIS
   CAPEL, THOMAS JOHN

CARLETON, DUDLEY WILMOT, 4TH BARON DORCHESTER
CARPENTER, MARY
CARR, JOSEPH WILLIAM COMYNS
CASSAL, CHARLES EDWARD
CATES, ARTHUR
CHAMBERLAIN, JOSEPH
CHAMBERLAIN, RICHARD
CHAPMAN, HANNAH <MRS.>
CHAPMAN, JOHN
CHRISTIE, - <MISS>
CLARK, C. W.
CLARK, SIR JOHN FORBES, 2ND BT.
CLARK, WILLIAM J.
CLARKE, THOMAS CHATFIELD
CLAYTON, ELLEN CREATHORNE <MRS. JAMES HENRY NEEDHAM>
COBDEN, JANE E. <MISS>
COLE, SIR HENRY
COLLINS, EUGENE
CONYNGHAM, GEORGE HENRY, 3RD MARQUIS OF CONYNGHAM
CORFIELD, WILLIAM HENRY
CORKER, H. D.
COXE, SIR JAMES
CRAIK, DINAH MARIA <MRS. GEORGE LILLIE CRAIK, nee
    MULOCK>
CRAWSHAY, ROSE MARY <MRS. ROBERT THOMPSON CRAWSHAY,
    nee YEATES
CROSSKEY, HENRY WILLIAM
CUNNINGTON, JOHN
DALDORPH, A.
DARWIN, CHARLES ROBERT
DARWIN, ERASMUS ALVEY
DAVIES, CHARLES MAURICE
DEADMAN, GEORGE
DE CHAUMONT, FRANCIS STEPHEN BENNETT FRANCOIS
DE LA RUE, WARREN
DICKSEE, SIR FRANCIS BERNARD
DIXON, GEORGE
DOMINIE, FRANK
DOMVILLE, WILLIAM HENRY
DRUMMOND, ROBERT B.
DRYSDALE CHARLES ROBERT
DUNBAR, SIR CHARLES GORDON CUMMING, 9TH BT.
DUNDAS, JOHN CHARLES
ELMORE, ALFRED
ERRINGTON, SIR GEORGE, 1ST BT.
ESCOMBE, - <MRS. FRANK ESCOMBE>
FAED, THOMAS
FARTHING, - <MRS. WILLIAM FARTHING>
FARTHING, WILLIAM
FAWCETT, HENRY
FIELDING, WILLIAM E.
FIRTH, JOSEPH FIRTH BOTTOMLEY
FLOWER, WILLIAM HENRY
FORD, FREDERICK A.
FRANKLAND, SIR EDWARD
FURNIVALL, FREDERICK JAMES
GLASSE, JOHN
GODWIN, GEORGE
GREY, MARIA GEORGINA <MRS. WILLIAM THOMAS GREY, nee
    SHIRREFF>
GROSVENOR, HUGH LUPUS, 1ST DUKE OF WESTMINSTER
GRUNDY, CHARLES SYDNEY
HANCOCK, CHARLES FREDERICK
HANSARD, SEPTIMUS COX HOLMES
HAWEIS, HUGH REGINALD
HAYNES, WILLIAM B. <"MAJ.">
HERKOMER, SIR HUBERT VON
HEYWOOD, JAMES
HOBHOUSE, ARTHUR, 1ST BARON HOBHOUSE
HOLL, FRANK
HOLLAND, SAMUEL
HOLYOAKE, GEORGE JACOB
HOPES, E.
HOPGOOD, JAMES
HOPPS, JOHN PAGE
HOPWOOD, CHARLES HENRY
HORSFALL, THOMAS COGLAN

HOWARD, GEORGE JAMES, 9TH EARL OF CARLISLE
HOWE, - <MRS.>
HUGHES, GEORGE
HUNT, MARION EDITH HOLMAN <MRS. WILLIAM HOLMAN HUNT,
    nee WAUGH>
HUNT, WILFRED
HUNT, WILLIAM HOLMAN
HUXLEY, THOMAS HENRY
JOHNSTONE, HARCOURT VANDEN BEMPDE, 1ST BARON DERWENT
JONES, ROWLAND J.
JONES, SIR THOMAS ALFRED
JOYNER, GEORGE
JUDGE, EMILY <MRS. MARK HAYLER JUDGE, nee SIMPSON>
JUDGE, MARK HAYLER
KINGSFORD, ALGERNON GODFREY
KINGSFORD, ANNA <MRS. ALGERNON GODFREY KINGSFORD, nee
    BONUS>
LAKE, WILLIAM
LAMBERT, BROOKE
LANKESTER, SIR EDWIN RAY
LA TOUCHE, JAMES DIGUES
LAWSON, HARRY LAWSON WEBSTER LEVY-, 1ST VISCOUNT
    BURNHAM
LAWSON, HENRY
LECKY, WILLIAM EDWARD HARTPOLE
LEE, ROBERT JAMES
LEGROS, ALPHONSE
LEHMANN, RUDOLPH
LEIGHTON, FREDERICK, 1ST BARON LEIGHTON OF STRETTON
LEON, GEORGE I. <OR GEORGE J.>
LETHEBY, HENRY
LINDSAY, SIR COUTTS, 2ND BT.
LINTON, SIR JAMES DROMGOLE
LONG, FREDERICK
LOWE, L. <MRS.>
LYTTLETON, WILLIAM HENRY
MACDONALD, ALEXANDER
MAITLAND, EDWARD
MARTIN, THOMAS H.
MATHER, SIR WILLIAM
MAXSE, FREDERICK AUGUSTUS
MEAD, W. H.
MEDLAND, JOHN B.
MILLAIS, SIR JOHN EVERETT, 1ST BT.
MILLSON, FRANK E.
MOCATTA, FREDERICK DAVID
MORLEY, HENRY
MUELLER, FRIEDRICH MAX
NASMYTH, JAMES
NATION, WILLIAM HAMILTON CODRINGTON
NOEL, ROBERT RALPH
OSWALD, EUGENE
PARSONS, ANNA F. <MISS>
PEACH, W. W.
PENNINGTON, FREDERICK
PERRIER, ANNA <MRS. JOHN PERRIER>
PICKERSGILL, EDWARD HARE
PICTON, JAMES ALLANSON
PILLANS, THOMAS D.
PLUMPTRE, CHARLES JOHN
POMEROY, JAMES SPENCER, 6TH VISCOUNT HARBERTON
POTTER, THOMAS BAYLEY
PRAED, SIR HERBERT BULKLEY MACKWORTH, 1ST BT.
PRATT, HODGSON
PRIMROSE, ARCHIBALD PHILIP, 5TH EARL OF ROSEBERY
QUIN, WINDHAM THOMAS WYNDHAM, 4TH EARL OF DUNRAVEN
RAMSAY, JOHN WILLIAM, 13TH EARL OF DALHOUSIE
RAWLEY, WALTER J.
READE, CHARLES
REED, DANIEL M.
RENNICK, CHARLES
REVELL, W. F.
REYNOLDS, WILLIAM HAMMOND
RICHARDSON, SIR BENJAMIN WARD
RICHARDSON, MARY E. <MISS>
RIVIERE, BRITON
ROEBUCK, JOHN ARTHUR

ROGERS, WILLIAM
ROMANES, GEORGE JOHN
ROMILLY, WILLIAM, 2ND BARON ROMILLY
RONNIGER, - <MADAME>
ROSCOE, HENRY ENFIELD
ROWLANDS, JAMES
RUTHERFURD, HENRY
SAINSBURY, - <MRS. SAMUEL SAINSBURY>
SAINSBURY, ALAN FOX
SAINSBURY, SAMUEL
SANDWITH, HUMPHREY
SCOTT, ROBSON J.
SEELEY, SIR JOHN ROBERT
SHUTTLEWORTH, HENRY CARY
SIEMENS, <CHARLES> SIR WILLIAM
SIMPSON, E. MARSH
SIMPSON, HENRY T.
SIMPSON, JANE H. <MRS.>
SIMPSON, JOHN H.
SIMS, F. MANLEY
SMITH, GEORGE VANCE
SMITHSON, EDWARD
SMYTH, J. D. HIRST
SOLLY, HENRY
SOUTTER, FRANCIS WILLIAM
SPENCER, HERBERT
SPOTTISWOODE, WILLIAM
STAFFORD, WILLIAM
STANLEY, ARTHUR PENRHYN
STANLEY, EDWARD HENRY, 15TH EARL OF DERBY
STANTON, CHARLES HOLBROW
STEELE, STEPHEN
STRANGWAYS, HENRY EDWARD FOX-, 5TH EARL OF ILCHESTER
STRUTT, EDWARD, 1ST BARON BELPER
SULLIVAN, SIR EDWARD, 1ST BT.
SWANWICK, ANNA <MISS>
TADEMA, SIR LAWRENCE ALMA-
TAYLOR, GEORGE G.
TAYLOR, HELEN <MISS>
TAYLOR, PETER ALFRED
THOMAS, FRANK R.
THOMAS, J. H.
THOMAS, W. CAVE
THOMAS, WILLIAM LUSON
THOMPSON, SIR HENRY, 1ST BT.
THOMPSON, JOSEPH WILLIAM
TREVELYAN, ARTHUR
TRIST, JOHN
TYNDALL, JOHN
VENTURI, EMILIE <MRS. G. A. VENTURI, nee ASHURST>
VOYSEY, CHARLES
WALTER, JAMES
WATSON, THOMAS HENRY
WATTS, GEORGE FREDERICK
WAY, ROBERT E.
WEDGWOOD, FRANCIS
WESTLAKE, JOHN
WHITE, WILLIAM O.
WHITWORTH, BENJAMIN
WILKS, JOHN MARK
WINGFIELD, MERVYN EDWARD, 7TH VISCOUNT POWERSCOURT
WOOD, JOHN DENNISTOUN
WOOLNER, THOMAS
WORBY, JOSHUA
YEAMES, WILLIAM FREDERICK
YOUNG, GEORGE H.

Travelling Tax Abolition Committee

BAKER, DANIEL
BEAL, MICHAEL
BELL, THOMAS EVANS
BOTT, THOMAS
BOURNE, T. J.
BRIGGS, THOMAS
BROADHURST, HENRY
BURT, THOMAS
CARSON, THOMAS
COLLET, COLLET DOBSON
COOPER, CHARLES R.
COWEN, JOSEPH
CRAWSHAY, GEORGE
DUIGNAN, W. H.
FRANCIS, FRANCIS
HILL, ALSAGER HAY
HOLYOAKE, GEORGE JACOB
HORN, W. WILSON
HOWELL, GEORGE
HOWELL, W. H.
HYDE, JOSEPH
JAMES, WALTER HENRY, 2ND BARON NORTHBOURNE
KIBBLE, A. W.
LEACH, JOHN
LITTLETON, HENRY
MARSDEN, MARK EAGLES
MAYALL, J. J. E.
MOORE, RICHARD
MURPHY, GEORGE MOLLETT
NOBLE, JOHN
NODAL, JOHN HOWARD
NOVELLO, JOSEPH ALFRED
POTTER, GEORGE
PRATT, HODGSON
RUSSELL, RICHARD
SHARMAN, WILLIAM
SHIPTON, GEORGE
SIMPSON, G.
SMITH, A. M.
THOMPSON, JOSEPH
TORRENS, WILLIAM TORRENS MCCULLAGH
WALHOUSE, EDWARD
WATSON, ROBERT SPENCE
WATTS, EDWARD HENRY
WATTS, JOHN
WRIGHT, THEODORE

Victoria Street Soc for Protection of Animals from
Vivisection

ADAMS, CHARLES
ADDINGTON, WILLIAM WELLS, 3RD VISCOUNT SIDMOUTH
ADLAM, SOPHIA HARFORD <MRS. WILLIAM ADLAM, nee
PARKER>
ADLAM, WILLIAM
ASHLEY, ANTHONY EVELYN MELBOURNE
ASHLEY, LADY EDITH FLORENCE
BELL, ERNEST
BERDOE, EDWARD
BLIGH, JOHN STUART, 6TH EARL OF DARNLEY
BONAPARTE, LOUIS LUCIEN, PRINCE
BROWNE, EDWARD HAROLD
BROWNING, ROBERT
BRUCE, ERNEST AUGUSTUS CHARLES BRUDENELL, 3RD MARQUIS
OF AILESBURY
BRYAN, BENJAMIN
BRYANT, OLIVE <MISS>
CANNING, EMMELINE ROSABELLE
CARLYLE, THOMAS
CHANNING, WILLIAM HENRY
CHARLOTTE EUGENIE AUGUSTE AMALIE ALBERTINE, PRINCESS
OF SWEDEN
CLARKE, JOHN HENRY
COBBE, FRANCES POWER <MISS>

CODRINGTON, SIR GERALD WILLIAM HENRY, 6TH AND 1ST BT.
COLERIDGE, BERNARD JOHN SEYMOUR, 2ND BARON COLERIDGE
COLERIDGE, JOHN DUKE, 1ST BARON COLERIDGE
COLERIDGE, MILDRED MARY <LATER, MRS. CHARLES WARREN
    ADAMS>
COLERIDGE, STEPHEN WILLIAM BUCHANAN
COOPER, ANTHONY ASHLEY, 7TH EARL OF SHAFTESBURY
COWIE, - <MISS>
DOUGLAS, SIR ROBERT PERCY, 4TH BT.
DUNDAS, JULIANA CAVENDISH, COUNTESS OF CAMPERDOWN
    <wife of 2ND EARL, nee PHILIPS>
ERSKINE, SHIPLEY GORDON STUART, 14TH EARL OF BUCHAN
FIRTH, JOSEPH FIRTH BOTTOMLEY
FRASER, JAMES
GIMSON, W. GIMSON
GORDON, - <MISS>
GOWER, ANNE SUTHERLAND LEVESON-, DUCHESS OF
    SUTHERLAND, COUNTESS OF CROMARTIE
GREEN, CHARLOTTE <MISS>
GUTHRIE, ELLEN E. <MISS>
HARRISON, GILBERT
HERVEY, ARTHUR CHARLES
HOLDEN, FRANCES <MRS. LUTHER HOLDEN, nee STERRY>
KELLY, SIR FITZROY EDWARD
KEMBALL, ANNA FRANCES, LADY <WIFE OF SIR A. B.
    KEMBALL, nee SHAW>
LEGARD, SIR CHARLES, 11TH BT.
LLOYD, - <MISS>
LOPES, HENRY CHARLES, 1ST BARON LUDLOW
MCDOUGALL, SIR PATRICK LEONARD
MACEVILLY, JOHN
MACKARNESS, JOHN FIELDER
MCKENZIE, COLIN
MALET, SIR ALEXANDER, 2ND BT.
MANNING, HENRY EDWARD
MARSTON, - <MISS>
MATTHEWS, J.
MELVILLE, ALEXANDER LESLIE-, 10TH EARL OF LEVEN AND
    9TH EARL OF MELVILLE
MONRO, - <MISS>
MORRISON, - <MRS. FRANK MORRISON>
MORRISON, JOHN CHARLES DOWNIE
MUNDELLA, ANTHONY JOHN
PAGET, WALPURGA EHRENGARDE HELENA DE HOHENTHAL, LADY
    <wife of SIR A. B. PAGET>
PENDER, - <MRS. JAMES PENDER>
PIRKIS, FRED E.
REES, ELLEN ELCUM <MISS>
REID, ROBERT THRESHIE, 1ST EARL LOREBURN
RYLE, JOHN CHARLES
SCARLETT, HELEN, LADY ABINGER <WIFE OF 3RD BARON
    ABINGER, nee MAGRUDER>
SEYMOUR, HUGH DE GREY, 6TH MARQUIS OF HERTFORD
SINDEN, R. H.
SOMERSET, HENRY ADELBERT WELLINGTON FITZROY, 9TH DUKE
    OF BEAUFORT
STANLEY, ARTHUR PENRHYN
STANSFELD, SIR JAMES
STRUTT, CLARA ELIZABETH LA TOUCHE, LADY RAYLEIGH
    <wife of 2ND BARON, nee VICARS>
STUART, JOHN PATRICK CRICHTON, 3RD MARQUIS OF BUTE
TEMPLE, GEORGIANA COWPER-, LADY MOUNT-TEMPLE <wife of
    1ST BN., nee TOLLEMACHE>
TEMPLE, WILLIAM FRANCIS COWPER-, 1ST BARON
    MOUNT-TEMPLE
TENNYSON, ALFRED, 1ST BARON TENNYSON
THOMSON, WILLIAM, 1ST BARON KELVIN
VAUGHAN, CHARLES JOHN
VERSCHOYLE, JOHN STUART
WALLOP, LADY EVELINE ALICIA JULIANA, COUNTESS OF
    PORTSMOUTH <wife of 5TH EARL>
WALLOP, ISAAC NEWTON, 5TH EARL OF PORTSMOUTH
WEBSTER, JOHN
WILMOT, SIR JOHN EARDLEY EARDLEY-, 2ND BT.

Vigilance Assn for Defense of Personal Rights

ARCH, JOSEPH
ARDEN, DOUGLAS
BAILY, J. S.
BLACKBURN, HELLEN
BRIGHT, JACOB
BRIGHT, URSULA M. <MRS. JACOB BRIGHT, nee MELLOR>
BUTLER, GEORGE
BUTLER, JOSEPHINE E. <MRS. GEORGE BUTLER, nee GREY>
EDGELL, EDGELL WYATT
GLOVER, - <MRS. R. R. GLOVER>
HAMPSON, ROBERT
KING, - <MRS. E. M. KING>
LEVY, JOSEPH HIAM
MCLAREN, WALTER B.
MALLESON, WILLIAM TAYLOR
MARSDEN, MARK EAGLES
SHAEN, WILLIAM
SHEARER, - <MRS.>
STUART, JAMES
TARRING, SIR CHARLES JAMES
TAYLOR, CLEMENTIA <MRS. PETER ALFRED TAYLOR, nee
    DOUGHTY>
TAYLOR, PETER ALFRED
TODD, ISABELLA<MISS>
VENTURI, EMILIE <MRS. G. A. VENTURI, nee ASHURST>
WOLSTENHOLME, ELIZABETH C.


Working Men's Comtee Promoting Separation Church and
State

APPLEGARTH, ROBERT
BROADHURST, HENRY
DEIGHTON, JOHN
FOSTER, W. H.
GUILE, DANIEL
HOWELL, GEORGE
LATHAM, R. MARSDEN
POTTER, GEORGE
SQUIRE, JAMES
WHETSTONE, F. J.


Working Men's Natl League for Abolition State Regulation
of Vice

DYER, ALFRED STACE
ELMES, EDWARD
GOULT, SYDNEY <OR SIDNEY>
GULLIVER, WILLIAM
HADLEY, SYDNEY CHARLES
JONES, EDMUND
JOYCE, JOSEPH
LUCRAFT, BENJAMIN
SIMMONS, ALFRED


Working Men's Protestant League

MCCLURE, THOMAS


Workmen's Natl Assn for Abolition Sugar Bounties

GILLMAN, L.
KELLY, THOMAS M.
MONTIETH, JOHN
PETERS, SAMUEL

Workmen´s Peace Assn

BAHNS, -
BAILEY, -
BEALES, EDMOND
BRITTEN, BENJAMIN
BURT, THOMAS
CREMER, SIR WILLIAM RANDAL
EATON, -
EVANS, HOWARD
GALBRAITH, -
HANCOCK, -
JOINER, -
KINGSTON, -
LUCRAFT, BENJAMIN
MATKIN, C.
MATKIN, W.
PAGE, -
PRATT, HODGSON
SAVAGE, -
WALKER, -
WATERMAN, -
WORLEY, W. C.